Chile in the Nineties

Originally published in Spanish as *Chile en los noventa*, 1998.

This English edition was published February 2000 by Stanford
University Libraries in cooperation with the Presidency of the
Republic of Chile. The Spanish edition was edited, printed, and
distributed in 1998 by Dolmen Ediciones S.A., Santiago, Chile.

Publisher: Michael A. Keller
Coordination: Roberto Trujillo
Managing Editor: Andrew Herkovic
Translation: Katty Kauffman and Patricia Linderman,
Link Profesionales Traducciones Ltda.
Technical support and supplemental translation: Ryan Max Steinberg
Cover painting: Santiago Aránguiz
Design: Kina Sullivan

ISBN: 0-911221-21-2

Printed in The United States of America

Chile
In the Nineties

Editors:
Cristián Toloza
Eugenio Lahera

STANFORD UNIVERSITY LIBRARIES 2000

Acknowledgments from Original Edition

This book has been sponsored by the Presidency of the Republic of Chile through its Research Office. The analyses and opinions expressed here are the responsibility of each author.

The editors would like to thank President Eduardo Frei Ruiz-Tagle for having stimulated an intellectual endeavor and open reflection upon our national situation, an effort that transcends the everyday demands of governing. We appreciate the fact that despite his demanding schedule, he dedicated time to meet with the authors, participate in some of the analyses, and comment upon the articles that make up this book.

Chile in the Nineties is the result of a collective effort. Each text was discussed in a workshop with approximately 10 invited participants, with comments made on the written versions and discussions of the central themes. The editors would like to thank the more than 200 professionals, experts, and social leaders who actively participated in these seminars. We would particularly like to recognize the individuals who made formal comments on the articles: Angel Flisfich, Alfredo Rheren, Sergio Galilea, Alicia Frohmann, Francisco Rojas, Emilio Meneses, Andrés Sanfuentes, Eduardo Bitrán, Ricardo Paredes, Juan Enrique Vega, Patricio Rodrigo, Raúl Urzúa, Dagmar Raczynski, Iván Núñez, Mario Alburquerque, José Bengoa, Inés Recca, Carlos Catalán, Hernán Courard, and Rafael Otano.

Manual Araneda assisted with the cover design. Verónica Baeza administratively coordinated the book's production, and Claudia Izquierdo organized the workshops. Paulina Matta and Rodrigo Pinto undertook the stylistic editing. Santiago Aránguiz graciously lent one of his paintings for the cover. To all of them, and to Dolmen Ediciones for their hard work, we express our appreciation.

Table of Contents

Economics

Society

Culture

Assessment and Outlook of the Concertación

Introduction

Introduction

The job of President of the Republic gives the citizen the opportunity to undertake a wide-range of dialogue, not only with the leaders of political parties and unions, but also with men and women of all walks of life, along the vast continuum of human and geographical diversity which constitutes our nation.

Democratic leadership calls for close attention to this continuing conversation between the country's citizens and the occupant of its highest office. This particular aspect of my job has made me a uniquely privileged witness of the transformations taking place across our country, in our living conditions, and among our people.

Many of the changes occurring in particular areas of national life have not been obvious to other Chileans. A groundbreaking transformation in a specialized field may be almost invisible to the wider society. City dwellers may be unaware of changing working conditions in mining or agriculture. Improvements in education may be reflected only in specialized statistical measurements.

In any case, we rarely have the chance to pause and reflect adequately upon the scope and implications of these changes. Emerging technologies become part of our daily routines, gradually transforming our way of life without our even noticing. Even the country's leaders are usually too occupied with the daily demands of their jobs to take note of these transformations on a global level. Yet Chile has changed dramatically, rapidly, and profoundly during the 1990s, and for this reason I felt it necessary to undertake a comprehensive and pluralistic assessment, based on solid evidence, of the events of this decade during which democracy has returned to govern our national community.

This period has been intense, challenging, and complex. We have seen our material wealth expand in unprecedented measure. Our country has become involved, more than ever before, in common undertakings with the rest of humanity. We have experienced the tensions inherent to a consolidating democracy. Our culture and way of life have changed, and continue to change, and every field of endeavor within our nation is modernizing with accelerating speed.

What has occurred in these years cannot be summed up in a series of dates and events; it has been, more accurately, a collective maturation process. As I have affirmed in the past, we are the generation of Chileans closest to achieving full development for our nation, a dream cherished by many of our predecessors. Yet, as we advance, we can also more clearly perceive the distance still separating us from our goal of creating a modern, developed, equitable, fully integrated, and profoundly democratic country. As we undertake this journey, we must constantly reflect upon the implications of our progress, recognizing what we have achieved as well as what has happened without our willing it. Only then can we proceed along the road to development with increasing insight and maturity.

With these goals in mind, I gathered together a team of professionals, technical experts, and intellectuals to undertake the wide-ranging reflections collected in this book. My intention was not to present an official version of the events of these years, but to provide a thoughtful, analytical assessment, avoiding the extremes of smug triumphalism and deepest pessimism which have become so entrenched in our national culture. The first of these attitudes imagines us as unique in Latin America, sole possessors of a formula by which one segment of the national community inexorably propels the rest toward modernization and development. The second state of mind denies the advances we have achieved, or dismisses them as the property of an extremely small group. Both perceptions deny the possibility of recognizing national development as a task shared by all Chileans, a task which requires us to apply our energy and resources to the construction of an integrated national community with a stable and confident vision of itself.

In calling for these reflections, I have acted in the belief that the arduous task of governing does not preclude the possibility of viewing our nation's achievements with a measure of detachment. While we properly promote and defend the progress made by our country, we cannot ignore the unfinished work and emerging challenges our national dynamism has set before us. Development itself brings new tasks, new expectations, and new social tensions which must be confronted.

I have especially hoped that this intellectual exercise would provide an integrated vision of Chile, one which includes its politics, economy, society, and culture. Thus, a broad perspective has been emphasized here, avoiding explanations emanating from a narrow or partisan point of view.

Since 1970, when Aníbal Pinto and other prominent authors wrote *Chile, hoy (Chile Today)*, there has been almost no other editorial effort of this nature. The importance of Pinto's work lay in its diverse, incisive, and complex vision of the national situation at that time. The guiding force shared by that work and the present one is the quest to comprehend the transformations affecting our nation. Yet since that era, our world has changed its face profoundly.

Today, in contrast to those days, our country finds itself fully integrated into the international system, as well as vitally involved in the restructuring of the global economy. The opening of our economy, our countless new commercial ties spreading out in all directions, and our renewed commitment to the diplomatic promotion of democracy — all these are signs of a closer relationship with the world than Chile maintained in the past.

The world order has changed; Chile has changed; our region has changed. We require profound reflections to help guide our steps through a world in rapid transition.

A New World

In our era we have witnessed the enshrinement of democracy as the basic foundation for political coexistence, as well as the universalization of human rights as a requirement of the human moral order. A strong humanist ethos has arisen, which recognizes the equality of the sexes, acknowledges the fragility of ecological systems, and understands that the common home we inhabit requires care and protection.

We have witnessed extraordinary scientific and technological progress, rising educational achievement, the advance of industrialization and economic growth, increasing urbanization, a worldwide communications explosion, and the development of an increasingly complex and diversified labor market.

We have experienced a modernization dynamic that has already become universal in scope. More fundamentally, change has been expressed in a profound revision of the conceptions of human happiness which have fed revolutionary utopias and attempts at social engineering. The world has undergone rapid and drastic change as a result of the collapse of the totalitarian ideologies.

Modes of social organization and coexistence have also changed, along with ideas about their relative success and desirability. There has been a revaluation of family time, daily routines, personal projects, and cultural life. Under this new value system, politics has ceased to be the focal point of life in society. Opportunities for personal and private development have expanded accordingly. Individual interests have become more complex, and the nation's collective identity has come to rest upon a less political and more cultural foundation.

This multifaceted transformation has led Chile in recent decades through an accelerated modernization process, transforming its productive, labor, and economic structure. Comparing the country's current situation with that at mid-century, we can observe that our economy is no longer based upon a single export; our industrial structure is no longer sheltered by the State; our formerly rigid social classes have dissolved; the majority of our workers are now employed in the service sector; women have been largely and successfully incorporated into the work force; and even our society's demographic structure has changed within this relatively short period. Our families are smaller, and our children receive an education which their parents did not possess and their grandparents could not even have imagined.

The articles presented in this work, along with a dialogue established with some of their authors, have led me to believe that Chile faces a promising, though complex, situation at this moment in its development. As in any country experiencing accelerated growth, the old and the new coexist in the same institutional structure. Old and new cultural strands crisscross each other, often producing logical and emotional contradictions. Old and new needs and aspirations demand to be addressed quickly and effectively.

As a society, we find ourselves obliged to confront unprecedented challenges arising from our very successes. At the same time, long-cherished aspirations continue to contribute issues to the public agenda. I believe that readers of this book will gain a better understanding of the urgency of addressing certain areas of continuing importance which have not been granted top priority in government policy considerations in the past.

Our Achievements Give Rise to New Challenges

Chile's economic growth, as all the statistics confirm, has been remarkable. In the 1990s we have experienced sustained GNP growth and continuously falling inflation, as well as significant increases in productivity and savings. We have enjoyed substantial budgetary surpluses, along with an acceptable and sustainable current account deficit. Today, our country exports almost 17 billion dollars' worth of goods and services, more than double the 8.1 billion exported in 1989. Chile's fixed capital investment rate is approximately 30%; more than nine hundred thousand new jobs have been created during the first seven years of this decade; and wages have increased in real terms by 34.7% in the private sector and 57.6% among public employees.

Yet these achievements themselves have given rise to new problems and challenges. When a society experiences continuous and impressive growth, as Chile has done, expectations for socio-economic improvement among its citizens rise dramatically. The success of political initiatives may lead to new demands, expose new contradictions, or carry us to a higher level of vision at which reality appears quite different.

Thus, for example, it is not enough simply to increase the volume of our country's exports. At the same time, export diversity, both in products and markets, must also be promoted. The base of export business must be broadened, particularly among small and medium-sized firms. This, in turn, cannot be accomplished without concurrent advances in worker training, business education, and technological modernization.

Another achievement that has brought new challenges into view has been our country's solid advance in the fight against poverty, which during the past nine years has permitted more than two million three hundred thousand people to escape from dire need and deprivation. This great step forward has illuminated the remaining task of reducing inequality in our society. Perceptions of inequity have been arising throughout our country and are expressed objectively in various indicators. Thus, if we hope for effective recognition of our advances in social justice and our population's living conditions, absolute reductions in poverty and marginality must be accompanied by an increasingly democratic distribution of social opportunities, as well as reductions in income inequality.

This way of thinking calls for new methods of assessing the impact of our social policies. The challenge of universal coverage has been successfully met, especially in the areas of health and education. Yet today it is necessary, while maintaining the levels achieved, to emphasize the quality of our social services, in order to reap greater benefits from the social investment which has absorbed an increasing amount of resources since 1990. The goal of achieving lasting improvement in income levels and quality of life for our society's poorest members obliges us to strengthen the management, financing, focus, decentralization, and evaluation of social programs.

Meanwhile, changes in our country's social structure have brought new vulnerabilities to light. As women have become more fully incorporated into the labor force and the family structure has been modified, the threat of a new kind of marginality has arisen among middle- and lower-income groups. The destruction of traditional social networks and support systems, placed alongside the demands of survival in a modern society, have made life more difficult for many families. The problems of single-parent families, female heads of household, and the elderly are becoming more pressing issues for society and the State.

New Issues Express Long-standing Aspirations

We have moved forward as a country. This is undeniable. Yet in the course of our advance, new issues have arisen on the social agenda which would have been inconceivable just two decades ago — or if they were imagined, they were discounted as problems of rich, highly-developed societies, having little relevance for poor nations. Today, however, issues such as environmental protection have become part of our own agenda. The environmental dimension has been recognized as an indispensable factor in development, indeed a condition for its advance, requiring the cooperation of the business community and the participation of the citizenry. This view recognizes that economic and political costs must be assumed by both social and business groups. It implies moving the debate beyond the economic maximalism that views environmental protection as a burden, making growth more difficult, as well as the ecological fundamentalism which sees the root of the problem in the basis of industrial civilization itself.

In addition, the country's growth and the changes in its development style have made certain institutional adjustments unavoidable. Foremost among these is the modernization of the State, aimed at reorienting Chile's government apparatus toward public service. As the State seeks to serve the common good more effectively, it will require regulatory and technical modernization and an improved institutional focus, as well as an enhanced capacity for action. These necessities transcend the stale debate over the size of government, and lead to a greater focus on its supervisory and regulatory responsibilities. In this role, the State must strengthen the institutions that safeguard the competitiveness and transparency of the market in order to promote economic effectiveness, as well as to ensure adequate respect for the rights of users and consumers. What the country needs is not merely a larger or smaller bureaucracy, but a government adequate to society's demands for social expenditures, the promotion of productive activity, investment in infrastructure where the private sector fails to provide it, support for fair competition, and effective regulation of monopolistic service sectors.

Clearly, the need to redesign public institutions is not confined to the economic sphere. There is a growing conviction that we must rethink many of the institutional structures we depend upon, since they have not kept pace with the dynamism of our society. This impulse has already led to the renovation of our legal system, and it must be extended to other spheres. Numerous political and public institutions, among which might be mentioned the electoral system and the political parties, must be redesigned to allow the more effective expression of our citizens' aspirations.

Similarly, we must continue to confront the complex challenges of decentralization with boldness and imagination. We have already made evident progress in this respect. We have democratized political power on the county level, and under my administration, the percentage of public investment under regional control is being increased from 21% to 42%. However, we can and must do more. We must also recognize that this challenge is not confined to the government. Our society must create and sustain an institutionalized capacity for regional development which, under the political and technical leadership of regional governments, can effectively harmonize political, social, and business forces on the local and regional levels.

Democracy, markets, and the State do not endure without change. As our democracy becomes more solidly established, we can, with greater peace of mind, with fewer fears, and with the experience gained from democracy and economic growth, reflect more deeply on the institutions which govern the Chilean people, seeking ways to make them more legitimate, more modern, and more inclusive. A family experiencing change also repairs and renovates its own home.

New Strategic Challenges for Development

The attempt to satisfy the expectations raised throughout society during the 1980s has obligated our country's democratic governments to focus on those matters appearing most urgent. Reversing the decline in public primary and secondary education, narrowing the housing deficit, improving health care for the population, and raising pensions for retirees have been among the concerns of the past two administrations.

However, as we approach the milestone of a full decade of democracy, we cannot shirk our duty to confront, with energy and resolve, additional subjects crucial to our country's development. Among these, higher education deserves particular attention. It is undeniable that Chile's universities have received increased government funding in recent years, while greater resources have also been devoted to enabling less-privileged students to earn a university degree. However, the entire system of higher education must become more coherent and integrated, in order to ensure its equity and quality over the long term.

The state of higher education in Chile today is profoundly different from that of less than two decades ago. To grasp the magnitude of the transformation, it is only necessary to consider that in 1980, Chile had a total of eight institutions of higher learning, while 16 years later there were 262. Clearly, a new framework is needed to govern the management, financing, and organization of our higher educational institutions, and also, more centrally, to strengthen their identity and mission. The universities' connection with regional and national development also deserves particular consideration.

Another example of a new challenge generated by change in our country is the increasing distance and skepticism felt by many of our citizens toward political activity. The great risk here is of a generalized discrediting of democratic institutions, even of democracy itself. The combination of this political disaffectation with the deeply-rooted interpersonal mistrust manifested within our culture leads one to think of the need to strengthen educational institutions and to develop a closer link between pedagogical practice and the valuation of democratic attitudes and practices.

Finally, and without pretending to exhaust the numerous topics addressed by the articles in this book, we can also point out that extremely intense and continuous changes, such as those undergone by our country, inevitably leave a profound mark upon the people and social groups involved. A clear example of this is seen in the union movement, which has lost some of the impetus sustaining it in previous decades. The challenge of rethinking systems of organization and action is not confined to the State or the government. When a country experiences profound and global change, every group in society must weigh two options: persisting on the course which previously defined its identity, or embracing with courage and imagination the possibilities offered by a new environment to redefine and renew its essential mission.

How much the country has changed since the beginning of the 1970s is illustrated by Aníbal Pinto's opening statement for the chapter on economic development and social relations in his now-classic book, *Chile, hoy:*

> Since its early days, Chile has shown relative advancement in its social organization and institutional structures, in comparison with its economic progress, a disparity which has tended to worsen over the past two decades.[1]

---

1   *Chile, hoy* (Santiago: Siglo XXI Editores, 1970), p. 5.

The asymmetry noted by Pinto almost three decades ago has reversed itself in the intervening years. Today we have witnessed extraordinarily dynamic transformations in the economic sphere, and with them the need for substantial reform of public and private institutions. A country that hopes to develop must sustain this development through the integration and harmonization of its various structures and institutions. Yet this challenge must be viewed against the broad backdrop of our country's continuing progress, since considering only the inadequacies that remain may result in paralysis in the hour of action.

Many books aim to impart the last word on a subject. This one, in contrast, aspires to be a starting point for a mature and balanced debate. Each article, after its own fashion, is a seriously developed argument inviting discussion, critical judgment, and thoughtful weighing of its suggestions.

I hope that this book will find a special welcome among the members of the Concertación coalition, who bear the ongoing obligation to broaden their horizons, to give concrete expression to the profound convictions they represent, and to ensure that our country's development process is characterized by democracy, justice, and solidarity. My hope for this work is that it will suggest new public policies, help to broaden our political imaginations, and above all, enrich our idea of Chile.

EDUARDO FREI RUIZ-TAGLE
President of the Republic

Politics

The Chilean Political System:
Characteristics and Tendencies

Mario Fernández

I. The New Chilean Democracy Since 1990

Today Chile is a democracy. It is imperfect, as all democracies are. These two definitive statements contain a vital and powerful message. At the same time, they provide a conceptually important starting point for politicological analysis. Affirming that "Chile is a democracy" is equivalent to stating that "the Chilean political system is democratic," thus taking two theoretical steps: first, dividing the category "political systems" into democratic and non-democratic subdivisions, and second, affirming that Chile belongs to the first group.

It is the standpoint of this essay that both of these assertions, regarding the theory as well as its validity in the Chilean case, are undeniable and indispensable for analysis of the country's situation. However, questions have been raised from diverse sources as to whether Chile has truly completed the transition from authoritarianism to democracy, and whether it enjoys democratic status today. This essay will discuss both the concept of the political system and its democratic nature in Chile.

1. DEMOCRACY AS A POLITICAL SYSTEM

As was pointed out in a relatively recent work, the concept of political system has become so current in the vocabulary of politics and political science that its meaning almost appears self-evident (Nohlen 1994:388). This situation has arisen after nearly a half-century of theoretical battles following the publication of David Easton's book, *The Political System*, in 1953.[1]

During that time, the concept "political system" competed with analogous terms such as "State," "governmental regimes," "power structures," "political institutions," and "means of production." The academic struggle surrounding these terms involved, fundamentally, the legitimization of political science as an autonomous discipline with its own conceptual and methodological framework, as opposed to those of law, sociology, or economics.

The current use of the expression "political system" emerged from this scientific quarrel among the social sciences over the past half-century. The perspective taken by

---

1 From the same author, David Easton, followed "An Approach to the Analysis to Political Systems," in *World Politics* 9 (1957):383-400, as well as *A Framework for Political Analysis* (Englewood Cliffs, NJ, 1965).

political science not only achieved a place for itself among the branches of knowledge about human society, but also it eventually imposed upon the others its basic concept for the analysis of political phenomena. This conceptual supremacy does not mean that the other scientific perspectives have lost validity, but simply that when addressing politics as an object of study, they restrict themselves to the limits of their respective disciplines. The national legislature, for example, is studied under constitutional law as a lawmaking body, in sociology as a segment of the elite, and in economics as a source of regulation and oversight for productive processes. Political science, however, is left to define its role as part of the decision-making structure, along with its relation to the political parties, the electoral system, the social and territorial structure of the country, the political culture, and the interests or demands of groups in society.[2]

Understanding that the concept of "political system" encompasses a kind of global view of political phenomena, we must assume that its counterpart in reality is equivalent in scope. Next our attention turns naturally to the category "democracy" (as opposed to non-democracies, which include totalitarian and authoritarian systems), which in the past decade has emerged as the unchallenged standard by which to measure modern collective life.

This association between political system and democracy has not always been so evident. In the period before the present decade, when antagonistic global political systems vied for ideological and organizational supremacy, the term "democracy" was loaded with diverse meanings and was subject to qualifications making it difficult to apply to existing societies. Thus, along with the overall grouping into capitalist, socialist, or non-aligned democracies, further classifications proliferated, such as formal democracies, real democracies, social democracies, and economic democracies. These conceptual complexities, arising from fragmented and biased points of view, impeded the identification of democracy itself as a political system, reducing it to lower levels such as "political regimes," in which the differentiating factors could be ascribed to institutional forms or value systems. This situation led to a certain reluctance to define democracy in the academic sphere, resulting in the adoption of alternative terms (Dahl [1989] called it "polyarchy"), alongside the rhetorical extremes of ideological antagonists, who assigned democratic status according to the faction in which a country acknowledged membership.

This confusion regarding political systems and democracy decisively marked the context of the Chilean political conflict of 1973 and beyond, and its effects are still discernible in political debate and practice. As we shall see, the lingering dissatisfaction in the 1990s with Chile's achievements in the area of democracy, compared to what remains to be done, as well as the continuing tendency to take refuge in an eternally stretched-out "transition," arise from this tradition of discussion and analysis of the most ideal extremes of formal and real democracy.

Notwithstanding these continuing effects, it is clear that in the context of the 1990s, the debate over democracy is restricted to identifying it as the only civilized political system, or at least the most civilized one. As Sartori has noted, the phenomenon in which democracy stands alone without opponents poses a question without precedent in the

---

2 This consensus in the use of the concept "political system," however, does not exclude the persistence of distinct connotations in Anglo-Saxon and European circles, arising from their differing legal systems and concepts of "State" or "government." See Von Beyme (1994), ch. 3, pp. 88ff.

modern world: "... while it becomes more and more difficult to resist democracy, will democracy know how to resist itself?" (Sartori 1994:319).

In other words, in the current global political climate, the great political questions are raised within democracy, or at least with respect to it, as it evolves in both negative and positive directions, and however complex a path of obstacles and uncertainties it must confront. This can be seen in examples such as the dualism of rights and liberties, where the level of coexistence and harmony is situated in the full exercise of pluralism, tolerance, and individuality, together with the equally full protection of the fundamental rights of persons through the legal and political systems.

Thus, during the 1990s, as the concept of "political system" became universal in theory, the concept of "democracy" became equally global. This premise provides a basic foundation upon which to describe and analyze the Chilean political system.

2. TRANSITION AND DEMOCRATIZATION

The change in government that took place in Chile on March 11, 1990, has not had a unanimous interpretation among academics or among those directly involved in the process. While it is true that events such as this are highly symbolic and signify neither the beginning nor the end of history, the inauguration of a government elected by the people signified for some the end of the transition, while for others that recent moment merely began the transformation from authoritarianism to democracy.

For the majority, in keeping with a national tendency toward caution, the transfer of power from Pinochet to Aylwin gave rise to a diffuse phase, described as the "unfinished transition" (Zaldívar 1995) or the "incomplete transition" (Garretón 1995). A collection of President Aylwin's speeches during his first two years in office is entitled *The Chilean Transition*, in spite of the fact that the same leader once stated that "the transition was the step from the authoritarian government to a democratic regime" (1992 Presidential Message). On the other hand, the then-Minister of the Presidency, Genaro Arriagada, stated in 1994 that Chile had "culminated a successful transition" and advocated a change from the "logic of the transition" to the "logic of modernization" (Arriagada 1994).

What is certain is that these conceptual ambiguities have a dual source. One is theoretical in nature, and the other political.

On the one hand, a strong transitional focus can be found in theoretical analyses of political change, according to which such change takes place in phases. The continuum of change is initiated with the collapse of democracy, followed by the installation of authoritarianism, the transition to democracy, and finally, the democratic consolidation. This evolutionary model was used to study the processes occurring in southern Europe at the end of the 1970s, in Latin America in the 1980s, and in Eastern Europe in the 1990s, in spite of the complexities posed by comparative analysis of such diverse societies. The suitability of the same model in the Chilean case has been extensively examined (Valenzuela 1989), with a better fit found for past phases and poorer results for the present. The breakdown of democracy in Chile and the authoritarian regime can be placed within this framework, but the model does not seem as useful to explain Chile's particular experiences of transition and democratic consolidation.

The weakness of the transitional focus for Chile resides in the fact that it is based too much on the nature of authoritarianism and too little on that of democracy. In other words, instead of focusing on the successes of emerging democracies, proponents of this theory emphasize the continuing relevance of the authoritarian legacy within them. Thus, in this model, authoritarian features are expected to be retained during the consummation of the transition, persisting as a latent threat of relapse to autocracy. This focus sets forth an ideal vision of democracy, making it impossible to identify the boundary between democracy and the authoritarianism which preceded it. In this model, the transition is always underway.

At the same time, the notion of the persistence of the transition is rooted in political ideas and debate. Various participants in the Chilean process evaluate it differently. Supporters of the military regime would place the first steps of the transition in the mid-1970s, with the institutionalization of the authoritarian regime. For them, this process accelerated in the late 1980s, with the creation of laws covering politics, parties, and elections, and with the plebiscite of 1988, finally culminating with the handover of the government in 1990. On the other hand, among members of the Concertación coalition, the idea predominates that the transition began at the end of the 1980s, but that it continued after 1990, due to the persistence of the so-called "authoritarian enclaves" in the Constitution and the Basic Law.

Both visions, derived more from politics than from political science, serve to weaken the notion of democracy. The first outlook minimizes the distance of the military regime from democracy and overvalues the institutional concessions of the late 1980s. The second view produces an artificial dichotomy between a positive evaluation of a successful transition which has passed through a consolidation phase, and a negative vision of the present, designed mainly for political and internal consumption, evidenced in the terms "unfinished" and "incomplete" mentioned above.[3]

Whatever its theoretical or political origin, this ambiguity about the significance of the transition does not contribute to the construction of an overwhelming and positive public perception of democracy, as would befit the massive efforts expended on its behalf since 1990. A dissatisfied or skeptical evaluation of democracy predominates, exacerbated by its inherent problems and the social costs extracted in the work of confronting them. To explain this sense of inadequacy, the historical excuse reappears, strengthening the phantom of the authoritarian past, which takes on legitimacy as it becomes a part of the democratic debate. Thus, a vicious cycle is initiated, based more on theory than reality, arising more from the heat of debate than the unfolding of historical processes.

It seems to us that the persistence of this focus is not only unfortunate, but also scientifically inaccurate. This focus is an unnecessary obstacle, denying democracy its full opportunity to unfold and to overcome its imperfections, and it does not take empirical account of the totality of the Chilean political process since 1990.

Our proposal is to speak of democratization rather than transition. With this step, we accept that the change from authoritarianism to democracy has already taken place, and the transformation at the heart of the political system is recognized and affirmed: democratic legitimization of power; functioning institutions; the rule of law; respect for public and individual rights and liberties; and competitive elections among

---

3   A vision equidistant from these positions, based on the dynamics of the political process, is expressed by Boeninger (1997):380. On this discussion as it relates to the Chilean transition, see also the Catholic University of Chile's special issue of *Revista de Ciencia Política*, Vol. 16, No. 1-2, 1994.

legally constituted political parties. At the same time, this notion of democratization implies acceptance of a concept of *real* democracy, incorporating its essential trait of eternal perfectibility.[4] In other words, Chile is currently in a state of democracy, however incomplete or unfinished, and not one of transition, a phase which ended, with whatever characteristics one may ascribe to it, on March 11, 1990.

In accordance with this line of argumentation, the so-called authoritarian enclaves must be understood as imperfections of democracy and must be addressed as such, using the logic appropriate to a democratic context. The same goes for limitations in labor law or the other legislative subjects being considered by the Constitutional Tribunal. From a comparative perspective, according to the notion of ideal democracy set forth under the transitional focus, West Germany could not have considered itself a democracy until the fall of the Wall in 1989, since it had not completely consolidated its sovereignty. Neither could the United States have been called a democracy before the establishment of civil rights for the black population in the 1960s.

As a final consideration in our comparison between the concepts of transition and democratization, it is useful to look back at the origin of both in the literature of political science. In the book *Transitions to Democracy,* published in 1970, author D. Rustow sought to identify "the conditions which make democracy possible and prosperous," and proposed a "framework of a possible model of transition to democracy." As can be seen, the concept of transition is associated with a desirable, future change, conceived when there is still uncertainty and insecurity regarding its realization. This helps explain its greater proximity to the initial condition (the non-democratic system) than to the endpoint (democracy). The same phenomenon is illustrated by the title of the other influential work on this subject: *Transitions from Authoritarian Rule* (O'Donnell, Schmitter, Whitehead 1986).[5]

Twenty years after Rustow's book, Samuel Huntington published *The Third Wave: Democratization in the Late Twentieth Century* (1991). The expression "democratization" was used to refer to processes leading up to the arrival point (democracy), which was emphasized more than the starting point (autocracy). This focus does not ignore the fact that authoritarian remnants are present during democratization, but their persistence does not negate the recognition that democracy has been instituted. If new democracies are not viewed in this light, one cannot consider the transitions in the ex-communist countries to have been successful until all totalitarian characteristics have disappeared from their political cultures, which will take decades.

It would be tedious and, finally, impossible, to pin down in theory the exact point at which democracy can be considered to begin. However, it is useful to take account of the statements of prominent contemporary thinkers on the subject of democracy's perfectibility (admitting, thus, its imperfect nature). At the end of his second great work on democracy, R. Dahl (1993:408) writes: "We can state that in the future, as in the past, the rigorous demands of the democratic process will not be fully satisfied, nor will many of the theoretical and practical questions which it poses be completely resolved." Similarly, G. Sartori

---

4   According to the work of Von Beyme and Nohlen, *Systemwechsel* (System Transformation), which is defined as a "transformation in the manner of exercising political power." See Nohlen (1995):765.

5   The Spanish version was published by Ed. Paidós, Barcelona, 1994 (4 volumes), under the title of *Transiciones desde un gobierno autoritario.* An exhaustive criticism of this work can be found in Bermeo's article (1990).

(1994:4) notes: "A democratic system is situated upon a democratic deontology (concept of what is right), and what the democracy *is* cannot be disconnected from what the democracy *should be*. A democratic experience develops astride the gap between 'should be' and 'is,' along the path signaled by ideal aspirations, which always go beyond real conditions."

Thus, the failings of a democracy cannot alter the fact of its existence; they can even be seen to legitimize it. The Chilean democracy is imperfect, as they all are. But it is a democracy. It has traits which are authoritarian, as seen in France after Gaullist domination; nationalist, as in Germany or Russia; classist, as in England; or clientelistic, as in Italy. Yet fundamentally, Chile has a democratic political system.

3. THE CONSTRUCTION OF DEMOCRACY

Aside from the theoretical arguments presented above, the democratic nature of the Chilean political system can be clearly seen in its current reality. Every sphere of society shows solid, democratic foundations, which are more strongly rooted and stable than its problematic, unhealthy, or even anti-democratic traits (those which Huntington terms "contextual problems of the transition"). On the other hand, taking a long-term perspective, Chile's historical democratic foundations can easily be confused with the phenomena of the past few decades, as well as the transformations in society and the economy, whose authoritarian origin does not negate their contribution to the country's renewed democracy.

This complex network of components, of diverse origin and tendency, which makes up Chile's current political reality is aptly described with the expression "construction," used by Presidents Aylwin and Frei in their respective first messages to the Full Congress in 1990 and 1994. In 1990 President Aylwin stated: "History teaches us that nations are constructed through the continued action of successive generations. Nobody begins from zero. Children inherit the realities which their parents pass on to them. Each new government takes charge of a country handed over to it by the preceding one." President Frei noted in 1994: "It is our urgent task to construct, with the spiritual strength of our nation, a common democratic foundation."

The expression "construction" carries connotations of a common heritage in Chile's political system shared by all of the country's parties, sectors, and generations over the past decades. And this shared legacy must include the controversial constitutional framework of 1980, the roots of which lie in the texts of 1833 and 1925, and whose reforms of 1989, 1992, and 1996 have enjoyed broad contemporary consensus. For this reason, the points of controversy in the debate over constitutional reforms in recent years have been limited to very specific and limited subjects — the so-called authoritarian enclaves — the eventual and necessary reform of which can only take place through an agreement between the government and the opposition, given the balance of power in the Senate on this issue.

Taking for example the question of liberties, a prerequisite for every democracy, we observe that the economic liberty generated by the neoliberal economic model imposed in the 1980s has been increasingly accompanied by political liberty, emerging out of the liberalization at the end of the 1980s and amply manifested from the start of the 1990s. This has been joined by cultural liberty, which is still struggling to find its place at the end of this decade. Taken separately, each one of these liberties evidences a separate point of origin and path of development, but when taken together, they constitute essential parts of an overall "democratic construction." If we accept the evocative phrase according to which democracy is a "task shared by all," we are describing exactly this constructivist idea of democracy, which in Chile's case is a reality difficult to recognize but impossible to deny.

With this vision, the present description of the Chilean political system has been formulated, based upon both theoretical concepts of democratization and the practical appreciation of democratic construction. With this dual foundation, it is possible to aspire to a double objective. This is first to describe the Chilean political system in a dynamic framework, taking account of the political process as it occurs today; and second, to formulate an affirmation of Chile's current democratic status without inhibitions regarding the origin of its supporting factors.

II. Chilean Political Culture

Although it is a conceptually difficult term, political culture can be said to refer to the subjective dimension of political activity, to "the ideas, written or not, and the value systems which regulate the political action of the members of a society" (Fenner 1995:565).

The importance of political culture has increased in Latin America with the transition to democracy throughout the region.[6] At the same time, the viewpoints of modernization theory undeniably predominate (Almond and Verba 1965), giving rise to a lack of confidence in the success of democratization in Latin American countries, especially those with low levels of socioeconomic development. At the same time, remnants persist, although in very diminished form, of neo-Marxist structuralist positions, in which the concept of political culture is subordinated to the idea of the "superstructure" determined by economic power relationships.

In Chile's case, the debate over political culture centers on the existence of democratic values and beliefs versus authoritarian ones, as a result of the processes tending in one or the other direction over the past decades. Here it is important to examine the cultural traits which shaped the political behavior of the main protagonists of the transition, as well as the effects of the phenomenon of modernity upon Chilean society.

1. DEMOCRACY VERSUS AUTHORITARIANISM

First Thesis: *The democratization process in Chile is sustained by the prevalence of democratic beliefs and values, deriving both from longstanding national traditions and the vitality of the pluralistic society emerging after 1990.*

After 1990, democratic beliefs and values outweighed authoritarian tendencies. This can be explained by the broad appeal of the democratic idea, which encompasses the entire political spectrum, and by the association of the authoritarian culture with the military regime.

Within this hypothesis resides the basis for considering Chile as a case of re-democratization, keeping in mind that a great part of the democratic culture is present in historical memory from the pre-1973 era. Because of demographic changes in the country and the length of the authoritarian period, this democratic memory is present in only a segment of

---

6 See Thesing (1995). For an analysis of the Chilean authoritarian culture as manifested under the military regime, see Brunner (1983).

the population, and the rest only received it secondhand from those who were adults before 1973. At the same time, a new democratic culture is evident in the country, which began to develop with the 1987 liberalization and expanded with the plebiscite of 1988 and the 1989 presidential elections. This new culture is based on firsthand experience and represents a certain break with the idea of democracy as it existed in 1973, to which are attributed negative experiences and defects that contributed to its own collapse.

Yet according to another historical-political school of thought, Chile presents an example of historical continuity since its founding as a republic. This vision is based on a comparison with other Latin American countries, but it is lacking in self-criticism with respect to subjects such as the constitutional suspensions of 1891 and 1924-32, or the lack of adequate political participation until the middle of the current century. However, this view is profoundly rooted among the population and among politicians, and it is a basis for Chilean national pride. Thus, since 1990, this vision of the nation has served as a support for the consolidation of democracy.[7]

The persisting adherence to democratic principles, as explained in the previous paragraph, gained strength after 1990 with the addition of the former supporters of the authoritarian regime now pledged to democracy, along with left-wing adherents of the renewed socialist movement. On the one side, those who had supported the military coup based their position on the need to defend democracy against the danger faced by the country in 1973. On the other side, those who voiced radical criticism of the formal democracy before 1973, and played a militant role in the Allende government or its unofficial support groups, came to recognize the importance of democratic institutions. Thus, in the 1990s, public support for democracy is extremely broad.

Authoritarian characteristics, on the other hand, are identified with the military regime and stand in conflict with the country's predominating culture. Even for those who believed that the 1973 coup was justified, the stability of the country's current situation does not warrant the persistence of authoritarian traits.

Second Thesis: *The persistence of cultural remnants of extremism and authoritarianism, which sometimes emerge when issues are raised regarding the confrontations before 1990, present a threat that is more apparent than real.*

While the collective trauma from the breakdown of democracy with its manifestations of violence continues to be felt, it is becoming attenuated as normal relations resume among the participants in the conflict and as interpretations of recent history become more objective.

The period beginning in 1990 has seen various tense episodes, arising out of some of the most complex issues of the transition. These have included civilian-military relations, institutional confrontations, the judging of cases of human rights violations, terrorist acts (such as the assassination of Senator Jaime Guzmán in April 1991), the actions of the so-called "Network Army" in December 1991, the dismissal of a justice of the Supreme Court in 1992, the military "boinazo" demonstration in May 1993, and the Letelier-Contreras

---

7   An analysis of the origins of "order" as a cultural attribute of Chilean political organization can be found
     in the work of A.M. Stuven (1997):259-311. Another vision of the Chilean legalistic tradition as it affects
     the country's legal-political structure can be found in B. Bravo (1996). On the effects of the military regime
     on political ideas, see Huneeus (1987).

case. These events have led to speculation about the vulnerability of democracy and the possibility of renewed conflict. The frightening prospect of a return to hostile confrontation leads some among the population, including political leaders, to an exaggerated perception of danger compared to the true gravity of the situation.

Along with the events listed above, commemorative acts, personal testimony, and constant appeals to avoid repeating the drama of 1973 have served to maintain the national trauma in collective awareness (equivalent to the "Never again!" of the Holocaust). However, the direct repercussions of the crisis have diminished with the practice of democratic politics and with greater knowledge of the facts, as the legal and cultural obstacles to their discussion dissipate. Literature and the arts, as well as politics, have also contributed to this gradual recognition of reality. In addition, there is an evident decrease in the emotional or subjective charge of various interpretations, brought about not only through the increasing distance of the participants from the events, but also through generational change and the rise of new leaders in many fields of activity who lack firsthand connection with the events of authoritarianism or with the transitional phase.

2. LEGALISM AND FORMALISM

Thesis: *The legalistic procedure followed in the Chilean democratization process was not merely imposed as an act of political engineering or a solution agreed upon by the political class; it is a manifestation of a Chilean cultural trait present throughout the country's history.*[8]

This legalistic tradition has played a supporting role in the Chilean democratization process, adding a "reassuring" factor to the perceptions of a population faced with an institutional restructuring of the country.

The legal path of Chilean political change, initiated with the acceptance of the Constitution of 1980 and the successive so-called "political" laws, can be explained with reference to politics (as discussed later in this essay), but also to the national culture. There is a widespread belief among the Chilean population in legal omnipotence and the need for every agreement to have a legal expression; thus, the execution of any type of socio-economic reform must be expressed in law. Even during the authoritarian period, extensive legislative activity was carried out to regulate the regime itself (constitutional acts), or its provisional reforms and privatization measures.

Public attitudes since 1990 have included a mixture of enthusiasm, anticipation of change, and uncertainty. The presence of a legal framework and the tradition of respect for its enforcement have helped reassure the public during the political normalization process. This effect has also been evident each time a public problem or conflict has been officially regulated, whether by the creation of a law or the application of law by the courts. From this point of view, Radbruch's prerequisites for legal security have been fulfilled in Chile: security of law and security before the law.

In addition, a positive perception of the law has become widespread, as legal reforms are associated with the welfare of the population, improved access to justice and the protection of individual rights.

---

8   On the expression of the consensualist tradition in the Chilean process of the 1980s, see Chapter 8 of
    Boeninger (1997):367ff. In contrast, a critical vision of consensus in Chile is found in Moulian (1997):37ff.

3. CONSENSUS AND PRAGMATISM

Thesis: *The idea of political consensus, which was limited to the political class during the transition, has been culturally extended to the majority of the Chilean population. The use of consensus to reconcile differences and regulate conflicts arises from two sources. First, it is a reaction against the extreme polarization of the past three decades; and second, it represents an extension throughout society of a tradition of the Chilean political class.*

The expression "consensus" became part of the Chilean political vocabulary during the mid-1980s, after the period of protests which represented the high point of confrontations between the government and the opposition. Gradually, despite resistance and prejudice within the parties and among their factions, the idea of consensus became internalized as a cultural instrument of the political class. The most graphic expression of this concept is found in the word "Concertación" itself, which not only became the name of the campaign alliance and governing coalition, but also served as an appeal to the citizenry to set aside confrontational thinking. Consensus replaced the mindset of conflict and polarization which had reigned in Chilean politics since the 1970s, and it became established as a kind of yardstick for behavior in post-1990 Chile. Each intra-coalition or intra-party confrontation occurring during the second Concertación administration required special explanations to justify its break with the consensual spirit.

Nevertheless, this consensus is founded upon the "accommodation" of positions, with concessions made on all sides. Thus, as the perception of the danger of political debate lessens, greater differentiation or polarization of positions may become evident.

Second Thesis: *The restriction of political promises to those which are possible to achieve, which has characterized political programs and management since 1990, is a reaction to the ideology-driven, pie-in-the-sky government plans and programs of the 1960s and beyond; it also expresses the responsible, pragmatic mentality incorporated into the culture of Chilean public service since the 1980s.*

The political culture of the Chilean population includes a widespread conviction that the 1973 breakdown was due in great part to the parties' tendency to put forth radical programs having little to do with reality. This tendency led to a situation where stated goals were not expected to be achieved, but simply served a mobilizing function aimed at destroying existing structures.

This outlook has remained strong among Chileans and has spread to the political class. The result has been that recent government programs have been designed to be both technically and politically viable, with highly concrete and well-defined goals. This focus derives not only from the lessons of the past, but from the technocratic mentality shared by the economic sector and the civilian officials of the military government, whose ethos was based on monetary and fiscal discipline. In this approach, the democratic administrations have exhibited a kind of continuity of behavior with the previous regime, regardless of the substantive public policy differences between them.

4. DIMENSIONS OF MODERNITY

First Thesis: *As political changes occurred in Chile, components of a type of modernization initiated in the country in the 1980s have developed in complementary fashion. Economic liberty arose from neoliberalism and privatization and reached its full expression in the middle of that decade. Political liberty emerged as a product of the liberalization after 1986, expanding with the electoral campaigns of 1988 and 1989 and the institutional reinstallation of democracy. Finally, cultural liberty (equivalent to the "destape" or "uncorking of the bottle" in Spain) has been coming into full flower since 1990, influenced by the environment of economic and political freedom.*

The phenomenon of modernity referred to here is not comparable to the tendencies manifested in countries with fully consolidated democracies and developed socio-economic structures. Instead, it is unfolded in stages within a heterogeneous society. The cumulative evolution of the diverse manifestations of liberty is highly specific to Chile, because its presumed foundation was economic liberalism, which set the stage for the development of the other dimensions, while maintaining itself at the base of the entire phenomenon. In other words, in Chile being modern "includes" being liberal in the economic sphere. Anyone putting forth proposals of state intervention or regulation in the economic sphere is not considered modern in Chile today.

Second Thesis: *The social models of modernity in Chile have been predominantly formed by the examples of North American "Reaganomics" (the push toward privatization), Southeast Asia (the "tiger" model, competitiveness, educational systems), and post-Francoism (relativism, secularism). The combination of these influences results in a framework which is broad (including conservatives and progressives), but also contradictory and ambiguous in the translation of its ideas into concrete policies and programs.*

This hypothesis presents one of the most complex and difficult problems arising from Chilean political change, and also one with weighty consequences for the course of this process. The influences mentioned above combine to present a multifaceted view of modernity, in which diverse cultural viewpoints are superimposed, all attractive and dynamic, but fundamentally contradictory. Chilean society and its political leaders do not address or do not recognize the negative side of this phenomenon. Since the country's results have been positive, it is maintained that these influences have been positive as well, discounting the possibility that their diversity of origin constitutes a negative. Nevertheless, a few difficulties have been recognized. For example, educational reforms or productivity measurements based mainly on Southeast Asian models have already presented various problems of adaptation to Chile's European traditions.

III. The Institutional Dimension

The importance of the institutional dimension in Chile's democratization process lies in the regulated character of its tradition and in the legalism inherent in Chilean political culture. In fact, the Chilean transition could not have occurred without a tacit agreement on the part of the opposition accepting the validity, while not necessarily the legitimacy, of the institutional structures set up during the military regime, especially the Constitution of 1980.[9] This understanding was seen as a concession on the part of the opposition, as well as a ratification of the government's intention to legitimize its hold on power until the completion of the established period. As is well known, the opposition was victorious in the plebiscite of October 5, 1988, as well as in the presidential elections of December 1989, confirming, paradoxically, the functional capability of the authoritarian institutionality to bring about the transition. Between these two events, government and opposition held public negotiations regarding the reforms which must be included in the Constitution and its related legislation, the results of which were ratified by an extremely broad majority through a plebiscite held in June 1989.

A clear description of the Chilean transit to democracy along an institutional path was provided by Antonio Viera-Gallo, writing in 1989: "The plebiscite of 1989 clarified the Chilean political process. On the one hand, it remained evident that the transit to democracy enjoyed broad support among the citizens. The majority of the country rejected the continuation [of the authoritarian regime]. At the same time, the specific form that the step from authoritarianism to democracy would take was outlined. The transition had to be undertaken within the current legal structure," (Geisse and Ramírez 1989:15).

Thus, Chile's institutional structures played a decisive role in its democratization. They not only provided a legitimate regulatory framework for the political process, but also they served as a channel for democratic debate and for the reform and improvement of their own laws and regulations. This is not to say that the reform of various aspects of Chile's institutionality was not necessary or urgent, or that the debate surrounding this reform was not accompanied in the following years by a certain degree of tension or conflict within the Chilean political system. Yet what is most significant is that the institutions' role was more central in Chile than in other countries that have undergone political transformations.

This institutional dimension must be contrasted with the role played by individual leaders in other political cultures. The difference can be seen in neighboring countries such as Argentina and Peru, where the presidential figure is the determining factor in the implementation of institutional changes, the intent of which is often to enhance the incumbent's own electability. In Chile, on the other hand, two reforms to the presidential term of office have been undertaken, both of which shortened it, and the subject remains on the public agenda (Cea 1993:221-226).

---

9   The starting point of the agreement on institutionality arose out of a seminar organized by ICHEH on July 27-28, 1984, entitled "A Constitutional Legal-Political System for Chile," lectures which were published in 1985 under the title *Una salida político-institucional para Chile*. On this occasion, Patricio Aylwin referred to the legitimacy of the 1980 Constitution, indicating the barrier it could pose to political consensus: "I cannot expect that General Pinochet will recognize his Constitution as illegitimate; neither can he demand that I recognize it as legitimate." He added: "How can this impasse be resolved without humiliating somebody? There is only one way: deliberately avoiding the topic of the transactional legitimacy of the transition, while at the same time demonstrating to the people the importance of legal standards to govern political processes."

1. THE FUNCTION OF THE CONSTITUTION

As noted above, the validity of the Constitution of 1980 during the Chilean democratization process contrasts markedly with the controversy surrounding its drafting and ratification, not only among the opposition to the authoritarian government, but also in circles close to the regime, which expressed reservations about the plebiscite mechanism and several of the articles. The persistence of this constitutional framework through almost a decade of opposition and political confrontation can be explained not only by its functionality at that moment in time, but also by the weight historically accorded to the Constitution in the Chilean political structure.[10] In 1925, the occasion of the previous constitutional plebiscite, the requirements for the constituent process were not followed with complete precision; yet the approved text not only guided the subsequent political normalization, but also remained in uninterrupted force for nearly a half-century.[11]

On the other hand, there was no other reasonable option for the opposition in 1987 than to accept the rules of the game dictated by the regime, which at least offered the possibility of electoral victory within its framework, as actually occurred. From the regime's point of view, the risk of losing was offset by the dividend of historical legitimacy in the democratic transfer of power, while the stability of the rules was guaranteed through the mechanisms of the Constitution itself, impeding the creation of an absolute counterweight to the president or radical reform of the Constitution and its fundamental political laws.

Nevertheless, at the end of the 1990s, a more focused confrontation has arisen with respect to the political effects of the constitutional articles. The designation of institutional senators at the end of 1997 and the decision of the commander-in-chief of the Armed Forces to exercise his right to a lifelong Senate seat have brought the constitutional question into the public debate on terms analogous to those of a decade ago. This new discussion was strongly influenced by the results of the 1997 parliamentary election, which consolidated the government-opposition equilibrium for the purpose of carrying out constitutional reforms.

First Thesis: *The continuing legitimacy of the 1980 Constitution has helped maintain political stability since 1990.*

Reservations about the Constitution's legitimacy of origin and public criticism of the so-called authoritarian enclaves have not affected institutional stability; indeed, they have fulfilled a useful function in the democratization process. However, the continued phenomena of political equalization in Congress and polarization of positions on the Constitution raise questions about the continuation of political stability on the same terms as seen up to 1997.

Once the question of the legitimacy of the 1980 Constitution was resolved through negotiations in 1987-89 between the authoritarian regime and the democratic opposition, the Constitution served as an institutional framework for the change in the political regime and the transfer of power to the first two democratic administrations.

---

10   Using the most integrated concept of a constitution, above and beyond its narrow rational-legal framework, the 1980 Constitution has played a political role which goes beyond the original debate as to its legitimacy. On the variety of constitutional concepts, see Merino Merchán et. al. (1995):80 ff.

11   For the historical-political context of the drafting and approval of the 1925 Constitution, see Volume III of Gonzalo Vial's Historia de Chile (1996):531 ff.

Since 1990, constitutional reform has consistently been a subject for political debate, along with criticism of the form and content of numerous constitutional articles. However, there is tacit acceptance of the validity of the Constitution and its organic laws, as well as the necessity for strict respect of this legal structure. Because of this requirement for valid rules of the game, the Constitution has been a fundamental element of Chile's political stability since 1990 and has served as a secure framework for the country's socio-economic development.

The constitutional debate has value in itself, since it touches upon the central issues of the political life of the community, under the assumption that they must be integrated in its fundamental laws. Thus, in spite of the intensity of the criticism of the 1980 text and the arguments that surround it, which arise from the ongoing reservations about its legitimacy of origin, this criticism has added vitality to the questioned constitutional text itself by stimulating discussion. In addition, during various crisis situations, the governing coalition has obtained institutional victories through appeals to the 1980 text, as with the impeachment of a Supreme Court justice by both houses of Congress in 1993.

The debate about the so-called authoritarian enclaves has advanced considerably since the second half of 1995. This debate has ventured into sensitive territory as it revisited the discussions of 1987, but the ensuing disagreements could at no time be classified as threats to overall stability. On the contrary, the results of these discussions have signaled that changes to the Constitution in these areas would enjoy broad acceptance. In other words, reforms to the Constitution will take place at some point because they are necessary and legitimate under conditions of national stability and normality. Yet, in the meantime, reform discussions are not a threat to stability; instead, they demonstrate the vitality of the democratizing debate, as they test the participants' capacity for consensus in working to construct a new framework of political relationships.

Second Thesis: *The current Constitution includes elements that reflect national traditions before 1973, the opportunistic needs of the authoritarian regime, and the requirements of the transition. Pressure for reform is directed at both the authoritarian and the traditional aspects.*

Excepting the so-called authoritarian enclaves, whose importance has already been mentioned, and new material such as constitutional guarantees and other expressions of legal modernization, the 1980 Constitution is chiefly a reflection of the Chilean constitutional tradition and accentuates tendencies exhibited in the reforms starting in the 1940s.[12]

For example, the pronounced presidentialism and the consolidation of a strong national government in spite of formal regionalization are integral elements of Chilean constitutional tradition. Similarly, the uneven nature of the text on the subject of reform follows the tendencies of 1833 and 1925 (Cea 1990:267ff.).

At the same time, it is evident that the so-called authoritarian enclaves make these historical tendencies more rigid, since they incorporate new provisions which neutralize rather than strengthen the president in a democratic context. Furthermore, the addition of the so-called institutional senators to a binomial system impedes constitutional reform, because the participation and cooperation of these senators is required to achieve the necessary quorum for reform.

---

12 The nature of the new Constitution, together with the persistence of traditional Chilean constitutional standards in the 1980 text, is explained in a comprehensive study by Silva Bascuñán (1997), Vol. III, pp. 243ff.

In any case, the 1980 text, applied in a democratic context, accentuates traditional Chilean constitutional difficulties. The text establishes a strong presidential regime, but one which is impotent in the face of entrenched opposition in the Senate, as well as surrounded by autonomous corporative bodies.

Thus, the need for present and future reform does not only arise merely from the constitutional remnants of authoritarianism, but also from longstanding imperfections of the Chilean constitutional order. It is possible that this reform must wait until both tendencies are clearly evident in order to achieve the necessary consensus for action without endangering political stability.

2. THE FORM OF THE STATE

Paradoxically, the impulse toward the decentralization of the Chilean state arose during the first months of the military government, sparked by a commission constituted for that purpose, the National Commission for Administrative Regionalization (Conara), which enjoyed the support of the United Nations Development Program. Of course the nature of the authoritarian regime and its determination to maintain the traditional unitary form of the State prevented the implemented reforms from bringing about a new territorial distribution of administrative authority in favor of regional and local governments, whose delegated power actually lessened in comparison to the situation before 1973.

However, within the framework of this initiative — known as the regionalization of the country — the military regime devolved social services, especially education and public health, to the municipal level, in accordance with the principles applied by the neoliberal technocrats to social policies. This process, arising out of the socio-economic sphere, became a decisive element in the democratic structuralization later achieved by local governments and administrations.

On the other hand, the dilemma of harmonizing the form of the unitary State with the functional and legal imperative of decentralization constituted an ongoing challenge for all the political parties, not only for the Concertación. The motto of bringing "decision-making to the people" implied improved democracy and greater effectiveness, along with the possibility of diluting the centers of power represented by the government and the opposition.

First Thesis: *In spite of reform efforts, the centralized tendency of the Chilean state has been maintained, both in decision-making authority and in political culture and behavior.*

Decentralization has been a representative and influential idea in Chilean development strategies for more than 10 years, evident in government programs, political debate, and technical-academic reflections (Boisier 1993). The authoritarian regime carried out regionalizing and decentralizing reforms in a merely formal manner (such as the transfer of services to the municipalities). However, since 1990, two great substantive reforms have taken place at the regional and county [comuna] levels (Nogueira and Luksic 1992; Varas and Mohor 1992).

Nevertheless, the tendency towards centralizing unitarism persists in decision-making and especially in political behavior. This phenomenon can be seen in the importance of ministers, as compared to regional leaders or mayors, in making fundamental decisions that affect public policy.

Second Thesis: *The 1991 constitutional reform addressing regional governments and county administration, along with the complementary measures of 1996 and 1997, constitutes the country's principal institutional democratization measure since 1990.*

The importance of this reform (Law No. 19,907 of November 12, 1991) resides principally in the democratization of the selection of local authorities. It established the popular election of mayors and council members, which took place for the first time in June 1992. At the same time, the reform created a regulatory framework for the municipalities, establishing them as public corporations with administrative autonomy, legal status, and independent resources.

Regional governments were also established, with various areas of autonomy and authority. These are presided over by the regional governor *[intendente]*, named by the president, and the regional council, elected by county-level representatives.

In its consideration of the reform initiative, the government specified that the measure "reaffirmed the unitary character of the structure of the State, while at the same time promoting its administrative decentralization."

In early 1996, a "reform of the reform" was undertaken, instituting the direct election of mayors, which began with the municipal elections held on October 27 of the same year.

Third Thesis: *The amalgamation of centralized structures and ways of thinking with decentralizing reforms and practices has produced institutional redundancy and administrative gaps.*

In practice, the opposing tendencies represented by centralized regulations and traditions, on the one hand, and decentralizing reforms and practices on the other hand, have produced confusion with respect to the authority and responsibilities of the various levels of government involved.

This phenomenon is especially evident in the large cities, where the magnitude of infrastructure projects or public service administrations leads them to be directed by the central government along with the regional and local administrations. This overlapping of authority produces imbalances, which can result in the concentration of power at particular levels (as in the case of some mayors who have become powerful figures). However, on the other extreme, some problems which are difficult to solve (such as pollution in Santiago) tend to fall between the cracks as no one takes clear responsibility for decision-making, with the consequent deficiency in public management.

3. THE PRESIDENTIAL REGIME

It is evident that interest in reforming the Chilean presidential regime declined as the transition advanced and its success was consolidated. It is interesting to note that the constitutional drafting body formed by the opposition to the authoritarian regime, the so-called "Group of Twenty-Four," officially approved the semi-presidential regime as the most suitable for Chile's democratic future, and that several of its leading members later served in the first democratic administration, during which the subject of the political regime was never called into question. These developments do not reflect the irrelevance of the issue but rather the capacity to foresee the tendency of the political culture, the need to accept the current constitutional order for the transition, and the advantage of the institution of the presidency in bringing about democratic normalization.

What is certain is that during the seven years of democracy since 1990, the only references to political reform have been isolated voices motivated by the necessity of balancing intra-coalition interests to achieve success in the presidential elections, since both the Concertación and its opposition contain two roughly equal political forces, each of which aspires to nominate a presidential candidate from their ranks. Thus, the motivation for reform is of an instrumental and electoral nature, unrelated to the presumed incompatibility between presidentialism and a multi-party system, as was postulated among the causes of the institutional collapse in 1973.

It is more useful to view the presidential regime in light of concrete political events in Chile since 1990 than through the theoretical prism prevalent during the authoritarian regime (Rehren 1993:15-38). From this perspective, it is possible to demonstrate not only the accomplishments of the institution of the presidency in Chile's normalization, but also the opportunities that may arise from the adaptation of its traditional form to the challenges of democratic governance. It should be added that governance in the Chilean context since 1990 must be evaluated according to the achievement of the protagonists' own objectives, especially those of the government itself.

First Thesis: *The current presidentialist structure has played a stabilizing role during the democratization process, because it is rooted in the democratic political tradition of Chile.*

In spite of the objections of various critics (Godoy 1992; Linz and Valenzuela 1994), Chilean presidentialism, accentuated by the 1980 text, has played a role in democratic stabilization, especially because the presidential figure is so closely identified with the Chilean democratic tradition. The authoritarian regime, in spite of its use of the presidential title, is viewed as an anomaly or exception within this tradition.

At the same time, it is generally agreed that the difficult political conditions after 1990, along with the challenge of institutional reconstruction, required a government embodied in a strong central authority. This is even clearer when one considers the multi-party framework of the governing coalition and the traumatic memories of disorder before the 1973 crisis.

Second Thesis: *The strength of the executive in government administration contrasts with its limitations in the legislative sphere, stemming from the party and electoral systems.*

After 1990, the much-studied contrast (Fernández Baeza 1991:129-149) between the president's executive strength and legislative weakness increased even further. The real cause, while not a formal one, of this widening discrepancy can be found in the country's party and electoral systems.

First, the multi-party system not only affects the president's legislative influence through the presence of an opposition seeking to block the government's initiatives, but also through the complexity arising within the governing coalition itself. The difficulty of achieving agreement on presidential initiatives in certain sensitive areas (laws addressing human rights or the privatization of utility companies, for example), has highlighted the weakness of the chief executive within his own coalition.

Furthermore, the binomial electoral system and the addition of institutional senators to the Senate have made it difficult in practice for the executive to achieve the majority necessary for passing legislation, especially in areas requiring a special majority.

Third Thesis: *The power of the National Congress, as opposed to that of the executive, may be defined as the capacity to block, rather than an oversight and control function.*

The traditional prerogatives of the legislature vis-à-vis the executive branch are specified under Chilean constitutional law: oversight by the Chamber of Deputies and political judgment in the Senate. However, these powers have little practical effect, as evidenced by the numerous investigative commissions constituted in the Chamber which have not resulted in sanctions. Instead, the parliament's true balancing power is found in its capacity to prevent a legislative proposal sent to Congress by the executive from being discussed. The majority held by the opposition in the full Congress is sufficient to achieve this as a result of the binomial system and the institutional senators. It occurred in practice with a package of legal and constitutional reforms sent to Congress by the administration in August 1995. This controversial package, representing the most extensive political-legislative battle since 1990, was never debated in the chambers of Parliament because the opposition was able to block discussion on the subject.

Fourth Thesis: *The power of the representative branches of government — the president and Congress — are excessively limited by the autonomous constitutional bodies, which include judicial, regulatory, economic, and corporate entities.*

The 1980 text expanded the number of constitutionally established entities and granted them greater autonomy and authority. The comptroller, the electoral administration and the Department of Justice had always enjoyed this status. To these were added numerous others: a new Constitutional Tribunal, much more powerful than that established in 1970; the Central Bank, redesigned following the model of the German Bundesbank; and the National Security Council, dominated by the armed and internal security forces and created through a specific constitutional statute. The function of this network of autonomous constitutional bodies has been analyzed to date only on a theoretical level. However, several practical manifestations of their power to limit other branches of government have been evident, such as the influence of the Constitutional Tribunal upon the legislative process.

Fifth Thesis: *Under the presidential regime, the Concertación of Parties for Democracy has operated as the most stable and successful pluralistic governing coalition in the history of Chile.*

Until the first quarter of the present century, Chile's political system was characterized by strong presidentialism and the existence of dominant parties, leading to the formation of governments in which the president exercised power personally with support from his party. Coalitions were relatively ephemeral and were constituted and dissolved in reaction to transient crises, for which cabinets were also formed. This situation was clearly evident in the poorly-named "Parliamentary Republic" between 1891 and 1924, when ministers were politically responsible before Parliament. Starting with the reestablishment of institutional normality in 1932, before the emergence of a strong constellation of parties, coalitions began to form, although under the dominance of the majority party at the time, the Radicals. Coalitions were also formed between 1952 and 1964, as well as during the Popular Unity government (1970-1973), when the Radical Party no longer commanded a majority. Yet none of these coalitions ever lasted for a full legislative period, nor was any alliance able to win two consecutive presidential elections, along with various parliamentary and municipal elections.

The Concertación arose out of the political liberalization of the second half of the 1980s (Ortega 1992), and it has survived to the present day. Its parties worked together on the governmental agenda, and from their ranks were recruited cabinet members and other high officials of the two democratic administrations. Nevertheless, the Concertación remains a pluralist conglomeration of the center-left, whose members have been mutually antagonistic during a great part of the Republic's history since 1932 and especially during the crisis culminating in 1973.

Sixth Thesis: *Since 1990, cabinet members of both administrations have been chosen through presidential confidence and supra-party considerations. The stability of the cabinets can be explained by the effectiveness of this selection method as well as the achievements of the governments themselves.*

The task of forming a coalition government in 1990 under a presidential regime during a phase of transition from authoritarianism was a difficult one, not only because of its unprecedented nature, but also because of the persisting trauma of the Allende government's "quota system," as well as the recent authoritarian experience of cabinets constituted through the distribution of areas of influence among the Armed Forces and the powerful technocratic groups developed under the military regime.

Respect for presidential prerogative in the naming of high officials of both democratic administrations was institutionalized in Article 32, No. 9 of the Constitution. According to this text, the president has the special attribution "to name and remove at his pleasure the ministers of State, undersecretaries, superintendents, and governors." In order to reconcile this authority with the parties' competition for positions and to examine the technical suitability of specific persons for particular functions, a committee was formed to propose candidates to the president, consisting of political representatives of the coalition's principal parties. Under President Aylwin, this team consisted of the ministers Boeninger (DC) and E. Correa (PS/PPD); under President Frei, the ministers G. Arriagada (DC), G. Correa (PS), and V. M. Rebolledo (PPD), who worked with party leaders as well as non-political groups supporting the government.

While both processes were similar, some differences can be noted. In 1990, the Concertación was a grouping of numerous parties, including various smaller ones, all of which were represented in the Cabinet. In 1994, the coalition had shrunk to four parties, divided into two subgroups. In addition, by 1994 the coalition had gained the benefit of experience during a period of government, and thus the new team understood more clearly the nature and duties of each position. Finally, the 1994 program, as we shall see, differed greatly from that of 1990, which was strongly influenced by the issues and pressures of the transition.

Seventh Thesis: *Compared to the pre-1973 period, the legislative power of the administrations since 1990 has been more limited, in spite of their expanded budgetary prerogatives.*

This circumstance, as well as being relevant to hypotheses about the presidential regime, is essential to the question of governance. The problem raised here is the government's ability to act, both to implement its program and to react to unforeseeable events.

Undoubtedly, the greater power lies in the preparation and execution of the budget. The executive branch possesses various advantages in budgetary formulation: the exclusive legal initiative for its discussion, the fact that the Congress cannot reduce spending levels, and the security that the budget will be accepted as proposed if it is not approved in Congress within 60 days. This last constitutional disposition (Art. 64) reversed the prerogative exercised by Congress at the beginning of the 1891 civil war, which was a continuing source of tension between the branches of government until 1973. And while Congress has been prevented since 1980 from reducing proposed spending levels, it is also prohibited from raising them, thus putting an end to the earlier Congressional tendency to approve budgetary deficits, with all of their inflationary consequences.

Legislative power, on the other hand, is more limited by the formal dispositions of the Constitution, according to which the executive possesses broad freedom of action only if it enjoys a sufficient parliamentary majority. To achieve this, proposals have been put forth with the goal of forming a party superstructure which succeeds in controlling more than 34% of Congressional votes, and thus is able to use the electoral system to its advantage.

Nevertheless, it remains necessary to examine other instruments of power possessed by the executive since 1990, whose real effect has been little studied. It must be kept in mind that the drafters of the 1980 text had in mind a political system dominated by an authoritarian figure, at least in the period before 1989. Thereafter, the powers conferred by the Constitution have been available to democratic leaders. Elements worthy of further study include presidential leadership and the regulatory capacities of the executive.

Eighth Thesis: *The number of public officials the president may directly appoint has been limited, and the democratic administrations have been obligated to work with a relatively independent civil service.*

On December 5, 1986, the authoritarian regime established the structure of public administration and the regulations governing its officials, through the Constitutional Organic Law on the Basis of Organization of the State. On September 23, 1989, as the regime neared the end of its era, it established the law known as the Administrative Statute, which regulated the vocation of public officials in detail. Common to both bodies of law, which complement the text of the 1980 Constitution, are the political restrictions placed upon government officials and the limitation on executive appointments, whereby only five hundred officials may be named by the president. This limitation is in line with usual practice among the civil services of large democracies. However, it was put in place only after an almost complete turnover of public officials, accomplished over 17 years, with the broadest possible discretional freedom.

In consequence, the democratic government found itself with a multitude of state bureaucrats, both at the national and local levels, who were appointed by the authoritarian regime and protected by rules against dismissal. At the same time, the government lacked the capacity to designate a reasonable number of political appointees. A reform to the law was achieved in 1990, increasing the number of political appointees to 1,000. Meanwhile, the government was forced to resort to hiring technical personnel as contractors in order to carry out its programs, a measure which provoked great debate among the opposition.

IV. Elections and Political Parties

As we consider the institutional framework of the political system, the importance of opportunities for citizen participation in political decisionsmust be taken into account. This may also be called "legitimization" — an essential element of Chile's political transformation resided in the operation of the parties and the holding of elections, which conferred democratic legitimacy upon the origin and exercise of power.

Since the beginning of the democratization process, general, presidential, parliamentary, and municipal elections have been held in Chile (1989, 1992, 1993, 1996, and 1997), organized and carried out under conditions of full normality. The political parties, regulated by law for the purpose of participating in elections, function legally and freely.

Paradoxically, scholarly studies of the Chilean political parties are not as numerous as the parties' importance in the political process would suggest, and researchers have occupied themselves more with the parties' formal and programmatic aspects than with analysis from the points of view of political science or sociology.[13]

Scientific attention has been focused on the characteristics of the binomial system (M. Fernández 1989) or the study of specific elections (Auth 1994; Friedmann and Micco 1992). Few studies systematically examine the variables of the party and electoral systems as they are manifested in the Chilean case.

At the same time, the periodicity of elections and the reliability of the official data easily permit systematic study, especially if one considers that three elections will have taken place in the course of less than four years (municipal in 1996, parliamentary in 1997, and presidential in 1999).

1. ELECTIONS AND THE ELECTORAL SYSTEM

First Thesis: *Chilean elections have been properly organized and carried out, which has helped legitimize the political process. Electoral participation, however, has gradually declined, as measured by rates of voter registration, attendance at the polls, and the casting of valid ballots.*

In Chile it is obligatory to vote (Art. 16 of the Constitution), but registration is not mandatory. In addition, the sanctions for neglecting to vote are not applicable in practice. In the past, it has been possible to sustain statistically that participation in elections is high, considering the percentage of registered voters among the total population. However, this proportion changed in 1997, as the voter rolls declined by almost a million people.

The organization of elections has been irreproachable, being subject to detailed regulations, supervised by independent bodies of constitutional rank, and linked to a long tradition of correctness in the country's elections, especially since the great electoral reform of 1957 ended the practice of bribery. The validity of election procedures is reflected empirically in the number of complaints presented in each election, which refer to votes nullified by manipulated results.

Given the above characteristics, Chilean elections have served a legitimizing function in the democratization process, giving those elected an indisputable mandate and promoting civic education and participation among the population.

---

13   See: García (1998), Scully (1992), and Saffirio (1994):63-113.

In the elections of 1997, however, the percentage of defaced and blank ballots was especially high, reaching one-sixth of total votes cast. This phenomenon has not been sufficiently analyzed, but it is presumed that it indicates growing dissatisfaction with politicians and the current practice of politics.

Second Thesis: *The binomial electoral system has not altered the multi-party framework, but it has compelled parties to form coalitions.*

The binomial system was first studied by the authoritarian regime in the mid-1980s, in the hope of bringing about a change in the Chilean system of multiple parties. Two points of view were already evident in the debate of that time (Cea et al. 1988; Fernández 1986:75-93). Adherents of Duverger's thesis of direct causation believed that a majority-based system would bring about the convergence of a two-party framework. This would remove two chronic causes of Chilean political instability: multiple parties and polarization. A competing theory, using an empirical and historical focus, held that in the Chilean case the system of multiple parties was too entrenched to be broken up through reforms to the electoral system; thus, the most effective remedy would be to adjust the electoral system to this reality, making corrections which would impede the excessive proliferation and segmentation of parties.

The regime set forth the binomial electoral system in a 1986 law (Law No. 18,586 of October 1) which was later adjusted, permitting inter-party agreements (Law No. 18,825 of August 17, 1989), a signal of recognition of the country's multi-party reality.

The exigencies of binomial candidacies and coalitions obligated the parties to establish national alliances with adjustments in each district, which became known as "coalitions by omission." Among the consequences of this approach was the impossibility of knowing how many votes each party could muster on the national level for parliamentary elections, since none was able to present candidates across the entire country.

Third Thesis: *The municipal electoral system permits a high level of proportionality and allows all parties of any significance to be represented.*

The system established for municipal elections in the 1991 constitutional reform democratizing local governments was defined as "proportional representation in the distributed total method," permitting "electoral sub-agreements among parties or federations within each list." The number of positions open for election varied between six and 10, according to the size of the municipality.

This system, similar to that applicable to parliamentary elections before 1973, allows great proportionality among the parties presenting candidates and prevents the exclusion of parties of any significance, as occurs in elections for the national Congress, especially with the Communist Party. Furthermore, while associations among parties are permitted, the so-called "coalitions by omission" are not found at this level, since the preference systems among the parties operate through the number of candidates on the list contributed by each party.

Fourth Thesis: *The continuation of the current electoral system will depend more on election results leading to shifts in majority status than on the political will to reform it.*

In spite of the disadvantages of the present electoral system and the opinion of the governing coalition on the subject, serious obstacles to its reform have arisen.

On the one hand, reform of the system would require a special majority and thus the concurrence of the opposition. However, the current opposition is not in favor of reform, since it sees itself favored by binomialism. At the same time, reform would imply altering the basis upon which all members of Congress have been elected. This argument is not explicitly made, but it can help explain the lack of enthusiasm for debate on the subject of reform.

The only viable impetus for reform of the electoral system would thus be a change in majority status, brought about by general elections, which would convert reform into a means of salvation for key decision-makers faced with a significant electoral loss.

The latest attempt at reform, with its proposal of "corrected proportionality," has met with repeated rejection by the opposition. The most effective option might therefore be a mixed mechanism, which would maintain the current system but add to it a number of parliamentary members elected through the distributed-total method (Fernández 1995).

2. PARTIES AND THE PARTY SYSTEM

First Thesis: *The multi-party structure of the Chilean system since 1990, which reflects the country's historical tradition, differs from the pre-1973 system in the context in which the parties operate.*

The number and distribution of parties since 1989 is practically identical to the picture presented before 1973: five leading parties — two of the right, two of the left, and one of the center — along with three parties of varying importance which are denied parliamentary representation by the binomial system, but which increasingly play a role in the political scene. This is especially true of the Communist Party, which in 1997 obtained 8% of the popular vote.

The great difference between the two systems is found in two complementary elements. The social context of 1973 led to increases in what Sartori terms "the distance between the parties," in an atmosphere charged with conflict, polarization, and inflexibility. This contrasts sharply with the climate of consensus and constructive participation prevailing since 1990. Similarly, the programmatic and ideological foundations of the parties changed radically between the two periods. The collapse of the socialist bloc, along with the globalization and privatization of the international economy, have decisively influenced the "renewal" of Chilean party platforms, with consequently greater opportunities for understanding among them.

Second Thesis: *In their internal organization and operation, the political parties exhibit the same traits as in 1973. The new organizations (the Party for Democracy or PPD, and the Independent Democratic Union or UDI) show more modern characteristics, although they are highly restricted by the traditionally dominant styles and by the origin of both parties, arising from historical political tendencies.*

In contrast with the transformations seen in the area of doctrine and programs, the Chilean political parties have not shown profound innovations in internal organization and operation. They maintain oligarchical and centralized procedures for recruiting and selecting leaders as well as for making important decisions. At the same time, little mobility is evident in party leadership positions, which are held by a small group of persons largely stemming from the pre-1973 elite.

The parties have had severe difficulties in opening themselves up to society and becoming receptive to its needs and opinions. Surveys show a gulf of separation and alienation between the parties and the population, along with an image of "self-barricading" by parties with respect to the subjects they address and the initiatives they undertake.

Third Thesis: *The legal framework governing the Chilean parties is more regulatory than functional, lacking fundamental rules such as those relating to public financing of parties and elections.*

The Political Parties Law was created under the authoritarian regime in 1987, when a restrictive vision of the function and even the doctrine of political parties prevailed. At that time, Article 8 of the Constitution was still in force, limiting pluralism and excluding specific groups according to their views.

The operation of the parties since 1990 and the holding of elections have exposed numerous gaps and imperfections in this legislation. In practice, the parties have attempted to skirt the regulations, or have adapted to them in a superficial manner, maintaining their own internal customs and designations. The most serious of the deficiencies is the absence of regulation and control of campaign financing, which is addressed in the law only through a prohibition on receiving foreign support. It is noteworthy that the highest levels of campaign spending, especially in parliamentary elections, are seen among the parties of the right. The substantial private donations received by these parties are subject to no limit or control.

Conclusions

The Chilean political system is currently undergoing a post-authoritarian democratization process. The use of the term "transition" would impute a provisional character to this system, thus disregarding the consistent democratic construction achieved by the country in a framework of political, economic, and social stability since 1990.

Without a doubt, the Chilean political system will undergo various changes in the near future, and it will be affected by tensions and adjusted through reforms. Yet these phenomena, aside from their emotional repercussions, do not necessarily imply the absence of democracy or the continuation of an intermediate situation of "transit" between authoritarianism and democracy. On the contrary, these are characteristics of democracy itself. Their outcome will not be a regression to authoritarianism, but a consolidation of democracy's true foundation on a higher plane of civilization.

This essay attempted to analyze, using a historical and empirical focus, the characteristics of the Chilean political system as it has been structured and as it currently functions, rather than how it should ideally be configured.

BIBLIOGRAPHICAL REFERENCES

Almond, G., S. Verba, eds., 1965. *The Civic Culture*. Boston: Little & Brown.

Arriagada, G., 1994. "Inauguración del III Congreso de la Asociación Chilena de Ciencia Política." Santiago, July 1994.

Auth, J., 1994. "Elecciones presidenciales y parlamentarias de 1993." *Estudios Públicos* 54.

Aylwin, P., 1992. *La transición chilena: Discursos escogidos 1990-1992*. Santiago: Ed. Andrés Bello.

Bermeo. N., 1990. "Rethinking Regime Change." *Comparative Politics* 22(3), April 1990, pp. 359-377.

Boeninger, E., 1997. *Democracia en Chile: Lecciones para la gobernabilidad*. Santiago: Ed. Andrés Bello.

Boissier, S. "Descentralización en Chile: Antecedentes, situación actual y desafíos futuros." *Contribuciones* 4(93).

Bravo, B., 1996. *El Estado de derecho en Chile*. Santiago: Ed. P. Universidad Católica de Chile.

Brunner, J. J., 1983. *La cultura autoritaria*. Santiago: Flacso.

Cea J. L. et al., 1988. "Sistema electoral y Congreso Nacional." *Revista de Ciencia Política*, special edition. Santiago, September 1988.

Cea, J. L., 1990. "Rigidez constitucional y estabilidad institucional." *Revista Universitaria de Valparaíso*, p. 267 ff.

——. 1993. "Implicancias constitucionales de la redacción del período presidencial." *Revista Chilena del Derecho* 20 (May-Dec.), pp. 221-226.

Dahl, R., 1989. *La poliarquía, participación y oposición*. Madrid: Ed. Tecnos. (Original version published by Yale University Press in 1971).

——. 1993. *La democracia y sus críticos*. 2nd ed. Barcelona: Ed. Paidós.

Fenner, Ch., 1995. "Politische Kultur." In: D. Nohlen, ed. *Wörterbuch Staat und Politik*. Bonn.

Fernández Baeza, M., 1986. "Sistemas electorales. Sus problemas y opciones para la democracia chilena." In: Fundación F. Ebert. *Sistemas electorales y representación política en América Latina*. Madrid: pp. 75-93.

——. 1989. "El proyecto de ley electoral chilena de agosto de 1988. Análisis de sus fundamentos y alcances." In: *Estudios Sociales* 59, Trimestre 1.

——. 1991. "El Primer Ministro dentro del sistema presidencial: Una propuesta para Chile." In: D. Nohlen y M. Fernández, eds. *Presidencialismo vs. parlamentarismo en América Latina*. Caracas: Ed. Nueva Sociedad Caracas, pp. 129-149.

——. 1995. "Binominalismo y proporcionalidad. Una fórmula viable para la reforma electoral del Parlamento chileno." *Papeles de trabajo* PEP 50. Corporación Tiempo 2000. Santiago.

Friedmann, R. y S. Micco., 1992. *Reforma municipal y elecciones comunales en Chile*. Santiago: CED.

García, A. M., 1998. *La ley orgánica de los partidos políticos*. Santiago: Ed. Jurídica de Chile.

Garretón, M. A., 1995. *Hacia una nueva era política: Estudio sobre las democratizaciones*. Santiago: F.C.E.

Geisse, F. and J. Ramírez, 1989. *La reforma constitucional*. Santiago: Cesoc.

Godoy, O., ed., 1992. *Cambio de régimen político*. Santiago: Ed. P. Universidad Católica de Chile.

Huneeus, C., 1987. *Los chilenos y la política: Cambio y continuidad en el autoritarismo*. Santiago: ICHE.

Huntington, S., 1991. *The Third Wave: Democratization in the Late Twentieth Century*. Norman / London: University of Oklahoma Press. Published in Spanish by Ed. Paidós, Barcelona, 1994.

Linz, J. and A. Valenzuela, eds., 1994. *The Failure of Presidential Democracy: The Case of Latin America*. Baltimore: Johns Hopkins University Press.

Merino Merchán, J.F. et al., 1995. *Lecciones de Derecho Constitucional*. Madrid: Ed. Tecnos.

Moulian, T., 1997. *Chile actual: Anatomía de un mito*. Santiago: LOM/Arcis.

Nogueira, H. and Z Luksic., 1992. "Algunos contenidos fundamentales de la descentralización regional y municipal." In: *Cuadernos de Jurídica*. Santiago: U. Diego Portales.

Nohlen, D. 1994. "Politisches System." In: D. Nohlen, ed. *Lexikon der Politik*, Volume 2. Munich: Verlag Beck.

Nohlen, D., ed. 1995. *Wörterbuch Staat und Politik*. Bonn: Bundeszentrale für Politische Bildung.

O'Donnell, G., P. Schmitter y L. Whitehead. 1994 [1986]. *Transiciones desde un gobierno autoritario*. 4 vols. Barcelona: Ed. Paidós.

Ortega, E., 1992. *Historia de una alianza política*. Santiago: CED/Cesoc.

Rehren, A., 1993. "La presidencia en el gobierno de la Concertación." *Estudios Sociales* 75, Trimestre 1, pp. 15-38.

Rustow, D., 1979. "Transitions to Democracy: Toward a Dynamic Model." *Comparative Politics* 2 (April): 337-363.

Saffirio, E., 1994. "El sistema de partidos y la sociedad civil en la redemocratización chilena." *Estudios Sociales* 82, Trimestre 4, pp. 63-113.

Sartori, G., 1994. *¿Qué es la democracia?* Bogotá: Altamir.

Scully, T., 1992. *Los partidos de centro y la evolución política chilena.* Santiago: Ed. Cieplan/Notre Dame.

Stuven, A. M., 1997. "Aproximación a la cultura política de la elite chilena: Concepto y valoración del orden social (1830-1860)." *Estudios Públicos* 66 (Fall), pp. 259-311.

Thesing, J., 1995. *La cultura política en América Latina.* Mainz: KAS.

Valenzuela, A., 1989. *El quiebre de la democracia en Chile.* 2nd ed. Santiago: Flacso.

Varas, P. and S. Mohor, 1992. *Reforma regional, provincial y municipal.* Santiago: Ed. Jurídica de Chile.

Vial, G., 1996. *Historia de Chile.* Vol. III. Santiago: Ed. Zig-Zag.

Von Beyme, K., 1994. *Teoría política del siglo XX: De la modernidad a la postmodernidad.* Madrid: Alianza Universidad.

Von Beyme, K. and D. Nohlen, 1995. "Systemwechsel." In: Nohlen 1995, pp. 765-776.

Zaldívar, A. 1995. *La transición inconclusa.* Santiago: Ed. Los Andes.

The Political Parties

Enrique Cañas

Introduction

T his essay presents a broad overview of the Chilean political party system during the 1990s. The most important characteristics of each party will be mentioned, along with its specific situation in Chilean politics: its effectiveness, its problems, and its prospects in light of its political, electoral, and internal development.

Political information was derived from our press archives. Electoral data were provided by the Ministry of the Interior. As well as examining the two most recent parliamentary elections (1993 and 1997), we present a comparative analysis of the municipal elections of 1992 and 1996, in which the election results are compared to the Human Development Index (HDI) of Chile's 52 most developed and least developed counties [comunas].*

The HDI was designed by the United Nations Development Program (UNDP) on the basis of six social variables measured during the census of 1992: population, school attendance, literacy, infant mortality, average per capita income, and general poverty rate. According to the UNDP index, Chile's counties of greatest human development exhibit values ranging from 0.951 (Vitacura) to 0.777 (Osorno). The HDI values of the 52 counties of lowest human development range from 0.636 (Molina) to 0.465 (Ranquil). Within the group of high-HDI counties, 2,392,916 valid ballots were cast in 1992, increasing to 3,130,608 in 1996. The group with the lowest HDI had 400,268 voters in 1992 and 391,403 in 1996.

This work also presents a comparative examination of voter behavior in 11 predominantly urban counties and in Chile's 157 rural counties. The classification of counties is based upon the 1992 census. The counties with the highest population density are considered urban. Rural counties are those in which more than half the population lives in rural areas, as defined by the Ministry of Planning and Cooperation (Mideplan). In the urban counties, the sample comprises approximately 2,205,000 inhabitants, and in the rural regions, some 1,675,000 persons, permitting global comparisons between the two groups.

---

* For a total of 104 counties.

Information on internal party operations was derived from interviews with party representatives: Milenko Mihovilovic (PDC), Francisco Aleuy (PS), José Auth (PPD), Tomás Duval (RN), Felipe Salaberry, and Andrés Tagle (UDI).[1]

I. General Profile of the Party System in the New Democracy

The Chilean political party system, which had reached a high level of consolidation and continuity before the intervention of the Armed Forces in September 1973,[2] underwent drastic change during the military government period.[3]

A tripolar party system can be seen to emerge from the parliamentary elections of 1989, 1993, and 1997, which is highly competitive and centrist in tendency. The leading political groups recognize allegiance either to the left (Socialist Party, PS; Party for Democracy, PPD; and Communist Party, PC), to the center (Christian Democratic Party, PDC; and Radical Social Democratic Party, PRSD), or to the right of the political spectrum (National Renewal, RN; and Independent Democratic Union, UDI). The Union of the Center-Center (UCC), which divided the vote of the right in the 1989 presidential election with the candidacy of Francisco Javier Errázuriz, appeared to be a movement of the right, but it positioned itself as a centrist party.

Thus far during the 1990s, all of the parties have confronted relatively similar problems and opportunities, as can be seen from analysis of the leading parties' current status. This has, in turn, influenced their ability to appeal to the voters and the relationship they maintain with the government.

Intense leadership competition has been the most visible characteristic of the Chilean party system, both within and among the various parties. This competition is generated from several sources: internal conflicts among networks of influence; disagreements over strategies and programs; and the process of choosing candidates, especially the presidential candidate or candidates within each of the leading coalitions.

---

1   For the processing of electoral data, I would like to express my appreciation of the efficient and faithful assistance of social psychologists Iván Armijo Rodríguez, of the School of Psychology, Catholic University of Chile, and Rodrigo Uribe Bravo, advisor to the Research Office of the Presidency of the Republic and consultant to the PNUD. I sincerely appreciate the valuable critical comments offered by Cristián Toloza Castillo, Ph.D. (Psychology), as well as the suggestions and editorial revision from Rodrigo Uribe Bravo and Sergio Contreras Villa, Ph.D. (Sociology). I am equally grateful for the contributions of historian Alfredo Lastra Norambuena and political scientist Marta Godoy Henríquez, who applied their respective knowledge to the sections on the Radical Social Democratic Party and the Communist Party of Chile.
2   Liliana De Riz, "Política y partidos políticos. Ejercicio de análisis comparado. Argentina, Brasil, Chile y Uruguay," *Síntesis* (Madrid) 2 (1987):39-62; J. Samuel Valenzuela, "Orígenes y transformaciones del sistema de partidos en Chile," *Estudios Públicos* 58 (1995):5-77; Arturo Valenzuela, "El quiebre de la democracia en Chile" (Santiago: Flacso, 1989); Patricio Chaparro, "Los actores sociales y políticos y el quiebre del sistema político democrático chileno," *Estudios Sociales* 37 (1983): 277-296.
3   There have been practically no systematic studies of the transformation of the political party system during the military government. Instead, works with a highly general perspective predominate. See Manuel A. Garretón, "La oposición política y el sistema partidario en el régimen militar chileno: Un proceso de aprendizaje para la transición," in Marcelo Cavarozzi and Manuel A. Garretón, eds., *Muerte y resurrección: Los partidos políticos en el autoritarismo y las transiciones en el Cono Sur* (Santiago: flacso, 1989).

As an unintended side effect of this leadership competition, the parties have found it difficult to promote programs of action which are attractive to the electorate. This in turn has hampered the development of a cultural discussion which would raise the perceived value of politics in society. The need for such a revaluation of politics is made clear by the results of the 1997 parliamentary elections. On that occasion, a broad majority of the population did not express loyalty toward the governing Concertación coalition, nor toward the opposition; not even, in fact, toward the mechanisms of democratic participation.

It should be added that both the current electoral system and the presidentialist model of government favor a high level of inter-party competition. Under the present electoral system, 50% of the contested positions can be obtained by means of the second majority, which gives rise to competition within the coalitions and not among them. The presidentialist style of government produces a high concentration of power in the party controlling the presidency, leading to an inevitable loss of influence among other coalition members.

As a new century approaches, the Chilean parties face challenges on three fronts: socially, with the need for greater equity; politically, with the necessity to consolidate democratic institutions; and culturally, with the imperative for politicians to inspire higher levels of credibility and democratic commitment among the citizenry. The task confronting the parties is to bring these factors into line with the country's economic development, which has proceeded quite consistently throughout the 1990s. How the various coalitions and the parties that make them up will fare in the confrontation of these challenges remains to be answered.

1. THE CONCERTACIÓN OF PARTIES FOR DEMOCRACY

Every political coalition in the world must confront obstacles as it seeks to maintain itself and endure over time. Certain situations of "difficult governability" within the Concertación can be explained, not by unresolvable internal conflicts, but by the political stage which Chile is passing through, which strongly increases the competition among political actors as they maneuver to gain powerful positions in the legislative and executive branches of government.

In addition, the Concertación's internal relations reflect the institutional difficulties of a coalition governing within a rigidly presidentialist political regime. At the same time, long-standing constitutional and political incompatibilities stand between party and parliamentary politics and the responsibilities of government.

The far-reaching cultural transformation of Chilean society is another important structural fact which helps explain the Concertación's occasional weaknesses. The affirmation of values such as the free market, individualism, pragmatic conduct, efficiency, and competition, as elements of a new "cultural logic," do not provoke as much debate among the opposition as among the governing parties themselves. Thus the historical quest for social justice and equality of opportunity, the driving force behind the Concertación's unity, has been partially permeated by the ideas and dynamics of this new "cultural logic," leading to a paucity of original definitions and long-term alternatives.

To this is added the fact that the Concertación includes culturally differentiated subgroups and factions, which can sometimes be highly volatile. Competition among the various currents of the coalition is especially evident during pre-election periods.

TABLE 1

VOTING EVOLUTION OF THE CONCERTACIÓN OF PARTIES FOR DEMOCRACY

Year	%	Votes	Total Valid Votes
1989	51.48	3,499,713	6,797,122
1992	53.32	3,422,807	6,419,807
1993	55.39	3,733,276	6,738,859
1996	56.08	3,464,329	6,176,827
1997	50.54	2,872,916	5,684,426

The achievement of institutional normalization, along with guarantees of social stability and economic growth, will be determining factors for the future of Chilean politics. The rapid transformations taking place in Chilean life obligate the members of the governing coalition to continually reformulate their alliance, actively adapting it to changes in society rather than being led by change. The Concertación recognizes the necessity to improve its mechanisms for internal conflict resolution, determining if disputes should be resolved by majority vote or by consensus, through parliamentary debate or within the individual parties making up the coalition.

The PDC, being the majority party, hopes to head up a third term of government. Many of its leaders believe that they were already quite generous with their policy of omission in the 1993 parliamentary elections, after which they recaptured their share of the vote in many districts in 1997. On the other hand, the socialists and PPD supporters also feel that they have been generous, since they have twice voted for a PDC presidential candidate. This leads them reasonably to claim their turn at the highest national leadership positions, especially considering that in the past few legislative contests, these parties were able to achieve relative electoral parity with the PDC.

For historical reasons, both the PS and the PPD show some resentment at the idea of continued "subservience" to the majority party. They also have high-profile leaders who, according to recent surveys, are very popular among the electorate.

The presidential election in 1999 will be Chile's last in the 20th century and the third since the democratic restoration in 1989. The election process, which is already underway, will culminate in the selection of one or two candidates endorsed by the Concertación. One possibility might be the nomination of a single Concertación candidate from the ranks of the PDC, which would thus aim for three presidential terms at the head of a governing coalition, lasting until March 2006, for a total of 16 years. Alternatively, the coalition might nominate a representative from the PS-PPD axis, who would probably also receive the support of the PRSD. There is also the possibility that two candidates might be presented, which would complicate the coalition's political viability and the continued stability of the government.

The central task faced by Concertación leaders is the design of a strategic mission to reactivate the team spirit that accompanied the coalition's birth and early political development. A proposal is emerging to redesign the platform of the ruling officials, in order to show that the coalition is capable of governing until well beyond the turn of the century. The repercussions for the country of a breakup of the Concertación cannot be predicted.

Even setting aside these possible costs to the nation, the coalition's leaders are aware that a split would devalue their historical accomplishments as a common government.

Public support for the Concertación has fluctuated in the five elections since 1989. The coalition increased its share of the vote from 51.48% to 56.08% in 1996, but then abruptly lost strength in 1997, receiving 50.5% of the national vote. This result was widely interpreted as a rebuke from the voters, especially in reaction to the tangled internal disputes within the governing coalition.

2.OPPOSITION ON THE RIGHT

Within the opposition, there is long-standing tension between those who favor a strategy of increasing criticism of the government, in order to bring about the collapse of the Concertación, and those who argue that the opposition must be constructive. The opposition is also aware of the complex challenges faced by the Concertación and the difficulty of presenting a viable alternative with a consistent and politically attractive plan for the country.

Some factions hope for the breakdown of the governing coalition, resulting in a 1999 presidential election polarized between left and right. Such a situation would favor the right, since significant numbers of centrist voters do not identify with leftist culture, and the Christian Democrats might be displaced into a minority position.

Other factions, representing the liberal democratic right, prefer not to pin their hopes upon a governmental crisis, since this would imply taking up the cause of chaos and flirting with the risk of a return to authoritarianism. The hypothesis supported by this group is that each modernizing step promoted by the president moves the country ideologically closer to the center-right and further from the Concertación's historical views. The result might be the *de facto* creation of a sort of super-coalition, higher than the Concertación and including some elements of the opposition, to which President Frei Ruiz-Tagle could appeal for support for the implementation of his plans, especially in the later stages of his administration.

The right has presented itself as playing a balancing role in the political system, as demonstrated in the candidacies of Hernán Büchi and Alessandri Bessa. However, the right has also divided its strength in presidential elections, by presenting the candidacies of Francisco Javier Errázuriz in 1989 and José Piñera in 1993.

Both phenomena raise the subject of internal governance on the right and its political effects. Cristián Larroulet, executive director of the Liberty and Development Institute, affirmed in late 1996 that "the right cannot govern until it learns to govern itself" (*La Segunda*, December 13, 1996). The truth is that the strength which the right managed to gain in the 1996 municipal elections was not sufficiently exploited to improve its political operations or to develop a coherent unified force. The situation may change in the near future, however, since the UDI gained electoral strength in the most recent parliamentary election and increased its parliamentary representation. These factors, along with the party's possession of a high-profile leader, may lead to a progressive dynamic of strategic convergence with the RN.

The leadership of the opposition has noted worrying signs in the results of recent elections in various districts and precincts. For this reason it is considered "urgent" to support cooperation between the RN and UDI. This would mean developing an alliance capable of

TABLE 2

EVOLUTION OF OPPOSITION ALLIANCE VOTING

Year	%	Votes	Total Valid Votes
1989	34.18	2,323,581	6,797,122
1992	29.66	1,903,871	6,419,807
1993	36.68	2,471,789	6,738,859
1996	32.49	2,007,346	6,176,827
1997	36.25	2,060,636	5,648,426

generating homogeneous policy alternatives, instituting primary elections for a common presidential candidate, and working together to present a political profile with more attractive and modern ideas than those emerging from the Concertación, a proposition which could be embodied in the pragmatic and achievement-oriented image of a leader such as Joaquín Lavín.

The crisis of confidence and lack of effective cooperation in this area of the political spectrum arose in part from the failed attempt at federation in early 1988. Seven years later, the rift was again evident in the debate surrounding constitutional reform. The heated disagreements provoked by this subject led to the suspension of the regular sessions held by the alliance to work out common positions.

During the water crisis of 1996, Andrés Allamand received Christian Democratic support to become the first opposition president of an investigative commission. In the Dipreca case, the RN supported the election of a DC member for the presidency of the Chamber of Deputies oversight commission. Both arrangements were criticized as counterproductive by the UDI, which claimed they weakened the role of the opposition.

The right has traversed a long and difficult path in its quest to present a real alternative to the electorate. Its most evident difficulty is the persistence of internal rivalry; this is quite similar, in fact, to the situation within the Concertación itself. According to some analysts, there are actually three right wings: the old right, represented by the National Renewal factions most strongly anchored in the authoritarian past; the extreme right, represented by UDI; and the liberal democratic and trade union right, represented by moderate leaders hoping to attract centrist voters from the UDI and RN. The evident differences in these right-wing sectors hinder public opinion from visualizing them as a coherent coalition.

From an electoral point of view, the opposition alliance has achieved better results in parliamentary elections than at the municipal level. The opposition received 36.68% of the vote in 1993. A similar level of support was achieved in the parliamentary election of 1997, representing a clear increase over the 1989 elections and the municipal races of 1992 and 1996.

II. The Parties of the New Democracy

1. CHRISTIAN DEMOCRATIC PARTY (PDC)

Political Development

The PDC, a party of Christian social origin founded in 1957, underwent significant cultural and institutional changes during the military government. The party's experience as an opposition group against the authoritarian regime added depth and complexity to its political plans and programs.

During the seven years since the re-establishment of democracy in Chile, the PDC has experienced a decline in internal cohesion and discipline, accompanied by sporadic disputes within the party, all of which have affected its standing in national politics.

During the government of Patricio Aylwin, the PDC became the key party of the Chilean political system, exhibiting an attitude of steady loyalty and cooperation toward the administration and the Concertación. The coordination mechanisms set up among the party, the government, and members of Congress in early 1990 contributed to this cooperative spirit. In addition, the strategy followed by the party from 1990 to 1994 emphasized the quest for consensus with other political and social forces. These factors, along with the characteristics of that period in Chile's history, contributed to the profoundly consistent quality of democratic governance achieved during that period.

As the country returned to democracy, the Christian Democrats initiated both programmatic and operational reforms to their party. Its active commitment to the complex tasks of the transition allowed it to partially meet those challenges. The experience of mobilizing its members for transition-related initiatives was also useful in the programmatic sphere.

Persisting disagreements within the party as to the model of development and concept of society it should support were addressed at the Fourth National Congress in November 1991. On that occasion, the party reaffirmed many of its historical concepts derived from Christian humanist ideas, along with its commitment to the people and to solidarity. Definitions adopted in the late 1960s and early 1970s, such as "communitarian" and "communitarian socialist," were abandoned.

Nevertheless, as time passed, divisive currents became more evident, as disagreements arose upon fundamental issues such as the social market economy, the governmental and electoral systems, the role of the private sector in development, and the social security model inherited from the previous regime. Internal disagreement emerged on issues related to culture and values, such as the divorce law, film censorship, and the anti-AIDS campaigns. Even the party's strategic role in the democratization process was disputed.

Although these disagreements did not seriously disturb the internal harmony of the party during the Aylwin administration, they became evident during the first four years under President Frei, resulting in somewhat strained relations among certain members of Congress, Christian Democratic leaders, and government officials.

The results of the 1997 parliamentary elections affected the party's self-perception, particularly with respect to its political future. Some apprehension may have arisen after previous votes, but only these last elections produced widespread recognition of a critical situation for the party.

Electoral Profile

TABLE 3

PDC: VOTING AND SOCIODEMOGRAPHICS

Parliamentary 1989	Municipal 1992			Parliamentary 1993	Municipal 1996			Parliamentary 1997
27.0	29.0			27.0	26.0			22.9
	52 counties w/ highest IDH *				52 counties w/ highest IDH			
	41.0				28.9			
	52 counties w/ lowest IDH				52 counties w/ lowest IDH			
	23.4				23.0			
	104 counties w/ lowest & highest IDH				104 counties w/ lowest & highest IDH			
	38.2				28.0			
	11 urban counties				11 urban counties			
	North	Central	South		North	Central	South	
	42.8	29.8	30.5		57.2	22.3	29.8	
	157 rural counties				157 rural counties			
	North	Central	South		North	Central	South	
	19.5	28.4	25.7		15.5	26	26.9	

*IDH (Human Development Index), PNUD, which uses as a base the 1992 census and incorporates six variables: population, education level, literacy, infant mortality, average per capita income and percentage of county poverty.

The PDC's current situation is especially delicate, since numerous parties of the present political spectrum have laid claim to centrist positions, meaning that none can stake out the center for itself. To this must be added the "exhaustion" effect of the Christian Democrats' long period in power as the leading party in the Chilean political system.

Internally, the party has faced two basic challenges in recent times: formulating a coherent policy consensus and managing the competition for leadership positions. Each of these issues is related in an essential way to the other, as well as to the electoral decline experienced by the party in 1997.

In the struggle to outline its program, the party grappled with a series of definitions until late 1997. This impeded the development of a differentiated thematic discussion capable of reactivating the party's growth in harmony with the social and cultural changes in Chilean society over the past 25 years. Factions within the PDC argued over whether the organization should be an "electoral machine party," occupied mainly with strategies for winning elections, or a citizens' party, primarily concerned with its own members' interests and the issues most directly affecting the country's citizens.

Similarly, after the parliamentary elections of 1993 and 1997, the party entered into two successive phases of renewal, as it attempted to adjust its discourse and political practice to the new realities and challenges of Chilean society. This affected the party's ability to respond to government initiatives.

Within the party there are leaders of great prominence for whom liberalism and the market economy are not an adequate set of instruments for achieving progress in the area of social justice. This vision clearly contrasts with the convictions of other leaders, who

FIGURE 1

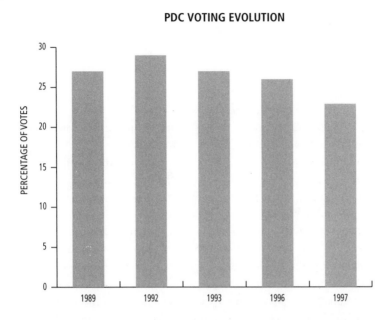

PDC VOTING EVOLUTION

are more closely aligned with the entrepreneurial spirit and private initiative, as well as more highly attuned to the business community and to the modernist sectors of the right. The struggle for internal leadership is influenced both by evaluations of the track record of current party leaders and the need to identify attractive candidates for office, especially for the 1999 presidential elections.

In recent years, the PDC has been forced to confront unprecedented difficulties in the process of selecting candidates for public office. These obstacles are associated with the characteristics of the binomial system, which severely restricts the electoral options presented to the citizenry.

The PDC's internal elections in April 1997 clearly demonstrated that internal conflicts among Christian Democrats center on personal and group leadership, as well as on differing conceptions of the party's role in the political process and the program it should pursue. According to some, the Christian Democrats must more energetically face the challenges presented by the emerging currents in Chilean society. The leadership issue is also involved; the party must have leaders who can comprehend and harmonize both the country's new social environment and the Christian Democratic culture. Further, the PDC must become a more inclusive party, capable of broadening its base and attracting new supporters.

Table 3 and Figure 1 show the overall electoral evolution of the PDC and its perceptible decline in areas with a higher Human Development Index. This had repercussions on the national level, as the party experienced a drop of 10 percentage points within the sample of 108 counties covered by this study. In addition, the party's overall average voter support in the rural counties diminished from 24.5% to 22.7%. All of this is congruent with the Christian Democrats' poor electoral showing in the 1997 parliamentary elections.

In the 1996 municipal elections, the PDC diminished its electoral strength from 28.9% to 26%, a decrease of 2.9%. This tendency continued with the results of the parliamentary elections of 1997, in which the PDC lost four percentage points compared to the 1993 results. Further losses can be confirmed in counties where declines in support were already evident in 1993.

Internal Situation[4]

In reaction to feelings of dissatisfaction within the PDC, the National Board in 1994 and 1997 initiated reforms to the organizational structure of the party, hoping to improve its effectiveness and gain increased support on the national level.

This modernizing effort focused on modifying internal statutes, improving coordination between the regional and county levels, strengthening the party tribunals, increasing member participation in internal operations, and improving the party's links to the electorate (membership rules, regularization of membership records, generation of leaders, election of candidates, ties with social organizations, lists of supporters).

Under Alejandro Foxley's management, the PDC was able to modernize a large proportion of its internal operations. The most significant modernization was carried out in the area of information systems, permitting party organizations to become interlinked throughout the country. The party can now keep local activists informed at all times of events on the national level, passing along information such as the content of National Council sessions.

The most important statutory modifications were those establishing the direct election of National Board members, starting in 1991. In addition, local supreme tribunals were established, which coordinate with the provincial tribunals, thus decentralizing the handling of internal disputes. Advances were also achieved in reproducing the structure of the National Board on the regional level, helping to democratize party operations.

At the same time, new rules were established to decentralize the system for admitting new party members. This is now managed by the county committees, without mandatory intervention from higher levels. The PDC currently has 108,000 members, 50% of which vote in party elections. Ten thousand new members were formally incorporated between 1990 and 1996. This represents a relatively small increase when compared to the growth rates of the 1960s and 1970s; nevertheless, it is a significant number if one takes into account the low level of enthusiasm for politics evidenced throughout Chilean civil society in the 1990s.

One of the principal internal problems of the PDC rests in the insufficiently fluid nature of its internal management, as reflected in the operation of the National Committee and the National Board. The party organization, as defined by its current statutes, does not permit the development of a linear work structure on the basis of defined plans; it also impedes harmonious interaction among the various subgroups of the party.

The PDC's highest decision-making bodies are the National Congress, National Committee, National Council, Board of Directors, and the Supreme Tribunal. The institu-

---

4   Information based on an interview with Milenko Mihovilovic, director of the Electoral Division of the PDC.

tion also possesses specialized technical commissions and a division focusing on electoral topics. The holding of a new National Congress is a central issue on the PDC's internal agenda for 1998. The National Committee meets once or twice a year and is composed of approximately 450 national delegates. These delegates select the National Council, which meets weekly and acts as the party's leading decision-making body, together with the board of directors.

The operation of the technical commissions requires more frequent meetings as well as ongoing interaction with the National Council, in order to provide effective support for the party in specific public policy areas. The electoral division is one of the most dynamic bodies of the PDC. The leaders in this area, as in other parties, exercise significant influence upon the party's political tactics.

The PDC's income derives in part from the payment of membership dues at the county level. Internal funds are used to maintain party headquarters in various locations. The income from some assets held by the party also help finance many of its activities.

With respect to its centers of thought and intellectual work, the PDC finds itself facing an evident challenge: empowering and utilizing the professional and technical talents at its disposal in order to recover the potent political-intellectual tradition enjoyed by the organization in its early years. It must be remembered that it was precisely this tradition which allowed the PDC to stand out from other parties and become a new historical focal point for Chile's development. Currently, there is no organization capable of independently and consistently projecting a specifically Christian Democratic set of ideas with appeal to both party members and the society as a whole. The result is a particularly delicate and challenging situation for the PDC as it faces the future.

2. SOCIALIST PARTY OF CHILE (PS)

Political Development
During the 1960s and early 1970s, the left debated various controversial strategies for political activity. While the Communist Party maintained the moderate positions to which it had adhered in the 1950s, the PS, at the Congresses of Linares (1965) and Chillán (1967), became radicalized, adopting Leninist frameworks for action on all levels.

Currently, Chilean socialism is in a transition stage from its extremist ideological roots toward a set of ideas reflecting the less rigid and more constructive character of contemporary politics. An empirical expression of this process can be found in the fact that the socialists have distanced themselves from their decades-old political and strategic alliance with the Communist Party and forged stronger ties to the PPD in the new democracy. This organization of the moderate left, inspired by liberal ideas, interacts with the socialists in an ambiguous relationship of cooperation and competition for the leadership of the Chilean Left.

It should be remembered that the Socialist Party includes supporters whose political vocations began in the old democracy, as well as others who joined party life more recently, during the socialist renewal toward the end of the 1970s and in the following decade.

The military government did not succeed in eliminating the main elements of the cultural model developed by the Allendist Left starting in the 1960s. However, while many components of this culture were maintained, great differences began to incubate within it, starting with the experience of exile, which endowed those who suffered it with intensely experienced and strongly differentiated customs and traditions. Thus it can be observed that some sectors of the socialist membership developed more sympathy for the prevailing liberal, pragmatic, and results-oriented discourse, while others maintained ties to the cultural and ideological nomenclature of the old democracy.

This situation led, at the end of the 1980s, to the creation of the PPD out of the PS, while the latter lost much of the rigidity which had characterized it in the past. The new flexibility enabled both parties to accept shared leadership and common political strategies in a spirit of teamwork and consensus. Nevertheless, the repositioning of the PS as a party "different" from the PPD, along with the self-definition of the latter as "independent" of the former, often resulted in a two-pronged approach and a confused competition of identities, as the parties sought to attract more or less the same voters.

During the Aylwin administration, relations between the PS and the PPD exhibited some strain, although the parties had formed a common bench in Congress and had established quite effective coordination mechanisms. The problems arose when the PS demanded an end to the practice of joint membership in both parties; at the same time, it plotted various political initiatives to bring about the PPD's dissolution. This strategy failed, and the PS-PPD bloc was obligated to design new mechanisms of interaction to mitigate conflict.

In spite of the tensions arising in the left wing of the Concertación, both the PS and the PPD maintained a loyal relationship with the first Concertación government. Unlike the internally divided socialist world of the late 1970s — when each variation formed its own party — during the 1990-94 period the party made a passable effort to maintain internal discipline and to pragmatically support the work of the Aylwin administration, one of whose most important ministries, that of economics, was headed up by a Socialist Party member.

This support contrasts with the party's actions during the first years of the Frei administration. The socialists, believing that the government would abandon the institutional issues of the transition, demanded that the executive "reinstate" these tasks and promote them alongside those related to social modernization. Recurring conflicts over plans and proposals led to a permanent polemical battle between the party and the Frei administration. Criticism of governmental management continued, and with the Cabinet changes in September 1994, the situation became truly tense. Some socialists began to raise the question of withdrawing support from the government (*Hoy*, no. 916, 1995). The party plunged into profound reflection about the appropriate agenda and political practice for the end of the century.

The PS in those years was always aware of the nature of its problems, which involved the broad spectrum of intellectual interpretations of socialism existing within the party. These ranged from those who acknowledged the benefits of the market economy, saw growth as a means to help resolve social problems, and recognized the subsidiary role of the State, to those who, without being categorically against the system, emphasized its weaknesses and structural contradictions, supporting the political strengthening of the government.

The president of the PS, Camilo Escalona, in his work "Society, Politics and Human Beings," [Sociedad, política y ser humano] took account of these competing visions and developed the idea of a "critical humanism" for the consolidation of democracy above and beyond neoliberalism. In Escalona's view, the PS should combine elements of Marxism along with tenets of secular humanism and Christianity. However, for other leaders, Marxism was no longer a component of socialism's ideological framework nor its essence (as reported in *La Época*, October 9, 1994).

One socialist senator, expressing criticism of his party, called upon it to renew itself and leave behind the historical symbols and messages of the past (*La Segunda*, April 18, 1995). Another member responded: "With all of the valuable achievements of the renovation process, it has not succeeded in producing an ethos, an emotion, a passion that brings people together and one that they can identify with. Without this ancestral spirit, which arises from its history, the atomization of the PS will end by dispersing the party entirely, or it will become a mass of competing leaders without followers," (*La Época*, May 4, 1995).

While political disputes among its larger factions have affected internal harmony, the party has actually exhibited a notable level of institutional cohesion and tranquillity in recent years, in contrast to the virulent conflicts experienced within other parties. The PS has also recognized that constant conflict with the executive and with the other parties of the alliance would lead it down precisely the wrong path, if their goal was to project an image of viable alternative leadership from the left, headed by a member of their own ranks.

If the acceptable level of harmony and governance exhibited within the socialist wing during the Frei years has sometimes resembled the model of internal government used by monolithic parties, this was not due to ideological unanimity, nor to the absence of potentially explosive disagreements. Rather, it was brought about by the necessity to act with "tactical pragmatism." The party has had significant success in exercising stern institutional self-discipline and producing coherence on the issues in order to project a credible political image among the citizens and to further bolster the popularity of the sector's political leadership, confirmed by public opinion polls since 1994.

The stewardship of Camilo Escalona in recent years has been favorable to these plans. Along with promoting unity and peaceful integration among its internal factions, the PS has carefully maintained its relationship with the government and the leadership of the PDC, with a view toward improving the prospects for consensus and strengthening the Concertación, as well as increasing the chances that a socialist may carry the coalition's presidential banner in December 1999.

The future of the PS will depend in great measure upon the type of internal consensus which its factions are able to reach, as well as the political relations it establishes with the PPD, a party which includes many ex-socialists and which, as we have mentioned, reflects the significant cultural transformations experienced by the non-communist left over the past few decades.

Table 4 and Figure 2 show the overall electoral evolution of the PS. The party has expanded its base of support in the counties of lower human development, increasing from 9.9% to 15.4%. This is comparable to the increase seen in the rural counties where the party's average share of the vote rose from 6.4% to 8.7%. In the most recent parliamentary elections, the PS maintained its electoral support at the 1993 level of approximately 12%.

In Figure 2, the electoral situation of the PS in 1989 is not presented, since it was included within the political umbrella of the PPD. The sharp increase between the municipal election of 1992 and the parliamentary races of 1997 is notable, in spite of the fact that the party's base of support has remained constant in the two most recent congressional elections.

Electoral Profile

TABLE 4

PS: VOTING AND SOCIODEMOGRAPHICS

Parliamentary 1989	Municipal 1992			Parliamentary 1993	Municipal 1996			Parliamentary 1997
	8.6			11.9	10.6			11.9
	52 counties w/ highest IDH				52 counties w/ highest IDH			
	9.9				8.6			
	52 counties w/ lowest IDH				52 counties w/ lowest IDH			
	9.9				15.4			
	104 counties w/ lowest & highest IDH				104 counties w/ lowest & highest IDH			
	8.4				9.4			
	11 urban counties				11 urban counties			
	North	Central	South		North	Central	South	
	8.2	7.3	13.9		6.3	6.4	21.1	
	157 rural counties				157 rural counties			
	North	Central	South		North	Central	South	
	5.6	5.7	8.0		8.0	9.3	9.0	

FIGURE 2

EVOLUTION OF PS VOTING

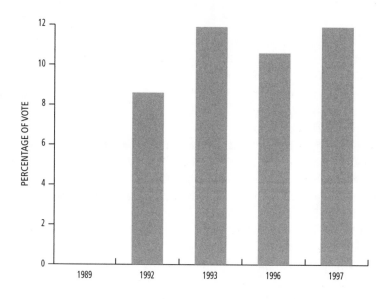

Internal Situation[5]

The PS's internal statutes are viewed almost as a sacred text. With the strongly legalistic nature of socialist culture, statutory discussions take on special relevance, illustrated by the fact that even the party's internal networks of influence are regulated by statutes.

In reaction to the experience of underground operation during the military government, the admission of new members is relatively unregulated; there are no intermediate categories such as provisional member or non-member supporter. This subject is also affected by the fact that the socialists have not even defined whether they are primarily an activists' or a citizens' party. The current rolls of the PS include 76,000 members, with 16,000 new members formally incorporated between 1994 and 1997.

The party's highest decision-making bodies are the National Congress, the National Council, the Central Committee, the Political Commission, the National Board, and the specialized secretariats and commissions. More solid structures are found as one moves up the organizational scale.

The National Congress, the body responsible for medium- and long-term policies, meets every four years and is made up of some 500 persons elected as regional delegates, along with the Central Committee and the regional and county presidents. The delegates elect a Coordinating Board of Directors for the congresses, which is distinct from the National Board. The principal difficulties confronted by National Congresses during the 1990s have involved basic ideological problems, upon which the socialists have temporarily agreed to suspend decision.

The National Council meets twice a year and is composed of the members of the Central Committee along with all of the regional, provincial, and county presidents. This is the body which exercises leadership between Congresses, defining party tactics over the short and intermediate terms. The Council operates through work groups focusing on a specific list of subjects. The results are reported to plenary sessions, which reproduce the debate of the commissions.

The Central Committee is elected by the members through a proportional representation system, as are other socialist officials. Made up of almost 100 persons who meet six times a year, the Central Committee's decisions are more far-reaching than those made by the National Council. This Committee is the body which best reflects the internal tendencies existing in the party.

The Supreme Tribunal is an autonomous and permanent internal structure, elected by the National Congress in a single open list. This body has authority over jurisdictional and disciplinary matters raised within the party. Its 12 members do not exercise party leadership positions, nor can they serve as candidates for election unless they resign from the Tribunal.

The Political Commission is made up of 20 to 25 members chosen by the Central Committee, and its task is to establish more specific plans of action than those emanating from the Committee.

Parallel to the PS's main lines of organizational authority, specialized secretariats and commissions provide technical advice to the party on numerous issues of public policy.

---

5   Information based on an interview with Francisco Aleuy.

On the internal level, the most important change introduced by the PS has been positive discrimination in favor of women. Currently, no list may be presented for an electoral
event that does not contain a minimum percentage of female candidates.

One of the most heated controversies within the party concerns internal political representation. Since the system allows democratic competition among counties with low
and high density, the strong counties tend to dominate over the smaller ones. In consequence, the opinions and influence of the leaders of smaller counties receive relatively less
weight, producing the sense of a lack of participation in party life. There have been protracted discussions about the best way to eliminate this distortion, and similarly, to redistribute the balance of influence to emphasize quality and not simply quantity in the origin
of the representation.

In its relations with the PPD, the PS dismisses any possibility of fusion into a single
organization. In the event that this seemed necessary, the PS would accept, at most, the joint
creation of a sort of Progressive Federation. The basic spirit and culture of the PPD is recognized as different from that of the PS. In addition, there is widespread fear within the PPD
that in any fusion or federation process, the PS could swallow up the PPD. Furthermore, the
PS does not rely upon strong personalized leadership, but upon its own institutional structure; in the PPD the phenomenon of "political bosses" is well-recognized.

The PS supports legislation on the issue of political financing and supports the establishment of spending limits. The party requires the payment of membership dues.
Congressional representatives and government officials contribute a fixed percentage of
their salaries. For other members, dues are set according to income levels. The PS possesses little real estate or other assets. No funds are available to pay party officials, except for
administrative personnel. This situation should be criticized, not on ethical grounds, but
as a deficiency in the area of organization.

In the intellectual sphere, debate within the Socialist Party has become more complex
in recent years. According to some of its analysts, associated with the Advance Center, the
party exhibits the trait of positivity, which implies seizing the initiative to debate upon
crucial historical moments. That is to say, the context of the party's intellectual reflection
suggests a cultural reconstruction of socialism congruent with and aimed at the current
era (*La Época*, August 25, 1994).

3. THE PARTY FOR DEMOCRACY (PPD)

Political Development
Free from atavistic commitments to the old traditions of Chilean politics, and endowed
with a new multicultural perspective, the PPD emerged from the socialist world in 1987
as a new kind of party, combining aspects of the modernizing impetus of the liberal sector of the PS with new policy ideas contributed by more traditional sectors of that party.

Within a very short time after its creation, the PPD generated unexpected enthusiasm
among diverse sectors of Chilean society. It proved especially attractive to young people
and independent voters who did not identify with the traditions of the Old Left and who
were attracted to a more pragmatic, less ideological ethos. The party aimed at being more
inclusive and capable of winning voters from both the center and the left, thus challenging
the political predominance which the Christian Democrats were poised to seize at the end
of the 1980s.

The PPD was initially conceived as an instrumental organization, formed to assemble the people, parties, and movements favoring a "No" vote in the plebiscite of October 1988. The party arose in great measure out of the Committee of the Left for Free Elections (CIEL). Very quickly, the organization was able to consolidate itself as an autonomous unit, affirming its will to remain on the national political scene.

The party possesses a contradictory set of definitions which place it variously on the left and in the center. In accordance with its declaration of principles, it conceives itself as a liberal-progressive movement, advocating a democratic socialism. Its strongly pragmatic inspiration allows it to project an identity somewhere between moderate leftism and pronounced liberalism, combined with support for multicultural societal action. For this reason, the PPD recoils from universalizing and abstract rhetoric, as well as absolute certainties and closed identities, gravitating instead toward political practices which recognize the multiplicity and variety of social life (see J. Molina V., "Elecciones en el PPD," *La Época*, September 3, 1994).

It is important to remember that the PPD emerged during a historical cycle when the self-referential ideological frameworks were beginning to enter into crisis. This was a time when the culture of industrialism, upon which leftist parties and movements had been based, was beginning to fade; a time when, in contrast, democracy, the free market and the spread of information were becoming universal; a time when technology was radically modifying traditional work and production methods; and a time when the individual occupied a more central position than the "masses," while politics was becoming a part and not the whole of the search for fulfillment of human aspirations (Antonio Leal, *La Nación*, May 19, 1995).

During the first four years of Concertación government, the PPD was not yet considered to be a party as such. When government officials were named, the status of the PPD as a member party was not widely acknowledged. In addition, since individual personalities played such a decisive role in the PPD, it displayed less discipline and loyalty to the Aylwin government than the other parties of the Concertación.

Between 1990 and 1994, the PPD gradually distanced itself from the PS and energetically and successfully promoted its principal political figures. The stage was set for ongoing competition among the parties, which in turn produced confusion among those holding a more closed vision of politics, closer to that of the traditional party activist (see report in *Hoy*, no. 865, 1994).

After the departure of the socialists in July 1992 and the PPD's consequent drop in numbers and loss of influence upon the new organization, the view was expressed that an overemphasis on personalities impeded the party from attracting voters with a coherent program. The PPD undertook a long period of internal reordering, which allowed it to present an identity to the electorate above and beyond that of its principal political figures.

With the holding of primaries and the proposal of a PPD nominee in 1993, the party gained an important opportunity for electoral negotiation, allowing it to elect the majority of its candidates to Congress. "The objectives of the campaign do not have to do with the PPD as an institution, how to increase its visibility and prestige or to try to reposition it," expressed the document prepared for the occasion, entitled "Leaders" (see report in *Hoy*, no. 865, 1994).

The party achieved a respectable level of voter support and was able to take on significant responsibilities in the Frei administration, with which it maintained change-able relations, ranging from full support to the rejection of some of the government's pro-posals. The organization continued to be viewed as a junior partner by the other parties of the Concertación. It was also seen as an amalgamation of voters from a wide range of polit-ical sectors and cultures, whose affinities appeared and disappeared in accordance with the objectives pursued.

In contrast to the other parties of the system, the PPD does not have internal factions. That is to say, the PPD does not include groupings of members centered on policy issues which have arisen over time. The PPD has a brief history and is more strongly marked by the diverse personal origins of its leaders and members. In place of factions are weakly developed impulses and points of emphasis: for example, the divide between some leaders who exhibit almost no ideological motivation and prefer the operational side of things, and others for whom an interest in programmatic content is fundamental and necessary.

The PPD possesses a hybrid rather than monocultural nature, allowing it to compre-hend diverse social expressions. The principal nucleus of electoral support for the PPD arises from "modern" middle-class sectors, through which it accedes to the leadership of relatively disorganized lower-middle class groups. This places it among the parties with the lowest level of pressure from interest groups and organized labor (*La Época*, November 3, 1994). However, this is also the cause of one of the most visible internal problems of the PPD: its low representation among union members and university students. The "accept-ed" parties among members of the nation's social organizations are basically the PDC, the PS, and even the PC.

The influence of leaders who have switched from traditional parties explains the spo-radic emergence of internal political "machines" in the PPD. This leads to conflict

Electoral Profile

TABLE 5

PPD: VOTING AND SOCIODEMOGRAPHICS

Parliamentary 1989	Municipal 1992			Parliamentary 1993	Municipal 1996			Parliamentary 1997
11.4	9.2			11.8	11.8			11.8
	52 counties w/ highest IDH				52 counties w/ highest IDH			
	12.4				12.6			
	52 counties w/ lowest IDH				52 counties w/ lowest IDH			
	10.5				10.2			
	104 counties w/ lowest & highest IDH				104 counties w/ lowest & highest IDH			
	11.6				11.3			
	11 urban counties				11 urban counties			
	North	Central	South		North	Central	South	
	7.0	11.4	7.2		7.9	15.6	5.9	
	157 rural counties				157 rural counties			
	North	Central	South		North	Central	South	
	13.7	6.9	8.2		10.4	9.3	9.0	

between party members who reject classical politics and those who want to practice new methods. Added to this is the excessive proliferation of personalized initiatives within the organization, reinforcing the theory of an artificial party of individuals in which a confused dialogue is produced between the old and the new, between politicians and those disenchanted with politics, between political operators and promoters of new issues, between technicians and public speakers, and so forth.

The PPD, like all the other parties, is experiencing a transition between old and new ways of practicing politics. Internally, two great tasks are debated which must be faced in a simultaneous and balanced manner: consolidating the structure and content of the party's message, and managing and channeling membership growth to produce a modern, efficient organization which can consolidate its support on the county and regional levels. The party has continued to examine basic internal questions over the past few years, such as its membership goal, whether it must have its own members as such, and its most appropriate structures and strategic content.

Until recently, the party continued to be governed under the liberal and personal style of Jorge Schaulsohn, a style which, at bottom, was simply the legacy of the artificial model conceived for the party during its founding. This has created feelings of frustration among some PPD leaders, who do not consider a party to be viable without an organic internal identity (*Hoy*, no. 944, 1995). Today, under the direction of Sergio Bitar, it is emphasized that party operations do not represent the personal exercise of power, but a focus on fundamental ideas about the best way to fulfill the needs of the citizenry.

Such is the importance of the organic theme in the PPD. Tension persists between two distinct visions of the organization: a party of issues preoccupied with specific development topics; or an organic citizens' party in which its members determine its program and operational style.

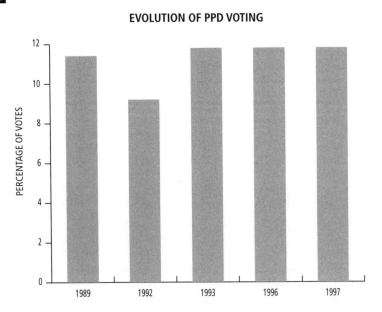

FIGURE 3

EVOLUTION OF PPD VOTING

PERCENTAGE OF VOTES

1989 1992 1993 1996 1997

The search for a clear posture regarding the issues on the national agenda does not signify greater articulation and coherence of the PPD's set of ideas; its leaders even point with pride to its ideological fragmentation. It is in this spirit of diversity that they wish to advance toward an identity as a movement of influences drawing from a cross-section of political sensibilities.

What is clearly and almost definitively discounted is the possibility of fusion with the PS, although the PPD recognizes the need to maintain good political relations with that party.

The hypothesis can be raised that the PPD tends to present itself as an "electoral machine" party which can grow not only by capturing support from modernized sectors of the left, but also by conquering segments of the center and the right, allowing it to compete for the space traditionally belonging to the Christian Democrats.

The overall electoral evolution of the PPD, which appears in Table 5 and Figure 3, shows a stable level of voter support throughout the period from 1989 to 1997, at a proportion approaching 12%. From a socio-demographic point of view, the PPD maintains a hard core of municipal electoral support, remaining at approximately 11% in counties with both greater and lesser HDI. In Chile's 157 rural counties, the PPD receives some 10% of the vote. All of these figures are congruent with the national vote results in the five elections since 1989.

Internal Situation[6]

At its founding in 1987, the party united around a Declaration of Principles whose central concept was the value of democracy and the rejection of continued rule by the authoritarian regime. Beginning in 1993, the organization revised its statutes, defining broad outlines of its views on social, political, economic, and cultural issues.

In 1989, the PPD was the first party in the Chilean political system to establish universal voting for the election of all of its leaders. Its organizational chart presents a relatively decentralized structure, although in some aspects it may still need adjustment to achieve greater effectiveness and efficiency in party operations and member participation.

Within the political hierarchy, the National Council, composed of 400 representatives elected by members on the provincial level, represents the fundamental authority of the organization and serves as a sort of legislative power. To this are added the National Board, the Political Commission, and the Board of Directors.

After the National Council is constituted, the election of the National Board follows. The Board includes 52 members who meet monthly: 13 regional presidents, 32 spokespersons, one youth president, and the six members of the board of directors. The National Board is charged with choosing the Political Commission. The 12 members of the Commission, along with the board of directors, adopt political resolutions. According to party statutes, the Board does not legally exist, since the main decision-making body after the National Council — which meets twice a year — is the Political Commission, which meets weekly. A situation of uncertainty prevails regarding the composition of the board of directors and the functions of the vice presidents. The PPD is still reflecting upon these issues.

---

6   Information based on an interview with José Auth.

The National Board chooses the members of the Political Commission and elects the national secretaries, who are also Board members and are in charge of supporting the party through the secretariats of Studies and Programs, Municipal and Regional Associations, International Relations, Training and Events, Labor and Social Issues, Communications, and the Internal Organization. Of these, the most complex and dynamic are Studies and Programs, along with Labor and Social Issues, which function as a grouping of subcommissions, the former presenting the highest level of activity. It should be noted, however, that the financial limitations of the PPD restrict the work of the executive secretariats.

Having been created as an open and informal organization, the PPD does not have rules for the entry of new members, nor does it offer provisional membership phases. Its membership level has shown steady growth and currently approaches 100,000, but only a fourth of this number participates in internal elections. The party's political training and development systems function only sporadically, due to financial constraints. Nevertheless, the party possesses a think tank, Chile XXI, which is dedicated to promoting debate in the social sciences and providing effective support to PPD representatives in Congress.

The PPD was the first party to formally institute positive discrimination to promote women's participation in party life. This measure has positively affected voter support for female candidates. The demographic structure of the PPD reveals that the party is composed mainly of young persons, predominantly between 30 and 50 years of age, who view themselves as being on the left, on the center-left, or progressive-liberal.

One of the PPD's main internal problems is the party's electoral system, which makes the election of leaders extremely complex and costly, especially since the vote is universal. The system does not recognize groupings or lists within the party, marking an important difference with the PDC and the PS. Since the PPD is a party of individuals and not of crystallized factions, internal elections are less polarized, and disputes are not as pronounced as in the parties mentioned above.

Because internal candidates are not grouped into factions, voters are confronted with the personalities of individuals whom they may or may not know, giving nationally well-known or "famous" leaders an important advantage. Nevertheless, *de facto* alliances sometimes form during election campaigns, which operate through lists representing groups, which in turn represent powerful political "bosses."

A central problem in the PPD's electoral system is its use of the multiple vote formula, which obliges members to use numerous slips of paper when voting. Numerous leaders are elected individually on a differentiated slate: various national council members, a provincial president, four candidates for the regional board, 16 National Board members, a party president, a secretary-general, three vice-presidents and a county president.

Thus, a system originally conceived to provide complete democratic transparency in party operations ends by distorting it. The organization has sometimes found it necessary to modify the current electoral mechanisms; for example, by diminishing the number of votes to which party members are entitled.

4. NATIONAL RENEWAL (RN)

Political Development

During the period immediately following the 1973 military intervention, the National Party, which had represented the traditional right since the mid-1960s, agreed to dissolve itself as a political force, thus accepting the new non-democratic conditions of national life.

As the authoritarian regime embarked upon a liberalization process in 1983, two political tendencies arose among supporters of the government, which gradually coalesced into two parties: the UDI, with its roots in the corporatist and social union movements; and RN, based on traditional republican currents.

Faced with the strongly polarized condition of Chilean politics in the first half of the 1980s, RN understood that a significant part of the authoritarian plan for overall "regeneration" of Chilean society was headed for failure. This led it to become involved in the search for formulas for a transition to democracy and to support calls for the regime to open itself up to constructive dialogue with the opposition.

With the defeat of the hard-line in the plebiscite of October 1988, RN aligned itself in a spirit of consensus with the democratic opposition, attempting to restore the democratic character possessed by the traditional right and to consolidate its leadership in that part of the political spectrum. The party sought to isolate the hard-line factions collected in the UDI and to attract centrist voters with the aim of gaining power in the general elections to be held the following year.

The heated disputes between the RN and UDI since their failed attempt at federation in a single organization in early 1988, along with the ongoing discord accompanying the constitutional agreement of May 1989 and the elections in December of the same year, increased public impressions of disunity in this part of the political spectrum. This was further confirmed by the rise of a third current on the right, the UCC, whose programmatic platform tended toward a vague and extravagant populism.

National Renewal did not achieve its goal of gaining presidential power, but it won a high percentage of the votes in the parliamentary elections of 1989, leaving the UDI and UCC in clearly subordinate positions and allowing the RN to enter the new democratic period as the principal player among the opposition.

During the first seven years of the new democracy, the right never managed to adopt a homogeneous strategy in opposition to the Concertación governments. Instead, a diversity of strategies were employed, some contradictory and competing. However, the nature of the electoral system obligated the organizations of the right to moderate their conflicts, to unite to a certain extent, and to form a coalition to share the sector's representation in Congress.

At the beginning of the Aylwin administration, RN continued its policy of consensus, which it called the "democracy of agreements." This strategy was a productive one, but it began to be perceived as principally favoring the government. Critics charged that it de-emphasized the RN and prevented the party from imposing its views within the Concertación or advancing its political prospects for 1993. Additional concerns included preventing the loss of voters to the UDI and increasing control over the party's own senators.

In response, RN adopted a more hard-line position with respect to the government, beginning to accuse it of resting upon the successes of the past without creating new plans for the future. This new policy, which was not critical enough to lose the label of constructive opposition, was called the "democracy of alternatives." It permitted the RN to suggest and impose its initiatives wherever the government showed weakness.

Nevertheless, during the Aylwin administration, RN never truly succeeded in replacing its policy of agreements with one of criticism and parallel proposals. The party had emphasized its desire for democratic stability from the beginning, since a merely obstructionist stance would have reproduced the unproductive, divisive policies used by the democratic opposition in its unsuccessful attempts to topple the military government in the early 1980s. In addition, the eight-year term of the presidency established by the 1980 Constitution, along with the low probability that a candidate from the right would be elected in 1993, increased the attractiveness of negotiation aimed at reducing this period to four or six years. Success on this point would obviate the waiting period of at least 12 years — the four of the Aylwin government plus the eight of the new term — until the right could hope to gain access to power, a situation which became the Achilles heel of the "democracy of alternatives."

The RN's "democracy of agreements" was a success in that it contributed to the country's stability during the Aylwin administration. In the economic sphere, this was expressed in almost universal agreement regarding the market economy's advantages as an instrument of Chilean development. Tax and labor reforms found broad support among business people, workers, and politicians, permitting progress in the social sphere to outpace the government's original plans. Agreement upon the reform of Article 9 of the Constitution allowed the executive to free political prisoners, contributing to defusing that explosive situation. With the agreement on municipal reform, also supported by the UDI, the right freed itself from accusations on the part of the government that it opposed democratic mayoral elections. The administration, for its part, moved forward in the RN-supported areas of municipal autonomy and the decentralization of the country.

A few weeks into the Frei administration, a new strategic pattern of opposition to the government and the Concertación emerged. The situation arose when the parties of the right and the designated senators combined their votes to displace the Concertación into a minority position in all of the Senate's sectorial commissions. The outcome of the political developments unfolding in Chile in early 1994 was still unclear, and the right was poised to propel its oppositional role into a more confrontational direction, in hopes of presenting itself as a viable leadership alternative.

However, during the first three years of the Frei government, the internal conflicts within National Renewal hindered its effectiveness in promoting itself on a national scale. Two different visions of the party and its political program existed within the organization: the first inspired by a progressive centrism distanced from the authoritarian culture, and the other inclined toward more corporatist and conservative postures, with a strong defensive attitude toward the work of the military government.

The more progressive fringes of the RN are aware that in current circumstances they have little chance of articulating viable policy proposals sharply distinguished from those of the Concertación. This fact has been one of the most significant obstacles to the creation of an effective opposition to the current government and to the "democracy of alternatives" strategy. The RN's own advisors have reminded the party of the broad consensus existing in Chile today regarding the value of political democracy and the effectiveness of the market economy, both of which are becoming part of the country's common political heritage.

Electoral Profile

TABLE 6

RN: VOTING AND SOCIODEMOGRAPHICS

Parliamentary 1989	Municipal 1992			Parliamentary 1993	Municipal 1996			Parliamentary 1997
18.2	17.9			16.3	18.6			16.31
	52 counties w/ highest IDH				52 counties w/ highest IDH			
	18.7				17.9			
	52 counties w/ lowest IDH				52 counties w/ lowest IDH			
	14.6				17.9			
	104 counties w/ lowest & highest IDH				104 counties w/ lowest & highest IDH			
	18.3				18.3			
	11 urban counties				11 urban counties			
	North	Central	South		North	Central	South	
	10.1	16.6	9.0		8.4	19.8	18.0	
	157 rural counties				157 rural counties			
	North	Central	South		North	Central	South	
	14.5	17.8	20.3		13.6	11.2	10.1	

Nevertheless, it would be a mistake to underestimate the capacity of the right to raise issues of public debate. They possess the means to do this, and they have demonstrated a keen tactical sense on certain occasions, responding immediately to problems which are socially very sensitive but supposedly neglected by the government authorities, such as the subject of public security.

National Renewal has sometimes attempted to lay claim to the modernizing concepts promoted by the Frei government. The idea is to transform these issues into an emblematic factor of the party's unity, a demonstration of its effectiveness and an instrument for weakening the government's base of political support. However, these expectations have not been consistently fulfilled. This is shown in the damage to the party's cohesiveness caused by the prickly polemics surrounding the proposal of eliminating the designated senators, a reform measure which in mid-1997 was rejected by the Senate with the votes of the RN's conservative minority. That is to say, neither the new board of directors, presided over by Alberto Espina, nor the Council, nor all the party's representatives could impose party discipline on this position favorable to the fortification of Chilean democracy.

This situation has hindered the emergence of clear political leadership enjoying broad support within the party. The RN's democratic leaders must undertake a profound renewal process reaching to the heart of rightist thought. They need all of the right and not just a part of it. One factor explaining the relative electoral impotence of the right, both in the old and the new democracy, may be its weakness in identifying and sustaining political leaders capable of imposing internal discipline and capturing social majorities. The right's debility as an electoral force is quite the opposite of its cultural and ideological influence upon the country, based on its control of the media, its economic legacy, its complex network of institutional connections, and its commitment to practical realism and technical performance.

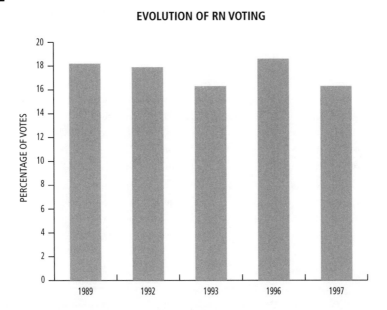

FIGURE 4

EVOLUTION OF RN VOTING

The overall electoral evolution of the RN, as shown in Table 6 and Figure 4, shows a reduction of approximately two percentage points in the period after 1989. Nevertheless, the party has maintained its base of support in the last two elections for the National Congress. From the socio-demographic point of view, a significant increase in electoral support can be seen on the municipal level in the counties of lesser HDI, rising from 14.6% to 17.9%. This is relatively congruent with the votes received by the RN in the 1997 congressional elections. In the rural zones, the party's average support paradoxically dropped from 17.6% to 11.3%, which is not at all congruent with the overall national average.

Internal Situation[7]
Since its creation in 1987, RN has held a succession of internal elections at the county, district, and regional levels. The excessive personalism that can be observed among its leaders in party elections strongly emphasizes the need to endow the party with greater levels of institutional organization. The statutes adopted in 1987 have been undergoing modification, especially regarding the regulation of internal elections, in which the regions demand more participation.

The RN's internal structure includes the General Council; the Political Commission; the National Board; the regional, district, and county leaders; and the Supreme Tribunal. On the regional, district, and county level, the internal structure of the RN reproduces the organizational model of the central leadership, varying only in the number of council members.

The General Council meets once or twice each year. Its 400 members, which include members of Congress and the board of directors, set the overall direction of the party, define its

---

7   Information based on an interview with Tomás Duval.

spheres of action and choose its candidates for Congress. General Council meetings are announced one month in advance, and their agenda is determined by common agreement among the board of directors and the Political Commission. The number of Council members may be increased or decreased in accordance with the votes received by the party in each district.

In contrast to the PPD's board of directors, whose members do not have formally established sectorial functions, the RN directors include a president and vice-presidents for politics, programs, elections, and communications, as well as a general secretary and a treasurer. The vice-presidents are empowered to execute the resolutions of the General Council.

The Political Commission is composed of 25 members, some of which are elected by the General Council and others by the party's congressional representatives. Added to these, to provide for internal democratic equilibrium, are the board of directors, mayoral representatives, the General Council members, and the regional presidents. The Political Commission is tasked with defining more immediate policy directions.

The Supreme Tribunal is elected by the General Council and meets once a month. Its five members — charged with resolving all of the party's statutory and regulatory disputes — remain five years in office. The members have the right to participate in the General Council but do not vote, and they supervise elections within the party.

Although RN defined its overall objectives in 1989, it remained undecided with respect to some programmatic issues. Progress was later made in this area by the General Council, in cooperation with the Liberty Institute, an academic research center which also advises RN's Congressional representatives and designs training and political development programs for the party's youth. RN does not have technical commissions to provide public policy advice, as do the PPD and PDC. The Liberty Institute fulfills this role, and the Political Commission formulates the party's responses to highly complex and specific issues.

The party's membership has grown from 60,000 in 1987 to 91,700 in 1997. Of these, only 50% work actively for the party. Every new applicant must be sponsored by two current members. The District Council makes the final decision on the admission of new members.

RN has a low level of representation in Chile's traditional popular organizations. It does not explicitly aim to penetrate union organizations such as the CUT, but it is well represented in the country's professional organizations, among bankers, and in some private unions.

The party enjoys a relatively comfortable financial situation. Members must be current in their dues payments in order to participate in internal elections. Individual regions and members of Congress finance their own headquarters and campaigns.

The main challenges faced by the party in recent times are solving internal political conflicts without sacrificing the party's fundamental coherence, and substantially reducing the excessive concentration of power in the board of directors and the Political Commission. The proposal has been made to deconcentrate power toward the regional level; progress was made toward this goal in the most recent municipal elections.

5. INDEPENDENT DEMOCRATIC UNION (UDI)

Political Development
Led by the imposing force of Jaime Guzmán Errázuriz, one of the most influential intellectuals of the military government, the *gremialistas* renounced the apolitical mentality they had held since the 1970s and entered the democratic transition process in 1983, uniting to form a political movement.

Until the end of the 1980s, conservative and liberalizing ideas vied for prominence in the UDI's internal debate. The party's dialogue with anti-regime forces was hampered by its inclination to reject any distortion of the legal-constitutional framework designed by the military regime. Later, without renouncing its strict fidelity to the work of Pinochet's government, it claimed a small but significant space for itself on the political spectrum of the developing democracy, claiming to be the only party represented in Congress without an attraction for the political center.

During the Aylwin government, the UDI rejected the RN's policy of agreements and became a more confrontational opposition party, although conserving its "independentist" style. When Jaime Guzmán was assassinated, it became a "fashionable" party, and its sudden growth was due in large measure to the emotional impact of that crime across broad sectors of society. UDI thought also aimed at bringing together rightist public opinion and the Pinochet contingents alienated by the RN's "democracy of agreements." The UDI's hope was, and is, to capture a consistent majority of the votes cast for General Pinochet in the 1988 plebiscite, positioning itself as the group most representative of the work of the military government. It positions itself as a modern, Christian, people's party.

In contrast to the moderate political ideas predominant in the RN, the UDI's internal unity is based on strongly-defended symbols and concepts, such as the 1980 Constitution, which it defends against modification, and Catholic traditionalism, which exercises broad influence among its members and disposes them to conservative political positions.

The hybrid nature of this party is expressed in its neoliberal economic ideas, its conservative cultural standpoint, and its populist reasoning in the political and social spheres. During a significant part of the new democratic period, the UDI exhibited oligarchical and messianic traits, not hesitating to develop sectarian attitudes based on its profound identification with the work of the military regime. Given such characteristics, it can be stated that this party is the one that most faithfully reflects the world of the right predominant in the old democracy.

The political profile of the UDI, as well as the ideological characteristics of the RN's conservative minority, are clear signals of the polyform nature of the right in Chile. It appears incapable of institutionalizing organic unity through cultural, behavioral, and moral consensus, and thus passing along its ideas to future generations and winning a greater and more consistent share of the electorate.

An incipient awareness of this situation is spreading within the UDI. Over the medium term, two broad internal currents can be expected to crystallize in the party: one of corporatist-democratic nature, aspiring to redefine itself and move beyond the ideas of the authoritarian regime, increasing its valuation of democracy and the "politics of social results"; and the other of corporatist-authoritarian nature, in which politics and democracy continue to be viewed in the light of the military government's historical project of societal regeneration.

The first of these factions would emphasize the integration of views about the past, on the condition of technical consensus regarding the future (J. Lavín, La Segunda, January 3, 1997). The second would emphasize a vision of politics derived from the spirit of authoritarian convictions about democratic effectiveness, expressed by the 1980 Constitution (La Época, October 2, 1995). The need to effectively integrate both tendencies may become a principal risk factor for the party's internal stability.

Electoral Profile

TABLE 7

UDI: VOTING AND SOCIODEMOGRAPHICS

Parliamentary 1989	Municipal 1992			Parliamentary 1993	Municipal 1996			Parliamentary 1997
10.2	11.4			12.1	13.0			14.4
	52 counties w/ highest IDH				52 counties w/ highest IDH			
	14.8				13.8			
	52 counties w/ lowest IDH				52 counties w/ lowest IDH			
	9.7				13.3			
	104 counties w/ lowest & highest IDH				104 counties w/ lowest & highest IDH			
	14.2				13.9			
	11 urban counties				11 urban counties			
	North	Central	South		North	Central	South	
	6.1	9.0	8.5		4.1	14.0	13.6	
	157 rural counties				157 rural counties			
	North	Central	South		North	Central	South	
	12.0	10.4	10.1		13.6	11.2	10.1	

FIGURE 5

EVOLUTION OF UDI VOTING

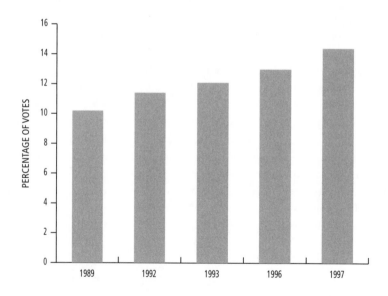

Currently, UDI continues to have evident difficulties in developing doctrinal and programmatic content independent of the legacy of issues from the military government, and thus in freeing itself from the influence of the so-called "factional powers." The party faces the pressing need to develop independence from the military. Sympathy still prevails between the Armed Forces and the UDI leadership who lived and worked with the military.

However, it is not clear that the party can continue to represent the ideas of new generations of military personnel (*Hoy*, no. 946, 1995). In any case, if the leadership of the UDI persists in anchoring itself in the defense of certain symbols and institutions associated with the era of military government, it is quite possible that the level of conflict with RN will increase, as that party delves into more practical subjects and more centrist positions.

The UDI's overall electoral evolution, summed up in Table 7 and Figure 5, shows a noticeable increase in voter support between 1989 and 1997. This increase has been discrete in its development, but sustained and consistent, which is clearly expressed in the comparison of the last two parliamentary election results. In municipal elections, the UDI increased its support from 9.7% to 13.3% between 1992 and 1996, a figure which is relatively congruent with the votes received in the 1997 parliamentary election. The observed decline is very slight but congruent with its base of electoral support exhibited in 1997. In the rural counties, the UDI experienced a slight increase, from 10.1% to 11.6%, in municipal elections.

Internal Situation[8]

As a relatively young political movement created in 1983, the UDI exhibits a still-developing internal structure. It was closely associated with the university social association tradition. In late 1988 the UDI was organized as a party, allying itself with the RN and adopting that party's statutes and declaration of principles, which had been devised by Jaime Guzmán.

All of the UDI's decision-making bodies are chosen every two years. The party's organic nucleus consists of a General Council, Political Commission, National Board, and Supreme Tribunal. The party also possesses an Electoral Commission and various technical advisory committees focusing on public policy issues.

The county boards and councils make up the regional councils, which elect the regional boards and national council members.

The General Council is composed of 405 elected members, one for each 200 members of the party. The Council in turn elects the National Board, Political Commission, and Supreme Tribunal. The General Council is empowered to provide direction to the board and the Political Commission. It also nominates the party's candidates for Congress and the presidency, and it can approve or reject the party program. The Political Commission, composed of 15 members elected by the General Council and the party's members of Congress, determines the political orientation of the party in agreement with the General Council, and considers initiatives to organize the party in other areas of the country. The National Board adopts decisions of an immediate nature, which may require the assent of the Political Commission. The Board is composed of eight members (a president, five vice-presidents, a secretary, and a pro-secretary). Its vice-presidents are not specialized by sector as in the PDC and RN. The Supreme Tribunal resolves statutory and ethical disputes at the request of any member. It also plays an obligatory role in internal elections. Its members may not have positions on the Board.

In spite of having organized an event of this kind in the early 1990s, the UDI does not possess by statute the institution of the Ideological Congress. Neither has it instituted — as in the PPD and PS — positive discrimination in favor of women. The party's female members oppose such a measure, considering it artificial, divisive, and feminist in nature.

---

8   Information based on an interview with Andrés Tagle and Felipe Salaberry.

A recent addition to the statutes has been the formation of the Joint Directive Council, the body charged with making the party's most important decisions. It is composed of the Political Commission, the National Board, the regional presidents, and the party's representatives in Congress.

The UDI has some 72,000 members, with a growth rate of 50% since 1989. There are no restrictions for entry; the only requirement is the sponsorship of two current members. The UDI membership is relatively young, with more than 50% of party members between 35 and 50 years old. Women are strongly represented (the party has more female than male mayors), as are lower-income groups. A significant increase in membership and voter support took place in 1991. Of the overall membership, only 30% participates actively in the party structure.

The UDI emphasizes the need to reinforce its organizational presence among youth, blue-collar workers, professionals (especially professors), and community groups (such as neighborhood associations and committees). The party has created functional fronts to promote itself in these areas of society.

In the area of technical and intellectual support, the UDI emphasizes training activities for young members. These are carried out by the Jaime Guzmán Foundation, which sponsors discussion circles in the style of grassroots community organizations. The Liberty and Development Institute provides technical advice to the party's members of Congress and to the board of directors, in coordination with the Guzmán Foundation. The UDI's technical committees issue standing invitations to researchers from both institutions to participate in advisory meetings. Any cases of disagreement are resolved by the party.

The UDI enjoys a comfortable financial situation. Its two regional headquarters, as well as its central office, are financed with resources received from mandatory dues and the contributions of members of Congress. The party opposes the regulation of political financing, believing that spending limits and ethical issues related to financing would be difficult to control in a fair and objective manner.

One of the central internal challenges for the UDI is modernization of the operation of the Political Commission through the institution of a more highly organized and planned agenda. Also discussed in recent times has been the need to increase the competitiveness of vice-presidential elections, avoiding the ongoing practice of closed lists. The party recognizes itself as being highly homogeneous and weak in structuring competition between parallel lists. There is also discussion of the fact that decision-making continues to be highly centralized. Only the largest regions (the Metropolitan Region along with the Fifth and Sixth regions) participate in decision-making events.

6. RADICAL SOCIAL DEMOCRATIC PARTY (PRSD)

Political Development

The origins of the Radical Social Democratic Party (PRSD) stretch back to the middle of the 19th century, with the formation of the first electoral assemblies. The earliest of these was constituted in the city of Copiapó on December 27, 1863. The birth of the assemblies was influenced by the European social struggles of 1848, especially in France, and by the legacy of the Society for Equality, of which they were considered a continuation. The number of electoral assemblies rapidly increased throughout the country, and they were considered the best means to influence the selection of congressional candidates under the 1833

Constitution. The assemblies, as a new form of political organization inherited from the French Republican clubs, evolved parallel to institutions created around the same time, such as the Volunteer Firemen's Association and the Masons. The membership of the latter included many ex-Equalitarians and future Radicals.

The Radical Party arose out of the social transformations occurring in Chile during the second half of the 19th century. The party was an organized manifestation of the feelings of dissatisfaction in the provinces acknowledged by the "reds" or Radicals. It is no accident that the first assembly was held outside the capital. Later, the middle classes of the larger cities joined the assemblies, making up the bulk of their membership. It is not an exaggeration to claim that the republic's most significant laws were developed under the influence of the Radical congressmen. Many of Radicalism's main tenets were implemented during the administrations of Radical presidents after the triumph of the Popular Front in 1938. Between that year and 1952, three governments were headed by Radicals.

Starting in the early 1970s, the Radical Party became a full member of the Socialist International. It was a founder of the Popular Unity movement and formed part of Salvador Allende's government. As a result of the political infighting of those years, a group of members critical of the Popular Unity government and its policies split off from the party. The dissidents created the Radical Left Party, and later the Chilean Social Democracy Party. Both parties supported the Democratic Alliance, the National Accord, the campaign for the "no" vote in Pinochet's referendum, and the formation of the Concertación.

In the new democracy, the two social democratic parties, with their similar roots, were able to overcome the differences of the 1970s. On August 6, 1994, the reunited party changed its name to the Radical Social Democratic Party (PRSD).

Radicalism has been characterized as a party of the center, although it is not strictly ideological in nature. Throughout its history, in its eagerness to maintain political equilibrium, it has formed governments with highly diverse coalitions, variously including both communists and conservatives. Over the past few decades, however, the Radicals have settled into a position on the center-left; as a result, many members with other points of view have left the party. Ex-Radicals have joined almost every party across the national political spectrum. The cabinet of President Frei, for example, included ex-Radicals now representing the other three parties of the governing coalition.

The composition of the current PRSD membership is very different from its profile when it was the country's leading political party and the central axis of all governing coalitions. With its current social composition, the PRSD can probably be considered the most "proletarian" party of the Concertación.

In its declaration of principles, the PRSD defines itself as a party representing lay humanism, democracy, rationalism, and solidarity. It acknowledges ideological roots in European social democracy as well as Latin American reformist movements.

The current binomial electoral system has accelerated the decline of long-standing Radical political practices. Traditional Radical political culture depended upon three institutions which today have nearly disappeared: the assemblies, Radical clubs, and conventions. Other hindrances to the party's development include the Political Parties Law, as well as the apparently more democratic form of universal internal elections, in which anyone on the electoral rolls who has declared support for the party may vote, whether or not they are active members or have paid their dues. While Chile's current political and institutional environment affects all the parties, it has apparently weighed more heavily on the

Radicals, who, with more than a century of tradition, have found it difficult to adapt to new situations.

Within the Concertación, the PRSD has not followed a strictly defined policy of alliances, but has reacted to particular circumstances as they arise. Its fellow members of the Socialist International, the PPD, and PS, would seem to be its natural allies. However, relations with these parties have been characterized mainly by competition for a similar segment of the electorate, in the party's constant effort to win more than 5% of the vote and thus maintain its validity as a party under the country's current laws. The PRSD must also continuously work to win voter support in order to avoid being absorbed by another party. The PRSD views itself as being closer to the PDC than are the other parties of the left.

The PRSD's membership in the Socialist International has led it to emphasize its concept of democratic socialism although, in contrast to European social democratic parties, the PRSD does not recognize its origins in the workers' movement. However, European events, starting with the triumph of Solidarity in Poland, have given rise to reflection among the new generations of Radicals. The party's reunification with the social democratic current, in which 19th-century traditions weigh less heavily, have reinforced these events. All factions of the party face the challenge of adapting their traditions to the requirements of the 21st century, incorporating the cultural values of new generations without turning their backs on the past.

Electoral Situation

The overall electoral development of the Radicals may be depicted as a gradual decline in political force. In the 1989 parliamentary elections, the Radical Party, before its alliance with the Social Democrats, achieved some 4% of the vote. After its agreement with the PSD in 1992, the PR increased to 5% of the vote, while the PSD received a meager 0.42%. In the 1993 parliamentary elections, the link between the parties was maintained, but support for the Radicals shrank to 3%, while the PSD remained on the brink of disappearance with 0.79% of the vote. In 1996, the fusion of the two parties under the name PRSD led to relative success, allowing the party to attract 6.5% of the electorate. However, this increase was dramatically reversed in 1997, when the new alliance received only 3.13% of the citizens' mandate. Such a signal from the voters may well have set the organization on the road toward disintegration and disappearance.

Internal Situation

The Radical Social Democratic Party, the current representative of the old Radical tradition, was hastily formed when both of its constituent parties faced the loss of legal recognition under the Political Parties Law, although their fusion had already been contemplated for some time. The new party was created under a certain time pressure, as a consequence of the limited period set by law for the registration of new political parties. Thus, there was no time for discussion of the new party's statutes and declaration of principles outside the merging parties' leadership. The new organization also lacked a program as such.

The party's rules for the admission of new members are relatively simple. Any citizen registered in the voter rolls may become a member of the PRSD. Prospective members must present an application, co-sponsored by two active members, to the county assembly where they are registered to vote. The current membership stands at around 87,000, of whom slightly more than 50,000 are women. Some 12,500 members participated in the last internal elections.

In traditional Radical culture, the assembly generated the party's political and programmatic initiatives. There are assemblies in every county of the country; however, they have currently lost their importance since their activity has been weakened by the Political Parties Law. The party currently exhibits a very low level of activity, mobilizing almost exclusively for elections.

Party organizations include the county assemblies, district councils, the General Council, the National Convention, the Political Commission, various national organizations and departments, the Supreme Tribunal, and the regional tribunals. The Central Board, considered to be the party's highest standing body, executes PRSD policies in all of their expressions. This body's headquarters in Santiago is referred to as the National Executive Committee (CEN). It is viewed as a superior political authority to the General Board, which is made up of General Council members elected by the district councils, which in turn are chosen through universal elections.

The National Convention, at which the National Board was formerly elected, has changed its character and is currently technically considered the highest instance of the party, charged with elaborating doctrinal, political, ideological, and programmatic proposals. By statute it must meet every two years. However, since the formation of the PRSD, the National Convention has never been convoked. This fact explains many of the internal, ideological, and political problems suffered by the party in recent years.

Since its unification, Social Democratic Radicalism has not undertaken the ideological and programmatic discussion necessary to adapt itself to the new political environment of the post-military government period. In practice, the PRSD has been programmatically dissolved into the Concertación. This has hindered it from presenting its own image to the country and the electorate, especially in the areas traditionally identified with Radical movements, such as secularism and education. Concurrently, the party's academic and policy research institutions, such as the Professional Department, the Political Commission, and the party's think tanks, have ceased to function or have lessened their activity.

In consequence, the PRSD maintains a low profile in the discussion of leading topics on the national agenda, although many brilliant professionals are associated with the party. Thus, among the current Board's highest priorities, supported by all internal factions, is the holding of a national convention to address both ideological and internal problems. Proposals have been raised for the reform, or even re-formulation of the party, to harmonize its program and internal structure with the requirements of political practice in the 21st century.

Like all political parties opposing the dictatorship, the PRSD was deprived of all of its assets, including its assembly sites and Radical clubs. Its current financial situation is quite unfavorable. In practice, it depends upon contributions from wealthy members, since the payment of dues is solely a moral obligation and not a condition of membership, a situation which tends to distort the member-party relationship. The PRSD supports governmental financing of political parties.

The National Executive Committee (CEN) is elected every two years through a proportional system granting the offices of president, one vice-president, general secretary, and treasurer to the winning list. The remaining positions are proportionally elected among all of the other candidates, who compete in a single list. The CEN is tasked with governing the party in accordance with its statutes, declaration of principles, voting, platform, and other guidelines provided by the General Council and/or the National Convention.

The Political Commission is an advisory, consultation, and research body, charged with informing the CEN and the General Council about any issue of interest to the party leadership. In addition to its president, the commission includes 11 members who are elected for a period of two years by the CEN and may be re-elected.

7. CHILEAN COMMUNIST PARTY (PC)

Political Development

The Communist Party of Chile, founded at the turn of the century by Luis Emilio Recabarren, has historically taken up the banner of the workers' movement. It reached its highest level of expression during the Allende government. The party suffered extreme repression under the military government but was able to resist more successfully than the PS. The communists had more experience in underground action, as well as a tradition of greater cohesion and internal discipline. During the authoritarian phase, the party acquired a cellular organizational structure, allowing it to maintain a certain unity of action and greater legitimacy among its internal leaders.

The PC's role on the national political scene in the 1990s has been influenced by a series of factors arising out of the country's experiences during the 1970s and 1980s, as well as by others of international character. The PC criticized the handling of the end of the military government and the transition to democracy, viewing it as a solution worked out by the military and the more moderate wing of the opposition. The new institutions preserve much of the order established by the Armed Forces and additionally place restrictions on the parties of the left. The Communist Party is also critical of the neoliberal economic model established in the 1980s, which in its judgment introduces a system of ideas and values contrary to the progressivist thought historically prevalent among the Chilean population. The Chilean Communist Party has also been affected by the fall of the socialist system in Eastern Europe, which has led to discouragement, disconcertion, and dispersion among members of leftist parties throughout the world.

The 15th Congress, held in May 1989, reaffirmed the party's Marxist-Leninist character, which was again ratified by the 16th Congress in 1994. It should be mentioned that beginning with this last Congress, the PC formally recognized its roots in the Socialist Workers' Party, founded in 1912, five years before the October Revolution. Thus the 16th Congress was transformed into the 20th Congress.

The PC supported Patricio Aylwin's candidacy and participated in the instrumental organization PAIS (Joint Party of the Socialist Left). Not being a member of the Concertación of Parties for Democracy, the Communist Party found itself marginalized by the government and Congress, a situation aggravated by the restrictions and exclusions established by the 1980 Constitution for parties not attached to coalitions. From this difficult position, the Communists practiced a policy of constructive independence toward the government, supporting all actions it saw as advancing the democratization of the country. Over the course of the 1990s, this stance gradually changed to active opposition, as the communists came to believe that the government's actions, rather than democratizing the country, were oriented toward consolidating the economic, social, and political system established by the military government.

While some PAIS members joined the Concertación after the 1990 elections, the Communist Party, together with other leftist groups, formed the Allendist Democratic Movement of the Left (MIDA). This organization remained active until the 1993 elections, for which it nominated Eugenio Pizarro. Later the organization participated in joint initiatives with the Humanist Party, when the latter separated from the Concertación, and factions splitting off from the Socialist Party, as well as other independent leftist groups. With some of these it formed, for the 1996 municipal and 1997 parliamentary elections, the alliance known as "The Left."

The Communist Party proposed to participate in the presidential and parliamentary elections of December 1999 within this coalition, signaling that these "will be a decisive landmark in the struggle for democracy only if the popular masses participate in them resolutely." [9]

The most recent initiative undertaken by the Communist Party to promote the democratization of the country has been its unsuccessful offer to the Concertación regarding the so-called National Democratic Accord, an electoral understanding for the 1997 Congressional elections. The offer was based on a four-point compromise: abolition of the binomial electoral system, approval of the Labor Reform proposal, improvements in income distribution, and justice in the cases of human rights violations occurring during the military dictatorship.

The PC's political action in recent years has been especially focused on workers and students, among which its standing has risen, as seen in the most recent university federation elections. The party is also working to articulate a distinct "alternative" to the neoliberal model. This program includes advocacy for solutions based on majority rights, the reaffirmation of the State's determining role in the economic and social spheres, the use of natural resources for the benefit of the country as a whole, and support for social justice. This "alternative," presented in the Party Program approved by the 20th Congress (1994) and in the Platform of the Left (1997), is beginning to find support among Chileans, as shown by the slate's achievement of 6.73% of the vote in 1997.

The party's actions have also propelled it into a leadership position on the Left, embodied in the Communist secretary-general, Gladys Marín. In her view, the great challenge that must propel the organization forward is to bring about the revolutionary transformation of society and counteract the defenders of "anti-democracy" through the pressure of social mobilization. Ms. Marín affirms that "if the social movement achieves not just a fragmented idea of its goals, but one which harmonizes with a global vision for all of society, we will have a plan valid for the workers, students, and finally for the left as a whole," (*Hoy*, no. 1.072, February 1998).

Electoral Situation

The 6.73% obtained by the Communist Party in the parliamentary elections on December 11, 1997, evoked surprise among some national and international political analysts. Many had assumed that the combined effects of the binomial electoral system and the party's scarce material and financial resources would limit its share of the vote to 5% or lower.

---

9   Report from the 15th Congress of the Communist Party of Chile, 1989.

Adding the votes cast for the New Popular Alliance and the leftist independents comprising the list of "The Left," the total reaches 7.47%, the highest figure achieved by the extraparliamentary left since the country's return to democracy.

For the 1989 presidential and parliamentary elections, the Communist Party joined with the Socialist Party-Almeyda Sector, the Historical Socialist Party, the Christian Left, the Revolutionary Movement of the Left (MIR) and the Radical Social Democratic Party to form an instrumental party called the Joint Party of the Socialist Left (PAIS), which was able to elect two congressional representatives. In the municipal elections of June 28, 1992, the Communist Party list (which included all of the candidates of the Allendist Democratic Movement, MIDA), obtained 6.7% of the national vote, although pre-election polls had not projected it to receive more than 3%.

A decline in support was seen in the 1993 parliamentary elections, in which it obtained 4.99%. In accordance with the rules of the binomial electoral system, this result did not permit it to obtain a single parliamentary seat, and in addition the party was obliged to re-register itself in various regions of the country. The Communist Party slightly increased its share of the vote in the 1996 municipal elections, achieving a figure of about 6% for "The Left" list in conjunction with independent leftist forces. Thus the Communist Party remains a significant force on the left wing of the country's political spectrum — similar to the 1938 Popular Front, as well as the process initiated with the 1951 formation of the People's Front, culminating in 1970 with the Popular Unity movement.

In the parliamentary elections of 1997, "The Left" and "Humanist" lists received a combined total of 10.35% of overall votes. Furthermore, the Communist Party, formerly without a single representative in the Senate or Chamber of Deputies, obtained the eighth largest mandate in the Senate with the candidacy of Gladys Marín. The 171,790 ballots cast for the Communist leader represented 15.69% of the vote in election district 7, West Santiago, surpassing the number of votes received by 16 elected senators.

Internal Situation

The end of the Communist Party's period of illegal operation during the military government came about through its fulfillment of the requirements set forth in the Political Parties Law, No. 19,603, of March 11, 1987, with the registration of more than 60,000 members throughout the country. The public expression of the party was thus legalized. The PC's internal structure and current operation are congruent with its conception of itself as a "revolutionary party," a trait it has claimed since its inception in 1912.

The party organization is guided by the principle of "democratic centralism." This is described as the participation of all members in the formulation, planning, and implementation of the party's political line. Resolutions arising from discussions at all levels are adopted by unanimous agreement or majority vote. The principle also requires that once a resolution is adopted, all members must act in accordance with it.

Democracy and centralization are also expressed in the selection of leaders of cells, county committees, regional committees, and the Central Committee. Any member may become a candidate for leadership through a proposal to his or her constituent body, which takes into consideration the candidates' characteristics, interests, and qualities, as well as the needs of the organization.

Through a resolution adopted at the first Conference, held in June 1990, the Communist Party acquired a new national structure. The cell, consisting of a small group of members from the same neighborhood, workplace or service organization, is the basic building block of the party. Above the cell is the county Central Committee, selected by all members of the county's cell, which works on political problems affecting its territory. Above the county level are the regional committees, which direct and carry out Communist political leadership in each region.

The National Congress, the party's highest body, meets every four years. Its participants include the delegates elected to the regional congresses, in addition to the members of the Central Committee. In the period between Congresses, the party's highest authority is the Central Committee, made up of 80 members elected at the National Congress. The Central Committee, which meets every two months, gives direction and force to the implementation of the party's political line. Between meetings, the Central Committee relies upon two subgroups: the Political Commission, made up of 15 of its members, and the five-member Secretariat. It also maintains the national commissions as auxiliary bodies, which research, elaborate, and promote actions in particular areas of social life. The national commissions include Unions, Agriculture, Population, Women, Professionals, Human Rights, Ecology, Indigenous Peoples, Communications, and others.

The PC once enjoyed the financial solidarity of the socialist world. Today its resources are limited to the contributions of its members. Neither the party's national fundraising campaigns nor the obligatory daily sales of five copies of the newspaper *El Siglo* [The Century] by each member are sufficient to cover the party's payroll and operating expenses. Not surprisingly, the PC strongly supports the return of confiscated assets to the parties, as well as government financing of political activity.

In 1997, Communist Party organizations covered all 13 regions of the country and 70% of Chile's counties. The party is currently preparing for the 21st Congress in 1998. This process is initiated in the cells and culminates, after several months of discussion, in the National Congress. The Congress will set the party's political line starting in March 1998, as it faces the challenges and responsibilities posed by the evolution of Chilean society. The support of Communist academic centers such as the Alejandro Lipschutz Institute of Sciences, whose work has a broad influence upon the political undertakings of the left in general, will be fundamental to this task.

Conclusions

All of the parties observed — with the partial exception of the PPD — have a commitment to formal debate and the development of ideological and programmatic definitions. There is evidence of an internal transition within the party system. As the information collected here shows, the Chilean system presents a high level of competition, developed in the framework of a qualitatively centrist political culture, with personalized leadership frequently observed. A significant characteristic of the party system in the 1990s has been the broadly dispersed set of values and ideas espoused within the most important parties and coalitions. This, together with the often reactive and unpredictable nature of the parties' political strategies, has tended to generate confusion and even disillusionment with politics on the grassroots level, resulting in imbalances of power between the parties and the executive branch. It should be mentioned that each party in the system shows some level

FIGURE 7

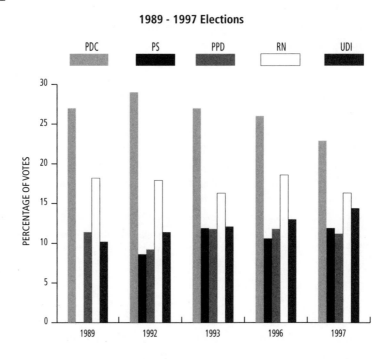

1989 - 1997 Elections

PDC   PS   PPD   RN   UDI

of concern as to its ideological position in the market economy, as many struggle to define a more nuanced vision of the development concepts offered by the world of liberal ideas.

In the electoral sphere, the Christian Democratic Party has diminished its share of the vote in relative terms but remains the system's indisputable majority party in parliamentary elections, although its situation is more precarious among some socio-demographic segments analyzed here in the comparison of counties according to the Human Development Index. The PPD-PS alliance has slightly increased or maintained its voter support on the parliamentary and municipal levels. The PC has increased its political relevance as its electoral strength has risen. On the right, the UDI stands out with a significant electoral force, aided by a powerful and clearly personalized leadership. RN has maintained itself as the majority party of the opposition and the second in importance within the Chilean system. In light of the municipal and parliamentary election results achieved by the country's five leading parties, on a macro scale, the most important political factor is voter motivation. Throughout all of the elections, with the exception of the 1997 congressional races, the PDC obtained approximately 26%, RN 18%, the UDI 12-13%, and the PS and the PPD between 10% and 11%. This relative continuity weakens the assertion that analytical comparisons between the parliamentary and municipal elections are impossible (see Figure 6).

Internally, the parties recognize the need for further institutional modernization, including decentralizing organizational structures and decision-making processes; promoting equilibrium in internal political representation and better coordination among internal bodies; and increasing member participation in party politics. The parties' think tanks and advisory bodies vary widely in their quality and influence, but the need to strengthen their effectiveness and impact upon political affairs is generally recognized.

The Decentralization Process

Jaime Ahumada

Introduction

Decentralization, as expressed in the proposals being developed in Latin America, takes two general directions. The first seeks to divide and compartmentalize social conflicts and demands, advancing toward privatization, a minimal State, reduced public expenditures, and a greater role for business. In contrast, the second seeks to promote the modernization of the State through political democratization, greater management effectiveness, and increased social participation. Thus, the notion of decentralization is a highly ambiguous one, due to the multiplicity of concepts which it suggests and the social and political heterogeneity of those who support it. Adherents of the most diverse schools of thought, from socialists to neoliberals, include it in their proposals and programs.

The experience of decentralization efforts in Chile can serve to illustrate the content and consequences of the Latin American decentralization impulse. The Chilean case, in its recent authoritarian and democratic phases, seems to confirm that both of these tendencies are present and influential.

In analyzing the Chilean decentralization process, four important topics must be considered:
- The context in which changes are carried out
- The contrast between the idea of decentralization during the military dictatorship and under the democratic governments, installed by popular vote starting in 1990
- The strengths and weaknesses presented by the municipalities, provinces, and regions for the implementation of the new policies, especially in the democratic phase
- The third effort being undertaken by the country in this area, in which discussion still predominates over action.

I. The Context of Change

After democracy was re-instituted in 1990, along with the rule of law, Chile continued its strong economic growth, sustained by its earlier model of trade opening, external financing, and integration into global markets. The Chilean government today aims at economic growth with social equity, while the country's business sectors play an increasingly active role in international economic relations and even in the political system. At the same time, the country is undergoing an internal transformation represented by decentralization, regionalization, and municipalization throughout its territory. While the latter process may sometimes conflict with the country's policy of external opening, it has continued its progress through the force of its democratizing character and the new opportunities for participation which it provides.

The export model, with its selective effect and the imbalances it produces on the subnational level, coexists with a political system promoting a greater role for the regions and counties [comunas], through the decentralization of governmental and social structures.

The State is beginning to change its historically centralized and authoritarian nature. Not only are the regions, provinces, and counties gaining more power, devolved upon them by the unitary State, but the government's own internal organizations are increasingly being urged to adopt decentralized and pluralist structures and functions. The national government has begun to subdivide itself and transfer powers, responsibilities, and resources to more local levels. The regions, provinces, and counties themselves are being impelled to legitimize themselves in their own jurisdictions, electing their own authorities and seeking participation mechanisms for society in their management and decision-making processes.

However, participatory democracy and decentralized development are arising in the midst of a great cognitive gap, with society lacking a decentralizing political and economic culture, and history weighing in on the side of centralism. Thus questions arise regarding compatibility between the market economy model, a concentrator of priorities and resources, and the political model of transition from a centralized and authoritarian State to a decentralized and democratic State. The answers can only be found in a synthesis between external opening and globalization and internal opening and decentralization, and between the opportunities offered by internationalization and the capacity of regions and counties to take advantage of them.

Thus Chile's aim is to enter the 21st century with active regional and municipal governments with greater resources and powers which effectively promote development plans, programs, and projects; which stimulate technical creation and innovation; and which have the capacity to balance the distorting effects of the country's market policies and external integration. This task will require both national and regional leadership, as well as dynamic coordination and cooperation between the central government and the subnational levels.

1. THE NEED FOR REFORM

Historically Chile has had a centralist structure, starting with the administrative and institutional framework established in the colonial period, and continuing with the installation of an authoritarian presidential regime in 1830, the influence of which has persisted through the 1980 Constitution. Other centralizing factors have included the territorial organization carried out during Chile's republican infancy in the previous century; the country's political, economic, and social development, marked by the sustained growth of Santiago and its concentration of decision-making powers; and the lesser growth rates and even regression of the regions. The weight of tradition and the greater strategic efficiency of centralist models have been invoked to support these developments. Reference is also made to the failure of the decentralization efforts and regionalist movements of the previous century, represented by Lircay (1830) and the states of exception established in 1851 and 1861. On the other hand, it is recognized that the country is not completely satisfied with the type of State prescribed by the dominant models.

In fact, antecedents of the current efforts to decentralize the State and even society can be found in the previous century, in the Constitution and Federal Laws of 1826, the 1828 Constitution, the regionalist movements emerging under President Manuel Montt, and initiatives taken by President José Manuel Balmaceda. The present century has seen the creation of the Provincial Assemblies in the 1925 Constitution, along with other proposals made at the founding of the Corporation for the Promotion of Production (Corfo) during the Popular Front, as well as the duty-free zones established under the government of General Ibáñez. Some of these initiatives were unsuccessful, while others were only partially carried out. It fell to the governments of Presidents Jorge Alessandri, Eduardo Frei, and Salvador Allende to undertake the nation's first period of authentic decentralizing efforts, which lasted until 1973.

After 1960, Chile focused greater resolve upon creating a new type of State; promoting action by the regions, provinces, and counties in order to populate and democratize the territories; creating a modern institutional structure; and involving the organized community in the management of national and subnational development.

The creation of the Consultive Committees for Economic Planning and Reconstruction (Copere) in the early 1960s, the founding of the National Planning Office (Odeplan) in 1967, and the strengthening of regional policies in the early 1970s were significant developments, setting the stage for the second decentralization effort, which unfolded under the military dictatorship starting in 1973.

The military junta first viewed this tendency more as administrative and authoritarian deconcentration than territorial and functional decentralization. In the period from 1973 to 1980, the military regime undertook the administrative reorganization of the State, creating the National Commission for Adlministrative Rationalization (Conara) and dictating numerous laws and statutes related to the country's regions and municipalities. Various initiatives were established to promote this process, including tax and customs exemptions, bonuses, loans, and social programs and funds, especially on the local level.

Later, the 1980 Constitution, with its neo-presidentialist formula enshrining an extreme concentration of power in the Head of State, became the legal foundation for the military government's authoritarian deconcentration as well as its so-called "territorial decentralization" policy, expressed in the municipal laws of 1988.

During his candidacy in the 1989 presidential elections, Patricio Aylwin pledged to facilitate the transition from authoritarian to democratic government and to transform the territorial and functional deconcentration process into an authentic decentralization strategy. This would be accomplished through municipal reform, improvements to the law of neighborhood associations, and democratization on the regional and local levels. As president, he persuaded the opposition to agree upon a parliamentary timetable which culminated with the new municipal and regional laws.

It was clear that neither the 1989 constitutional reforms, nor the political mechanisms available during the post-plebiscite period, could alter the foundations of a system granting the President of the Republic the sole power to name regional governors [intendentes], provincial governors, and mayors, and to control the most important aspects of regional and local administration. Unquestionably, this had been a strategic consideration for the military regime, looking ahead to a period in which they would need more subtle support mechanisms, as occurred between 1990 and 1992. The regime viewed the subnational level as a kind of safeguard, providing a replacement contingent for the nation's political elite as well as a sort of protective shield for the military government's achievements and historical reputation.

The governments of Presidents Aylwin and Frei chose a path of negotiation, consensus, and limited confrontation with the opposition forces, especially during the constitutional and legal reform process from 1990 to 1993. These reforms paved the way for the municipal elections of June 1992, the configuration of regional and provincial governments, the holding of elections for regional councils, and the later renovations of the country's institutional, economic, and financial architecture.

2. THE *SUI GENERIS* NATURE OF THE CHILEAN TRANSITION

As the Chilean transition unfolded, it revealed its *sui generis* character. While decentralization was considered a pressing objective within the modernization and reform of the national State, it did not yet enjoy the necessary impetus. It was hindered by resistance deriving from the country's centralist history and culture, insufficient general knowledge of the initiative, and a lack of community participation in public life.

Political action centered on elections and the strengthening of a democracy dominated by political parties. The concern for a deeper integration of political and economic forces at all levels remained secondary. Democracy was underpinned by sustained and balanced economic growth, favorable fiscal accounts, and an almost exaggerated rigidity in the assignment of resources. These resources were controlled by the Ministry of Finance, and subnational demands were processed by the Ministry of Public Works, in particular the chiefs of services, ministerial regional secretaries (Seremis), and the Undersecretariat for Regional and Administrative Development (Subdere).

These limiting factors for decentralization were accentuated by the breakdown of the municipal system; the "capital-centered" effect, of which Santiago is the best exponent and the regional capitals its subordinate "clones"; and the institutional imbalances permeating the entire subnational level.

Nevertheless, further reforms have recently been introduced to improve local election processes, and regulations covering municipal administration are being formalized, along with those related to the work of the regional councils and municipal associations. There is a tendency on the local level to emphasize personal leadership over political operations, a factor which introduces very concrete needs and problems. Recent proposals have included instituting the direct election of regional governors and regional council members; strengthening the role of the provincial governors; and empowering the Regional and County Councils. The most recent presidential messages have emphasized a frontal attack on centralism, and thus a devolution of decision-making power to the people. These aspirations must form the essence of Chile's decentralization process.

A similar phenomenon is seen in the significant projected increases in the percentage of public investment under regional control, as well as the expansion of funds to finance decentralized projects. The work of the National Fund for Regional Development (FNDR) during the period 1990-94 was carefully evaluated, and new mechanisms such as the Sectorial Investments under Regional Assignation (ISAR), the Regional Investments under Local Assignation (IRAL), and the Program Agreements were established. In addition, the new municipal revenue law and the reappraisal of non-agricultural real estate have clearly increased the resources available to the country's municipalities.

3. AS THE SUBNATIONAL GOVERNMENTS ARE STRENGTHENED, NEW PROBLEMS APPEAR AND THEIR MANAGEMENT BECOMES MORE COMPLEX.

Chile's regional, provincial, and county administrations are being significantly strengthened. The regional planning law; the formation of administrative and decision-making structures at these levels; advances in the coordination of provincial governments; and the emphasis among the municipalities on improved administration are eloquent examples of a process struggling to advance within an environment of regional imbalances, provinces still searching for political and institutional identity, and counties lacking in administrative expertise.

It is encouraging to note that the groups accompanying presidential visits to other countries of the region have included not only business leaders, but also regional governors and other subnational leaders. This participation is fundamental for the development of more active and globalized international economic relations, as well as for the external integration of the regions. At the same time, subnational officials' increasing interest and experience in the formulation of strategic guidelines and development plans will aid in the formation of a regional leadership class with broader political horizons and a better understanding of how to govern their regions and empower local forces.

Progress in decentralization and the modernization of institutions and management methods will demand determined action and creative attention to areas of weakness and deficiency. Currently, only mayors and council members are elected by popular vote, since the regional governors and provincial governors are named by the president, while the regional council members are chosen in second-degree elections. At the same time, community participation in the determination of policies and programs at the regional, provincial, and county levels is still low, confining itself in practice to the election of local authorities, in spite of attempts made by the central government and the regions and counties themselves to increase it.

Aside from these weaknesses, however, certain inroads have been made. The Cabinet has held meetings in many regional capitals and prominent cities and has even proposed development plans and annual agenda in the subnational territories, as with the Arica and Austral Plans and the recent Temuco Agenda. The institutions of the municipalities and regional councils have been put into place, and they have begun to raise new demands and issues to be addressed in public policy. Specific regional mobilizations have arisen which do not reach the level of general demands but provide opportunities for improved interaction with the central government. The Arica Plan of 1994, the Arica Law of 1995, and the recently approved Austral Plan are initiatives to support further development of the remote territories, although they are still insufficient for these communities.

In other words, the goals of spatial and political pluralism, the consolidation of the democratic state, and the pluralist exercise of popular participation recently began to be glimpsed on the horizon of the decentralization process. At the same time, the necessity for great institutional and societal changes has appeared as a condition for success in this inspiring experience of building a country.

4. THE DEBUT OF SUBNATIONAL DEMOCRACY

On June 28, 1992, municipal democracy was formally inaugurated with popular elections, clearing the way for new and significant municipal responsibilities in the preparation of their own development plans and budgets, as well as an increase in community participation and the expression of local aspirations.

On November 18 of the same year, the Chilean Association of Municipalities (Achimun) was created, assimilating models from other countries. During the Aylwin administration, this association came to resemble a lobbying group representing municipal interests and helping to increase awareness of local problems in the executive branch, Congress, and public opinion.

The President of the Santiago Mayoral Council, Jaime Ravinet, not only formulated the structure of this organization and contributed to creating its atmosphere of consensus reaching across party lines, but also had a strong impact on its internal policies and international ties. Ravinet presided for a period over the International Union of Local Authorities (IULA), and his reelection as the highest authority of the capital city catapulted him into a position as a leader with national impact.

The current president of Achimun, Gonzalo Duarte, seems to be focusing his leadership on internal aspects of municipal politics and an active liaison with the central government, aiming above all to overcome deficiencies in the municipalized services and to secure financing for growing local budgets.

During these years, the municipal level has clearly gained prestige and influence, and its successful example has helped spur the formation of regional governments and the founding of the National Association of Regional Council Members.

The election of the regional councils on April 3, 1993, underlined the will to continue the decentralizing tendency. Several kinds of decisions ceased to be made by the central government, and tasks were passed to the regions such as the elaboration of strategies and development plans, the preparing of the regional budget, and the allocation of regional investment funds.

That date, April 3, 1993, was considered a milestone in the pluralization of national power. For the first time in the country's history, regional governments were headed by regional governors named by a democratic president, alongside elected regional councils with regulatory, decision-making, and budgetary powers. The regions were also supported by fiscal mechanisms such as the Fund for Regional Development, the Investments under Regional and Local Assignation, and the Planning Agreements.

The principal responsibilities of this level of government have been to administer regional development; manage a significant percentage of public investment; supervise the organization of the territory; promote productive activity; and coordinate social policies such as anti-poverty programs, which require a high level of cooperation between governments at the municipal and regional levels.

The inauguration of the regional governments has been an incontestable advance in decentralization. However, interventionist currents persist in the central government and Congress, in addition to the reflexive demand throughout society that every problem must be solved, in the final instance, by the President of the Republic, the regional governor, the provincial governor, or the local mayor. The centralizing effect of the capitals and the national, provincial, regional, or county institutions permeates the fabric of the Chilean socioeconomic structure.

Meanwhile, a lack of confidence can still be noted among authorities of the national government toward the municipalities and regions, and at the same time, weaknesses and insecurities persist among subnational leaders regarding the exercise of their functions and responsibilities. The bold, definitive step toward local control has still not been taken, and the momentum still favors recentralizing forces.

5. THE DIFFICULT PATH FROM THEORY TO PRACTICE

Chile's democratic governments have supported the consolidation of sub-national governments, along with a higher level of regionalization and municipalization, in a difficult and complex framework of free-market economic policies. These policies favor regions better endowed with natural resources, and especially the Metropolitan Region. This region, with its advantage of including the national capital, enjoys a highly disproportionate share of services as well as private and public investment. Addressing this problem will require greater inter-ministerial coordination and an improved framework of inter-governmental and subnational relations for the elaboration and execution of public policies.

A new distribution of labor is needed within the country's official structures, as well as greater involvement of the population in the tasks of development and national construction. This may lead to the elaboration of a supporting body of law, and even the creation of a Ministry or Secretariat to channel and promote the overall development process.

The structure of the regional governments has been developing in a process of successive approximations since the 1980s, with the Regional Development Councils (Coredes); the 1991 modifications of the 1980 Constitution's 13th chapter, on the Government and Administration of the State; the 1992 Organic Constitutional Law of Regional Governments; the election of the regional councils in 1993; and the May 1995 law delineating the structure of the regional governments.

Various levels of sub-national government are being configured at the same time, although, it has been argued, without the necessary coordinated and simultaneous character. The regional level is governed by an indirectly elected regional council and a designated regional governor, integrating the phenomena of deconcentration and decentralization. At the provincial level, regulatory and bureaucratic difficulties are encountered in the coordination of public services. The municipalities, whose leaders are elected by popular vote, are advancing most rapidly in the political-institutional decentralization process and have broadened their management powers due to the new reform just approved by Congress.

Examples of successful county administration, often praised in the media, can be seen in Iquique, Santiago, Las Condes, La Serena, Huechuraba, Rancagua, Concepción, Temuco, Puerto Montt, and Punta Arenas. All of these counties are distinguished by the search for innovative planning and management techniques. Iquique has focused on the issue of transoceanic corridors. In Santiago and Las Condes, emphasis is placed on empowering the mayoral council and on the concept of businesslike municipalities achieving a positive cost-benefit balance for society. In La Serena, Huechuraba, and Concepción, large tourism projects have been implemented, as well as proposals for social integration, community development, and strategic alliances with the private sector. In Rancagua and Temuco, local economic development networks have been formed, along with active neighborhood initiatives. Puerto Montt and Punta Arenas have focused on community participation, public-private convergence, and greater territorial decentralization. Further examples of dynamism on the local level are found in jurisdictions such as Antofagasta, Coquimbo, Bernardo O'Higgins, Concepción, and Los Lagos.

Despite decades of effort, however, many goals still appear distant, due to political, economic, and cultural impediments. The Corporation for the Regionalization of Chile (CorChile), at the Fourteenth National Regionalization Day celebrated in October of this year in Arica, insisted upon a state monopoly for the decentralization process, both from the budgetary and the decision-making point of view. The president of CorChile, Claudio Lapostol, noted that United Nations reports continue to confirm great differences between the quality of life in Santiago and in the regions. He also emphasized many municipalities' reiterated attempts to return responsibilities such as education and public health to the central government due to a lack of resources.

Studies by the Freedom and Development Institute in 1997 showed that the investment controlled by regional authorities is growing sluggishly compared to the rest of the investment budget. Within the National Fund for Regional Development (FNDR), the fastest-growing budgetary category is the so-called provisions, which are allocated by the central administration.

The regional economic analysis entitled "Productive Development of the Regions," recently published by the Ministry of Economics, gives evidence of the great economic disparities among the regions. Almost 50% of Chile's GNP is concentrated in the Metropolitan Region. If the regions of Bio-Bio and Valparaiso are added to this figure, the total represents some 70% of GNP concentrated in these three of the country's 13 regions. This worrisome situation, already exploited with effect in various political campaigns, is beginning to weigh heavily upon local and regional leaders, as they seek to reconcile current legal requirements with the daily problems of their populations and territories.

In the quest to confront regional inequality in the promotion of development, the subject of decentralization has arisen more urgently in public opinion and political discourse. The national and Santiago press, principally influenced by the company "El Mercurio" and the Journalistic Consortium of Chile (Copesa), have highlighted decentralization efforts in their columns and editorial pages. The regional media allot even more space and attention to this issue, since it constitutes more relevant "news." Coverage includes reports on the particular region's own problems, anti-capital protests, and developments favoring other provinces and regions. The daily newspaper *El Mercurio* is prominent in this area, maintaining in-depth coverage of opinions and news pertaining to the decentralization process.

The provincial and regional press has consistently emphasized problems related to imperfections in the country's political-administrative division. Provincial claims receive significant coverage in regionally deconcentrated media outlets. Criticism of the Arica and Austral Plans, reports on the persistent deficiencies in municipalized education and health services, and the complaints of agricultural producers and environmental groups also find a receptive audience. A spirit of anti-capital resentment is manifested, along with open accusations of abandonment of the outlying territories on the part of the central authorities.

II. Authoritarian and Democratic Types of Decentralization

Decentralization is a complex process. It implies a profound transformation of the State and society, and one of its most central characteristics is the consultation, mobilization, and participation of a multiplicity of forces throughout the country.

The democratization of political and social relations lends legitimacy to the decentralization process and deepens the transformations occurring within it. Yet this was precisely the limitation of the efforts made by the military government: the regime advanced toward territorial deconcentration and economic deregulation but did not institute democratic elections for subnational authorities. The Concertación coalition governments have moved toward spatial and political pluralism and territorial democracy, although they have not as yet shown the necessary political will to create a new form of State endowed with full social equity.

1. MILITARY DECENTRALIZATION

Decentralization had been a latent subject on the national development agenda when the military government began to focus upon it. The regime created a new institutional infrastructure under which subnational governments began to function. It channeled its decentralizing efforts through the municipalities, granting them greater powers and resources. Funds were created to finance this activity, which followed the principles of territorial deconcentration and economic deregulation. The tenets followed by the regime included the primacy of the market, political authoritarianism in the selection of leaders, administrative deconcentration, and a strict central authority.

As is well known, the decentralization undertaken by the military government cemented itself into a vertical decision-making system, lacking regional or local democracy. Regions were established through the demarcation of borders, the granting of deconcentrated functions, and the creation of an infrastructure for regional and local governments.

The implicit intention of the military government was the geopolitical and geostrategic utilization of territories susceptible to external threats or internal unrest. However, the deconcentrating dialectic led to unexpected effects in the territories: the formation of a new regional consciousness, accentuation of the municipalities' importance as local forces, and even the appearance of a certain type of military leader with regionalist impetus and inspiration.

The Austral Highway is the greatest achievement of the military period and, from a geopolitical perspective, it constitutes an example of conquest of the internal frontier, especially in the Region of Aysén.

2. DEMOCRATIC DECENTRALIZATION

A close look at the democratic period reveals two decentralization phases which stand out sharply. The first included the Aylwin administration's legal-institutional proposals, the related parliamentary negotiations, and the early implementation of the Constitutional Organic Laws on municipal and regional government (May 1990 - April 1993). The second, a time of adjustment and consolidation, was initiated with the election of the regional council members and the installation of the regional governments throughout the country. It extends to the present day, with the new county reforms, the municipal revenue law, the regional planning law, and the political commitments to significantly augment the percentage of public investment under regional control, from 21% in 1994 to some 42% before the end of President Frei Ruiz-Tagle's term in office.

Reforms under President Aylwin

In the 1990-93 period, the constitutional reforms and the municipal and regional laws approved by Congress permitted substantial advances in the transition to democracy and the consolidation of a State under the rule of law.

These reforms, while limited, aimed at bringing about substantive changes to both the State and Chilean society. The regional, provincial, and county levels were firmly established within a new system of vertical relations. The regional, provincial, and county authorities were installed, with new powers, resources, and responsibilities.

The regions, provinces, and counties have increasingly adopted deconcentrated and decentralized functions and structures, gaining in identity and organization, legitimizing their territorial spaces and advancing toward a new territorial democracy which must involve active mechanisms of consultation and citizen participation. This calls for overall modernization and institutional reforms to provide direction to the process as a whole and lend transparency to decentralization efforts. The goal is a framework which can adapt flexibly to new situations; promote a capacity for innovation; value human resources and their development; and establish fluid information and communication networks within and among the diverse instances and levels of territorial management.

The path uniting development and decentralization leads from regionalization to regionalism and finally to full regional government, and from municipalization to county empowerment and ultimately to authentic local government. It is a search for identity, development, and truly democratic government on the part of the territories, within a greater national system.

In general, it can be maintained that regionalization has not yet moved forward to regionalism nor authentic regional development, and that the regional government remains a quasi-government. The municipalities do not feel connected to this process, and compartmentalization, even segregation, substitute for social and democratic integration and construction of the regions. Chile today has regional quasi-governments, municipalities with mayoral councils, universities which call themselves regional, and regional newspapers deconcentrated from their headquarters in the capital, but its economy and society still have not reacted to this opportunity with the energy required.

An emblematic statement from this first phase of the democratic period was given by President Aylwin in his last Message to the Nation in May 1993. He indicated that the transition from a long authoritarian regime to a functioning democratic community had taken place without trauma or damage, but not without problems and difficulties. He pointed to poverty as the greatest of these problems, and regional and county decentralization as one of the most pressing tasks of his administration.

In this message, as in his previous addresses, county and regional decentralization occupied a primary place. Its strategic nature was reaffirmed, as well as its integration in a broader political undertaking, its importance to effective government and governance, and its decisive role in reversing the public policies of the authoritarian period.

Under the Aylwin government, the previous regional and municipal model was reformulated, with the democratic election of local authorities and the assignment of resources for these levels. Not without hesitation and even resistance, regional government began to be viewed as a key structure for the transfer of powers and resources, as well as a gatekeeper for possible protests against the necessary regulations of a difficult transition.

The Aylwin administration's territorial decentralization efforts were clear in their starting point, but their advance highlighted various problems. In the political system, decision-making remained centralized. In the economic system, the dysfunctionalities and imbalances generated by the external opening of markets hindered the achievement of overall equilibrium. In the social system, participation mechanisms were still lacking, while marginal and impoverished areas remained. Natural disasters and other crises underscored the fragility of market allocations and the human weaknesses of many in the business world.

This first moment of the democratic process, coinciding with President Aylwin's period of government, manifested the complexity of the democracy of agreements and the increasing difficulty of implementing strategic reforms. The task was still incomplete with regard to regional and local management, the decentralization of public services and resources, and the education and training of administrative personnel and the political class at the subnational level.

Change and Innovation Under President Frei

The second phase of the democratic governments, one of adjustment and consolidation, began with the inauguration of the regional governments on April 23, 1993, nearly coinciding with the current presidential term. The reforms to the Chilean constitutional system undertaken during this period represent a serious and strategic effort to improve inter-governmental and inter-level relations, the integration of public administrations, and the country's political and bureaucratic culture itself.

Decentralization has clearly moved forward during this phase. Full territorial and political decentralization in the counties is combined with partial territorial decentralization in the regions and provinces. The advances in municipal decentralization have become a model for the social and political construction of the regions, as the country seeks to reinvent the art and science of regional government and exercise it on a human scale.

a) Issues and Commitments Under the Frei Administration

As it moves toward a more participative democracy, Chile's government has chosen a slow and gradual path to facilitate the great cultural change signified by this transition. The pace and coordination of this process are still unclear. Its advance raises questions of regional identity, the construction of the new institutions, the type of development and its financing, and the necessary "know-how" in the management of inter-governmental and inter-level relations. Additional questions concern political plans, the capacity of government, democratic governance, political leadership, and social participation in the territories.

The political system's deficiencies are also thrown into relief, including centralized parties, a lack of regional and local consciousness, and a political class permeated by traditional views of the country and the territories. The business class is essentially concentrated in the capital, and although it has gained international experience, it hesitates to break the umbilical cord of state protection and support. Meanwhile, the universities lag behind in the education and training of regional and municipal administrators and elites, although efforts in this direction are being made by the Catholic University and the Universities of Chile, Santiago, and Los Lagos. Neighborhood groups are often managed in an excessively bureaucratic manner, and local leaders continue at times to place personal ambition over the interests of the community.

Complex issues are raised, including productive development, the fight against poverty, environmental protection, and regional and municipal concerns regarding finance and administration. Other urgent questions arise as well. What identities do our regions have? What role is played by the historical names for our old provincial units? Why is the first Region not simply "Tarapacá," the Twelfth "Magallanes," and so forth? What political proposal and what strategic scenario will guide the decentralized development of the regions? Are they pivotal regions, associative regions, or virtual regions? Macro-regions, meso-regions, or micro-regions? Strategic regions, tactical regions, or support regions?

What leaderships, what alliances, what plans, what political and social resources will activate the territories? How can we resolve the question of integration, so fundamental in this era of globalization? What is implied by the governing capacity of a region? Is it only a circuit running from planning to budgeting, or does it also involve the capacity to intelligently imagine the future; lead a society; exercise effective authority; and make appropriate, collective, and consensual decisions? How is politics related to techno-political concerns?

What role should be assigned to regional governments? That of conducting politics and promoting socioeconomic and cultural activity? Do the regions, provinces and counties enjoy the necessary levels of political leadership and social participation to achieve this? Must the county be the fundamental political cell in the construction of the regions and our development as a nation? All of these questions are crucial for our country's passage into the third decentralizing phase, which is now taking shape.

b) President Frei's Important Proposal: "to significantly increase the percentage of public investment managed at the regional level ... to accelerate and consolidate the regionalization and decentralization of the country."
As noted by the President, "starting in 1991, a gradually increasing portion of the investments of the Ministries of Housing and Urban Affairs, Public Works, Interior, and others began to be allocated by regional bodies, until 21% of the central government's public investments were controlled by the regions, in order to finance projects identified and prepared by municipalities and regional institutions."

Thus, the President proposes that to accelerate and consolidate the regionalization and decentralization of the country, investment is necessary both in the regions and by the regions. He strengthened this proposal in his message to the nation on May 21, 1994, making a commitment to raise investment under regional control to 42% before the end of his term in office. This will be accomplished through increased financing for the National Fund for Regional Development; the identification of new areas suitable for investment under regional control; investment planning agreements between regions and ministries; and other specialized mechanisms.

This is not a program imposed from above by condescending authorities. Rather, it is an attempt to integrate the institutional decentralization promoted by the Aylwin administration with President Frei's fiscal decentralization efforts and development policies. In the same message, President Frei described other aspects of his plan for further decentralization:

- Improve and strengthen regional governments, so that they will be capable of formulating guidelines for the development of their regions; prioritize the use of resources under regional control; effectively manage human and financial resources; implement regional plans; and coordinate with the counties and municipalities
- Transform the municipalities into efficient community services by providing them with greater resources; support approval of the municipal revenue law in Congress; provide them with the flexibility to effectively administer resources for education, health, and other areas; and improve their management and technical skills
- Ensure that the transfer of responsibilities and resources to municipalities does not simply reproduce centralist mechanisms at local levels
- Promote decision-making by regional, provincial, and county officials, and transfer the necessary authority to these levels

The central challenge emerging from these plans is the coordination of political, institutional, and fiscal decentralization. The education and training of human resources at subnational levels may also be added to this list.

The Frei administration, inaugurated in March 1994, has made a programmatic commitment to share the job of government with the people. Yet the broadening of democracy, territorial and political decentralization, and the active participation of the community in the development process must be harmonized with other national goals such as macroeconomic stability, internationalization of the economy, increased investment, economic development, sustainable and equitable growth, and environmental quality.

Reaching these goals will involve the reform of the State, the active participation of regional and local leaders, and the modernization of public administration on decentralized levels. This will require the harmonization of institutional and fiscal decentralization; the achievement of equilibrium among powers, functions, institutions, and resources; and the creation of fluid and participative inter-governmental relations.

c) Regional Governments and Fiscal Decentralization

In Chile's decentralization process, the most appropriate issues for local governments have been considered those related to social policies and services. For regional governments, these have been increased control over public investment in the region; territorial organization; and the promotion of productive activity. These have led to fiscal decentralization in favor of regional governments; coordination between the municipalities and regions; and local and regional economic development.

Fiscal decentralization is a basic component of the decentralization and regionalization process, as regional governments gain the power and skills to acquire, assign, and utilize budgetary resources. This so-called "investment under regional assignation" is administered by an array of organizations and mechanisms: the National Fund for Regional Development (FNDR), Sectorial Investments under Regional Assignation (ISAR), Regional Investments under Local Assignation (IRAL), and, most recently, the Planning Agreements. All of these programs aim at the transfer of funds with the participation of regional governments. The regions may determine the investment projects to be funded, as with the FNDR, the ISAR, and the Planning Agreements, or may oversee the intra-regional distribution of the resources, with the investment priorities by project being locally determined through the IRAL.

There have been setbacks in the use of regionally controlled resources in the years 1994, 1995, and 1996, especially within the FNDR. However, it currently appears that these deficiencies are being overcome, as a result of the implementation of the regional plans, the municipalities' progress in formulating projects, and the improved management of regional development.

One of the variables used by the government to evaluate regional leadership is the effective use of the FNDR, the regions' principal investment tool. It is used to finance initiatives in various sectors of social and economic infrastructure, in order to promote coordinated and equitable territorial development. Ninety percent of FNDR funding is distributed in accordance with territorial coefficients and socioeconomic indicators, 5% is shared among the regions to stimulate effectiveness, and the remaining 5% is reserved for emergencies such as droughts and natural disasters.

Measures of effectiveness in the use of FNDR resources include the manner in which assigned resources are spent during the year in question; the percentage of resources assigned to poor communities; the percentage assigned to pre-investment activity (such as preliminary studies and engineering designs); and the percentage assigned to projects receiving favorable economic recommendations.

Paradoxically, the FNDR principally finances municipal projects. Furthermore, its complexity makes its management difficult, limiting its effectiveness as a decentralizing fund and raising questions about the allocation of its expenditures.

The management of this fund involves a great part of the public administration apparatus. The regional governments and regional councils select the investment projects to be implemented and control the investment through their subsidiary offices. The municipalities and local governments generate project proposals. The Ministry of Planning and Cooperation (Mideplan) and the regional secretariats for planning and cooperation evaluate and coordinate the process. The Ministerial Regional Secretariats (Seremis) assist in the diagnosis and generation of sectorial projects. The Regional Comptrollers and the Ministry of finance are involved in budgetary control; the Undersecretariat for Regional and Administrative Development (Subdere) in the distribution and assignation of resources; and the Subdere's Regional Control Units in consulting and evaluation. Further participants include the National Council for Narcotics Control (Conace); the National Energy Commission (CNE); the Ministry of Education (Mineduc), for the distribution and management of supplies; the deconcentrated services of the Ministry of Public Works (MOP), and the Ministry of Housing and Urban Affairs (Minvu); and finally the electric, water, and sewer utilities.

As can be seen, the public administration units involved are numerous and also geographically dispersed, suggesting that the decentralization process still faces many difficult bureaucratic obstacles.

Between 1990 and 1996, the regional governments' investment instruments were diversified. At the beginning of the democratic period, only the FNDR existed (Decree Law #575 of 1974). In contrast, the regions currently possess eight ISAR programs corresponding to the ministries, as well as two IRAL programs, while work is beginning on the Planning Agreements, with nine agreements already concluded in eight regions, primarily with the Ministries of Public Works and Housing and Urban Affairs.

In 1996, the FNDR accounted for 50.6% of the total Investment under Regional Assignation and 11.2% of total public investment, exhibiting real growth of 18.8% from 1994 to 1996. The ISAR's share of Investment under Regional Assignation was on the order of 36.2%, accounting for some 8.1% of total public investment, with an increase of 3.8% from 1994 to 1996. The IRAL's proportion of Investment under Regional Assignation was 9.1%, comprising 2.0% of total public investment, with an increase of 44.3% from 1994 to 1996 (also including the ISAR-Fosis share). The Planning Agreements accounted for some 3.9% of the total of Investment under Regional Assignation and 0.9% of total public investment.

In 1997, the influence of the Planning Agreements upon the Investment under Regional Assignation began to rise, as a result of negotiations between the Ministries and the regional governments. With all of the advances achieved, however, further efforts remain necessary, since progress toward President Frei's goal of doubling the share of Investment under Regional Assignation within total public investment still appears quite slow.

Inter-ministerial coordination has been advanced in recent months, as demonstrated by an initiative developed by the Inter-Ministerial Committee on Productive Development. This policy seeks to enhance Chile's capacity to compete as a country through the territorial deconcentration of public services and state agencies such as the Corporation for the Promotion of Production (Corfo), the Technical Cooperation Service (Sercotec), the National Training and Employment Service (Sence), the National Tourism Service (Sernatur), and others.

The 1997 Report on Global Competitiveness from the World Economic Forum ranks Chile's competitiveness as clearly superior to that of its larger Mercosur partners, Brazil and Argentina. This is especially the case in comparisons of the roles of government and infrastructure, as well as in the evaluation of commercial sectors in the 1997 Ranking by Factors.

Although these statistics do not present a definitive picture, the Investment under Regional Assignation grew between 1990 and 1993 from 10.7% of public investment to 19%, advancing from 27.5 billion pesos to 59.7 billion. From 1994 to 1997, it expanded from 21.2% of public investment to an estimated 26%, advancing from 78 billion pesos to 227 billion.

The Under Secretary for Regional and Administrative Development, Marcelo Schooling, stated to the newspaper *El Mercurio* (October 18, 1997) that 33.34% of public investment would be subject to regional control in 1998. This represents approximately 388.6 billion pesos, principally provided through the FNDR and the Ministries of Public Works, Housing, Health, and the Interior. It is additionally expected that Public Works will contribute a larger share of resources to this mechanism in 1998.

The Under Secretary of the Secretariat-General of the Ministry of the Presidency, Sergio Galilea, has stated that in the coming century, half of public investment will be controlled by regional bodies, counting the investment mentioned above along with that provided to the municipalities.

The municipalities' own revenues expanded from 368 billion pesos in 1994 to 550 billion in 1996, exhibiting real growth of 22%, a higher rate than the country's economic expansion over the same period. Budgetary transfers for education increased from 258 billion pesos in 1994 to 354 billion in 1996. Today the municipalities receive over one trillion pesos through transfers, representing twice the 1990 figure.

As can be seen, an intensive effort has been made during the democratic period to activate regions, provinces, and counties, but problems still persist, especially in the areas of health, education, and the management capacity of subnational governments and administrations. During 1996 and 1997, unions in these areas have mobilized for higher pay and better working conditions.

To reach the country's goals in this area, it will be necessary to accelerate the substitution of decentralized investment for centralized funds, especially those of the Ministries of Public Works (MOP) and Housing and Urban Affairs (Minvu) which between them control a high proportion of public investment. The Planning Agreements, instruments with a high growth potential for the support of regional development strategies, must also be utilized to the maximum extent. Finally, a specific timetable of ministerial commitments is required to ensure the expansion of allocations for the Investment under Regional Assignation in the country's future budgets, which also implies increasing total public investment through the FNDR, since this fund represents more than 50% of the Investment under Regional Assignation.

As Chile seeks to harmonize the political-institutional development, planning, and human resources required for decentralized investment, the reform of the State and the modernization of public management appears as a fundamental necessity. Capacities for leadership, coordination, planning, and strategic vision must be developed on the county, provincial, regional, and national levels. This will involve an initiative undertaken by the country as a whole.

In January 1996, President Frei called upon the private sector to invest in roadways, railways, water and sewer systems, and ports, calling for the empowerment of the regions and the implementation of the Arica and Austral Plans. During 1997, he issued a challenge to the entire country to assume rights and responsibilities in the decentralization and construction of Chile.

Currently, the regional planning and municipal revenue laws have been approved, and municipal management reforms are being deliberated by Congress. To these advances can be added the experience acquired from the territorial and political decentralization process in the counties and partial territorial decentralization in the regions and provinces. Reflections arise from this experience on the strengths and weaknesses of the municipalities and regions as they seek to meet the challenges of the new policies.

III. Strengths and Weaknesses of the Municipalities and Regions Affecting the Decentralization Process

1. SUBNATIONAL STRENGTHS

Since the 1970s, the municipalities have played a unique role in the daily life of Chileans. Few areas of community life are untouched by the municipal corporations. Primary health care, education, environmental protection, city infrastructure, urban roadways, the maintenance of secondary roads, attention to social problems, and other equally important areas are among their responsibilities.

The municipalities have a dual administrative structure, with a mayor and a council representing the executive and legislative branches, respectively. To this is added the Social-Economic Council, an advisory body representing leading local organizations.

The municipalities, with their proximity to the people, should permit the greatest level of community participation in the tasks of government and local development. Decentralization appears virtually impossible without active local participation. The municipalities currently manage some 1.5 billion dollars annually, representing 2% of GNP; if the regional governments' resources are added, this reaches 3.5 billion dollars, approximately 5% of GNP. In the world's leading democracies, municipalities manage between 7% and 10% of GNP, as noted by Mayor Ravinet in 1995, based on figures provided by the IULA (International Union of Local Authorities).

A dual system of government was also chosen for the regions, similar to that of the municipalities. The regional governor interacts with a regional council, a collegial body with significant powers in the determination of regional strategies, development plans, and budgets. Regional governors are advised by regional cabinets, which include the regional council, the ministerial regional secretariats, and the provincial governors.

Another strength at the subnational level is the financing system already in place, including the FNDR and the Municipal Common Fund.

The regions' intermediate position in the country's political, administrative, and geographic structure positions them to take full advantage of the powers, responsibilities, and resources transferred by the central government and to become a driving force behind regional and national development.

On January 31, 1996, the political parties and the Association of Regional Councils convened a roundtable discussion to promote a new agenda, aimed at delivering more decision-making power to the regions and promoting decentralization, as referred to in the presidential message of May 1997.

2. SUBNATIONAL WEAKNESSES

Weaknesses at the subnational level that may impede decentralization efforts are mainly found in the gaps or "gray areas" in the exercise of powers and responsibilities. The Chilean system has often been characterized by delivering more functions and responsibilities than resources.

At the last Municipalities Congress in May 1997, Mayor Duarte, elected president of that body, stated that municipal deficits are alarming, amounting to 22 billion pesos in 1996, or some 500 million dollars. These deficits derive from the devolution of functions without the necessary financing, he noted. Furthermore, the decentralized education and health services required 58 billion pesos from municipal budgets last year to continue their operations.

Meanwhile, officials at the national level have expressed fears of possible macroeconomic imbalances or movements toward federalism with demands for greater autonomy and powers. Concern has also been expressed regarding deficits, especially on the municipal level, where 300 municipalities are in the red. A further area of deficiency is the education and training of human resources, which affects the level of political, managerial, and technical expertise on the subnational level.

The most sensitive points lie in the areas of autonomy, municipal-regional coordina-tion, human resources, budgetary decentralization, and the financing of the decentraliza-tion process. One of the most intractable issues has been the relationship between the cen-tral government and the municipalities in the areas of education and health. In some regions, and at the recent Municipalities Congress, the suggestion has even been raised of returning responsibility for these services to the central government.

The current president of Achimun has declared his intention to propose the cre-ation of a single committee to coordinate the financing of the devolved services, the effective decentralization of political power, and full municipal autonomy to structure effective local governments. The Minister of Health, Alex figueroa, recognizes that municipal health services and the national system function in a disjointed and poorly integrated manner, mainly because of mutual mistrust. He reports the widespread con-viction among public health officials that all clinics should be returned to the national system. In turn, the municipalities show a lack of confidence in the national level (*La Época*, October 5, 1997).

This array of subnational strengths and weaknesses raises numerous questions for the further development of decentralization in Chile.

3. *What Do We Have in Chile: Municipal government or municipal administration?*
Regional government, quasi-regional government, or semi-independent regional administration?
These questions are central to the Chilean decentralization process, since they affect all areas of regional and local administration.

During 1996 and 1997, numerous political parties, including the Socialists, the Party for Democracy (PPD), the Independent Democratic Union (UDI), and National Renovation (RN), have called for the popular election of regional governors and regional council members. The Chilean Association of Municipalities has requested clarification of the role of the municipal executive in government and administration.

The mayor of Temuco, René Saffirio, in *Política y Espíritu* (April-May 1996), maintains that advances in democratization and the increasingly prominent role of the municipali-ties have led to the need to transform the municipal corporations from simple providers of services into authentic local governments with the powers, responsibilities, and resources to meet the needs of modern communities.

In Chile, the county level paradoxically appears as the most decentralized, with its elected authorities, a highly refined set of regulations and much-discussed legislation. In contrast, the regional governor is designated, the regional councils are the product of sec-ond-degree elections, and the Seremis are specialized secretariats deconcentrated from the national ministries, with double dependency and unclear functions. The provincial governors have poorly-defined roles and highly restricted autonomy in decision-making and the assignment of resources.

Fiscal decentralization lags behind other developments, and the current government, as we have noted, is undertaking efforts to substantially increase the Investment under Regional Assignation and the activity of the National Regional Development Fund and the Municipal Common Fund.

4. THE LATIN AMERICAN AND CHILEAN EXPERIENCE

It is recognized, both in Chile and across Latin America, that:

- Municipalities are currently considered an important level of government, not simply administrative units.
- Greater political autonomy, enhanced institutional capacity, and an increasing voice in the generation and use of resources is being granted to them.
- Their authorities are elected by popular vote.
- The separation of powers is established in the municipal structure, emphasizing the classic or dual system.
- There is a political and legal tendency to encourage municipalities to raise their own revenue and to rationalize the transfer and distribution of resources through the Common Municipal Funds and other forms of financing.
- Both local planning and community participation have acquired new legitimacy in recognition of the favorable conditions for their development at this level.
- The democratic and social construction of the regions calls for solidarity and coordination among the regional and local levels on cultural and political issues, giving them impetus from below.

These advances move in the opposite direction from the old tendencies, such as the tactical weakness of the municipalities, seen in the fact that among Latin America's 15,600 municipalities, not more than 400 could be considered valid partners of the central governments. Other limiting factors have included the municipalities' persistent internal centralism; the relative nature of their powers and responsibilities; their lack of human and financial resources; their difficulties in providing adequate services and generating their own revenue; and their incapacity to generate sustainable projects and attract international technical and financial assistance.

Reactions to these deficiencies have included the so-called "reform of the reforms"; the creation of technical advisory institutions for international relations; the creation of financial cooperation mechanisms to attract funds and finance projects; the adoption of new methods of intersectorial and intercommunity management; the new emphasis on municipal associations; and improved human resources development programs.

The overwhelming majority of Latin American municipalities, some 12,000, are rural or rural/urban. It is here that municipal weaknesses are expressed most dramatically, along with legal and regulatory deficiencies, ineffective financing policies, and the lack of true democratizing will on the part of national governments. Last May, Chile's current government, through the Committee of Ministers for Urban Development and Territorial Organization, announced plans to promote the real estate and tourism sectors, non-polluting industries, the construction of social housing and settlement creation for 223 rural counties of the country having less than 25,000 inhabitants. Similarly, it is creating incentives for the eradication of marginal settlements and is working intensively on its program for the nation's 900 poorest schools. Starting in 1998, these schools will provide full coverage in primary education, whereupon the initiative will enter its second phase, covering the fifth to eighth grades.

New initiatives and responses are constantly arising, and talk of reinventing government becomes more insistent: reinforcing the role of the regional governor as a protagonist of the deconcentration and decentralization processes; providing strong techno-political support to the regions, whether through the regional governor's office, a regional decision-making system, or a territorial advisor; redefining the regional governor's role as a supporter and coordinator of services and municipalities; establishing metropolitan governments; creating incentive and reward systems for good management; improving the image of regions and municipalities; elevating the quality of creative teams for political action and negotiation; creating crisis administration centers; providing work stations for advanced computing; developing think tanks, and so forth.

Some observers even maintain that every municipal government includes two basic elements: autonomy and localism. These factors drive the quest for political and financial independence and active community participation in the establishment of self-managed structures and development networks.

The issue of community involvement is always present, emphasizing the proximity of decision-makers to the people and the possibility of establishing authentic social participation mechanisms for the solution of local problems. This also implies the decentralization of political parties and advancement toward more democratic forms of political participation. A similar situation is seen in the provinces and regions, although a stronger identity exists at the provincial level and a lesser emphasis on regionalism.

5. MUNICIPALITIES AND DECENTRALIZATION

Historically, municipalities can be viewed as an expression of the decentralizing impulse rooted in the national spirit, involving the right to administer one's own community and the aspiration to participate in local government.

It is important to recognize the municipality as a historical level of administration. Beyond this recognition, however, various questions arise regarding the territorial distribution of power and authority and the degree of decentralization of the regions and provinces. These are some of the "gray areas" in inter-level relations which favor the effects of capital-centeredness. A case of decentralization in law but recentralization in fact is seen in the new centralism of the capital cities, whether national, regional, or provincial, with their tendency to reconcentrate power and resources.

The institutional architecture on the municipal level raises numerous questions: the election of mayors, the number and role of the council members, the role of the Social-Economic Councils, the role of the regional governor, the election of the Regional Council, and so forth. Effective training will be necessary for municipal administrators and other local officials. It can safely be said that more work lies ahead than has been accomplished.

The devolution of public services from the central level to the regions and municipalities and a commitment to user participation is integrally linked with governance and governing capacity in the regions and counties. Regional and local claims against the national government must be managed effectively. Furthermore, coordination is necessary among local interest groups, non-governmental organizations (NGOs), the private sector, and the municipalities.

6. REGIONAL IMBALANCES AND MUNICIPAL DIVERSITY
CONTRAST WITH REGULATORY AND LEGAL UNIFORMITY

Chile has 13 regions, 51 provinces, and 345 counties. The 13 regions are not equal among themselves, and the Metropolitan Region exhibits the greatest differences with respect to the others. The province of Santiago does not have a governorship, and its importance surpasses that of any other province.

The subject is complex. In the case of the Metropolitan Region (RM), Chile's national issues overshadow the region's problems, and the capital-centered effect affects local, provincial, and national development. Santiago covers both the metropolitan area and the region. This produces a sort of non-region, with an excessive economic, demographic, and urban concentration.

It is said that "Santiago is Chile," and the Metropolitan Region tends to overlook its own problems, its unique characteristics, and its need to decentralize in order to further its social and political development.

Yet the decentralization of the RM will be difficult to attempt. Can the growth of Santiago be decelerated without affecting the growth of the country? The Metropolitan Region is home to nearly 43% of Chile's population, while its surface area represents 2.04% of the country. It produces 47% of the country's GNP. The RM accounts for 26.3% of Chile's public investment projects, 21.5% of private investments, and 60% of national consumption. It is the headquarters of 46 important economic groups and 71% of the country's large companies; 80% of bank deposits are held in Santiago. These statistics overwhelmingly confirm the centralism and capital-centeredness of our country.

The management of the city of Santiago, with its dual nature of national and metropolitan capital, impacts strongly upon the rest of the nation as it extracts resources from the regions through fiscal policy and reinvests the proceeds of productive activities located in the territories. While until 1984 the RM experienced deindustrialization as a result of free market policies, it is currently undergoing a recuperation and reactivation process. This is due in part to the political initiative of the present mayor of Santiago to coordinate national strategies involving the regional and local levels and the central government itself. The current proposal to transform Santiago into a regional financial center for Latin America and the world is also linked to the mayor's initiative.

The population of the RM is 5,236,321, of which 97% or 5,092,721, live in urban areas, concentrated in the city of Santiago, with the most populous counties being La florida, Peñalolén, Las Condes, El Bosque, Recoleta, Maipú, Cerro Navia, Ñuñoa, and Conchalí.

The per capita product in the RM slightly surpasses the national average. Regional output represents 41% of national GNP, with the following sectors contributing most heavily: services (34%), manufacturing industries (24.8%), and trade (22.3%). The regional product has fluctuated since 1982, with periods of highs and lows, but has not regained its 1981 level (42.3%).

The 345 Chilean counties spread across the nation are extraordinarily heterogeneous. Again, the most populous and wealthiest counties are located in the RM: to those listed above must be added Providencia, Santiago, Vitacura, and La Reina, especially for their overall and per capita income levels. No comprehensive municipal typology has been undertaken, and their territorial, functional, and demographic differences have not been the object of political negotiations.

According to international experts, the Metropolitan Region has been excellently positioned for economic growth and for attracting investments during the period 1992-2000 (Fabril-Sofofa Promotion Society). This situation qualifies the RM as a leading force in the globalization and internationalization of the country. However, this privileged position has been constructed upon a foundation of internal colonialism, which must be addressed by providing compensation and greater equity to the other regions.

IV. A Balanced View of Options for the Future

More than seven years of this difficult, complex, and almost unprecedented process of democratic transition have passed. Political, economic, and social paradoxes have multiplied, as new pluralist initiatives exist side by side with powerful remnants of authoritarianism. Perplexed, we observe a succession of phenomena which seem unthinkable in a democratic country: the electorate's low regard for politics; fundamentalist economic policies supporting the "infallible" market and a triumphant business class; neoliberal vetoes of already-restricted labor policies; and the lack of alternative proposals from an organically and politically weak working class. Even the territorial decentralization in progress does not serve to mobilize the public. Its discussion remains confined to expert and intellectual circles and appears more prominently in the communications media than in election campaigns.

However, "something is moving," and there is striking unanimity about the necessity to undertake a strong decentralization program and continue the progress already achieved. Both the government and the opposition have reiterated their determination to advance in this process, although they emphasize different aspects of the decentralizing impulse.

The government considers its most outstanding achievements to be the full functioning of the regional governments and councils; the implementation of the related personnel plans; and the incorporation of the Sectorial Investments under Regional Assignation and the Planning Agreements into the National Budgetary Law as new instruments of fiscal decentralization.

President Frei, in his May 1997 message to the nation, stated that the government will continue to advance in the coming years toward its targets for investment under regional control, as well as in other areas, such as reforms to the Constitutional Organic Law on Regional Government and Administration; the deconcentration of the ministries; new forms of budgetary deliberation; additional economic promotion measures within the FNDR; and the strengthening of the municipalities.

The September 1996 issue of *Mensaje* magazine presented the opinions of Mayors Jaime Ravinet of Santiago and Esteban Valenzuela of Rancagua, along with council member Lily Pérez and Congressman Carlos Montes, both of La florida. All of these leaders emphasized the municipalities' role as agents of change, driving forces behind economic and social development, and platforms for local participation and ongoing democratic innovation.

All of the political parties represented in Congress have reiterated their support for further decentralization and the promotion of the regions, provinces, and counties. Most prominent among these are National Renovation, the Christian Democrats, and the Socialist Party.

The president of Sofofa, Felipe Lamarca, in a diagnosis of the Chilean economy, provided to *Qué Pasa* magazine (August 1997) and in an appearance before the Fourteenth National Meeting of Businesses (Enade) on October 28, emphasized the necessity to decentralize the powers concentrated in the Metropolitan Region and alluded to the regions' great imbalances in human resources, technology, competitiveness, and investment levels. He indicated the necessity to form authentic regional governments, elected by the people of each region. Regional and provincial governors should be supported by a council or directorate and should have the capacity to make decisions related to social problems, infrastructure, growth, and economic competition. Responsibility for defense, economics, security, and international policies in the regions would continue to fall upon the President of the Republic.

In his speech, Lamarca referred to regionalization as one of the 10 essential areas for the country's development, maintaining that "the revolution begins with the regions," since a regional spirit already exists, and the wise use of this spirit will help bring about the decentralization of decisions and resources.

Chile today faces the challenge of advancing toward higher levels of democracy, decentralization, and development; the creation of new opportunities; and the elaboration of a new pact between the State and society encompassing the shared responsibilities, liberties, and knowledge necessary for a country in the 21st century.

The more than 14 million Chileans must be incorporated into the democratic exercise, participating actively in the government of the various territorial and administrative levels. Economic and social equilibrium must be established as the country offers greater opportunities to the population, providing sustainability to a society imbued with solidarity, shared responsibility, and justice.

The proximity between governors and the governed is a strategic point raising various proposals:

a) Democratization, decentralization, growth, local and regional economic development, regionalization, municipalization, and popular participation must be integrated in a strategy to define subnational levels of government. Political, social, and geographic stabilizing factors must be created to correct the action of the market, along with a subnational policy consistent with internal and external integration. As the country faces the globalization of markets and the internationalization of its economy, which are breaking down national borders, it becomes increasingly essential to create real local and regional governments, capable of dialogue, negotiation, and integration into the new dynamic.

b) The democratic governments are on the verge of redistributing significant power from the top to the bottom, which will create new political classes, social groups, business, and union elites, as well as new forms of participation, in spite of the problematic initial situation.

c) The strengthening of counties and municipalities necessarily entails the empowering and consolidation of the regions, the national economy, and Chilean democracy itself. The impulse to devolve power from the top toward the bottom, which persists in spite of some regional and national resistance, will lead to democratization at all levels and improve the effectiveness of the national government.

d) Regional-local solidarity, coordination, and mutual support demonstrate an interesting synergy. Here, the regions have advantages of scale (in economics, infrastructure, science and technology, diversity, and support for inter-county relations), while the counties allow greater proximity of the population to those making decisions and carrying out public policies.

Coordination of the territories and an appropriate division of labor will help transform the subnational levels into new and effective participants in the international competition for capital, technology, and markets, aside from creating optimal conditions for satisfying development objectives.

Currently, the coordination between regional governments and municipalities is very weak. It is lacking in participatory mechanisms as well as contact among technical and professional colleagues.

e) Municipal management has become a strategic factor for increasing governmental capacity and the governance of the nation and the regions.

To confront this challenge, Chile must:

- Reform the State, reinventing it in accordance with the country's advancing decentralization and unique geopolitical and geoeconomic situation to create a new regionally democratic State, with a clear division of labor among the levels of government and the flexibility to react to the challenges of development
- Define municipal management practices that will produce quality, efficiency, effectiveness, and participation, tailored to the particular environment of each municipality
- Develop mechanisms to promote local programmatic, financial, technological, and educational action, recognizing that decentralization is a strategic factor in a revitalized concept of nationhood
- Promote the active and cooperative commitment of the private sector to local and regional development within a new, more democratic regulatory framework and a development model of productive transformation, social equity, and political liberty and equality
- Provide incentives to harness the community's political and creative energy to support local development projects
- Redefine the county as the motor of national and regional policies, plans, programs, and projects

Chile must complete this process of municipal and regional transformation in spite of recentralizing currents within the central government, including organized pressure groups linked to the conservative establishment. The goal is not to advance toward an expanded State or a constantly mobilized society, which would produce unnecessary conflict. The goal of decentralization, in Chile's case, is to lay the foundation for a common project of national and international integration, based on the unique characteristics of our population, geography, resources, and culture. This new and effective national structure will derive strength and viability from regional governments endowed with ample powers and resources, as well as a spirit of community autonomy and territorial and political pluralism.

Final Remarks

This paper, which attempts to describe the complex and fascinating process of decentralization in Chile, hopes to provide points of reference and analysis to spur progress in the elaboration of policies and actions aimed at establishing a truly decentralized democratic State and a pluralistic and participative society.

An extensive bibliography was consulted in the course of this effort, of which I will mention the most outstanding authors, media, and institutions, allowing the reader to explore this material without dry references and tiresome explanatory footnotes.

This work derived great benefit from the studies and opinions of Eduardo Palma, Juan Cavada, Sergio Bossier, Carlos de Mattos, Rolando Franco, Jaime Gatica, Gonzalo Daniel Martner, José Antonio Ávalos, José María Saavedra, Arturo Aylwin, Reinhard Friedmann, Felipe Lamarca, Felipe Ortega, Luis Lira, Jaime Ravinet, Lily Pérez, Carlos Montes, Ricardo Núñez, Patricio Cotal, Luis Hernández, Claudia Serrano, René Saffirio, Ignacio Irarrázaval, and Juan Enrique Sierra.

Documentation from United Nations sources was also consulted, including the Economic and Social Planning Institute of Latin America and the Caribbean, the United Nations Economic Commission for Latin America and the Caribbean (ECLAC), and the United Nations Development Program (UNDP). Other information was provided by the University Promotion Corporation (CPU), the Economic Research Corporation for Latin America (Cieplan), the Freedom and Development Institute, and the Frei Foundation, as well as the Chilean Ministries of Planning (Mideplan), Interior (Undersecretariat for Regional Development and Administrative Undersecretariat for Regional and Administrative Development), Economics, Health, and Education.

Finally, valuable information was obtained from the newspapers *El Mercurio*, *La Época*, *La Segunda*, and *La Tercera de la Hora*, in addition to the magazines *Qué Pasa*, *Hoy*, *Mensaje*, *Ercilla*, *Política y Espíritu*, *Cuadernos de El Avión Rojo*, and the journal *Democracia Regional y Local* published by the Undersecretariat for Regional and Administrative Development (Subdere).

Chile's International Integration

Alberto van Klaveren *

D uring the 1990s, four factors contributed to defining Chilean foreign policy. The first of these, unquestionably, is the historical tradition accumulated over more than a century and a half of independence. The basic principles taking root during this time shaped the country's image in the world and are especially reflected in Chile's territorial structure, its relations with its neighbors, and its participation in international organizations. The second factor is the legacy of the military regime, which left a very deep scar upon Chile's international relations, and the subsequent democratic restoration. The third is the country's economic opening, which was initiated during the authoritarian regime and soon became part of a general trend throughout Latin America. The fourth consists of the great political and economic changes occurring in the world, which have had a decisive impact on Chile's foreign policy and Chilean society itself.

The goal of this chapter is to present an overview of the changing course of Chilean foreign policy during the years of restored democratic government. This evaluation will not confine itself to the context of Chilean politics. Instead, it starts from the premise that the sweeping changes in the international environment — globalization, the end of the Cold War, economic multipolarity, strategic unilateralism, and the revitalization of regional integration processes — have deeply affected international relations, modifying traditional foreign policy definitions and altering the conditions for both public and private action.

Rather than providing a chronological account of the evolution of Chilean foreign policy, this essay seeks to identify the principal areas of change and to point out the challenges and emerging tendencies faced by the country today.

I. A Complex Legacy

Chile's foreign policy contains elements of both permanence and change. Generally, during periods of internal stability, the enduring factors have predominated. Conversely, in times of rapid internal or external change, innovative factors have tended to rise in importance. Some of the enduring elements in Chilean foreign policy are related to the territorial questions arising through the years. These have largely been a product of the poorly-defined borders typical of the colonial period and the resulting demarcation disputes,

---

* The research underlying this article received funding from Fondecyt-Chile (Project #1961201). The author appreciates the assistance of Rodrigo Ruiz Ortiz in the preparation of the accompanying charts.

which have persisted even up to very recent times. The historical legacy also includes intense and complex relations among neighboring countries, in which periods of cooperation and regional solidarity alternate with times of competition and even diplomatic and military conflict. These problems have occasionally affected Chile's policies toward the great powers, which in the past were generally subordinated to South American concerns (Burr 1965:261; Meneses 1987:7-55). During the previous century, Chile, like other Latin American nations, operated within a regional balance of power based on territorial, economic, strategic, and political issues. Particular importance was assumed by the evolution of our relations with Argentina, Bolivia, and Peru, as well as the historical relationship established among these neighbors.

The history of Chile's foreign policy and those of its nearest neighbors is not very different from that observed in Europe, with the exception that armed conflicts predominated in the Old World with more force and until much more recently. However, the current form in which this legacy is expressed can hardly be more different. In Western Europe, a history of rivalry and conflict has acted as a driving force behind one of the most advanced integration processes being undertaken in the world today. Territorial claims have been relegated to the past, and while sentiments of rivalry and affinity may persist, arising from long-standing conflicts and alliances, these do not serve to mobilize public opinion, with the possible exception of audiences at sporting events.

In Latin America — and Chile is no exception — lingering effects of old conflicts and territorial questions continue to represent a central element of foreign policy which, paradoxically, must be reconciled with the region's drive toward greater cooperation and the challenges imposed by globalized economies. In Chile, as in neighboring countries, historical events and the visions and interpretations surrounding them still powerfully influence the perceptions of influential foreign policy figures as well as public opinion.

For example, Argentine nationalism has been fed by perceptions of territorial injustice which do not appear warranted in historical terms.[1] No Argentine government has been able to refute these historical perceptions, and as seen in the Campo de Hielos Sur dispute, even the Left enthusiastically adds its voice to more nationalist positions. Paradoxically, in Chile, supposedly a beneficiary of the losses suffered by Argentina, perceptions of territorial plunder and historical rivalry are practically symmetrical and similarly deeply-rooted in public opinion. According to periodic opinion surveys, Chileans retain a strong sense of nationalism and a significant degree of mistrust toward their eastern neighbor.

History also continues to play a significant role in our relations with Bolivia and Peru. One of the most influential Peruvian diplomats in recent decades, Carlos García Bedoya, has emphasized the tragic impact of his country's defeat in the War of the Pacific and its struggle to reconstruct a sense of national unity and a new international image free of the "mortgages" of the past. (Bedoya 1981:52). Peru's relations with Chile are still influenced by the results of this 19th-century war and especially by Peru's territorial losses. In Bolivia, the quest for an outlet to the sea, through territories that are an integral part of Chile, has constituted a fundamental foreign policy objective for a hundred years, although other priorities[2] are gradually becoming evident.

---

1   This is the thesis of Carlos Escudé, Argentine specialist and former advisor to Foreign Minister Guido Di Tella, (1987).
2   For a recent Bolivian perspective, see Gómez García-Palao (1995).

These legacies are not expressed in an unchanging manner. One cannot speak of determinism in this area, as shown by the advances in relations among neighbors in the present decade. However, historical sensibilities are an element of certain continuity in foreign policy, and due to their nature, they are easily exploited for domestic political purposes, as has repeatedly been observed among our neighbors and within Chile itself.

The political debate on territorial questions tends to be intense. But precisely in this territorial and strategic area, greater continuity is observed, as well as higher levels of consensus regarding the basic principles and definitions of Chilean foreign policy. This has remained true despite the abrupt political changes experienced by the country. No impartial observer can maintain that the Concertación governments' attitudes toward border disputes have been substantially different from those of the military regime, or even the Popular Unity government. There has been continuity in Chilean responses to the Bolivian claims, which date far back into our history, although it should be noted that the military regime actually made the most progress in negotiations for sovereign Bolivian access to the sea, which unfortunately ended in failure. The negotiations begun in 1992 to complete the fulfillment of the 1929 treaty between Chile and Peru have a direct antecedent in a similar, though unsuccessful, process initiated in 1985 under the military regime. The framework for current initiatives with Argentina is the Peace and Friendship Treaty signed in 1984. Continuity has also been observed in Chile's positions in recent decades regarding border disputes such as the Laguna del Desierto or the Campos de Hielo Sur.

This coincidence does not appear surprising. It is based upon a vision of relations with Chile's neighbors widely shared across diverse sectors of the population. This is confirmed in the recent White Book on National Defense (Foreign Relations Ministry 1997), prepared by experts and representatives of a very broad political spectrum, along with civil and military authorities. Even experts in territorial questions from neighboring countries tend to emphasize — and sometimes lament — the continuity observed in this area of Chilean policy.

Thus, no analysis of Chilean foreign policy can ignore the historical burden remaining from the previous century; neither can it disregard the impact of the country's recent political evolution upon foreign policy. Due to a series of factors, the links between domestic politics and foreign policy have become more pronounced in Chile than in other countries of Latin America and the world.

Starting in the 1930s, Chile enjoyed a long period of democratic continuity, during which it developed a moderate and stable foreign policy. This policy was heavily oriented toward regional relations, grounded in legalism and aimed at the projection of Chile's democratic values in the international system.[3] The country focused primarily on relations with its Latin American neighbors and with the United States. While tendencies toward cooperation predominated in the region, long-standing border disputes also demanded a significant amount of attention. Although ties with the United States were relatively close, and Chile remained a loyal ally of Washington during the greater part of the Cold War era, these relations were not free from friction and underwent

---

3   For a brief but useful analysis of the evolution of Chilean foreign policy between 1946 and 1979, see Wilhelmy (1979).

a profound deterioration with the advent of the Popular Unity government in the early 1970s (Muñoz and Portales 1987). During the 1960s, closer ties were also established with the European countries, based on significant political and cultural affinities. Chile's democratic stability during this period became an important foreign policy resource.

In the economic sphere, foreign policy reflected the "developmentist" concepts in vogue during the period. The practically comprehensive protection of the economy was considered desirable. There was no great concern for the production of exportable goods, or for the effect upon these of indiscriminate import substitution policies or recurring setbacks in the real exchange rate. Viewing the State as the virtual motor of the economy, Chile actively pressed for Latin American unity, supporting a development strategy based on import substitution on the national and regional levels. Strongly influenced by the set of ideas then current in the United Nations' Economic Commission for Latin America, which had installed its headquarters in Santiago, Chilean leaders saw integration as a sort of bulwark against the negative effects of the world economy. They promoted the protection of emerging domestic industries, very gradual and regulated trade liberalization, and greater controls on investment flows. These tendencies are especially reflected in the composition of the Andean Pact, an integration mechanism created in the late 1960s with active Chilean support.

At the same time, Chile placed great hopes in its participation in international economic organizations, aligning itself with the rest of Latin America and with the African and Asian countries in the construction of a new international economic order.[4] The country participated enthusiastically in the Group of 77 and supported a series of initiatives aimed at the industrialized countries. During the Popular Unity government, Chile also joined the Non-Aligned Movement (see Fermandois 1985).

Chile's turbulent evolution made it into a sort of political laboratory, evoking interest among the international community. The reform process undertaken by President Frei Montalva attracted the attention of reformist circles in Europe and Latin America and also awoke considerable interest in the United States, due to its similarities with elements of President Kennedy's Alliance for Progress. The revolutionary experiment of the Popular Unity movement provoked interest and sympathy among leftist groups throughout the world, who identified with its success or failure.

The 1973 military coup and the repressive policies of the authoritarian regime marked a profound break in Chile's process of integration into the international system. Chile became an emblematic case in the international struggle for democracy and human rights. The military regime became politically isolated, scorned by international public opinion and the object of frequent condemnations from the principal international organizations (Muñoz 1986). This ostracism contrasted with the solidarity provided to the political and social forces of the democratic opposition.

The military regime initially justified itself in national security terms, linking the country's internal political conflict to the international East-West confrontation. The regime's foreign policy in its early years was thus marked by the radical nature of the internal

---

4   The distinguished Chilean diplomat and participant in many of these efforts, Hernán Santa Cruz, discusses some of these claims in his book, Cooperar o perecer (1993).

struggle against the democratic forces, directing itself not only against the Soviet Union and its allies, but also against Western and Third World political forces which criticized the human rights situation in Chile. In this veritable ideological crusade, General Pinochet's regime concentrated a great part of its political energy on the defense of a regime which, not without justification, viewed itself as a "fortress under siege."

After having enjoyed the initial support and active assistance of the United States, the military regime was forced to confront a progressive deterioration in its relations with the superpower, as a consequence of a new preoccupation for human rights in Latin America as well as the assassination by agents of the Chilean regime of ex-minister Orlando Letelier in Washington. This growing distance led to the application of trade and financial sanctions, including Chile's exclusion from the Generalized Preference System, the suspension of public guarantees on investments, and an arms sales embargo. Relations with Europe and the rest of Latin America suffered a significant chill; various countries broke diplomatic ties with Chile or distanced themselves from Chilean authorities and diplomats.

This hostile political environment weighed heavily upon foreign policy and the work of the Foreign Ministry. National security was also affected. Relations with neighboring countries became highly strained. Ties with Peru deteriorated, exacerbated by the commemoration of the Pacific War centennial and by a rather enigmatic incident in Peru leading to the expulsion of a distinguished Chilean ambassador. Negotiations aimed at providing Bolivia with an outlet to the sea reached a dead end. Relations with Argentina were overshadowed by that country's rejection of arbitration in the Beagle case, the breakdown of subsequent bilateral negotiations and the threat of an outbreak of war. Chile felt forced to develop a defensive external strategy, accompanied by a substantial increase in the military budget, which had also increased significantly in nearby countries. If in the past democracy had been a resource that fortified international action, during the 1970s and 1980s its absence became a severe limitation. Throughout the 1980s, the nature of the authoritarian regime impeded Chile's incorporation into the regional coordination mechanisms then gaining strength in Latin America.

Economic relations were also affected by the coup, due to the interruption of then-significant flows of assistance, as well as the initial reticence of some investors, above all Europeans. In 1976, Chile withdrew from the Andean Pact as a consequence of that group's close association with protectionist economic doctrine. As time passed, the broad economic opening and liberalization process advanced by the regime allowed the country to compensate in part for the effects of its political isolation. Chile opened its market to the outside world, reduced tariffs unilaterally, and adopted regulations much more favorable to foreign investment, while a wide-ranging privatization program attracted international interest.

The recovery and internationalization of the Chilean economy were not free of complications. The country exhibited extremely high levels of external debt, along with cyclical crises which continued until the early 1980s. Starting at that time, however, Chile began to enjoy increasing prestige in international economic and financial circles.

It was natural that the new democratic government coming to power in 1990 in a peaceful and consensual transition established the country's reintegration into the international system as its principal foreign policy goal. However, in light of the profound changes which had occurred on the international scene and in Chile's economy and society, the new democracy's foreign policy could not limit itself to recovering the positions held during the previous democratic era. Replicating these stances would have meant a return to earlier

models of integration adopted in the region: attaching the country to Third World movements which were now in frank decline, or promoting a traditional and closed regionalism
incompatible with the considerable diversification achieved in the country's international
economic relations. Thus, the concept of reintegration was not limited to the normalization
of pre-existing foreign relations, but included an active strategy of revising and strengthening the country's principal ties. Foreign policy was forced to adapt to the profound changes
which had occurred on the global, regional, and domestic levels.

Similarly, the continued opening of the economy required a more active concept of
international integration, complementing the unilateral approach favored by the previous
regime with a policy of trade negotiations.

II. Economic Diplomacy: The Quest for Open Regionalism

The Concertación faced an internal and external economic situation very different from
that experienced by previous democratic governments.

First, the weight accorded to economic issues in foreign policy had increased enormously, as a logical consequence of the degree of internationalization already exhibited by
the economy, as well as the opening process still underway. Second, the government's
vision regarding the nature of the international system had been revised, especially with
respect to the previous democratic period. Various examples in Asia, and to a lesser extent
in Latin America, including Chile itself, seemed to demonstrate that structural dependency would not impede the country's development.

At the same time, the unsuccessful attempts to reform the international economic
system which had evoked such enthusiasm in the late 1960s and early 1970s were followed by more nuanced and realistic visions. Although Chile maintained its membership
in the groups representing developing countries, this area of multilateral politics had
become much more moderate in tone and orientation and carried less weight in foreign
policy. In addition, the growing success of Chile's exports called for much more intense
action in defense of the country's trade positions, under the constant threat of protectionism in the principal destination markets. Unsurprisingly, the country's increasingly
powerful business sectors placed great emphasis on this last point, publicly and privately
demanding governmental intervention and assistance each time a threat was detected in
an external market.

Thus, the consolidation and broadening of Chile's export markets became a fundamental objective. By 1990, Chile already enjoyed significant diversification in both destination markets and export offerings. The first Concertación government aimed at maintaining and strengthening these tendencies and, later, promoting increased added value
among exports. It was precisely for this reason that Chile assigned such importance to
world trade liberalization. Retrogressive tendencies, as well as interest group pressures
within the principal world markets, represented obstacles to this objective. In the government's view, the drive toward free world trade seemed to slow in the early 1990s, when
protectionist practices flared up again in many markets. A worrisome contradiction arose
between the economic opening recommended to the country and the increasing restriction of access to the markets of the very countries making these recommendations. For
this reason, the country placed great expectations in the culmination of the Uruguay

Round, although in full consciousness of its imperfections and limitations.

The Concertación's trade policy came to represent one of the leading foreign policy innovations of the past few decades. During the 1970s, the same factions that later came together to form the Concertación had, with rather limited success, channeled a portion of the country's trade policy into the Latin American integration process underway at the time, with special emphasis on the Latin American Free Trade Association (Alalc) and the Andean Pact. However, the actual liberalization achieved through these integration schemes of the early 1970s was very modest, due to their numerous exceptions and the negotiation methods chosen. In addition, since the country's most significant trade flows were outside Latin American markets, trade policy retained in practice the defensive and selective character which had placed Chile among the most protectionist countries in Latin America (Ffrench-Davis 1989:51). The military regime altered this situation drastically, opting for the unilateral opening of external trade and concentrating its efforts to open other markets upon the multilateral environment of GATT.

This unilateral opening was a key element in the economic success which began to be observed in Chile during the 1980s. Yet it suffered the obvious limitation that, by definition, it lacked reciprocity and thus did not contribute to the opening of other markets. Multilateralism, in theory representing an ideal option, since it raises the hope of concerted liberalization across all of the world's markets, also had its limitations. The commitments actually taken on by many countries in the Uruguay Round were highly gradual and restrictive in nature. Various sectors were exempted from multilateral negotiations. The problem of graduated tariffs, which affected Chilean products of greater added value, especially manufactured export goods, was not eliminated.

Thus it became necessary to combine Chile's previous trade policy, based on unilateral opening, with multilateral negotiation and more active integration into the increasingly globalized world economy. In this effort, the search for effective bilateral or regional mechanisms ceased to have substantive importance. Instead, Chile needed to ensure its access to the great global and regional markets; neglect in this area would allow others to obtain advantages that would displace Chilean products.

The first Concertación government thus began to develop a trade policy combining unilateral, bilateral, regional, and multilateral strategies.[5] This option gained increasing prominence and was especially oriented at the beginning toward Latin America, taking advantage of the legal framework provided by Alalc's successor organization, the Latin American Integration Association (Aladi). The first free trade agreement negotiated by Chile within this strategy was with Mexico in 1991. It should be noted that although the Latin American integration process had been going on for 30 years, this was the first authentic free trade agreement signed in the region.

Nevertheless, the negotiation of further accords was criticized from two perspectives. Some neoliberal economists warned of possible trade distortions arising from these agreements; additionally, more in private than in public, they viewed the rest of Latin America with mistrust and a certain disdain. On the other hand, many government leaders considered it more useful and relevant to concentrate their negotiating efforts on what was then considered a crucial element of Chile's international integration: a free trade agreement

---

5   A good analysis of Chilean trade policy during the first two years of the Concertación government is found in Butelmann and Meller, eds. (1992).

with the United States, whether bilateral or in the broader framework of the recently negotiated NAFTA agreement among Canada, the United States, and Mexico. The perception, which later proved to be erroneous, that the seemingly imminent free trade accord with the United States would somehow be incompatible with further Latin American agreements slowed the pace of the latter for some time.

The strong interest in NAFTA shown by the economic team of the first Concertación government, with the support of some prominent political ministers, can be explained on both economic and political grounds. On economic grounds was the need to ensure access to the country's most important market, as well as the seal of economic prestige which this link would confer upon the country at a moment where some uncertainty still prevailed about the democratic government's ability to continue the economic successes achieved during the military regime. On political grounds was the view that NAFTA would help cement Chile's commitment to the market economy model, which even now meets with reservations among some factions of the Concertación itself. Similarly, it was believed that NAFTA would contribute to strengthening Chilean democracy, since it would be strongly conditioned upon the continuation of the democratic system.

The apparent contradiction between Latin American negotiations and the hopes for an agreement with the United States was further complicated by a sort of regional division of labor among the country's ministries. Thus, while the Foreign Ministry, and to a lesser extent the Ministry of Economics, preoccupied themselves with Latin America, the Ministry of finance addressed the United States, while the Ministry of Economics dealt with various European issues (Martini 1994). As tends to happen, this parallel structure became a source of discord,[6] affecting negotiations with several Latin American countries, the United States, and less frequently, the APEC countries of Asia.

Domestic considerations impeded the United States government from initiating trade negotiations during the Aylwin administration, draining credibility from the proposal for a hemispheric free trade zone announced by President Bush in 1990 within the framework of the Free Trade Initiative of the Americas. However, this negotiation delay had the virtue of eliminating the false dilemma between NAFTA and Latin America. The policy of pursuing negotiations within Latin America was strengthened with the signing of free trade agreements with Venezuela (1993) and Colombia (1994), to which must be added the economic complementation agreements negotiated with Argentina (1991) and Bolivia (1993), which fell short of the full liberalization of mutual trade.

The second Concertación government was able to definitively transcend the NAFTA/Latin America dilemma, clearly establishing Latin America as its priority. This was expressed in the continuation of free trade negotiations, leading to the signing of an agreement with Ecuador (1995) and the initiation of treaty negotiations with Peru and Panama.

However, Chile's most important step in Latin American policy was its association with Mercosur. The agreement, signed after intense debate in Congress, called for the gradual liberalization of all of Chile's trade with its two leading Latin American partners. In associating itself with this highly promising structure so near its borders, Chile renewed its participation in the Latin American integration process. The complex negotiations for this

---

6   See the editorial by Roberto Pizarro, then the Foreign Ministry's Bilateral Economic Assistant Director, "Nuestra política exterior," *La Época* newspaper, March 2, 1993, as well as Guillermo Turner, "Quién manda este buque," *Hoy* magazine (Santiago), March 7, 1994, pp. 39-42.

agreement first required persuading the member countries to establish the category of associate member. This option, which had not been initially contemplated by the group, met with resistance precisely because it was hoped that Chile would join as a full member.

From the Chilean perspective, the agreement with Mercosur not only revitalized the country's commitment to Latin America, but also responded to a strong economic necessity. Over the medium term, the accord would provide a stable framework for the region's increasing physical integration, as well as promoting industrial development which had been restrained by the limited size of the Chilean market. The link with Mercosur also took on strategic importance, because of the close proximity of this integration process and its direct implications for the country's security.

If this is so, it may be asked why Chile did not become a full member of Mercosur. The answer is quite simple. Mercosur became a Customs Union: that is, a free trade zone with common tariffs toward third countries. Considering the average level of Mercosur's tariffs, Chile's full participation would have required elevating its own external trade barriers and thus reducing the openness of its economy, as Paraguay and Uruguay had effectively been forced to do. This option lacked support in Chile, demonstrated by the fact that during the Congressional debate on precisely this subject, the Frei government made the commitment to continue the gradual reduction of external tariffs. It is interesting to note the contrast between this decision and the agreement between Brazil and Argentina to raise tariffs in 1997, in response to the financial turbulence threatening both countries. This demonstrates continuing differences of focus between Chile and Mercosur in the area of economic opening and seems to rule out the possibility that Chile will soon join the Customs Union. In addition, Chile's single tariff structure contrasts with the differentiated tariff schedule maintained by Mercosur. finally, full participation in Mercosur would have obliged Chile to act in concert with all of the other members when negotiating trade agreements with third countries, a requirement which did not appear compatible with Chile's other commercial interests.

The clear Latin American priority established by the second Concertación government did not imply its neglect of relations with other regions. This explains the government's insistence upon preserving its autonomy to negotiate individual agreements, allowing it to strengthen its ties with non-Latin American markets, which continue to absorb more than 80% of Chilean exports. As shown in Tables 2 and 3, Chile's high level of diversification in destination markets is a central characteristic of its external trade. The same phenomenon is observed for imports. From a strictly commercial point of view, the country has not had, and does not now have, a natural trading partner. It should not be forgotten that Chile exports more to Japan than to Brazil, more to the United Kingdom than to Argentina, more to Korea than to Peru, and more to Holland than to Mexico. This diversification is one of the strengths of the Chilean economy, since it helps cushion the effects of the cyclical crises affecting the world's great markets.

The growing globalization of the economy provided the opportunity for Chile to consolidate its participation in the Asia-Pacific Economic Cooperation (APEC) framework. Thus Chile gained a foothold, lamentably still very exceptional for a Latin American country, in the fastest-growing area of the world economy. Chile also signed a new agreement with the European Union (EU), an important step on the still-long path toward a political and economic association with the 15 European nations forming the world's largest integrated market. This instrument strengthens Chile's historical links with Europe, while aiming at rapid progress in the liberalization of trade in goods and services.

A free trade agreement with Canada was ratified in 1997 as part of Chile's strategy of developing closer ties to North American markets. The accord was markedly innovative, due to the breadth of subjects included as well as the fact that it eliminated injurious anti-dumping measures between the signatories, something that could not be achieved within NAFTA itself. All of this was accomplished without removing Chile's restrictions on short-term capital movement, which had been among Canada's initial demands. Certainly, a free trade agreement with the United States or with NAFTA remains a desirable goal, taking into consideration that Chile already has an accord with Canada and is negotiating an updated agreement with Mexico. However, at this point in time, such an agreement is not imperative, nor is it especially urgent for our country.

With its policy of integration and multiple memberships, Chile has a strong interest in the convergence of the trade agreements it has signed in the hemisphere. This would help produce a certain uniformity in commerce, coinciding with trade liberalization on a global scale. Thus, the negotiation of a Free Trade Area of the Americas (ALCA), whose beginnings are hoped to be announced at the Second Summit of the Americas in Santiago, will be more important for the country than a bilateral accord with the United States. Certainly, this process, expected to culminate in 2005, will be extensive and complex. Yet it represents an instrument of very special value to the country of the region which has already negotiated the highest number of agreements with the FTAA's future members.

The concept of open regionalism best sums up Chile's current trade policy. The concept has multiple meanings, and it is not free of contradictions. In Chilean practice, the open character of regionalism is expressed in three ways. first, the various options of regional integration are not viewed as mutually exclusive, but rather as tending to complement each other. Thus, there is no incompatibility between Mercosur and ALCA, or between membership in APEC and closer ties to the EU. Second, the agreements are open to the incorporation of new members. And finally, regional frameworks are strengthened in a manner compatible with world trade liberalization, avoiding the raising of new barriers against goods and services imported from other areas of the world. This last point is perhaps the most fundamental characteristic of open regionalism, but it is at the same time the most difficult to achieve, since by definition a preferential trade agreement tends to discriminate against third countries.

Attracting foreign investment has been a basic objective of the Concertación governments. It was believed that external capital would not only increase the country's investment rate, but also would facilitate its integration into the increasingly international business world, bringing positive side effects such as access to new technologies, participation in established trade networks, and so forth. As shown in Table 5, Chile succeeded in attracting a substantial flow of investment from abroad during the 1990s. The country's economic stability, the peaceful and consensual nature of its democratic transition, and the constant improvement in its competitiveness indicators contributed to this achievement. At the same time, Chile adhered to an internationally recognized mechanism to resolve investment disputes and signed a series of investment promotion and protection accords.

The increasing activity of Chilean businesses abroad has presented a new dimension for the country's international integration. This activity was not the result of any government strategy, but the perceived need of a highly representative group of domestic companies to expand and internationalize their operations. The great majority of this capital flow was initially concentrated in our three neighboring countries, especially in Argentina and Peru. However, as shown in Table 7, Chilean investment was gradually extended into other countries such as Brazil, Colombia, and Venezuela.

Chilean foreign policy gradually began to take account of this new situation. Investment agreements, traditionally conceived to facilitate the establishment of foreign companies in Chile, began to be seen as a framework for the operation of Chilean businesses abroad. Chile's diplomatic representatives abroad, as well as the Foreign Ministry itself, began to play a supporting role in the promotion and defense of economic interests, a phenomenon common to all investment-exporting countries. The fact that a very significant part of these investments was concentrated in neighboring countries presented an additional complication, since their presence could arouse mistrust; or conversely, any foreign action prejudicial to these investments could be construed as a hostile action against Chile. However, this risk, a version of which is seen even in major sporting events, is reduced if both sides share a full understanding of the nature of the problem as well as the difference between conflicts of economic interest and those of a more political and strategic nature.

The presence of substantial Chilean investments abroad places another perspective on the treaties concluded to avoid double taxation of business income. In the past, only those countries with considerable investments in Chile, or those planning to undertake them in the future, had shown interest in this option. Today, the interest is shared by our own tax authorities with respect to the operation of Chilean businesses abroad. Until very recently, Chilean tax law presented barriers to the conclusion of agreements of this kind. However, this was changed in 1997, permitting negotiations to begin for an agreement model very closely following the practice of the Organization for Economic Cooperation and Development (OECD), which includes the world's most advanced economies.

III. Policy Toward Chile's Neighbors: The Two Agendas

The criticism is heard with some frequency that the Concertación's foreign policy has been excessively driven by economics. While no one can fail to recognize the great importance taken on by economic diplomacy, it is no less certain that other historical foreign policy priorities have retained their force. This is especially clear in the area of relations with Chile's neighbors, which remain a central priority for the Foreign Ministry and the government in general.

Realizing that isolationist strategies were no longer viable, the democratic governments undertook a pragmatic and realistic policy of seeking closer ties to neighboring countries and the rest of Latin America. A precursor to this strategy was exhibited in the last years of the military government, except that the regime possessed less room to maneuver, and its negotiations with neighboring countries were more sporadic and did not appear to derive from a more integral plan. In addition, the hostile environment confronted by the country during the late 1970s had left a very significant imprint upon the leaders of the Armed Forces.

Within a much more favorable environment, the Concertación believed that a stable foreign policy called for satisfactory relations with the country's neighbors. For national security reasons, as well as the promotion of sustained development, it was essential to resolve the lingering conflicts of the past and construct close economic, cultural, and political ties, leading to a regional environment of mutual confidence and cooperation. A "good neighbor policy" began to be mentioned, aiming at resolving long-standing border disputes, with full adherence to the traditional principles maintained in this sphere, and providing a new framework for relations of growing interdependence with Chile's regional partners.

Chile's agenda with its neighbors included both traditional and new issues. The traditional issues included historical concerns focusing on border issues. The new issues arose from the new tendency toward interdependence and cooperation which was visibly strengthening, stimulated by Chile's economic development and its drive toward regionalization and globalization. Thus, historical concerns were combined with an agenda of integration, understood not as a utopian political project, but as the consequence of economic and social phenomena quite independent of government action, in which the driving forces were the country's entrepreneurs, or to a lesser extent, the various regions of the country.

None of Chile's bilateral relationships expresses the realities of interdependence as clearly as our ties with Argentina. As the countries' relations became increasingly multifaceted and complex, the Concertación expended great efforts to change the character of this bilateral relationship historically characterized by periodic disputes and mutual distrust. The need was obvious to resolve the border disputes which traditionally had increased the tension of bilateral relations and which, on a very recent occasion, had brought the two countries almost to the point of war.

In August 1990, Presidents Aylwin and Menem took the initiative of identifying every border issue still in dispute between Argentina and Chile, with the goal of finding a definitive solution for all of them. After intense work, during which special care was taken to consult the National Congress, the armed forces, and the political parties, 24 problem areas were identified in the demarcation of the international border (Foreign Relations Ministry 1994). Through a Presidential Declaration on Borders adopted by both leaders in Buenos Aires on August 2, 1991, 22 problems were directly resolved. The Laguna del Desierto controversy was submitted to international arbitration, in conformity with the requirements of the 1984 Peace and Friendship Treaty. The remaining dispute, the border demarcation between fitz Roy Mountain and the Daudet Hill, known as Campos de Hielo Sur in Chile and Hielos Continentales in Argentina, was resolved through an agreement between the two governments, which was submitted for parliamentary approval in both countries.

From the Chilean point of view, the Laguna del Desierto arbitration aimed at regaining a portion of national territory which had been the object of dispute for almost a century, which had provoked serious incidents and great tensions in the 1960s, and which during the past three decades had been physically occupied by Argentina. Arbitration was the only option, excluding the use of force, for reasserting Chilean rights to the area. The Tribunal considering this question consisted of five Latin American judges agreed upon by both governments, a matter which would later be strongly questioned by opposition circles in Chile. In 1994, the Tribunal handed down a decision entirely favorable to Argentina. This case represented a painful and difficult episode for Chile's government, although the affected territory had not been in Chilean hands for several decades, and the events underlying the dispute lay far back in history. The government accepted the decision, invoking the country's tradition of respect for international law, although it pursued an unsuccessful attempt at appeal through the same Tribunal. Although criticism of the results was widely expressed, relations with Argentina continued to improve, and significantly, no faction questioned this development.

Meanwhile, parliamentary approval was still pending in early 1998 for the definitive border negotiated by both countries for the Campos de Hielo Sur area. In both Chile and Argentina, opposition leaders have expressed reservations about the pact, claiming that valid borders already existed, although of course these alleged borders do not coincide. This delay has not impeded the advance of bilateral relations, nor has it caused public unrest in either country. Since a negotiated agreement exists, respected until now by both governments, this is a very different question from the Laguna del Desierto issue. However, the lack of a parliamentary decision, explained especially by the Argentine political situation, leaves open, at least from a legal point of view, a matter which may return to disturb bilateral relations in the future. This is especially true considering that the 24 points making up the 1991 Presidential Declaration were always understood as a single package from which no issue could be deleted.

Yet relations between Chile and Argentina are far from being reduced solely to historical border questions. In recent years, a truly qualitative leap in bilateral relations has been seen, without precedent in history. Bilateral trade has increased substantially, although a somewhat cyclical tendency is still observed. Hundreds of thousands of Chilean citizens live in Argentina. Tourism from Argentina has become a highly significant source of income for Chile, on a level with our country's most dynamic export sectors. Investments by Chilean businesses in Argentina surpassed six billion dollars in 1997, representing more than 40% of the total. These investments are shared among some 160 enterprises. In the area of energy integration, important advances have included the Tierra del Fuego gas pipeline, the joint petroleum operation at Este de la Boca Oriental in the Magellan Strait, and the Neuquén-Concepción oil pipeline, as well as the Gas Andes, Transandino, Transpatagónico, and Norte de Chile gas lines.

In 1997, both countries signed a major mining integration accord which will benefit the mining sector in both countries as well as the regions of the Chilean North. This accord outlines obligatory exit routes for the products of new Argentine mining operations. In the area of physical integration, the countries have created six Border Committees and implemented a Master Plan for Border Crossings, aimed at reconstructing or reinforcing official services at the crossings of Jama, Sico, San Francisco, Agua Negra, Cristo Redentor, Pehuenche, Pino Hachado, Cardenal Samoré, Huemules, Coyhaique Alto, Integración Austral, and San Sebastián.

This new era in bilateral relations has required and will continue to require ongoing evaluation of the framework and bilateral instruments in use. Presidential meetings have multiplied and have given rise to meetings of the ministers most closely involved in the bilateral relationship. Occasionally, these meetings have been held outside the capitals, symbolizing the enormous importance of these relations for the regions and provinces of the two countries.

Meanwhile, the increasing interdependence between Chile and Argentina has given rise to new necessities in the areas of infrastructure and physical integration, especially as Chile has set the strategic goal of becoming a bridge between the Atlantic and the Pacific, supporting the interchange between the Southern Cone of Latin America and the great

Asian markets. Providing transport and intermediation services between two of the world's most important emerging markets, Latin America and Asia, may produce great benefits for our country. At the same time, these services will facilitate the transit of Chile's goods and services to these two regions. Obviously, Argentina will play a central role in the fulfillment of this objective. Yet very careful revision is still needed concerning the quality of the connections uniting us with that country, applying obvious criteria of economic feasibility. Equally, the quality and flexibility of the commercial, financial, and port services which can be offered to Argentine businesses must be evaluated, along with methods to facilitate the transit of people and merchandise across the country.

During the 1990s, Chile was able to improve its relations with Bolivia, creating opportunities for dialogue to address various issues on the bilateral agenda. The Presidents of Chile and Bolivia met twice after 1990. The Permanent Mechanism for Political Consultation was established in 1994 and has held five meetings since that time. Additionally, an Economic Complementation Agreement was signed in 1993, aimed at broadening the flow of trade. The idea of a free trade agreement had to be discarded, since it could further accentuate the bilateral surplus in Chile's favor. In the area of physical integration, two Border Committees were set up for the crossings at Tambo Quemado and Colchane. Advances were also made in the facilitation of customs processing and tourist transit. Efforts on both sides led to the pavement of the Arica-La Paz highway, the only paved road uniting Bolivia with the outside world. This achievement has contributed to a substantial increase in the flow of tourists to Arica and Iquique.

The amount of Bolivian cargo passing through Chilean territory has risen, and an Aeronautical Agreement has substantially increased the frequency of air traffic between Bolivia and the cities of the Chilean North. Similarly, the broadening of the tariff sections of the Economic Complementation Agreement and the signing of a Phyto- and Zoo-sanitary Convention resulted in an increase of Bolivian exports to Chile. These are expected to amount to some 80 million dollars within a few years, thus reducing the Bolivian trade deficit to a ratio of 3 to 1, in comparison to 13 to 1 in 1993. Chilean investments in Bolivia are beginning to be balanced by a Bolivian counterpart, as demonstrated in the concession of the Chilean section of the Arica-La Paz railway to a company of Bolivian majority ownership. The new Port Law approved by the Chilean Congress and the grant of the necessary infrastructure, combined with Arica's existing foreign investment facilities, provide attractive business opportunities for Bolivian companies and investors.

Undeniably, throughout this period Bolivia has maintained its quest for a sovereign outlet to the sea as one of its main foreign policy objectives. This historical objective has not diminished in importance, although each Bolivian administration has defined and expressed it in a different manner. The extreme sensitivity shown by Bolivia in its bilateral relations with Chile has also continued undiminished, exhibited in virtually all of the rapprochement efforts occurring between the two countries. This situation has obviously limited Chile's options with respect to Bolivia and has required very careful evaluation of the steps to be followed with this neighbor. Problems of mutually contradictory perceptions and expectations have also been in evidence. On more than a few occasions, Chilean initiatives have been interpreted by La Paz as steps toward maritime negotiations, while Santiago tends to consider them as a means for reducing the pressure for these same claims. The evolution of bilateral relations has also been affected by political changes in Bolivia. Thus, the advances observed during the government of President Sánchez de

Lozada contrast with the attitude of the new Bolivian government since August 1997, which has led to greater distance between the two countries and even to Bolivian denunciations of Chile.

On the other hand, the Bolivian authorities have applied a different standard to commercial and economic subjects, showing the intention to continue developing these ties. Thus, frequent references are made to Bolivia's central location on the continent and its capacity to facilitate transit between the Atlantic and Pacific Basins, even in recognition that its landlocked condition does not give it access to ports. However, old problems have also been exacerbated, such as claims related to the movement of storage facilities for Bolivian minerals from populated areas in Antofagasta and Arica to sites outside the urban radius, which have added to the costs of transport but which have been necessary due to the protests of residents living near these storage areas.

The Concertación similarly undertook significant foreign policy efforts to resolve remaining disputes from the 1929 treaty between Chile and Peru. These consisted of the construction of a seafront dock on Arica's bay for the use of Peru, along with a Peruvian customs office and a station for the Tacna railway. The promised works were constructed in the middle of the last decade, with Peru's previous approval and to its satisfaction (Foreign Relations Ministry 1994:56). However, the continuing lack of agreement upon the legal framework governing this infrastructure prevented the resolution of the matter. In 1992, negotiations were initiated aimed at fully executing the remaining provisions of the 1929 Treaty. This process culminated in May 1993 with the signing of the Lima Conventions, including a new legal framework applicable to these works. However, in the face of criticism in the Peruvian Parliament and from other quarters, the Conventions were withdrawn by President Fujimori. Currently, both countries hope to reinitiate talks in order to proceed with the delivery of the works and to determine the legal framework for their utilization. Chile does not feel great pressure to do so. As affirmed by Foreign Minister Insulza, the country does not consider itself to be in a state of debt, nor even negligence (Insulza 1998). In any event, these works must be handed over in full recognition of their location in a territory over which Chile exercises full sovereignty, and their administration must be compatible with this fact. Significantly, Peru has publicly recognized that the legal nature of the remaining issues does not involve a question of borders.

The recovery of the Peruvian economy and the recent privatization process has generated broad new opportunities for bilateral economic ties. Trade between the two countries has grown considerably, more than doubling between 1990 and 1997. An increasing flow of people has also been observed. A significant number of Peruvian citizens reside in Chile, ranging from entrepreneurs and professionals to workers in the informal sector. Chile is also an important source for the dynamic Peruvian tourism sector.

Similarly, this neighboring country has become a highly important destination for Chilean investments abroad. The frequency of air traffic and other travel between the two countries is rising. Chile and Peru are currently negotiating an Economic Complementation Agreement to liberalize bilateral trade. Peru has become the third market for our exports within Latin America, and there is evident interest in establishing clear ground rules for this commerce. At the same time, the accord will be of great benefit to Chilean investors in Peru. Although these trade negotiations have progressed more slowly than those with other Latin American nations, the signing of an accord in 1998 is an achievable goal. From the Peruvian perspective, this negotiation is seen as even more viable than the country's initiative toward Mercosur, which seems to demonstrate that the obstacles encountered are due more to threats perceived by the business sectors of both countries than to political or historical considerations.

IV. Latin American Policy: Renewed Regionalism

Until the 1970s, Chile had a long history of supporting Latin American integration efforts, playing a leadership role in initiatives such as the Andean Pact. However, later evaluation of these experiences, the political problems affecting the country during the 1970s and 1980s, the new economic model, and the transformations in the regional and world environment led to the modification of traditional concepts regarding Latin American integration.

Chile naturally continued to maintain close economic ties with the rest of the region, which were not strictly limited to the commercial plane. After declining during the 1980s, Latin America's share of Chilean external trade again increased. While Latin America received 12.2% of Chilean exports in 1990, by 1997 this figure had risen to 17.5%. The region likewise began to represent a major market for Chilean exports of higher added value. This tendency was accentuated as the effects of the crisis which had struck Latin America during the previous decade began to abate (Sáez 1993).

As discussed above, Chile negotiated a series of accords after 1990, aimed at creating free trade areas, promoting physical and energy integration, and developing new forms of regional cooperation. Chile attempted to advance consistently in this direction, while keeping clearly in mind that its opening to the world was irreversible and that it must avoid integration options hindering the strengthening of ties with other regions.

In very general terms, it was held that regional integration schemes must not merely be an expression of political will; nor should they aim at unrealistic and overly ambitious goals. Instead, they should lead to significant trade flows in goods and services, the adoption of compatible economic politics, economic stability among member nations, the use of collective mechanisms, and enhanced competitiveness. Integration must be driven by pragmatism and rest upon a real and solid economic basis. It is believed that as other Latin American economies reach levels of stability and liberalization similar to Chile's, our participation in regional integration will increase, not only because of affinity and goodwill, but also in order to reap its concrete benefits. Chile's association with Mercosur confirms this conviction.

In the pursuit of these goals, Chile's foreign policy has regained its long-standing Latin American priority. Special emphasis is placed on its nearest neighbors, which are considered the central framework of a strategic alliance for participation in the global system, promoting the region's competitiveness and raising its international profile. This regional emphasis, reflecting an important departure from Chile's stance during the military regime, is justified not only for reasons of solidarity and brotherhood, but also because of changes in the economic and political environment (Figueroa 1994).

Apart from Chile's immediate neighbors, two additional Latin American nations occupy a fundamental place in Chile's newly redefined regional policies. The first is Brazil, which had traditionally held a place of great importance in Chile's international relations, both in political and economic terms.[8] The Aylwin government sought a strengthening of

---

8   The potential for the future of Chilean-Brazilian relations is analyzed in the volume compiled by J. Garrido
    Rojas and P. Álamos Varas (1992).

ties with this major partner. However, a series of circumstances prevented the completion of negotiations for an economic complementation agreement. This failure was largely caused by that country's complex and sometimes chaotic political and economic situation during the early part of the decade. Yet doubts also existed in Chile about the advisability of negotiation with an economy viewed as unstable and excessively subsidized. These limitations were transcended with the stabilization of Brazil's economic and political situation. The earlier bilateral trade talks were supplanted by negotiations with Mercosur. Yet a new bilateral understanding was achieved in the political sphere, further stimulated by President Fernando Henrique Cardoso's strong commitment to Chile, as well as the institution of annual presidential visits.

The second country of great importance for Chile is Mexico. The two countries' resumption of diplomatic relations in 1990 was quickly followed by the intensification of mutual ties. This was spurred on in part by the dynamism of the Mexican economy, the existence of important areas of foreign policy agreement between the two countries, and shared interest in the creation of a hemispheric free trade zone.

In the 1990s, Chile began to develop horizontal assistance programs with Central American and Caribbean nations. Chile's International Cooperation Agency (AGCI) became an instrument for implementing this policy, although at its creation it had placed much more emphasis on receiving rather than providing international assistance. While endowed with modest resources, as shown in Table 10, these horizontal cooperation programs earned widespread recognition and helped cement Chile's ties with Central America and the Caribbean. Similarly, during the Frei administration, Chile began to participate in trilateral cooperative experiments in Central America, in connection with various European countries and Japan.

On the regional level, Chile's return to democracy permitted it to join the Rio Group, thus overcoming a serious barrier to relations with the rest of the region. Chile became a full and active member in this interesting and innovative regional mechanism, acting as Secretary Pro Tempore during 1993 and organizing the group's Seventh Presidential Summit (Secretaría Pro Tempore, Grupo de Río 1993). Chile's contributions were especially oriented toward the defense of democracy, the harmonization of regional integration and cooperation frameworks, and the strengthening of interchanges between Latin America and the other countries and regions of the world. During Chile's time as secretary, a dialogue was initiated between the Group and Japan, in addition to the institutionalized dialogue already maintained with the European Community, for which the 1992 annual meeting had taken place in Santiago.

Chile's Latin American policy was not limited to the economic sphere. The global and regional context appeared propitious for progress in regional security. Aside from being favorable to Chilean interests, this policy could permit overall regional reductions in military expenditures over the long term. The Concertación governments began to pursue a prudent and gradual policy of security negotiations, focusing on progressive steps rather than overly broad, ambitious, or abstract frameworks, which were not considered to be viable. Chile, together with Argentina and Brazil, contributed actively to the reform of the Treaty of Tlatelolco for the proscription of nuclear arms in the region. Thanks to this reform, in January 1994 Chile was able to subscribe fully to the legal regime established by this groundbreaking treaty. Chile also concluded the Mendoza Compromise with Argentina, Brazil, and Uruguay to outlaw weapons of mass destruction. Steps such as these not only contribute to creating a more stable and secure environment in the region, but also address growing world concerns about arms proliferation.

In 1995, Chile hosted an Inter-American Conference on Mutual Confidence Measures. The conference focused on the identification and application of all military and non-military measures to strengthen mutual confidence in the region. Similar efforts have been undertaken on a bilateral level, as demonstrated by the periodic meetings between Chilean and Peruvian military leaders, as well as the agreements reached by the foreign ministers of Chile and Argentina in Zapallar, Chile, in July 1997. Recently, Chile was one of the four countries acting as guarantors for the resolution of the dispute between Ecuador and Peru. This was an extremely delicate task, in consideration of the complex historical ties maintained by Chile with both neighbors. However, the diplomatic management of this delicate problem, which even required presidential intervention at various stages, earned public recognition from both Ecuador and Peru.

In the new climate taking hold in Latin America, Chile also found it necessary to insist on the maintenance of traditional balances in the region. This implied accepting the possibility that all regional partners might strengthen their military forces, but that this reinforcement would take place under conditions of equality. Thus Foreign Minister Insulza noted the inappropriateness of introducing into Latin America institutions foreign to the region and more suited to the Cold War era, a direct allusion to the status obtained by Argentina of a special non-NATO ally of the United States.[9]

The return and consolidation of democracy in Latin America starting in the 1980s was a key element in the success of regional political cooperation. Closely linked to this democratic renewal, the protection of human rights arose as a regional concern. Numerous mandatory conventions led to the rise of a truly new regional regime, a new set of rules, and institutions imposing concrete commitments and obligations upon the countries of the region (see Van Klaveren 1993). Chile joined this initiative, although it was obvious that its own government would have to confront cases of past human rights violations within the new inter-American institutions, and that its current policies would be subject to scrutiny. Although some factions within the country are not yet accustomed to this new international jurisdiction, it is accepted as completely natural in regions such as Europe, where states with as strong a democratic tradition as the United Kingdom are subject to the European Court for Human Rights.

In addition, the Concertación coalition's concern for the protection and promotion of democracy in the region led the Aylwin administration to support the adoption of the "Santiago Commitment to Democracy and the Renewal of the Inter-American System," along with Resolution 1080 on "Representative Democracy," at the Twenty-first General Assembly of the Organization of American States (OAS), held in Chile's capital in 1991. These instruments established an automatic response mechanism for cases of unlawful interruption of the democratic process in any OAS nation. In practice, the Rio Group has followed a similar line, including the automatic suspension of any member country rejecting democracy. Like other Latin American countries, Chile has faced various dilemmas in its attempt to harmonize the promotion of democracy on the regional and global levels with the principle of non-intervention. Likewise, other objectives such as economic

---

9   From the coverage in the Santiago newspaper *El Mercurio* of the appearance of Foreign Minister Insulza before the Defense and Foreign Affairs Commissions of the Chamber of Deputies, August 21, 1997.

advancement or the good neighbor policy have sometimes clashed with this goal. Lacking a definitive solution, Chile has sought to establish a delicate equilibrium between its support for democracy and other foreign policy interests.

Democratic governance was a central topic at the Sixth Ibero-American Summit of Heads of State and Government held in Santiago in 1996. Debate centered not only on support for democratic processes in Latin America, but also on the substantive improvement of regimes still showing serious deficiencies. These systems must move toward governance and transparency in order to effectively serve the interests of the citizens who elected them (Frei Ruiz-Tagle 1996).

V. North America: The Complexities of a Great Power and the Discovery of New Partners

It is commonplace to state that relations with the United States represent a central priority for Chilean foreign policy, not only because of the preeminent position occupied by the United States on the regional and global levels, but also due to the history of bilateral relations, which have been strongly marked by our own political evolution (Sigmund 1993). Our relations with the superpower are also a subject of preferential attention in Chilean political circles, overshadowing interest in Europe and Japan, although these have similar importance from an economic point of view.

As confirmed by recent experience, any decision by Washington, D.C., affecting our country, whether in the political or economic sphere, will be submitted to more exacting scrutiny than other foreign policy topics. This arises in part from the lower level of domestic consensus on many of the issues involved in our relations with Washington. The strong symbolic weight of these ties, their considerable impact on domestic politics, and the undeniable attraction on the part of the communications media toward everything occurring in the United States must be taken into consideration in the design of our policy toward that country. This remains true despite the fact that the economic and political importance of the United States to our country has gradually diminished over the past decade, as a consequence of the diversification of our external ties and the rise of other priorities. Relations with the United States are still a central element of Chile's foreign policy, but they are not a defining factor, as they have been in the past.[10]

The often bumpy trajectory of our bilateral relations can be summed up with the concept of an aloof friendship (Muñoz and Portales 1987), remaining in force during President Frei Montalva's last years in office, the Popular Unity government, and the military regime, when Washington's initial support was replaced by increasingly tense relations. This shift left a strong imprint upon Chilean military circles and the civilians who supported them.

With the democratic restoration, Chile saw the chance for the first time in more than 20 years to overcome the conflicts and tensions of the past and to establish more mature and normal relations with the United States, in harmony with Chile's other foreign policy priorities. The majority of the questions that had remained unresolved for many years

---

10 An interesting contrast may be noted here with Argentina, where in recent years great emphasis has been placed on the alliance with the United States. See De la Balze and Roca (1997).

were now cleared up. As a symbol of the new era in relations, President Bush paid an official visit to the country in 1990, the first by a U.S. president in 30 years. Chile was reincorporated into the Generalized Preference System. The Kennedy Amendment provisions prohibiting arms sales were lifted. Relations were reestablished in the area of defense cooperation. The case of the assassination in Washington of ex-Foreign Minister Letelier was resolved in a fully satisfactory manner, both as to the government of Chile's responsibilities regarding this terrorist act, as well as to the conviction and later imprisonment of the principal persons involved.

During the Aylwin administration, Chile was mentioned as an exemplary case in the context of the Initiative of the Americas, and the possibility of negotiating a free trade agreement — whether bilaterally or within the NAFTA framework — appeared very real. However, this hope was frustrated due to internal disagreements in Washington, as the U.S. Congress refused to grant the necessary negotiation mandate, or fast-track authority, to the executive branch. Additional problems eluded resolution, such as the question of indemnity in the contaminated-grape dispute, but these were not sufficient to overturn a frankly positive evaluation of the relationship.

The second Concertación government has had a similar experience. Bilateral relations continue on an excellent footing, as confirmed during President Frei's state visit to the United States in 1997. Bilateral trade is dynamic, the United States continues to be the principal source of foreign investment in Chile, and Washington has observed Chile's transition process and democratic consolidation with great respect and consideration. Cooperation in the area of defense has been intensified, and although Chile did not solicit it, Washington lifted the embargo on the sale of state-of-the-art combat aircraft to Latin America.

The two countries have cooperated effectively on a series of regional and global issues, based upon a foundation of respect for Chile's own positions in some especially sensitive areas, such as the Helms-Burton law and the treatment of the Cuban question in general, the focus on drug trafficking and the methods used to combat it, and some questions related to hemispheric security. finally, Chile's hosting of the Second Summit of the Americas remains significant, especially since the first meeting, held in Miami, was unilaterally convoked by the United States. In addition, an impressive level of cooperation was achieved between the two countries for the organization of the Santiago meeting.

Notwithstanding this favorable balance, areas of frustration for Chile still remain. first, the solemn invitation extended to Chile by President Clinton at the Miami Summit in 1994, together with President Zedillo of Mexico and Prime Minister Chrétien of Canada, to negotiate its membership in NAFTA, has not been able to be fulfilled. Chile took the initial steps to begin the negotiation process. The teams were assembled and the first technical meetings held. More than three years later, the lack of agreement between the U.S. legislative and executive powers for the approval of fast-track negotiation authority has impeded further progress. These events were surrounded by an environment of sporadic announcements and rumors, while being complicated by the intervention of numerous governmental agencies and a plethora of private actors offering their lobbying services and implying that the subject was practically one of life or death for the Chilean economy. This situation contrasts with the uncomplicated and goal-oriented negotiations for Chile's free trade accord with Canada and our updated agreement with Mexico.

Second, there have been serious episodes of protectionism, such as the threat of sanctions against Chilean salmon exporters in late 1997, which fortunately was mainly neutralized through the joint action of the private sector and the Chilean government, or the restrictions affecting some wood exports, a very complex subject since it does not depend directly upon the U.S. President.

Third, with the conferring of the status of special non-NATO ally upon Argentina, Washington clearly introduced a new element into the always-delicate regional balance of the Southern Cone. However, in reality the measure has a mostly symbolic character and does not involve the transfer of sophisticated weapons, as alleged by some misinformed Chilean commentators.

Does this mixed balance mean that Chile's friendship with the United States continues to be an aloof one? Is this an area of foreign policy failures, as the opposition charges? We do not share these impressions. It is closer to the truth to say that the problems we have faced are simply the complications of relations with the leading global power and probably the most complex national partner in the world. It must be kept in mind that, in contrast to the presidentialist democracies of Latin America or the parliamentary governments of Europe, in Washington the conduct of foreign policy is shared between the executive and legislative branches. The great number of individuals and groups influencing the great power's international relations must be remembered, along with the often paralyzing deadlock which can be produced among them.

Paradoxically, the imperial power of our times does not maintain a coherent foreign policy, characterized by clear goals and timetables. U.S. foreign policy only becomes truly cohesive in the face of crises affecting national security, or on subjects of extremely high priority. Chile, more for good than for ill, is not in this category. Trade problems are a lamentably normal occurrence in a market such as that of the United States, as is well known by the Canadians, Mexicans, Europeans, and Japanese, who have had to confront greater problems than Chile's. In spite of everything mentioned here, the United States continues to be one of the most open markets for our country, and bilateral relations are much more positive than those observed in many other Latin American countries.

Yet relations with North America are not limited to the United States. During the 1990s, Chile established a truly exemplary relationship with Canada, one of the most developed and powerful economies in the world and the second largest source of foreign investment in Chile. The free trade agreement between Chile and Canada is one of the most innovative instruments ever negotiated in the hemisphere.

This relationship covers both the economic and political spheres. Since 1995, meetings between the two countries' heads of government have become annual in frequency. A notable level of cooperation has been achieved within international organizations, as demonstrated by Chilean support for the Canadian initiative to ban anti-personnel mines. One of the largest communities of Chileans abroad is found in Canada. The true breakthrough represented by this special relationship illustrates the potential of the new era now underway in the hemisphere.

Relations with Mexico have followed a similar path. The obviously strained relations during the military regime were followed by consistent increases in political and economic cooperation. A keystone for the new relationship was the bilateral free trade agreement, which entered into force in 1992 and facilitated a trade increase from 270 million dollars in that year to 1.45 billion dollars in 1997. Mexico is now among the five principal providers of imported products to Chile. The success of this accord led to its extension into new areas such as services. At the same time, Chile and Mexico have acknowledged their agreement on a series of political issues as well as a highly similar vision of Latin American regionalism. This explains Chile's strong interest in avoiding North-South polarization in the Americas, which has sometimes emerged among members of Mercosur and in the United States itself.

VI. Europe: Affinity and Renewal

Particularly rich historical and cultural ties, a strong current of political affinity, and considerable shared economic interests have ensured that Western Europe, and especially the countries comprising the European Union (EU), has been one of the principal focal points of Chile's international relations during the 1990s.

Europe has always exercised a special attraction across diverse Chilean political and intellectual circles. European models and doctrines have served as sources of inspiration for numerous political parties and movements, and institutional developments in the Old World have invariably awakened interest among politicians and academics. The fact that the Chilean political spectrum was traditionally configured quite similarly to that of Europe led to the establishment of close ties between Chilean parties and the leading European political movements.

Chile's foreign policy leaders over the last few decades have emphasized the country's links with Western Europe, although with varying methods and results. This was especially evident in the foreign policy establishment prior to the military regime, which exhibited a moderate and Western orientation. The Popular Unity government's foreign policy also placed a high priority on the strengthening of ties with Western Europe, in spite of its more Third World and revolutionary orientation. And although the most extreme groups of the Chilean right historically shared few interests and values with a democratic, pragmatic, and pluralist Europe, closer links have been forged in recent years between the more moderate factions of the Chilean right and their European counterparts. Military ties between Chile and the EU countries have also retained their traditional importance, in spite of the vicissitudes in political relations.

The dramatic political events in Chile beginning in the 1960s evoked considerable attention from Western European governments, internal political forces, and public opinion, apparently out of proportion to the country's economic, strategic, or demographic importance.

After the country's democratic restoration, the first Concertación coalition government gradually redefined its policies toward Europe. The change in government had removed the principal obstacle to improved political and, to a lesser extent, economic ties, allowing the country to move from a defensive posture to a more active and multidimensional one, integrating both economic and political elements.

Chile's strategy was basically to transform existing affinities, especially in the political sphere, into a both qualitatively and quantitatively improved relationship. In a period when the EU was strengthening its own structure and reexamining its links with nearby countries, the Chilean authorities considered it opportune to raise the question of an association with the EU. Even if this objective did not prove viable, the strategy would help reinforce institutional ties between the EU and Chile.

At the same time, Chile sought to increase its presence in priority EU countries, emphasizing economic aspects without neglecting political ones. Thus efforts were made to establish dynamic relations with Germany, Spain, the United Kingdom, France, Italy, the Netherlands, and the Scandinavian nations. Consultative mechanisms among the respective Foreign Ministries served to further this objective. Relations with these countries were not only restricted to the search for preferential trade treatment, but also aimed at furthering economic ties, cooperative efforts, and political interests.

Some difficulties were encountered in this effort. These included the continued presence in Chile of the veritable concentration camp known as Colonia Dignidad, which for good reason was seen, especially in Germany, as an unacceptable phenomenon within a democratic regime. However, the German authorities placed great confidence in the protracted and still-inconclusive legal battle fought by the Aylwin and Frei administration against the Colony's successor entities, cognizant of the legal system's limitations in confronting a phenomenon which had persisted for such a long time with the complicity of so many people. Another incident affecting Germany was the Chilean government's decision to grant asylum in its Moscow embassy to the former head of the collapsed German Democratic Republic, Erich Honecker. However, the later unfolding of this episode, including Honecker's acquittal by the Bonn government itself, helped to legitimize the Chilean position in the eyes of the German authorities. Meanwhile, relations with France were strained by that country's nuclear tests in the Southeast Pacific, which provoked great alarm in Chile.

Over time, as political normalization occurred and the weight of economic diplomacy increased, the politicized character of relations between Chile and Europe tended to diminish. This did not mean that political factors had become unimportant, but simply that internal Chilean politics no longer represented the main influence upon relations with Europe, nor their principal driving force.

Western Europe remains among the highest-priority areas for Chile's international economic relations. The EU is one of the two principal regional markets for Chilean external trade, absorbing some 22% of total exports in 1997. However, a significant decline has occurred compared to the early 1990s, in contrast with the growth of Chilean exports in other markets.

While Chilean exports to the EU have been characterized by cycles of increase and decline, Chilean imports from Europe have steadily increased, from 1.561 billion dollars in 1991 to 3.161 billion dollars in October 1997. This trade almost exclusively comprises high-added-value products. Trade with the EU may rebound moderately as the European countries continue their recovery from the recession of the early 1990s, which has now spread to Asian markets.

Chilean exports have confronted protectionist threats in Europe, as elsewhere. Among these was the dispute over apple exports during a great part of the Aylwin administration, which was finally resolved in a direct manner, although only after Chile announced its decision to take the conflict to the World Trade Organization (WTO). Temporary problems were observed in the fishmeal market, and the threat was raised that copper would be identified as a harmful substance in drinking water, a classification which could affect pipes made from that metal. However, these difficulties did not justify the perception in some business and political circles that the EU represents a highly protectionist market for Chile. The great majority of Chilean products are subject to very low tariffs, and the country's exports do not face the barriers affecting products such as wheat and meat from Argentina and Uruguay. On the other hand, Chile has been called before an EU panel due to its tax system for alcohol which, in Europe's view, discriminates in favor of domestic pisco.

Close to one-fourth of accumulated foreign investment in Chile has come from Europe. This proportion is significantly higher in such vital industries as services, industry, construction, agriculture, and transportation. Spain, the United Kingdom, Holland, and finland are among Chile's most important sources of foreign investment. Prominent European financial groups, representing both pension funds and banks, have maintained a significant presence in Chile. Meanwhile, strategic alliances are beginning to form among Chilean and European companies, aimed at achieving coverage in both markets as well as joint operations in third countries.

Europe's sympathy for Chile's return to democracy brought forth a generous flow of assistance during the first years of the Concertación coalition government. Although Chile's status as a country of intermediate development restricted its capacity to attract aid, it was assisted by a disposition among donor countries to support the democratic consolidation, as well as the creation of a new and flexible structure to channel the flow of funds, the International Cooperation Agency (AGCI).[11] The EU accounted for half of the international aid received by Chile, mainly consisting of support for social and educational programs, science and technology, the strengthening of civil institutions, and environmental protection. Some European countries joined Chile in triangular cooperative programs with Central America. At the same time, Chile showed interest in the development of new methods of international cooperation, oriented toward the promotion of new businesses, human resources development, the modernization of the State, and innovation in science and technology. However, as had been foreseen, these flows have diminished considerably in recent years, as Chile's rising income ended its eligibility for certain types of funds.

Chile strengthened its ties first with the European Community (EC) and then with the EU. In May 1991, the Aylwin administration signed a Cooperation Framework Agreement with the EC. As the new EU began to develop a new generation of agreements, the Frei government signed a new instrument in 1996, preparing the way for the final objective of a political and economic association with the EU and its member states.[12] This instrument not only provides for high-level political dialogue, but also contains numerous economic, trade, and cooperation provisions which will have important consequences for Chile's development. In the long run, the accord will serve as an indispensable step toward trade liberalization between Chile and the EU, ensuring access for Chilean exports to the vast common market. This is envisioned to be achieved around the year 2000.

It should be noted that, through a declaration attached to the accord, Chile reserves the option of advancing toward the objective of an association with the EU either through bilateral negotiation or jointly with Mercosur. Although some EU Commission representatives and certain member countries do not hide their preference for joint negotiation with Mercosur, Chile's interest in keeping both options open was respected. The concept of "bridges" between EU negotiations with Mercosur and those with Chile was facilitated by Chile's association with that group, signed in the same week as the framework agreement with the EU.

---

11 See the article by the then-Ambassador for International Assistance Coordination and current Foreign Minister, José Miguel Insulza, "Cooperación internacional y política exterior," (Insulza 1992:15-38).

12 For a justification of this interest, see the article by the Under Secretary for Foreign Relations, Mariano Fernández A. (1995).

VII. The Asian-Pacific Region: The New Frontier

Although historical antecedents demonstrate Chile's advanced interest in the Pacific Basin (Orrego Vicuña 1972), the country has generally tended to look more toward the rest of Latin America, along with North America and Europe. Only in the past few decades has a systematic effort been made to achieve closer relations with the Pacific Basin. Initially, this impulse came from the academic sector and the Navy. Yet beginning in the 1970s, this effort became a foreign policy priority, supported by hard geographic facts: Chile's strategic location in the Southeast Pacific, its Polynesian presence represented by Easter Island, and its long-standing trade ties with Japan.

The military regime developed a policy of outreach toward the Pacific Basin. In addition to the obvious trade and strategic considerations, it was believed that significant areas of political agreement might be found between the dictatorship and authoritarian regimes in various Asian countries. This perception was not always correct, as evidenced by the embarrassing cancellation of General Pinochet's visit to the Philippines in 1980, communicated only during the flight to Manila. Yet despite this incident, the policy continued to be maintained, leading to the opening of a series of embassies and consulates in some countries, the establishment of diplomatic relations in others, and numerous high-level missions and meetings to coordinate this opening to the Pacific.

The maintenance of full relations with the People's Republic of China, the strong commercial ties already existing with Japan, and Chile's growing relationship with the Republic of Korea and the members of the Association of Southeast Asian Nations (ASEAN) all contributed to the success of this policy. At the same time, Chile began to participate in the Pacific Basin Economic Council (PBEC), a prominent Southeast Asian business organization. In 1983, PBEC held its annual international assembly in Santiago, supported by the University of Chile's Institute of International Studies, which had organized seminars on the Pacific Basin since 1970 (Armanet, Álamos, and O'Shea 1996:24). Chile's presence in this forum served as a precedent for our participation in the Pacific Economic Cooperation Council (PECC), which was initiated informally in the early 1980s.

The first Concertación government did not squander these efforts. Although its initial priorities were oriented more toward the Americas and Europe, areas more familiar to the new government leaders, a key group of high Foreign Ministry officials, with support from colleagues in other ministries and from academic and business circles, very soon began to strengthen the Pacific policy initiated by the previous regime (Wilhelmy and Lazo 1997:12-17). The economic facts supported this focus. By the early 1990s, Southeast Asia already represented one of the most dynamic areas for Chilean foreign trade (Gutiérrez 1997). In fact, it had displaced Europe as the leading regional market for Chilean exports. Japan alternated with the United States as the top individual market for Chilean goods; Taiwan and Korea were among the world's principal buyers of our products; trade with the People's Republic of China reached record levels; and commerce with the ASEAN countries increased strikingly.

Diplomatic representation in the area was also reinforced. In 1992, President Aylwin became the first Chilean president to undertake an official tour of Southeast Asian countries. This effort was followed by additional visits, and since then no year has passed without a presidential trip to the area. In a region where economics is closely tied to politics, these contacts at the highest level not only served to narrow the political and cultural gap between Chile and Asia, but also provided a new impulse to commercial, financial, and investment links with the opposite shore of the Pacific.

In May 1991, Chile became a full member of the PECC, a tripartite, unofficial organization including representatives from the public sector and the business and academic communities. In 1992, the government promoted the restructuring of the Chilean National Committee for Pacific Cooperation (Chilpec), an advisory body covering all aspects of Chile's participation in Pacific cooperative frameworks. At the beginning of the Frei administration, the Foreign Ministry proposed the establishment of the Chilean Pacific Foundation. The Foundation's mandate includes supporting Chile's participation in the PECC, creating a Center for APEC Studies, and developing other initiatives to strengthen Chile's presence in the Asian-Pacific region. In 1997, the Foundation was chosen to organize the Twelfth General Meeting of the PECC, which became the first prominent Asian-Pacific event ever held in a Latin American country.

The Concertación government's next objective was to obtain membership in the prestigious forum of APEC, a high-level governmental entity considered the nucleus of regional organization efforts. Chile already participated in the PECC and met the prerequisites established by the organization: maintaining strong economic ties to the Asian-Pacific region; sharing the objectives and principles of APEC, which included a deep commitment to open economies and trade liberalization; and possessing a healthy economy. However, Chile confronted resistance from many members against opening the incipient organization to Latin American nations, which were considered unstable and far removed from the Asian-Pacific region.

The Chilean government undertook an active campaign to overcome this initial hesitation. The skeptics were led by Prime Minister Keating of Australia, one of the forum's founding countries, who supported consolidating the organization's framework before inviting new members to join. This reticence was shared, to varying degrees, by other prominent Asian countries as well as in circles close to Chile, such as the United States and Canada. In contrast, the Chilean initiative met with enthusiastic responses from Malaysia and other ASEAN countries, followed by China and New Zealand. Mexico had also presented its candidacy, with the distinction that it enjoyed the strong backing of the United States in the atmosphere of initial enthusiasm surrounding NAFTA, which had also led Mexico to join the Organization for Economic Cooperation and Development (OECD). United States interest in the Mexican case finally led to a formula satisfying the United States, Canada, and others with the entry of Mexico, Australia with the admittance of the weak but nearby economy of Papua New Guinea, and Malaysia and ASEAN with the incorporation of Chile, which, significantly, was postponed until 1994 (Wilhelmy and Lazo 1997:30-31). This result, largely attributable to the Foreign Ministry, has been one of the Concertación's most spectacular foreign policy achievements.

Chile's Asian policy was not limited to the multilateral and economic spheres. Significant efforts were also undertaken to consolidate bilateral ties. The Foreign Ministry recognized that the Asian-Pacific region presented great economic, political, and cultural diversity, including highly developed countries and developing countries; advanced democracies, authoritarian regimes, and one-party systems; and ancient civilizations as well as cultures with clearly Western roots. Thus a differentiated focus was maintained toward the area. The long-standing relationship with Japan, a country which had always placed extraordinary value on the stability of bilateral ties, was further consolidated.

Relations with the People's Republic of China required special attention due to Beijing's enormous sensitivity toward any implied sign of recognition for the Taipei regime. The need to develop strong relations with Korea became evident, as that country transformed itself within only a few years into Chile's second leading Asian partner.

The progress of the ASEAN economies, along with the advance of that regional entity, drew Chile's attention to relations with its members, in particular with Malaysia. Prime Minister Malathir's strong international leadership and his view of Chile as a special partner within Latin America evoked reciprocal interest from our country. Revitalization of our relations with Australia and New Zealand was also necessary. Ties with Australia had suffered a serious setback during the authoritarian regime, and a large Chilean community, mostly composed of political exiles, had become established in that country. Chile's goal with New Zealand was to cultivate a set of affinities in the commercial area — New Zealand also pursued an active and innovative trade policy — and on the multilateral level, where the two countries shared similar Antarctic, maritime, and environmental interests. finally, Chile's South Pacific presence and the location of Easter Island also required attention to that region (Cousiño 1997).

VIII. Multilateralism: Chile's Global Responsibilities

Participation in the multilateral system has always been a fundamental aspect of Chile's foreign policy and its integration into the world. Conscious that a country such as ours cannot hope to change unfavorable regional or global circumstances by itself, Chile's foreign policy leaders have emphasized joint action through international organizations and other collective mechanisms. As a small and developing nation, Chile had placed great expectations in multilateral politics, becoming a particularly active member of a number of regional and global organizations, contributing its own vision and creative ideas. The fact that this tradition had sheltered rather utopian visions did not preclude the achievement of highly practical objectives, including the extension of Chile's maritime borders, the protection of its Antarctic interests, and a flow of technical assistance of great importance to the country at the time. This historical tradition was restricted during the military regime, especially with respect to the international political assemblies. Chile continued to participate in technical bodies highly relevant to our national interests, such as the United Nations Conference on the Law of the Sea, in which the country continues to play an active role. However, in general terms, the country's multilateral politics were weakened by the military regime, as its authorities reacted negatively toward the international bodies that criticized them.

The new democratic government reestablished Chile's presence in multilateral forums and institutions, placing great emphasis on the country's new global responsibilities. This change of direction cannot be explained simply by the precedent of the earlier democratic period. It was also obvious that a new role for the international organizations was emerging from the profound transformations in the international system. A series of problematic events in our country called for multilateral treatment, as international agreements were being modified in such crucial areas as peace and security, the defense of democracy and human rights, trade, environmental protection, the fight against drug trafficking and terrorism, and cooperation for economic and social development. In several cases, multilateralism was reinforced by the direct participation of civil society in international forums. This represents a little-recognized expression of globalization itself, which is far from a merely economic phenomenon.

It is clear that the high initial expectations for the emergence of a new multilateralism were not fully satisfied. Yet it is equally clear that significant reforms and renewal occurred, in which Chile began to participate. Chile supported the United Nations' new post-Cold War role in the prevention and resolution of international conflicts. As in earlier periods, Chile looked naturally to the United Nations in response to international crises of the 1990s. Thus, instead of seeking an individual role in crises such as the Gulf War, the North Korean nuclear threat, the conflicts in Africa's great lake region, or the recent situation in Iraq, Chile has defined its positions with attention to the U.N. consensus.

After several decades of absence, Chile was elected by an overwhelming majority as a non-permanent member of the U.N. Security Council for the 1996-97 period. Interestingly, this candidacy was the object of considerable domestic discussion, due to worries that it would entail a political cost and expose us to highly complex pressures. Yet these fears were unfounded; Chile carried out its function admirably and without incident, fulfilling a principle of international responsibility expressly designated in its Program of Government.

Other sectors associated with foreign policy have also pledged themselves to this principle. Thus, during the 1990s, the Chilean Armed Forces participated in U.N. peacekeeping operations in Kuwait (Air Force), El Salvador (Carabineros), and Cambodia (Navy). The results of these experiences were generally satisfactory, signaling a new dimension of international action for a country which had held itself aloof from such initiatives for many years. During the Frei administration, the Carabineros participated in U.N. forces serving in Bosnia, and an Air Force detachment was assigned to the Iraq crisis, acting as relief forces for a German contingent. This rising level of activity, to which the Army will soon be added, has led to the elaboration of a Presidential Directive outlining the conditions for Chile's participation in peacekeeping forces. The ministers of Foreign Affairs and Defense have also developed a relationship of close cooperation for this purpose.

Chile's foreign policy in the 1990s has strongly emphasized support for current or prospective treaties dealing with disarmament and the prohibition of weapons of mass destruction. Chile participated actively in the establishment of the International Organization for the Prohibition of Chemical Weapons and has taken the necessary steps to comply with the stringent provisions of its underlying treaty. In 1995, the country finally signed the Nuclear Non-Proliferation Treaty, abandoning its previous doctrinaire stance which had rejected the agreement because its tenets did not apply to pre-existing nuclear powers. This position had initially been supported by other nations around the world, but it gradually became more isolated and even contradictory, since Chile strongly shared the general interest in avoiding the emergence of new nuclear powers.

Similarly, Chile became one of the first signatories of the Total Nuclear Test Ban Treaty in 1996. The country had a very special interest in this instrument, due to the large public protests and other expressions of concern throughout Chilean society after France's nuclear explosions in the South Pacific. In the same year, Chile joined the Disarmament Conference. In 1997, the country was one of the original signatories of the Convention for the Proscription of Anti-Personnel Mines, one of the most innovative and widely-publicized disarmament instruments of recent years. This commitment, adopted after consultation with all of the officials involved, called for the removal of these weapons from our own borders, with all of the associated costs. In short, within a few years Chile not only ceased being an outsider to global disarmament and denuclearization efforts, but came to join the vanguard in this area.

Chile's multilateral policies continued to address its Antarctic territory, as well as the maritime and air spaces in which it exercises sovereignty or whose adequate protection affects the country directly, issues which have always been fundamental for our country (Wilhelmy and Infante 1993:111-112). During the past decade, the Antarctic Treaty system has dealt intensively with the question of environmental protection, giving rise to new agreements and forums on the issue. Special mention should be made of the Madrid Protocol, signed in October 1991, which Chile views as the most valuable source of commitments achieved in this area. It stipulates that any activity on the Antarctic continent must undergo an environmental impact study, thus imposing additional costs. It should be noted that through the Antarctic System, Chile fully accedes to the international order. In no other forum does our country exercise prerogatives equal to those of the great powers, such as veto rights and full participation in the administration of such an extensive area. Chile is now seeking to make further progress through the strengthening of relevant domestic institutions and the implementation of a true national Antarctic program.

In the area of maritime rights, Chile finally ratified the United Nations Convention on the Law of the Sea, thus culminating a diplomatic effort initiated in 1947, in which each successive administration had participated. This instrument represents one of the clearest examples of the emergence of a new international legal regime, in which Chile and other small- and medium-sized countries have been able to make a decisive contribution. Yet the instrument also has its limitations, such as the treatment of transzonal and highly migratory fish species found outside the 200 nautical mile limit, which are not sufficiently protected under international rules. This problem will require special attention in coming years, in consideration of the vital economic role played by Chile's fisheries. Recently, Chile has been seeking areas of concrete agreement with other countries on this subject, principally within the framework of the Permanent Commission of the South Pacific.

Multilateral policy faced a new challenge as the issue of environmental protection emerged onto the international stage. Environmental questions affect a very broad spectrum of our international relations, including maritime and Antarctic policies; economic negotiations; commodities exports; the transport of toxic substances, potentially dangerous cargo, and nuclear materials; waste disposal; foreign investment; public works; and forestry policy. Multilateral policy is also closely linked to the welfare of indigenous peoples, an extraordinarily complex subject which has only begun to arise in our foreign relations. Not surprisingly, an array of global non-governmental organizations — Greenpeace is an eloquent example — have begun to have a significant impact on foreign policy in many countries, as well as on domestic affairs.

Chile has enthusiastically participated in the leading environmental forums, such as the historic Summit Conference on the Environment and Development, held in Rio de Janeiro in 1992, and the Summit on Climate Change in Kyoto in early 1998. Due attention has also been paid to more technical gatherings focused on forest conservation, desertification, hazardous waste, the transport of nuclear materials, and other issues. The growing importance of these topics recently led the Foreign Ministry to express the goal of defining an environmental foreign policy. The projection of a national position on the subject has been hampered in the past by an internal lack of definition and confusion of authority. These problems are being resolved; however, the principal participants in this debate will inevitably continue to raise the level of their demands. The fact that protectionist subterfuges, little-informed activists, or sponsors with less-than-altruistic interests are sometimes found behind these demands does not diminish the seriousness of the problem.

Multilateralism has not only been a question for the state. It has also permitted highly diverse elements of civil society to express their demands and aspirations on a global stage, leading to the adoption of international regulations which are later enacted on the domestic level. This dimension of globalization tends to be passed over by analysis focusing more on economics. A good example of this civil multilateralism is found in the treatment of gender issues, or if one prefers, women's issues. Chile became fully engaged in the international debate on this subject during the 1990s, participating actively in conferences such as the Fourth World Conference on Women, held in Beijing in 1995. At the same time, the new international norms arising in this area had a decisive influence on our own country, reinforcing long-standing demands and providing a new impulse to the activity of the National Women's Service and many other organizations.

Similarly, multilateral foreign policy reflected a strong interest in social development. This led to the World Summit on Social Development, organized through an initiative of the Aylwin government and held in Copenhagen in March 1995. From Chile's point of view, the cruel imbalance persisting within and among the various nations of the world represents a source of insecurity which cannot be ignored. The Summit was the first conference within the United Nations system to treat social issues within an integrated perspective. The close association between democracy, human rights, the environment, and equitable economic development was examined in detail, and a program of action was adopted which received significant support from the international community.

Conclusions

The priorities described here do not by any means exhaust the foreign policy undertakings of the Concertación governments. Chile also maintained a presence in other areas of the world, including the Middle East, North Africa, Central Europe, and Russia. Chile developed a new relationship with South Africa, after the fall of the apartheid system and the initiation of that country's transition to democracy, which showed some similarities to Chile's own situation. The country occupied itself with numerous issues in a wide range of forums and institutions. However, it was also increasingly capable of ordering its foreign policy priorities, never an easy task for a relatively small country, constantly subject to the interplay of internal and external forces, as well as lobbies which mobilize in support of extraordinarily diverse interests.

Chile's intense international activity required the adaptation of its foreign policy instruments. This necessity was obvious within the Foreign Ministry, but it also extended to other areas of the government and even the private sector. The Concertación governments faced the challenge of making the foreign policy apparatus more effective, modern, and integrated. Concretely, this required the reorganization of the Foreign Ministry in accordance with geographic areas and broad functional topics, transcending the traditional division between political and economic affairs. The search for highly qualified diplomatic and professional personnel, as well as innovative management techniques, was also intensified.

In a highly legalistic country such as ours, the quest to improve the foreign policy structure was rapidly mistaken for a proposal to create a new Organic Law and statutory framework for the Foreign Ministry, a subject which had been brought up several times during the 1990s. In practice, however, significant organizational and management changes were possible without the need for new laws. A gradual restructuring has taken place within the existing framework, leading to better integration between the political and economic areas; the creation of new units and the dissolution of others; a significant and little-recognized rationalization in budgetary management; the establishment of an information network; the development of new training programs; the creation of highly professionalized economic negotiation teams; the renewal of ProChile; and the establishment of the International Cooperation Agency (AGCI), which was later directly linked to the Foreign Ministry.

Much remains to be done, and profound changes are needed. Yet it is also important to evaluate what has been accomplished to date. Today, the country's involvement in an ongoing process of international economic negotiations seems quite natural, but it is important to remember that the teams leading this effort hardly existed at the beginning of the decade. Foreign affairs management has been professionalized to an extent that usually goes without recognition. The level of professionalism in our foreign service is fully comparable to that of more established diplomatic services in the region, and it has been complemented by the contributions of highly knowledgeable specialists.

Certainly, much more innovation is still possible. Yet it is important to keep in mind that legal reform of the Foreign Ministry will require a forceful political commitment, so that it does not simply become part of a factional struggle. This is not an easy condition to fulfill. In addition, reform is necessary throughout the public sector, of which the Foreign Ministry is an integral part, and due to the complexity of the task, the thoroughgoing reform of the Chilean state is not a current priority. finally, experiences in other countries and partial reforms to other Chilean ministries reveal that institutional change processes are highly complex and often lead to conflict with unions and other groups. All this underlines the necessity for a very solid internal consensus, in order to avoid high costs for an agency which is busy confronting urgent external challenges.

In today's world, many policies which do not fall under the exclusive, or even the principal, jurisdiction of the Foreign Ministry require an integrated vision which can only be provided by the nation's foreign affairs agency as it seeks to maintain the coherence of external actions. Thus, various coordination mechanisms must be established in the foreign policy area. The International Economic Negotiations Committee, established during the Aylwin administration, has played a highly valuable technical role. Under President Frei, the Foreign Policy Ministers' Committee was created to fulfill a more political function. The private sector's inevitable role in foreign policy considerations also requires new mechanisms, such as the Private Sector Participation Committee, which has complemented the highly efficient informal channels accompanying every economic negotiation process. Through the Foreign Affairs Council, an advisory body created in its Organic Law, the Foreign Ministry has maintained an ongoing liaison with the country's ex-foreign ministers, various political factions of the government and opposition, and specialists in international topics.

Unquestionably, the foreign policy of the two Concertación governments presents a favorable balance. Nearly all public opinion polls reveal especially positive impressions of the Concertación governments' foreign relations, making this one of the areas meeting with the highest public approval. This approval does not derive from one or two specific issues, but from the country's overall achievements. The result may be surprising, considering that the first Concertación administration opted for a low-profile international policy, pursued, as President Aylwin has recalled, "in a minor key," (Bengoa and Tironi 1994:19). Similarly, the second government placed its emphasis on pragmatic diplomacy, eschewing the pursuit of international leadership or prestige.

Certainly, the balance is not equally favorable in all areas. Policies toward Chile's neighbors have confronted objective limitations. In contrast to optimistic expectations, some historical disputes remain unresolved, especially border questions, although mainly because Chile's three neighbors have preferred to keep them open. Our relationship with Mercosur includes some uncertainties, stemming from our own decision to continue defining Chilean economic integration and other policies in an individual manner, as well as our divergent positions on hemispheric trade liberalization and the opening of our own markets. At times, we have harbored excessive expectations in our relations with the United States, as demonstrated by the long and frustrating experience of the fast-track negotiation issue, which was overemphasized within Chile itself. Our relations with Europe have also sometimes been affected by an excess of optimism. Our growing economic ties with Asia have not been accompanied by comparable efforts in the political and social spheres, so that the region remains relatively remote from Chilean society.

However, the general balance is broadly positive. Our foreign relations have undergone a qualitative change, transcending both the reintegration envisioned in the early 1990s and the return to venerable historical traditions somewhat nostalgically foreseen during the years of opposition to the military regime. We have not simply recovered a tradition; we are integrating ourselves in a new and unique manner into the world.

Foreign policy projects values and is, to a great extent, a reflection of domestic policy. Yet it also fulfills the essential function of adaptation to changing conditions within the international system, as we are reminded by one of the few Chilean theoreticians in the field of international relations (Tomassini 1989:155). The experience of these eight years confirms that our country is adapting itself to its new external context, and that precisely this necessity constitutes the principal source of changes in policy. Foreign policy responds more to external stimuli than to the demands of domestic policy or the characteristics of a particular government.

Nevertheless, a series of initiatives is planned for foreign policy in the coming years, including the modernization of the State; improvement of an infrastructure which has become inadequate for the country's new international integration; greater regional participation in foreign policy; and above all, the realization of necessary cultural changes in a nation which until recently was highly insular and inward-looking. Chile's success in confronting these challenges will determine its ability to build upon the achievements of this very productive decade.

Appendix: Tables and Charts

TABLE 1

EVOLUTION OF FOREIGN TRADE
(Figures in millions of dollars)

Items	1985	1990	1991	1992	1993	1994	1995	1996	1997
Exports (FOB)	3,804.1	8,309.9	8,929.4	10,123.6	9,415.0	11,643.4	16,444.7	15,396.2	16,875.4
Imports (CIF)	3,268.3	7,677.6	8,093.7	10,128.7	11,125.4	11,824.6	15,914.1	17,827.5	19,659.8
Global Exchange	7,072.4	15,987.5	17,023.1	20,252.3	20,540.4	23,468.0	32,358.8	33,223.7	36,535.2
Gross Domestic Product (1)	28,104	30,183	42,253	43,703	52,163	67,300	71,905	75,000	
Global Exchange Relative to GDP (%)		56.89	56.40	47.93	47.00	45.00	48.10	46.20	48.71

(1) Estimated information, not official

SOURCE: Banco Central de Chile.

TABLE 2

PRINCIPAL DESTINATION COUNTRIES OF EXPORT SHIPMENTS FROM CHILE
(Figures in millions of dollars)

Countries	1985	1990	1991	1992	1993	1994	1995	1996	1997
USA	870.7	1,469.2	1,596.3	1,649.4	1,655.2	2,012.1	2,375.0	2,559.1	2,504.7
Japan	392.5	1,388.2	1,644.0	1,707.3	1,502.3	1,976.2	2,906.4	2,495.7	2,467.4
United King.	256.2	558.7	408.4	571.5	554.4	523.0	1,076.0	886.5	1,022.0
Korea	64.9	259.3	263.2	242.8	413.4	583.7	896.5	864.1	953.9
Brazil	209.7	487.4	447.6	450.9	407.1	604.7	1,056.8	934.5	880.9
Taiwan	38.5	279.8	395.3	490.9	407.7	538.5	703.2	629.1	747.8
Argentina	84.5	113.5	257.4	461.6	588.9	637.1	585.6	700.9	715.1
Germany	370.6	941.3	709.4	603.7	486.5	582.4	837.4	742.3	665.0
Italy	197.2	406.2	344.8	388.2	330.3	359.3	608.8	475.3	463.0
France	144.6	402.3	389.9	395.6	373.7	404.0	508.2	392.8	440.7
Holland	142.4	314.8	362.9	333.7	260.3	345.5	437.6	393.6	398.3
Spain	74.4	268.3	345.5	366.5	240.7	219.1	319.5	281.8	324.2

1997 figures correspond to the period between January & November

SOURCE: Banco Central de Chile.

TABLE 3

PRINCIPAL DESTINATION MARKETS FOR CHILEAN EXPORTS
AND PERCENTAGE OF TOTAL PARTICIPATION
(Figures in millions of dollars)

Trade Block	1985		1990		1991		1992		1993	
	Amount	%	Amount	%	Amount	%	Amount	%	Amount	%
Aladi (1)	536.1	14.10	1,014.3	12.20	1,238.6	13.87	1,620.3	16.00	1,786.8	18.98
Mercosur	312.1	8.20	652.0	7.85	770.0	8.62	990.5	9.78	1,089.2	11.57
North America (2)	946.5	24.88	1,525.4	18.36	1,649.4	18.47	1,713.1	16.92	1,716.3	18.22
European Union	1,226.0	32.22	3,203.1	38.54	2,881.3	32.26	2,931.7	28.96	2,443.9	25.96
Asia-Pacific (3) (4)	706.4	17.20	2,245.9	26.42	2,639.6	29.35	3,147.1	30.90	2,901.1	30.45

	1994		1995		1996		1997 (5)	
	Amount	%	Amount	%	Amount	%	Amount	%
Aladi (1)	2,338.2	20.08	2,990.5	18.18	2,915.8	18.94	2,782.7	17.55
Mercosur	1,352.3	11.61	1,774.7	10.80	1,759.8	11.43	1,551.1	9.78
North America (2)	2,082.5	17.88	2,471.0	15.03	2,698.7	17.52	2,431.4	15.33
European Union	2,830.0	24.30	4,448.3	27.05	3,680.2	23.90	3,548.2	22.37
Asia-Pacific (3) (4)	3,799.1	31.96	5,587.9	33.33	5,153.0	32.81	5,045.1	33.61

(1) Includes Mercosur
(2) Canada and the U.S.
(3) Countries include: Australia, Korea, China, Philippines, Hong Kong, Indonesia, Japan, Malaysia, Singapore, Thailand,
    and Taiwan.
(4) For the year 1985, figures are only available for China, Korea, Hong Kong, Japan, and Taiwan.
(5) Figures from 1997 correspond to the period between January & November

SOURCE: Banco Central de Chile.

TABLE 4

PRINCIPAL TRADE BLOCK DESTINATIONS FOR CHILEAN EXPORTS

1990

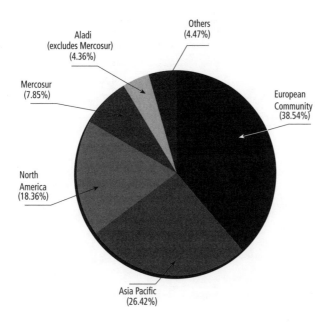

Others (4.47%)
Aladi (excludes Mercosur) (4.36%)
Mercosur (7.85%)
European Community (38.54%)
North America (18.36%)
Asia Pacific (26.42%)

1996

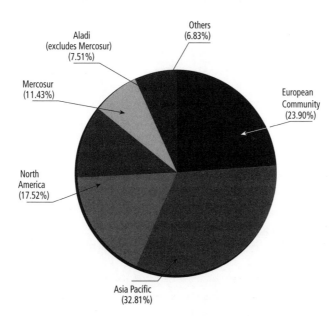

Others (6.83%)
Aladi (excludes Mercosur) (7.51%)
Mercosur (11.43%)
European Community (23.90%)
North America (17.52%)
Asia Pacific (32.81%)

TABLE 5

MATERIALIZED FOREIGN INVESTMENT
(Figures in millions of dollars)

Year	Capital Contributions (A)	DL 600 Associated Credits (B)	Total DL 600 (A+B)	Cap. 14 (1) Capital Contributions (C)	Total Contributions (A+C)	ADRs (1) (D)	Total Capital Investments (A+C+D)	Total Investment (Capital + Credit
1990	510.7	809.6	1,320.30	35.7	546.4	104.6	651	1,460.60
1991	572.5	409.4	981.9	93.4	665.9	8.5	674.4	1,083.80
1992	691.8	307.1	998.9	149.8	841.6	292	1,133.60	1,440.70
1993	890	839.8	1,729.80	204.2	1,094.20	818.1	1,912.30	2,752.10
1994	1,554.40	976.7	2,531.10	410.2	1,964.60	1,647.90	3,612.50	4,589.20
1995	1,789.50	1,238.50	3,028.00	409.6	2,199.10	884.4	3,083.50	4,322.00
1996	3,929.20	871.3	4,800.50	445	4,374.20	1,148.10	5,522.30	6,393.60
Jan-Dec 1996	3,929.20	871.3	4,800.50	445	4,374.20	1,148.10	5,522.30	6,393.60
Jan-Dec 1997	3,730.00	1,311.20	5,041.20	920.8	4,650.80	2,130.40	6,781.20	8,092.40
Increment	-5.10%	50.50%	5.00%	106.90%	6.30%	85.60%	22.80%	26.60%

(1) Information supplied by the Banco Central de Chile. Provisional Figures.

TABLE 6

MATERIALIZED FOREIGN INVESTMENT VIA D.L.600 BY COUNTRY OF ORIGIN
(Figures in millions of dollars)

Countries	1974-1989	1990	1991	1992	1993	1994	1995	1996	1997	TOTAL
USA	2,248,157	270,945	350,524	300,066	623,701	996,343	1,549,255	2,263,788	913,377	9,516,156
Canada	494,085	252,913	91,916	222,107	480,503	755,501	530,794	359,828	678,821	3,866,468
Spain	527,298	32,152	46,820	7,136	103,404	17,627	55,091	489,695	1,497,786	2,777,009
UK	384,254	240,984	105,724	16,975	17,846	36,045	90,347	231,716	185,034	1,308,925
South Africa	41,601	1,950	0	100,373	13,242	84,376	219,264	74,318	448,188	983,312
Australia	241,002	219,338	32,851	23,880	23,724	16,204	27,417	108,633	181,056	874,105
Japan	144,298	56,681	78,407	78,231	78,401	66,048	15,862	147,531	154,403	819,862
Holland	177,324	10,965	42,421	9,142	13,160	10,667	39,671	121,198	362,173	786,721
Cayman Islands	5,414	90,563	11,378	5,785	4,252	15,564	48,478	215,036	215,975	612,445
Finland	133	436	10,588	6,912	20,851	198,262	120,933	59,390	12,964	430,469
Italy	20,728	1,373	12,559	3,292	2,490	7,857	5,173	324,897	18,547	396,916
Argentina	32,766	2,675	9,230	12,384	48,744	63,435	41,484	96,856	59,546	367,120
France	95,080	20,883	7,911	40,228	12,277	27,115	26,272	65,771	56,015	351,552
Switzerland	56,402	6,230	30,802	30,678	75,366	48,197	4,999	28,800	45,228	326,702

(*) Provisional figures; 1997 corresponds to the period between January and December.

Note: These figures include transfers between countries during the year in which they were produced.

TABLE 7

WORLD WIDE INVESTMENT OF CHILEAN CAPITAL
(1990 - July 1997)

Country	Materialized Chilean Investment	% Participation	Total Project Sum in Millions of US$	% Participation
Argentina	5,939.80	43.6	10,985.20	42.2
Peru	1,814.80	13.3	3,861.90	14.8
Brazil	1,471.00	10.8	4,813.20	18.5
Colombia	981.5	7.2	1,482.70	5.7
Mexico	499.8	3.7	647.7	2.5
Panama	387.5	2.8	390.4	1.5
Guernsey (Channel Island)	298.1	2.2	298.1	1.1
Bolivia	246.7	1.8	301.5	1.2
Grand Cayman Island	241.4	1.8	241.4	0.9
Venezuela	185.9	1.4	534.8	2.1
Russia	153.2	1.1	303.2	1.2
British Virgin Islands	138.9	1	138.9	0.5
Aruba	96	0.7	213.7	0.8
Paraguay	78.2	0.6	93	0.4
England	76.2	0.6	76.2	0.3
United States	48.2	0.4	88.2	0.3
China	46.1	0.3	76.2	0.3
Cuba	37.8	0.3	46.3	0.2
Thailand	30	0.2	30	0.1
Uruguay	28.7	0.2	35.9	0.1
Ecuador	27.5	0.2	54.5	0.2
Liberia	24.7	0.2	24.7	0.1
Curazao	23	0.2	23	0.1
Latvia	15	0.1	50	0.2
Switzerland	10	0.1	10	0
Costa Rica	6.2	0	6.2	0
Sweden	5.5	0	5.5	0
France	5.4	0	5.4	0
Malaysia	5	0	5	0
Turkey	4	0	4	0
Liechtenstein	3.6	0	3.6	0
Belgium	2	0	2	0
Denmark	0.8	0	0.8	0
Canada	0.5	0	0.5	0
Poland	0.3	0	0.3	0
Germany	0	0	0	0
Dutch Antilles	0	0	0	0
Bermuda Islands	0	0	0	0
Bosnia	0	0	0	0
Croatia	0	0	0	0
United Arab Emirate	0	0	0	0
Philippines	0	0	0	0
Guinea Bissau	0	0	0	0
Japan	0	0	0	0
Others w/o investment	702.7	5.2	1,173.40	4.5
Total	13,635.90	100	26,027.30	100

Source: Foreign Investment Committee, Executive Vice President; prepared by same using press materials.

TABLE 8

OFFICIAL STATISTICS CONCERNING COOPERATION GRANTED TO CHILE
FIGURES FROM FINANCING SOURCES
1990-1996

Financing Sources	Donation in US$	# of Projects	Credit in US$	# of Projects	Total in US$	# of Projects
1. BILATERAL						
Germany	101,316,338	97	728,55,739	6	174,172,077	103
Belgium	5,129,213	46			5,129,213	46
Canada	20,114,559	28			20,114,559	28
Korea	140,726	2	39,500,000	5	140,726	2
Denmark	15,000,734	14	18,757,505	3	15,000,734	14
Spain	28,348,755	70			67,848,755	75
Finland	1,291,440	12	40,000,000	2	1,291,440	12
France	37,700,997	50	190,800,000	3	56,458,502	53
Holland	46,104,039	29	7,486,039	1	46,104,039	29
England	8,882,961	27	10,000,000	3	8,882,961	27
Israel	1,331,500	15	46,000,000	1	1,331,500	15
Italy	29,481,515	24	48,000,000	3	69,481,515	26
Japan	144,475,395	59			335,275,395	62
Luxembourg	7,461,344	8			7,461,344	8
Norway	16,179,757	31			23,665,796	32
Sweden	41,804,527	73			51,804,527	76
Switzerland	8,592,773	31			54,592,773	32
United States	92,888,220	91			140,888,220	94
Total Bilateral	606,244,793	707	473,399,283	27	1,079,644,076	734
2. MULTILATERAL						
EC	164,986,716	112			164,986,716	112
OAS	647,000	13			647	13
UN	194,703,213	185			29,069,497	185
Total Multilateral	29,069,497	310	0	0	194,703,213	310
Total	800,948,006	1,017	473,399,283	27	1,274,347,289	1,044

TABLE 9A

OFFICIAL STATISTICS CONCERNING COOPERATION GRANTED TO CHILE
FIGURES FROM FINANCING SOURCES
1990-1993

Financing Sources	Donation in US$	# of Projects	Credit in US$	# of Projects	Amount in US$	# of Projects
1. BILATERAL						
Germany	72,779,445	57	72,855,739	6	145,635,184	63
Belgium	3,500,000	1			3,500,000	1
Canada	15,912,167	18			15,912,167	18
Korea	40,726	1	28,500,000	4	40,726	1
Denmark	14,387,109	10	18,757,505	3	14,387,109	10
Spain	17,499,317	34			45,999,317	38
Finland	1,049,074	3	20,000,000	1	1,049,074	3
France	21,434,555	28	190,800,000	3	40,192,060	31
Holland	44,605,514	24			44,605,514	24
England	4,412,570	14	10,000,000	1	4,412,570	14
Israel	813,500	7	38,000,000	2	813,500	7
Italy	22,780,504	7	41,000,000	2	42,780,504	8
Japan	89,605,395	29			280,405,395	32
Luxembourg	773,603	2			2,773,603	2
Norway	15,941,828	28			15,941,828	28
Sweden	34,522,283	42			44,522,283	43
Switzerland	2,099,596	2			40,099,596	4
United States	85,293,114	52			126,293,114	54
Total Bilateral	449,450,300	359	419,913,244	22	869,363,544	381
2. MULTILATERAL						
EC	99,003,458	62			99,003,458	62
OAS	647,000	13			647	13
UN	24,986,578	104			24,986,578	104
Total Multilateral	124,637,036	179	0	0	124,637,036	179
Total	**574,087,336**	**538**	**419,913,244**	**22**	**994,000,580**	**560**

TABLE 9B

OFFICIAL STATISTICS CONCERNING COOPERATION GRANTED TO CHILE
FIGURES FROM FINANCING SOURCES
1994-1996

Financing Sources	Donation in US $	# of Projects	Credit in US $	# of Projects	Amount in US $	# of Projects	Amount in US $	# of Projects
1. BILATERAL								
Germany	28,536,893	40			28,536,893	40	174,172,077	103
Belgium	1,629,213	45			1,629,213	45	5,129,213	46
Canada	4,202,392	10	11,000,000	1	4,202,392	10	20,114,559	28
Korea	100,000	1			100,000	1	140,726	2
Denmark	613,625	4			614,000	4	15,000,734	14
Spain	10,849,438	36	20,000,000	1	21,849,438	37	67,848,755	75
Finland	242,366	9			242,366	9	1,291,440	12
France	16,266,442	22	7,486,039	1	16,266,442	22	56,458,502	53
Holland	1,498,525	5	10,000,000	1	1,498,525	5	46,104,039	29
England	4,470,391	13	5,000,000	1	4,470,391	13	8,882,961	27
Israel	518,000	8			518,000	8	1,331,500	15
Italy	6,701,011	17			26,701,011	18	69,481,515	26
Japan	54,870,000	30			54,870,000	30	335,275,395	62
Luxemburg	4,687,741	6			4,687,741	6	7,461,344	8
Norway	237,929	3			7,723,968	4	23,665,796	32
Sweden	7,282,244	33			7,282,244	33	51,804,527	76
Switzerland	4,493,177	27			14,493,177	28	54,592,773	32
United States	9,595,106	39			14,595,106	40	140,888,220	94
Total Bilateral	156,794,493	348	53,486,039	5	210,280,532	353	1,079,644,076	734
2. MULTILATERAL								
EC	65,983,258	50			65,983,258	50	164,986,716	112
OAS	4,082,919	81			4,082,919	81	647,000	13
UN							29,069,497	185
Total Multilateral	70,066,177	131	0	0	70,066,177	131	194,703,213	310
Total	226,860,670	479	53,486,039	5	280,346,709	484	1,274,347,289	1044

TABLE 10

SUMMARY OF NATIONAL RESOURCES MOBILIZED
FOR THE CHILEAN HORIZONTAL COOPERATION PROGRAM
YEARS 1992-1998 (*)
Value in dollars

CTPD Resources Mobilized by AGCI	1992	1993	1994	1995	1996	1997 (*)	1998 (*)	Accumulated Total
Annual Total	660,990	2,966,370	1,869,491	1,863,475	2,563,710	2,681,126	2,772,956	15,378,117

SOURCE: Memoria Institucional, 1992, 1993, 1994, 1995, 1996. An exchange rate of 1 US$ to 430 pesos was applied to the budgetary assignments from 1997 and 1998.

BIBLIOGRAPHICAL REFERENCES

Armanet, P., P. Álamos, and L. O'Shea. 1996. Las relaciones de Chile con los organismos multilaterales de la Cuenca del Pacífico. Santiago: Institute of International Studies, University of Chile and Chilean Pacific Foundation.

Bengoa, J. and E. Tironi. 1994. "Una mirada retrospectiva: entrevista a don Patricio Aylwin Azócar." Proposiciones 25 (October). Santiago: Ediciones SUR.

Bergsten, C. F. 1997. "Open Regionalism." The World Economy, Vol. 20 (August 5), pp. 545-564.

Burr, R. N. 1965. By Reason or Force: Chile and the Balancing of Power in South America, 1830-1905. Berkeley: University of California Press.

Butelmann, A. and P. Meller, eds. 1992. Estrategia comercial chilena para la década del 90. Santiago: Cieplan.

Cousiño, J. A. 1997. Política y estrategia en el Pacífico Insular. Santiago: Institute for International Studies, University of Chile.

De la Balze, F. and E. A. Roca. 1997. Argentina y EE.UU.: Fundamentos de una nueva alianza. Buenos Aires: Banking Association of the Republic of Argentina and Argentine Council for International Relations.

De Martini, M. I. 1994. "Las claves de la Cancillería." La Época newspaper, April 3.

ECLAC (Economic Commision for Latin America and the Caribbean [Spanish: Cepal]). 1994. El regionalismo abierto en América Latina y el Caribe. Santiago: Cepal, United Nations.

Escudé, C. 1987. Patología del nacionalismo. Buenos Aires: Ed. Tesis, Instituto Torcuato Di Tella.

Fermandois, J. 1985. Chile y el mundo 1970-1973: La política exterior del gobierno de la Unidad Popular y el sistema internacional. Santiago: Ed. Universidad Católica de Chile.

Fernández Amunátegui, M. 1995. "Estado actual de las relaciones entre Chile y la Unión Europea." In: Various authors. Relaciones con la Unión Europea: una visión latinoamericana. Santiago: Celare.

Ffrench-Davis, R. 1989. "Bases para una estrategia de comercio exterior chilena." In: H. Muñoz, ed. Chile: política exterior para la democracia. Santiago: Pehuén Editores.

Figueroa, C. 1994. "Una política exterior para una región en cambio." Estudios Internacionales 106 (April-June), pp. 252-265.

Foreign Relations Ministry. 1994. Política exterior vecinal del gobierno del Presidente Aylwin 1990-1994. Santiago: Foreign Relations Ministry.

Frei Ruiz-Tagle, E. 1996. Ideas para el diálogo democrático. Special edition for the Sixth Latin American Summit. Santiago: Dirección de Contenidos de la Presidencia de la República.

García Bedoya, C. 1981. Política exterior peruana: Teoría y práctica. Lima: Mosca Azul Editores.

Garrido Rojas, J. and P. Álamos Varas. 1992. Relaciones Chile-Brasil en la década de los noventa. Santiago: Institute for International Studies.

Gómez García-Palao, V. 1995. "Las relaciones económicas entre Bolivia y Chile: limitaciones y oportunidades." In: R. Barrios et al. Política exterior boliviana: Tendencias y desafíos. La Paz: Udapex/Ildis, pp. 291-329.

Gutiérrez, B. H. 1997. "Las relaciones económicas de Chile con los países de Asia-Pacífico." Report presented to the Latin American and Caribbean Meeting of the Pacific Asia Research Center, Latin American Economic System (SELA). Caracas, July 17-18.

Insulza, J. M. 1992. "Cooperación internacional y política exterior." In: CINDA. Cooperación Internacional: La experiencia chilena 1990-1991. Santiago: Ed. CINDA, pp. 15-38.

Insulza, J. M. 1998. Presentation Before the Commissions for Foreign Relations, Inter-Parliamentary Affairs and Latin American Integration of the Chamber of Deputies, Valparaiso, January 6.

Meneses, E. 1987. "Coping with Decline: Chilean Foreign Policy During the Twentieth Century, 1902-1972." Doctoral thesis, Balliol College, Oxford University.

Muñoz, H. 1986. Las relaciones exteriores del gobierno militar chileno. Santiago: Ediciones del Ornitorrinco.

Muñoz, H. and C. Portales. 1987. Una amistad esquiva: Las relaciones exteriores del gobierno militar chileno. Santiago: Pehuén Editores.

National Defense Ministry. 1997. Libro de la Defensa Nacional de Chile. 1997. Santiago: National Defense Ministry.

Orrego Vicuña, F. 1972. La participación de Chile en el sistema internacional. Santiago: Ed. Gabriela Mistral.

Pizarro, R. 1993. "Nuestra política exterior." La Época newspaper, March 2.

Sáez, R. E. 1993. "Chile-América Latina: Relaciones económicas y negociaciones bilaterales." Cono Sur (Flacso, Santiago de Chile) 12(1) (January-February), pp. 9-14.

Santa Cruz, H. 1993. Cooperar o perecer: El dilema de la comunidad internacional. Santiago: SRV.

Secretariat Pro Tempore, Rio Group. 1993. VII Cumbre Presidencial Chile, 1993: Actividades del Mecanismo Permanente de Consulta y Concertación Política. Santiago: Fondo de Cultura Económica.

Sigmund, P. E. 1993. The United States and Democracy in Chile. Baltimore: The Johns Hopkins University Press.

Tomassini, L. 1989. Teoría y práctica de la política internacional. Santiago: Ed. Universidad Católica de Chile.

Turner, G. 1994. "¿Quién manda este buque?" Hoy magazine (Santiago), March 7, pp. 39-42.

Van Klaveren, A. 1993. "El apoyo a la democracia en América Latina: ¿Hacia un nuevo régimen internacional?" Síntesis 21 (July-December), pp. 17-36.

Wilhelmy, M. 1979. "Hacia un análisis de la política exterior chilena contemporánea." Estudios Internacionales 48 (October-December), pp. 440-471.

Wilhelmy, M. and M. T. Infante. 1993. "La política exterior en los años 90: el gobierno del Presidente Aylwin y algunas proyecciones." Estudios Sociales 75 (Trimester 1).

Wilhelmy, M. and R. M. Lazo. 1997. "La política multilateral de Chile en Asia-Pacífico." Proyecto Fondecyt 1950834. Manuscript.

National Defense and the Armed Forces

Gonzalo García

Introduction

The context from which I write calls for initial clarification. From March 1994 to August 1997, I served as an advisor to the Minister of Defense and had the honor to participate from beginning to end in many of the Ministry's initiatives. This experience underlies many of the opinions expressed here, but it does not compromise the article's central principles in any way. This article does not pretend to be a history of the period, since it lacks the comprehensive vision necessary for such a project. It aims at an analytical focus; however, it has been hampered by the scarcity of literature about the period, along with the inapplicability of many previous patterns of analysis from political science and sociology to a period such as the 1990s. Thus, the text cites relatively few sources, since practically none exist on the topic as it will be discussed here. Especially useful to me have been the conversations I have had during these years with highly engaged intellectuals who have contributed significantly to the advance of understanding in this area, including Rodrigo Atria, Emilio Meneses, Sergio Micco, Francisco Rojas, and Eduardo Saffirio. It should be noted that my opinions do not necessarily represent their points of view.

I. "It depends upon the lens you are looking through."

In politics, it is always important to possess a world view regarding the various aspects of national life. This world view furnishes basic concepts on a subject and allows its holder to interpret phenomena through the lens of these concepts. Even in less ideologized periods, conceptual frameworks are always present, assisting in the interpretation of events and, above all, the formulation of proposals for improvement. Frameworks represent basic elements of political socialization. Thus, it is natural to expect that such frameworks will exist in an area such as national defense and, in particular, the role of the military in a democracy.

Looking behind particular arguments to discover this conceptual nucleus can lead to a better understanding of the diverging opinions on a subject, as well as to improved prospects for achieving consensus. This is especially useful in areas which are not on the immediate public agenda. Exploration of the sociological and psychological underpinnings of the predominant political actors may explain the type of problems and expectations found in an area such as defense.

At least five paradigms can be identified in the treatment of Chilean military topics during this century, although this does not pretend to be an exhaustive list. I have associated these paradigms with their date or period of origin, without implying that these were the dominant ideas of their time. As I will show, paradigms generated in one era often maintained their force in later political discussions. Some paradigms are even built upon others, according to their own internal logic.

The first paradigm was an outlook of the 1930s, advocating the Armed Forces' return to their barracks. This disposition is expressed in both a negative and a positive manner: first, stipulating what the Armed Forces should not do, and second, limiting the actions they should undertake. The first sense includes the convictions that the Armed Forces have no other role but the preservation of external security, and that their political and public visibility should be not only minimal but zero. This view seems to connect the idea of retreat to the barracks with a certain connotation of political defeat. From a positive perspective, this paradigm delimits the military's sphere of action, above all in its relationship with politics. This is the paradigm of abstention.

The second paradigm is a view popular in the 1950s and 1960s, which encouraged the use of the Armed Forces for national development. In an era of intense activity to promote development, with the apparatus of the State seen as its natural motor, the idea appears obvious to involve the Armed Forces in this high-priority national effort. The logic behind this paradigm is the effective use of the Armed Forces' excess capacity in the absence of external conflicts. A classic example of this tendency was the creation of the Military Work Corps during the democratic government of General Ibáñez. This view may even extend the concept of national development to the preservation of public order and internal security, granting the Armed Forces a role as the guarantor of last resort of the country's fundamental stability. We may call this phenomenon the paradigm of utility. This utility does not involve the weighing of costs and benefits, but the broadening of the Armed Forces' functions in an innovative manner. Utility is measured politically and not economically.

Third, we find the paradigm of politicized arbitration. Starting in the late 1960s, but above all during the 1970s, it was empirically shown that the Armed Forces can play a role in ending internal conflicts, acting as arbiters or referees.[1] The nature of arbitration also implies that these military actions are given a political definition, first from outside the institutions and later from within.

The Armed Forces were the focal point of the resolution of our democracy's conflicts that led to its end. There are differing versions of the paradigm of arbitration among leftist and rightist observers of the period. For the Left, the Armed Forces were the instrument that tipped the balance of power against the supporters of the Popular Unity government, destroying the country's weakened equilibrium. In contrast, for the Right, the Armed Forces acted as a guarantor of institutional integrity and generic protective power above

---

1   The principle is evident that domestic conflict cannot and must not be resolved through the arbitration of the Armed Forces. Such an occurrence would place in question the political development of the country involved. Thus, with much effort we discover this phenomenon in politically underdeveloped nations of post-colonial Africa. In recognition of our republican history, it is not enough to indicate the pure factual condition of a grave internal conflict as a prerequisite for intervention. For the Armed Forces to be granted even a marginal role as an arbiter, it must be proved beyond any doubt that this would be the proper mechanism to achieve a solution within the democratic framework. Since this is virtually impossible, as our own experience demonstrates, the option of military arbitration is not only unacceptable, but inadequate.

the democratically elected public authorities. The vision of the Left is more that of a coercive arbitration by the Armed Forces of a particular political project. In contrast, the Right sees a delegated arbitration; that is, an abdication of one's own political will in the form of a blank check to the Armed Forces.[2]

The next conceptual framework to arise was the paradigm of political-military relations. This is a vision from the late 1980s and early 1990s, dominated by the twin goals of establishing or reestablishing bridges between civilians and the military and designing clear regulations for the relations between these groups, guided by the principle of military subordination to civil authority. This legitimate proposition arose from the conflict between the military government's Copernican alteration of the Armed Forces' constitutional position and the requirements of the new democratic environment.

However, the continued validity of this controversial constitutional framework forces this paradigm to focus on the organizational structure of defense and the Armed Forces' role in non-military spheres. The emphasis is placed upon the tone of relations, which may range from praise to castigation. Perhaps the clearest precedent to this paradigm is the Portales vision that inaugurated a highly significant era in Chilean institutional development. It seems natural that this paradigm arises in periods of democratic restoration.

Finally, it appears that a new vision has emerged, the national interest paradigm of the late 1990s.[3] This paradigm views the Armed Forces in their classic and professional role as defenders of external sovereignty. Contributing to this vision has been the changing nature of defense topics in the region and the world, which has enormously expanded the basic debate, introducing new threats, risks, and opportunities for nations in a new world order. At the same time, this paradigm is consistent with Chile's more active role on the international stage and, above all, in the hemispheric community. The translation of the national interest paradigm into a defense strategy in service of a dynamic foreign policy seems to be the intention and orientation of our current defense system, as it seeks to modernize and improve its conceptual framework.

These paradigms, some contradictory and others complementary, have contributed to forming the opinions of various political actors. Behind the polemics sometimes heard on defense issues lie paradigms such as those explained here. It is obvious that all of them have some degree of validity.

Some observers have assumed that the military regime's electoral failure necessarily obligated the Armed Forces to adopt the paradigm of abstention. This position is prob-

---

2 As I have described, the distinction between coercive arbitration and delegated arbitration conceptually divides the Left and Right of the era. The Left's tactical view of the Armed Forces and the Right's strategic one have had a profound historical impact which is still felt today, making these concepts difficult to compare, even if they can be described analytically.

3 This paradigm can also be understood as inherent to all of the Armed Forces' institutional functions since the 19th century. However, since it lacks its own content, its historical adaptability is both essential and unclear. Thus, this paradigm can be conceived as an essential requisite for all of the others. Some would even sustain that the Armed Forces' intervention in 1973 was in the national interest. However, appealing to the idea of national interest today means debating the foundations and manifestations of public defense policy, in synthesis with our country's new national and international environment. This is what is profoundly new.

lematic because it fails to recognize the transactional nature of our transition to democracy. Nevertheless, the success of the transition and the establishment of a culture of normality — although without changes to the constitutional rules for the sector — lead us to expect that this paradigm will have continued validity.

At the same time, the Armed Forces' ability to contribute to national development is widely acknowledged, and reflections on this subject are becoming more complex. The paradigm of utility is emerging with renewed force. However, the challenge will lie in the definition of the military's role in national development: whether it serves as a direct actor, exercises a protective function for these new interests, or takes on some kind of intermediate role. Meanwhile, the type of development Chile seeks is still in debate. The discussion at any seminar on the subject will provide an idea of the multiplicity of viewpoints in this area.

As long as the Constitution includes the Armed Forces' mission of guaranteeing the institutional order of the Republic, the paradigm of arbitration will be relevant for a significant segment of public opinion. It will be claimed that even without this Constitutional rule, a valid appeal to empirical evidence can still be made. However, this paradigm ignores the course followed by the democratic process in the 1990s and throughout almost all of our republican history. We will return to this point at the end of this paper.

The viewpoint of political-military relations extends to every time and period, since the legal framework regulating the relationship between political leaders and the Armed Forces is both necessary and imperfect.

Finally, the national interest paradigm, in an era of increasing reflection on defense topics, will be the natural and professional outlook as the country faces new defense and security issues. Yet since this paradigm has not yet been extended throughout society, it will continue to struggle for a long period against other points of view such as those described by the paradigms above.

The categorization of particular politicians and parties according to their views on defense issues, and the identification of the paradigm or combination of paradigms best suited to the institutional interests of the Armed Forces, are subjects upon which it does not behoove me to comment, as they remain matters for study and discussion.

Some of the principal distinctions between the paradigms should be pointed out, in order to highlight their complementary relationships. Clearly, the paradigms offer different views of the Armed Forces' organization and goals. The paradigm of abstention, in its positive sense, limits the action of military forces, establishing above all their natural boundary with politics. Thus, it defines the space granted to the national defense authorities. This is a framework that permits action, but does not establish guidelines or contents for the concrete defense of a country. Accordingly, the national interest paradigm may be used to establish the primary goals of defense in a particular context, while the paradigm of utility may supply ideas for the secondary or alternative functions of defense institutions in general and the Armed Forces in particular. At the same time, the paradigm of political-military relations can help to complete the picture of positive abstention described by the first paradigm. This is a line of reflection permitting the linking of some of these ideas. Other combinations are possible, but I have the impression that democracy itself might become one of the variables at risk. Meanwhile, this analysis leads us to identify by exclusion the paradigm representing a contradiction to the others: the paradigm of arbitration. Thus we conclude our taxonomic reflection.

Starting from the assumption that these ideas or paradigms exist, we shall analyze snapshots of two moments in the recent evolution of defense policy. These will help illuminate the variations in focus exhibited during the 1990s, which were such a complex and difficult period for our democracy.

II. Snapshots of Two Moments: 1990 and 1997

National defense during these years was in the public consciousness not so much due to its essential content, but because of the issues surrounding it. The main actors of our country's recent history have mostly come from the military world, and the military regime has left its imprint on our new democracy and contributed to forming its cultural contradictions. Thus, it seems natural to examine the recent development of the national defense sector, and in particular, one of its privileged protagonists: the Armed Forces.

However, we can naturally achieve little distance as observers of the history of the last eight republican years, which makes this intellectual exercise more difficult. The instability of the period may lead us into a series of reckless judgments as to the actions of the era's main figures, undertaking a sort of journalistic analysis of winners and losers which is not conducive to understanding what has really happened during Chile's transition to democracy. Therefore, I would like to propose a rather more naive but practical vision, which is to observe the changes in the defense sphere during the 1990s through the analysis of two moments in time: March 1990 and December 1997. In this approach, the importance of the period's main actors is devalued — a position I have long advocated, with a certain renunciation of high-level politics — while a closer look is permitted at the changes occurring in our democracy. While these snapshots are necessarily somewhat subjective, I hope they will contribute to an understanding of the condition of Chile's institutions in the past and their situation today.

The following analysis will focus on the two relevant groups making up the world of defense: the civilians with responsibilities in this area and the military itself. The predominant tendencies of each group will be identified, along with their most important distinctions.

1. TRANSFORMATIONS FROM 1990 TO 1997:
THE MILITARY WORLD VIEWED FROM OUTSIDE

This section will attempt an analysis of the Armed Forces from outside, including the external manifestations of its complex set of symbols. The Armed Forces will be viewed as an indistinguishable whole, with appropriate exceptions as indicated. This work will focus, as much as possible, upon the Armed Forces' fundamental professional orientation as a guideline for their evolution, without discounting their political role, but also without placing undue emphasis upon it.

From Partisanism To National Support
The first characteristic calling for analysis is the Armed Forces' status as a political actor. The actions of the military regime culturally framed this status and will continue to frame it for years to come, giving the Armed Forces a historical legacy they cannot escape. No matter how many theoretical distinctions are made, the evidence indicates that generations of

Chileans will view national defense through the lens of the military regime, and this must be accepted as part of reality.

The Armed Forces' link with the traditional Right, the birth of a new modernizing-authoritarian Right, and the establishment of liberal policies confined to the economic sphere constitute the point of departure from which the Armed Forces entered into the democratic system governed by the 1980 Constitution. This legal framework represents the Armed Forces' political ideas, its institutional convictions, and its points of reference. Clearly, as the democratic transition advanced and became consolidated, the centrality of the Armed Forces as political participants in this process gradually diminished.

The right-wing factions elected to Congress in 1989 were always conscious of the fact that they did not fully capitalize upon the cultural impact of the military regime. Thus, their natural tendency was to court the electorate assembled under the figure of General Pinochet. Pinochet's status as commander-in-chief of the Army allowed the legitimate continuation of his special and privileged relationship with this military branch. The tenuous link between historical loyalty and the need for electoral success stood at the center of debate among right-wing circles. Arguments over perceived devaluation of the military regime's achievements hindered the prospects for growth in the sector. This phenomenon is again evident in the results of the 1997 parliamentary elections and the accession to Congress of figures associated with the military government.

Thus it is undeniable that, from the perspective of 1990, the Armed Forces were an axis around which the political parties revolved in opposition, as they had opposed each other during the military regime.

In the 1997 snapshot, some of these political characteristics can still be perceived. However, the hard data from 1997 show a decline in the Armed Forces' political role,[4] a visible, though slight, loosening of the 1990 party configurations, and the rise of new leaders with a different understanding, not of the Armed Forces' past, but of their present and future functions.

One of the central aspects of the new situation is the Concertación coalition government's pledge not to involve the Armed Forces in tasks outside of defense, despite their broad constitutional mandate. The effect of this guarantee is to strengthen the services' focus on public defense policy, and this is the direction in which they have advanced in recent years. Thus, a healthier relationship is being developed between the Armed Forces and some parties of the Concertación, in particular the Christian Democrats, although this represents more an initiative of President Frei himself than of the party apparatus.

This revival of the Armed Forces' national mission is especially reflected in legislative support for the sector's proposals, which have recently met with little or no opposition.[5]

---

4 Here it should not be forgotten that the secretive and illegal interference of Army intelligence agents in party politics, as in the Charly and Piñeragate cases, caused damage to these institutions, compelling them to establish prohibitions against such actions.

5 The best demonstration of this is seen in the evolution of legislation on defense subjects. Initially, the few laws proposed in this area (such as the modification of military courts' jurisdiction and changes to the regulations covering the retirement of generals) met with little discussion and were rarely approved. Today, we find a profusion of proposals (including the Armed Forces health law, the special readjustment, the new Personnel Statute, studies of obligatory military service, and so forth), which have met with more vigorous discussion and analysis, concluding with full Congressional approval.

However, excessive conclusions cannot be drawn from these facts, since it is possible that many of these projects were approved due to criteria of strict political responsibility, the desire to maintain good relations with the military, or out of mere tolerance, but without substantive agreement with the proposals involved. While it is easy to state that the Armed Forces belong to the nation and that defense is a task of all citizens, the full realization of these affirmations constitutes a serious challenge which the country must continue to face, and which in recent decades has been only sparsely in evidence.

From Internal To External Security

The displacement of the Armed Forces from internal to external security has continued with its own momentum since the regime left power. However, some characteristics of the former remain in the snapshot of 1990, where various uncertainties are visible in this regard. In particular, the actions of the military intelligence services and the use of directly obtained or residual information remained an unresolved issue. In the 1997 snapshot, however, the completed transit from internal to external security has led to the uncovering of two apparent dilemmas.

First, it appears that some people believed that external security would be satisfied only through the paradigm of the return to barracks. In contrast, others insisted upon the logic that the defense of external sovereignty presupposes the integration of society, given that defense is a task shared by all. It is possible that this tension will persist among us for years. Some disagreement is natural in democratic countries; in some, the divide almost seems to be between those who believe in the necessity for defense and those who discount it. The latter could leave the State practically defenseless. In contrast, others, perhaps more numerous, have no alternative vision of defense policy and take refuge in a certain realism, recognizing the need for countries to have Armed Forces, but preferably remaining within their barracks and without the need for obligatory military service.

The second dilemma involves the military's participation in internal security measures, which led to a refusal to consider any role for the Armed Forces in this area.[6] In the 1990 snapshot, this refusal was total. In contrast, in the 1997 view the level of rejection remains high, but the policies actually practiced exhibit much of the contrary. Military participation in the control of electoral processes,[7] their incidental but legally recognized role in the fight against drug trafficking, and their activity during catastrophes at the margin of a state of constitutional exception are functions strongly supported by common sense.

Here I would like to follow the logic of this subject a bit further. It seems obvious that this pragmatic vision calls for adjustment of our constitutional and legal mechanisms to legitimize this participation. In the area of catastrophes, above all, it seems logical to pool increasingly scarce state resources to coordinate preventive and organizational measures aimed at these phenomena, while always respecting the powers of the democratic authorities, who are ultimately responsible for the success or failure of such actions. Including these functions among the Armed Forces' responsibilities does not involve the granting of

---

6   This perception was reinforced by military officials' participation in preemptive and repressive political operations, which was confirmed with the absorption of the CNI into the DINE and later attenuated by the exclusion of all ex-CNI agents.

7   This is a historical reaffirmation of a role they have played since 1938, under the famous Olavarría Law. To date, nobody has consistently opposed the Armed Forces' continued exercise of this function.

police powers, or even imply that the Armed Forces can substitute for the police.[8] These considerations reaffirm the need to eliminate some powers of the military which are confusingly laid out in the Organic Law of States of Constitutional Exception, in order to let the political responsibility fall upon those who must direct the response to a catastrophe.

From Narrow To Globalized National Interest

The above debate has also led to a search to redefine the Armed Forces' classic mission in the new context of the 1990s.

It was impossible to capture, in a single principle, the force of the almost simultaneous coincidence of the return of democracy and the end of the Cold War. The orientation of the Armed Forces — and toward them — was basically predetermined by the democratic restoration and the military services' integration into the new political system. However, from a cultural point of view, the transformations in the international order were professionally challenging for the defense sector. For a while, a healing variety of idealist internationalism prevailed. Yet after a few years, new topics began to arise on the international agenda: new conflicts and their implications not only for countries, but for subregions and regions. A synthesis began to be developed among international cooperation, security, national identity, and integration.

In the early 1990s, a certain doctrinal vacuum regarding this new phenomenon prevailed within the Armed Forces, with the exception of the Navy. The latter constructed a theory of sea presence which acknowledged this global transformation to a certain degree.

By 1997, however, recognition of global changes had spread widely throughout the defense sector, manifesting itself in a relative opposition of priorities with those domestic leaders strongly supported by the export-driven model of growth through the opening of markets. Here a contradiction arises between right-wing political loyalties and rightist business circles. In general, the Armed Forces' position stands in opposition to liberal culture across the entire Chilean ideological spectrum. Some liberals hold a disparaging view of the role played by defense in this area, promoting the notion of the military as an obstacle to development.

Today, coherent doctrines have been developed regarding defense and the development of its institutions. Meanwhile, efforts have been put forth for some time to transcend narrow debates and achieve consensus. The decisive step toward uniting the democratic and post-Cold War agendas was the Chilean military's extensive participation in U.N. peacekeeping operations. Their first assignment was on the Iraq-Kuwait border, followed by operations in Cambodia, El Salvador, Iraq, and Bosnia. Chilean military observers were assigned to the conflict between Peru and Ecuador. As a result of these deployments, Armed Forces personnel have been direct witnesses to and participants in the changing international agenda, and they have conducted their missions in accordance with a new and complex understanding of national interest.

The central point is this: national interest has been broadened, and to the concept of territorial sovereignty has been added a commitment to international peace and concern for the new challenges of development. Thus, a transcendent change has taken place: throughout Chile's 20th-century history, each time defense clashed with development, the

---

8 However, the Armed Forces do have a role in this area in the case of a collapse of the State, although always under the previous authorization of the relevant democratic authority.

first prevailed, giving rise to the protectionist and import substitution models of internal development. Today, when conflict arises between defense and development, the latter predominates. Some are satisfied simply with having brought about this change in priorities. Yet true national responsibility will only be achieved when defense is instructed how it should behave in the face of the new risks presented by development: the opening of markets and border crossings; increased environmental interdependence; shared control over essential goods and services; the free flow of commercial transportation, and so forth. Adapting defense policies to this new environment remains a challenge for the future.

From Autonomous To Partially Consensual Operation

After the failure of the 1988 plebiscite, the Governing Junta's legislative commissions brought about a transfer of power marked by a lack of confidence in the new democratic authorities and their methods. They rapidly established a series of unprecedented institutional, political, economic, and social security prerogatives for the Armed Forces, which in some cases contradicted the regulations in force during almost all of the regime's years in power.

One of the most important of these changes was the incorporation of the Organic Constitutional Law of the Armed Forces into the 1989 constitutional reform. This measure established the legal guidelines for the military and set a minimum level of economic benefits for Armed Forces personnel.

This body of law, together with the dispositions of the Constitution itself, established a kind of bridge between the executive branch and the military institutions. The institutional autonomy of the military weakened the historical powers of the president and abrogated those of the Senate. This debate has become sufficiently well-known through later attempts at constitutional reform.

Nevertheless, it should be noted that from the perspective of 1997, the criticism of these regulations has become slightly more restrained, for two main reasons. first, the government has won administrative recognition for presidential prerogatives, for example in the issue of the president's "disposition" over personnel appointment, promotion, and retirement. Similarly, opposition to presidential appointments on the part of military leaders have led, in practice, to adverse impact upon the professional careers of the objecting officials, while the presidential nominees remain in their appointed positions. Certainly, this career damage has not taken place as a punishment for specific actions, but it has been manifested in evaluations for promotion occurring months and even years later.[9] Finally, and naturally, the weight of presidential power increases with its exercise.

---

9   It should be remembered that the power of a president to order the retirement of a high official or general of the Armed Forces because of extraordinary circumstances does not exist in our legislation. An important case related to this subject is that of Brigadier Lepe, whose proposed promotion to the rank of Brigadier General was denied by President Frei, causing political controversy. It is categorically true — supported by official declarations of the Corps of Generals of the Army — that the president had the full and absolute right to reject the promotion. This is not the place to examine the case in depth; however, some commentary may be useful. The objection to the promotion was Brigadier Lepe's alleged participation in the death of Carmelo Soria, imputed to a DINA brigade although judicially unproven. The 1978 Amnesty Law extinguished any penal responsibility. That is a fact. The debate centered on Brigadier Lepe's irreproachable official service record and the presumption of innocence in his favor. That is another fact. However, to believe that granting the rank of general of the Republic exclusively on the basis of this last

Second, the conviction has become widespread that external interference with or politicization of institutional and career development within the Armed Forces must be avoided. Thus, it is probable that support will increase for the constitutional body of law permitting the most qualified members of each military service to rise to the High Command. Here, respect for the hierarchical, disciplined, and professional nature of the Armed Forces translates into political confidence in their senior officials. As such, the State abstains from intervening in the advance of military careers from the lowest ranks up to colonel.

The prospects for economic stability within the military institutions themselves remain an important issue. The Governing Junta elevated the Law of Reserved Copper Funds No. 13.196 to the constitutional organic level, while increasing its minimum floors and adding a State guarantee in the case that these minimum levels were not reached. (In practice, the law has worked well, with the State guarantee invoked only once, in 1995, as a result of falling copper prices and with minimal budgetary repercussions.) The 1989 budget was frozen as a floor for future expenditures, and its growth was linked to inflation rather than to a determined percentage of GDP.[10]

Thus, taking advantage of the constitutional restrictions upon the legislative powers, the Armed Forces established an autonomous budget providing an adequate level of military funding with minimal opportunity for the government to modify these expenditures.

The issue of economic autonomy led to a certain political withdrawal from military questions, since budgetary discussions focused only upon marginal details. Dialogue was also impossible regarding arms acquisitions financed by the Copper Law, due to the technical nature of the subject, the military officials' reluctance to discuss it, and the lack of Congressional authority in the area. The political parties and their representatives in Congress lacked viable alternative proposals. Even the Minister of National Defense has not been able to promote reflection on defense topics, since he has emphasized the fulfillment of his policies, within which approving the budget continues to be one of the most relevant. He cannot afford to give up one of his few political-administrative strengths: approving the budget of these institutions sheltered by favorable regulations. Finally, the atmosphere of prudence observed during the political transition represented another reason to avoid debating these issues.

However, from the perspective of 1997, the macroeconomic structure of the Armed Forces has significantly altered, and thus a new basis can be found for reflection upon it.

Since 1994, military expenditures have exhibited a real increase of 12.5%, today reaching a total of 530 billion pesos, including the income from Reserved Copper Funds Law, but without the social security funds budgeted through the Ministry of Labor and Social Security.

---

fact is a degradation of what it means to be a general or admiral. These highest of ranks are beyond the reach of a standard professional career, which officially terminates with 30 years of service at the rank of colonel. Granting the honor of general requires the most thorough reflection and judgment, since it affects the leadership and destiny of the Corps of Generals as a whole. The use of presidential power confirms that the military career cannot be governed exclusively by internal criteria, as all of our Constitutions establish. The risk faced here is called corporativism, and that is also a fact.

10 If the 1989 defense budget's share of GDP had been chosen as a basis, today's defense spending would represent more than 3% of GDP and not the current 1.7%, according to figures provided in the National Defense Book of 1997.

Thus, defense spending has remained relatively stable, with a real growth rate of approximately 4% annually: less than the economic growth of the country, but surpassing by far the minimum levels established in the law. In political terms, this signifies that the government has maintained and even increased its concern for the defense sector, providing the means for it to sustain its operational capacity, in accordance with our country's current situation.

Changing tendencies can be seen in the internal distribution of these expenditures. A decrease from 23% to 20% is observed in the share of the budget deriving from the Copper Law, as well as an increase from 51.1% to 54.3% in overall personnel expenditures. Since 1994, the growth in defense spending has been concentrated in the area of personnel, exhibiting a real increase of 20.7%, similar to the country's rise in GDP over the same period. Thus Chile's economic development over the last few years has been reflected to a certain extent within the Armed Forces. A report issued by the Chamber of Deputies in 1995 found the Armed Forces to be in a state of relative deficiency, which has been largely remedied since that time.

This growth is explained by three factors: the annual salary adjustments for public sector employees; the 7% special readjustment granted to the Armed Forces in 1996, including payments under the Armed Forces Health Law; and finally, the natural increase in compensation for personnel whose average age is rising each year, as they acquire rights associated with seniority and career advancement. In 1994, the average annual expenditure for each member of the Armed Forces was 4,343,000 pesos. Today, this figure is 5,401,000 pesos. This amount does not include the spending which will be mandated by the new Personnel Statute of the Armed Forces (16.5 billion pesos), nor the funds needed to return the depleted Pension Fund to a sound financial footing. The breakdown of this system was caused by a large increase in benefits payments, accompanied by a decline in the funds available to meet these obligations.[11] This has been probably one of the most short-sighted policies in the sector, producing a pervasive crisis in the Armed Forces' social security system since 1995.

These figures demonstrate that budgetary discussions no longer focus on the fulfillment of the minimum levels set forth by the Constitutional Organic Law of the Armed Forces. They now permit analysis of the budget on its own merit, a question in which slow but steady progress has been made. This development, supported by the information exchange policies promoted by the Ministry of National Defense, is what has made possible the increases in resources for Armed Forces personnel.

Of course, this process has not yet been completed, since it has been dominated by the gradualist spirit common to all the sectors. Clearly, no one is disposed to influence the budget of a particular sector without a thorough technical understanding of its income, expenditures, and how they are utilized. These objections are especially valid in the area of defense.

However, some likely future tendencies may be suggested through two final analyses of defense economics.

First, determination of the amount of the defense budget requires an additional conceptual definition. It is not merely an academic exercise, but highly useful, to measure defense spending in relation to GDP. Using 1996 values as a baseline, in 1990 defense

---

11 The most important aspect of this pension modification was the increase of the base for severance pay in early 1990 from 24 to 30 months. In 1995, due to the elimination of fixed rates, the Pension Fund could no longer continue to be self-financing.

spending represented some 2.7% of GDP, gradually falling to 1.56% of GDP in 1997. Measured as a percentage of the overall budget, the figure has decreased from 15.6% in 1990 to 8.94% in 1997. In political terms, this represents a clear demonstration of governmental priorities. In 1990, defense spending stood at a level equal to 95% of education spending. By 1997, it only reached 53% of that amount. Defense spending in 1990 in relation to health spending was 270%. In 1997, it is 122%. This decrease is only relative, but it must be recognized that the defense function is being carried out at a static level of funding, while facing new complexities which will lead in the coming years to debate over the effective functioning of the minimum funding floors. Meanwhile, government and parliamentary powers will be strengthened if they take the initiative to raise these spending levels.

Second, the Copper Law can be expected to experience a similar evolution. Its share of the defense budget remains low, at the same time that the cost of acquisition and maintenance of new weapons systems is rising due to technological advances. The pressure on Copper Law resources from recent purchases will affect equilibrium in this area, above all in the Army and Air Force, in spite of these services' highly effective financial management. It is a fact that the option of abolishing this law and moving military financing to the regular budget would not only affect the military's macroeconomic stability, but would probably also lead to increased defense spending. In addition, this would be accompanied by pressure to allow Congressional influence in the military acquisitions process, although the institutional strength is lacking for healthy debate on this subject. In other words, the country's political institutions have not reached the necessary level of professionalism to sustain this technically complex discussion, involving highly sensitive matters.[12] Thus, except for pressure for the privatization of CODELCO, the radical modification of this body of law does not appear to be an option for the near future, in the absence of a professional culture able to undertake these debates.

Symbolic Identity: From Corporative Defense To National Unity

Symbols in hierarchical institutions are highly significant. For the military, they represent a code of references and meanings. With their perpetuation of national symbols, the Armed Forces have carried out the historical function of preserving fundamental traditions for the State of Chile since its independence.[13]

---

12 Here it is useful to remember the recent debate over submarines. The discussion, lacking any strategic content, simply reproduced the arguments of competing providers, as illustrated by the public statements of representatives of the companies in question. However, it is quite probable that such technical difficulties exist in any legislative area, and that waiting for our Congress to gain the necessary expertise would be a good pretext for weakening the budgetary power of our democracy. Here it appears that one of Chile's principal institutional weaknesses is the delicate issue of transparency in the links between public and private interest. This is the truly important question, and as long as it is not resolved, public policy will suffer. In the concrete case of defense, except for the Congress of the United States, which has the power to authorize certain purchases and especially arms sales, the acquisitions of arms systems remains rooted in the executive branch of Western democracies, aside from later phases of control and even cancellation.

13 The role of symbols presupposes the existence of a national identity and a manner of conceiving it. This point is found, both in intellectual and military circles, to be closely connected with the debate over the relation between the State and society; the fundamental nature of the Army; the existence of a national strategy; and in general, with any ideas related to the collective definition of a people as a historical subject. All of these aspects greatly exceed the scope of this work, but they are basic for an understanding of this point.

Thus, the Armed Forces' relationship with national symbols is inextricably linked to their classic function. However, the military regime exhibited a certain tendency to use these national symbols in the service of its own political program.

Nevertheless, in a highly significant adaptation process which has received little or no attention, the fight over these symbols has been nearly abandoned, and the sense of national unity behind them has increased. The reason for this is the spread of the conviction that defense is a task shared by all Chileans, a patriotic duty requiring the commitment of each citizen, beyond factional affiliations.

In addition, the presence of democracy itself has contributed to raising the country's political-strategic stature,[14] an assertion which is supported by and incorporated into official military doctrines.[15] One of the advantages of this principle is that it has led to the valuation of democracy as a solid foundation for defense.

2. TRANSFORMATIONS FROM 1990 TO 1997: THE POLITICAL WORLD VIEWED FROM WITHIN

An additional dimension of change is represented by a development discussed above: the new vision arising from the political world, a vision which has only matured over the last two years. More precisely, these changes have arisen in the government's view of defense, promoting a new outlook for the sector.

In this section, I hope to show the central motivations of Chile's political leaders for this change in vision, which involves a new and innovative spirit.

From Political-Military Relations To Defense Policy

It was evident that in the face of the military's own distrust of democratic decision-making processes, the political authorities in the area of defense, with their relative lack of power, would exercise a certain vindictive logic in the promotion of presidential authority over the Armed Forces. In consequence, defense debate focused on the question of who exercised power in the area, and not whether the functions and policies of defense were desirable on their own merit.

It is also obvious that this debate over supremacy, equilibrium, or subordination led to an ongoing state of rivalry in civilian-military or political-military relations. Both civilian and military leaders took a confrontational approach, in the belief that these relations contained the key to the democratic transition. For this reason, I do not wish to present a criticism of the protagonists of the democratic restoration, but rather a self-criticism for the constant underestimation of the Armed Forces' prospects for development, above all those of the Army.[16]

---

14 Political-strategic stature is a state's degree of influence in the international sphere, as a result of the effective development of its national strength, as well as its will and capacity to employ this asset in the promotion and defense of its interests. It is the international image projected by a country, according to the Glossary of the 1997 National Defense Book.

15 The National Defense Book proclaims Chile's new democratic ideas and values and describes the country's objectives and strategies for their defense. Thus it supersedes previous debates, such as that surrounding the new-defunct National Security Doctrine.

16 It is clear that actions and reactions obeying the same logic dominated the codes of conduct in these relations. By the end, the Aylwin government tended toward delicate criticism of the Ministry of Defense, as if the Army officials had not had any part in the political-military conflicts, with an attitude clearly demonstrating the low expectations for cooperation prevalent during this period.

However, the continuing legal, institutional, or purely political conflicts finally led to the recognition that the focal points in civilian-military relations had to be changed. Thus, since 1993, the attempt has been made to center the debate on the military's own subject: defense policy itself. With this, an adversarial relationship is being transformed into one of institutional development. Conflicts over power are being replaced by opportunities for cooperation and leadership. Points of contact between civilians and military personnel, on subjects of mutual interest, are being increased. Conflicts are being defused and referred to the appropriate instances for resolution. It is being recognized, as advocated in earlier periods of our history, that legal disputes belong to the sphere of justice, while professional attitudes belong to the sphere of defense.[17]

This new vision had a powerful effect: not actually preventing the foreseeable conflicts between political and military interests, but channeling them and confronting them more effectively. No one can deny that the judicial problem of the Letelier case was a highly explosive one, but it was resolved with very encouraging results for Chilean democracy.

Thus, the new focus on defense policy was not adopted as a concession to the military, nor was it the result of a historical vision blinded by amnesty. On the contrary, it aimed at reducing conflict, guiding it toward resolution, and ensuring a professional perspective on the part of Chile's military institutions. This attitude began to take hold in 1996, and it seems likely to continue on its present course, in spite of the historic changes in protagonists which are occurring.

Behind this process stood the government's recognition of the Armed Forces' natural mission, with all of its consequences and necessities. The point of no return to the previous political treatment of defense was reached in the adoption of a lexicon, incorporating the terminology of defense itself, with its notions of threats, hypothetical conflicts, political-strategic global estimations, mutual confidence measures, and so forth, along with the commitment to work seriously to reduce the probability of conflict and guarantee the continued security of our State.

From a Culture of Military Secrecy To One of Transparency
One of the fundamental innovations of President Frei's administration was the aforementioned establishment of defense policy as the focal point in discussions of military affairs. This focus depends upon a basic prerequisite: knowledge of the country's current defense policy or its development if it is lacking.

Thus, from the beginning of President Frei's term in office, the proposal was made to publish a National Defense Book, which would clearly lay out the foundation and instruments of Chile's defense.

This proposal met with broad success. Significantly, the challenge of creating the National Defense Book required the formation of the beginnings of a defense community. A community of this nature is a group of civilians and military leaders, including government officials and academic experts on the subject, who provide the technical and political points of reference and the fundamental orientations of the defense sector, who recognize its challenges and are loyal to its goals. In developed democratic societies, these groups not

---

17 See the first address by the Minister of National Defense to the War Academies in 1995, published by the Secretariat of Communication and Culture of the Ministry of the Governmental Secretary-General.

only develop initiatives for improving defense policy, but also they provide the basis for sustaining it over time as a durable and authentic national vision, non-partisan and independent of the particular administration in power.

On August 20, 1997, the National Defense Book was published, the first of its kind in Latin America. Since that time, it has increasingly become the natural prototype for policies promoting confidence and transparency in the sphere of defense. A country that clearly explains the foundations, structure, and implementation of its defense enterprise is in a position to tolerate wide-ranging debate on the subject.

With this, Chile has taken a great step, displacing the subject of defense from the specialized technical journals — financed by interest groups representing the arms industry — to the open forum of citizen reflection on public policy.

At the same time, the country has gained the benefit of a common vocabulary shared by experts and civil authorities in the field of defense. This book provides a basis for future defense policies and sets the guidelines for this sphere for the years to come.

From the international point of view, the National Defense Book represents a point of strength for our foreign policy and a radical commitment to peace through transparency. As it is read beyond our borders, it must challenge the other countries of our region to demonstrate convincingly why defense spending in Latin America is the lowest in the world.

This rejection of the culture of military secrecy will increase our citizens' consciousness of their rights and duties in the defense of their country. In addition, it is a natural requirement of our democracy.

Finally, it is true that the practice of representative democracies around the world is marred by growing indifference to public policies, not only because of their technical content, but also due to the lack of opportunities for participation in their formulation and commitment to their goals. However, Chile's preparation of a National Defense Book through a year and a half of effort, with the help of more than 130 representatives of military, parliamentary, executive, academic, and other civilian circles shows that even policies from which little is expected can provide the opportunity to lend a broader and deeper context to our democracy.

From International Military Contact To High-Level Cooperation

Military institutions share common orientations which can be observed across the most diverse cultures. Thus it is almost inevitable that military branches will discover affinities with the corresponding services of other countries, even among potential adversaries.

This special relationship can become a natural vehicle for the exchange of experiences, training methods, and other information which can be applied as each country seeks to modernize its own professional development strategies.

Chile's international isolation during the 1970s and 1980s hindered and bureaucratized these relations considerably. However, commercial relations were not subject to equivalent restrictions. This provided a privileged link to companies in the arms industry, who were free to pursue negotiations for new weapons systems with a quarantined Chile throughout the era of the military regime. The Armed Forces' institutional modernization and adaptation processes suffered structural changes which were economically very costly, even if they provided the basis for a certain liberation from monodependency.

The democratic government has taken the necessary steps to extend the current fluidity of our international relations to the realm of defense. Thus, Chile has signed a Memoranda of Understanding with a series of countries, which can make significant contributions to our defense policies and practices.[18] These relations have usually been established between the countries' respective Ministers of Defense and then extended to other areas, thus expanding inter-military contacts to the whole of the bilateral relationship.

These formal agreements have led to highly concrete benefits such as the opening of markets, the lifting of restrictions on the use of particular sophisticated technologies, joint venture opportunities, direct negotiations without intermediaries, the obtaining of politically-based prices for certain weapons systems, and so forth. At the same time, the traditional exchange programs which have always been so useful have been strengthened. Opportunities have even arisen for participation in joint operations with other countries, with alliances such as NATO or in U.N. peacekeeping operations, with all the possibilities offered by agreements of this nature.[19]

From Threats of Subordination To Opportunities for Leadership

In the preceding pages, the author has come close to representing a Ministerial perspective, appearing to have lost his bearings and become absorbed in officialist self-complacency, as if his horizons did not stretch beyond the Diego Portales Building. I have already mentioned the context of this article.

I would like to report that my apparent forgetfulness of the relevance of other political actors to this subject is not what it seems to be. The omission is deliberate. There is no doubt that in recent years the Ministry of National Defense has acquired a central position in the management of defense policy, and that this is only understandable due to the initiatives generated from within the Ministry itself. The environment is different because the logic is different; a strong stimulus to the civilian side of defense has come from the central level; transparency and the spread of information have been promoted from the same source; and the Armed Forces' legislative and budgetary initiatives have been strongly backed by the Ministry, which has helped make their proposals viable and has stood up for their needs.

The centrality of the Ministry is related to the nature of its mission. The president's supremacy of power in this area is exercised through the Ministry. One of the evident results of this process, in contrast to what is seen with other State policies, is the concentration of management and supervision authority in the Minister of Defense. This is what makes the difference between mere formal power and its exercise. It is the difference between leadership and subordination. It seems obvious to acknowledge the institutional deficiencies of the

---

18 To date, Memoranda of Understanding or general agreements have been signed with the United States, France, Germany, England, Spain, Sweden, Belgium, Italy, the Russian Federation, and Malaysia, and will shortly be signed with Israel and South Korea. Far from being pro forma statements, these accords have led to far-reaching initiatives and improvements. Perhaps the most important of these is the agreement between Chile and Spain for the joint development of a terrestrial observation satellite.

19 A recent and notable example is the agreement by the Ministries of Foreign Relations and Defense of Argentina and Chile to carry out joint military exercises in 1998. The implementation of this proposal is already underway. Today, international contact between Ministries must become more frequent, due to the increasing pace of innovation in the sector. This is demonstrated, for good or ill, in the debate over the U.S. decisions — characterized as the "candy policy" — to lift restrictions on sophisticated armaments for Chile, to grant special non-NATO ally status to Argentina, and to support Brazil's accession to the U.N. Security Council as a new permanent member after the Council's reform.

subordinating powers. Yet it seems our duty to recognize that such deficiencies are relative, as well as to recognize what is demonstrated in the practical exercise of Ministerial powers. With prominent civil leadership behind it, the principle of subordination acquires vitality. In the lack of such leadership, subordination hardens in the complacent conviction that it controls the Armed Forces, without knowing why and for what purpose.

This centrality of the Ministry is not only applicable to the Armed Forces but also to the defense community, which seeks to understand, debate, and extend the sector's policies. In particular, the members of the Defense Commissions of both the Senate and the Chamber of Deputies have become the official interlocutors of the political parties in these technical debates, often supported by information supplied to them by the Ministry.

Meanwhile, the new National Defense Book does not simply contain international proposals or descriptions of the current state of defense. In addition, it establishes the ground rules which will guide the sector's development, providing a common frame of reference to those who wish to promote improvements in the sphere of defense. The issue of mandatory military service is a good example of this. There is undeniable pressure to modify, improve, or abolish this system, for very diverse reasons. However, recently-introduced innovations explore all of the possible alternatives within the model of obligatory military service and the draft. The effectiveness thus achieved, measured by a significant increase in voluntary compliance, has restrained calls for a change of framework, such as conversion to a fully professional Army.

It seems necessary to promote constitutional reform initiatives in order to cement the principle of subordination in a definitive manner. However, the essential prerequisite for this task will be continued leadership of the area with a fundamental commitment to the country's defense, and with the political initiative to maintain the viability of defense in a context of rapid global change.

In the process of reconstructing our democratic institutions, we must address some legacies remaining from long ago. One of the most significant for this area is the absence of a legal framework for the Ministry of National Defense. To rectify this omission seems a logical and necessary step, which would mark the end of the first great stage of recuperation of civil leadership in the area of defense.

Continued speculations are possible about the principal tendencies arising in the area of defense today, such as the most appropriate defense model for Chile; the ongoing education and training of military personnel; improvement of inter-functional skills and experiences; tightening of the link between defense and foreign policy; identification of defense prospects in the context of Mercosur, and so forth. However, the development of each of these aspects will follow a path which appears more and more obvious: a strengthening of the ties between the military and other institutions, and the use of strategies of cooperation to advance State policy in the area of national defense.

Final Remarks

Beyond the processes described here, additional circumstances have arisen which signify the completion of a cycle of our history. Since late October 1997, an unprecedented flood of news has issued from the world of defense. During the past year, along with the naming of the institutional High Commands — accompanied by the above-mentioned Army incident involving the promotion of Brigadier Lepe — the new commanders-in-chief of the Army and Navy were nominated: Major General Ricardo Izurieta and Admiral Jorge Arancibia.

These nominations, counterbalanced by the retirement of General Augusto Pinochet in March 1998, as well as that of Admiral Jorge Martínez, who has been a designated senator for the National Security Council, mark the beginning of a new period which must be judged in both a military and a political sense.

Militarily, the end of a transition has been reached. Its success has been guaranteed for some time, as measured by its achievement of a state of normalcy, independent of the lingering public uncertainty surrounding some issues, such as the exact date of General Pinochet's retirement. The tense atmosphere expected to accompany the military succession never materialized. Even the Lepe incident did not lead to a protracted conflict, nor did it damage relations among the actors involved, although it cast a temporary shadow over the well-planned pathway of change.

The key to this phenomenon is explained, to my understanding, by an ongoing tendency of underestimating the power held by the Ministry of National Defense. As a result, the Ministry was able to act with considerable confidence in light of pundits' underrated view of its capacity. Meanwhile, the Army had had enough time to prepare itself institutionally for the moment when General Pinochet would step down, thus reducing the trauma of change. This is not to deny that the new Commander-in-Chief will face numerous challenges. It is probable that he intends, without public fanfare, to undertake needed institutional renovation and modernization efforts, following plans approved by the Army. It is significant to note the recognition imparted to General Izurieta by all of the military branches, a phenomenon which — and here I make a leap of faith — will increase over time, providing considerable support for his leadership.

At the same time, Admiral Arancibia's command of the Navy seals the transition in the military world and brings to an end a period marked by a certain millenarian dogmatism.

It should also be noted that the retirement of the Minister of Defense, Edmundo Pérez Yoma, a both surprising and logical development, marks the end of a phase of conceptual and institutional preparation in the political world in relation to defense. The content and direction resulting from this preparation will gradually become more evident in the coming years. In the meantime, my comments are intended to help explain certain tendencies and project them into the sphere of defense. The following analysis emerges in part from the phenomena discussed above, but it has much more to do with our country's recent political history.

Politically, at the end of 1997 and the beginning of 1998, important questions are being raised regarding Chile's political climate. I believe that while developments in this area will have some impact upon the subject of defense, they will be irrelevant for the sector's progress. For this reason, I will judge this political climate with political arguments, although I include this phenomenon here because of the actors involved and their connection to the military world.

For some time, the democratic transition has been described as an extended process, and there seems to be no clear means to put an end to it. Some have identified specific moments as the end of the transition. However, for many others, defense issues and the political involvement of General Pinochet have prevented a declaration that the transition was over. Many — above all in the Concertación coalition — point to the need for constitutional reforms to complete the political transition. Others will believe that our democratic consolidation will commence with the termination of General Pinochet's senatorial position or with his retirement.

However, what sense does it make to declare the end of the transition? In my judgment, this is nothing more than a model designed by political engineers, with an ending that can never be reached. The transition cannot be simply concluded, since its phenomena have a historical nature, and there is still much unresolved history that awaits legal and constitutional reforms. A belligerent debate might arise on this subject, but it will take place within a tremendously stable country in some essential aspects. And such a debate, while unpleasant, may lead to recognition of what has really happened: the transition ended a while ago, at the moment when it was no longer viable to reverse the democratic process.

Nevertheless, we are witnessing a degradation of Chilean democracy which does not derive from the presence of certain political figures in Congress, but from the persistence of basic constitutional laws not suited to their time. The strict application of non-democratic constitutional law in a culturally democratic period will result not in a crisis of the rules — which can easily weather any attempt at reform — but rather a crisis of society. The instrumental consensus of 1989 was enough to permit the inauguration of the democracy of the 1990s, but it did not have the capacity to create a stable and enduring democratic society, and this lack has been evident for years now. The Concertación seems to understand this well, although it is wrong in insisting upon a single way of reforming the Constitution. But the Right, at present, does not grasp the fact that if these regulations are applied to them as a government — a natural possibility in a democracy — they could not govern Chile, but only administer it.

If no mechanism is found to make our Constitution compatible with democracy, we will witness the continuing degradation of our political system. In my judgment, this is the true legacy of admitting certain leaders of the military regime to the Senate. Yet, since institutions may also accomplish miracles, the exercise of democratic debate may carry us toward a genuinely national and republican view, toward a future which may either lie very far away, or closer than we imagine.

Economics

Chile's Development Strategy:
Growth With Equity

Joaquín Vial

Introduction

This paper seeks to contribute to the debate about the economic development strategy that will most effectively promote both economic growth and social equity. Over the past year, uncertainty about the proper economic model for Chile has become increasingly widespread. This is more than a little ironic, since the rest of Latin America looks to Chile as a model in the economic sphere.

The first section of this paper provides a brief overview of Chile's economic performance over the last decade, comparing it with that of earlier decades. The second section discusses the current sense of unease and disillusionment with the country's economic model. Next, we seek to determine the reasons for this disillusionment. As we shall see, some aspects of this unease are caused by the economic model itself; some are the result of long-term historical conditions which can be modified only gradually; and some represent temporary failings which can be addressed by government action to bring about greater equity in our society. The last section of this work presents some public policy considerations to be taken into account as our country faces the challenges of economic progress and equity.

I. Chile in the 1990s: A Clear Case of Economic Success

The classic indicators unmistakably reflect outstanding performance on the part of Chile's economy, both in relation to the past and in comparison with other countries.

Under the two administrations of the Concertación coalition, the economy has grown at an average annual rate of 7%, resulting in real per-capita income growth of more than 5% annually. Inflation has fallen from an average of 30% in the 1980s to single-digit levels in the 1990s. This trend may soon permit Chile to lower its inflation rate to the world average for the first time in over a century. Unemployment, which stood at 15% just a decade ago, has now dropped to 6%, considered by some to represent full employment.

This overall progress has led to significant improvements in living standards for the Chilean people, particularly the neediest groups. Income levels for the poorest Chileans have been rising at a rate equal to or greater than overall income. The proportion of the population living beneath the poverty line dropped from 45% in 1987 to 23% in 1996.

Perhaps the most encouraging aspect of these developments is the fact that, compared to earlier periods, Chile's economy now shows signs of being able to maintain this economic progress in the future. Domestic savings rates as a percentage of GDP have doubled compared to earlier decades; the fixed capital investment rate is close to 30% of GDP; foreign debt is falling; and direct investment as a percentage of all foreign capital flows is very high, compared to historic levels in Chile as well as rates in the rest of Latin America. Chilean companies are expanding and are beginning to invest abroad. Chile is internationally recognized for its high level of competitiveness, not only among developing countries, but on an international level, where it stands out clearly from the other economies in the region.

Among the factors responsible for Chile's stable and sustained growth, the most important has been the rise in domestic savings rates. Historically, Chile maintained a relatively low savings rate, forcing the country to depend on external financing to raise funds for investment. These foreign funds were channeled through the public sector, allowing the government to influence private investment activities with special offers of subsidized credit. In addition, interest rates were often subsidized indirectly through high levels of inflation.

The untenable nature of this situation became obvious with the repeated exchange rate crises in the post-war period, which continued up to the 1970s. A typical cycle in the Chilean economy would start with an abundance of dollars, derived, for example, from a successful foreign debt renegotiation or a rise in the price of copper. This permitted an expansion in investment, along with a rising exchange rate to limit inflation. The greater

TABLE 1

EVOLUTION AND COMPOSITION OF SAVINGS
(Percentage of GDP)

Year	Total Savings	External Savings	National Savings				
			Government	FEC	Public Companies	Remainder	Total
1985	17.2	9.4	0.4	0.0	n.d.	n.d.	7.8
1986	18.9	7.3	1.3	0.0	n.d.	n.d.	11.5
1987	22.2	5.0	3.0	0.5	n.d.	n.d.	17.3
1988	22.8	0.5	2.3	3.0	n.d.	n.d.	22.3
1989	25.5	1.8	3.0	3.7	n.d.	n.d.	23.7
1990	26.3	2.0	2.5	2.3	2.2	17.2	24.2
1991	24.5	0.4	3.7	0.7	1.7	18.0	24.1
1992	26.8	2.0	4.9	0.3	1.9	17.7	24.8
1993	28.8	4.8	4.8	-0.2	1.7	17.6	23.9
1994	26.8	1.4	4.8	0.2	1.2	19.2	25.4
1995	27.4	-0.2	5.3	1.0	1.3	20.0	27.6
1996	27.7	4.4	5.6	0.3	1.3	16.1	23.3

SOURCE: Central Bank and Budget Administration Office.

economic activity spurred by higher investment led to rising imports, which, after absorbing the temporary surplus of hard currency, began to put pressure on cash reserves. This would be followed by an exchange rate crisis, higher inflation, and a sharp drop in investment, induced by internal adjustment. More restrictive monetary policies would be implemented, and external savings flows would decline, driven away by the exchange rate crisis.

The structural changes in Chile's economy have broken this vicious cycle, which had reached a point where external savings stood at less than 2% of GDP. Internal savings began to grow, thanks to the government's promotion efforts and to the significant accumulation in individual savings through the social security system. The country's dependence on external savings was eliminated. In fact, the tremendous investment expansion of the 1990s was mainly financed with domestic funds. This turnaround has been so dramatic that external exchange rate shocks, such as those occurring in 1993, have had little or no effect on Chile's economic activity or its inflation rate.

TABLE 2

INDICATORS OF NATIONAL SOLVENCY
(Percentage of GDP)

Year	Checking Account Debt	Total External Debt	International Reserves	Net External Debt	Central Government Surplus
1980	6.9	25.1	14.3	25.1	5.9
1981	13.9	45.8	11.1	34.7	2.7
1982	9.0	67.1	10.1	57.0	-3.2
1983	5.5	89.4	10.0	79.3	-2.5
1984	10.8	100.4	10.5	89.9	-2.8
1985	8.6	124.6	11.3	113.2	-3.6
1986	6.3	110.2	9.4	100.8	-0.8
1987	3.9	99.8	9.0	90.8	1.9
1988	1.0	78.5	10.6	67.9	1.0
1989	2.5	62.1	10.5	51.7	1.4
1990	1.8	61.1	17.6	43.5	0.8
1991	-0.3	50.3	19.3	31.0	1.5
1992	1.6	44.4	21.1	23.3	2.2
1993	4.6	43.1	21.4	21.7	1.9
1994	1.2	41.7	25.8	15.9	1.7
1995	-0.2	32.4	22.0	10.4	2.5
1996	4.4	34.6	25.0	9.6	2.2

Sub-Period Averages

1980-85	9.1	77.8	11.2	66.5	-0.6
1986-95	2.2	62.4	16.7	45.7	1.4
1990-95	1.4	45.5	21.2	24.3	1.8
1986-96	2.4	59.8	17.4	42.4	1.5

A second group of key indicators also illustrates the solidity of the current growth process. Table 2 shows the accumulated external debt in Chile's economy, as well as figures for the public and private sectors, all expressed as a percentage of GDP.

The indicators presented here give evidence of the country's external solvency. The most important flow indicator is the current accounts deficit, which measures the degree of dependence on external savings. A country like Chile should generally maintain this figure at between 3% and 4% of GDP; this is the authorities' goal when setting macroeconomic policies. The table shows an impressive drop from the unsustainable deficit of 9% of GDP in the first half of the 1980s to an average deficit lower than 2% during the 1990s. The pattern exhibited by external assets and debt clearly reflects this turnaround. Foreign debt, which at its peak rose higher than 100% of GDP, is now only one-third of GDP, which is considered low by international standards.

International reserves have also increased, stabilizing at a level higher than 20% of GDP. This has caused the net international reserve debt to fall to a mere 10% of GDP. For the first time in decades, the external sector is no longer an impediment to economic growth, and the servicing of foreign debt has ceased to be an excessive burden on the Chilean people.

Notable progress has also been made in another long-standing problem area for Chile's economy: by 1996, the government had enjoyed an entire decade of budgetary surplus. These surpluses have enabled Chile to reduce its public external debt from almost US$18 billion in 1986 to just US$5.3 billion in 1996. They have also allowed the government to take money out of circulation, thus simplifying the work of the Central Bank. If this had not been possible, the Bank would not have been able to maintain its exchange rate policies — or it would have been forced to relax its monetary policy, with the resulting effect on inflation.

The evidence is sufficiently clear to justify the conclusion that after decades of searching for a formula for rapid and sustainable growth, Chile has finally found one. The country has overcome its economic backwardness, which Encina remarked upon in 1911 and which led Pinto to call Chile a case of "frustrated development" in the 1960s.

A market economy of sorts operated in Chile during the 1960s, with the private sector playing an important, though repressed and highly regulated, role. Yet it was clearly the economic reforms implemented by the military regime which brought about a radical change in the country's development model. The private sector became the dominant force in the economy, and the state limited itself to protecting fair competition and introducing corrective measures to counterbalance the country's highly unequal distribution of wealth, accentuated by the government's own economic reforms, the sale of public property and the financial measures implemented before the 1982-83 crisis.

The return to democracy was accompanied by a renewed focus on social equity, which had been absent from the economic models and policies dominant during the military regime. The first Concertación administration coined the slogan "Growth with Equity" to reassure those concerned with social issues and to provide a new standard for economic policy.

It is interesting to note that the Concertación retained the basic structural characteristics of the military regime's economic system. The new democratic government emphasized respect for private property, allowed the free market to continue operating with minimum interference, continued the privatization of state companies (although at a slower pace), and promoted the international opening of the economy. The government hoped that certain small but strategic changes in the economic structure, aimed at greater equity in labor relations and more effective regulation in areas of clear market failure (as in pollution, overfishing, and similar cases), would allow the economy to maintain its dynamism and become more equitable at the same time. Budgetary policy was also re-oriented, with a strong emphasis on the promotion of equity.

During the eight years of Concertación administration, the country's performance has justified the government's hopes. Economic progress has continued, while impressive strides have been made against poverty. Nevertheless, a feeling of unease is currently growing among members of the Concertación parties. Most people are satisfied with Chile's growth and macroeconomic accomplishments, but they are still skeptical about the country's progress in reducing inequality, protecting the environment, and resolving the growing daily problems faced by the population. These include urban congestion, crime, drugs, and drug-related violence. Many feel that Chile has made great progress, but that the lives of its people have not improved.

Within the leadership circles of the Concertación, there is general acceptance of the economic strategy which has brought so much material progress to our country. Yet the contrast between this strategy and the ideals cherished by many of these leaders in their younger years remains a sore point. It seems that even though the Concertación's policies have been largely successful, they still do not satisfy numerous leaders within the coalition.

In recent months, this dissatisfaction has been expressed through the criticism of continuing imbalances in the distribution of wealth and the apparent lack of progress in this area. More frequently than the quality of the data would merit, World Bank statistics are cited which show that Chile has the most unequal income distribution among similar countries in the region, implying the need for immediate and drastic action (see De Gregorio and Landerretche, 1998).

The statistics seem to show a highly unequal distribution of income in Chile, which has changed very little in recent times. When equivalent measurements are used, however, Chile does not seem to be worse off than the majority of Latin American countries. An important factor in comparing Chile with other countries is the high proportion of wealth concentrated in the richest segments of the population. The poorest groups in Chile earn a proportion of national income similar to that received by the poor in other countries. However, the richest earn a considerably higher share (almost 10% of all income) than in other, more egalitarian countries, at the expense of the middle class.

Anxiety over this issue has caused great tension within the government and the Concertación parties. The parties have become sounding boards for citizen concerns, while the administration, driven to achieve results, generally supports leaving the system as it is, while attempting to fine-tune its policies to respond to specific problems.

If these concerns over equity are to be translated into public policies, or into a proposal for a new model of development, the government must first identify alternatives to current policies. It must then determine whether these alternatives are viable within the existing economic system, and whether it is worth risking the economic progress already achieved in order to implement them.

II. Development Strategies and Society

One of the first things economics students learn is that the market system is much more neutral than one might think. Basically, it ensures the efficient use of resources within a given set of preconditions: the existing distribution of wealth, personal preferences, society's values and attitudes, available opportunities, production techniques, and so forth. A common viewpoint among economists, especially within academic circles, is that the majority of undesirable results which are usually attributed to the market are actually due to these preconditions. That is, they simply reflect the underlying values and social conditions which are the basis of individual decisions to buy and sell.[1] However, there are also many areas in which the market needs to be directed, corrected, or even repressed, in order to avoid serious inequalities and imbalances in the distribution of resources.

Socialist systems represented an attempt to construct a fairer economy without using market mechanisms. Their most serious shortcomings stemmed from the fact that socialist planners could not change certain fundamental aspects of human behavior. Because of the resulting proliferation of waste and inefficiency, these systems were not viable.

The option of replacing the market system itself can thus be rejected. The obvious alternative is to introduce corrective mechanisms to ensure the system's proper operation. This calls for a careful examination of poorly-functioning areas within the market system. Government analysts have tried to determine which of the emerging problems in Chilean society are related to the market system, and which stem from deeper dilemmas. These deeper problems will require targeted solutions which may or may not involve economic policy.

1. MARKET FAILURES AND THE COSTS OF PROGRESS

A brief review of the issues now gaining prominence on the public agenda will demonstrate the impact that market failures can have on the quality of life.

A frequent criticism of the current economic system involves the sense of helplessness felt by people burdened with the negative effects generated by others' pursuit of wealth. There are numerous examples: abuses (real or imagined) within public utility companies previously owned by the state; the disturbances caused by Gas Andes construction projects on the perimeter of Santiago; the destruction of native forests to produce wood chips for export; growing pollution problems in cities; and many more. In all of these cases, individuals or companies, in the interest of profit, undertake actions which cause harm to people who do not benefit from these actions and are not compensated for the damage caused. What almost all these cases have in common is a negative "externality" which is not corrected and thus will lead to socially undesirable decisions if left exclusively to market forces. The only exception is the natural monopoly held by public utilities; here, consumer exploitation is an inherent risk which must be avoided through appropriate regulatory mechanisms.

---

1 To be fair, we should mention that in a balanced economy, the salary levels of those participating in the productive process are a result of the system itself, which is why the system has such a big influence on income distribution. We will return to this point later.

An "externality" is nothing more than the simultaneous production of two or more goods, at least one of which is not marketable. For example, an industry might produce both wood pulp and toxic liquid waste. A car offers transportation services to its owner, but it causes congestion and delays for third parties, as well as emitting noxious exhaust. In these cases, something "bad" is associated with the production of a "good," and the producer of the good thing derives benefits from it but does not shoulder the costs of the "bad" things.[2] These are cases of market failure, since they encourage excessive production of the "bad" things along with the "good." This is a standard conclusion of conventional economic theories, recognized by even the strictest neoliberal economists.

When a country embarks upon an accelerated development process and experiences rapid material and economic progress, problems such as pollution and traffic congestion also arise. Quite often, these side effects associated with progress are the consequences of market failures, and they are not always recognized and penalized as they should be.[3]

Many of these problems only become evident once the economy begins to experience dynamic growth. In a stagnant economy, all of these problems are present, but they are more localized and do not evoke general concern. However, when the number of vehicles in a country, for example, begins to grow at annual levels higher than 10%, the social costs of the externalities associated with vehicle use quickly become evident.

The most difficult task is to find an effective way to correct for these negative effects. One proposed solution has been to nationalize companies, so that they will produce for the common good rather than for profit. This model has failed everywhere in the world, since it does not provide incentives for companies to efficiently produce the "good," and in the majority of cases it does not even encourage them to limit production of the associated "bad" effects.

The attitude taken toward these market failures is an important distinguishing element among various development theories. The neoliberal tendency is to play down these failures and their effects, pointing out that the costs of state regulation and intervention in such cases may be higher than the benefits achieved. The Concertación governments have emphasized the need to find more efficient corrective mechanisms. These may involve the promotion of more effective competition or market regulation through fixed prices, fees, technical standards, or other measures.

The modern tendency is to create institutional mechanisms, forcing private companies and consumers to take account of the cost of the "bad" things they produce into their decisions. Rather than substituting for the market, this approach seeks to support its operation, correcting for the presence of externalities. This sounds relatively simple, but it is not. It is a complex political and technical problem, which must take into account the characteristics of the legal system, the country's customs and traditions, its institutional capacities, the balance of power, and so forth. The recent controversies surrounding the

---

2 The opposite may also happen: an additional, non-marketable "good" may be produced simultaneously with a commercially valuable product. In this case, people tend to invest less than the socially desirable amount in these activities. One example of this is a tree plantation, which not only produces wood but also captures carbon dioxide from the atmosphere and protects soil and watersheds.

3 It should not be assumed that these are the only types of problems associated with development. Material progress tends to create a link between the idea of success and the improvement of one's economic status, leading to modifications of traditional values and customs.

passage of the fisheries and Native Forests bills, to mention two recent cases involving environmental regulation, suggest how difficult it is to establish corrective mechanisms when markets fail due to externalities.

A second area of criticism of the market system focuses on the unequal distribution of income. This issue became a worldwide concern in the 19th century, with tremendous political repercussions. Early critics maintained that the market undervalued the contribution of labor, and alternative theories arose to explain the value of goods and services. Over the years, this point of view lost ground, in the face of evidence that attempts to pay workers more than the indicated market value led to serious distortions in the distribution of resources as well as burgeoning unemployment, especially among unskilled workers and other disadvantaged groups.

A later theory pointed to market failures caused by the huge power imbalance between employers and employees, which allowed the owners of capital to appropriate an unfair share of profits. This line of thought led to worker protection mechanisms such as unions and labor legislation. These fully-justified measures have been implemented in all Western economies, where unions have become powerful and influential. However, in many places, these organizations have expanded beyond prudent bounds, leading to lower rates of job creation and competitiveness, and even to increased corruption in some countries. It is not surprising that there is a tendency throughout Latin America to support more flexible labor systems, while simultaneously maintaining legal protections for workers' basic rights, including the opportunity for collective bargaining in the workplace.

During the post-war era, in both the developed and developing world, the state assumed a much more active role in the distribution of wealth. Governments provided direct subsidies to the poor and expanded their support for services such as health care, education, and social security. This heightened social activism was financed by increased taxation, which in the majority of European countries had a strong redistributive slant. Unfortunately, in developing countries, with their weak institutions and meager resources, attempts to construct welfare states produced large budget deficits, destabilizing the economy and hindering growth.[4]

A wide range of policies aimed at improving income distribution have been applied in different countries at various times. In Latin America, with its highly unequal distribution of both wealth and income, these policies have clearly emphasized the redistribution of assets: agrarian reform, nationalization of mining companies, and income tax rates intended to be highly progressive.[5]

One of the biggest merits of these asset-based policies is that they break the exclusive link between equity issues and the operation of labor markets. In the 1960s and 1970s, governments begin to emphasize the importance of narrowing the existing gaps in income and human capital, and thus the redistributive efforts within the labor market gradually began to lose their central place as a focus of public policy.

---

4 Developed countries have also experienced budgetary imbalances in their attempts to finance the welfare state, due to disparities between the dynamic evolution of income sources and the rising costs of health care and education, and also due to perverse incentives generated by social security systems and unemployment benefits.

5 In practice, tax rates have not been progressive, because they are distorted by numerous legislative and administrative mechanisms.

In the 1970s, and even more so in the 1980s, governments begin to emphasize the goal of poverty reduction, by means of accelerated economic growth and public policy measures aimed at the neediest groups. The issue of inequality itself was pushed to the back burner, especially in developing countries.

2. THE MARKET AND SOCIETY'S FAILURES

A common criticism of market systems is their "unfeeling" nature, since, in order to operate effectively and generate employment, they supposedly "require" the existence of salaries which are insufficient to provide a dignified living. The root of the problem is that a person's need for income and the value of his or her contribution to the productive process do not necessarily coincide. In some cases, this may simply be a "natural" reflection of the innate capacities of each person. However, it may also stem from deeper problems in society, such as a shortage of opportunities for individuals to develop marketable skills.

Unfortunately, this problem is complicated by the fact that in a market economy, opportunities are closely linked to existing wealth. The wealthy enjoy better health care starting in the womb, along with better educational opportunities, resources which stimulate and facilitate personal development, and so forth. This produces a natural tendency whereby income discrepancies (which are inevitable when people are paid according to their contribution to the productive process) become differences in opportunities, not only for those who earn the income, but also for their descendants. The situation is exacerbated by the accumulation of wealth through the generations.

Some might think that this problem only affects developing countries with cultural traditions that severely limit social mobility. However, it is a much more general phenomenon. In countries with considerable social mobility, such as the United States, studies have shown that children of high-income families tend to earn higher incomes than those who come from poor households (For example, Naga 1996).

Thus, the allocation of resources in a functioning market depends in part on the pre-existing distribution of wealth and opportunities. If these "initial conditions" are distributed in an unequal fashion, the market tends to perpetuate these inequalities. The challenge is consequently to correct the initial conditions. For the most part, a society's failure to satisfactorily resolve its equity problems points to underlying deficiencies in its values and forms of organization.

How far can redistributive policies advance before they begin to hamper general progress? There are no objective limits. If individualism predominates in society, and success is measured by individual material well-being, public acceptance of voluntary or compulsive redistributive actions will be very limited. On the other hand, if social solidarity predominates, and people are valued for who they are and not for what they have, philanthropy will be more common, and people will be more likely to tolerate tax increases for redistributive efforts.

Table 3 shows information about income distribution by quintile, according to the 1994 Casen survey. These figures demonstrate the importance of autonomous income compared to subsidies at all income levels, even the lowest. This suggests that even a substantial increase in direct subsidies is not enough to significantly change income distribution.

A second notable aspect is the importance of indirect transfers to the poor, through

TABLE 3

COMPOSITION OF INCOME, BY QUINTILE : 1994

(Monthly averages of household income in 1994 pesos)

	INCOME QUINTILE				
	I	II	III	IV	V
I. Autonomous Income	64,102	122,813	180,879	274,214	860,242
Income from work	56,899	106,295	150,174	218,908	708,634
Other autonomous income	7,203	16,518	30,705	55,306	151,608
Retirement and Pensions	5,233	13,578	24,293	38,305	75,261
Capital Income	358	1,011	4,071	12,498	69,503
Other Income	1,612	1,930	2,342	4,504	6,844
II. Monetary Subsidies	3,582	2,986	2,108	1,408	653
Unemployment Subsidy	65	66	42	28	4
Family Allocations	1,458	1,448	1,028	744	373
PASIS	1,175	1,114	884	514	146
SUF	855	332	122	47	24
Other Subsidies	29	27	33	76	107
III. Total Monetary Income	67,684	125,799	182,987	275,621	860,895
IV. Attributes of Social Cost	35,774	25,594	17,951	9,359	8,940
Education	20,974	15,667	10,988	8,137	4,470
Heath	14,800	9,927	6,963	1,222	4,470
V. Total Income	103,458	151,393	200,938	284,980	869,835

SOURCE: Ministry of Planning and Cooperation, 1994 Casen Survey.

social spending on health and education. This spending is a vital contribution to social equity, because it creates opportunities for the children of the poorest families, yet it is not included in the traditional measurements of income distribution.

A third aspect, important in this case because it points to a weakness in the information collected, is the surprisingly low level of capital returns within the income figures provided by this survey. This is striking when one observes the functional income distribution obtained from the National Accounts, showing that employee salaries constitute around 35% of all income, representing some 42% of total profits. One possible explanation of this disparity is that Casen's measurements may include non-salary income under the category of paid work. This income may be highly significant in the case of the self-employed, professionals, and entrepreneurs.

The lesson from these figures is relatively simple: if income consists principally of payment for contributions to the productive process (work and capital), and if these contributions are mainly predetermined, changes in primary income distribution (the distribution of autonomous income) will necessarily be slow.

Of course, there are exceptions to the rule. In revolutionary periods bringing about massive changes in property ownership, or in periods of far-reaching structural reform accompanied by equally profound changes in the relative price of assets, it is possible to rapidly alter income distribution. However, there is no cause for enthusiasm about this option, since such transformations are highly traumatic, putting the democratic political system itself at risk. Additionally, the high level of instability in these situations leads to uncertainty about property rights, which can have lasting effects on investment, seriously compromising the country's prospects for growth.

Thus, while there is a good amount states can do to construct more egalitarian and fair societies, there are real limits as to their ability to alter income distribution over the short term. History has repeatedly proven that individuals' expectations of material success for themselves and their descendants are one of the strongest motivations in life, influencing a great number of personal decisions. All parents hope to secure improved health care and educational opportunities for their children. A society which is very strict in ensuring equal opportunities will probably strangle its principal motor of economic and material progress. This option may be valid for very rich countries, but it is certainly not for poor ones. Thus, it is the very societies with the most marked inequalities which find it harder to impose redistributive measures on assets and income, thus perpetuating their poverty.

Building up human capital among poor and middle-class groups through social spending on education and health care seems to be the most effective way to create more equal opportunities. These measures, of course, run up against the limits of taxation that middle and upper-income groups will tolerate, restricting the resources available.

Finally, it should be pointed out that the will to act is not enough; measures must also be highly effective and efficient. Few countries will tolerate tax increases to fund social programs if results are not observed over time and the resources appear to be wasted.

3. WHAT CAN WE ASK OF THE ECONOMIC SYSTEM?

Every economic system includes a mechanism for allocating resources as well as a set of institutions and regulations. The allocation mechanism should provide incentives and feedback in order to distribute resources efficiently and achieve stable, long-term growth.

In our society, as in most of the world, market mechanisms are used to allocate resources. Historical evidence clearly demonstrates that the market is the most effective instrument for this purpose, when it is supported by regulations and institutions to protect property rights and the validity of contracts. These are the minimum requirements for the efficient operation of the market. Furthermore, in order for the system to operate well, the market must also reflect the opportunity costs of goods and resources as clearly and transparently as possible. This means that competition must be present, and it must be easy to transfer goods between various regions of the country and different branches of the economy. The denser the economic activity, and the higher the number of participants in the market, the better the market will represent the true value of the goods traded.

Experience has shown that the majority of countries choosing market mechanisms have enjoyed comparatively rapid growth and have thus been able to make inroads against poverty. However, a passive state attitude is not enough. Ongoing action is necessary to ensure effective competition, protection, and expansion of property rights, and correction of the deficiencies which often impede the market. An efficient market needs an active and vigilant state.

An economic system producing steady growth should allow systematic gains in living standards at all levels of society. There is no "economic law" stating that market economies lower the quality of life for middle- and lower-class groups. The oft-cited "Kuznetz Curve," which points to an increase in inequality during the early stages of economic growth, has been theoretically refuted and shown to lack empirical evidence (Bruno, Ravallion, and Squire 1996).

However, it is not sufficient simply to maintain growth rates and keep income distribution from worsening. If intolerable inequality is the starting point, and a high proportion of the population lives in poverty, a "neutral" system promising "long-term" change is not enough. Moral considerations and even the pursuit of other social goals demand advances in poverty reduction and the correction of the most severe inequalities. This is not an easy task.

Can we demand that growth be accompanied by a reduction in social inequality? Strictly speaking, a pure market economy does not adequately ensure that this will happen, even if the state intervenes to correct distortions produced by externalities and inadequate competition. As we have seen, inequalities are the product of a poor initial distribution of physical, human, and financial resources, along with social and cultural structures that impede social mobility. The market itself tends to perpetuate these conditions rather than alter them. This is universally recognized, and even the strictest neo-liberal economists acknowledge the state's role in ensuring access for the poor to basic public goods such as education, health care, and social security.

Thus, public policies must be used to bring about a more egalitarian society. Furthermore, the state's responsibility increases according to the magnitude of the problems faced by a society, such as the number of people living below the poverty line, the level of access to quality education and health care, and people's capacity to save for retirement. If these indicators are unfavorable, and if they are accompanied by a high concentration of property in the hands of the rich, the construction of an egalitarian society will be extremely difficult, and results will likely appear only over the long term. How fast a country can make these changes also depends on its values and institutions. This is where political action plays an important role. Social priorities and institutions are not immutable, and those who wish to see rapid advances toward greater equity must strive to win broad acceptance for their point of view.

In summary, in a thriving economic system with healthy prospects for growth and development, wages must reflect real contributions to the productive process. Growth will help reduce poverty, but it is not likely be sufficient, since many poor people lack the initial resources to participate in a market economy. This is where public policies to combat poverty are needed, consisting of direct income transfers to the poorest groups, along with programs to help the poor successfully integrate themselves into the economic system. However, efforts aimed at increased equity should not be limited to the very poor. Inequalities in living conditions, political participation, and access to education, justice, health care, and social security are broader problems. Governments should thus promote policies to create equal opportunities throughout society.

Therefore, when we speak of "growth with equity," we mean that promoting growth is fundamental to our country's development strategy, but it must be accompanied by poverty reduction and increased opportunity. Harmonizing these two objectives is not easy, and states should concentrate their efforts upon the areas where growth and equity are most compatible, such as investment in education. Experience has clearly shown that drastic measures to correct income distribution over the short term can have extremely negative effects on economic growth. These measures tend to produce large budget deficits or rising taxes, along with uncertainty over property rights, which discourages investment.

4. CHILE'S PROGRESS TO DATE

As we mentioned in the first section of this paper, it is undeniable that Chile's recent economic performance has been highly satisfactory, and that the country's social programs have also achieved impressive results, most clearly demonstrated by the significant reduction in poverty during this period. Yet criticism has recently become more intense, focusing on two issues in particular: social and environmental policies.

While Chile is faced with serious environmental problems, we believe there are reasons to be optimistic in this area. It can be argued that Chile did not possess the institutional strength to effectively regulate a dynamic market economy; thus, the country was not able to prevent environmental problems from arising. Yet during the past decade, Chile has acted to modernize and improve its institutions. There are grounds for hope that development will begin to have a positive rather than a negative effect on our country's ecosystems and natural resources.

On the social front, the most frequent criticism is that the government has not fulfilled its pledge of linking increased growth to more equitable income distribution. However, if we examine certain indicators, especially within the labor market, we see that the system has created favorable conditions for increased equality. Unemployment rates have fallen, salaries have improved, the poor are better represented in the labor force, and public sector and minimum wages have significantly improved in real terms. It is doubtful that one can expect much more. While it is true that injustices are still numerous, including violations of labor regulations, it would have been difficult for employment levels and real salaries to have grown faster than they did over the past five years. The clearest demonstration of this is the fact that real salaries and average worker productivity increased at a similar rate. Attempts to raise salaries faster than this would likely stall the pace of job creation.

Table 4 shows employment patterns over the past few years and demonstrates the increase in overall employment, especially among women.

TABLE 4

JOB MARKET INDICATORS 1989-96

Year	Thousands of Jobs			Employment Rate			Unemployment Rate		
	Total	Men	Women	Total	Men	Women	Total	Men	Women
1989	4,412	3,098	1,314	52.6	75.8	30.5	7.9	6.8	10.6
1995	5,192	3,521	1,671	54.8	76.7	34.0	7.3	6.3	9.5
1996	5,249	3,600	1,649	53.3	74.2	33.1	6.3	5.6	7.9

SOURCE: National Statistics Institute.

TABLE 5

EVOLUTION OF REAL WAGES, 1989-96
(Base: April 1993 = 100)

YEAR	GENERAL	PRIVATE	PUBLIC	MINIMUM INCOME
1989	88.2	89.7	83.8	84.2
1995	111.0	108.7	117.1	116.5
1996	115.0	111.7	123.9	121.4
% CHANGE				
1989-1995	25.9	21.2	39.8	38.3
1989-1996	30.4	24.6	47.9	44.1

SOURCE: National Statistics Institute.

Table 5 shows the increase in real wages, which grew by 28% in the period covered by the chart. The "government, community, and social services" category, including almost the entire public sector, has enjoyed the most impressive gains. Thus, the downward trend in public sector salaries during the 1980s has been reversed. The minimum wage, which directly or indirectly affects 16% of the employed work force, has risen at above-average rates. In fact, it has regained the exceptionally high levels of the early 1980s, yet with the difference that the overall rise in productivity in today's economy indicates that these figures are not merely a symptom of instability.

One important issue that has not received enough attention from researchers is the unequal income distribution among salaried workers. It has been suggested that these inequalities are on the rise, and that employment is becoming more "informalized." However, no systematic examination of empirical evidence has yet been undertaken to confirm these conclusions. In one of the few scholarly contributions to this debate (Meller and Tokman 1996), the authors show that salary differences between white-collar and blue-collar workers are greater in the 1990s than they were in the 1970s; however, this differential was reduced during the greatest surge in exports (starting in the second half of the 1980s). Related studies (such as Meller and Escobar 1996) demonstrate a convergence in the salaries paid by large companies in Santiago and in the regions, which has not occurred among small companies.

It should be noted, however, that the question of equity does not end with the labor market. Other economic sectors must be examined, especially returns on capital investment and related public policies.

The period of democratic reconstruction has affected returns on capital in two significant ways, which may not be repeatable in the future. The first was a sharp rise in the value of existing capital, as a result of the consolidation of the market economy system and the elimination of uncertainties in property transactions after 17 years of military rule. The second factor has been the high real interest rates, especially in relation to the rest of the world, deriving from government attempts to contain the inflationary pressures associated with rising investment, which expanded from 21% of GDP in 1988 to more than 27% in 1995.

TABLE 6

FINANCIAL CAPITAL YIELD
(Real annual averages)

Year	15 year Mortgage Bills (and longer)	Average Rate of Return Pension Fund Yield	Real Stock Prices % Change in General Stock Price Index
1985	8.6	13.4	-3.0
1986	6.8	12.3	63.9
1987	6.7	5.4	52.4
1988	6.4	6.5	7.6
1989	7.5	6.9	27.6
1990	8.2	15.6	21.6
1991	6.4	29.7	83.3
1992	6.9	3.0	21.5
1993	7.0	16.2	-2.2
1994	6.4	18.2	39.8
1995	6.5	-2.5	-4.2
1996	6.6	3.5	-11.6

SOURCE: Stock Exchange and AFP Superintendent.

In normal circumstances, both factors would have resulted in impressive capital earnings favoring the wealthiest groups in society. However, the workers also profited in this case, since a considerable proportion of the country's pension funds were invested in stocks and thus enjoyed a strong appreciation in value. This helped to diffuse the distinction between workers and capitalists; what would normally have caused a strong concentration of property instead expanded capital ownership to middle- and lower-class groups.

Another way to examine equity is to track the progress of the poverty rate. The results here have been good, with a relatively high number of people rising out of poverty for each percentage point of economic growth, compared to other countries (De Gregorio and Cowan 1996). This trend became even more favorable during the 1990s, as the job market stabilized and government social spending increased.

Analysis of progress in the quest for equal opportunities is a bit more complex, because it is difficult to obtain systematic data on this subject. To point to a lack of equal opportunity, analysts generally use income distribution figures. In Chile, these show that income is highly concentrated in the hands of the rich, a tendency which has hardly changed in recent years. However, this is only one part of the problem, and equal opportunity studies based on these statistics alone are neither dynamic nor complete. The biggest problem is that these indicators are not designed to show social mobility. There are no data to tell us if those identified among the poorest groups in the Casen survey are the same people who were living below the poverty line in 1987, 1992, or 1994. Nor do we know how many households have moved from one income quintile to another. Yet mobility among income levels is a key factor for evaluating the egalitarianism of a society. Highly unequal income distribution with considerable movement among quintiles is not the same as the identical distribution with no mobility.

TABLE 7

INDICATORS OF EQUITY IN THE EDUCATIONAL SYSTEM

	1988	1994	1996
% performance on SIMCE math test			
- Municipal	48.3	65.4	67.9
- Subsidized Individual	54.7	71.4	73.2
- Paid Individual	73.3	86.4	85.6
Monthly subsidy by student (1996 dollars)	8,867.0	11,297.0	15,408.0

NOTE: Refers to fourth year basic student performance.
SOURCE: Compendium of Statistical Information, Education Ministry.

Available data also provides no information about mobility between generations. How many of today's rich come from middle- and lower-class families? We currently have no way of knowing, and we will not know until institutions begin to carry out surveys tracking individuals and households over the years. Some incomplete statistics show significant progress in a few areas; for example, we can see that the children of poor families today receive more years of schooling than their parents did, especially in rural areas.

We also have evidence of change in the quality of public services for middle- and lower-income groups. It is true, for example, that children at subsidized private schools perform better on standardized (SIMCE) tests than public school students, and that children at full-tuition private schools achieve the highest scores of all. Thus, we can assume in general that poor children are receiving a lower-quality education than rich children. However, this gap in educational quality has decreased over time, because performance at public schools has improved at a faster rate than performance at the other types of schools. This can be explained in part by an average increase in real government spending per student.

These improvements are even more noticeable in the 900 schools singled out for special government support because of their relatively poor performance and the poverty of the communities they serve. Although their students' average test scores are still lower than those at other schools, they have improved significantly in recent years, from 54.7% in 1988 to 67.7% in 1994. This demonstrates the decreasing gap in quality among Chile's three types of educational institutions. The proposed lengthening of the school day will principally benefit middle- and lower-income students, since the majority of full-tuition private schools already operate on a longer schedule.

Examining health care, we can also see a narrowing gap between spending per patient in public versus private health care, although very little is known about the objective standards of care in each of these areas. Public health care is still viewed as inadequate and overburdened, but waiting periods appear to have shortened. Infant mortality and deaths in childbirth have dropped significantly, which clearly reflects better public health care, as well as better coverage of the groups at highest risk.

The figures presented above indicate that Chile's economic system, which is made up of both market and public policy components, is moving in the right direction. Overall, employment is at satisfactory levels. The public sector, however, still shows a serious inability to provide high-quality social services. Chile's population still suffers from extreme imbalances in opportunity, and a high percentage of the population lives close to or below the poverty line. The improvements mentioned above represent advances, but today's situation remains far from ideal. The central question, however, is whether there are other, substantially different paths the government might take which would bring faster results. The answer is clearly no.

Certain specific aspects of government policy can certainly be improved. Yet all indicators show that the current economic system, combined with our country's determination to build a more equal society, will be sufficient to simultaneously bring about accelerated improvements in the standard of living of the population and a gradual reduction in inequality, especially in the opportunities provided to our nation's children.

III. Constructing the Society We Deserve

We have seen in the previous sections that a market economy open to foreign investment, in which the private sector plays an important role, is capable of generating dynamic growth as long as certain basic institutions, such as the legal system, are operating effectively. We saw that the system can even significantly reduce poverty, if the poorest groups are able to gain access to the job market. Yet we have also seen that these conditions have not been sufficient to significantly improve social equity. This is a serious problem in a country such as Chile, not only for ethical reasons, but also because it casts a shadow of doubt over the existing economic and political systems.

It is also very clear that the market alone does not resolve resource allocation issues, especially where many negative externalities are present. The escalating problems of air pollution and traffic congestion in Santiago are obvious examples. These situations call for state intervention; however, if state programs are poorly designed or executed, they can worsen the situation, as has been the case with vehicle restrictions.

1. DEMYSTIFICATION OF RESOURCE ALLOCATION MECHANISMS

The reflections above make clear that a country's economic model should be dissociated from ideological considerations. In the past, being pro-market was equated with being pro-capital and anti-worker. To support state action, on the other hand, was to be for the workers and thus for the poor. These associations arose from causal connections which are now obsolete. Resource allocation mechanisms such as the market should be viewed simply as instruments to achieve improvements in well-being. Considerations of equity and fair distribution are fundamental for the evaluation of these instruments. Yet these considerations do not necessarily lead to a slant in favor of state interference in markets or state production of goods and services.

The selection of instruments cannot be separated from budgetary policy aimed at correcting social problems. For example, a realistic charge for household water services, permitting an acceptable return on capital, is a prerequisite for inducing the private sector to invest in this area and offer its services to the community. Yet poor families may not be able to pay the market price. Chile's solution, which seems to be the most appropriate, has been to provide subsidies to the poorest families, identified through CAS cards. Thus, governments can use policy remedies to compensate for the burden on poor families represented by the market cost of water services.

This is an interesting example, because it also reflects the market's inability to assure an adequate supply of this resource. The distribution of drinking water to households is clearly a natural monopoly; leaving this market open to the arbitrary fluctuations of supply and demand would lead to the exploitation of consumers through unnecessarily high prices and inferior service. Therefore, in cases like this the state must intervene by fixing prices, not for redistributive reasons (the wealthy are large consumers of water), but to counteract the distortions caused by the monopolistic nature of this service.

The case of water also offers an interesting lesson about misguided public policy. The cost-free concession of perpetual water rights is a grave market distortion which has favored the concentration of ownership of a scarce and vital resource. This has had a severe impact on efficiency in key sectors such as power generation, agriculture, and mining. It has also caused a concentration of wealth, with the obvious negative impact on overall income distribution.

Thus, our first proposal for the economic system is the demystification of resource allocation mechanisms. The market almost always offers the best solution to problems of resource allocation, leading to the most efficient methods for producing and distributing goods and services. In exceptional cases, this is not enough, and the state must impose regulations or other mechanisms to resolve the problem (Bitrán and Sáez 1998).

2. PUBLIC POLICIES MUST PROMOTE EQUITY

A second conclusion arising from the foregoing analysis is that public policy, and specifically budgetary policy, cannot be neutral on the subject of equity. Government policies should be aimed at assisting society's poorest groups, as well as improving the distribution of wealth, income, and access to opportunities. Thus, more "efficient" policies are not necessarily the best ones, unless they are accompanied by compensatory measures.

Pro-market policies aimed at accelerating growth, for example, must be justified by the fact that they provide better opportunities for the poor to enter the job market, or that they generate the resources necessary to provide assistance and services to the needy. We must remember that growth has its costs, and in many cases, such as the environment, these may be significant. Growth is not the ultimate goal, to be prioritized above all others.

When governments design public policies to create a more egalitarian society, they must take special care with measures that redistribute capital assets or that significantly affect the value of resources. We have already seen that altering income flows and distribution is quite difficult, since they are predetermined by the existing distribution of wealth. When authorities take measures that lead to the redistribution of real assets, they should pay close attention to the consequences, since these will be permanent. For example, when the government gives free perpetual water rights to a select group; when it hands out fishing quotas for free; when it alters soil use regulations; or when it pardons debt or waives payments for the construction of irrigation systems, this helps the rich get richer. This is the inevitable result of such action in a market economy, and care must be taken to minimize it. If the state wishes to offer public goods to the private sector, it should sell them at auction, and the selling price should reflect appropriate compensation for the rest of society. The same is true for mining concessions, and so forth. The state must also be extremely rigorous in collecting on loans it has granted.

Changes in regulations inevitably trigger capital gains and losses. The neo-liberal solution — eliminating regulations altogether — has the same effect, but instead of depending on the regulatory discretion of public servants, it depends on the initial distribution of assets and on chance (although, of course, those who start with nothing cannot hope to gain).

Full transparency, along with strict prosecution of cases of illicit influence, are prerequisites for effective state regulation. The government must also design a tax system that adequately taxes capital gains and earnings. Thus, it is completely unacceptable for the government to postpone property appraisals year after year, especially those for farmland.[6] If certain sectors are experiencing hard times, this will be directly reflected in the value of assets. A regular and flexible appraisal system is the best way to assist those facing the devaluation of their assets as a result of systematic, rather than individual, problems.

3. THE NEED FOR STATE EFFICIENCY AND MODERNIZATION

In its quest to help create a more equitable society, the government must rigorously examine the effectiveness and efficiency of its activities. Poorly-spent funds are resources diverted from the highest-priority task, which is to promote fair and equal opportunities for the entire population to advance. Every peso taken from taxpayers must be spent for the benefit of all. This calls for a systematic analysis of state income and spending.

This may sound similar to neo-liberal thinking, but there is a big difference. Neo-liberal analysis calls for increased state efficiency and a reduced tax burden in order to diminish not only the state's productive role and its capacity to "interfere" in the market, but also its capacity to redistribute income and to invest in programs aiding the poor. In our case, on the other hand, efficiency is recognized as a vital tool in the promotion of social equity.

4. NON-ECONOMIC EQUITY CONSIDERATIONS

A common problem with economics-centered ideologies is that they tend to stress economic factors in defining personal well-being. While these factors are important, they are not the only relevant elements in the search for equity. For example, the creation of a swifter, more efficient, and more accessible justice system is a fundamental imperative for a democratic system which hopes to uphold human dignity.

When public policy alternatives are evaluated, the government must take these non-economic factors into account. Intense political battles have been waged to achieve marginal improvements in the economic situation of the middle and lower classes, but comparable efforts have not been undertaken in other areas that directly affect human dignity and the quality of life.

Chile's recent history offers examples of governmental measures in support of the lower and middle classes which transcend economic considerations. Justifying agrarian reform, such as that carried out in the 1960s in purely economic terms, has become increasingly difficult. However, that reform gave a fundamental boost to farm workers'

---

6 It should be remembered that the tax rate is based on presumed income, which in turn is based on the appraised value of the property.

dignity and self-respect, as well as furthering their integration into the rest of society. Initiatives such as "Promoting the People" and many others have helped to create a sense of community and have facilitated grassroots participation in solving everyday problems. These are examples of investments in equity and well-being which go far beyond simple economic considerations.

5. AS MUCH EQUITY AS POSSIBLE

The great failure of the socialist systems was that their naively populist theories did not take medium- and long-term consequences into account. Socialist policies ultimately did more harm than good because their effects were immediate but transitory. Chile has learned this lesson, as evidenced in the phrase which has become a cliché in our country: "While we must preserve macroeconomic equilibrium, we must also . . . "

This maxim must be followed without compromise if we are to avoid undesirable consequences. An economic order must be established and preserved that allows improvements to be permanent, not fleeting. No country can advance toward equity by consciously sacrificing "a little bit of macroeconomic equilibrium."

Of course, the methods for maintaining this equilibrium are not chiseled in stone. New disagreements constantly arise among macroeconomists as to the feasibility and effectiveness of certain measures, although they may all agree on the goals. Yet this does not imply that authorities may deliberately relax macroeconomic discipline to pursue the goal of equity. Economic theory, international experience, and Chilean history show that any advances gained thereby will be ephemeral ones, and the final result may even cause harm to the very groups with the least ability to defend themselves against adverse economic conditions: the poor.

Thus, policymakers must be both hard-headed and responsible when evaluating how far and how fast a government can advance in the achievement of equity. They must also be cautious when choosing among competing policies. The attempt to solve too many problems at once can be dangerous and even counterproductive. The overreaching activism of the Left in general, and the Latin American Left in particular, may itself be a significant obstacle to the reduction of poverty and the expansion of opportunities in society.

6. EXPANDING THE BOUNDARIES OF THE POSSIBLE

An economist should be aware of the limits of what is possible in the achievement of equity. However, when economists propose a particular path to be followed in a country's development, this proposal should also include ways to gradually expand the range of possibilities for the achievement of equity. In a relatively poor country such as Chile, chances for advancement among the poorest groups is limited by the population's cultural and consumption patterns, especially among the middle and upper classes.

In a society where individualism predominates, and progress is considered to be synonymous with the expansion of personal consumption, the spread of egalitarianism will be very slow. Political representatives will press for gradual reductions in the tax burden, and public policy will promote growth at all costs. A society like this, at the end of the 20th century, faces an ongoing risk of social unrest or the emergence of populist movements which may produce economic instability and even endanger the democratic system itself.

Our proposal must include an appeal to the people to moderate their lifestyles and their economic aspirations. This is necessary in order to finance investments in human capital as well as income transfers to poorer groups. Excess consumption not only offends and harms the poor, but also degrades the environment and diverts investment from worthier projects. Changes in lifestyle are also necessary to ensure the sustainability of economic growth (see Escudero and Lerda 1996). This is a tremendous challenge at a time when the whole world seems to be promoting individualism.

Chile has been a pioneer in many ways over the past decade, and many consider our country a model to be followed. But this "model" may yet fail, if it does not produce a shared commitment to solidarity capable of reducing the gaps in power, income, and opportunities that currently divide our society. The only way to achieve this is through a profound change in values. We must increase our respect for each other and for the environment, while restraining the hedonist appetites which have led to ballooning consumption and the severe stress of excessive indebtedness for many Chileans. The public sector must exercise strong leadership in this regard, and politicians must set an example by making their own lifestyles more restrained and by expressing greater solidarity.

If appeals and examples are not sufficient, it will be necessary to review the tax structure for ways to improve the allocation of resources and to discourage conspicuous and unnecessary consumption. Luxury taxes, for example, might someday serve their intended purpose, although today they are nothing but a source of wealth and privilege for those who can benefit from their loopholes.

If our goal is to maintain an economic system which generates greater levels of wealth and distributes that wealth more fairly, we must foster a sincere and profound concern for equity at all levels of society. Those who currently enjoy luxury should make their lifestyles more austere. We may dream about the "perfect" system, but if our values do not change, any system we implement will remain distorted, serving the interests not of the many but of the few.

BIBLIOGRAPHICAL REFERENCES

Bitrán, E. and R. E. Sáez. 1998. "Mercado, Estado y Regulación," in R. Cortázar and J. Vial, eds. *Construyendo opciones*. Santiago: Cieplan-Dolmen.

Bruno, M., M. Ravallion, and L. Squire. 1996. "Equity and Growth in Developing Countries." Policy Research Working Paper 1563. World Bank.

Cortázar, R. and J. Vial, eds. 1998. *Construyendo opciones*. Santiago: Cieplan-Dolmen.

De Gregorio, J. and O. Landerretche. 1998. "Equidad, distribución y desarrollo integrador." In: R. Cortázar and J. Vial, eds.

De Gregorio, J. and K. Cowan. 1996. "Distribución del ingreso y pobreza en Chile: ¿Estamos mal? ¿Ha habido progresos? ¿Hemos retrocedido?" Table No. 5. Santiago: Ministerio de Hacienda. Mimeograph.

Escudero, J. and S. Lerda. 1996. "Implicancias ambientales de los cambios en los patrones de consumo en Chile," in O. Sunkel, ed.: *Sustentabilidad ambiental del crecimiento económico chileno*. Santiago: Universidad de Chile.

Escudero, J. and J. Vial. 1998. "El medio ambiente como una nueva dimensión del desarrollo," in R. Cortázar and J. Vial, eds.

Meller, P., ed. 1996. *El modelo exportador chileno. Crecimiento y equidad*. Santiago: Cieplan.

Meller, P. and A. Tokman. 1996. "Apertura comercial y diferencial salarial en Chile." In: P. Meller, ed.

Meller, P. and B. Escobar. 1996. "Efecto regional del modelo exportador: evolución del diferencial salarial entre regiones y Santiago." In: P. Meller, ed.

Naga, R.H.A. 1996. "Family Background, Intergenerational Mobility and Earnings Distribution: Evidence from the United States." Lausanne: Lausanne University. Mimeograph.

Productive Transformation:
Competitiveness and Job Creation

Osvaldo Rosales

I. Principal Traits of Chile's Economic Development

The Chilean economy has enjoyed vigorous and uninterrupted growth over the last 14 years, the longest growth cycle the country has ever recorded.[1] Since 1990, the country has moved from conditions of external debt, high unemployment rates and poverty to sustained growth, macroeconomic stability, record levels of savings and investment, strong increases in productivity, and considerable trade growth. This change has resulted in annual real salary increases of about 4%, reduced unemployment, and significant progress in eliminating poverty.

The gains in investment and productivity stem in part from the economic policies and reforms carried out by the previous government, particularly the overhaul of the export sector it began in 1985. The military government implemented policies intended to correct inconsistencies in macroeconomic policy, reinforce the foundations of fiscal stability and low inflation, and increase savings, investment, and exports. These trends have continued to bear fruit during the 1990s.

The current debate is over how to convert the successes of an open and competitive economy into more progressive income distribution and attain greater reductions in the breadth and intensity of poverty. (Other chapters of this publication address these issues.) Chile's income distribution has remained practically constant despite more than a decade of growth and actually worsened slightly in recent years. This has occurred despite progressive-minded government policies. Income redistribution policies have shown some progress in transferring wealth to the poorest 10th of the population. Nonetheless, there has been less progress in transferring productive resources to the poorest Chileans; that is, in primary income distribution. The government will have to pay more attention to the evolution of the labor market, productivity, and wages to offset the entrenchment of extreme disparities in primary resource distribution, as these disparities are gradually reversing the gains made by other redistribution policies. The current, extended growth cycle (1984-96) has two distinct phases. The first, from 1984 to 1989, was based on the use

---

1   Between 1984 and 1995 Chile grew at an annual rate of 6.6%, whereas the world economy grew at a rate of 3.3%, Latin America at 2.8% and developing countries at 5.3%. The group of thirty Asian countries grew at a rate of 7.8%. In the same period, the per capita product grew at an annual rate of 4.9%, resulting in an increase of 78% for the entire period. If this growth rate persists, we can expect the 1984 per capita GDP to double by 1998.

TABLE 1

PRODUCTION & INFLATION

	1984-89	1990-96
GNP Growth [a/]	6.5	6.8
Per Capita GNP [a/]	4.7	5.1
Actual/Potential GNP Gap (%)	9.2	1.2
Inflation [a/]	20.4	13.9
Real Interest Rate %	8.4	9.5

SAVINGS, INVESTMENTS & EXPORT RATES

	1984-89	1990-96
Investment [b/]	19.2	25.2
External Savings [c/]	5.8	2.0
Internal Savings [c/]	14.9	24.8
Exports (% GNP) [b/]	29.0	36.1
Real Exchange Rate (1985=100)	138.7	97.4
Nominal Tariff (%)	20.1	11.0

SOURCES OF ECONOMIC GROWTH

	1984-89	1990-96
Real Export Variation [a/]	9.8	9.8
Real Investment Variation [a/]	16.1	9.7
Real Consumption Variation [a/]	4.3	7.6

EMPLOYMENT, WAGES & PRODUCTIVITY

	1984-89	1990-96
Unemployment Rated [d/]	10.5	6.7
Employment, variation [a/]	4.8	2.5
Real Wages, variation [a/]	1.0	4.0
GNP / Occupation, variation [a/]	1.6	4.2
Minimum Legal Income, variation [a/]	-1.8	5.5

SOURCE: Originally from O. Londerretche, Research Division of the Ministry of Finances. Updated by the author.

[a/] Average annual variation rate.

[b/] As percentage of GNP to 1986 constant prices.

[c/] As percentage of GNP to current prices

[d/] % above work force.

of idle capacity. Consequently, this phase exhibited less investment and a greater differential between real production and potential production. Unemployment was also running high, so real wage hikes were limited and growth policies were aimed more at creating jobs than bolstering productivity.

During the 1990-96 period, by contrast, growth levels were closer to productive capacity and therefore a smaller gap between real and potential production ensued. Growth during this period has required more investment and domestic savings. The labor market has been closer to full employment, demanding greater increases in productivity.

The increased dynamism of the Chilean economy is based on macroeconomic stability, high levels of savings and investment, and, above all, a sustained expansion in the export of goods and services. The latter has been the engine behind the country's economic growth. Between 1984 and 1996, fixed capital formation (FCF) has grown an average of 12.5% annually. The FCF coefficient consequently rose from 19.2% of Gross Domestic Product (GDP) between 1984 and 1989 to 28.3% of GDP in 1996 (with an average of 27.3% from 1994-96). Meanwhile, exports have expanded an average of 9.8% annually, increasing their real share of GDP to 38.7% by 1996.

The 1984-96 period has shown not only high GDP growth (6.6% per annum), but also investment and export growth that outpaced GDP. This reflects the consolidation of the country's expansion process; productive capacity has increased consistently while a more export-oriented focus has developed progressively.

The most dramatic change in the Chilean economy is the sharp rise in domestic savings, which spiraled from 14.9% of GDP between 1984 and 1989 to 24.8% in the 1990s. The country's accelerated investment and export mechanisms are founded in part on national savings (which in turn limits the need to borrow money abroad).

Chile now faces "a structural change in its growth dynamic." In the second half of the 1980s, significant improvements in the terms of trade and a considerable rise in the real exchange rate (RER) fueled growth. These changes elevated the competitiveness/price ratio of the nation's exports. In that period, growth consisted basically of recovering unused productive capacity; i.e., bridging the rather large gap between real and potential production. In the 1990s, the country has used up its most easily incorporated productive capacity, and subsequent growth has had to depend more on investment and gains in productivity and efficiency.[2]

Economic growth over the last 13 years can also be divided into two other phases, this time looking at expansion by industry. In the first period, 1985-89, the trade goods sector had the highest competitiveness/price gains. Exports boomed during the period, particularly in agriculture, forestry, fishing, and manufacturing. Some non-tradable areas, like construction, retail, and telecommunications, also expanded considerably. Some studies indicate that this process was tied to the export dynamic (ECLAC 1994; Table 6 and 26, 29).

During the second period, from 1990-95, a consistent decline in the real exchange rate meant that non-tradable sectors acquired greater importance. These included utilities (electricity, gas, and water), retail, transportation, and communications. Overall exports, especially non-traditional ones, have continued their strong expansion due to productivity gains. The situation described is reflected in the trajectory of the real rate of exchange, which has declined continuously in the 1990s. This trend exemplifies the difference between Chile's expansion in productivity and that of the rest of the world. In fact, the country's recent growth contrasts with the expansion of the late 1980s, when the real exchange rate increased constantly as a result of Chile's trade deficit.[3] The chances of a recovery in that rate or a slowing of its decline will depend on bolstered domestic savings and higher productivity growth in the non-tradable sector. These goals require that Chile limit its balance of payments surplus (capital accounts) to levels compatible with macroeconomic stability. In the context of a deteriorating rate of exchange, the challenge for macroeconomic policy and productive development is to "increase productivity gains."

The Chilean economy has historically exhibited low growth in "total input productivity." Between 1950 and 1980, this factor increased only 1.1% annually, less than the Latin American average of 1.2% and less than half that of Asian countries or the other member countries of the Organization for Economic Cooperation and Development (OECD). Now, in the 1990s, Chile's productivity growth of 2.5% stands at twice that of the Latin American average, although it is still less than half of Asia's (ECLAC 1996; 70, Table III.1).

---

2   Between 1985 and 1989, average productivity per worker grew at an annual rate of 0.2%, while it grew at an average annual rate of 3.5% between 1990 and 1994. Total Input Productivity grew at an annual rate of 1.7% in the first period and 2.2% in the second.

3   In 1995 and 1996 the real rate of exchange accentuated its fall (5.7% and 4.7%, respectively). Up until the month of September, 1997, the twelve month rate of decline is 8.9%. This represents a delicate situation that, in its persistence, would constitute a certain pitfall for the export dynamic, specifically non-traditional exports.

Chile lags behind international leaders in productivity economy-wide, so this challenge extends to almost all sectors. Our average productivity per worker is one third that of North America, although different industries, companies, and regions vary significantly. Productivity per worker in small companies is 38% that of large companies; the productivity of the power, gas, and water sector is nine times that of the agricultural sector; and, in manufacturing, the productivity of the industrial chemicals area is five times that of textiles and clothing (García 1997).

Greater work force flexibility would enable Chile to more efficiently assign its labor resources. This flexibility entails the following: facilitating movement from lower-productivity jobs to higher-productivity ones; reducing the transaction costs associated with searching for and changing jobs; and expanding the coverage of training programs. The country still needs to improve links between training programs and conversion programs. Chile also must improve unemployment insurance and provide more information to workers about the labor market.

The increasing participation of women in the labor market is a potential stimulus to growth, one that demands a special public policy effort. The appropriate policies should encourage women's participation by avoiding discriminatory practices, reducing cultural and economic barriers, and making work norms and schedules more flexible. Increased productivity, the implementation of unemployment insurance, and the greater role of women in the work force all directly help to reduce poverty and distribute income more equitably.

II. Exports and Competitiveness

The Chilean economy's trade aperture has utilized neutral incentives, with low and equal tariffs. This has enabled us to reallocate resources based on comparative advantages, and stimulating investment in, and production and exportation of, natural resources. These products retain a dominant role in the export basket and the growth dynamic.

1. EXPORT DYNAMIC

The current coefficient of export aperture is on the order of 38% of GDP, measured in terms of real goods and services exports. This coefficient is significantly higher than the Latin American average of around 23%. Two decades ago Chile's exports barely exceeded 12% of GDP and were considerably less than the regional average. The country's leading export product, copper, accounted for more than 70% of exports at the start of the 1970s. Today it accounts for less than 40%.

Export activity has been the linchpin of the Chilean economy's dynamism, growing an average of 7.6% each year between 1980 and 1995. Natural resources continue to dominate the structure of the export basket, although the country has made significant progress in processing those resources within Chile.[4] In 1985, 75% of exports were unprocessed natural

---

4   The First to the Fourth Regions primarily export mineral products; the Fourth to the Sixth Regions, or the central zone, fruit; the Seventh to the Tenth Regions, or the southern region, forestry products. Ocean products are added to the First and Fifth Regions, as are products derived from fish add to the Eighth, Tenth, Eleventh and Twelfth Regions (PNUD 1996).

TABLE 2

EXPORTING DYNAMISIM

DYNAMIC	1965-70	1985-90	1990-96
Exports of Goods & Services / GNP (%)	12	30	35
Real Annual Growth Goods & Services Exports (%)	3	11	9
Copper Exports / Goods Exports (%)	74	46	39

SOURCE: Meller & Sáez (1995), Díaz & Ramos (1997).

resources, 22% processed natural resources, and just 3% other industrial products. In 1996, those figures were 57%, 32%, and 11%, respectively. Clearly, non-natural resource-based industrial exports and processed natural resource exports are growing. Natural resource exports, although still predominantly mineral (55%), are diversifying. They include fruit (20%), fish and marine products (13%), and forestry products (11%).

Diversification also occurs within each of these industries. To the extent that exports depend heavily on access to natural resources, the export process exhibits a certain decentralization of production. The period in question shows a sustained increase in exports, greater than both Chile's GDP growth and trade growth worldwide. Chilean exports have increased their share of international commerce and imports of OECD countries. The progress in the latter two areas is minimal, however, since the country's exports are concentrated in relatively non-dynamic sectors of world trade.

Export Diversification

An interesting diversification process has accompanied the strong export dynamic. Products and markets have diversified and the industrial export base has expanded. In 1990, 4,100 exporters sent 2,300 products to 129 markets. In 1996, 5,840 exporters sold 3,890 products to 180 markets. (The number of exporters has tended to stagnate in the last three years, however.) Diversification is also evident within each sector of natural resource exports. The forestry sector, for example, has gone from exporting 61 products in 1973 to 385 products in 1996. Raw materials exports exhibit a prominent trend toward diversification and technological modernization. Rapid technological innovation and significant productivity increases have played a role in the strong export dynamic. This is true of both raw materials exports and those that incorporate primary and secondary natural resource processing.[5] Notable examples of primary natural resource processing include salmon, hake, fruit, and cellulose.

Achieving competitiveness in some of these sectors is a technological challenge in terms of production, administration, quality, presentation, shipping, and marketing. It is therefore inaccurate to associate such primary exports with technological backwardness. Examples of

---

5   These expressions were used for the first time in the 1997 Díaz and Ramos document. The export of trunks, logs and chips correspond to primary export. Cellulose corresponds to the category of primary natural resource processing, while wooden boards, furniture, paper and diapers correspond to secondary natural resource processing.

sectors that are technologically advanced are salmon farming and the forestry industry.

In the case of salmon, the industry's notable achievements include: the adaptation of farming technology; developing studies of disease in salmon hatchlings; creating genetic varieties adapted to Chile's environment; disease control; monitoring and reacting to red tides, which salmon farmers deal with by submerging the flotation cages or moving them elsewhere; analyzing environmental impacts; controlling quality, packaging, and presentation mechanisms; and using cold storage or refrigeration in shipping the product or holding it in port facilities (Achurra 1995). Each of these areas presents significant technological challenges. Remaining competitive requires being at the forefront of technology in all areas.

Services, which represent nearly 20% of total exports, have grown rather dynamically. Non-financial service exports have grown 16.6 times between 1987 and 1995. Transportation and tourism account for 70% of service exports. Other significant areas include port services, shipping, and insurance. Among the emerging sectors are health care, higher education, social security services, audiovisual services, and consulting. The latter services are often not recorded or appear annotated in records of goods exports. Chile does not have proper records of these booming modern professional services, or of other highly dynamic service sectors (Figueroa 1997). Trade aperture in the service sector has been unilateral up to now, so the evolution of trade agreements could have a significant effect on the future of the services trade.[6]

In the framework of diversification, manufactured goods are increasing their relative weight in the export basket. This is true both of goods based on natural resources and of those that are not. Between 1985 and 1995, the volume of raw materials exports grew 11.7% annually. Exports of natural resources with primary processing grew 15.8%, and those with secondary processing grew 23.6%. In short, all these types of exports grew faster than GDP, non-traditional exports grew more than average, and the highest-growth exports were those with the most processing. In regard to processed exports, the high growth rates have something to do with their low initial volume. Still, the important thing is that these sectors have maintained these high growth rates for a number of years.

Specialization and Export Markets

The pattern of specialization varies according to the target market. The European Union and Asia are the most active in acquiring our natural resources. Asia, in particular, absorbs one-third of our natural resource exports, processed or unprocessed. Latin America receives a marked concentration of our industrial exports. Non-natural resource-based industrial products are sold mainly within the region, first to the Andean market, followed by the Southern Common Market (Mercosur). The nature of export specialization by market and its impact on each industry in the productive apparatus are important issues in Chile's trade agreements (See Table 3).

Chilean exports' share of the OECD market continues to be minimal. It grew from 0.23% to 0.26% between 1980 and 1994, albeit with noteworthy changes in composition. Our share of the natural resources market rose from 0.26% to 0.75%, while our share of manufactured goods fell from 0.21% to 0.11% (ILO 1998).

---

6   ProChile estimates that 1997 service exports will reach 3.5 billion dollars, though the effective figure could reach close to 6 billion dollars, given the underestimation of these services.

TABLE 3

COMPOSITION OF EXPORTS DESTINED FOR PRINCIPAL TRADING BLOCKS : 1995
(Percentages)

	MERCOSUR	NAFTA	E.C.	JAPAN	ASIA W/O JAPAN	ANDEAN GROUP
Natural Resources	40.68	62.07	70.68	56.03	68.82	22.28
Mining	32.76	41.05	62.92	54.88	62.27	13.06
Fruit	5.36	20.66	7.07	0.66	2.06	7.00
Agriculture	1.83	2.22	1.41	0.42	0.05	1.66
Cattle	0.70	0.09	0.14	0.01	0.07	0.54
Forestry	0.04	0.07	0.35	0.22	4.27	0.03
Fishing	0.00	0.20	0.21	0.27	0.11	0.00
Processed Natural Resources	30.97	29.10	24.39	43.10	28.80	38.51
Food Industry	14.04	19.84	11.13	26.59	12.12	19.65
Pulp/Paper Industry	15.79	1.97	12.48	4.98	13.63	17.89
Forestry/Furniture Industry	1.13	7.29	0.79	11.53	3.05	0.98
Industrial Products Not Based on Natural Resources	28.35	8.83	4.93	0.87	2.38	39.21
Textile, Garment & Leather Industry	2.70	1.89	0.46	0.02	0.31	5.42
Basic Iron & Steel Industry	0.32	0.81	0.66	0.01	0.22	2.58
Chemical Production Industry	10.92	3.15	3.08	0.74	1.12	15.26
Machinery & Metal Production Industry	12.77	1.41	0.31	0.06	0.12	1.80
Non-specific Manufacturing	1.64	1.41	0.31	0.06	0.12	1.80
Total Exports (mill. US $)	1,768,363	2,516,387	4,354,697	2,889,831	2,531,748	1,081,255

SOURCE: Headquarters of International Economic Relations, I. Figueroa (1997)
"Principales rasgos de la inserción de Chile en la economía mundial".

Our performance in the Latin American market was less satisfying, as our share fell from 1.61% to 1.18% during the same period. Chile even declined in natural resources, with a relative increase in mineral exports offset by a fall in agricultural products. The country performed much better in Mercosur, with our export share rising from 1.53% to 2.57%. This result was due primarily to natural resource exports, particularly agricultural products, which rose from 2.8% to 5.94%.

The impact of the real exchange rate differs according to export market. The competitiveness of Chilean exports fell among the North American Free Trade Agreement (NAFTA) countries, but improved substantially among Mercosur countries, as a result of Argentina and Brazil's exchange rate difficulties on several occasions during the 1990s.

The impact of the exchange rate also differs among industries. The relevant real exchange rate for the manufacturing industry has fallen markedly, relative to the last few years of the 1980s. Productivity increases for this industry are below the economy-wide average and its labor costs exhibit above-average growth.

In any case, the debate about the pattern of specialization continues. The five leading products still account for almost half of exports. Copper's share has declined but it still accounts for 40% of all goods exported. Chile's internationally recognized products — those in which it has more than 15% of the global market — are fishmeal, copper, grapes, and salmon.

Chilean exports have improved their relative position in world trade, growing faster than worldwide exports as a whole. Nevertheless, Chile's exports are concentrated in low-growth areas of international trade. To use ECLAC's terminology for international insertion, Chile is improving its "efficiency" without achieving good "positioning"; that is, without moving into highly-dynamic industries (ECLAC 1992). Thus, Chile's excellent export performance, highly dependent on natural resources and achieved by displacing competitors, is vulnerable to protectionism.

The structure of the export industry is highly concentrated. Ten companies, two of them state-owned, account for about 40% of exports. According to 1992 figures from the Ministry of the Economy, the companies with the greatest sales volume constituted 34% of exporters and accounted for 95% of total exports. Medium-sized companies represented 11% of exporters and 2% of exports, and small companies represented 55% of exporters and barely 3% of exports.

The majority of companies (59%) export less than US$100,000 worth of goods, and only 25% export between US$100,000 and US$1 million. The export business has a high turnover rate, meaning companies enter and exit the business frequently. This undermines the advantages of learned expertise in trade and technology and makes it difficult to build strategic networks and partnerships with clients and suppliers.

This rate of turnover is greater among smaller companies. Addressing this problem is therefore a significant part of the export development strategy and is necessary in order to help small and medium companies in the export business achieve stability.

2. COMPETITIVE POSITION

Many highly regarded reports on international competitiveness acknowledge that Chile has a solid footing in world trade, even better than that of several industrialized nations. The methodologies of these reports may be highly questionable but all provide proof that Chile has made significant progress in various aspects of its economy. In general, the reports cite the following as Chile's leading assets: its dynamic growth, savings, and investment levels; its low inflation; its export orientation; the predominant role of the market; the assumption of individual risk; and the tendency toward large strategic alliances. The reports also give positive marks to the Chilean government's small size, fiscal policy, and limited intervention. However, they do question the government's lack of progress in modernizing.

According to the reports, Chile's competitive weaknesses include its small market, limited domestic technological capacity, and the economy's overall productivity. They also mention the country's weak export base of industrial commodities and its limited production of capital goods. Furthermore, they say, Chile has a vulnerable transportation infrastructure and is behind in education and job training. They also mention that Chilean companies do not spend enough on research and development. With regard to public institutions, the greatest shortcomings are the inefficient justice system and the lag time in implementing anti-trust, environmental, and consumer protection legislation.

3. THE SECOND EXPORT PHASE

Chile seems to have done a poor job of defining and debating what is known as the "second export phase." In practice, different camps argued for practically exclusive emphasis on either natural resources or manufactured goods. More recently, services entered the debate. None of the camps considered our competitive advantages in terms of our natural resources and a decade of sustained economic growth.

Perhaps it would be more effective to debate the challenges of a "mature export development" strategy that enables us to use our competitive advantages and reduce our liabilities. We cannot deny the magnitude of the technological challenges we face in the exportation of natural resources with primary or secondary processing, and in production, administration, quality control, presentation, shipping, and marketing. The challenge in several of these areas is more pronounced than it is in our services and manufacturing sectors.

Our strategy should not be to turn our back on natural resources, but rather to facilitate their use. This requires that we establish as many profitable links in industry as possible, up and down the production chain. In order to take advantage of natural resource clusters, we must carry out research to define the magnitude and costs of the technology gap and to identify the expertise of industries that could potentially join together to manage a particular natural resource. The country also needs to adapt its policies on productive development and export promotion to meet these goals.

If Chile is to progress, it must further promote quality standards, create technical training institutes, adapt and strengthen job training efforts, and alter the territorial distribution of productive development.

From this perspective, a "mature export development" strategy has more to do with diversifying products and markets and widening the export base than with giving "a priori" preference to determined export sectors. It would not be appropriate for us to give a detailed analysis of the necessary export policies here, but the following is a list of activities Chile could promote: the formation of export/trading companies; foreign investment in marketing and distribution chains; joint operations by domestic companies in export markets; and the installation of importers of Chilean products in our main foreign markets, in partnership with local investors there. The prominent traits of export development should also include a stronger emphasis on export promotion, quality, branding, and insurance. This development could be based on natural resources but also incorporate technology and know-how into the links between those resources and manufacturing and services (Rosales 1995).

Likewise, Chile's export growth should assure a greater and more stable presence among small and medium companies by providing incentives to indirect exporters and service exporters. These incentives (in accordance with World Trade Organization (WTO) norms) could be an appropriate means of making our export industry more dynamic and equitable.

III. Employment

From 1986-96, GDP grew 7.6% annually and employment 2.9%, the best performance in the region. In recent years, however, employment has risen just slightly more than 1% each year. As we have already noted, the macroeconomic and production systems have performed differently at different times during the growth cycle. In the 1990s, lower employment growth has been accompanied by decreases in unemployment and informal employment, and by increases in real wages and labor productivity.

Labor productivity is greater because of the stronger capital/labor ratio and improvements in the work force's training, expressed in terms of average educational levels. According to Mideplan (1996), 35% of the jobs generated between 1986 and 1989 were informal jobs, a figure that fell to 29% between 1990 and 1995. This figure is impressive if we consider that, during the 1990s, 80% of the jobs created in Latin America have been in the informal sector (ILO 1996). We need to study further the causes of lower job growth and the link between productivity and wage increases. Most importantly, we need to study more in order to have a clearer picture of the labor market, one that shows the labor situation by industry and region.

The government's recent revision of employment statistics tempers our optimism about the labor market. The government has replaced its previous estimate of unemployment, 4.9% per year from 1992-95, with 7.1%, a figure too high to be explained only by frictional unemployment. The reality of unemployment among young people and lower-income groups continues to be an important challenge for economic policy.[7]

1. OCCUPATIONAL STRUCTURE

We see a change over the last decade in occupational structure, with fewer jobs in farming and in community, social, and personal services (Table 4). Due to the fact that these sectors have the lowest average production per worker, we could interpret this change as a gradual movement of the labor force from low-productivity areas to more productive ones. In the last three years, however, employment has fallen in the tradable goods sectors and has increased in only the energy, financial services, transportation, and communications sectors, as well as in community, social, and personal services. The latter three services have shown the highest rate of expansion.

Table 5 compares job creation to data on industry production and productivity. In the years 1986-96, the most dynamic sectors in terms of job creation were financial services and construction. The increases in employment were similar to or greater than the increases in production, indicating that the increase in productivity was marginal or negative. In the financial sector it was negative. The most dynamic sectors in terms of production were transportation and commerce. Job growth in these sectors is not low, but it is significantly lower than production growth. Consequently, productivity growth here is above the economy-wide average.

---

7   In 1997 (trimesters accumulated through the month of August) national unemployment has averaged 6.1%. Over the course of 15 to 19 years, unemployment has been 18.9%; over 20 to 24 years it has been 13.6%. Of the unemployed youth, almost 65% correspond with 40% of lower income groups. This indicates that youth unemployment rates among the poorest groups exceed 30%.

TABLE 4

STRUCTURE OF LABOR FORCE BY BRANCH OF ACTIVITY
(percentage of the employed population)

	1986	1990	1996
Agriculture	20.6	19.2	15.2
Mining	2.2	2.3	1.8
Industry	13.6	16.1	16.3
Power	0.6	0.5	0.7
Construction	4.7	6.4	7.8
Wholesale/Retail Sales	16.7	17.7	17.9
Transport	5.9	6.9	7.5
Financial Services	4.0	4.5	6.8
Community Level Enterprises	31.5	26.3	25.9
Total	100.0	100.0	100.0

SOURCE: National Statistics Institute, employment surveys.

TABLE 5

PRODUCTION, EMPLOYMENT, & PRODUCTIVITY BY SECTOR *

	PERIOD 1996-86			PERIOD 1996-90		
	GNP	EMPLOYMENT	PRODUCTIVITY	GNP	EMPLOYMENT	PRODUCTIVITY
Agriculture	5.7	0.3	5.4	4.1	-1.4	5.5
Mining	5.1	1.1	3.9	6.1	-1.5	7.7
Industry	6.1	5.0	1.0	6.0	2.8	3.0
Power	6.6	5.2	1.4	10.2	10.7	-0.5
Construction	8.8	8.4	0.4	8.2	6.1	2.0
Wholesale/Retail Sales	9.6	3.7	5.7	10.4	2.8	7.4
Transport	10.0	5.3	4.4	10.2	3.6	6.4
Financial Services	7.4	9.0	-1.5	6.7	10.0	-3.2
Community Level Enterprises	2.6	1.2	1.4	3.0	2.6	0.3
Total	6.6	3.2	3.4	6.9	2.7	4.1

SOURCE: INE.

*Here productivity refers to the average productivity of a job; in other words, the ratio of a sector's production and the people it employs.

TABLE 6

CHANGES IN PRODUCTIVITY, 1986-96

	1986	1990	1996	Change 1996-86
Agriculture	37.9	42.5	46.3	69.2
Mining	502.9	433.4	531.8	46.6
Industry	137.0	116.5	109.8	11.0
Power	430.2	467.3	356.7	14.9
Construction	104.1	87.9	78.8	3.9
Wholesale/Retail Sales	88.6	91.6	110.9	73.5
Transport	109.3	106.7	121.5	54.1
Financial Services	318.5	306.5	198.2	-13.8
Community Level Enterprises	43.9	45.4	36.4	23.8
Total	100.0	100.0	100.0	38.5

SOURCE: INE.

In the most recent period, 1990-96, the financial system accentuates its pattern of high growth with heavy job absorption and a decline in average productivity. The same occurs in the power sector. These two sectors are the only ones in which average labor productivity falls.

Mining, retail, and transport exhibit strong productivity increases. The intense growth of these sectors has not been accompanied by similar growth in jobs, so the productivity increases are much higher than average. This indicates rapid investment growth in these sectors. Also, in the retail sector, the productivity increase indicates a marked organizational change from low-sales volume outlets to large stores. These three sectors thus account for a large part of GDP expansion. But as long as their high growth rates are based on significant investments, organizational changes, and capital-intensive technologies, they will continue to create few jobs.

The energy sector is the most dynamic in job creation, but has little importance (less than 1%) in the employment structure. If we disregard this sector, employment grows 6% annually in construction and financial services. Employment based on financial services, transport, and communications is practically equal to that of non-mining natural resources sectors or to that of all industrial manufacturing.

Chile may need to change its employment policies, traditionally linked to the primary and secondary sectors, to include a greater concern for the services sector. The relative significance of the social, communal, and personal services sector, for example, has declined drastically in recent years, compared to the mid-1980s. This decline has slowed in the last three years, during which time this industry has exhibited the strongest job growth. The relative importance of jobs in public administration, defense, and personal and home care services has fallen, while jobs in health care, dentistry, entertainment and recreation have increased. The latter jobs are associated with higher productivity and better wages.

2. PRODUCTIVITY BY INDUSTRY

From 1986-96, the gap in labor productivity expanded at each end of the scale. The shift reflects differences in the intensity of factors and in the organization of productive processes, also known as soft technology. Retail and agriculture exhibited the greatest productivity gains, followed by transport and mining. Productivity gains have been marginal in construction, and productivity has declined in the financial sector. In the aggregate, however, the disparities have diminished. The relative improvements in farming, retail, and transportation offset the decline in manufacturing, power, and financial services. An analysis of the distribution of productivity within an industry, based on the varying size of companies, is a pending task.

Table 6 shows the productivity variations among industries by average labor productivity.

Upon examining average production per industry, we see that agriculture, despite its rapidly climbing productivity, remains far behind the national average. The industry's strong productivity growth nonetheless enables it to move out of last place in production per worker. Replacing agriculture here is the social, community, and personal services sector, which employs almost one-fourth of the working population.

In 1986, the average productivity of the mining sector was 13.3 times that of agriculture, whereas in 1996 it was only 11.5 times. The opposite occurred with the social, community, and personal services sector. Here, the difference in average productivity between mining and this sector grew from 11.5 times in 1986 to 14.6 times in 1996. This fact will be cause for concern if social, community, and personal services (the sector with the lowest productivity per worker) continue to exhibit the greatest job growth of any sector, as we noted previously.

The evidence on the causes of lower job growth, in spite of high economic growth, is mixed and requires further research. Likewise, Chile should also examine in greater detail the relation between productivity and wage increases. This research should be done at the microeconomic level, analyzing said relation by industry, region, and company size. At present, however, this data is unavailable.

What we do know is that the training mechanisms for people changing jobs or for young people entering the job market appear to be weak. As in all high-growth situations, companies and jobs in Chile are created and eliminated with great frequency (Engel 1997). In addition, the productivity differential shows no signs of declining with growth, which indicates that the job opportunities created in the leading industries could be underutilized. Chile might not have the base of unemployed workers with the new skills required by technological changes and competitive adaptations. This also explains the expansion of the wage range on the basis of qualifications.

Young people account for 36% of the unemployed. We will not improve their job opportunities with growth alone, since the supply of and demand for skills do not coincide. If we are to achieve a more harmonious relation between wages and productivity, we must improve the skills of those who work in low-productivity industries. This will allow them to gradually move away from jobs that can be eliminated or automated toward jobs that directly or indirectly contribute to expanding industries with competitive potential.

The most pronounced change in Chile's labor market, the decline in farming jobs, is explained exclusively by the drastic fall in youth employment. Another issue for future research is finding out whether this situation is the result of a natural or desirable migration to the city and to more productive activities, or whether it is the result of a premature and accelerated migration that obliges young people to take on precarious urban jobs.

TABLE 7

TOTAL FACTOR PRODUCTIVITY
(Average annual rates of growth)

	1950-80	1980-94	1989-94	1950-94
Latin America	1.2	-0.8	1.1	0.6
Asia	2.6	3.1	4.4	2.8
OECD	2.5	0.7	0.4	2.0
Chile	1.1	0.6	2.5	0.9
Brazil	1.2	-1.5	-1.6	0.3
Argentina	1.0	-0.3	4.5	0.6
Mexico	1.5	-1.2	0.1	0.6

SOURCE: Hofman (1996).

TABLE 8

GNP, EMPLOYMENT, & PRODUCTIVITY *
(Average annual rate of variation)

	1984-89	1990-95	1984-95
Employment	4.8	2.4	3.6
Production / Employee	1.4	4.3	3.0
GNP	6.5	6.7	6.6

SOURCE: Research unit, Ministry of Finance
* Average job productivity.

TABLE 9

SOURCES OF PRODUCTIVITY GROWTH BY EMPLOYEE
(Average annual percentage change)

	CAPITAL/LABOR	TFP	PRODUCTIVITY BY EMPLOYEE
1980-84	0.5	-1.2	-0.7
1985-89	-1.5	1.7	0.2
1990-94	1.3	2.2	3.5

SOURCE: Research unit, Ministry of Finance.
TFP = Total Factor Productivity.

IV. The History of Chilean Productivity

Historically, the Chilean economy exhibits low growth in Total Input Productivity (PTF). This growth is slightly below the Latin American average, which itself increased only 1.2% each year from 1950 to 1980.[8] That is less than half the productivity growth of Asia or the OECD countries, indicating a technological backwardness that after 30 years explains a good part of the differences in income and well-being among the regions.

Thanks to the early recovery of the Chilean economy in the 1980s, its PTF did decline, as in the rest of the Latin American region. In the 1990s, Chile has achieved a PTF similar to that of Asia from 1950-80, and double the Latin American average. Asia's PTF, nonetheless, continues to be almost twice that of Chile.

If we examine recent economic growth in terms of supply, we see in the 1990s a reorientation of growth toward a stronger productivity base. From 1984-89, GDP growth was reflected more in employment increases than in productivity gains. In the 1990s, the opposite has occurred. The first period's growth was based on absorbing unused labor and on taking advantage of existing productive capacity. In the second, growth has required more investment, efficiency, and productivity.

Maintaining growth, therefore, demands a strong element of productivity. This requires preserving the country's dynamic investment in fixed capital and further improving Total Input Productivity, which acts as a measure of the economy's overall efficiency.

In the 1985-89 period, we see a virtual stagnation in average labor productivity, due to a decline in the capital/labor ratio (employment increased 6.3% annually, while capital increased only 2.5% annually). In the recent period, by contrast, average labor productivity increases as much due to relative growth in capital (6%, versus 2.8% for employment) as to a greater rise in Total Input Productivity.[9]

The Chilean economy's productivity challenge is twofold. First, it is economy-wide, as its demands are valid for all industries. Our productivity gap with the industrialized world is considerable and does not show signs of narrowing. Second, our answer to this challenge must involve reducing our internal productivity gaps. These seem to have widened a great deal and do not appear to be closing.

Data from 1993 shows that average productivity per worker in a small company was 38% that of a large company, while for medium companies the figure was 69% (Table 11).

The productivity of the energy, gas, and water sector is nine times that of the agricultural sector and more than four times that of the manufacturing industry. This high productivity differential recurs in each industry and among regions. One of the government's main concerns is accelerating the dissemination of technology among all lagging regions, industries, and companies. This concern explains the policies the government has submitted for the debate over how to revitalize our competitiveness.

---

8   Total Input Productivity is a measure of the economy's overall efficiency. It refers to the growth in GDP that is not explained by increased utilization of productive factors, and therefore has to do with technological change and greater efficiency.

9   It is difficult to isolate the components of Total Input Productivity, which is normally associated with intensity of technological change. It is possible that the biggest stress of commercial aperture is the operation of effects of scale, productive capacity use, technological transfer, managerial efficiency, and modifications in business management that foreign commerce demands.

TABLE 10

AVERAGE EMPLOYEE PRODUCTIVITY:
INTERNATIONAL COMPARISON

	1950	1973	1980	1989	1994
Argentina	41	40	45	32	38
Brazil	18	24	30	26	24
Chile	32	35	35	30	33
USA	100	100	100	100	100

SOURCE: Innovation Program, "Study of TFP in Chile," draft, Ministry of Finance (1997)

TABLE 11

AVERAGE EMPLOYEE PRODUCTIVITY
(Average productivity 1993-95 = 100)

Electricity, Gas, Water	460
Mining	434
Financial Services	210
Transport & Communications	106
Manufacturing Industry	102
Wholesale & Retail Sales	92
Construction	72
Agriculture & Fishing	51

SOURCE: Research unit estimates, Ministry of Finance.

On a related issue, the real exchange rate fell an average of 5% in both 1995 and 1996, less than the average increase in labor productivity. Given the marked differences in productivity by industry and company size, it is evident that a good part of the productive apparatus cannot handle the necessary competitive adaptation. The mix of economic policies that push the exchange rate down and raise interest rates exacerbates the competitive pressure on those companies that do not have the option of international financing. This is not a neutral economic policy. Larger companies have access to external credit at a lower cost than domestic credit and thereby avoid the cost of the exchange, passing it on to the smaller companies that cannot acquire this cheaper credit. In other words, the aforementioned policy mix has promoted the internationalization of large companies with inexpensive financing, while restricting the competitiveness of others by driving up the price of credit and lowering the exchange rate. This undermines the profitability of some companies' exports and allows imported competition to lower prices. While the political discourse might defend even-handed, non-discriminatory policies, the macroeconomy favors large companies that can acquire inexpensive foreign financing and punishes companies that export goods not associated with natural resources. When we compare the macro-economic amounts involved here with the macroeconomic amounts distributed across the board to support production, it is evident that, in the aggregate, equity does not pre-dominate. Thus we see the urgency of a more committed effort to promote production. The government must limit the decline of the exchange rate enough to compensate small and medium companies with production assistance.

V. Macroeconomic Impacts on Production and Employment

Despite initial fears, Chile's transition to democracy has practically established itself on the basis of macroeconomic achievements. The legitimacy of the governing coalition has infiltrated the economy gradually. Its spectacular achievements in growth and stability have slowly earned the recognition of the business community and the world.

The government's basic economic goals are important but, thus far, limited. They include reduced inflation and stable growth based on the economy's potential. To these ends, the government watches over domestic savings, monitors a current account deficit that is sustainable over time (an estimated 3% to 4% of GDP), and adjusts interest rates to keep spending from exceeding by too much the evolution of potential production.

In practice, the government has developed a peculiar and unorthodox focus that favors a holistic vision of macroeconomic equilibria. The recent Chilean experience exhibits a macroeconomic environment of fiscal savings, low and falling inflation, a moderate and sustainable current account deficit, and a GDP that does not greatly exceed its potential (an estimated 6.5% to 7% annually). Government officials watch closely the gap between spending and production, establish timely corrective measures, and take advantage of the reasonable opportunities for growth afforded by the gains of trade. Chile's macroeconomic strategy favors these criteria without overemphasizing any single objective (e.g., reducing inflation) at the cost of others (e.g., growing current account deficit, exchange rate decline, or unstable interest rate adjustment). This stable growth scenario promotes adequate savings and a complementary relation between foreign and domestic savings. In the absence of these policies, external savings would tend to have an adverse effect on domestic savings, particularly when the former exceeds its typical value (ECLAC 1996).

The best strategies for achieving high savings and investment, and sustained increases in the productivity of inputs, have proven to be the following: provide incentives for domestic savings; gradually reduce inflation while taking advantage of increases in savings and productivity; limit the current account deficit to a sustainable level; and keep relative prices at a level that provides for stability in the key macroeconomic variables. This approach has enabled Chile to strengthen its institutions, which in turn promote macro-economic stability and incentives to capital formation and growth.[10] The institutional

---

10 Highlighted here is the autonomy of the Central Bank and its express objective to reduce inflation to inter-national levels in a gradual manner yet also in a comparatively short amount of time. In the achievement of a fiscal surplus, the technological solidity of the budgetary and tributary authorities should be highlighted.

traits that complement this focus include rigorous supervision and prudent regulation of the financial system, and mechanisms for promoting competition in markets characterized by natural monopolies. Admittedly, the government still faces considerable challenges in the latter area.

1. IS THE HOLISTIC VISION ERODING?

In recent years, the holistic macroeconomic vision we described has faced new realities and seems to have faded. The objective of economic policy was to limit the decline in the real exchange rate to 2% annually, but this indicator actually fell 5% in 1995 and in 1996 even exceeded the adjusted goal of 4%. Domestic savings stagnated at about 23% of GDP, an insufficient amount for the country to continue growing at 6%-7% annually without undermining the stability of the current account deficit. The consensus about the sustainable level of external debt weakened. During the first half of 1997, the government also showed signs of public disagreement about exchange rate policy.[11]

In addition, the discussion about Chile being a "financial center" is wearing down leaders' confidence in the system of short-term capital reserve requirements and calling into question the speed with which capital accounts are opened. Finally, and no less important, the country's impressive reduction of inflation has made further reduction a greater priority of economic policy. Our solid and persistent reduction of inflation has created the temptation to abandon the gradual approach to controlling it. Consequently, there is a partial disregard of other economic objectives, or at least a predisposition to sacrifice them in the name of greater progress against inflation.

This is not only a debate about economic policy. To maintain growth of more than 6% with falling inflation — which will decrease to 2% in two or three years with the current mix of economic policies — is only the tip of the iceberg. As the iceberg comes to the surface, other issues of greater import emerge. In technical areas, the issue is the need for a mix of fiscal, monetary, and exchange policies that can counteract an abundant flow of external resources. In substantive matters, the issues are tax reform, tariff reduction, and fiscal and social policy in the next government. The decisions we make in response to these issues will play a role in defining our place in the global economy.

In the 1990s, Chile reduced inflation more than ever before in its history. In 1997, the country completed four straight years of single-digit inflation below the rate of GDP growth. The fall in the real exchange rate of 5% per year has played a decisive role in this process. It is true that average worker productivity has grown at a similar pace, but this fact is valid only in the aggregate. The averages hide a widening of the gap between productivity and wages among different industries and different size companies. This gap creates a tremendous obstacle to progress in equitable distribution and threatens the viability of many productive sectors.

The current account deficit has averaged 2% of GDP each year since 1992. Chile has financed its current account deficit with capital inflows on the order of 6% of GDP. The difference goes to accumulating reserves that are, relatively speaking, among the highest in the world. The cost is a quasi-fiscal deficit in the Central Bank of 0.8% of annual GDP, or approximately US$600 million.

---

11 In the second half of 1997, in any case, we see economic authorities exhibiting more concern about this issue, reflected in their search for ways to limit the decline of the exchange rate.

The policy mix provides declining inflation but is heavily dependent on reducing the exchange rate. This undermines one of the pillars of the export diversification strategy. The country seems to have set aside the "second export phase" without having carried out a serious debate about what type of productive and export specialization strategy to pursue. Clearly there are a variety of well-founded opinions on this issue, but to opt for certain opinions without debate is foolhardy.

2. THE BUSINESS COMMUNITY'S PROPOSALS

The discourse of business leaders focuses on the possibility of accelerating the rates of GDP growth and inflation reduction simultaneously by taking advantage of access to external financing. These leaders have suggested that a current account deficit of 6%-8% is acceptable and would enable the country to raise its investment coefficient to 30% of GDP.[12] In addition, they argue that facilitating greater capital inflows to finance the current account deficit will tend to further depress the exchange rate. This would in turn correct the reduction in the price of tradable goods and accelerate the decline in inflation.

If such an opportunity were in fact available, and the costs did not exceed the benefits, we would have no other choice but to take advantage of it. Unfortunately, this option carries with it considerable risks as clearly proven by recent experiences inside and outside our region. In this context, our macroeconomic alternatives have heavy implications for the development of production, exports and labor.

The current mix of economic policies may have worn out its usefulness. Signs of this include the excessive decline in the exchange rate, the stagnation in domestic savings, and the continued use of reserve requirement mechanisms that, some say, may be retarding the internationalization of the Chilean economy. The economy could grow more than the government has estimated if it has access to external savings greater than the 3.5-4% of GDP recommended by the Central Bank. Current policy restricts external financing and thereby limits investment and growth. The economy has a potential growth on the order of 8 or 9%. In order to take advantage of it we must deregulate the capital account, lower taxes and adjust interest rates to a level compatible with international rates. This would enable us to reduce the pressure of speculative capital flows as long as we make a stronger effort at fiscal austerity.

Some analysts suggest there is serious reason to believe Chile is facing a permanent shock of external financing on the order of 5 to 6 points of GDP annually. They say the country could take advantage of available external savings and raise the growth rate above the 7.4% we have had in the 1990s. This would require relaxing restrictions on capital flows and allowing for a higher current account deficit, which the country would then finance with the resulting greater investment.

Likewise, some analysts argue that such a high current account deficit would not be a problem because the country could substitute public savings for external savings, taking advantage of the greater access the economy would have to the latter.

---

12   This text was completed before the Asian financial crisis. Clearly, given the financial turbulence at the end of 1997, no one still publicly defends external imbalances of six points of GDP. This is exactly the government's point: limiting the current account deficit to a natural level, precisely in order to avoid overexposure during times of instability in the financial markets.

In short, the suggested mix, according to Larroulet (1997), would be:
- Reach a current account deficit (CAD) of 6-8% of GDP.
- Reduce tariffs to 5% without subsidies.
- Lower tax pressure by a couple of points of GDP without subsidies.
- Bring interest rates into parity with international rates.

Proponents of this policy are fully conscious of the formidable pressure it would exert on private spending, so they adjust government spending. The think-tank Libertad y Desarrollo says that for this plan to work, public savings must increase by two GDP points, in addition to current savings. By comparison, let us suppose that the tariff reduction (from 11% to 5%) reduces government revenues by 1.5% of GDP. This means that additional public savings have to be 3.5% of GDP (2 points of marginal savings and 1.5% to compensate for the reduction in tariff revenues). As public savings were 5.6% of GDP in 1996, this policy would require an overall public savings of 9.1% of GDP, with a marginal savings of four GDP points, more than total public spending on education (which is 3% of GDP).

The following notions support business' position:
- a greater potential GDP than that estimated by the government
- stable access to a higher current account deficit than that estimated by the Central Bank
- a faster and broader aperture of the capital account
- compensation for reduced public savings with increased external savings

This position, which is widely accepted in business circles, ultimately puts at risk public savings, the pillar of the high-yet-stable growth strategy. The turbulence of the international financial and exchange markets is well known, and the volatility of international capital has affected economies that are much wealthier and much more stable than Chile's. As such, to substitute public savings with external savings (with a greater current account deficit) would be more than an ideological statement; it would be an act of macroeconomic irresponsibility.

The weakness of the business position is based on the high risk of macroeconomic instability and the "stop and go" cycles, which reality shows behave erratically when it comes to external savings (Mexico, 1994; Czech Republic, 1997; Thailand, 1997). Loosening the macroeconomic focus that has predominated in the 1990s and adopting the aforementioned approach would probably raise the growth rate above 8% and bring inflation down close to zero within one or two years. But its costs would include aggravating the decline in the exchange rate and raising the current account deficit to unsustainable levels, to the point of requiring an interest rate adjustment to calm investors and avoid capital flight.

From the standpoint of production and labor, this strategy would favor imports over exports, undermining domestic savings and pushing the exchange rate down even more. All this, in consequence, would decrease employment in tradable goods sectors. Under these conditions, we could reasonably expect to see a high concentration of workers in retail, construction, and financial services, which would make the labor structure more susceptible to economic cycles.

3. MACROECONOMIC ALTERNATIVES AND THE PRODUCTIVE PROFILE

In the mid-1990s, the emerging Chilean economy is experiencing difficulties controlling inflation and spending, although it has a low-risk rating and a great capacity for attracting foreign capital. The marked growth of spending — which exhibits frequent cycles of over-expansion — is basically due to the great availability of foreign capital, which in turn takes advantage of the high return on domestic investment.

First-generation, non-industrialized countries (NICs) did not experience this difficulty, both because they established severe capital controls and because financial globalization operated on a lesser scale. Second-generation NICs have faced these problems when they have exceeded a cautious level of current account deficit, the most recent example being the economic crisis in Thailand.

Net inflows of outside capital (8 to 10% of GDP) are incompatible with a sustainable CAD (of 3-4% of GDP). This is the principal problem of exchange rate policy.[13] The Chilean economy seems to have reached a point where it needs to adopt a new exchange rate policy, given the decisive role this mechanism plays in defining production, labor and exports.

Both theory and empirical evidence indicate that an RER and real interest rates that achieve internal and external equilibrium in an emerging economy — with a sustainable CAD and low inflation — can result in net inflows of destabilizing capital. This convergence occurs via a gradual accumulation of real capital and the consequent increase in the capital/labor ratio in the recipient economy (Held 1996). Attempts to accelerate this convergence with high financial inflows create a well-known situation:

- an overall revaluation of assets (the wealth effect)
- a decline in domestic savings, derived from the wealth effect
- a reduction of the real exchange rate
- a rise in the CAD
- expectations of currency devaluation
- ultimately effective devaluation, and a costly adjustment in the balance of payments
- financial crisis

This was the recipe for the Mexican crisis of 1994, Thailand in 1997, and Chile and Argentina at the beginning of the 1980s. The correct path, then, is to persevere in maintaining a sustainable CAD and an RER that is compatible with an export orientation, managing net capital inflows when necessary.

Policy suggestions for this orientation include:

- raise the domestic capital component in D.L. 600 investment guidelines[14]
- plan real foreign investments, including the associated credits, for a period of three years, requiring approval of capital inflows not previously announced (Agosin 1997)
- introduce variable marginal reserve requirements for investment capital inflows, fixed one year in advance, according to the projected balance of payments situation

---

13   This situation would continue even if the CAD rose two points and net capital inflows declined by the same amount. At this point, though, the problem would become a dangerous CAD by international standards.

14   Gathered from the recent Foreign Investment Committee's decision to raise, from 30 to 50%, the domestic capital component of the D.L.600 protection operations.

- limit placement of secondary American Depository Receipts (ADRs) (Rosales 1994; Ffrench-Davis 1997)
- review tax incentives for foreign mining investment in new projects (Arriagada 1997)
- expand investment opportunities for the Pension Fund Administrators (AFPs) to include: real infrastructure projects; risk capital; issuance of government bonds (with the Production Development Corporation, Corfo, as a second-tier bank) to provide small and medium businesses (SMBs) with credit and funds for technological modernization; and issuance of government bonds for public investments pertaining to systemic competitiveness (infrastructure, ports, export development, science and technology, training and education)
- extend the foreign capital reserve requirement period from 12 to 24 months, thereby reducing interest rate arbitrage (Bitar 1997)
- establish a reserve requirement for supplier credits or, failing that, establish a 90-day coverage period for imports, thereby promoting demand for foreign currency (Bitar 1997)
- raise taxes on interest repatriated abroad (today 5%) to 15 or 20% in order to reduce the incentive to bring funds in as credit and repatriate the interest at the 5% rate, instead of the 35% that applies to revenues (García 1997)

Chile cannot address the gravity of the peso revaluation process with a single measure or with a limited set of economic policies. We must enact measures that stimulate domestic savings, along with others that stimulate demand for foreign currency, while restricting the money supply. Meanwhile, we need to examine the viability of some of the measures proposed. Excess foreign capital manifests itself in excess consumer spending, so it is also fundamental that the government expand its set of tools for regulating spending cycles in accordance with the economy's potential. An effective defense of the exchange rate requires the use of anti-cyclical tax measures (Rosales 1994; Zahler 1995) or of marginal rates of social security taxation, contingent on the economic cycle and diverted into individual accounts (Rosales 1994).

These measures may be unorthodox but they are a serious effort to counteract economic distortions. At the same time, these policies would help prolong the country's long growth cycle. This goal demands that we reinvigorate our non-traditional exports, broaden our export base by involving more companies, reduce disparities in productivity, and better extend the benefits of growth to the labor market. From this perspective, we can examine the specific aspects of economic policy that have a decisive role in the export dynamic.

Inflation Deceleration

In the current context of globalization, our inflationary goal is undoubtedly to achieve the lowest rate of inflation possible, but in a manner that is stable and minimizes the direct or indirect costs on other macroeconomic variables. At the current inflation level of about 5%, additional reductions will have an ever-increasing effect on production and employment levels. The impact of high capital flows on aggregate demand will obligate the government to work in medium-term periods, employing high interest rates and requiring a constant effort to reduce the national budget. These measures are especially necessary given that fiscal policy will, in the next three years, face a set of income and spending factors that threaten to lower current domestic savings (Dipres 1996).

Reducing inflation more quickly, without altering the flow of foreign capital, will aggravate the decline in the real exchange rate. The value of the currency already has fallen almost 5% annually for five years. At the same time, an impending tariff reduction and a series of trade agreements are about to further increase the competitive demands on the tradable goods sectors, particularly those that compete with imports.

In this scenario, high interest rates (particularly for SMBs and microlenders) will persist and the exchange rate will continue to decline for some time, lowering the profitability of non-traditional exports and the viability of many productive units.

Anti-inflationary policy options are debatable in and of themselves. Nonetheless, we would do well to keep in mind the ongoing vulnerability of the export basket in the face of variable terms of exchange and protectionist pressures. This is our distinct asymmetry: an inflationary performance similar to the OECD countries and a third-world export structure, highly vulnerable to external cycles. If we redouble our efforts against inflation, external shocks will have stronger repercussions. As the gap between real and nominal variables narrows, each adjustment will have a harsher impact. The effect will be especially pronounced in the labor market, where unemployment will likely increase in order to stabilize the economy under its new conditions.

Priorities in the Relationship Between Inflation and the Exchange Rate

It would be risky for the government to continue revaluating the peso at the pace it has done for the last three years. This policy would adversely effect production and labor and destabilize our external accounts. In fact, there are no known examples of export success accompanied by a sustained rate of revaluation. The exception would be if a nation had consolidated its exports and achieved a current account surplus, which could occur after at least two decades of vigorous export development.

Let us recall that anti-inflation policy thus far has aimed to lower inflation while taking advantage of domestic savings and productivity. In the last two years, savings have stagnated and productivity gains have probably come from the reduction of manual labor in leading industries. As such, it would be more sensible for us to recover the holistic vision of macroeconomic equilibrium, while expanding the lens with which we evaluate the performance of economic policy.

The Speed of Capital Account Aperture

The 1990s have demonstrated a government preference for opening the current account, as seen in the approach to exchange rate policy, the disincentives to short-term capital, and incentives to medium- and long-term capital aimed at improving technology and productive capacity.

The debate about a "financial center" tends to modify these priorities. Theory aside, we cannot easily imagine a "financial center" that imposes a reserve requirement on short-term foreign capital, does not allow free conversion, and maintains the current system of prudish regulation and supervision. But if the country were to maintain these conditions, it would in truth be doing nothing more than extending an international financial policy that is sensible and sensitive to the dangers posed by financial globalization. Such a policy is designed to limit the importation of risk and minimize external shocks.

We should expect the government to update its proposals for furthering the country's financial insertion into the global marketplace, incorporating the lessons of Hong

Kong's stock market and financial crises and their impact on the rest of the world. In particular, we should note here that countries whose current account imbalances exceed 5% of GDP face limitations in the international financial market.

VI. Greater Equilibrium Between Macroeconomics and Productive Development

High and stable growth is a central part of achieving equity, but it alone is not sufficient. It must be complemented, on the one hand, by more effective social policies. These should offer broad coverage and adequate financing, and focus on promoting opportunities and investment in human resources. On the other hand, growth must be accompanied by productive development policies that have a greater relevance for resources and for the institutional framework. The latter policies must include training, technical support, financing, and technology to modernize the production of small and medium enterprises, which provide the majority of jobs.

The public and private funds currently assigned to training, productive development, and dissemination of technology are insufficient to meet our challenges. If we do not make significant progress in these areas, we will lag behind in employment and in the social benefits of growth.

Neoliberalism has never questioned its support for production gains. Nevertheless, a good part of the governing coalition still entertains serious doubts about the necessity or urgency of more rapid progress in this area. The government believes that the mere performance of markets and horizontal development policies can adequately address the formation and modernization of our technological, entrepreneurial, and human resource bases. These elements are essential to improving our international competitiveness and positioning.

The key questions here are: does structural heterogeneity matter or not? Does it decline with growth? If not, are horizontal policies sufficient to close the gap, or at least diminish the most conspicuous differences (like backward regions or industries that are not economically viable but have a significant share of manual labor)? What alternative tools are available that can close gaps in productivity and income, and at the same time enhance productivity?

If there are doubts about the technical effectiveness of such tools or about the ability of institutions to resist protectionist pressures, we have operational solutions for both. The performance evaluations the country has already implemented point in the right direction. However, we detect a great asymmetry in the government's numerous performance measures for productive development tools but few or none for other areas of public spending that are far more important in dollar terms.

Our central argument, then, is that the country's successes in macroeconomics and international arena have brought us to a turning point. We are starting to perceive the need for a stronger commitment to productive development and job quality. The debate is just beginning. It could start with the consolidation of our macroeconomic equilibrium, which we must preserve with great care, regardless of the scenarios we face. The key factor could be preserving the holistic vision of our macroeconomic equilibrium while paying closer attention to the macroeconomy's varying impacts on different industries and on the level and quality of employment.

BIBLIOGRAPHICAL REFERENCES

Achurra, M. 1995. "La experiencia de un nuevo producto de exportación: los salmones." In: P. Meller and R. Eduardo Sáez, eds. *Auge exportador chileno. Lecciones y desafíos futuros.* Santiago: Cieplan, Dolmen.

Agosín, M. 1997. Speech at Asexma seminar: "The Export Model and the Exchange Rate." Santiago, August 20.

Arriagada, G. 1997. "La tributación minera." El Mercurio, p. A-2, December 14.

Bitar, S. 1997. Speech before the Senate, regarding the report by the President of the Central Bank to the Senate, September 9.

Díaz, A. and J. Ramos. 1997. "Apertura y competitividad." In: R. Cortázar and J. Vial, eds. *Construyendo opciones. Propuestas económicas y sociales para el cambio de siglo.* Santiago: Cieplan.

DIPRES (Budget Director's Office, Finance Ministry). 1996. "Aspectos macroeconómicos del proyecto de ley de presupuestos del sector público del año 1997." Santiago: Budget Director's Office, Finance Ministry.

ECLAC. 1992. "Equidad y transformación productiva: un enfoque integrado." LC/G.1701(SES.23/3), February, pp. 112 to 120.

ECLAC. 1994. "El crecimiento económico y su difusión social: el caso de Chile de 1987 a 1992." LC/R.1483, December, Santiago.

ECLAC. 1996. "Fortalecer el desarrollo. Interacciones entre macro y microeconomía." LC/G.1898(SES.26/3), March.

Engel, E. et al. 1997. "Dinámica de empleo y productividad en manufactura: evidencia micro y consecuencias macro." Industrial Engineering Department, University of Chile (mimeo).

Figueroa, I. 1997. Principales rasgos de la inserción de Chile en la economía mundial. Año 1996. Santiago: General Directorate of International Economic Relations, Chilean Ministry of Foreign Relations, May.

Ffrench-Davis, R. 1997. Speech at Asexma Seminar: "The Export Model and the Exchange Rate." Santiago, August 20.

García, A. 1997. "The Importance of Productivity To Economic Growth and Income Distribution." Ministry of the Economy conference at the Second International Workshop on Economy and Administration, Santiago.

Held, G. 1996. "Notas sobre política cambiaria." Santiago: ECLAC (mimeo), August.

Hofman, A. 1996. "Economic Growth and fluctuations in Latin America. The Long Run." Work presented at the conference on "Development strategy after neoliberal economic restructuring in Latin America." Miami, North-South Center, University of Miami.

ILO. 1996. "Panorama Laboral 1995." ILO Report 2. Lima.

ILO. 1998. Chile. *Crecimiento, empleo y el desafío de justicia social,* pp. 248 to 250. Based on M. Mortimore, América latina frente a la globalización. Serie Desarrollo Productivo 23. Santiago: ECLAC.

Larroulet, C. 1997. Speech at Asexma seminar. "Political Economy and Export Development." Santiago, May 15.

Meller, P. and R. Sáez. 1995. *Auge exportador chileno. Lecciones y desafíos futuros.* Santiago: Cieplan, Dolmen.

Mideplan. 1996. *Balance de seis años de las políticas sociales, 1990/1996.* Santiago: Planning and Aid Ministry, August.

Ministry of the Economy, Chile. 1997. "Estudio sobre productividad total de factores en Chile," (mimeo).

Rosales, O. 1994. "Tipo de cambio y modelo exportador." *El Diario,* column on December 21.

Rosales, O. 1995. "Política industrial y fomento de la competitividad." ECLAC magazine 53, August.

UNDP. 1996. Desarrollo humano en Chile 1996, September.

Zahler, R. 1995. Speech on the 70th anniversary of the Central Bank of Chile.

The State of Economic Processes

Francisco Javier
José María Fuentes

Introduction

T he subject of the size, role, and effectiveness of the State reemerged prominently in Chilean political debate during the final months of 1997. In part, this was because the issue represented a clear point of distinction between government and opposition supporters in the campaigns for the December Congressional elections. While the former pointed to their achievements and called for increased resources, the latter identified unsatisfied demands and tied them to deficiencies in government management or to an oversized or excessively active State.

While the debate has at times been heated, the issue is clearly not a new one. In fact, during a significant portion of this century, the topic of the State's role in the economy has been at the forefront of ideological debate both in Chile and around the world.

In Chile, the extent of the State's economic activity has most frequently been determined by the political orientation of the government in power. The most extreme examples were manifested in the period from the 1960s through the 1980s, when the Chilean State reached its maximum and minimum levels of economic activism in the 20th century.[1]

In recent years, however, the polarization of these positions has decreased dramatically. Political stances are no longer "all or nothing," and broad areas of consensus exist. One sign of this was that despite the democratic opposition's continual criticisms of the military government's economic model, when the Concertación came to power it did not reverse the policy of curtailing the State's active role in the economy.[2] Although the State has significantly increased its role in fostering social development, promoting growth, and regulating the economy, all of the country's mainstream political currents acknowledge the private sector as the driving force behind Chile's economic expansion. They further agree that the State should not function as a producer of goods and services that can be adequately supplied by the private sector.

---

1 For example, in 1973 some 596 companies were owned or managed by the State. That figure dropped to 47 in just 10 years.
2 For example, of the 45 companies owned or managed by the State in 1989, only 38 remained in government hands by 1994. Government spending as a percentage of GNP fell from 21% in 1990 to 20.5% in 1995.

Nonetheless, the apparent similarity between the democratic administrations and the military regime diminishes considerably when we look more closely at concrete actions taken by the State during the 1990s. The difference is particularly evident in the democratic governments' goal of growth with equity and their willingness to compensate for short-comings in market operations.

The State can be understood as "a set of social institutions that establish order in a given territory and are supported by the threat of centralized coercive force." Thus, this concept is much broader than that of government, which is the entity tasked with defining public policies and administering the State apparatus. Despite this distinction, and the title of this paper, the authors will focus on the role that government, as the State's administrative entity, has played during this decade. This does not exclude the discussion of topics applicable to the State as a whole, but simply implies a focus on the government's role in addressing those subjects. More specifically, we will seek to highlight the actions that have had the strongest repercussions in the economic system, although their influence on political, social, and cultural affairs may be equally profound.

The State is unquestionably responsible for furnishing the legal order that facilitates the interaction of the country's various social, economic, and political forces. In a democratic context, upholding the rule of law becomes a critical State function which cannot be delegated. While a general analysis of this function is far beyond the scope of this paper, it is nonetheless evident that a large portion of the State's economic action involves the creation and execution of laws. This process requires the participation of the three branches of government. However, this paper will mainly focus on the role of the administrative branch in promoting legislation compatible with its economic goals. We will also describe the conceptual framework for the State's economic action, as well as the efforts undertaken by government to ensure both the technical and social effectiveness of this action.

The extent of governmental participation in a nation's economic affairs varies enormously. While in some cases this action is limited to legislative measures, in others it extends to direct participation in the production of goods and services. Many governments, however, fall somewhere in between: encouraging private sector action through taxes, subsidies, and regulations, or contracting with private entities to implement public policies under the supervision of State agencies.

This paper is not organized on the basis of specific State interventions. Rather, it is structured according to the type of tasks carried out by the government, as the State's administrative body, in order to increase efficiency and equity in the economy. It also seeks to address how the Aylwin and Frei administrations have met these challenges from 1990 through 1997.

Along with the public policy priorities and achievements during that period, it is important to note the obstacles the democratic administrations have faced, particularly those related to politics and internal management. The former include restrictions placed on executive branch activity by Congress and the judiciary. These limitations are not addressed here but are discussed extensively in other chapters of this book. The subject of the government's efforts to increase efficiency in its internal operations, however, will be reviewed.

The Economic Role of the State

It is interesting to note that almost complete consensus reigns among economists of vary-ing political persuasions on the theoretical foundations of the welfare economy. The con-cept is that when conditions for perfect competition exist, the free operation of markets will lead to the "optimum" allocation of resources (according to Pareto's definition). In other words, artificial improvements to one factor will negatively affect another. Nevertheless, the distribution of income is determined by the education, skills, technology, capital, and other resources possessed by people when they enter the market. Therefore, even if markets were competitively perfect, society could determine that the resulting dis-tribution of income is unsatisfactory and request that the State take action to redistribute income or wealth. This is achieved primarily through tax and social welfare policies.

The identification of equity as a policy objective is one of the important differences between the governments before and after 1990. The Concertación coalition, during its eight years in office, has maintained a consistent policy of striving for a more equitable dis-tribution of income and wealth. This policy is discussed in Section 1 of this paper.

Aside from these efforts to improve the distribution of wealth, it is important to rec-ognize that the prerequisites for perfect competition are not present. On the contrary, significant market deficiencies are seen in various sectors of Chile's economy. From an economic perspective, this means that markets are operating inefficiently. Welfare theory calls upon government to counterbalance this inefficiency.

The Chilean government has shown much more determination to compensate for these shortcomings during the past decade than in the preceding years. The decisions adopted and the methods used to confront particular problems in market operations have been a source of controversy. Conceptual and practical aspects of the Concertación admin-istrations' quest for greater efficiency in imperfect markets are discussed in sections 2 and 3. Section 2 also examines the government's production of public goods and its efforts to compensate for negative externalities. Section 3 reviews the regulation of monopolies and the State's promotion of fair competition.

The evidence will show that during the 1990s, the government of Chile has been com-mitted to both efficiency and equity. However, it is not sufficient for the administration to identify needs and design policies to satisfy them. Rather, the government must also carry out this action in the most effective and efficient manner possible, deriving maximum utili-ty from taxpayer-provided resources. As it faces more complex challenges, the government must seek to improve its efficiency as a manager. Thus, Section 4 addresses the govern-ment's current efforts to modernize public administration.

Interestingly, the dual objectives of equity and efficiency are not necessarily contra-dictory. While Chile's recent history clearly shows that significant progress can be made in one area if enormous sacrifices are made in the other, economists, politicians, and Chilean society in general appear to have taken a lesson from this experience. During the 1990s, therefore, public policy has sought to satisfy both objectives simultaneously. Similarly, the public and private sector should not be perceived as rivals but as complementary forces as they seek to confront the challenges of development. For these reasons, the discussions below cut across these lines and are separated here solely to facilitate their presentation.

I. The State's Search for Equity

The CASEN survey of December 1996 revealed that 23.2% of Chile's inhabitants — some 3.3 million people — live in impoverished households, defined as those in which per capita monetary income falls below the poverty line. Of this total, approximately 841,000 are truly indigent.

This situation was much worse at the beginning of the decade. In 1987, poverty affected 45.1% of Chileans, or some 5.5 million people. That figure fell by just 500,000 individuals over the following three years (through December 1990). During the next six years, within a democratic system but with similar rates of annual GNP growth, nearly two million Chileans escaped from poverty.

In spite of this progress, Chile's poverty rate continues to represent a problem which the entire nation must contribute to resolving. While growth has been the leading factor behind reductions in poverty, the State has also contributed actively with its social policies.

Despite Chile's achievements in fighting poverty, the country's income distribution remains highly unequal. The wealthiest 10% receives some 40% of income, exceeding the earnings of the most impoverished 10% by a ratio of thirty to one.

The figures show that little progress has been made in this area in recent years. The country's efforts have succeeded only in preventing further deterioration, not in reversing the trend. However, it must be recognized that in rapidly-expanding market economies such as Chile's, an increase in the concentration of wealth is frequently observed, since the system highly compensates those who contribute most to the process (investors, entrepreneurs, and skilled laborers) and provides them with expanded opportunities.

It can be argued that poverty and income distribution are two different issues, and that only the former calls for government intervention. However, in the view of many experts, especially those associated with the Concertación, the pronounced imbalances among different social groups are equally worrisome. These imbalances lead to differing interpretations of the concept of poverty on both sides of income gap. Dissatisfaction is common among those unable to attain levels of income and consumption they believe to be "average." Thus, the unequal distribution of income may give rise to excessive indebtedness, job dissatisfaction, or excessive overtime work. Sociopolitical phenomena are also attributed to the gap, especially resentment of a system perceived as inequitable, humiliating, and encouraging the abuse of power and privileges.

Unlike the fight against poverty, which involves relatively direct and targeted policies, the quest to improve income distribution lacks flexible, politically viable mechanisms which are clearly compatible with the country's growth. The national distribution of income stems from structural factors in the economy and can only be altered by long-term changes or through drastic and traumatic measures such as expropriation or high taxes. In the latter case, experience shows that such a "minimum common denominator" approach can, after a few years or decades, lead to stunted growth and to income distribution as unequal as it was before (although potentially supplemented with other entitlements).

In addition to promoting growth-oriented policies, the Concertación governments have encouraged reforms aimed at improving income distribution in a gradual and politically viable manner. The Concertación has recognized that these policies represent medium- to long-term measures which may not show immediate results.

Within these efforts, three main areas of policy and action can be distinguished, although they are intertwined to a certain extent. The first set of measures involve the direct or indirect modification of income levels. The second set includes government efforts to improve the future distribution of skills and resources through social investment. Finally, policies are promoted to provide economic support to society's most disadvantaged groups.

1. POLICIES AFFECTING INCOME DISTRIBUTION

Because of its clearly redistributive nature, this first category of policies has generated considerable controversy. The Aylwin administration, upon taking office, nonetheless felt strongly that these reforms needed to be on the agenda to counterbalance legislation established prior to March 1990. The previous system protected corporate concerns to the detriment of workers and State interests. Examples include labor legislation strongly tilted toward employers, a tax system with low personal and corporate income tax rates (as well as numerous loopholes), a repayment system for subordinated debt favoring private banks over the Central Bank, and a lack of legal protection for consumers.

The incoming administration found its hands tied in any attempt to modify the legal framework in place in 1990. During the eight years of democratic rule, the presence of designated Senators and the effects of the binomial electoral system have combined to give the opposition ongoing control of the Senate. Since bills require approval by both houses to be enacted, any new law must be supported by at least a portion of the opposition.

Tax reform was one legal modification implemented by the first Concertación administration. The changes targeted four areas. The basis used to calculate corporate tax was expanded. Flat and complementary tax rates were increased. The tax basis for agricultural, mining, and transportation industries was changed from assumed income to real income, and the value added tax (VAT) was increased from 16% to 18%. These modifications generated an additional US$600 million per year in revenues, thereby enabling the government to increase social spending by 9.3% in real terms between 1990 and 1991 and an additional 10.5% the following year.

As a result of negotiations conducted with opposition Senators from the Renovacion Nacional party, the new tax schedule was temporary, expiring at the end of 1993. However, new negotiations that year allowed the VAT level to remain at 18% during 1994 and 1995, and the president was authorized to maintain a rate of between 16% and 18% in 1997.

The labor reforms approved between 1991 and 1993 represented another legal modification attained as a result of agreements between the government and the opposition. Although the reforms were considered insufficient by leading union organizations such as the CUT, as well as by the government — which proposed a revised bill in 1997 without success — they clearly constituted significant progress and served to further empower workers.

The labor reforms included an increase in maximum severance pay for laid-off workers from five to eleven months of wages; the creation of a system of indemnity for household servants; improvements to the vacation system based on years of service; tightening of employers' responsibility to ensure compliance with labor and social security laws among subcontractors; establishment of minimum conditions for seasonal agricultural workers; legal recognition for syndicated unions; and the creation of a fund for training union leaders.

Along with these tax and labor reforms, the government achieved eventual success with a consumer rights bill submitted by the Executive to Congress in 1991. This law, which took more than five years to be negotiated through the legislative process, regulates the relationship between vendors and consumers. It also provides consumers with tools to defend themselves against potential vendor abuses.

The main features of this legislation include the enumeration of consumers' basic rights and obligations; the definition of consumers' rights as inalienable; authorization for the creation of consumer organizations; specification of vendors' obligations; regulation of standard-form contracts; procedures for establishing liability; penalties for breaches of contract or severe deficiencies in goods or services; and legal procedures to enable consumers to defend their rights.

Lastly, the law establishes a simple mechanism allowing consumers to exercise their rights either by filing a complaint with the National Consumers' Service (SERNAC) or with the local courts. In the latter case, suits must be filed in writing before a judge, but need not be presented by an attorney.

The veto power of the right-wing opposition, thanks to its majority in the Senate, was a constant consideration during the negotiations for all of the above-mentioned reforms (tax, labor, and consumer rights), since these changes threatened to affect the interests of the most powerful groups in Chilean society. Nonetheless, the government and a portion of the opposition were able to reach agreement on these three important efforts, within a context of strong public pressure for reform. Although contributions from the floor of Congress have enhanced the bills in some cases, the usual pattern was that the bills suffered such drastic modifications that their final text differed radically from the original proposal.

In the December 1997 elections, the moderate opposition circles whose cooperation made progress on these reforms possible lost ground to those taking a harder line against redistributive policies. Thus, the negotiating room for further agreements leading to a more equitable distribution of income has become even more limited.

2. SOCIAL INVESTMENT POLICIES

A second type of policy has focused on providing greater equity in social investment. In keeping with commitments made in the early 1990s to "pay the social debt" and "invest in people," more than two-thirds of the public budget throughout the decade has been allocated to so-called social spending, primarily represented by health, housing, social security, and education. Social spending rose from 12.6% of GNP in 1989 and 12.8% in 1990 to a stable figure of some 13.5% between 1993 and 1997. In real terms, this translates to a 77% increase in the funds allocated to these areas.

While keeping public finances in order, the democratic administrations have also increased real wages for civil servants and significantly expanded their benefits. Particularly noteworthy achievements have been made in the area of pensions, housing, health, and education. Due to the importance of human resources in the latter two areas, both in sheer numbers and because of their direct contact with the population, special emphasis has been placed on raising the previously meager wages for workers in these fields.

Increasing the productivity of present and future workers has been another important goal as the government has sought to correct income imbalances in a stable and self-sustaining manner. These measures have also contributed to economic efficiency, as explained below.

Educational reform has been critical to this effort. Better-educated children are better prepared for life and become more productive workers. Real spending on education nearly doubled between 1990 and 1997.

In the area of training, the resources provided to the National Training and Employment Service (SENCE), including scholarship programs, grants, youth training, contracts for worker training, and so forth, increased by 900% in real terms between 1990 and 1997, thus reaching 10 times their previous level. During the same period, SENCE's salary expenditures rose by just 51%.

Policies aimed at promoting microenterprises and improving small businesses' access to credit, training, and technical advice also dovetailed nicely with efforts to expand GNP and enable new players to benefit from the country's dynamic growth. Although these policies continue to receive limited public funding, they represent a dramatic shift away from the traditional system of subsidies. The old methods tended to favor specific sectors, and the powerful businessmen in them, leading to a greater concentration of wealth rather than a more equitable distribution of prosperity.

Interestingly, in addition to a net increase in the resources allocated to social investments, efforts have simultaneously been made to improve their coverage and efficiency. Thus, the private sector has been brought in to implement numerous social programs under the oversight specialized government agencies. Under this approach, the government focuses on designing and evaluating the programs to ensure that its social goals are being met.

Although evaluation methods in this area are still limited, available studies suggest that the strategy of outsourcing these projects to the private sector has expanded coverage and raised standards. Evidence is even more limited in the areas of supervision and impact evaluation. However, some examples of poor administration have emerged, suggesting that the government needs to play a stronger role in the oversight of these projects.

Significantly, these social investment policies do not exclusively target the poor. They also help to improve conditions for the middle class, whose gradual weakening largely accounted for the broadened income distribution gap observed during the military regime.

3. SUPPORT POLICIES FOR THE NEEDY

The third type of government action in the social sphere worthy of special mention is the effort to steadily improve conditions for the many disadvantaged Chileans for whom no effective support mechanisms previously existed.

In addition to the political and legal benefits obtained by needy Chileans during the 1990s, it is important to note that specific policies have been implemented to provide greater economic advantages to indigenous peoples, the physically challenged, female heads of household, retirees and senior citizens, youth, minimum wage earners, and the residents of isolated and remote areas.

II. Economic Efficiency in Providing Public Goods and Compensating for Negative Externalities

According to the basic tenets of economic welfare theory, the State can contribute to increasing efficiency if the economy does not operate under truly competitive conditions.[3]

Goods and services are understood to be provided in an economically efficient form when their number and price are consistent with what the society overall is willing to buy.

Since this rationale stems from a conceptual framework widely accepted by economists, it serves as a solid foundation for a discussion of those areas where the State is called upon to correct inefficiencies. Thus, we will provide additional commentary on the subject of market deficiencies before turning to the corrective actions taken in Chilean markets during the 1990s.

Two types of market shortcomings are the so-called "externalities" and the presence of "public goods." While the two situations are completely different, they are presented together here because they often appear simultaneously and tend to respond well to similar public policies.

4. THE CONCEPTS OF PUBLIC GOODS AND EXTERNALITIES

Public Goods

A public good is defined as a product or service with the following characteristics: first, the cost of an additional person using the good is practically zero; second, it is difficult or impossible to prevent an additional person from accessing the good. In other words, the status of "public good" largely depends on the inability to exclude potential beneficiaries. We speak of pure public goods when that exclusion is neither appropriate nor easy to effect.

Because of these features, public goods tend to be unattractive to private sector suppliers. In essence, the private sector is uninterested in offering a service for which no one is willing to pay, since everyone will wait for a third party to fund the good and then make use of it at no cost. For this reason, the market tends to generate a number of public goods which is below the socially desirable level; that is, the form and number society overall is willing to finance. These features do not mean that the public good is free or inexpensive. On the contrary, in many cases, these products or services are quite costly.

The need for public goods is one of the primary reasons for State intervention in the economy, even where the market is relied upon to allocate most resources. Pure public goods might include national defense, public security, public health (such as the control of epidemics), environmental protection, political stability, macroeconomic stability, an appropriate international image, or a reasonable distribution of income. In addition, other public goods exist which are not quite so "pure" because exclusion is possible, although expensive or inappropriate. This may been seen in State support for highway infrastructure or health care facilities.

---

3   Of course, government intervention in areas of market imperfection does not guarantee an increase in efficiency. For this to occur, the cost of such government action must be less than the cost of the deficiency it seeks to correct.

Externalities

Externalities occur when the actions of an individual or a company affect other people or organizations, but no compensation is made by either side for the resulting harm or benefit. Externalities can be either negative or positive.

In the case of a negative externality, an economic agent harms third parties by transferring (or externalizing) part of the cost of that action to society. Thus, persons making the decision to produce or consume a good or service do not consider this cost in their actions. A fully free market tends to generate a larger amount of negative externalities than is socially desirable.

The classic example of this is pollution. A factory that releases toxic gases generates costs such as discomfort, medical expenditures, reduced productivity, and even reduced life expectancy, but it does not pay the price for those effects. In this case, the social cost of the factory's production is greater than the private cost, since the latter includes only labor, raw materials, and capital investment. Since producers compare their cost with the value (price) society places on the good, it may appear to be profitable to manufacture a large quantity of products using environmentally-damaging processes. However, if we compare the benefits to the overall cost to society, it appears more efficient to produce less of this particular product.

In other words, in the case of negative externalities, since private players are not responsible for the entire cost of their actions, they tend to conduct them in excess.

Positive externalities may also occur and involve economic actions that benefit third parties. For example, a beekeeper and an apple producer generate mutually beneficial externalities. The logic of negative externalities is inversely applicable in these cases: the market tends to produce less than the socially optimum level when positive externalities are present.

5. CORRECTIVE ACTIONS IN THE 1990S

Clearly, these shortcomings in the marketplace are not mutually exclusive, and public policy may need to address both situations simultaneously. For this reason, the following description of corrective actions does not attribute the need for such measures to a particular economic phenomenon.

Macroeconomic Stability and Non-Distorting Policies

Chile's levels of inflation, fiscal surplus, unemployment, foreign trade, and economic growth place it among the best-managed nations in the world. Furthermore, the policies aimed at promoting exports and overall production are designed in such a fashion that they do not introduce distortions or interfere with the efficient allocation of resources.

In many ways, the 1990s can be considered the decade of Chile's highest economic performance this century. In fact, if the evolution of poverty and other social indicators are added, the progress achieved this decade stands unprecedented in the nation's entire history.

Although the macroeconomic details are analyzed in other chapters, it is important to note here that these policies have been perceived as a core function of the State, and that the government has shown leadership and initiative in their application. Furthermore, although the Central Bank is an autonomous agency not subject to the whims of the administration in power, it does form part of the structure of the State.

Investment in Infrastructure

The spectacular growth of Chile's foreign trade and particularly of natural resources exports has placed enormous pressure on the nation's domestic and international transportation network. For this reason, the continued success of Chile's export model depends upon the nation's roadways, bridges, tunnels, seaports, airports, and other infrastructure. Deficiencies in this network may produce a severe bottleneck for Chile's economic growth.

With this in mind, the democratic administrations have implemented an ambitious infrastructural investment plan. From 1990 through 1997, the government's budget for public works practically doubled in real terms. This enormous increase in the volume of investment was attained without staff increases at the Ministry involved.

Furthermore, the use of private capital through public works concessions and legislative reforms in the areas of seaports and sewage treatment systems will permit these services to broaden their coverage and achieve higher levels of efficiency.

Public Works Concessions   During the 1990s, the government of Chile has made consistent efforts to provide incentives for private sector participation in the development and maintenance of domestic public infrastructure through a system of concessions.

Neglect of the country's infrastructure during the 1980s created an enormous public works deficit and revitalized demand for investments to correct the problem. Funds have also been required in the 1990s to replace worn-out infrastructure and to finance new projects emerging in response to economic growth.

To meet current demands, annual public works investments in Chile must total some US$1.4 billion to US$1.5 billion through the late 1990s and into the coming century. In the early 1990s, it was widely believed that 50% of those funds could be raised through a concession program, and that the remaining 50% would be financed directly by the State. Although current forecasts of private sector involvement have been revised downward (to some 20%, or 300 million dollars), this contribution remains highly significant.

The concessions mechanism seeks to attain a series of simultaneous goals:
- expanding and improving the nation's infrastructure through renewed investment
- increasing efficiency in the use of resources
- introducing user fees to cover the cost of infrastructure (thus improving both financing and the allocation of costs in the economy)
- increasing user satisfaction

The concessions system is based on a call for bids from all interested companies. Bidders present economic proposals including fees to be charged and payments to the State, in accordance with minimum project specifications and other conditions. The successful bidder must create a company dedicated exclusively to implementing the project. That firm becomes the concessionaire.

Significantly, ownership of the concession project remains in the hands of the State from the beginning. The concessionaire is granted permission to use the project and to charge appropriate fees, once the State has inspected and approved its installations. The company must continue to comply with the project specifications, meet specific maintenance standards, and provide the services under the conditions established in the contract.[4]

---

4   The two preceding paragraphs are taken from PAL's Legislative Bulletin, November 1994.

Despite the key role taken on by the private sector in certain public works, the State remains highly active in this area. The government:
- undertakes the lion's share of investment (some 80%)
- retains responsibility for the long-term planning for infrastructure projects, to promote the public interest
- retains significant rights over the projects granted by concession

Among the latter is the ownership of the project, as noted above. In addition, the State reserves the capacity to influence the concessionaire's implementation of the contract, to collect information about the concessionaire and oversee its work, to modify the contract — subject to certain rules and limits — when necessary for the public interest, and to penalize the concessionaire for failure to meet its obligations.

While some of the foundations for the concession system originated in the mid-1980s, this strategy has flourished in the 1990s. During this decade, the system has come of age in legal terms (thanks to legal and regulatory modifications throughout the decade) as well as in its practical application, with the implementation of the first projects.

Modernization of Seaport Legislation   The development of Chile's seaports stands at a crossroads. On the one hand, Chilean ports tend to be small and to be situated in urban areas, making expansion difficult. On the other, the cargo moving through public ports has more than tripled since 1980, straining their current capacity as well as the access routes which serve them.

To rectify this situation and ameliorate port conditions, government policy has aimed at the following objectives:
- strengthening the efficiency and competitiveness of seaport operations
- promoting competition among ports and reinforcing competition among suppliers within them
- providing incentives for private investment
- modernizing the state-run sea port system
- creating an institutional framework permitting coordinated action by the State and the private sector
- ensuring that port systems are developed in harmony with their environment

To achieve these goals, three new policy approaches have been devised:
- a new regulatory framework for the seaport sector
- a system of seaport fees
- the modernization of the state-owned Chilean Port Company (EMPORCHI)

The new regulatory framework for the port system includes a set of revised concepts and operating rules for the sector in accord with the objectives noted above.

The new legislation includes the following elements, among others:
- the process for requesting and granting maritime concessions for the use of ports
- the rights and responsibilities of the concessionaire and the State
- requirements for licensing fees
- conditions for the cancellation of a concession
- regulations preventing monopolistic practices and promoting open competition

In its fee structure, the new system promotes competition wherever possible and calls for tariff regulation where competition is not viable.

Three types of activities can be distinguished which are subject to differing treatment. The first group includes loading and offloading services, the movement of cargo from the port to the ship and vice versa, and portage to private facilities. These activities, which are currently conducted by private firms in a strongly competitive framework, will continue in private sector hands, and port authorities will be excluded from carrying them out. Second, cargo storage and other secondary services will be free from tariff requirements. The third group of services, including the supply and operation of basic infrastructure required for cargo transfer; services provided to ships in protected waters; and other common port services will be subject to regulation.

The modernization of EMPORCHI will be effected through major structural and staffing modifications. Both changes aim to improve efficiency in port management. The structural change will involve breaking down the current state-owned company into a series of private corporations, each operating one or more ports. In the area of personnel, staff will cease to be civil servants and become employees of the private firms, through legal alteration of their contracts.

The modernization process also includes a series of requirements and restrictions to promote a higher level of professionalism and independence among the Boards of Directors.

It is hoped that this set of changes will improve the efficiency of the nation's ports, adapt them to the infrastructural requirements of current economic activities, and foster investment by the private sector. The new rules also seek to maintain and encourage competition in all areas of port activity where it is possible.

New Legislation for Water and Sewage Services   New legislation for water and sewage services was approved in late 1997. The law strengthens sectorial regulation and allows the private sector to acquire sewage companies currently owned by the State. The topic of regulation will be further discussed below.

With its limited resources, the State is currently unable to provide certain services. It is hoped that these activities may represent economically viable opportunities for the private sector, attracting an influx of private capital. Sewage treatment is an excellent example of this possibility.

Investment in the Promotion of Production

A third area of State contribution to markets where the private sector's investment is insufficient can be found in the promotion of production.

The State's efforts to bolster exports fall into this category. In 1995, reimbursements to exporters (approximately US$120 million), tax refunds on capital goods (some US$28 million), and ProChile's export promotion activities (some US$16 million) accounted for 41% of total expenditures on production promotion.

In addition, subsidies granted for job training (approx. US$68 million), technological innovation (US$40 million), auto assembly (US$28 million), irrigation (US$24 million), and forestry (US$16 million) represented 44% of public spending in this area.

The remaining 15% was spent on improving productivity and competitiveness among mid-sized, small, and micro enterprises. US$20 million was allocated to small-scale agriculture through the Instituto Nacional de Desarrollo Agropecuario (INDAP). Small and mid-sized mining operations received US$12 million through the Empresa Nacional de Minería (ENAMI). Small and mid-sized urban businesses were supported by the Corporacion de Fomento de la Produccion (CORFO) at a level of US$12 million. Other programs included the normalization of real estate ownership (US$4 million) as well as the support for microenterprises provided by the Solidarity and Social Investment Fund (FOSIS). Between 1991 and 1995, FOSIS assisted some 60,000 microentrepreneurs by providing training, consulting, and credit. In 1997, some US$14 million was allocated for FOSIS programs.

Environmental Externalities

A fourth area of government action worth noting is its correction for negative externalities affecting the environment. The market has been unable to achieve a socially desirable balance for problems such as pollution, the over-exploitation of natural resources, and congestion in major cities. These undesirable effects hamper the economy's long-term growth capacity and produce inefficient bottlenecks.

Over the past seven years, the Concertación governments have made notable progress in developing the necessary legislation, resources, knowledge, and institutions to address this emerging issue. The National Environmental Commission (CONAMA), created in June 1990, is tasked with coordinating action in the environmental field and formulating initiatives to improve the quality of the nation's environment.

The government sent a bill entitled "General Foundations for the Environment" to Congress, and the new law was enacted in March 1994. In concert with that effort, a set of presidential instructions for the preparation of environmental impact assessments was issued in 1993. Regulations establishing environmental quality and emissions guidelines were published in the Official Gazette in 1995. Regulations establishing procedures and timetables for prevention and cleanup plans went into effect in October 1995. In 1996, the legislation implementing the environmental impact assessment system was enacted. As a result of this law, all significant investment projects, both public and private, must present an environmental impact study or statement.

In addition to these regulations, which fall under the general framework law, specific regulations and measures have been established and enforced in the areas of air pollution, water pollution, solid waste management, the environmental deterioration of the Metropolitan Region, and the over-exploitation of natural resources. In the latter category, the 1991 Fisheries Law and the legal protection for native forests are particularly significant.

Regulations on the Administration of Third-Party Property

Although economic theory assumes that owners control their companies, in reality this economic premise is only partially correct. In fact, many minority shareholders may have a stake in corporations, along with shareholders who have ceded their rights to other entities. In the case of Chile's private pension fund administrators (AFPs), a small group of managers is responsible for assets belonging to thousands of workers.

The State is responsible for regulating and supervising the activities of these companies in such a manner that the rights of all interested parties are respected.

A unique challenge in this area is the growing activity of holding corporations and consortia. These conglomerates are composed of several companies interrelated by ownership, control, and/or association. Their features include:

• common, centralized management of finances and investment policies

- unified management policies throughout the conglomerate
- loyalty and a sense of belonging to the same team among the conglomerate's high-est-ranking executives, even if they work for different companies or areas
- clear and recognized central leadership
- a strategy focused on maximizing returns for the holding corporation over the long term rather than a focus on profits in each member company

Until the financial crisis of 1982, Chile's holding corporations were closely associated with banks. Furthermore, they used the banks' pools of deposits as sources of funds for their projects. The crisis showed that it was preferable for the banks to serve the community at large rather than being tied to a specific economic group. Chile's banking laws were changed to restrict operations among related people and companies and those involving shared ties of ownership.

During the 1980s and 1990s, a significant portion of the nation's savings has been accumulated in pension funds administered by the AFPs. Since the AFPs are authorized to invest in stocks, they have become increasingly influential on the boards of the nation's leading companies. While the AFPs participate in selecting board members, various laws have been enacted during the 1990s to ensure that their choices are limited to people unaffiliated with the holding groups controlling individual companies. The idea is that these board members will push individual firms to maximize their returns, thereby raising the value of pension funds and of the shares held by workers in the AFPs.

Important progress has been made in the 1990s in preventing holding companies or individual owners from acting to the detriment of minority shareholders. Measures in this area have included a ban on the use of insider information as well as restrictions on business operations that are incompatible with the interests of either minority or majority shareholders.

One example of this type of problem involved the Enersis conglomerate. In that case, a group of executives which held only 0.06% of the company's shares, but which held the positions of Chairman and General Manager, negotiated an agreement with Endesa Espana in which the aforementioned group would receive 33% of Endesa Espana's investment in the Chilean consortium. Strong opposition from individual shareholders and the AFPs, along with objections raised by the government supervisory agencies for AFPs and securities, thwarted the operation. As these lines were written, the outcome of this incident was not completely clear, although the executives involved had already resigned. Among the tools used by the government watchdogs, as well as by the minority shareholders and AFPs seeking to defend their interests, were the State regulations dealing with conflicts of interest and the use and availability of information.

III. The State Seeks Efficiency by Regulating Monopolies and Fostering Competition

From a theoretical perspective, the presence of monopolies is unanimously recognized as a justification for government intervention in the marketplace. Monopolies occur when one company or a small group of companies is able to control market prices. Such conditions are considered a deficiency in the market, since most of the virtues associated with a free market appear only in vigorously competitive environments; that is, when each company controls only a small segment of the market. Within a monopoly, the amount traded is below the social optimum, while the price charged exceeds it.

Monopoly situations can be resolved by promoting competition, for instance, by removing legal barriers that prevent the entrance of competitors. This approach has been used in cases such as the long-distance telephony market, where access was opened to numerous carriers. Another means of fostering competition is to open the economy to international trade, forcing domestic producers with no local challengers to compete with overseas manufacturers.

These solutions, however, do not work against natural monopolies in the area of services, where it is not feasible to open the market to additional players nor to introduce international competition. Examples include local telephony, electric and gas utilities, water and sewage services, the subway, railroads, etc.

Historically, Chile has confronted these monopoly situations by creating state-run enterprises that operate their services and charge fees in accordance with public policy objectives. Nonetheless, the current consensus is that the production of goods and services should primarily lie in the hands of the private sector. Thus, we are witnessing a gradual withdrawal of the State from its entrepreneurial role in dealing with monopolies and a shift toward a regulatory focus. In other words, the State is now concentrating on creating appropriate conditions to allow privately-run monopolies to provide services in the amounts and at the prices deemed to represent the social optimum. For example, the mechanisms for determining rates for local telephony, electrical distribution, and water and sewage services are established by law. In determining these prices, the regulators seek to identify rates compatible with the efficient operation of a model company.

Theoretically, this regulatory method faces limitations that can make it very expensive, potentially even more expensive than keeping the monopolies under the wing of the State. The regulatory cost will be higher if the market for the good or service is subject to numerous contingencies; if those contingencies are difficult to predict; if it is hard to monitor the established rates and ensure quality control; and if there are significant asymmetries in the negotiating capacities of the parties involved.[5]

Clearly, the movement against the "entrepreneurial State" commenced during the military government. However, the privatization policies implemented at that did not sufficiently address the problem of regulating private monopolies.

There were three problem areas worth mentioning:

First, the initial privatization program led to monopolies in some sectors where competition would have been possible.

One example is the power sector, where as a result of the privatization process (1978-88), the Empresa Nacional de Electricidad SA (ENDESA) secured 70% of the nation's power generation capacity, water rights to future hydroelectric projects, and the transmission grid in the central-southern part of the country. In addition, CORFO sold ENDESA the Pehuenche power company and thus further concentrated ownership of the nation's power generation capacity.

This almost complete concentration took place even though most experts agree that this type of activity can easily be competitive. In fact, the regulatory framework for this

---

5   This classification, as well as some of the examples given, are taken from E. Bitrán C. and E. Saavedra C., "Rol Regulador y Empresarial del Estado" in *Hacia el Estado Regulador* (Santiago: CIEPLAN, 1992).

industry (DFL 1 of 1982) establishes a system providing generating companies with unlimited access to the country's transmission and distribution grids using a system of tolls. However, some 60% of Chile's power backbone (the Central Interconnected System) is owned by ENDESA and Pehuenche, 83% of transmission is controlled by Transelec (an ENDESA subsidiary), and 14% by STS (of which ENDESA owns 40%). In addition, ENERSIS participates in the ownership of ENDESA and Chilectra (the main distribution firm). These conditions place other power generators at a distinct disadvantage in comparison with ENDESA.

A further example of an unnecessary monopoly was exhibited in the telecommunications industry, where for years long-distance calling remained in the hands of a single firm.

A second set of problems arose from ambiguities in the regulatory frameworks. Examples can be found in the power industry, telecommunications, and water services. The primary problem lies in asymmetrical information about the costs involved, a key component in determining the rates that a "model" company should charge.

A third set of obstacles was found among the regulatory agencies. According to Bitrán and Saavedra, "in Chile, regulators have been subject to influences and pressures of a political nature or from interest groups that keep them from adequately exercising their regulatory role."[6] The limited independence of these agencies stems in part from their organizational structures. They are often located within government ministries which are subject to consistent political pressure.

Furthermore, regulators frequently perceive their jobs as temporary — a consequence of low public sector wages — and tend to envision their professional futures on the other side of the regulatory fence. This may influence their decisions and thus severely hamper the State's regulatory capacity.

Finally, it comes as no surprise that major political and economic players can be extremely influential when it comes time to draft or vote on a law or regulation that affects their interests. One example noted by Bitrán and Saavedra to demonstrate the impact of political pressure in Chile is the difference between the legislation regulating the fisheries and public transportation industries, where the situation in need of regulation is conceptually similar. The fishermen, thanks to their strong lobbying capacity, were able to ensure that only a small number of fishing quotas are allocated through a public bidding process. The bus owners, however, having more limited political power and a poor public image, ended up with a system in which bus routes are determined exclusively through competitive bids.

The Concertación governments have actively worked to expand the State's regulatory capacity. Numerous new or modified regulations have been designed, developed, and implemented over the last seven years.

In some cases, the methodology has consisted of separating processes and creating opportunities for competition in activities that were previously absolute monopolies in overall terms. Examples include the separation of long distance telephony (currently competitive) from local calling (still a monopoly), and the separate administration of cargo and passenger trains (where competition is possible) from track management (still a monopoly). In addition, the new EMPORCHI legislation will facilitate competition among seaports.

---

6   Bitrán C. and E. Saavedra C., 1992.

Regulations are still being drafted in other cases, such as the electrical and gas utilities.

In the area of water and sewage services, in 1990 the State divided the Servicio Nacional de Obras Sanitarias (SENDOS) into 11 different autonomous corporations. Each of these new companies was organized to serve a particular region, in the areas from Region I through IV and XI through XII. (The Metropolitan region and Region V already had their own companies, EMOS and ESVAL, respectively).

Simultaneously, regulations were issued to control the rates set by these companies, and the first round of new rates was established that same year. The newly-adjusted rates, designed to allow the companies to operate at a profit without government subsidies, resulted in a price increase. To offset this social burden, the government implemented a new set of subsidies for low-income consumers.

In early 1995, the administration sent a new bill to Congress in an effort to introduce changes into the water industry's regulatory framework.

Designed to strengthen the State's regulatory capacity, the new law sets up a Superintendency of Water Services. High-level employees of the Superintendency are banned from providing services such as consulting, either directly or indirectly, to the companies under their supervision while they hold the post and for three months after their departure. In addition, the Superintendent is empowered to reorganize the institution based on changing and emerging oversight needs, within existing staff and budgetary allocations.

Competition is also being fostered in sectors where ownership is concentrated in the hands of a few companies. For example, the delivery of natural gas from Argentina will facilitate thermoelectric power generation, thereby reducing the monopoly power of the current hydroelectric producers.

Examples of market simulations through public bids can be seen in public transport and, to a lesser extent, in the fisheries industry.

In those industries that remain monopolies, the State establishes a rate similar to those that would exist under competitive conditions, based on estimates for a model company.

As noted in the preceding paragraphs, the democratic administrations have energetically used their resources and political will to address market imperfections in the areas human capital, infrastructure, production, and the environment, as well as the lack of competitive conditions in some markets. Although many tasks remain unfinished, the government's resolve to confront the areas neglected by the State before March 1990 remains evident.

It is interesting to note that the State's role in producing public goods, countering externalities, and regulating monopolies is included in all basic economics textbooks and should have been taken into account in the implementation of the economic model that inspired the military government. These functions were omitted for two main reasons: a strong ideological commitment to an overall reduction of the State's role in the economy, and the short-term conflict of such measures with the objectives of the business community's major players.

IV. The State Seeks Internal Efficiency

Although, as described above, the Chilean government has been successfully confronting new, demanding tasks, it is nonetheless weak when compared to the dynamism and innovation of the private sector.

Clearly, change is afoot in the areas that traditionally linked the State to economic processes. The arenas in which the State enjoyed broad legitimacy and wielded considerable power are shrinking daily. The State is no longer an entity that absorbs idle labor, nor an inexhaustible source of political patronage. State-owned companies are being privatized or downsized. The central government increasingly depends on the private sector to implement its policies, and regulations and enforcement are becoming more stringent. Public sector pay is comparatively unattractive.

The State is confronted with situations it is ill-prepared to face. Administrative decentralization has shifted responsibilities to the regional and local levels. These newfound duties are approached tentatively, without experience and with limited skill. Meanwhile, the "war on poverty" declared by political officials leads the needy to continue perceiving the State as their primary beacon of hope.

The challenge posed by regulation may best illustrate the State's relative weakness. The sectors that remain unregulated are the economy's most dynamic, endowed with abundant and high-quality human and technical resources, as well as significant lobbying capacity, whether directly or through the media. On the other hand, most of the State's regulatory agencies lack sufficient qualified personnel. When such staff members can be found, the State is hard-pressed to keep them in service. As noted above, the private sector has a keen ability to "co-opt" regulators, either by open and legal means (asymmetry in access to technical information, pressure from public opinion, job offers) or through secret and illegal mechanisms (personal networks, interest groups, or corruption).

These disadvantages on the part of the State are not only present in monopoly situations. Similar conditions exist in the oversight and enforcement of labor laws, forestry legislation, fishing regulations, and so forth. Although inspectors' pay is somewhat higher than that of other civil servants, their oversight capacity suffers from severely limited resources.

The widespread perception is that government service is not a desirable career. This, combined with a gradual loss in public appreciation for the work performed by civil servants (within an increasingly individualistic and materialistic culture), has served to fuel the flight to the private sector.

Experience in many countries indicates that regulation is only effective in the presence of solid oversight institutions. In budgetary terms, this means increased expenditures (usually above strict statutory limits) and the perception of a "larger" State. The business community reacts with public denunciations of an increase in red tape and "backsliding" from the worldwide trend to streamline government operations.

Structural transformations, such as changes to institutions and personnel systems, would require legal modifications which are not feasible given the opposition's majority in the Senate. The government has therefore chosen a path which does not require immediate legal change. It seeks to improve the management of public institutions within the current institutional framework. The calls to "modernize management" fall within this context. This means moving forward toward result-based administration, as well as gradually increasing the autonomy of "public managers" so that the public sector may take advantage of techniques proven effective in private organizations. These include the concept of a customer/user with rights (who also serves as an external evaluator of public service), allocation of budgetary resources according to output and effectiveness, and merit-based promotions and pay raises.

In the face of resource restrictions and institutional barriers, it is imperative to sustain the sense of duty and dedication felt by many of Chile's civil servants. Their can-do attitude will be crucial in enabling the State to play its rightful role in the economy, a role focused on protecting social interests, enforcing appropriate regulations, and fostering growth. This can only be attained with a solid team of efficient, committed, well-paid civil servants, along with private citizens who fulfill their obligations and demand their rights.

Final Remarks

The 1990s has been a decade of economic progress, as exhibited in high growth rates, low unemployment and inflation, reductions in poverty, and other indicators.

Although the private sector is acknowledged as the primary driving force behind the nation's growth, the State has nonetheless played a crucial role, promoting efficiency and fostering equity at the same time.

Equity, a key ingredient in the policies of the two Concertación administrations, has gradually become incorporated into Chile's economic advance. In marked contrast with the two preceding decades, the State has dramatically increased its investment in people, particularly among the most impoverished and vulnerable of its citizens. Similarly, efforts to impart marketable skills to workers, youth, and small business owners reflect a desire to create equal opportunities and see them blossom over time.

During this decade, the State has sought to improve the operation of the market. By supplying public goods, counterbalancing externalities, regulating monopolies, and encouraging competition, the State has increased efficiency and corrected market shortcomings which would otherwise have led to lower production levels, higher prices, and the entrenchment of privileged, inefficient industries.

Particular importance must be placed on the calls made to the private sector in the 1990s to carry out and fund public tasks, from the implementation of social programs by specialized private organizations to the use of private capital for the construction of roads, ports, and pipelines.

This aim of expanding the market economy coincides with so-called neoliberal schools of thought. However, at the onset of the decade, these tasks had been all but abandoned, in all likelihood due to pressure from a business community enjoying the benefits of a lack of regulation, as well as the ideological conviction that a strong State means a weak market and the stifling of the private sector.

That a center-left coalition should decisively seek to improve market operations is a sign of our country's consensus on the need for a model which is viable over the long-term, one which combines efficiency with equity. Despite this general consensus, the State's ability to back up its approach with concrete action is hampered by the political context in which the Executive lacks a majority in the Senate.

This Congressional obstacle is not the only one the State must confront in its efforts with regard to the economic process. Despite considerable progress, areas of weakness persist.

The State as a regulator is subject to enormous pressure from the groups it regulates. The ability of business leaders to influence political life is manifested in at least two key areas: their well-recognized role in funding political campaigns, and the incontrovertible power of the media controlled by business interests. Furthermore, as noted earlier, the public sector's pay scale severely limits its ability to attract and retain qualified, professional personnel. This increases the risk that Chile's civil servants will be co-opted by the companies they are called upon to oversee.

In the social sphere, dynamic economic success has led to rising expectations among the nation's most disenfranchised citizens. In light of these shifting demands, increased government spending still fails to meet people's hopes. Additional resources are needed, along with improved public management and strengthened program oversight.

Enormous tasks have been undertaken between 1990 and 1997. Despite the immense sums allocated to them, they remain incomplete. This is the case with educational reform and the remaining gaps in the area of health care. Other issues have emerged as a result of growth itself, such as the pollution and congestion in our major cities, and the relationship between the rational use of natural resources and environmental protection.

The tremendous range and diversity of the tasks that lie ahead suggest that, far from shrinking, the State must grow stronger, gaining technical skills and political legitimacy. This is the greater challenge before us, one which must be faced as Chile pursues its goal of environmentally, politically, and socially sustainable development over the long term.

Modernization, Development, and the Environment

Tonci Tomic
Fernando Toledo

Introduction

The world today is in the midst of a process of change, marked most distinctively by globalization. It is a true change in paradigm and as such is accompanied by a sense of crisis, from which Chile has not escaped. Empirical evidence indicates that such systemic transitions create winners and losers, good times and bad times, accentuated social differences, and not a small measure of frivolity and ostentation. Yet, history has taught us that once the new socio-institutional model is in place, paradoxically it bears little resemblance to the transition process that preceded it (Perez 1997).

Under such circumstances, the greatest challenge before us is to identify which aspects of the transition will become fundamental elements of the new scenario. Already we can assert that concern for the environment as a determining factor of quality of life will be one of these fundamental pillars. Recent debates over world development give us reason to affirm that an important aspect of the new socio-institutional model will be its resemblance to a natural system;[1] that is, a type of techno-ecosystem.[2]

This transformation process, known in Chile as modernization, cannot be completed until we fully confront the issue of the environment. In other words, transformation will not be feasible unless economic and social development follows a sustainable route, taking into account the parallel objectives of growth, equity, and natural resource preservation. This is a challenge for the State, political parties, and civil society. The incorporation of the environmental dimension in development will affect the rate of the modernization process for the country as a whole, both in the public and private spheres.

---

1   That is, a structure with large, medium, and small industries, occupying specific floors or niches, with explicit interdependence, mutually beneficial interrelationships, networks of high flexibility and adaptability, recycling, "co-ompetition" (cooperation and competition), "glocality" (global and local action); in short, one of great systemic efficiency.

2   A new publication of the MIT Press, the *Journal of Industrial Ecology*, has already raised this possibility.

I. Theoretical Considerations

1. A BRIEF LOOK AT A SHORT HISTORY

The November 1997 special issue of *Time* magazine is devoted entirely to the environmental issue, under the cover story "Our Precious Planet: Why Saving the Environment Will Be the Next Century's Biggest Challenge." This is an indication of the surprising evolution experienced by the environmental issue within a short period of time. While concern for the environment and nature have been evident throughout history, only during the last 25 years has it emerged as one of the most driving and mobilizing issues of modern society, and it is certain to become a central topic for the coming century.

Neither the concern expressed by modern society for nature and the environment, nor the real danger of degradation facing our environment of which so many have warned, sufficiently explain the force with which this issue has burst upon the scene. We need to explore in greater depth the context in which this concern has come to hold society's attention, at times obsessively, in its grip. That is, how in such a brief period of time we have shifted from believing factory smoke to be "the smell of progress," to the conviction that smog is the number one enemy of the health of the urban population of the planet.

In truth, we are talking about a concern for mankind itself, based on a negative diagnosis for its future, which has caused the environment to become such a widespread and growing concern. From this point of view, the fragility of the development model is due precisely to the failure to envision a sustainable pattern of production and consumption for all mankind based on the use of natural resources.[3]

Thus, the problem is not merely one of redefining the relationship between mankind and the natural environment. It is not a question of altering primarily technical variables — although technology is, undoubtedly, the focus of the change — but rather of establishing more harmonious ways for mankind to relate to the environment. The point of departure for this must be a change in relations among human beings themselves, a restructuring around a "new common sense" and greater solidarity, founded upon freedom and respect for life — in all its forms — which encompasses our species in its planetary wholeness.

It is this sphere of experience that explains the omission of landmark developments on the environmental issue from texts on ecology or environmental science; instead, these can be found in narrations of modern history. Distinguished figures such as Einstein and Gandhi not only placed in doubt the capability of societies to bring peace, justice, and well-being to all, but also the possibility for human beings to attain happiness in a world such as the one whose foundations were laid in the first half of the century.

Another landmark development was the international youth protest movement in 1968, a manifestation of an existential loss of faith in the possibility of a revolutionary transformation of society. This process gave birth to the ecology movements and green parties, which channeled this frustration by endowing the rebellious spirit with a new objective.

Since then, concern for the environment has spread throughout the world and has often been submitted to radical and fervent debate. However, in the second half of the

---

3   Simply stated, if all mankind were to attain the average standard of living of the wealthiest upper percentile, at the current state of technological progress, the natural resource reserve would collapse, since the demand for natural resources would be far greater than the world supply of those resources.

1990s, the environmental factor is no longer a hindrance. Rather, it tends to converge with economic principles in which sustainable development — economic growth in harmony with the efficient use of natural resources and environmental restoration — has begun to be a real possibility.

An incipient change is likewise evident in certain societal values, an essential pre-requisite if the objectives of sustainable development are to be achieved. A new ethic and a new esthetic outlook seem to be spreading throughout the world, contributing to the creation of the "new common sense" mentioned previously. This outlook assumes that the environmental dimension is an important factor in development, because mankind believes it to be so. Certainly, this does not guarantee success, but it is a basis for a good beginning.

Until recently, in Chile, as in the majority of developing nations, environmental degradation was seen as a problem stemming from excess progress, a characteristic of industrialized nations. Our countries had, it was said, more pressing problems, such as poverty and the lack of economic growth.[4] While there is some truth to this argument, countries such as Chile do have serious environmental problems: air pollution in cities such as Santiago; the contamination of rivers, lakes, and bays; soil erosion; and losses of biodiversity, to give just a few examples. The degree of environmental deterioration in the country is significant and must be confronted and reversed. Government officials have come to recognize the problem and have taken measures in this direction.

Environmental concerns first emerged as a social movement in Chile in the 1960s, but took firm hold during the period of authoritarian government that began in 1973. The active role acquired by the Catholic church as a social force during this era coincided with a new expression of civil society — the non-governmental organizations (NGOs) — in which academics and frustrated politicians, mainly from the center-left, formed an insti-tutional and intellectual foundation for the environmental movement.

Influenced by the church, universities, and political parties, the NGOs structured themselves upon the values characterizing these three institutions. Together they were able to bring about a horizontal rupture of the vertical relations between State and civil society. It was in this social context that environmental proposals, understood as part of the so-called "alternative" path, began to coalesce (Tomic 1988).

Towards the end of the 1980s, when the process of transition from authoritarian rule to democracy had begun, these movements took on the form of political parties, similar to their European counterparts. Thus was born the Humanist Party, which later split, with one faction becoming the Green Party. As in Europe, the Chilean environmental-ecology movement spread far beyond the boundaries of political parties. Although these parties have relatively low membership levels, they have achieved widespread social recognition.[5]

---

4   Although concern for natural resources existed in Chile, as can be seen in the enactment of the forest law, the creation of national parks, the development of water legislation, and so forth, this was by no means a generalized or global concern.

5   In all likelihood, this can be explained by the fact that voters are generally aware of the criteria necessary for governing a country, which small political parties, such as the Greens, are not able to guarantee, although they evoke a certain level of support from the population. Votes cast in their favor may also represent a protest against conventional parties, rather than true ideological preference. For the same reason, they are heavily supported by younger voters, a social group which is often attracted to movements for change.

The concept of protecting natural resources and the environment evokes great support among the population. They perceive the environmental issue as something related to their own lives. The environment affects them directly, particularly in relation to health and the quality of life for present and future generations.

Currently, in conjunction with the rather diffuse social movement organized around concern for the environment, there is a relatively solid network of NGO environmentalists, with international connections, which for the most part represents a genuine expression of civil society. Furthermore, all of the major political parties express concern for this subject and frequently issue statements on environmental matters, although the Party for Democracy (PPD) has come to be identified most closely with the topic. Finally, the Concertación coalition governments have counted environmental protection among their major initiatives since the beginning of the decade, although with varying degrees of success. At the very least, this issue has undeniably become established as a central topic for national debate.

2. THE NATURE OF THE ENVIRONMENTAL PROBLEM

Environmental degradation may be the consequence of various types of actions: production, urban development, infrastructural works, and so forth. It is an unintended consequence of the use of natural resources and physical space. In economic terms, this unintended effect is known as an externality — in this case a negative one. One characteristic of an externality is that its existence does not affect the initial decision to produce or consume from which it stemmed. By definition, market forces do not detect externalization, and therefore it is not corrected by the pressure of private costs upon production or consumption.

One major barrier to the solution of environmental problems is the difficulty of identifying their exact origin. Many observers contend that natural resource deterioration can be traced to the style of development itself. Consequently, on many occasions, what is known as "the environmental problem" is not treated within a strictly ecological context, with different spheres such as the economy and politics entering into play.

A second consideration is the fact that it is unclear how this conflict will be structured. Explicit knowledge is lacking of the various socio-political players involved and their possible strategies for resolving the problem.

Third, the environmental issue's extension in time complicates action. Sustainable development requires that natural resources are use in a manner consistent with the needs of present and future generations.[6] Yet it is not clear who represents the "future generations." If the fundamental question concerns the acceptance or rejection of environmental destruction and deterioration, the answer is obvious. Not so obvious, however, is the choice of environmentally sustainable alternatives which society is willing to implement, in light of their costs and benefits and the social distribution of the same.

In addition, individual protagonists often perform a dual role: as citizens protective of the interests of their community and as economic players who must work and produce. Rushing into the necessary changes to development strategies may lead to losses in profits

---

6 The concept of transcendence in time can be deduced from various definitions of sustainable growth, particularly the one enjoying the highest level of consensus: that developed by the Burndtland Report commission.

and jobs, or even to the disintegration of an entire social group. It is preferable to find ways to compensate for such drastic changes, since the choice of sustainable development is being made by society as a whole.

It is within this social context that we consider the environmental issue. Due to the wide range of interests involved, the subject is ripe for conflict among various elements of civil society and between these and the State. The political weight and influence of the parties to these conflicts differ significantly. The complexity of this situation further increases as a result of the dual roles of protagonists, and the low stage of development of conflict resolution mechanisms in this area. The identification of the problem is an extremely important step. Clarity is needed regarding the positions of the various protagonists if realistic proposals are to be developed and implemented as part of a negotiation process which receives its legitimacy from the country's legal-institutional structure.

3. DIFFERENT APPROACHES TO THE ENVIRONMENTAL ISSUE

Various approaches have guided the emergence of the environmental issue and its relation to development. Although this is by no means exhaustive, empirical observation distinguishes three approaches, which we denominate as a) neoclassic-restrictive; b) eco-physical; c) techno-structural.

The Neoclassic-Restrictive Approach

This is the most common institutional approach employed by governments and businesses. It is the model generated through the modernization of production. This proposal represents the interests of an open economy and competitive markets. It advocates indirect economic policies applying homogeneously to all socioeconomic groups, and it focuses State programs on the objective of economic growth.

This proposal endows the State with a relatively important role in economic development, in keeping with the classic model. However, this role declines systematically over time in relation to its involvement in the market. Its restrictive nature is seen in the fact that the environmental element is perceived as an externality and is therefore incorporated as a restriction to the model. Environmental initiatives focus on the implementation of prohibitions and disincentives intended to inhibit the system from undertaking processes that degrade the environment, but they do not prevent such processes from taking place. The majority of programmatic proposals within this model represent attempts to define a legal-institutional framework for environmental action. While necessary, this approach still falls short of adding considerations of sustainable development to the prevailing development strategy.

A second set of restrictive actions is observed in the enforcement of public health regulations. This approach has the potential to bring certain aspects of the system into harmony with environmental goals, leading to direct quality improvement in an array of consumer goods as well as the restriction of certain materials and means of production that pose risks to the health of the population.

Finally, various restrictive regulations are often implemented for the purpose of reducing the emission of substances harmful to the environment.

The Eco-Physical Approach

The ideological basis for this approach is found in the ecology movement, and its institutional support is provided by action-oriented non-governmental organizations. These NGOs advocate various proposals and promote a range of programs. Regardless of their particular points of view, all play an important role in the environmental debate, since they represent an aspect of societal conscience.

Their general approach, which we term eco-physical, includes a set of proposals in which environmental-ecological aspects are central, even taking precedence over factors which today appear essential to the economic, social, and political order. Most of these strategies include a strong social equity component in addition to their environmental focus. They seek a more sensitive approach to the complexities and heterogeneous nature of society, with the aim of establishing sustainable growth as a central characteristic of development, along with other considerations such as nutritional security, biological stability, and balanced urban development. In short, they embrace a certain notion of physical balance in the world as a whole.

This basic focus is shared by Chilean native forest defense organizations, indigenous culture preservation movements, and nuclear disarmament groups, among others.

The Techno-Structural Approach

This theoretical approach views a sustainable development model not as the by-product of a set of restrictions, but as part of a positive strategy of development. In other words, its objective is to incorporate the environmental factor as a strategic variable in the decision-making model. Much of the programmatic content of this proposal can be found in the Rio de Janeiro Summit accords, known as Program 21, which was endorsed by every country represented at the conference, including Chile.

One objective of the techno-structural proposal is the design of an environmental administrative system, along with market mechanisms and regulations, which grant priority to the environmental variable while also participating in the political decision-making process. This approach contends that acute macroeconomic imbalance endangers the stability required for effective environmental decision-making and the implementation of medium- and long-range policies. The approach argues that a balanced macroeconomic framework, accompanied by low inflation rates, is a prerequisite for the creation of feasible sustainable development programs.

The opening of markets is desirable as part of an external trade development strategy, since such conditions tend to create greater opportunities for growth and economic vitality by expanding supply and demand in a competitive climate. However, this should not be taken to be either an automatic or universal formula which, on its own, will guarantee favorable conditions for sustainable development.

At the center of this debate are the simultaneous goals of economic growth, social equity, and sustainable environmental policies.[7] From a theoretical standpoint, the achievement of these objectives strongly depends upon sustained productive growth, which in turn is based on the systematic incorporation of technological advances. The theoretical premise is that a strategy tying competitive development to technology will

---

7   A. Schejtman, citing F. Fajnzylber, "Inserción internacional e innovación institucional," *Revista de la Cepal* 44 (Santiago 1991).

allow labor to become an object of competition, wherever technological complexity requires skilled operators. Thus, the labor factor may be transformed from an expense that must be reduced into a kind of capital deployed for the greatest competitive advantage. This will foster social equity through sustained wage increases, while also boosting worker productivity.

A relationship of this kind also allows for the effective and intelligent management of renewable natural resources, since exhaustive exploitation is inefficient in the underlying model. When natural resources are depleted, a major source of production potential is lost, while technology raises the value of these resources. Economic depletion of natural resources occurs before the actual value of the potential flow is equal to zero.

II. Progress and Achievements

After the Concertación's 1988 victory and the election of Patricio Aylwin as president, the new government had to face the accumulated environmental deficit resulting from years of official neglect. The new administration was aware that in the brief space of four years it would only be able to put into place certain key elements of the legal and institutional structure needed to sustain environmental policy.

The military government had ignored problems such as illegal garbage dumps, the lack of water treatment plants, Santiago's chaotic traffic and heavy smog, and the growing environmental imbalances in a country making extensive use of its natural resources. These situations, with their high potential for conflict, were a key part of the country's political scene when the new administration took office.

1. EFFORTS TO SET UP A LEGAL-INSTITUTIONAL FRAMEWORK

Initial government actions focused on what were perceived to be the most urgent areas: air pollution in Santiago, pollution caused by mining, water pollution, and the impact and management of forestry and fishing activities.

Air Pollution
Santiago still holds the dubious honor of ranking among the world's most polluted cities, along with Mexico City and Sao Paulo. This situation arose from unchecked urban and industrial growth, exacerbated by the city's particular topographic and climatic characteristics. The Andean foothills that ring Santiago foster the polluting-trapping phenomenon known as thermal inversion, especially during the winter months of June and July. In 1990, only 100 days of good air quality were recorded in the entire year.

A government decree in 1990 created the Special Commission on Metropolitan Region Decontamination (CEDRM), with the specific mandate of fighting Santiago's pollution problems. From its inception, one of the commission's priorities was the improvement of air quality in Greater Santiago, viewed as a highly urgent issue by the population.

The CEDRM acted primarily by presidential decree to establish emission standards and air quality monitoring and warning systems. In conjunction with government ministries and mayoral offices, it not only sought to upgrade the public transportation fleet but also to manage traffic patterns in the capital. The decrees regulating emission levels for fixed industries (Supreme Decree No. 4, 1991) and vehicular emissions (Supreme Decree No. 211, 1992) were particularly important.

These legal tools quickly affected daily life in the city: new public transportation emission regulations were enacted, and catalytic converters became mandatory for all new vehicles in Santiago. Incentives coupled with strict laws forced transportation companies to replace their old fleets of buses. Despite resistance from bus company owners and drivers, the government, backed by public opinion, was able to transform this sector's chaotic "open market" into a system of public bids for city transportation routes.

At the same time, strict limits were placed on large industrial sources of pollution as well as certain small and medium-sized firms, which were compelled to shut down during emergency air quality situations. Restrictions on vehicles without catalytic converters in Santiago are the most well-known of the pre-emergency measures. The last digits of the vehicles' license plates determine the days of the working week on which they are barred from circulating. At times, this restriction has affected up to 40 percent of all registered vehicles.

Because the expansion of public transportation is considered one of the few long-term options for reducing the flow of private vehicles in the Metropolitan Region, the government has made plans for a third subway line. President Eduardo Frei, who as a Senator had been one of the project's major proponents, inaugurated the new subway line in 1996.

Although these and other measures implemented by the government have had a positive effect on Santiago's air pollution, the problem persists. Critics within the Concertación coalition complain that the government focuses too heavily upon emergency programs rather than preventive measures, a weakness still seen during the Frei administration. However, structural changes, such as providing Greater Santiago's homes, industries, and power plants with natural gas via the trans-Andean pipeline between Argentina and Chile, paving the many dirt roads in the capital, and granting concessions for public transportation routes, will probably produce tangible results before the end of the decade.

Recently, the Metropolitan Region authorities took the step of declaring Greater Santiago a "saturated zone," paving the way for the development and implementation of the Metropolitan Region De-Contamination Plan, aimed at improving the area's air pollution problem.

Contamination Caused by the Mining Industry

A great proportion of the environmental damage caused by mining is the result of liquid discharges into rivers and lakes, along with toxic gaseous emissions such as arsenic and sulfur dioxide. Despite its small population and economy, Chile is one of the world's 10 countries most highly contaminated with sulfur dioxide. The State's high level of involvement in the copper mining industry has made it the largest polluter, which is a complicated role, considering its responsibility for environmental protection.

In 1992, Mining Decree No. 185 created the Interministerial Air Quality Commission (CICA) and set regulations for facilities throughout the country that emit sulfurous gases, arsenic, and particulates. The objective of these regulations was to restrict emissions and establish decontamination plans for existing plants. Based upon regulations of the Environmental Protection Agency (EPA) of the United States, the decree sets standards at least as stringent as the EPA guidelines, and in some cases more so. Aimed primarily at the copper industry, Decree 185 was intended to gradually reduce hazardous emissions over time from industrial metallurgical plants and mines by the year 1999. These efforts have had considerable effect. A great number of sulfuric acid plants have been built based on emissions-reducing designs, albeit at a very high cost, estimated by Codelco and Enami to run into the hundreds of millions of dollars.

Water Pollution

Water pollution, as a consequence of human and industrial activity, is unquestionably one of the country's most serious environmental problems. Chile has almost no facilities for the treatment of industrial and mining wastes and by-products. Waste is discharged directly into rivers, lakes, harbors, and other bodies of water, strongly affecting the irrigation supply for agriculture as well as lake and coastal waters.

Created in 1990, the Health Services Superintendency enforces a new set of regulations, all established by decree, aimed at banning or restricting the discharge of some 30 hazardous substances, particularly heavy metals and hydrochloride compounds. These regulations distinguish between discharges into sewage systems and those made directly into rivers and other bodies of water.

In 1992, the government began construction of a wastewater collection system in Santiago. Under the Frei administration, public works have been completed for the control of coastal contamination in Viña del Mar. The next step will be to construct water treatment plants. Given the immense costs involved and the State's limited budgetary capacity, this undertaking will necessarily depend upon assistance from the private sector. In 1997, the Frei administration won congressional approval for key legislation to initiate this process, which will also involve massively expanded access to clean drinking water for rural communities.

Forestry and Fisheries

Issues related to the use and preservation of Chile's native forests and the expansion of forestry activities were part of the public debate even before the recovery of democracy. Various groups expressed concern for the loss of the country's natural heritage, the displacement of rural communities due to the expansion of forest plantations, and contamination from the waste and by-products of pulp plants and other forestry-related industries.

One of President Aylwin's first initiatives was to prohibit the felling of century-old araucaria trees by declaring this native species a national monument. Additional issues in this area were accompanied by intense debate within the government and the Concertación coalition. These included the rejection of the private Terranova project near Valdivia; the Golden Spring case in Chiloe during the Frei administration; and the Native Forest Recovery and Forestry Promotion Bill of 1992, which aimed at setting the groundrules for the lumber industry.

Chile's share of the international wood products market is not insignificant. In 1994, Chile ranked third in wood chip production, after the United States and Australia. The many years during which the Native Forest Recovery and Forestry Promotion bill has remained on the congressional agenda are an indication of the issue's complexity. The Frei administration has been called upon to make sensitive decisions regarding the management of these resources. The most notable cases are the Pumalin Park preservation project of U.S. citizen Douglas Tompkins; the Trillium forestry project in Tierra del Fuego involving the lenga species; and the recent case of the Rio Cruces pulp plant near Valdivia.

Far-reaching reform was also undertaken in another extractive industry: fisheries. Chile is one of the major players in the international fisheries industry, ranking third in total output in 1990, after Japan and the Soviet Union. However, intense pressure on fishing resources, characterized by cycles of over-exploitation and excess extractive capability, has compelled the government to draft new regulations to control this market. The General Fisheries and Agriculture Law was enacted for this purpose in 1992. A recent event generating much controversy was the decision by the Undersecretary for Fisheries to ban the *American Monarch* from entering Chilean territorial waters. A veritable fishing factory, the ship has the capacity to capture and process enormous quantities of fish in a very short span of time.

Among the provisions of the General Fisheries and Agriculture Law were limits upon the total catch of various fish species, as well as a mechanism of individual quotas, initially assigned through bids, which can be transferred or traded. The law's focus on production drew criticism, but it did provide the government with certain tools to prevent over-exploitation and resource depletion.

Finally, electricity generation, while not an extractive industry, has become an emblematic case among Chile's environmental issues. This is seen in the Upper Bio Bio river valley project, where an energy-producing company proposes to construct a series of dams. The first of these has already been constructed at Pangue, with permits pending for the next dam at Ralco.

2. FURTHER REFORM

Although the first Concertación government implemented short-term measures to ease certain environmental problems and attempted to define rules to regulate the area, the scope of these problems demanded reform of the national environmental system itself.

On June 5, 1990, President Aylwin issued a decree creating the National Environmental Commission (Conama) for the purpose of defining an environmental policy and proposing a legal framework and institutional structure to support this effort.

Conama spent nearly two years in drafting a legislative proposal. When the Christian Democrats introduced their own bill in late 1991 — known as the "Frei bill," since then-Senator Eduardo Frei was its major proponent — the government was compelled to speed up the process, appointing the then-Secretary General of the Presidency, Edgardo Boeninger, to oversee its progress.

The government finally introduced a bill in August 1992, which, after heated discussion and negotiation in Congress, became law in March 1994, a few days before President Frei took office at the helm of the second Concertación government. President Frei later ratified the four bodies of regulations contained in the law, known as the Basic Law of the Environment (No. 19,300).

Systemic Problems
The need for this new set of regulations derived from an institutional assessment that confirmed environmental policy flaws evident since the early 1990s.

When the new democratic government took office, it lacked basic knowledge about the tools the legal system might offer the executive branch. Specific authority was dispersed among many legal bodies and regulatory systems. The new administration was also compelled to consider the numerous power structures that the various authorities had established over the years. More than 70 government services, agencies, and ministries

exercised some degree of at least nominal authority over environmental issues, with no type of
coordination or overall supervision of the area.

This situation was not only detrimental to
adequate environmental planning. From a strictly
economic standpoint, it was also a barrier to
national development. The exercise of multiple,
dispersed, and often conflicting authority might
well become a nightmare for certain economic
enterprises.

During the years of the military government,
the common response to this dilemma was simply a hands-off approach from the various
authorities, as the government sought to reduce
the national budget and the size of the State apparatus. Yet this option was not viable for a government subject to democratic and constitutional
checks and balances. Certain economic sectors,
particularly those sensitive to changes in international markets and the increasing participation of
foreign investment, soon realized that a change
from a system of multiple environmental authorities to one with clear rules would be a better
option — a lesser evil for some, compared to the
possible discretionary exercise of authority over
environmental matters by local governments.

> **THE BASIC LAW OF THE ENVIRONMENT, NO. 19,300**
>
> The Basic Law introduced in the Senate in September 1992 spelled out the global per-spective guiding the democratic govern-ment in its treatment of environmental issues. The following principles are worthy of note:
> - The principle of prevention
> - The principle that the polluter pays
> - The principle of gradualism
> - The principle of responsibility, which holds that those responsible for environ-mental damage must compensate the victims of those damages
> - The principle of participation, one of vital importance, which calls for the parties affected by environmental problems to take an active part in solving the problem
> - The principle of effciency, according to which the measures taken must carry a minimum social cost and allow a more effective use of resources

Another reason for change, but one whose
importance is often overlooked by observers outside of Chile, was the country's expectation that it would be admitted to the North American Free Trade Agreement (NAFTA).
The U.S. Congress was expected to demand the enforcement of certain minimum environmental regulations in Chile before its president would enter into negotiations with our
country. Thus, the prospect of access to NAFTA reinforced the need for clearer structures
of authority and regulatory mechanisms.

A Legal Framework

The Basic Law of the Environment is fundamentally a statement of commitment, criticized by industry as well as environmental organizations. In contrast to environmental
legislation in Mexico, Colombia, and Peru, it only endeavors to establish certain general
rules. This was intended to avoid what a former Conama executive secretary has described
as the common Latin American tendency to enact specific regulations which are soon
superseded and ignored.

The Law established a basis for the creation of a complex network of environmental
quality regulations, aimed at pollution control as well as general environmental protection
and resource management. In 1995, the Frei administration enacted two key sets of regulations under the law, related to air quality and emission standards as well as preventive
measures and decontamination plans.

ENVIRONMENTAL ISSUES FOR SUSTAINABLE DEVELOPMENT

Major environmental issues the country needs to tackle include the following:

• Integrated water resource management
• Preservation and sustainable use of biological diversity
• Definition of policies and administrative systems for renewable natural resources
• Environmental quality certification and accreditation for Chilean products
• Regulation of territorial management and land use
• Improvements to the quality of life in urban areas
• Implementation of environmental policies for mining
• The role of energy production
• Taking charge of environmental liabilities
• Commitments to global environmental problems and their effects on Chile
• Monitoring and enforcement of environmental regulations
• Environmental education and cultural change
• Achieving a balance between private rights and the public interest in environmental matters and
• Introduction of environmental considerations into instruments of economic policy

The Law provided for civil responsibility in cases of environmental damage. It further consolidated Conama's legal foundation as the government agency responsible for coordinating national environmental policy, under the supervision of the General Secretary of the Presidency, acting on behalf of the nation's president.

One of the Law's most significant contributions is its requirement that all major projects, whether governmental or private, must submit an Environmental Impact Study (EIA) or Environmental Impact Statement (DIA) to Conama or the Regional Environmental Commission (Corema), which has the final authority over the approval of these evaluations.

Regulations under the Basic Law of the Environment

During the second Concertación administration, President Frei has enacted further regulations under Law No. 19,300. These included the following: the Charters of the National Commission Advisory Board and the Regional Environmental Commissions; procedures and timetables for the Prevention and Decontamination Plans; and Environmental and Emission Quality Standards, all of which were ratified on October 26, 1995. In addition, an Environmental Impact Evaluation System was ratified on April 3, 1997.

3. ENVIRONMENTAL POLICY FOR SUSTAINABLE DEVELOPMENT

Environmental policy for sustainable development is based upon the goals of raising the quality of life; seeking an improved balance between socioeconomic development and the environment; and acting decisively and collectively to achieve social equity and defeat poverty (Conama 1998).

Among the most notable principles guiding public policy are the development of an environmental consciousness; greater State and private sector involvement in the issue; participation; sustainable growth; responsibility; prevention; stability; gradual and continual improvement; institutional enhancements; and responsibility to the international community.

The government's environmental timetable sets forth three basic objectives: first, establish a plan and specific environmental policy commitments for the year 2000; second, determine priority tasks for improvement of the national environmental system; and third, identify the major environmental issues the country needs to tackle.

III. Expectations and Frustrations

It is common that the expectations for an emerging issue such as the environment are greater than the realistic possibilities. The pace of adjustments to institutions, legislation, personnel systems, and financing mechanisms, among other areas, is inevitably slower than one would hope. This seems even more the case in an area of such great appeal and importance for the future of humanity.

It is also common that once the original design — in this case, for the treatment of environmental issues — is put into practice, unforeseen situations and problems arise. However, the fact that some problems may be unforeseen is no justification for the failure to recognize flaws and errors that could have been avoided, as in all human endeavors. This is a responsibility that must be shouldered from the start.

We recognize the great effort represented by the creation of an institutional and legal apparatus, as in the case of Conama and the Basic Law of the Environment, which essentially started from scratch, since nothing but scattered provisions had previously existed. Yet, it has been the insufficiency of precisely this institutional-legal foundation which has produced the greatest frustrations. These weaknesses have hindered the country's progress down the path of sustainable development, as well as the possibility for complete fulfillment of the constitutional canon of the right of every citizen to live in a pollution-free environment.

Another flaw is the manner in which environmental policy, thus far, has centered on a set of general guidelines, complicating the development of a comprehensive environmental strategy that puts forth objectives and the mechanisms for achieving them.[8] It is important to define this overall strategy in order to prioritize objectives, in view of the impossible task of achieving all of them in a relatively brief period of time. This, in turn, would provide a frame of reference for different public entities directly or indirectly involved in environmental matters.

We believe it is essential to adopt a comprehensive environmental policy. Rather than simply compensate for market flaws through regulatory intervention, this policy must analyze the variables affecting market operations and determine how to create the conditions for their optimization, whether through subsidies, taxes, or the setting of prices for environmental goods to which the market generally assigns no value.

Interministerial Coordination

At the beginning of the decade, when the Concertación discussed the appropriate institutional foundation for protecting the environment and promoting sustainable development, two distinct proposals emerged. The one which was ultimately chosen involved the creation of an oversight body within a political agency directly under the president's office. The other called for the creation of an Environmental Affairs Ministry derived from the present National Property Ministry. Both alternatives were backed by solid arguments.

The alternative of choice led to the creation of the National Environmental Commission (Conama), a body run by a Council of Ministries and headed by the Secretary

---

8 This situation is presently under review. The government has already presented the nation with the document "Environmental Policy for Sustainable Development," approved by the Board of Conama Ministers on January 6, 1998.

General of the Presidency. It was felt that this course addressed both fundamental dimensions of the environmental issue: environmental protection and the promotion of sustainable development. The first would be achieved through direct action by Conama and its regional offices, as mandated in Law 19,300 and its accompanying provisions for the Environmental Impact Evaluation System, Standards and Regulations, Prevention and Decontamination Plans, and the Advisory Council. As for the second, it would be achieved through interministerial coordination on the environment with representatives of the Conama Advisory Board.

While this was probably a typical case of unrealistic expectations, it took a massive effort to get Conama off the ground, and only after the regulations had been enacted was it possible to provide the entity with an operational structure and set it in motion. An initial frustrating experience has been the limited extent of the government's "environmentalization" in terms of concrete action, beyond genuine expressions of good intentions.

The Institutional Framework and Environmental Conflicts

In several instances, the institutional foundation was shown to be lacking in tools to address certain issues at the heart of environmental conflicts, showing that there is still much to be accomplished in constructing a legal framework for environmental matters.[9] In some cases, generally large-scale investment projects or those that adversely affect large segments of the population — as with the pipeline that would bring natural gas from Argentina to Chile or the hydroelectric plant construction on the Upper Bio Bio River — the system was simply unable to respond. This was a consequence of the absence of certain legal provisions, as well as Conama's recent installation in regions that lack the financial or technical conditions to absorb and support vast projects involving several million dollars of investment. A channel exists for resolving such situations within the central government, but the idea has been to give preference to decentralized operations.

In other cases, citizen mobilization tested the system, forcing regional and national authorities to intervene in order to reach a solution satisfactory to all parties.

The Environmental Management Problem

The interministerial and multidisciplinary nature of the environmental area, established in existing law, tends to undercut political authority.[10] While Cabinet ministers who head each ministry bear political responsibility for the thematic area they direct, this is not the case with environmental authority. The executive director of Conama has authority at that agency, and the title indicates the nature of the job: an executive position. Political authority, then, resides in the Secretary General of the Presidency who presides over the Conama Board of Ministers.

While the current institutional base is adequate — despite its advantages and disadvantages, which should be completely explicit so as to avoid mistakes — that base does not

---

9 Conama itself has proposed modifications to some regulations and has indicated its willingness to propose changes to Law 19,300, if need be.

10 The highest decision-making authority is vested in the President of the Republic or the Secretary General of the Presidency, but the nature of these positions means that the environment represents only a small fragment of their concerns.

automatically convey responsibility for environmental management. In response to this situation, in May 1996, the president issued an executive order to designate the appointed regional governors as being responsible for environmental management.[11] This executive order clarifies two matters: first, that the governor holds political responsibility for environmental management, which is consistent with the overall model, since the governor presides over the Corema; and second, that the regions are the territorial basis for this management structure. Remaining to be defined are the environmental management model the country intends to adopt, as well as the needed actions to complement the Environmental Impact Evaluation System, as this does not suffice as a legal basis from which to set up a management model.

In situations of environmental conflict, it is a troubling fact that the disputing parties — project supporters and those adversely affected by the project — have often discounted the administrative route as a means for solving the problem, preferring to appeal directly to the courts. This has resulted in a kind of "judicialization" of the environmental issue. It has tended to drain legitimacy from the pertinent administrative bodies, since the courts should only intervene once the administrative route has been exhausted, and when one of the parties alleges harm caused by an administrative decision. Otherwise, the system created for environmental management could become merely a referral service, and the resolution of conflicts, which in most cases requires highly technical and complex information, could remain in the hands of judges, who rule according to the law without consideration for the actual environmental impact at the heart of the conflict.

Legal Inadequacy

Along with an adequate management model, the solution to the problem discussed above lies in defining and designing new and better legal tools for environmental management. The Environmental Impact Evaluation

DUMPS AT LO ERRAZURIZ AND CERROS DE RENCA

Countries that adopt significant new environmental policies have faced a dilemma: local communities reject measures intended for the common good of all but having a specific impact on their own surroundings. This situation, known as "not in my backyard" (NIMBY) has posed a serious obstacle for the implementation of countless environmental projects. An example, although not strictly environmental, occurred with the closing on December 31, 1996, of garage dumps at Lo Errazuriz and Cerros de Renca, which received 80% of all garbage produced in Santiago.

Ongoing social mobilizations took place throughout adjacent areas, demanding that the dumps be closed immediately. Every location proposed as a new site for the dump sparked social conflict, as occurred in Lampa and Til-Til. The law failed to establish the authority of mayors and governors in this area, further complicating the situation as the closing date approached with no solution in sight. The city stood at the brink of a health and environmental emergency.

The deadline arrived with still no solution at hand, compelling officials to postpone closing the dumps. Thanks to the action taken by the former governor, who became directly involved in the case, a solution was found in the northern section of Santiago, allowing the old waste dumps to be closed. However, the "not in my backyard" syndrome soon spread to the localities and municipalities which were forced to operate as temporary stations before the garbage dump's transfer to its permanent location.

---

11 Speech by President Eduardo Frei Ruiz-Tagle during the 1996 signing ceremony for the presidential order on regional environmental management.

LAND USE MANAGEMENT AND ENVIRONMENTAL REGULATION

Examples exist abroad, as in the case of Germany, where the conjunction of these two instruments has been extremely effective as a frame of reference to define what may be undertaken in a given territory (land use management) and what effects upon this territory may be permitted (environmental regulation). This would allow great savings, for example, in the Public Works Ministry's infrastructural development programs. The Ministry would be able to rely upon a global frame of reference for what may be done in a given space and reject projects beforehand, eliminating the need for long and costly feasibility studies before ruling them out.

This would provide an excellent way to complement the Environmental Impact Study, which contains highly subjective elements such as cost estimation. In the case of the Upper Bio Bio River, it is impossible to avoid asking how a cost can be assigned to the archeology, culture, or tradition of the Pehuenche people who have lived in the areas for centuries. How, concretely, can one assign a cost to the area's scenic beauty, or an archeological site such as the indigenous cemetery?

System is perhaps the central legal instrument for any environmental management model, but its underlying objective is merely to "regulate" potentially negative effects upon the environment caused by large-scale projects. Consequently, a legal vacuum leaves unregulated a great many smaller and medium-sized projects, the sum of which may result in effects as detrimental or worse than those of large projects. In the future, it will be necessary to study new legal instruments for environmental management, such as land use regulation in both urban and rural areas.[12] Other measures may include promoting citizen participation as a central element of environmental management; setting up a national environmental information system; and providing greater support to firms retooling their operations to reduce pollution.

Precedents can be found in other countries, particularly in Europe, where the environmental impact study is not considered the central tool for environmental management. These countries have an explicit land use policy, the result of consensus and flexibility, that makes it possible to maintain certain land use regulations, similar to urban regulatory plans. They also have clear, unambiguous environmental regulations for both emission control and quality.

Citizen Participation

There is a virtually national consensus that citizen participation is a key element in attaining sustainable development, as set forth in Law No. 19,300. There have been two basic forms of citizen participation or expression with respect to environmental issues: spontaneous protests against a given project or certain aspects of it, and the kind of systematic participation addressed by Law No. 19,300. It should be said in passing that this is one of the country's laws that most fosters citizen participation.

Experience has shown that spontaneous actions tend to be unruly and exceed regulatory bounds. Yet they often cause a project to be abandoned or lead to direct negotiation between the parties in conflict, which is a highly positive outcome. One problem that has

---

12 A spatial regulatory plan would make it possible, for example, to save large sums on studies, as the plan would identify various land use zones.

emerged in these negotiations, however, is that environmental goods and non-environmental goods have been treated as if they were interchangeable. For example, adverse environmental impact has been accepted in exchange for payments or other types of goods and services. This undermines the reason for the conflict and creates a poor precedent as a method for social action. This situation gives rise to the question: if a project has no negative environmental effects, perhaps due to its technology, should this compensate for harmful non-environmental aspects of the project? In our opinion, if environmental factors can be interchanged with other types of project impact, whether economic, archaeological, social, or of another kind, it will be simply impossible to structure an operational environmental management system.

One reason for the low level of citizen participation observed in this area is that the current legislation maintains confidentiality in the information used in developing Environmental Impact Studies. Communities have no access to this information and therefore have little opportunity to affect the final decision on whether to proceed with the project. Citizen reaction after the fact thus remains the only option. Nevertheless, it is not easy to devise a broad and permanent system for citizen participation, as this would only led to a type of anarchy on the subject, and over the long run it would discourage beneficial investment projects.

THE CAJON DEL MAIPO PIPELINE

A case that received extensive coverage in the press, the Cajon del Maipo project rallied neighbors, NGOs, and area congressional representatives in opposition to a pipeline which was to supply natural gas to much of the central region of the country and especially to thermoelectric plants.

After a series of technical debates and public controversies, an agreement was reached to change the route from the southern to the northern shore of the Maipo River, causing relief among some protesters and anger among others, mainly residents of San Jose de Maipo. After expressing their rejection of the new pipeline path, these citizens initiated negotiation leading to a settlement of one million dollars paid by the company to the community.

This negotiation with Cajon del Maipo residents is one of the most well-known cases of compensation for negative environmental impact with non-environmental values such as money, houses, scholarships, etc.

In all likelihood, rather than proposing a radical change in mechanisms for citizen participation — independent of the possibility of settlements — it is more advisable to move ahead with more efficient and effective administrative models for land use that involve citizens from the very start of a project. In this way, social pressure would be less intense and would be spread out over the course of a more coherent and interactive management process involving the affected parties and those responsible for environmental management.

Parallel to this, reforms explicitly fostering a climate favorable to negotiation must be introduced. Reforms should even propose a methodology for advancing toward a negotiated solution. Unlike the current system, this would be strictly limited to the environmental context, and the various parties will not feel the need to turn to the courts prematurely.

IV. Tension and Conflict

Tension involving environmental issues can generally be traced to three sources: first, the apparent contradiction between economy and environment; second, community perceptions of harm from a project; and third, a new source of tension: society's frustration over situations which appear to have no solution.

All these sources of tension must also be considered in the context of the active role played by environmental NGOs in supporting community interests. This is a positive development, since most environmental issues involve highly technical components which are more accessible to a specialized group than to the residents of a community, especially if it is impoverished.

The positions taken by certain NGOs in cases such as Trillium, the Upper Bio Bio, Rio Cruces, the gas pipeline, or the Renca thermoelectric project may appear exaggerated. Yet the opportunity to gather a broad spectrum of positions at the bargaining table should not be disregarded. In this manner, a higher level of participation, more information, and different points of view would be brought to the process, which might delay some projects but would be justifiable for the purpose of reaching a better solution and, unquestionably, for increasing the democratic content of the process.

The Economy and the Environment

Tension between the economy and the environment occurs because of the belief that there is a contradiction between an efficient economy and the reduction of the negative impact of productive activity upon the environment. It is important for economic entities to take responsibility for the negative impact upon the environment which traditionally falls upon society as a whole, just as the private sector takes credit for the benefits derived from economic activity. It is true that when a company takes responsibility for the environmental impact of its waste products and emissions, there is an added net cost for production.

Despite the competitive advantages offered by environmentally-oriented management, the need to take responsibility for negative externalities has generated tension among business executives, who perceive it to be an additional burden, and in some cases a change in the rules of the game. The issue is a complex one for small and medium-sized firms with relatively meager resources, as well as for long-established companies burdened with outmoded technologies. Whereas a startup company can incorporate environmental considerations in its design, major refitting efforts

THE PROMOTION OF CLEAN PRODUCTION

The Ministry of the Economy recently announced a new policy aimed at reducing emissions and/or discharges while simultaneously increasing competitive capacity. Clean production will result from the following five courses of action:
- Minimized and effcient consumption of raw materials, energy, and water
- Minimization of toxic and/or hazardous materials
- Minimization of the volume and toxicity of emissions
- Recycling and reuse of residual materials to the greatest extent possible
- Reduction of the environmental impact of products during their useful life and when discarded

For this purpose, support mechanisms maintained by Corfo may be utilized, such as Profo (Promotion Projects), FAT (Technical Assistance Funds), Premex (Export Management Support Program), and Fontec (National Technological and Productive Development Fund), as well as special lines of credit.

are needed among older companies which did not take account of environmental criteria in their construction or operations.

A major challenge for the so-called "megaprojects" is the approval of their Environmental Impact Studies. It is not easy to justify the impact of these giant projects, particularly the majority which employ natural resources. Their environmental impact is generally significant, and a series of highly subjective factors must be taken into account, such as cultural value and scenic beauty. Additional pressure is generated through public opinion campaigns and efforts by environmental groups to alert the national and international community to the issue. The resulting delays and economic losses may even induce companies to lose interest in pursuing the project.

A future approach to such situations should bring together the parties in conflict, since compelling and valid reasons support both positions. For this to occur, environmental legislation and the legal framework for environmental management must be improved, in order to create more expeditious and objective methods for conflict resolution, based upon adequate information, broad participation, and effective compensatory mechanisms.

Despite these government efforts, it is not feasible for all companies to develop clean production systems, nor are all companies capable of taking charge of their environmental impact. New companies will do so, as will large firms that can hire expert consultants, conform to an environmental quality certification system, and make the necessary investments. But a great many of the small and medium-sized firms that are the focus of the clean production policy will be left on the sidelines or will not be able to meet the new challenges.

The contribution of small and medium-sized companies to the national economy and the job market is significant. Therefore, we must give our full attention to this issue and, if necessary, create a special program to support these firms' conversion to cleaner technologies, following the example of the special promotional programs for agricultural irrigation.

Citizens and the Environment

The environmental issue is one of the spheres of interest in which civil society is most active and involved, which is a very important fact. However, citizen participation in the environmental sphere has a tendency to enter into conflict with certain aspects of the national development model, particularly in the strongly-defended area of property rights. Besides guaranteeing the fundamental right to own property, this tradition imposes practically no restrictions on property use. Thus it is necessary to consider the vague boundaries between individual and social rights, as actions in one area tend to affect the other, and these effects are not always positive. It is understandable that the invocation of property rights frequently evokes strong reactions from those who feel harmed by certain projects. These last may undertake actions that exceed the bounds of the law and existing participatory mechanisms, which appear incapable of containing expressions of conflict within appropriate channels.

Citizen protest principally stems from two main sources. First, citizens may react to a government decision that they feel is harmful to them. A classic example of this situation is the decision to install a garbage dump or sanitary landfill in a particular, a project that never fails to meet with community opposition. Second, the participation process may break down even after the Environmental Impact Study is presented to the community and the community has had the chance to analyze its findings, if local citizens are

THE COSTANERA NORTE CASE

This case is a classic example of citizen mobilization around a project with significant environmental impact: the construction of a high-speed freeway along the north shore of the Mapocho River, crossing Santiago east to west through the north Pedro de Valdivia and Bellavista neighborhoods of Providencia. Many similar highways have been built throughout the country and have met with opposition, but the Providencia neighborhood affected in this case was an upper-middle-class community with the resources and organizational skills to exert considerable pressure, and therefore the conflict has received greater attention in the media.

The problem is the same as in all similar cases: the impossibility for citizens to react within the given sixty days to the several volumes that comprise the Environmental Impact Study, most of which is of a highly technical nature, often incomprehensible to the layman in its content, conclusions, and implications.

In this specific situation, the Providencia municipal government supported the community by hiring environmental consultants, who "translated" the contents of the Environmental Impact Study into understandable terms. The question immediately comes to mind: what happens when a comparable situation arises in Lonquimay or Canela Baja, or any other poor community in the country?

An alternative may be the practice followed in some industrialized countries, such as the United States, where the company proposing a project must finance the process of translating technical studies into ordinary language.

not satisfied either because they expected the project to be rejected or they expected some type of compensation.

Regarding the Environmental Impact Evaluation System, it is important to note that a certain perception of inequity often arises among affected communities with respect to the project promoters. This is based on the fact that project proponents theoretically have all the advantages, consisting of ample information, technical know-how, economic resources, and unlimited time to prepare their study, while the community lacks all of the above and must state its case within an inflexible period of 60 days.

If a community is able to present its point of view convincingly, the Environmental Impact Study may be rejected or approved with objections. But, whenever the project is not rejected, the community feels that it has not had a real say in the decision and has only been invited to contribute information to the process.

Current regulations being incorporated into the Environmental Impact Evaluation System may pose a solution, which is the active and effective incorporation of citizens into the phase of Environmental Impact Study preparation for investment projects. In this manner, a true negotiation process between project promoters and the community would be underway from the start, rather than, as was common before the regulations came into effect, at the end of the process as a sort of presentation of facts after decisions have been made. This must be taken into account in the overall design of an environmental management system.

The Eco-Fundamentalist Movement

Various groups of activists have emerged, particularly from the non-governmental organizations, who are influenced by an eco-fundamentalist philosophy that questions the country's present development model, and who comprise a kind of environmental defense movement. These groups have been involved in several cases in which tensions have been aroused over environmental issues, and they have joined forces with the social-environmental movement in the country's most prominent environmental conflicts.

They are active both as participants in the social movement and as private organizations.

The emergence of these groups has been a positive development, and it carries with it two implications. First, it implies the arrival of a new player, with a different perspective and a role that can be identified as defense of the nation's environmental heritage. Second, these organizations represent a source of information and support for citizen groups, which often lack sufficient knowledge and organizational ability to undertake negotiations or exert pressure in favor of their interests or points of view. This has been the case with the Bio Bio Action Group (GABB) in the defense of the Upper Bio Bio River, the Forest Alliance in the Trillium case, and CorPirque with the gas pipeline, to name a few.

Even though conflict over specific environmental problems is a positive phenomenon, in that it contributes additional considerations and positions, it is also a source of growing tension as more investment projects are proposed and carried out. Many of these organizations connect environmental problems with the development model itself and therefore tend to hold strong anti-system view. In their association with the social movement, environmental groups often move beyond their ecological stances to join a protest movement that seeks to break with the current organization of society. This image attracts social segments that feel their needs and demands are not fully met within the present system.

As for this movement's potential at the polls, the initial successes of the Humanist Party were repeated only faintly, and since the Green Party split from the latter, it has represented a limited electoral base. Nevertheless, the last presidential election campaign included a candidate running on an environmentalist platform, although in actuality he represented the anti-system factions in general, with the exception of the Communist Party. The European experience indicates that "green" parties generally capture between 5% and 6% of the vote, which they are able to use as a bargaining chip. In a binomial electoral system such as Chile's, this force would be very weak if its support fell below the legal minimum for the constitution of political parties, but if it surpassed the minimum, an environmentalist party could eventually become a swing vote between opposing political coalitions.

The Weight of Inertia

The considerations briefly discussed above were related primarily to the environmental impact of projects initiated since the enactment of Law 19,300 and, more specifically, after the enactment of the regulations for the Environmental Impact Evaluation System.

A natural question, however, is what to do about all of the facilities constructed before the existence of this environmental legislation, a problem more complex than even the largest investment project. Examples include the chaotic growth of the city of Santiago over 17 years' time and the large number of industries operating with older, polluting technology. Some neighborhood groups have blocked roads during rush hours to draw attention to their opposition to the growing congestion and to the granting building permits in densely-populated areas that lack adequate infrastructure or green spaces. Similar citizen protests have occurred, as we have seen, around the issue of garbage dumps.

While the protests described above represent major issues with wide publicity, they have been accompanied by a large number of small-scale local protests against such phenomena as the emissions of a medium-sized factory, breaks in pipelines, the release of effluents into bodies of water, the indiscriminate use of agrochemicals, and so forth. These

THE NEED TO STRENGTHEN THE ENVIRONMENTAL EDUCATION SYSTEM

Environmental experts have noted that Chileans feel a need to educate and inform themselves on environmental issues. No single entity has responded to this need with a structured, integrated, and coherent proposal. Generally, environmental issues become known through the mass media, which are interested in the most newsworthy items. This leads to the presentation of those ecological issues which appear most striking, controversial, or unusual. At best the media can offer an incomplete view of a problem. These reports accustom people to a way of viewing and appreciating facts which is not necessarily the most desirable from the standpoint of objectivity, and which tends to incite ill-informed and even radical actions.

An example of this situation can be seen in the controversy surrounding the proposal for a wood pulp plant on the border between the Ninth and Tenth regions, which would dump its treated wastes through a pipeline stretching 35 kilometers into the Mehuin bay. Residents and fishermen of the coastal village, in a community mobilization marked by a certain fundamental rejection of progress, have tried to stop experts from taking water samples needed for various analyses required by the Environmental Impact Study.

controversies each affect limited numbers of people, but taken together, they undoubtedly involve a significant part of the population.

While these type of actions, due to their localized nature, have not caused significant social tension, they do contain an incipient element which must be considered. If responses are not forthcoming to local problems stemming from a recalcitrant business sector, these protests will eventually ignite far greater discontent and a social movement which is more difficult to control.

V. Major Challenges

We have witnessed countless achievements and progress in environmental matters over the course of the decade. It is undeniable that this issue has been given higher priority during the two terms of Concertación government. However, numerous and significant challenges still lie ahead as Chile seeks to follow an environmentally sustainable path founded upon consideration for the quality of life of its people, and to present an environmentally responsible image to the world.

Promotion of Environmental Consciousness

Any change begins by creating awareness of the conditions for that change. Any individual or collective action that seeks to impress the environmental issue upon national consciousness must be based upon accurate information, broad and democratic dissemination of this information, and education of the population as a whole.

Preparing and communicating relevant information should be based upon a foundation of equilibrium and consensus. The final objective is to ingrain the habit among the population of recognizing causal relations in human actions that affect the environment. That is, a cognizance of how our actions affect the environment and what their ultimate results will be, both in the near and the distant future.

This causal relationship must form the basis for a multi-faceted system to promote a sense of environmental consciousness. It must be aimed at society as a whole, as well as specific communities, particular target groups, and even individuals, since human beings constantly interact with the environment on all these planes.

Environmental education should be reinforced and should be included as part of the current environmental reform. It should be incorporated into regular education programs, both formally and informally, and on all educational levels: in kindergarten activities, elementary and high school programs, adult education, and so forth.

Within the models the country is constructing, education, information, and training represent key factors for development. These models are predominantly demand-oriented, and those who are doing the demanding must be in a better position to guide the process.

Institutional Structure and Policy
It is of utmost importance to raise the environmental issue beyond the National Environmental Commission and incorporate it throughout the entire governmental system. Ministries and agencies at the regional, provincial, and local levels must become involved with the issue so that their actions can reflect the environmental dimension and contribute to the development of a comprehensive environmental management system.

If this is to take place, the government must have an explicit environmental policy, which not only sets forth its principles and objectives — as it is currently in the process of doing — but also spells out the results it hopes to achieve for each entity affecting the environment in some way. Naturally, it will not be possible to undertake everything at once therefore, after defining the expected results, timetables, and those responsible for carrying out the programs, various environmental challenges will have to be prioritized politically, dividing them into short-, medium-, and long-term goals.

The Regional Environmental Commissions (Corema) are presently being administratively strengthened. At the same time, an environmental director is being assigned to each government ministry with direct or indirect environmental responsibility, as is the case with Mining, Agriculture, Housing, Public Works, and others. Over time, the influence of the environmental director should lead to the internalization of the issue within each ministerial department. This process will be reinforced by the new government-wide environmental policy, leading to a greater and more explicit commitment from political authorities in each case.

Although the degree of inter-ministerial coordination is still insufficient, the Corema has been able to devise an efficient structure for review of Environmental Impact Evaluations. Government ministries involved in study reviews are Agriculture (Cattle and Agricultural Service, SAG and National Forestry Corporation, Conaf), Public Works (Water Administration, DGA), Housing, Mining, Health (Metropolitan Environmental Health Service, Sesma), Defense (Maritime Territory Administration, Directemar), and Transportation (Transportation Secretary, Sectra).

Efforts are underway to relate the environmental issue to particular territorial areas. The presidential directive vesting regional governors with administrative responsibility for the environment is a step toward this objective. Municipal governments have also become more deeply involved, particularly when they are directly affected by significant environmental problems.

The Economy and Sustainable Growth
Global change in environmental matters has been reflected in the world economy. Two notable phenomena have been the environmental issue's influence upon trade relations

and the new world economic order and trade relations, as well as changes in technology. These developments signify a qualitative change in demand. Consumers are increasingly concerned about the environmental effects of the products they buy, and environmental certification systems have been developed to address this consideration.

At the conclusion of the Uruguay Round of the GATT talks, and with the subsequent formation of the World Trade Organization, the environmental issue was explicitly cited as a variable that world trade must take into account (FAO Seminar/World Bank 1996). Other international agreements explicitly refer to the environmental issue in the context of trade relations. In the case of NAFTA, a complementary accord addressed environmental regulations.

A substantial change has also been noted in consumers' criteria in their choice of products. Particular sensitivity is exhibited in the selection of primary goods, such as food or other products that could have toxic effects, including paint, toys, or other materials with which there is directed and prolonged contact. Commercial value is no longer the only criterion in choosing or acquiring a product. Consumers also consider health value that is, whether a given product may be harmful to the health and environmental value; that is, how the product was made and what impact its manufacture may have had upon the environment.

The change in consumer habits has led to a growing technological response. Current technology may be used to diminish the environmental effects of production, as well as to process wastes. Perhaps most interesting, however, is the emergence of an environmental business management process that is introducing the concept of the three "Rs" to the industrial system: reuse, recycling, and reduction in the use of raw materials.

Including the environmental issue as a factor in business management makes it possible to harmonize concern for the environment with economic interests. The application of the three "Rs" also produces cost savings, since firms pay a high price for waste. Initiatives such as the Economy Ministry's Clean Production Promotion Project and the programs of the Technological Research Corporation (Intec-Chile) (Corfo 1997) are already actively promoting this new approach and its advantages to business.

Perhaps one of the greatest challenges ahead is that of incorporating this perspective throughout the business world, so that environmental considerations become an integral element of domestic and international competition.

Some companies have received environmental management certification through the adoption of regulation ISO 14,000, which grants them international recognition for their adherence to environmentally sound management principles. However, this certification is not within the reach of all businesses, as its implementation is fairly expensive, and it has been primarily conceptualized for large export firms, such as mining and forestry companies.

A shift in environmental policy has been observed toward the problem of urban pollution. This urban focus has persisted despite the growing problem of natural resource depletion, which, since these natural resources constitute Chile's economic base, threatens to become as serious a problem as pollution.

Territorial Equilibrium

The achievement of territorial equilibrium involves a more balanced use of environmental space in accordance with its capacity. Its great influence upon the quality of life is evident. The manner in which space is used, both nationally and locally, has been decidedly imbalanced in our country. Despite the relative growth of regional capital cities, the degree of Chile's population concentration is surprising: the central zone, comprised of the Fifth, Sixth, and Metropolitan regions, is home to nearly 80% of the total national population.

The significant changes in people's expectations in a climate of globalization and modernization is increasing migration from rural to urban areas. This phenomenon presents the opportunity to redefine a population settlement policy, founded upon a mechanism of economic, social, and environmental structuring through intermediate cities, such as the provincial capitals, which channels the migration process to some extent. Such a measure would help halt the hypertrophy of large cities (Santiago and the regional capitals), which has brought with it serious pollution, congestion, overstretched services, and, in general, an accelerated deterioration in the quality of life.[13]

The unregulated use of space is also seen within the cities, as they spread chaotically, without regard for the quality of life and their capacity to satisfy basic needs. In many cities, traffic circulation has become increasingly difficult, accompanied by increasing waste production and noise levels. The shortage of green areas and recreational spaces has become critical. All of this points to a pressing need to re-think city development and to devise new ways to use urban space.

Social Participation

As the government has recognized, social participation is essential if a real solution to the environmental problem is to be found and if the country is to follow a course of sustainable development. Throughout this text, we have made numerous references to the issue of citizen participation, and there are several reasons for this. Most centrally, citizens must have opportunities for input — contributing their opinions and decisionmaking capacity — into the process of incorporating the environmental variable into the model proposed for society. The democratic system requires that societal problems be resolved in this manner.[14]

The government has made a significant effort to include citizens in environmental management. The degree of citizen participation contemplated in existing environmental legislation is unprecedented, yet even this is not enough. We must construct a fully participatory society, as it cannot be participatory in environmental matters but not in health, education, or other areas.

It is important to differentiate between freedom and democracy, although the shades of difference may be small. Modern societies tend to grant much individual freedom, which is certainly desirable, but this has not always gone hand in hand with democracy (paradoxically, they have even clashed at times), understood in the sense of the collective expression of social will and aspirations.

---

13 Under present circumstances it is very difficult to believe that Santiago's environmental problems will go away on their own. Increasingly, the solution appears to lie in fostering economic development in other regions.

14 Unlike inflation or unemployment, which are indicators of problems affecting the entire nation, most environmental problems are local in character. Therefore, citizen participation in identifying problems and finding solutions is essential, especially considering the State's democratizing intent to share its duties

This should lead us to careful reflection. The citizen participation envisioned in environmental legislation is limited to a system in which citizens are told what is going to happen — in this case a project affecting the environment — and they are given a chance to air their views.[15] Yet under no circumstances do the people have a real say in the approval or rejection of a project. In practice, there is no true participation in environmental management, with the exception of pressure exerted through protest demonstrations.

A long road still lies ahead. As we have defended the market economy because we believe it is the best system for organizing the national and international economy, and not for ideological reasons, we are also convinced that people must come first. We must be careful not to fall prey to any type of populism or institutional anarchy, but neither must we accept a kind of market autocracy, which is equally de-stabilizing, erodes the country's social foundation, and may give rise to fundamentalist and fanatical attitudes.

A solution will be reached when people are able to participate from the beginning of a process in an active and informed manner. In a context of negotiation between interested parties, people will work to ensure that projects are carried out in the most effective manner, to the benefit of the country, of the company involved, and most definitely, of all the people.

Modernization Policies and the Environment

The pace at which the environmental dimension is being incorporated into the development model, as well as the possibility of leading our economy along a sustainable route, are intimately related to the progress of the modernization of the State, in particular, and of the private sector, in general. Thus, it is not unusual that many of these issues first appear in internal discussions and often remain on the level of proposals or expressions of intention.

Public and private entities that are more organizationally modern — those that are more flexible in management, more horizontal in structure, and more versatile — are able to incorporate this issue more genuinely in their operational system. They will have a department in charge of the issue, and environmental factors will be consid-

---

A PROPOSAL FOR PARTICIPATORY TERRITORIAL ENVIRONMENTAL MANAGEMENT

We propose exploring an institutional level of our country's territorial structure which represents a true bridge between the regional and municipal governments: the Provincial Governors' Offices. The advantages for channeling citizen participation through these entities include:

• The provincial governor's role as a direct partner with the regional governor in the management of regional affairs
• The fact that the provincial governor is appointed by the President of the Republic rather than elected to office
• The provinces' positions as intermediate territorial entities facilitating coordination among the municipal and regional governments
• The fact that the provincial governor is a member of the Regional Environmental Commission (Corema)
• The fact that the responsibilities and duties of the provincial authority are relatively less convoluted than those of municipal governments

---

15 We must bear in mind that a project becomes subject to the Environmental Impact Evaluation System because it will definitely have an impact upon people. Participation is legitimate because a particular community will be affected by the project.

ered in the determination of priorities and actions. Environmental criteria will also be incorporated into management considerations as well as operations.

However, this modernization process takes place in a specific social and political context. In Chile's case, this context includes a still-developing civil society and, as elsewhere, a political party system whose role as society's representative at the highest levels of power is in crisis. These political parties are themselves engaged in a modernization process. Their statements on environmental issues are often simply campaign rhetoric, rather than the expression of an endogenous strategy stemming from genuine concern. This is related to the parties' weak structural link to society, which has resulted in declining party membership. And this, paradoxically, also appears to be a sign of modernization.

BIBLIOGRAPHICAL REFERENCES

Conama (National Environmental Commission). 1998. "Una política ambiental para el desarrollo sustentable," approved by the Conama Ministers Advisory Board in its January 9.

Corfo (Production Promotion Corporation). 1997. "Guía empresarial del medio ambiente," Santiago.

Fajnzylber, F. 1991. "Inserción internacional e innovación institucional." *Revista de la Cepal* 44, Santiago.

Pérez, C. 1997. "The Social and Political Challenge of the Present Paradigm Shift." Paper prepared for the Norwegian Investor Forum, based on a presentation to a seminar on "Evolutionary Economics and Spatial Income Inequality." Oslo.

FAO/World Bank Seminar. 1996. "Implementación del Acuerdo de la Ronda Uruguay en América Latina: el caso de la agricultura." Santiago.

Speech of President Eduardo Frei Ruiz-Tagle, during the signing ceremony for the presidential directive on regional environmental management. 1996.

Time Special Issue. 1997. "Our Precious Planet: Why Saving the Environment Will Be the Next Century's Biggest Challenge." November.

Tomic, T. 1988. "Elementos de la dinamización social, para la aplicación de tecnologías alternativas en Chile." In Cepal/FAO. *Desarrollo agrícola y participación campesina*, Santiago.

Society

Social Stratification in Chile
at the Close of the 20th Century

Arturo León
Javier Martínez

Introduction

The topic of social inequalities has been repeatedly pointed to as the main shortcoming of the Chilean style of development.[1] The confirmation of a concentrated and regressive income distribution usually accompanies these observations.

Nonetheless, a sizable conceptual gap exists between the notions of regressive income distribution and social inequality. The latter refers to the generation of obstacles to mobility towards the interior, obstacles that tend to form groups which, for a variety of reasons are typically differentiated not only by possibilities for reproduction, but also in terms of lifestyle and cultural ethos. From this perspective, the important question is not so much the size of the difference in the share of wealth between certain individuals or households, but rather how that share superimposes certain positions or roles that systematically affect probabilities for mobility. Thus, questions are raised as to the types of inequalities that tend to develop over longer periods of time and their foreseeable consequences, above and beyond obvious quantitative differences in current consumption capacities.

In this study we approached this question from the point of view of the occupational structure and the diverse subgroups that have been identified in that structure during the various stages of the nation's development. With this approach we intend to continue an interpretation that was initiated a decade and half ago, in the midst of far-reaching changes in the Chilean economic structure, changes that were followed by a no less decisive political and institutional transformation which restored the democratic legitimization of power. Our current examination will enable us to assess, with a greater historical perspective, the aspects of the occupational structure that changed, remained the same, or were extended after these important transformations.

---

1   We deliberately use the term "style of development" in keeping with Aníbal Pinto's that refers not only to the economic growth model but also to the accompanying and conditioning institutional and participatory dimensions.

The selection of this point of view should not be construed as taking a rigid doctrinary stance vis-a-vis other equally useful approaches to the problem of inequality in Chilean society (for example, approaches that select as crucial data the kinship relations of the dominant groups in society, more than property relations, or based on property ownership rather than trade relations given the entrenched "tiering" of landholdings in Chile. Rather, it means assuming the two-pronged methodological supposition that: (1) given the economic structure's degree of differentiation, other forms of inequality in social relations will tend to be expressed by means of the distribution of occupational opportunities; and that (2) the occupational structure provides an adequate field of evidence for assessing transformations in different social classes, *including the most populous*, which turns out to be of particular importance when one wishes to assess the transformations as a whole.

The Bases From Which "Class Structure" Will Be Examined
Social class is the term that corresponds to a vision of social inequality based on the occupational structure. Two powerful theoretical bases (Marxist and liberal) have used this vision to respond to two substantially different types of questions: questions pertaining to *mobilization* and questions dealing with *mobility*.

As Goldthorpe has pointed out, "Marx's class theory is mainly concerned with the formation of classes, and, in particular, with the occurrence and forms of collective class action,"[2] while the liberal theory occupies itself with an apparently inverse question: why and how is it that in industrial societies (not only in capitalist societies) "class formation is replaced by the disintegration of classes to the degree that the mobility between classes increases and unequal opportunities linked to class affiliation are substantially reduced."

On the other hand, as Goldthrope argues, the events of history raise other kinds of questions: given that neither of these theories' basic predictions has transpired (the formation of revolutionary proletariat in capitalist societies or the formation of open industrial societies with high cross-class social mobility), they are references to the persistence of inequalities between members of different social classes.

Our objective is to examine, from these three points of view, the transformations that have occurred in the Chilean socio-occupational structure over the last 25 years.

I. The Social Category Matrix

This study of the changes that have occurred in the social structure during the last quarter century is based on a data matrix that enables the identification of a wide group of social categories. These categories are indicative of shared situations that have historically been the "objective foundation" for constructing the country's important social actors. We used these same analytic categories in a prior study on the main changes that occurred between the late 1970s and mid 1980s.[3]

The criteria for constructing these social categories are more complex than the broad associations of "social class." They also have a greater historical weight than merely

---

2   John H. Goldthorpe, "Class analysis and the reorientation of class theory: the case of persisting differen-
    tials in educational attainment," in: *The British Journal of Sociology* 47(3) (September 1996), pp. 481-505.
3   See Javier Martínez and Arturo León, "La involución del proceso de desarrollo y la estructura social," CED,
    Materiales de Discusión 53 (Santiago, November 1984).

analytical constructions of socioeconomic "strata" based on continuous variables such as income or education. It is a process that uses a comprehensive list of social "actors" to identify the potential base of positions in the occupational structure.

Obviously, with this approximation it is only possible to work with "class-based" actors; that is, actors mainly defined by their position in social labor relations, since the majority of information comes from various data on employment.[4] Actors such as "the Church," or "political parties," for example, are inevitably excluded from consideration.

The process of constructing social categories resulted in the identification of segments of social classes, using not only economic classification criteria, but also according to the historical "layers" or "generations" that make up the "classes." In an economy and a society characterized by a relatively short history, in which the development process has been fundamental to the construction of the Nation and the State, one cannot be limited to the purely formal classifications of economic activity that are usually used for the differentiation of class "fractions." On the contrary, the development of certain sectors or branches of the economy and the emergence, transformation, or dissolution of certain social actors follows each stage of the growth process. If each class can define itself in terms of the existence of shared positions or roles in the system of production and exchange relations, it does not mean that they are perfectly homogenous: on the contrary, each class consists — like the earth — of different "layers" or "generations" that correspond to different moments in the course of economic activity. Therefore, during the construction of categories, we attempted to roughly distinguish these "layers" or subgroups, thus opening up the possibility of relating the study's results to other investigations with broader historical perspectives.

We believe that this approximation will facilitate an improvement in the current standoff between two of the country's intellectual stances that have developed independently. Many times, they have fueled opposing ideological constructions: (1) the persistence of a 19th-century representation of the Nation, the product of both conservative tradition and a hefty part of Chilean literature and national customs. According to this vision, the Nation is expressed in terms of three dominant groups — large-scale agricultural landowners, miners, and merchants. The history of this century is nothing more than the never-ending transformation of this dynamic of domination and the permanent resistance of such groups to social changes rising from modernizing forces with little hegemonic consistency; and (2) the intellectual production of the 1960s and 1970s (emanating especially from "anti-establishment" historiography and sociology) that, heavily influenced by a crude Marxism or by structuralist formalism, did not take into account the emergence of different social categories and tended to evaluate the country's modern history based on industrial capitalism's class categories, redefined by the circumstances of dependency.

---

4   The information used for the construction of social categories and the grouping of these categories in sectors and social classes comes from employment surveys conducted by the National Statistics Institute. These surveys have the advantage of ensuring a high degree of intertemporal comparability of information relating to the characteristics of the workforce. They cover a longer period of time than the National Socioeconomic Characterization (Casen) surveys and, like the Casen surveys, they provide reliable information on the population's incomes.

Undoubtedly, the matrix of social categories that we have once again adopted in this study is only a step in that direction, which looks to retake, for the exclusive purpose of an analysis of the changes of the last quarter century, the productive road of the analysis of history, opened by Aníbal Pinto almost 30 years ago,[5] and which our generation, influenced by all types of ideologies, did not give the attention it deserved.

The categories and social actors used in the study appear in Table 1; their descriptions can be found in Appendix I.

TABLE 1

NUMERICAL BREAKDOWN OF SOCIAL CATEGORIES
1995
(Thousands of people)

Social Categories in Agriculture, Forestry, Hunting, and Fishing	796.2	Social Categories Outside of Agriculture, Forestry, Hunting, and Fishing	4479.4
Agricultural Entrepreneur	**30.1**	**Non-Agricultural Entrepreneurs**	**141.0**
Export Agricultural Enterprises	12.2	Commercial Bourgeoisie	42.2
Non-Exporting Agricultural Enterprises	3.6	Capital-based Industrial Entrepreneurs	27.0
Landowning Bourgeoisie	8.9	Capital-based Service Sector Entrepreneur	18.5
Other Agricultural Enterprises	5.4	Other Capital-based Entrepreneur	53.2
Salaried Agricultural Labor	**421.7**	**Middle Echelons Wage-earners**	**1492.1**
Central Zone Agricultural Proletariat	199.5	White Collar Employees	243.6
South Central Zone Agricultural Proletariat	91.2	Upper Echelons Traditional Public Servants	13.1
Wheat Zone Rural Salaried Employee	20.5	Middle Echelons Traditional Public Servants	53.9
Southern Cattle/Dairy Company Proletariat	31.3	Lower Echelons Traditional Public Servants	57.6
Magallanes Livestock Proletariat	2.8	Upper Echelons Modern Public Servants	22.1
Remainder of the Agricultural Proletariats	20.1	Middle Echelons Modern Public Servants	151.8
Salaried Fishermen	17.9	Lower Echelons Modern Public Servants	63.8
Forestry Proletariat	38.5	Upper Echelons Modern Private Service Sector	99.2
		Middle Echelons Modern Private Service Sector	186.4
Peasantry and Poor Settlers	**344.4**	Lower Echelons Modern Private Service Sector	600.7
Norte Grande Indigenous Peasantry	5.7		
Norte Chico Poor Peasantry	16.0	**Independent Middle Groups**	**431.8**
Central Zone Peasantry	24.0	Retailers	211.8
South Central Zone Peasantry	90.2	Upper Echelons Independent Professionals	24.8
Araucanian Peasantry	51.7	Other Independent Professionals and Technocrats	45.9
Southern Zone Peasantry	29.6	"Modern" Craftsmen	55.8
Peasantry from Chiloé	15.1	Small-Scale Transport Bourgeoisie	93.4
Poor Settlers	4.3		
Other Peasants	40.6	**Traditional Craftsmen**	**285.5**
Metropolitan Zone Peasantry	22.7	Pirquineros (Independent Manual Labor Miners)	7.4
Small-Scale Fishermen	31.4	Traditional Craftsmen	196.5
Independent Carpenters	13.2	Construction Craftsmen	81.6

5   In particular his article, "Desarollo económico y relaciones sociales en Chile," various editions.

Social Categories Outside of Agriculture, Forestry, Hunting, and Fishing, *continued*	4479.4
Working Class Miners	**42.9**
Large Copper Mining Proletariat	4.1
Public Sector Coal Miners	0.0
Small and Mid-Sized Coal Mining Proletariat	4.4
Small and Mid-Sized Copper Mining Proletariat	18.0
Remaining Small and Mid-Sized Mining Proletariat	16.3
Industrial and Construction Working Class	**694.5**
Traditional Industrial Working Class	290.0
Second Phase Industrialization Industrial Working Class	166.5
Strategic Industries Working Class	8.7
Construction Workers	219.8
Traditional Public Sector Salaried Industrial Employees	3.7

Second Phase Industrialization Public Sector Salaried Employees	2.4
Public Strategic Industries Salaried Employee	0.5
Public Salaried Construction Employees	3.0
Retail and Service Sector Working Class	**795.5**
Retail Employees	31.8
Private Transport Salaried Employees	156.2
Service Sector Employees	262.7
Salaried Public Transport, Storage and Communications Employees	8.8
Public Tertiary Sector Salaried Employees	38.9
Private Office Service Personnel	278.0
Public Office Service Personnel	19.1
"Marginal" Groups	**596.1**
Marginal Retailers	169.6
Marginal Service Sector Workers	135.0
Domestic Servants	291.6

Source: Special tabulation of data from the National Institute of Statistics' October 1995 Employment and Unemployment Survey (Encuesta de Empleo y Desempleo)

II. The General Content of the Transformations: A Reexamination

1. THE MOBILIZATION FACTOR

Towards the mid-1980s, the evolution of the socio-occupational structure tended to be explained, almost naturally, by means of the mobilization model. In effect, in the midst of the ascent of the "capitalist revolution," which was driven by the power of an authoritative government, the questions of to what degree the restructuring was aimed at the constitution of actors capable of pitting a social force against the authoritative power, and to what degree it distorted the historic constitutive bases of classist actors or generated entirely new structural conditions, turned out to be central to an exploratory analysis.

A general view indicated a period strongly marked by *destructuralization* trends, in which neither "citizen" actors, typical of a society characterized by economic dynamism, nor "community" actors, indicative of static social orders, showed clear probabilities of coalescing. Previously, the probabilities leaned towards the dilemma of either a "rioting" of masses against the political powers or the atomization of civil society and the consequent conformity of the individual.

There were three basic factors that led to this interpretation, conceptually expressed through the notions of *inorganicness*, *exclusion*, and the *impermeability* of the socio-occupational structure.

The concept of *inorganicness* alludes to the weak "degree of collectivization involved in the social relations networks that accompany the different socio-occupational positions." That is, the low degree to which the dominant positions in the new structure "entail, for those who occupy them, a frequent and intense interaction with their peers, in the setting of complex and formalized institutions."[6] The "organicness" of the predominant positions in the socio-occupational structure seemed to be a key criteria for the constitution of "very classist classes," to use Hobsbawm's famous expression (whose characteristic model is the industrial working class), due to the fact that such positions "positively facilitate the formation of a 'sense of affiliation' among the people who occupy them, in relation to either the rest of society (...) or to the other social categories that make up their counterparts in the labor structure."[7]

The percentage of salaried workers in the active population turned out to be a simple indicator of inorganicness, considering that the organization of manual labor in complex productive units and the bureaucratization of administrative work historically accompany the salarization of the work force. A systematic fall in job rates, such as that observed throughout the 1970s and into the early 1980s, is clearly indicative of a growing inorganicness in the occupational structure.

The concept of *exclusion* refers to the expansion of a marginal mass that cannot be understood merely as a "reserve industrial army" but rather indicates the emergence of "a population, excluded to an unprecedented degree, that developed together with a deindustrialization process, that implies, in many cases, the disappearance of the technical foundation that would enable the incorporation of such sectors into new expansion cycles." Also resulting from this situation was a new increase in this mass due to overlapping recessive crises, and it "cannot be affirmed with the same certainty that [this mass] has been definitely excluded from employment possibilities in a new expansion cycle." At the time, we indicated, "as an overall effect" the formation of "an 'overpopulation' mass that performed the clear function of salary depression, while its function as a 'reserve' is frankly weak and doubtful." This translated into "a strong pressure on the active work force, which further enhances the effects of the inorganicness of the positions that come to dominate the formal employment structure."[8] A simple exclusion indicator turned out to be the proportion of unemployed individuals, workers in the special Minimum Employment (MEP) and Work for Heads of Households (POJH) Programs and household employment and marginal workers in trade and services to the active population as a whole, a proportion that increased noticeably during the 1970s and the first third of the 1980s.

Finally, the concept of *impermeability* refers to the economic system's very low ability to absorb *new* groups that, for biological, cultural, or historical reasons, were only recently initiating their incorporation into the active labor arena. (These groups had to be distinguished analytically from the mass of active workers forced out of employment and that constituted additional evidence of the excluded's superficial role as a "reserve.") The quotients between the increases in the active female and youth populations in formal jobs and the total increases of the active female and youth populations during the period were the empirical indicators that expressed this "impermeability." A simpler reading can be

---

6   Martínez and León, op. cit.
7   Ibid.
8   Ibid.

TABLE 2

"MOBILIZATION" KEY:
DIMENSIONS OF CHANGE IN THE CHILEAN SOCIAL STRUCTURE, 1971-95

	1971	1980	1982	1987	1990	1995
1. Disorganization ("Inorganicness"):						
Percentage of Salaried Employees in the Active Workforce	53	45	38	45	49	54
2. Exclusion:						
Percentage of Those "Excluded" (a) from the Active Workforce	13	25	36	23	18	16
3. Impermeability:						
Percentage of "Excluded" (b) Active Young People	20	39	51	31	26	17
Percentage of "Excluded" Active Women	32	40	50	41	35	29

(A) Unemployed; PEM and POJH; domestic work and marginal retail and service sector workers.

(b) Active population between the ages of 15 and 24.

Source: Special tabulations from the National Institute of Statistics' October - December trimester National Employment Surveys (Encuestas Nacionales de Empleo [ENE]).

made based on the percentage of "excluded" youth and women over the total youth (or women) in the active population, which during the period also tended to grow at an alarming rate.

A preliminary examination of these indicators, which were key throughout most of the last 25 years, facilitates an assessment of the magnitude of the changes that have taken place since then.

At first glance, Table 2 leads to a surprising conclusion: the indicators depict, through 1995, after a long downward trend, a situation almost identical to that of 1971. Does that mean that after 25 years we have ended up where we started? From the point of view of the employment structure's "organicness," exclusion, and impermeability, the answer would have to be strongly affirmative (at least to the extent implied by the indicators used). However, if the internal composition of the indicators is examined according to the social categories indicated, one can see that the underlying structure is very different from that of 1971.

First, in terms of the recuperation of "organicness" in the employment structure (measured as the salarization in said structure), there was a persistent increase in the *middle* salaried sectors during the period in question. These sectors grew from 18% in 1971 to 27% in 1995 (with intermediary percentages of 24% in 1980, 22% in 1987, and 24% in 1990): the age-old trend of *bureaucratization* continued to hold strong and, although it stopped equaling growth in public sector employment, it moved with even more dynamism to the *private* sector.[9] This sector's growth, much more than that of the

---

9   It is not possible to break down bureaucratic employment between the public and private sectors for 1971; between 1980 and 1995 public administrative employment decreased from 9% to 6.8% of the PEA, while in the private sector it rose from 15.3% to 21.3%.

independent middle groups (which only increased their participation in the employment structure by three decimals), is what explains the *urban middle sectors'* growth of nine points in the occupational structure.

The relocation of middle salaried groups in the private sector has had a strong cultural impact on such groups' orientation towards social mobility: important differences persist between the public and private sectors in terms of job stability (with "flexibility" being the distinguishing characteristic of the private sector and "rigidity" that of the public sector), the magnitude of remuneration differences among different positions in the pay-scale ("continuous" scales in public administration compared with scales that have "great leaps" in private administration), and the predictability of promotions and incentives, due to the nature of the criteria usually used for such awards (less importance in the private system is given to factors such as seniority and formal education and achievement definitions are based more directly on short-term productivity). These incentives for individualization are a powerful difference in terms of the probabilities of collective action and, consequently, qualify the characteristic of "organicness" theoretically attributable to salaried jobs.

A second major change that took place during the period in question was a drop in the prominence of the *working class*, particularly the *industrial working class*, in the occupational structure: between 1971 and 1995 the working class' participation in overall employment fell by six percentages points (from 34.5% to 28.9%). However, this figure hides the sector's restructuring: through 1971, 25.8% of the sector was represented by blue-collar positions in industry and construction; this participation fell to 13.1% in 1995 — a decrease of 13 points. "Blue-collar" employment (manual and salaried) in *trade* and *services*, on the other hand, increased from 7.4% to 15% of the economically active population (EAP) during those same years (a consistent trend throughout the period in question).

In light of the magnitude and importance of these changes, it is necessary to interpret the shifts that occurred in exclusion: it seems clear that the changes in the magnitude of exclusion throughout this period were due entirely to the unemployment variable, while the proportion of the "marginal" employment categories remained relatively constant: 10% in 1971, 10% in 1980, 12% in 1990, and 11% in 1995. However, if at the same time unemployment stemmed primarily from productive, salaried positions (as in effect it did) and did not return to this sector but rather to administrative salaried jobs, it is equally clear that the group excluded throughout the period of crisis and conversion in the Chilean economy was not a "reserve *industrial* army" (nor did it come to enlarge a "structural" or permanent "marginal mass"). Nonetheless, the data appear to indicate that this was not an opportunistic "exit and re-entry" phenomenon affecting the same work force group, but rather a restructuring through the "exit" of old groups and their "replacement" by new groups with different characteristics: the system's new *permeability* to the entry of youth and women, evident in Table 2, indicates the route by which this replacement occurred.

Apart from the economic significance of these changes, it is interesting to note that the reduction of blue-collar workers, the bureaucratization and division into three sectors of salaried jobs have tended to provoke an enormous impact on *unionism* (without considering changes in institutional contexts where such activities rose sharply), which historically appealed to an ideological legitimization based on the notion of *producers* and

TABLE 3

NUMERICAL BREAKDOWN OF SOCIAL CATEGORIES
(Thousands of people)

Social Categories-Large Groupings (including the unemployed)	Period				
	1971	1980	1987	1990	1995
Social Categories Within Agriculture, Forestry, Hunting, and Fishing	539.9	525.3	855.5	889.0	796.2
Agricultural Entrepreneurs	8.4	15.7	38.2	41.7	30.1
Salaried Agricultural Labor	299.8	236.9	473.1	469.0	421.7
Poor Peasantry and Settlers	246.0	272.7	344.1	378.3	344.4
Social Categories Outside of Agriculture, Forestry, Hunting, and Fishing	2416.0	3110.3	3477.8	3861.7	4512.8
Non-Agricultural Entrepreneurs	39.6	51.9	102.0	150.2	141.0
Industry	12.9	10.7	21.6	29.5	27.0
Wholesale/Retail Trade	6.9	21.7	32.9	39.2	42.2
Service Sector and Remainder (includes construction)	19.8	19.5	47.5	81.5	71.8
Middle Echelons Sectors	775.2	1217.8	1264.7	1489.2	1923.9
Salaried Public Employees	543.9(*)	327.2	315.1	325.9	362.3
Salaried Private Employees		557.1	694.6	865.5	1129.8
Independent	231.3	333.5	254.9	297.8	431.8
Traditional Craftsmen	183.7	190.5	206.5	247.1	285.5
Working Class	1018.5	738.0	1145.5	1329.7	1532.9
Mining	39.6	46.3	34.2	46.7	42.9
Industry and Construction	761.3	404.1	490.4	576.1	694.5
Trade and Services	217.6	287.6	621.0	706.9	795.5
"Marginal" Groups	282.4	376.5	571.0	595.9	596.1
Domestic Servants	159.3	206.9	298.4	306.7	291.6
Marginal Retailers	58.0	107.6	160.9	158.2	169.6
Marginal Service Sector Workers	65.1	62.0	111.8	131.0	135.0
Unemployed (**)	91.8	524.0	186.4	47.5	32.5
Not Classified	24.8	11.6	1.7	2.1	1.0
Total	2955.9	3635.6	4333.3	4750.6	5309.1

(*)   Includes public and private salaried employees.

(**) Includes people looking for work for the first time as well as PEM and POJH workers.

Source: Special tabulations from the National Institute of Statistics' October - December trimester National Employment Surveys (Encuestas Nacionales de Empleo [ENE]).

TABLE 4

NUMERICAL BREAKDOWN OF SOCIAL CATEGORIES
(Percentages)

Social Categories-Large Groupings (including the unemployed)	Period				
	1971	1980	1987	1990	1995
Social Categories Within Agriculture, Forestry, Hunting, and Fishing	18.3	14.4	19.7	18.7	15.0
Agricultural Entrepreneurs	0.3	0.4	0.9	0.9	0.6
Salaried Agricultural Workers	10.1	6.5	10.9	9.9	7.9
Poor Peasantry and Settlers	8.3	7.5	7.9	8.0	6.5
Social Categories Outside of Agriculture, Forestry, Hunting, and Fishing	81.7	85.6	80.3	81.3	85.0
Non-Agricultural Entrepreneurs	1.3	1.4	2.4	3.2	2.7
Industry	0.4	0.3	0.5	0.6	0.5
Wholesale/Retail Trade	0.2	0.6	0.8	0.8	0.8
Service Sector and Remainder (Includes Construction)	0.7	0.5	1.1	1.7	1.4
Middle Echelons Sectors	26.2	33.5	29.2	31.3	36.2
Salaried Public Employees	18.4(*)	9.0	7.3	6.9	6.8
Salaried Private Employees		15.3	16.0	18.2	21.3
Independents	7.8	9.2	5.9	6.3	8.1
Traditional Craftsmen	6.2	5.2	4.8	5.2	5.4
Working Class	34.5	20.3	26.4	28.0	28.9
Mining	1.3	1.3	0.8	1.0	0.8
Industry and Construction	25.8	11.1	11.3	12.1	13.1
Trade and Services	7.4	7.9	14.3	14.9	15.0
"Marginal" Services	9.6	10.4	13.2	12.5	11.2
Domestic Servants	5.4	5.7	6.9	6.5	5.5
Marginal Retailers	2.0	3.0	3.7	3.3	3.2
Marginal Service Sector Workers	2.2	1.7	2.6	2.8	2.5
Unemployed (**)	3.1	14.4	4.3	1.0	0.6
Not Classified	0.8	0.3	0.0	0.0	0.0
Total	100.0	100.0	100.0	100.0	100.0

(*) Includes public and private salaried employees.

(**) Includes people looking for work for the first time as well as PEM and POJH workers.

Source: Special tabulations from the National Institute of Statistics' October - December trimester National Employment Surveys (Encuestas Nacionales de Empleo [ENE]).

that later (since the foundation of the Central Única de Trabajadores in 1952), based its actions on an alliance between *public servants* and *industrial workers* in defense of salaries threatened by inflation (which today is not the most relevant of problems): if the "working class lifestyle" was predominant 25 years ago, the mesocratic lifestyle is predominant today.[10]

THE MOBILITY FACTOR

The changes of the various social categories' relative positions in the distribution of income and the evolution of absolute income levels in the most populous classes are basic evidence for an interpretation of the transformations in Chile's social structure that we have called the "mobility" factor. Education, traditionally considered to be the main mechanism for individual mobility, is also evidence in this respect, due to the growing value that society places on educational wealth, and because of education's effects in terms of concrete possibilities for ascent in the occupational and income scales. We will focus our attention, however, on long-term changes related to income and will analyze changes in education in the following section. Education is a decisive variable in determining opportunities for well-being and the mobility of individuals from different social classes. We have called this factor the "persistence of cross-class inequalities."

In cases such as Chile's, where the last 25 years have been characterized by large variations in income levels and an increase in the number of individuals that make up each social stratum, an analysis of upward or downward movements in terms of the incomes of individuals in different social strata can only be made using a scale that permits the *relative positions* held by those individuals to be examined. This is achieved by maintaining the size for the compared income layers fixed throughout the period being examined. For this study we used quintile income distribution.* The variations in the proportion of individuals from each social category in the upper segments of this relative scale (in the two highest distribution quintiles, for example) and in the lowest income segments (the bottom quintile), allowing for changes in the size of the social categories being compared, provide indications of ascent or descent via income.

Three general trends clearly emerge from a study of relative mobility through income in the various social categories: (1) the distancing of the working class from the middle sectors; (2) faster improvements in income in the categories of independent workers in comparison with salaried positions; and, consequently, (3) a change in the social composition of poverty, with poverty being measured on the basis of an income threshold or poverty line.

---

10 Perhaps a percentage-based expression is not sufficient to assess changes in the relative weight of the different sectors and their impact on the probability of the dominance of different models for collective action. Therefore, it is valuable to note that in raw figures these changes meant that in the 25-year period being examined, middle salaried positions increased from 550,000 to 1,400,000, blue-collar jobs in industry and construction decreased from 760,000 to 700,000, and blue-collar jobs in trade and services grew from 220,000 to 700,000. If we assume that each one of these jobs corresponds to roughly one household, we can get an approximate idea of the impact of these changes on the lifestyle of the national urban population.

*   This refers to dividing the distribution of income into five groups, each of which contains 20% of all working individuals.

TABLE 5

MEMBER DISTRIBUTION OF EACH SOCIAL CATEGORY BY INCOME GROUP

Social Categories	1971			1987			1990			1995		
	Poorest 20%	Next 40%	Richest 40%	Poorest 20%	Next 40%	Richest 40%	Poorest 20%	Next 40%	Richest 40%	Poorest 20%	Next 40%	Richest 40%
Social Categories Within Agriculture, Forestry, Hunting, and Fishing	34	50	16	28	49	23	36	49	15	39	43	18
Social Categories Outside of Agriculture, Forestry, Hunting, and Fishing	14	37	49	18	38	44	16	38	46	16	40	44
Non-Agricultural Entrepreneurs	-	5	95	-	2	98	-	2	98	-	1	99
Middle Echelons Sectors	5	26	69	5	23	72	6	26	68	7	28	65
Salaried Employees	2	24	74	4	23	73	4	26	70	7	32	61
Public	n.d.	n.d.	n.d.	1	13	86	2	20	78	3	28	69
Private	n.d.	n.d.	n.d.	5	28	67	5	29	66	9	33	58
Independent	12	30	58	8	24	68	13	24	63	5	18	77
Traditional Craftsmen	32	43	25	31	41	28	40	38	22	19	39	42
Working Class	8	50	42	11	58	31	9	56	35	17	60	23
Mining	1	35	64	4	38	58	5	31	64	4	29	67
Industry and Construction	8	52	40	9	63	28	7	60	33	16	61	23
Trade and Services	11	46	43	13	52	35	11	53	36	18	61	21
"Marginal" Groups	51	40	9	46	42	12	52	39	9	46	38	16
Domestic Servants	52	46	2	46	54	-	47	53	-	51	47	-
Marginal Retailers	53	26	21	44	29	27	53	26	21	44	25	31
Marginal Service Sector Workers	44	40	15	50	33	17	64	24	12	38	36	26

Source: Special tabulations from the National Institute of Statistics' October - December trimester National Employment Surveys (Encuestas Nacionales de Empleo [ENE]).

Increasing Discrepancies in the Income Scale between the Working and Middle Classes

The first confirmation of this trend is evidenced by the distinct evolution of the percentages of blue-collar and middle sector workers with low incomes (lowest 20%) and upper-middle and high incomes (highest 40%)[11] between 1971 and 1995. While the share of blue-collar workers with upper-middle and high incomes fell by nearly 50% (from 42% to 23%) and the percentage of blue-collar workers with low incomes doubled (from 8% to 17%), the position of the middle sectors as a whole in the distribution of income remained fairly constant: by the mid-1980s, two out of every three of the sectors' members continued to belong to the top two income quintiles, and only one in 20 was part of the neediest quintile. Thus, throughout this period, incorporation into

---

11 It should be noted that with very little variation during the years in question, the average distribution of income stood at around 60% of personal revenue. Therefore, the two highest quintiles of said distribution include employed individuals with incomes above average.

TABLE 6

MAKEUP OF THE POOREST 20% a/ BY SOCIAL CATEGORY
(Percentages)

Social Categories	Year			
	1971	1987	1990	1995
Social Categories Within Agriculture, Forestry, Hunting and Fishing	33	31	30	28
Non-Agricultural Entrepreneurs	-	-	-	-
Middle Echelons Sectors	7	7	8	11
Salaried Employees	2	3	4	9
Public	n.d.	-	-	1
Private	n.d.	3	4	8
Independent	5	4	4	2
Traditional Craftsmen	10	10	9	5
Working Class	10	7	11	21
Mining	-	-	-	-
Industry and Construction	4	3	4	10
Trade and Services	6	4	7	11
"Marginal" Groups	27	33	30	24
Domestic Servants	16	17	14	13
Marginal Retailers	5	10	8	7
Marginal Service Sector Workers	5	6	8	4
Unemployed	13	12	12	11
Total	100	100	100	100

Source: Special tabulations from the National Institute of Statistics' October - December trimester National Employment Surveys (Encuestas Nacionales de Empleo [ENE]).

a/ Refers to the poorest 20% of income distribution.

common middle sector occupations meant, with a high probability, the obtainment of incomes that were greater than the national average. This represented a clear rise in the social scale if the individuals taking such jobs came from marginal groups or working class households.

Two categories exhibit a trend different than the one described within the two most populous classes: among the working class, the salaried workers in the copper mining industry, and among the middle sectors, public servants. The former, traditionally the bloc with the greatest negotiating power, managed to raise their participation in the high income strata by nearly 10 percentage points beginning in the mid 1980s. It thus compensated for the relative setbacks experienced since the mid-1970s. Government employees, in contrast, saw their relative position in the income scale worsen due to the stagnation of public sector wages, which accompanied a strong reduction in the sector's participation in overall employment. Information on the setbacks experienced by salaried, public servants is not available for the period 1971-95. However, it is possible to verify that between 1987 and 1995, there was an important increase in public employees in the lower-middle stratum and a decrease of such workers' participation in the top two income quintiles.

TABLE 7

MAKEUP OF THE TOP 40% OF INCOMES, BY SOCIAL CATEGORY
(Percentages)

Social Categories	Year			
	1971	1987	1990	1995
Social Categories Within Agriculture, Forestry, Hunting, and Fishing	7	13	8	7
Non-Agricultural Entrepreneurs	4	6	8	7
Middle Echelons Sectors	46	54	54	59
Salaried	35	44	44	43
Public	n.d.	17	14	12
Private	n.d.	27	30	31
Independent	11	10	10	16
Traditional Craftsmen	4	3	3	6
Working Class	37	20	24	16
Mining	3	1	2	1
Industry and Construction	21	8	10	8
Trade & Services	13	11	12	7
"Marginal" Groups	2	4	3	5
Domestic Servants	-	-	-	-
Marginal Retailers	1	3	2	3
Marginal Service Sector Workers	1	1	1	2
Unemployed	-	-	-	-
Total	**100**	**100**	**100**	**100**

Source: Special tabulations from the National Institute of Statistics' October - December trimester National Employment Surveys (Encuestas Nacionales de Empleo [ENE]).

a/ Refers to the top 40% of income distribution.

The increasing discrepancies between working and middle class sector incomes, coupled with the increase of the latter and the decrease of the former in terms of their representation within all social categories, resulted in a pronounced change in the "classist" composition of the upper, upper-middle, and lowest income distribution segments.[12] In 1971, close to two out of every five members of the top two quintiles came from the working class, but by the mid-1980s this ratio had fallen to one in five; by 1995 it stood at one in six. In contrast, middle sectors' share of the top two quintiles was 46% in 1971: it increased to 54% in the 1980s and then to 59% in 1995.

The working class' presence in the lowest quintile doubled (going from 10% in 1971 to 21% in 1995) and its center moved towards marginal groups (household help and marginal workers in trade and services). The presence of the middle sectors, on the other hand, grew moderately from 7% to 11%, a low figure given the quintile's remarkable growth.

---

12 It is important to remember that relative and not absolute changes are being analyzed here. As will be seen below, since the mid-1980s, the vast majority of social categories show significant increases in their average real incomes due to the economy's high growth rate.

TABLE 8

MAKEUP OF THE TOP 40% OF INCOMES, BY SOCIAL CATEGORY
(Percentages)

Social Categories	Period		
1987 Index=100	1987	1990	1995
Social Categories Within Agriculture, Forestry, Hunting and Fishing	100	97	140
Agricultural Entrepreneurs	100	120	153
Salaried Agricultural Labor	100	107	129
Poor Peasantry and Settlers	100	70	153
Social Categories Outside of Agriculture, Forestry, Hunting and Fishing	100	110	159
Non-Agricultural Entrepreneurs	100	108	179
Industry	100	116	179
Wholesale/Retail Trade	100	92	182
Service Sector and Remainder (Includes Construction)	100	120	185
Middle Echelons Sectors	100	98	138
Salaried Public Employees	100	95	111
Salaried Private Employees	100	100	124
Independent	100	96	209
Traditional Craftsmen	100	107	214
Working Class	100	109	136
Mining	100	104	147
Industry and Construction	100	114	146
Trade and Services	100	105	126
"Marginal" Groups	100	99	173
Domestic Servants	100	115	158
Marginal Retailers	100	88	167
Marginal Service Sector Workers	100	89	198
PEM and POJH	100	231	0
Not Classified	100	103	203
Total	100	109	160

Source: Special tabulations from the National Institute of Statistics' October - December trimester National Employment Surveys(Encuestas Nacionales de Empleo [ENE]).

During this period, important changes occurred at the national level in the "classist" composition of the income distribution profile. These changes are not evident when only aggregate distributive changes are examined through deciles or other divisions of the population.

Faster Improvement in Earnings in Independent Categories Than in Salaried Jobs
Although this was a characteristic trait of a good part of the period, it crystallized beginning in 1990 with the continuation of the economy's rapid growth. In this period,

TABLE 9

PROPORTION OF EACH SOCIAL CATEGORY FOUND IN CONDITIONS OF POVERTY a/
(Percentages)

Social Categories	Year			
	1971	1987	1990	1995
Social Categories Within Agriculture, Forestry, Hunting, and Fishing	34	44	39	27
Non-Agricultural Entrepreneurs	-	-	-	-
Middle Echelons Sectors	5	12	11	6
Salaried Employees	2	11	9	6
Public	n.d.	6	8	6
Private	n.d.	12	10	6
Independent	12	19	17	6
Traditional Craftsmen	41	46	40	15
Working Class	9	44	36	26
Mining	-	-	-	16
Industry and Construction	8	47	37	28
Trade and Services	11	42	35	25
"Marginal" Groups	51	39	36	28
Domestic Servants b/	...	...	...	...
Marginal Retailers	54	38	36	22
Marginal Service Sector Workers	44	52	48	38
Total c/	100	100	100	100

a/ Refers to the percentage of people from each social category that live in households with incomes at or below the poverty line.

b/ Excluded because a high percentage live in their place of employment.

c/ These percentages don't agree with official poverty figures because they refer to the active workforce, not the country's total population.

Source: Special tabulations from the National Institute of Statistics' October - December trimester National Employment Surveys (Encuestas Nacionales de Empleo [ENE]).

and even since the mid-1980s, non-agricultural businessmen, independent groups within the middle classes, and other categories of low income, non-salaried workers (craftsmen and independent workers from marginal groups) achieved absolute increases in income that were much greater than those obtained by the salaried sectors. The same thing happened in the agricultural sector, where not only entrepreneurs, but also the peasantry, witnessed greater relative participation in income increases than the sector's salaried workers. Thus, while the average incomes in the non-salaried categories (entrepreneurs and self-employed workers) increased by 90% in real terms between 1987 and 1995, the average income in the salaried social categories increased by close to 40%. The average income of working individuals as a whole grew by 60% during this period. From the vantage point of the "mobility" factor, however, this disparity in the evolution of wages, consistent with the logic of an economy that has grown at high and sustained rates, has not constituted a means of upward mobility in the income scale since, as indicated above, salaried and independent jobs are the positions that have grown the fastest.

Changes in the Social Composition of Poverty

The two characteristics of the "mobility" factor served to modify the social composition of the population living in poverty, primarily due to the very different rates at which poverty was reduced within each category.[13] Although poverty rates decreased as a whole between 1995 and 1971 (falling from 20% to 18%), they increased relatively more among salaried workers than among independent workers.[14] The most important changes are as follows: a notable increase in poverty in all of the working class categories; a decrease in poverty in the agricultural categories; and an even more pronounced decrease among traditional craftsmen and marginal workers from the trade and services sectors.

These changes have important consequences for social policies and also lead to doubts as to whether poverty levels will continue to decrease with the same speed as they did during the recent period of economic recuperation and rapid expansion. The new poverty scenario suggests that poverty is no longer mainly associated with excluded social categories in urban areas and the peasantry and poor settlers in rural areas, as occurred during the late 1970s. Poverty increasingly affects wide sectors of the working class, a sector traditionally considered "included." Twenty-five years ago, one out of 10 members of the working class lived in poverty, by 1995 that ratio had increased to one in four. Marginal groups, on the other hand, have tended to exit poverty quite quickly, at a rate even greater than that of working class groups: in 1970, half of the sectors that were "socially excluded" fell within in the poverty strata; currently, only about 28% of the sector are in this situation.

The Persistence of Cross-Class Inequalities

Education and, in more general terms, the educational capital[15] that individuals of different social categories attain is a crucial factor in analyzing cross-class inequalities. Therefore, empirical evidence about the persistence, or lack thereof, of unequal access to education and the way in which it is passed on from one generation to the next is vital. As Goldthorpe points out: "The degree of stability in the time of classist differences in educational achievement constitutes a genuine, not spurious *explanandium* of class theory."[16]

---

13   The various changes in each social categories' incomes are not the only factor that explains the changes in poverty which affect continuously less households, although it may be the most important. Differences among social classes in terms of the rate of reductions in productiveness and rising participation in the "secondary" labor market, among other factors, are circumstances that have also contributed, over the long term, to the modification of the composition of the population living in poverty.

14   The figure for poverty rates for 1995 corresponds to a conservative estimate and was reached by assuming that a decrease had occurred between 1994 and 1995, but less than the one registered between 1992 and 1994. At the time this document was written the poverty estimates with information from the 1996 Casen survey were not available.

15   We use this term to include not only the number of years that an individual studies, but also the quality and appropriateness of the education to which the individual had access and the educational level of his or her home.

16   John H. Goldthorpe, "Class Analysis and the Reorientation of Class Theory: The Case of Persisting Differentials in Educational Attainment," op. cit., p. 487.

TABLE 10

EDUCATIONAL PROFILE OF SOCIAL CATEGORIES, 1995

Social Categories Percentages	All Ages				Age Groups							
	Total	0 to7	8 to 11	12 and over	15 to 24				45 and over			
					Sub-total	0 to 7	8 to11	12 and over	Sub-total	0 to 7	8 to11	12 and over
Social Categories Within Agriculture, Forestry, Hunting, and Fishing	100	65	25	10	100	45	42	13	100	87	7	6
Agricultural Entrepreneurs	100	33	20	47	100	3	31	66	100	44	17	39
Salaried Agricultural Labor	100	63	29	8	100	44	43	13	100	89	8	3
Poor Peasantry and Settlers	100	71	21	8	100	47	39	14	100	91	5	4
Social Categories Outside of Agriculture, Forestry, Hunting, and Fishing	100	21	27	52	100	10	33	57	100	42	21	37
Non-Agricultural Entrepreneurs	100	11	18	71	100	5	3	92	100	18	19	63
Industry	100	10	14	76	100	0	0	100	100	13	17	70
Wholesale/Retail Trade	100	11	16	73	100	0	0	100	100	17	16	67
Service Sector and Remainder (Includes Construction)	100	11	20	69	100	18	8	74	100	20	22	58
Middle Echelons Sectors	100	8	14	78	100	1	16	83	100	21	17	62
Salaried Public Employees	100	3	9	88	100	1	10	89	100	5	13	82
Salaried Private Employees	100	3	12	85	100	1	16	83	100	9	14	77
Independent	100	26	26	48	100	5	32	63	100	43	23	34
Traditional Craftsmen	100	43	34	23	100	22	47	31	100	64	23	13
Working Class	100	27	38	35	100	14	40	46	100	57	28	15
Mining	100	22	36	42	100	13	33	54	100	43	38	19
Industry and construction	100	31	39	30	100	17	40	43	100	64	23	13
Trade and Services	100	24	38	38	100	12	40	48	100	52	31	17
"Marginal" Groups	100	42	36	22	100	20	53	27	100	66	21	13
Domestic Servants	100	45	40	15	100	20	59	21	100	72	21	7
Marginal Retailers	100	35	33	32	100	15	40	45	100	54	25	21
Marginal Service Sector Workers	100	47	29	24	100	25	51	24	100	69	15	16
Unemployed (*)	100	10	32	58	100	11	31	58	100	32	51	17
Not Classified	100	10	55	35	100	0	55	45	100	15	65	20
Total	100	28	27	45	100	16	34	50	100	50	19	31

Source: Special tabulations from the National Institute of Statistics' October - December trimester National Employment Surveys (Encuestas Nacionales de Empleo [ENE]).

(*) Includes people looking for work for the first time as well as PEM and POJH workers.

TABLE 11

A YOUNG (AGES 20-24) PERSON'S PROBABILITY OF
ATTENDING A MINIMUM OF 8, 12, AND 15 YEARS OF SCHOOL
BROKEN DOWN BY FAMILY INCOME QUINTILE

Family Income Quintile[a/]	Percentage of 20-24 year-olds that will attend at least:								
	8 years of school			12 years of school			15 years of school		
	period			period			period		
	1987	1990	1995	1987	1990	1995	1987	1990	1995
1 (Poorest)	64.3	63.8	75.4	23.1	19.1	38.0	1.1	1.1	3.6
2	72.5	76.8	82.5	29.5	30.8	46.2	1.8	3.0	5.4
3	80.4	85.3	89.4	37.2	42.2	59.1	3.5	5.0	6.3
4	87.0	90.3	94.4	51.4	53.1	74.3	7.9	7.2	15.0
5 (Richest)	93.0	96.7	98.3	70.6	83.4	91.8	29.3	35.5	38.3
Total	78.4	81.6	87.8	39.9	42.5	60.7	6.8	8.2	12.4

Source: Special tabulations from the National Institute of Statistics' October - December trimester National Employment Surveys (Encuestas Nacionales de Empleo [ENE]).

a/ Per capita family income was used to construct the five groups.

The educational levels attained by young people entering the job market largely depends on the income level of their homes or the educational level of their parents. These characteristics are distributed unequally among social classes and thus provide an indication about the intergenerational reproduction of social inequalities and their relationship with society.

Given that the economy's rapid expansion raises the educational levels necessary to attain a given job, it is necessary to first examine how educational differences have evolved among different class groups throughout the period. Although we do not have information of the breakdown of educational levels by social category for 1971, the information for 1995, split up into age groups, gives us an idea of how the different social categories participated in rising education in that period.[17] The comparison of social category educational profiles in the 45 years old and over group (those people who in 1971 were part of the 20 years old and over group) with the current profile and with that of individuals entering the work force (the 15 to 24 age group) indicates a relative reduction in the educational disparities among social categories.

If one considers that the educational discrepancies among social categories in the oldest age group reflect the differences prevalent 25 years ago, the distances that today

---

17 Education's strong expansion, especially in the rates of secondary education between 1971 and 1995, changed noticeably the educational profile of the active population. For example, the percentage of the active population with 10 or more years of formal education increased by 117% to 48%, while the percentage of this population with less than six years of education decreased from 42% to 19%.

TABLE 12

A YOUNG (AGES 20-24) PERSON'S PROBABILITY OF ATTENDING A MINIMUM OF 8, 12, AND 15 YEARS OF SCHOOL BROKEN DOWN BY LEVEL OF PARENTAL EDUCATION

Parental Education [a/] (Number of School Years Completed)	Percentage of 20 - 24 year-olds that will attend at least:									Percentual Distribution of Young People (Between 20 and 24) by Parental Education Levels		
	8 years of school			12 years of school			15 years of school					
	period			period			period					
	1987	1990	1995	1987	1990	1995	1987	1990	1995	1987	1990	1995
0 - 2	49.7	53.8	61.4	14.5	15.0	24.4	0.1	0.2	1.3	20.6	18.2	12.3
3 - 5	75.4	77.8	78.7	20.1	29.4	39.7	1.2	0.8	2.3	31.0	28.7	23.1
6 - 9	90.8	91.7	93.7	46.9	47.4	61.7	5.2	5.5	7.4	32.6	33.1	35.1
10 - 12	95.7	95.3	98.7	72.0	72.6	87.2	23.2	20.6	20.7	11.4	14.6	19.1
13 and more	97.2	98.3	99.1	93.4	95.7	98.1	48.4	57.1	49.7	4.4	5.4	10.4
Total	78.4	81.7	87.8	39.9	42.6	60.7	6.8	8.2	12.4	100.0	100.0	100.0

Source: Special tabulations from the National Institute of Statistics' October - December trimester National Employment Surveys (Encuestas Nacionales de Empleo [ENE]).

a/ Refers to the average number of school years completed by the head of a household and his spouse.

separate the middle sectors from the blue-collar sectors have been slightly reduced.[18] Thus, for example, the difference in the percentage of individuals who study for at least 12 years has decreased from 47 to 43 percentage points. This did not happen in marginal groups where, despite an increase in educational levels due to the universalization of primary education, the distances that separate these groups from the most populous classes did not decrease: the enormous differences that separate them from the middle sectors (close to 50 percentage points) remained the same; these differences increased with respect to the working class.

When the current educational profile of young people (the 15 to 24 age group entering the work force) is examined, once again very pronounced cross-class differences are evident: while more than 83% of youth from middle sectors join the work force with at least 12 years of formal education, among the working classes this percentage only reaches 46%, and it falls to 28% for youth from marginal groups.

Although it is easy to accept the validity of the argument that there are inherent inequalities that largely explain the way in which education is distributed among different social classes, it is more difficult to find empirical evidence that adequately explains the magnitude of these inequalities and their evolution through time.

---

18 Obviously, the extent of the reduction in the educational discrepancies among categories is not independent of the educational strata used to establish the comparisons. Raising of the lower limit of the highest group from 12 to 15 years would probably result in a smaller decrease in the distances among the groups compared.

In this study we had access to data that enabled us to link the characteristics of one generation (parents) with the educational levels achieved by the members of the following generation (children). Thus we can provide evidence of the importance of a family's income and the parents' educational levels (a household's educational capital) in determining how many years young people will study. Nonetheless, apart from verifying the existence of differences in young people's educational opportunities as a function of their social origin, we are also interested in determining if there have been any changes in the way these inequalities have been reduced, or if, on the contrary, these inequalities have actually persisted or increased.

Although between 1987 and 1995 there was a very pronounced increase in youth education levels in all income segments (the percentage of individuals that completed secondary education rose from 40% to 61%), differences in the probability of reaching that level did not significantly decrease. In 1987, the percentage of youth from the neediest quintile that completed secondary education was 23%, 17 points below average; in 1995, the percentage of these youth that attained said education had increased to 38%, a notable change given the short time span. However, this increase also meant a relative relapse for this group, since the distance with respect to the average grew from 17 to almost 23 percentage points.

The evidence seems to indicate that the educational levels attained by parents[19] are more important than the family's income in determining children's levels of education, which leaves no doubt about *how opportunities and disadvantages are reproduced between generations*. It can be shown that in the 20 to 24 age group, the increase in the average level of education between 1987 and 1995 did not reduce the large differences in opportunities among young people coming from homes with differing educational capital.

On the other hand, we can also see that, to the extent that educational levels are raised and progress is made towards the universalization of secondary education; that is, to the extent that the probabilities that young people from the lower and middle classes complete secondary education rise, inequalities among classes will shift toward higher education. In 1995, less than 5% of young people belonging to households the bottom two income quintiles managed to complete 15 years of education; this percentage increased to 38% for youth belonging to households in the top income quintile. Between 1987 and 1995, the differences between the classes compared did not decrease.

As R. Urzúa has stated, "Although educational differences among households have always contributed to the maintenance of a certain degree of educational inheritance and also, therefore, to the inheritance of opportunities for social mobility, this role appears to have intensified with the raising of the thresholds that must be reached in order for education to make a difference in terms of opportunities for social mobility."[20]

Therefore, clear indications of the persistence of cross-class inequalities exists. The new generation's educational achievements continue to be dependent, to an important extent, on both the distribution of income and the adult generation's educational capital.

---

19 For this analysis we consider educational capital to be the average number of years studied by both parents and not only the education of the head of the household, as has been done in other studies of this nature.

20 Raúl Urzúa, "Globalización, modelo económico y transformación social: Una mirada parcial," (mimeo, Centro de Análisis de Políticas Públicas-CAPP, Universidad de Chile), p.20.

Conclusion

Chilean socioeconomic evolution has left behind the traits of inorganicness, exclusion, and impermeability that characterized the social structure until only a decade and a half ago, when those traits appeared to be the basic trends of a development style rather than elements of a critical transformation period. In 1995, job salarization and exclusion rates were similar to those that existed around 1970, during the end of a period of import substitution industrialization. However, the class structure that emerged from the profound socioeconomic transformations that have occurred since then presents notable differences with the previous structure: a sharp decline in the importance of the blue-collar working class and the bureaucratization and division into three parts of salaried, private sector jobs are the changes that have had the greatest impact. The vindictive logic of the mobilization of social actors, which translated into unionism's strong presence in the national landscape, has been replaced by a mesocratic lifestyle shaped by market forces.

The importance of the industrial working class and public servants in the employment structure has sharply declined, and these sectors have clearly lost participation in the distribution of a growing income mass. Today, there is a much greater income discrepancy between blue-collar workers and individuals from the middle classes. Although salarization regained strength with the reformalizing of employment, the categories of independent workers have improved their incomes faster than salaried workers have. As a result, today poverty has a much higher salaried component than it did 25 years ago and it is no longer mainly a problem of the disintegration of "marginal masses" (groups that appear to demonstrate a greater capacity than blue-collar workers to adapt and meld into the new scenario of market opportunities). The relative pauperization of blue-collar workers and public servants may, eventually, translate into the orientation of actions resistant to the consolidation of the new order.

Cross-class differences in total income have been very weakly offset by a reduction in educational differences, despite the notable overall improvement in nation-wide educational levels. The educational discrepancy between the current generation of blue-collar workers and the middle classes is slightly less than it was for the previous generation; the educational distance between the middle and working classes and marginal groups continues to be enormous. Within the new generation, cross-class differences in education continue to be very pronounced and still represent significant barriers to social mobility. Parents' educational levels, more than a family's income, appear to be the main factor in determining the education levels reached by children; this indicates the persistence of mainly inherent sources of inequality. Consequently, the great sideways social mobility that has occurred in Chilean society over the last 25 years seems to have resulted in very little net upward mobility. The overlapping of concentrated distributions of income and educational opportunities, even in the context of the accelerated growth of the respective available masses, points toward the persistence of cross-class inequalities and the resurgence of traditional forms of clashes of interests, rather than the emergence of egalitarian forms of citizenship capable of founding new social relationships characterized by solidarity.

Appendix: Description of Social Categories and Actions

For the purpose of describing social categories we feel it useful to begin with those categories derived from the three main activities that formed the foundation of Chile's economy during the agro-mining-export period, and upon which the bases of modern economic activities were later founded. That is, the social categories linked to agriculture, mining, and trade, just as they appear today. Below, we describe the social categories associated with the key modernization agents and processes —the State, urbanization and industrialization— and, finally, those categories that appear linked to the "deformations" of these processes and to certain specific transformations of the last 10 years.

Social Categories in Agriculture[21]

The agrarian reform process, and its subsequent reorientation, ended the social structure of the *hacienda* and gave way to a comprehensive segmentation of agricultural social groups, which were mainly a result of the external opening of the Chilean economy. In keeping with the new trends of Chilean agricultural development, the distinction among agricultural social categories is based on the criteria of regional differentiation.

We attempted to identify the following segments among the business categories: an *agricultural exporters* category, made up of agricultural entrepreneurs from the Norte Chico and the Valle Central who have been able to adopt export strategies and who focus on the production of fruits; a category of *non-exporting, agricultural entrepreneurs*, partially located in the Valle Central and in southern Chile and who have adopted profitable production lines for the domestic market or agro-industry (mainly beef and dairy livestock); and the "*landowning bourgeoisie*," agricultural producers unable to move toward exports for either ecological-ideological reasons or because they lack access to sufficient capital to adapt their land to other uses (the production of wheat, beats, potatoes, vegetables, etc.).

There are other agricultural proletariat and subproletariat segments articulated through direct production relationships: *the agricultural proletariat of the central zone, the agricultural proletariat of the south-central zone, the proletariat of the southern beef/dairy companies, the rural salaried workers in the wheat zone, and the Magallanes livestock proletariat.* Although this classification oversimplifies the complex diversity of salaried agricultural workers, it does cover the larger groups that can currently be identified from the point of view of rural working conditions, salaries, and lifestyles. In addition to these groups there is the *forestry proletariat*, which works under very precarious conditions (low wages, isolation in reforestation areas, employment instability) and which is mainly located in the Concepción, Maule, and Arauco areas.

Following this regional criteria, we identified categories within the *peasantry* that reflect, to a certain extent, the broad diversification and segmentation processes resulting from the agricultural changes that have occurred in Chile. These categories are as follows: *the indigenous peasantry from the Norte Grande, the poor peasantry from Norte Chico, the Araucanía peasantry, the southern peasantry, the peasants of Chiloé, and poor settlers*, each of

---

21 In this section the classification proposed by José Bengoa, *El campesino chileno después de la Reforma Agraria* (Santiago: Ediciones SUR, Colección Estudios Sociales, 1983) is strictly followed. We would like to thank the author for the patient aid he gave us in the construction of the operational definitions for this empirical analysis.

whom represents communities that are ethnically and geographically distinguishable. The *central, south central,* and the *Metropolitan Region peasantry* (which include the majority of the Agrarian Reform's allottees) were added to these categories. We also identified the categories of *small-scale fisherman* and *independent carpenters,* which, due to international economic activity classifications, are often confused with peasant categories.

Mining Social Groups

The oldest social group that coalesced in Chile in terms of the mining industry was that of the *pirquineros* (independent, manual-labor miners), from which other groups later emerged. After their origin as a general category, the *pirquineros* became a specific sector comprised of miners mainly located in the Norte Chico. More important than this group is the mining proletariat made up of *coal miners, miners in the Large Copper Mines* —the segment of the Chilean working class that has been the main foundation for the kind of unionism associated with the State's large strategic companies—, and the *miners in the Small and Medium Copper Mines,* whose working and negotiating conditions are inferior to that of their peers at the Large Mines and who are often in relations with employers other than the State, another reason for treating them as a different social category.[22]

Social Categories In Formal Trade

With respect to business activities, the *commercial bourgeoisie* should be mentioned first. This category, due to the growth of cities and improvements in the means of transportation, is located in the country's main urban centers. Complementary to this category and undertaking the same activities are *white collar employees and blue-collar workers.* The main social category in business activities continued to be that of small business owners or *retailers,* a social group that first developed in the shelter of a strongly protected and controlled domestic market, one that has shown a surprising ability to adapt to new market conditions. The growing differentiation in social representation among the different kinds of trade and services entrepreneurs makes it necessary to treat these categories separately, even though in the past they have participated together in common actions or organizations. Due to an inevitable association of ideas, and above and beyond the economic activity performed, retailers and the category of *small-scale transport bourgeoisie* were situated together.

Administrative and Professional Categories

The study of the growth and transformations of the State apparatus, as well as the social groups that have been favored by the development of public organisms at different times, is a key element to understanding the country's history. Therefore, when constructing this matrix of social categories we sought to identify the different groups and classes that make up the public service sector and that form an important part of the country's middle classes. When examining the different functions and positions within the public apparatus, we distinguished between the *traditional public servants* and the *modern public servants.* The former are associated with positions held by those tasked with administering

---

22 Unfortunately, the classifications did not permit the identification of the other significant category of miners, the workers in the *Iron Mines,* mainly located in the Third and Fourth Regions. As in other cases, here it was important to construct a residual category in conjunction with other workers in the mining industry.

the government's main local services, justice, and defense. The latter is comprised of those employees linked to activities that emerged and coalesced during the second phase of the State's development: social and welfare services, plus economic reform and other state agencies. In both segments we distinguished between the *upper echelons* —public servants who perform managerial functions and that are primarily professionals— and the *middle and lower echelons*, composed of technicians and unskilled workers.

Similarly, economic development allowed for the growth of important private institutions and businesses in which the increased complexity of administrative tasks, mainly in the area of services, gave rise to a *modern private services sector*, within which it is also necessary to distinguish among different strata (high, middle, low), according to the occupational hierarchy. It is important to examine the evolution of these social categories due to their rapid expansion. The specific activities of these categories (except for the technocrat segment) is not clearly defined.

The Country's Industrial Social Categories

When constructing social categories in the industrial sector, we sought, as with the cases of agriculture and mining, to include the sector's different development phases, especially in the case of blue-collar industrial workers. With the recognition of the existence of at least two phases of industrialization, the "easy substitution" phase (linked to the emergence of mass consumer goods industries) and the "difficult substitution" phase (linked to the development of industries that produce mass consumer goods with greater technological components, intermediaries, and capital), we identified *the capital-based industrial entrepreneur* and the following categories within the industrial blue-collar working class: the *traditional industrial blue-collar working class*, the *blue-collar working class of the second phase of substitution industrialization,* and *the strategic industries blue-collar working class*. In addition to these three categories (and within them, the public and private segments), we identified the *construction workers class* and *salaried transportation workers*.

In contrast to the majority of studies, which only consider categories that have reciprocal relations —cooperative or conflictive— within the industrial system, we allowed for the fact that industry displaces or subordinates diverse categories of craftsmen. First, industry affects *traditional craftsmen*; that is, people who are self-employed and whose work is related to the production or repair of consumer goods (cobblers, tailors, leather workers, etc.); second, industry affects the *construction craftsmen*, who organize only as needed for each job; and, last, industry affects the *modern craftsmen*: workers who, on their own or in small shops, work primarily in the repair of consumer goods with greater technological components (electronics shops, mechanics, etc.).

Categories of Urban Poverty

It is well known that the country's social and economic development has been a deformed and contradictory process in which, together with many of the social categories mentioned that represent the world of "incorporation," a great number of other categories, traditionally associated with the world of "marginality," appear. Nonetheless, the sharp increase in poverty rates during the 1970s and through the mid-1980s, and their continuous decrease since then, make it necessary to identify a plurality of categories in which the world of urban poverty and social exclusion are segmented, in order to analyze the effect that these changes have had on each of these categories. The *"blue-collar workers" of the service sector* and the *service personnel in public and private offices* are located in the sector closest to "inclusion," due mainly to greater probabilities for job stability, and for all effects of empirical classification we have considered them to be part of the "included" segment of society. The same criteria cannot be used for categories closer to *servants* (despite their formal "salaried" status) such as *household help*, or to those that are subject to social degradation, as was the case for the workers in the Minimum Employment Program (MEP) and the Occupation Program of Heads of Households (POJH). Also included among the most specific categories of urban poverty were the *marginal merchants* and *marginal workers in services*. Finally, the *unemployed* were also included in this category.

Integration and Development:
A Vision of Social Policy

María Pía Martin

Introduction

This essay seeks to outline the evolution of social policies in Chile over the past few decades. These policies underwent a profound transformation during the military regime, particularly as compared to previous periods. The policies of the 1990s partially continue and partially break with those implemented during the authoritarian period. An overview of social reforms between 1973 and 1989 will assist in highlighting recent changes in various areas of social policy.

Since 1990, social policy has been a key component of the government's strategy of growth with equity. This strategy contrasts with the military regime's traditional welfare policies. The Concertación has implemented a variety of new initiatives, such as training programs, the promotion of productive activity, and low-income community development programs, as well as programs supporting small businesses, agricultural producers, fisheries, and small-scale mining operations. These efforts have been accompanied by more traditional measures in the areas of health, education, housing, and social security. In addition, new programs have been directed toward vulnerable groups and geographic areas.

The fruits of this social strategy have included a gradual reduction in the country's poverty rate. Other factors have also contributed to this positive result, most notably the country's dynamic economic growth and increases in overall social spending. The state has allocated greater resources to the social sector, implemented numerous social programs, expanded access to services, and improved efficiency. The path toward equal opportunity and a fairer and more equitable society is a long and arduous one. Any increase in the impact of social policies constitutes a step forward along this path.

Meanwhile, significant inequalities persist today in the areas of health, education, housing, and social security. Additional policy efforts are required to maintain and extend present coverage and to increase the quality and fairness of current programs.

In the first part of this article, we will review the nature and impact of the social reforms implemented by the authoritarian regime. The second section will examine social strategies from 1990 to the present and their effects on the poverty rate and the distribution of income. The third part analyzes social policies and their effects on the quality of life, especially in the areas of health, education, housing, social security, and equal opportunity. Finally, we will address the primary challenges for social policy in the future.

I. The Change from Universal to Targeted Policies under the Military Government

During the 1950s, 1960s, and the early 1970s, the state exercised a monopoly in the creation, implementation, and financing of social policies. The central government carried out national policies in the areas of health, education, housing, and social security. Most programs sought to satisfy the basic needs of the population as a whole, with universal coverage as the ultimate goal. Under a vision of the "benevolent state," social policies became highly developed, and a complex institutional framework for social programs was created (Schkolnik and Bonnefoy 1994).

In spite of the aim of universal coverage, social policies benefited mainly salaried employees, to the detriment of informal and marginal workers, since many benefits such as health coverage, housing, and social security were channeled through the formal employment system. The groups with the greatest capacity to lobby the state (the middle classes and organized workers) were the most successful in gaining acceptance for their demands. This regressive system with its spiraling welfare benefits nonetheless succeeded in improving the nation's overall social development indicators, including the infant mortality rate and primary education coverage. Ongoing demands for more benefits and services, however, resulted in a continued expansion in social spending which was higher than the rate of GDP growth. This led to sustained financial deficits and macroeconomic imbalances (Raczynski and Cominetti 1994).

This model of social policy changed radically under the military regime. The break with democracy also marked a break with the universal social policies in place since the 1920s, which had become well-established between 1950 and 1973. With the change in economic approach from import substitution to a neo-liberal model, the new regime placed a much higher priority on macroeconomic objectives, reducing the state's activity in the productive and social spheres, and letting the private sector take a dominant role in development. The market was seen as the best mechanism for the allocation of resources; therefore, the state should reduce its role in providing and paying for services and confine itself to an essentially regulatory and supervisory function to ensure the correct operation of the market.

One of the first neo-liberal policies in the social sphere was the reduction of social expenditures to help curb inflation. The economic crises of 1975-76 and 1982-83 led to further cuts in social spending. The quality and coverage of social benefits and services underwent a progressive deterioration.

The shrinking of the social budget was associated with the idea of reducing social policies to a purely economic function. A state with a high level of activity in the social sector was replaced by one with a subsidiary role; intervention was only justifiable in cases where private sector action was not feasible. This orientation led to radical changes in the state's institutional structure as well as its social policies. Many reforms were carried out in an undemocratic manner, giving affected groups no opportunity to participate in the design of social policies nor to express their disagreement with the measures adopted.

During this period, no specific policies were created to reduce poverty, since the government believed that this would occur naturally through economic growth. The so-called "trickle-down policy," which assumed that economic successes would filter down from privileged groups to the rest of the population, obviated the need for redistributive policies or those specifically aimed at overcoming poverty. Limited social programs were aimed at ensuring minimum subsistence conditions for the poorest Chileans. A social safety net of subsidies was developed, mainly consisting of direct monetary assistance (the Family Subsidy or SUF; social aid pensions; and unemployment benefits, among others). These subsidies, administered by the municipalities, were targeted toward the neediest groups, seeking especially to ameliorate the effects of the economic crisis. In addition to the subsidies, employment programs such as the Minimum Employment Program (PEM) and the Employment Program for Heads of Households (POJH) were created, aimed at reducing the social effects of unemployment. The CAS (Socioeconomic Category) system, established to classify households by economic situation and target the most impoverished, was also implemented by the municipalities.[1]

Through the CAS formula, extreme poverty was treated as a concrete and measurable field of action. Using the CAS as a technical instrument, poverty levels could be quantified and evaluated. This in turn enabled social spending to be more effectively targeted. In the late 1980s, the National Socioeconomic Category system (Casen) was devised to define a limit of absolute need (Mac-Clure and Urmeneta 1995). It should be noted that the targeting of social spending and the introduction of measuring mechanisms were meant to increase the technical component of social policy.

The shift to subsidy-based programs, coupled with overall reductions in social spending and the focusing of resources on the most impoverished, meant the loss of many previous entitlements among middle and lower-middle income groups. These people were now forced to seek the social services they needed within the market, supposedly more efficient in the allocation and provision of resources.

Under the assumption that the private sector was more efficient and provided higher-quality services, the pay-as-you-go social security system was replaced by an individual capitalization scheme, administered by the private sector through Pension Fund Administrators (AFPs). Meanwhile, those who remained in the state system saw the value of their pensions fall. For health care, high- and middle-income groups switched to the private sector system through the Health Insurance Institutions (Isapres), which also contributed to financing public health care.

Meanwhile, decentralization measures began to be implemented in health and education, which would eventually end in privatization.[2] Public school administration was handed over to local city councils, and changes in the financing system opened the way for private investment. In health care, primary care centers were transferred to the municipalities. In both cases, co-payment systems were implemented. Private services enjoyed greater resources and focused on offering higher levels of quality. At the same time, the services offered by the public sector deteriorated due to shrinking levels of funding.

The housing subsidy system was changed, granting the private sector (the capital market and real estate firms) a greater role in the construction and financing of new homes. At the same time, massive relocation programs were implemented to move poorer

---

1   The CAS form was later redesigned, and CAS II (currently in use) was created. CAS II now considers housing conditions, including water and sewer connections, as well as employment and household income.

2   The reforms were not fully implemented, and the State continued to be responsible for setting policies for most social services, as well as for their technical and financial supervision. Furthermore, the majority of the population continued to use the public health care system and state-subsidized schools.

residents out to the periphery of cities. These policies produced a growing number of *allegados* (otherwise homeless people who reside with family members) and reshaped the population patterns of Chilean cities. A clear socio-spatial segregation developed, with the poorer members of society being confined to specific areas.

The crises resulting from these far-reaching changes were felt by a large portion of the population. During this period, unemployment rates were consistently higher than at any other time in the country's history, and real wages did not rise for 15 years afterward (García and Schkolnik 1995). In addition, the relocation measures pushed many workers formerly active in the informal labor market into unemployment.

As a result of the high unemployment rate and falling wages, the number of people living in poverty increased. According to a Casen survey conducted at the end of this period, 41.5% of the population was living in poverty, and the distribution of income had become significantly more imbalanced.[3] Furthermore, middle- and low-income groups were also affected by the deterioration in public services (Vergara 1990). The equity gap in society had grown wider, not only in monetary terms, but also in the quality of social services available to the needy.

II. Social Policies between 1990 and 1997

From 1990 to the present, social policies have exhibited elements of both continuity and change with respect to the previous period (Vergara 1993). The decentralized health care and educational systems have been maintained, but the link between decentralization and privatization has been broken. The decentralization of both of these services can be understood today as part of a democratization process. Local governments, with democratically-elected mayors and council members, are responsible for directing and administering these services. In education, advances have been made in the devolution of decision-making functions to local councils and to the educational establishments themselves. The constitutional reform of the municipalities gave greater decision-making powers to local councils in general. Another significant event was the 1996 establishment of the Regional Investment Fund under Local Assignation (IRAL), which includes municipalities and local communities in decisions about the management and allocation of regional resources.

Difficulties have been faced, however, in both the financing and the local management of social policies. Regional and local governments still show serious deficiencies in the management of monetary and human resources and in the effective implementation of health and education policies.

Nevertheless, with the return to democracy, participatory processes have been strengthened, involving both community organizations and the users of social programs in the decision-making process. With this, the country has moved beyond the neo-liberal line of thought which equates participation with co-payment. Starting in 1994, numerous participative forums were created (the National Council for the Elderly, National Council for the Eradication of Poverty, National Commission for the Modernization of Education,

---

3   According to the survey of household income in Greater Santiago between 1978 and 1988 by the National Statistics Institute (INE), the wealthiest quintile increased its share of income from 51.0% to 54.9%, while the poorest quintile's share decreased from 5.2% in 1978 to 4.4% in 1988. For more information, see Mideplan (1991).

and the National Council for the Control of Narcotics). These bodies allowed the community and the state to work together to set policies for areas previously lacking them, or
where public consensus is vital for their implementation.

During this period, the state's regulatory role was reinforced by measures aimed at
eliminating the distortions and inequalities produced by the privatization of social services, especially in health care and social security. Although these measures have tempered
the imbalances of the social reforms introduced during the military government,
significant disparities still persist in access to social services, as well as in their quality.

1. THE PAYMENT OF THE "SOCIAL DEBT"

In the early 1990s, high poverty rates, shrinking social benefits (especially for middle and
low-income groups), the uneven distribution of income, and the poor quality of social
services were considered part of a "social debt" which must be repaid. Consequently,
maintaining sustained economic growth, reducing poverty, and increasing social equity
were added to the task of strengthening democracy.

The neo-liberal strategy, based on the "trickle-down" theory of pure growth, had
already demonstrated its ineffectiveness in dealing with the problems of poverty and
inequality. Combining equity and economic growth became a central policy theme for the
new government. When the first Concertación administration took office, Chilean society
contained opposing extremes of economic success and poverty, raising the image of a
country divided between those who enjoyed the benefits of the modernization process and
those who had been left behind. The solution to this division, from the government's
point of view, was a more inclusive modernization process. Hence, the main innovations
in the new government's proposals were in the social sphere (Martínez 1995).

Since 1990, the international opening of the economy has been accompanied by policies aimed at promoting economic growth and preventing macroeconomic imbalances. At
the same time, the state resumed an active role in the social sphere, creating new programs
as well as providing increased resources to traditional social services such as health, housing, and social security. Thus, the democratic governments have attempted to combine
macroeconomic stability with sustainable social policies.

In 1989, the Concertación acknowledged the successes attained in economic development, but it also emphasized the pressing need to strengthen state action in the social
realm (Concertación de Partidos por la Democracia 1989). Social policies, now a central
aspect of governmental action, have pursued three basic objectives: improving the quality
of life for the entire population, ensuring equal opportunities, and bringing about the
social and economic integration of marginalized members of society.

Fulfillment of the pledge to expand social action was made possible by the 1990 Tax
Reform,[4] which permitted spending increases in the high-priority areas of health, education, and housing. During the following years, the portion of the budget allocated for
social spending rose progressively, from 59% in 1989 to 71% in 1996. Annual increases in
social spending have been consistently higher than increases in total public spending.

---

4   In 1990, the budget was set by the military government, with a 7.8% decrease from the previous year. The
    tax reform expanded the budget, prevented major cuts in programs, and paved the way for increased social
    spending between 1990 and 1992.

While public spending rose by 6.4% from 1995 to 1996, for example, social spending increased by 8% during the same period. In 1997, the Budgetary Law increased public spending by 5.6%, while social expenditures were expected to grow by 7.5%.

This increase was sustained in part by a change in the focus of the state's social action. The Concertación administrations have moved away from the concept of separate economic and social policies; they have come to consider social programs as part of their economic development strategy, viewing social spending as an investment in the people. Social policies are understood to encompass many different types of assistance, not simply the issuing of welfare checks. Under the democratic governments, social policies have become diversified and have moved in new directions. Universal policies, which help build up human capital, are combined with focused assistance for the poor, as well as selective policies aimed at promoting equal opportunities for disadvantaged groups (Schkolnik and Bonnefoy 1994).

Policies with universal coverage are viewed as investments, since if the whole population has access to adequate social benefits and services, they will be better able to serve in the labor force and work toward the country's development. The government has made efforts to improve quality and equity in these universal programs, especially in health, education, and housing. The aim is to provide equal opportunities for all social groups, especially the neediest.

Concrete social assistance programs for the poor were continued, using the data on impoverished households obtained from the 1987 Casen survey. The social safety net and the mechanisms for measuring poverty (the CAS form and the Casen survey) were also maintained. The budget for social assistance subsidies was increased, allowing increases in welfare payments as well as other subsidies and family allowances. Furthermore, the targeting of subsidies was improved (Mideplan 1996), and in 1996, subsidies were linked to incentives aimed at improving opportunities for the poor. An example of this was the extension of the Family Subsidy to cover students up to age 18. This new strategy represents an interesting combination of social aid policies and the promotion of opportunities.

In 1990, the government began to implement policies designed to improve opportunities for groups such as women, children, and the disabled, who are not necessarily living in extreme poverty, but who suffer from discrimination in society. Discrimination not only affects the ability of these groups to exercise their citizenship rights, but also their access to the benefits of development. Between 1990 and 1997, several plans were created to promote increased opportunities for these groups, including the Equal Opportunities Plan for Women, the National Plan for Children, and the National Care Plan for People with Disabilities.

Selective and targeted programs were also developed for groups identified as socially and economically vulnerable. The 1990 Casen survey identified several social categories whose members need assistance from specific programs to rise out of poverty. These groups are: female heads of households, underprivileged youth, children in difficult circumstances, and the elderly. Apart from this social targeting, a territorial focus was also introduced. The resulting programs, directed at areas of concentrated poverty, include the National Program for the Eradication of Poverty and its Special Municipalities Program, as well as the Program to Strengthen Impoverished Localities.

A new institutional framework was created to support these efforts to improve opportunities for vulnerable groups and those suffering discrimination. In addition, the programs designed for these groups are coordinated among different ministries, representing a new generation of multi-sector policies (Mideplan-UNICEF 1993).

Other notable new policies include those formulated to improve disadvantaged work-ers' job skills and economic productivity. These programs focus mainly on training individ-uals, including youth, and promoting small businesses. Qualifying small businesses may receive financial support (through private banks) and assistance with market access and technical training. The government considers these to be investment policies, since they generate opportunities and combine social policies with economic development measures.

In 1994, the elimination of extreme poverty was set as a priority goal, to be achieved by the beginning of the next millennium. Education was identified as the main tool for promoting equal opportunity and social equity; the country's educational system is cur-rently undergoing reform and modernization (Concertación de Partidos por la Democracia, 1994).

In summary, the 1990s have seen both sustained economic growth and significant progress in achieving the principal objective of the nation's social policies: the reduction of poverty. The socioeconomic strategy of growth with equity, based on factors such as economic growth, higher employment rates, rising pay, low inflation, and the reduction of poverty, has achieved positive results. Between 1989 and 1996, Chile's GDP rose by 60%. The country registered an average annual growth rate of 7% (one of the highest in Latin America) and achieved significant increases in the savings rate, which rose to between 27% and 28% of GDP. Inflation has been reduced from 30% at the end of the military gov-ernment to single-digit figures, enabling the country to maintain an overall macroeco-nomic balance and to increase the buying strength of domestic consumers. These achieve-ments have been reflected in dynamic job creation rates and the consequent drop in unemployment levels. Between 1990 and 1996, 840,000 new jobs were created, causing unemployment to drop from an average of 11.7% during the military regime to 5.3% in 1996 (excluding the PEM and POJH programs). While employment rose, wages also increased. Pay rose by 30% between 1989 and 1996, while the minimum wage increased by about 44% between 1990 and 1996 (the General Secretary of the Presidency 1997; Mideplan 1996). During this period, the poverty rate steadily declined, as will be further examined in the following section.

2. REDUCING POVERTY

Chile's advances in the fight against poverty have been brought about by a number of fac-tors, including the implementation of policies designed to promote equal opportunity as well as those which stimulated economic growth and therefore job creation. Chile's pover-ty rate has fallen significantly (see Table 1). According to the Casen surveys, the percentage of Chileans living in poverty fell from 45.1% to 23.2% between 1987 and 1996. At the same time, the rate of extreme poverty or indigence also dropped significantly, from 17.4% to 5.8% (Mideplan 1997a). In absolute figures, between 1987 and 1996, some two million Chileans were able to escape from poverty.

Since 1992, the rate of indigence has been reduced significantly, but at a slower pace than that of overall poverty. Indigence is more difficult to eliminate, since it represents a more entrenched kind of poverty, with a wide range of causes. Households affected by it also tend to be more dispersed.

The distribution of poverty varies between urban and rural areas (Table 2). Urban areas have the highest numbers of people living in poverty and indigence in absolute terms, whereas

TABLE 1

EVOLUTION OF RATES OF POVERTY AND INDIGENCE, BY POPULATION : 1987-96
(Percentages)

	1987	1990	1992	1994	1996
Indigent	17.4	12.9	8.8	7.6	5.8
Non-Indigent Poor	27.7	25.7	23.8	19.9	17.4
Total Poor	45.1	38.6	32.6	27.5	23.2
Non-Poor	54.9	61.4	67.4	72.5	76.8
Total	100.0	100.0	100.0	100.0	100.0

Source: The Ministry of Planning and Cooperation's 1987, 1990, 1992, 1994, and 1996 Casen Surveys.

rural areas demonstrate a proportionally higher percentage of indigence. The inhabitants of rural areas are also more dispersed, and in most cases, rural poverty is not only associated with deficiencies in access to basic services, such as health and education, but also with factors such as the lack of access to jobs, agricultural competition, and irrigation shortages. All these factors make the eradication of poverty in rural areas more difficult and complex.

Chile's regions show varying levels of poverty and indigence: according to the 1996 Casen Survey, the Ninth, Eighth, Seventh, Fifth, and Fourth Regions exhibit the highest rates of poverty and indigence, with figures exceeding 30%. The Second and Twelfth Regions, as well as the Metropolitan Region, have a lower proportion of poverty, with figures of 16% or lower.

Analysis of these figures tends to confirm the importance of job creation for the elimination of poverty (Gérmines Consultores 1995; Larrañaga 1994). The country's sustained economic growth has generated an ongoing increase in employment levels. Between 1990 and 1996, the average annual growth rate for employment climbed to 3.1%, a figure which exceeds the growth of the work force, which showed an annual average expansion rate of 2.6%.[5] This increase in employment has benefitted all income brackets, although work force growth has been greater in the lowest two income quintiles. During this period, employment levels in the lowest income quintiles grew at a rate greater than the national average. Between 1990 and 1996, the first (lowest) quintile showed an annual average growth rate of the employed work force of 3.7%, while the second quintile posted a rate of 3.9%. Both of these figures are superior to the total annual average growth rate in the employed labor force, which was 3.1%. Furthermore, the number of income earners per household increased, causing total household incomes to rise (Mideplan 1997e).

Although economic growth has had positive effects on the generation of employment and income, and thus contributed to reductions in poverty, it is not possible to attribute this success to growth alone. Other factors must also be recognized, such as the implementation of a wide range of social and economic policies which have benefited the neediest sectors of society. There is a correlation between economic growth and social policies. The

---

5   The workforce includes the population of individuals 15 years and older, employed or unemployed. The employed workforce includes individuals 15 years and older who are currently employed.

TABLE 2

EVOLUTION OF RURAL AND URBAN RATES OF POVERTY: 1996*

	Poor**		Indigent	
	Thousands	%	Thousands	%
By Household				
National Total	706.1	19.7	174.3	4.9
Urban Zones	561.3	18.5	130.4	4.3
Rural Zones	144.8	26.0	43.9	7.9
By Population				
National Total	3,288.3	23.2	813.8	5.8
Urban Zones	2,587.6	21.8	597.9	5.0
Rural Zones	700.7	30.6	215.9	9.4

Source: The Ministry of Planning and Cooperation's 1996 Casen Survey.

* After the 1996 change of definition of a rural zone, it is no longer possible to make comparisons with earlier Casen surveys.

** The total number of poor includes the indigent.

development of policies promoting the development of human capital played a fundamental role in the reduction of poverty during the 1990-1996 period. Access to government-subsidized education, health care, and other programs provided many Chileans with the opportunity to enter the job market and to rise above the poverty line (Durston 1994).

In spite of the increases in employment among the poorest segments of society, these groups continue to register unemployment levels above those of higher-income groups and above the national average. In 1996, the poorest quintile had an unemployment rate of 15.6%, compared to 1.5% in the richest quintile and a national average of 5.8%. Comparing employment levels between income deciles, the 1996 unemployment level in the poorest decile was 21.8%, 10.7% in the second decile, and 7.7% in the third decile (Mideplan 1997a). Although access to employment for the neediest Chileans may have risen, the jobs available to them are of low quality, with low productivity and remuneration.

In spite of the country's low unemployment levels, which stood at around 6% between 1996 and 1997, as well as the increase in employment among the neediest groups, a significant percentage of the population remains mired in poverty. This is explained by the difficulty experienced by these citizens in gaining access to better-paying jobs.

Improvements in the educational system and expanded job training programs have been undertaken to promote employment opportunities among the poor. Economic development programs, directed at microenterprises and small- and medium-sized companies, have also been developed. These companies make up 98% of the businesses in Chile and employ 80% of the work force (Göske and Traub 1996).

Access to employment is determined by many factors, such as disparities in opportunity among regions, as well as reduced employment opportunities for women and youth, reflected in the high levels of unemployment among these groups. The insecure nature of

TABLE 3

DISTRIBUTION OF HOUSEHOLD INCOME BY PERSONAL INCOME DECILE
1987-96*
(Percentage)

Personal Income Decile	Distribution of Personal Income				
	1987	1990	1992	1994	1996
1	1.2	1.4	1.5	1.3	1.3
2	2.6	2.7	2.8	2.7	2.6
3	3.4	3.6	3.7	3.5	3.5
4	4.2	4.5	4.7	4.6	4.5
5	5.3	5.4	5.6	5.5	5.4
6	6.2	6.9	6.8	6.4	6.3
7	8.1	7.8	8.1	8.1	8.2
8	11.0	10.3	10.4	10.6	11.1
9	16.1	15.2	14.8	15.4	15.5
10	41.9	42.2	41.9	41.9	41.6
Total	100.0	100.0	100.0	100.0	100.0

Source: The Ministry of Planning and Cooperation's 1987, 1990, 1992, 1994, and 1996 Casen Surveys.

(*) Live-in domestic servants and their nuclear families are excluded.

employment for many small business owners, casual laborers, and small agricultural producers demonstrates the need to strengthen programs aimed at improving opportunities
and incomes for these categories of workers.

3. INCOME DISTRIBUTION

The two main objectives of the Concertación's social strategy between 1990 and 1997 were
the eradication of poverty and the achievement of greater equity in society. Reducing
inequalities in income distribution is a vital component of the "growth with equity" strategy implemented at the beginning of the 1990s (Concertación de Partidos por la
Democracia 1994). Both redistributive strategies and equal opportunity policies are vital
for the achievement of a more equitable distribution of income. Income advances among
the poor should not depend solely upon direct or indirect state subsidies.

Equitable income distribution is particularly significant today. Surveys indicate
significant citizen dissatisfaction with the current development model and a widespread
belief that it has not helped the poor.[6] The majority of the population, however, support
the country's economic model and recognize the improvements in the quality of life that it

---

6   According to the December 1996 CERC survey, 74% of the people surveyed stated that economic development had not benefited them. This figure was higher in poorer areas, reaching 85%. Additionally, the October
1996 CEP survey showed that 42% of the people surveyed believed that the poverty level had remained the
same over the last few years. However, during the last four years, the number of impoverished homes possessing color televisions, automobiles, VCRs, and water heaters has nearly doubled.

has generated. Yet income distribution remains greatly imbalanced, raising questions about the model's ability to fulfill its promises of equity.

In late 1996, when the Casen survey was carried out, income distribution remained highly concentrated (Table 3). While the wealthiest 20% of households received 56.4% of personal income, the poorest 20% received only 3.9%. This means that the share of the wealthiest 20% is about 14 times that of the neediest quintile.

This concentration of income is higher in urban areas than in the countryside. In the former, the wealthiest quintile receives 56.4% of personal income, as opposed to 4.0% in the neediest quintile. In rural areas, the richest quintile accounts for 50.8% of income, while the neediest receives 4.9% Comparing the situation in 1996 to previous periods, one sees that there have been practically no changes with regard to the distribution of income.

The meager advances made in income distribution are principally due to unequal access to employment in general and especially to high-quality jobs. There is a growing consensus that investing in education is a fundamental way to improve the distribution of wealth over the long term. The consistent disparities in equality demonstrate the existence of mobility barriers which will not be resolved over the short term. These barriers mainly consist of unequal opportunities (especially in health care and education), disparities in job quality, and age and gender discrimination in access to employment. Thus, policies intended to improve the distribution of income must take into account a wide range of factors, not just education alone.

Gender stands out sharply as a contributing factor to income imbalances. The incorporation of women into the work force over the last 30 years has occurred at a slow but steady pace. In 1960, women accounted for 25.3% of the work force, while today the figure is close to 35%. However, women earn, on average, 25% less than men. Furthermore, women's participation has not been equal. According to the 1996 Casen survey, the participation of women in the wealthiest quintile is greater than that of women in the neediest quintile (52.1% compared to 19.1%). Furthermore, the participation of women in the wealthiest quintile is increasing, while that of women in the poorest quintile is decreasing. This affects the distribution of income, which is measured by household. At the same time, it reflects the fact that inherent elements of inequality persist in Chile (Beyer 1997).

III. Social Policies and the Quality of Life

1. THE IMPACT OF PUBLIC SPENDING

During the 1990s, public spending has been focused more on income-generating programs than on welfare measures, with health and education representing the main line-item increases in public spending. Investments in health and education have made the greatest contributions to eliminating the poverty and indigence that affect many Chileans. The incomes of needy households increase considerably when state contributions are included in measurements of personal income. The distribution of monetary income also improves, since some 70% of Chileans, almost all of whom are from low-income groups, use the public health system, and more than 90% of students are in the subsidized educational system (60% of these students attend municipal schools that mainly serve children from low-income families).

TABLE 4

DISTRIBUTIVE IMPACT OF SOCIAL SPENDING*
(Percentages)

	Income Quintile						
	I	II	III	IV	V	Total	Ratio V/I
a. Personal Income	4.0	8.0	11.8	18.5	57.6	100.0	14.3
b. Monetary Subsidies and Social Programs [a/]	35.2	25.5	18.3	14.1	7.0	100.0	0.2
Income Totals [b/]	6.3	9.3	12.3	18.2	54.0	100.0	8.6

Source: Ministry of Housing, "Las polìticas sociales del gobierno. Elementos, efectos, y desaflos," (Santiago, September 1, 1997)

* Based on the 1994 Casen Survey and information from the Budgetary Headquarters of the Ministry of Housing.

a/ Distribution by monetary subsidy spending (social assistance, subsidies, family allowances) and health and education spending quintile.

b/ Distribution by personal income quintile plus the monetary subsidy and social programs (education and health) quintile.

TABLE 5

DISTRIBUTION OF HOUSEHOLD INCOME BY PERSONAL INCOME DECILE
1996*

Personal Income Decile	Personal Income [a/]		Monetary Income [b/]	
	$	%	$	%
1	49,949	1.3	57,693	1.4
2	102,955	2.6	108,908	2.7
3	139,324	3.5	145,083	3.6
4	178,552	4.5	183,341	4.6
5	216,158	5.4	220,568	5.5
6	251,560	6.3	254,964	6.4
7	324,216	8.2	326,740	8.1
8	439,103	11.1	440,951	11.0
9	615,385	15.5	616,399	15.4
10	1,654,002	41.6	1,654,518	41.3
Total	397,170	100.0	400,966	100.0
20/20**		14.6		13.8

Source: Ministry of Planning and Cooperation, 1996 Casen Survey.

* Excludes live-in servants and their nuclear families.

** Ratio between the percentage of income earned by the richest 20% of households and the poorest 20%.

a/ Personal income: Income from productive factors, such as a wage, salary, retirement, investments, or interest.

b/ Monetary income: Personal income plus monetary transfers from the public sector (Social Aid Pensions, Family Subsidies, family allowances).

Public spending has had a direct impact on the incomes of the poor through monetary subsidies from the social safety net. These include the Family Subsidy (SUF), Social Aid Pensions (Pasis), the Potable Water Consumption Subsidy, housing subsidies, and others. Further supplemental income derives from pay subsidies for workers such as family allowances, unemployment benefits, maternal subsidies, and social security and health care benefits.

Since 1990, the value of monetary subsidies has progressively been raised, and benefits have been expanded for vulnerable population groups. The targeting of the social safety net's main subsidies has also improved. Family allowances are now calculated on a sliding scale which is inversely proportional to the beneficiary's income. In addition to extending the coverage of current benefits, new benefits have been created (such as a winter supplement for those receiving social aid pensions, and SUF for students up to 18 years of age). People capable of holding a good job have not become dependent on the social safety net, due to the low levels of benefits granted as well as the programs' targeting procedures.

An immediate effect of public spending on the quality of life for the poor was the improvement of monetary incomes and the distributive impact of social spending (Table 4). When cash transfers are considered in conjunction with the impact of social programs, the poorest quintile increased its income share from 4.0% to 6.3% by 1994, while the share of the richest quintile decreased from 57.6% to 54%.

If personal incomes are added to public sector cash transfers to the neediest sectors — the Family Subsidy, family allowance, and social aid pensions — the result is an increase in incomes in the first deciles, representing the poorest groups in Chilean society (Table 5).

According to the 1996 Casen survey, the average monthly income of households in the first decile increased from 49,949 to 57,693 pesos; in the second decile it increased from 102,955 to 108,908 pesos; and in the third decile from 139,324 to 145,083. In general, the poorest sectors experienced an improvement in their incomes due to state monetary subsidies. Social spending also produced a slight correction of the overall income distribution imbalance, providing a greater share of national income to the neediest Chileans.

However, the granting of monetary subsidies is a compensatory and temporary solution. It increases family income, but it does not represent an answer to the problem of extreme poverty. Families are able to rise out of conditions of extreme hardship (indigence and serious undernourishment) thanks to a number of subsidies and programs, but true improvements are generated through autonomous and self-sustained actions that ensure permanent progress. Policies concerned with overcoming poverty must include monetary subsidies to improve the living standards of impoverished families, but they must also provide opportunities for these families to raise their income levels on their own. Training programs that provide the poor with the necessary skills to join the labor force or to improve upon their current jobs are vitally important in overcoming extreme poverty (Mac-Clure and Urmeneta 1995:47-50).

2. COVERAGE AND QUALITY OF BASIC SOCIAL SERVICES

The implementation of universal social policies throughout Chile between 1950 and 1973 gave the majority of the population access to state social services. After 1973, the military regime reduced social investments and initiated a process of political and administrative restructuring. Universally-oriented policies were replaced with social aid policies with an exclusive focus on extreme poverty, although the social safety net remained in operation. The democratic governments since 1990 have increased public sector spending and again expanded social services coverage to the entire population.

This widespread coverage of social services has produced positive results. Chile's indicators are currently improving in areas such as infant mortality, educational coverage, and access to safe drinking water. This reflects the government's efforts to reduce poverty and improve the quality of life. In an international context, Chile climbed three places in the Human Development Report, put out by the United Nations Program for Human Development (UNPHD), between 1996 and 1997. It thus became the top-ranked Latin American nation, standing 30th in a list of 175 countries in terms of human development.[7] However, increases in the standard of living have been much slower and slighter for some social groups, such as the poor, small farmers, isolated rural inhabitants, indigenous peoples, and poor women and children. These groups are at a disadvantage in their access to goods and services, as well as in the quality of the goods and services they manage to obtain.

The country's ongoing development, as reflected in its social policies and its achievements in health, education, and basic infrastructure, presents new challenges to the social sector: to evolve from a goal of coverage to a goal of quality, as well as to shift from simple increases in spending to the improvement of management and the elimination of inequalities between privately- and publicly-provided social services.

Eliminating inequalities in the coverage and quality of social services will require more efficient public management, further decentralization, reductions in bureaucracy and red tape, improved targeting techniques, and new evaluative mechanisms. Alternative sources of financing must also be found, and relations with users must be improved.

EDUCATION POLICIES

Changes to the Educational System during the Military Regime
The military regime progressively reduced public spending on education. In 1985, these expenditures dropped to 4% of GDP. In 1986, they fell further to 3.4% of GDP, and they continued to fall until 1990, when they reached their lowest point during the last 20 years: 2.3% of GDP (Mideplan 1996). These budget reductions brought about a progressive decline in teacher salaries and a deterioration in educational infrastructure and equipment.

In the early 1980s, reforms were undertaken which transferred primary and secondary educational establishments to the municipalities. A new system of financing was introduced; schools received a per capita subsidy based on student attendance during the previous month. These reforms also opened the way for the creation of private schools, partially financed by public contributions, which enjoyed greater flexibility in the administration of their financial resources. The school system thus became a mixed system, featuring decentralized schools, government financing, and the involvement of both the private sector and the municipalities. Purely private, full-tuition schools were also created, mainly directed at the upper classes.

This decentralization process was actually more a case of administrative deconcentration, since the Ministry of Education remained central to the educational process. Neither responsibilities nor resources were passed on to municipalities for the implementation of

---

7   The UNPHD establishes a ranking according to the HDI (Human Development Index), which is based on
    three variables: life expectancy, education levels, and income.

decentralization. Indeed, decentralization was carried out in an authoritarian manner by mayors appointed by the military regime. Thus, this process represented municipalization rather than true decentralization. The principal modification accompanying the transfer of education to the municipalities lay in the financing system. The objective underlying municipalization and the establishment of a demand-side financing system was the eventual privatization of education. Greater private sector participation would, it was believed, increase competition and result in higher-quality services.

The transfer of education to the municipalities had progressed substantially by the end of 1981, with 87% of schools being municipalized. However, the 1982 recession forced the suspension of transfers, and the process was not resumed until 1986. At the beginning of the municipalization process in 1981, the municipal system served 80% of the population, while the subsidized private system had a 14% share. By 1989, this proportion had changed to 60% and 33%, respectively. The private full-tuition sector maintained its relatively small share of around 7% (Raczynski and Cominetti 1994).

During the municipalization process, the Ministry of Education maintained control of educational, technical, and curricular standards, as well as the evaluation of the educational process. Municipalities were responsible for the construction and maintenance of schools. Teacher employment and wage negotiations were decentralized; salaries steadily declined, and teachers lost the job-related rights they had previously acquired (Raczynski and Cominetti 1994). Educational organizations and the Parent and Student Centers lost their influence and had no official place or voice in the new educational system.

The municipalization of education did not include participation by the municipalities in the management of services. No technical decentralization measures were implemented which would have encouraged local pedagogical proposals. Although the municipalities acquired new powers, primary and secondary schools were not given autonomy or permitted to participate in an effective decentralization of education.

The reforms did not produce any changes in curricular organization or teaching methods, which are essential to the modernization and improvement of education. Quality deteriorated in the most disadvantaged areas, where the municipalities were receiving progressively lower levels of state funding and did not possess autonomous financial strength or the ability to attract investment income.[8] This led to great differences in quality among municipalities as well as according to the type of school, with full-tuition private schools and subsidized private schools ahead of municipalized schools.

Education in the 1990s

In 1990, when the new government took office, the country's educational system, the product of more than 30 years of effort and investment by successive governments, still exhibited several positive elements: the school system's broad coverage, the ongoing reduction of illiteracy, and a gradual increase in the average years of schooling completed by Chileans. However, the system also showed negative indicators in the areas of quality and distribution. It further suffered from serious management problems, such as low teacher salaries and the neglect of school infrastructure and equipment. These were a direct result of the lack of investment during the military regime (Mineduc 1996).

---

8   In Chile, almost 90% of students receive state subsidies. Of these students, some 60% attend municipalized schools, and the remaining 40% are in subsidized private schools.

Under the Aylwin and Frei administrations, public spending has increased, while the number of students in the educational system has remained relatively constant. Educational expenditures increased by 100% in real terms between 1990 and 1997, allowing educational subsidies to be doubled and investments in educational infrastructure to be increased by six times. Expanding resources also led to the doubling of teacher salaries as well as improvements in school texts and other classroom materials (Secretary General of the Presidency 1997).

Since 1990, the government's strategy has been to improve the quality and equity of the school system, while maintaining the basic financial and institutional structure of the 1980s. The system of subsidies based on student attendance has been maintained, as has administration at the municipal level and by local patrons. However, the role of the state has changed, and the government has begun efforts to improve educational quality and equity. Under the Concertación governments, the state has taken on a fundamental role in the creation of strategies and programs designed to produce improvements in these variables.

The educational policies of the 1990s are principally concerned with enhancing educational processes and learning outcomes. The new policy of equity is based on the principle of positive discrimination. In other words, offering truly equal opportunities to heterogeneous groups requires the allocation of greater resources and special attention to those groups which have been most socially and culturally disadvantaged in the past. As a result, special programs have been created which are directed at the neediest schools and students.

Increased attention and resources have also favored teachers, who have benefited financially from salary increases, as well as professionally from improved training and the enactment of legal reforms.

Between 1990 and 1994, the state's main concerns were to correct the deficiencies that had been produced by funding reductions and to move forward in the implementation of equity policies, especially in primary education. Educational policy since 1994 has continued to extend the reach of the equity improvement programs, which are selective programs targeted toward the neediest schools. Examples of such initiatives are the Education Quality and Equity Improvement Program (MECE), the Rural MECE, and the 900 Schools Program (P-900), which serves the 10% of schools identified as the most vulnerable and lowest-performing.

During this period, priority on the public agenda has been expanded to both primary and secondary education, with an emphasis on improvement and modernization. The priority placed upon education is based on its fundamental role in harmonizing the objectives of growth and equity. Education is seen as the most effective way to create opportunities for the population's social and economic development. Better education means greater productivity, higher incomes and a better chance to prosper in work, social, and cultural environments. Conversely, unequal access to high-quality education is the principal cause of the perpetuation of social inequality in our country (Mineduc 1996).

Conclusions

During the 1990s, the municipalized educational system has been maintained, but its orientation has been changed. The connection between decentralization and privatization, formed during the military regime, has been severed. Decentralization is now understood as a way of democratizing educational decisions and bestowing greater decision-making autonomy upon schools and the educational community. As a result of the policies carried out since 1990

TABLE 6

EDUCATION COVERAGE BY INSTRUCTION LEVEL: 1990-96

Instruction Level	1990	1992	1994	1996	Average Annual Rate of Growth
Preschool	20.9	24.7	26.9	29.8	6.1
Primary	96.8	97.4	97.6	98.2	0.2
Secondary	80.5	82.2	83.9	85.9	1.1

Source: Ministry of Planning and Cooperation's 1990, 1992, 1994, and 1996 Casen Surveys.

TABLE 7

AVERAGE AMOUNT OF SCHOOLING FOR PERSONS
OVER 15 YEARS OF AGE, BY POVERTY LEVEL*: 1996

Poverty Level	Urban	Rural	Total
Indigent	7.6	5.7	7.1
Poor, Non-Indigent	8.3	6.1	7.8
Non-Poor	10.5	6.4	9.9
Total	10.0	6.3	9.5

Source: Ministry of Planning & Cooperation's 1996 Casen Survey.
* Excludes live-in domestic servants and their nuclear families.

(Table 6), the proportion of school-aged children and youth outside the coverage of the educational system has decreased, and coverage at all educational levels has expanded.

The 1996 Casen survey shows that preschool education exhibited the highest average annual growth rate. This is explained by the fact that preschool coverage is still low; thus, it has a greater growth potential than primary or secondary education. Between 1990 and 1996, increases in primary and secondary education coverage brought 30,000 children and 51,000 adolescents into the educational system. Nonetheless, coverage is still higher in urban areas than in rural areas. This trend is especially pronounced in preschool education, where coverage rates are 32.6% in urban areas and 15.3% in rural areas. Marked differences also appear in secondary education. Urban coverage at this level reaches 89.9%, while in rural areas it is 68.5%. The gap in primary education is narrower, with coverage standing at 98.8% and 94.6%, respectively. These figures demonstrate the need to continue extending the reach of current rural education support mechanisms, as well as to create new assistance programs for students and schools in rural areas.

The 1996 Casen survey shows that 76.1% of children under the age of six do not attend any educational establishment. For children of primary school age, the figure is 1.1%, and at the secondary level it is 13.6%. In order to improve preschool attendance, especially for children of low-income families, legislation is required to address the coverage and operating hours of day care facilities in the workplace.

Absences from preschool, primary, and secondary education are greater in rural areas than in urban areas. Indigent communities register the highest occurrence of absences from the educational system. There is a direct positive correlation between family income and school participation. The high rate of absences among primary and secondary school students — 13.3% and 21.4% respectively — can be explained by the participation of young people in the work force; this calls for improvement of the country's child labor laws.

Illiteracy has been reduced, and the total number of students in the educational system has increased. The illiteracy rate dropped from 6% in 1987 to 4.4% in 1994, and rose slightly to 4.9% in 1996 (see Table 7). In both urban and rural areas, illiteracy has shown a downward trend, although illiteracy rates are four times greater in the latter (Hardy 1997a).

The average years of schooling completed by persons over 15 years of age has increased from nine years in 1990 to 9.5 years in 1996. However, this average drops to 7.8 years among low-income groups, and to 7.1 years among the indigent. The rural population also shows significantly lower levels of schooling. There are considerable differences in average years of schooling according to both age and income level, although the difference in schooling levels between the first and fifth quintile has been diminishing in each generation. The elderly population (65 to 74 years of age) of the neediest quintile has received just over one-third of the schooling enjoyed by the equivalent age group in the wealthiest quintile (3.4 and 9.9 years respectively). In contrast, the younger the population group, the smaller the differences in schooling. In the 15-to-24 age group, the average schooling of the neediest quintile is equivalent to three-quarters of that of the wealthiest (9.1 and 12.7 years respectively) (Mideplan 1997f).

Educational inequality becomes more apparent at the higher levels of the system, with greater coverage enjoyed by the richest quintiles. Differences in coverage, alongside the aforementioned disparities in equality between private and municipal schools, point to inequalities in educational opportunities and unequal chances for future social mobility, given the correlation between schooling and income levels.

State-supported primary and secondary schools suffer from serious quality problems. This limits their ability to promote the cultural, social, and economic integration of the population, besides representing a loss of value to society. Also worthy of mention are the shortage of preschool education and the lack of relevant training designed to prepare young people for the job market, both at the secondary and university levels. Effective training must be responsive to the demands of the labor market and the requirements of the country's development over the medium term.

HEALTH CARE POLICIES

Changes in Health Care during the Military Regime
In the early 1980s, the precept of the state's subsidiary role served as a guide for the transformation of the country's health care system. The decentralization of the system and the transfer of decisions regarding productivity and financial management to the private sector followed this line of thought. The municipalization of health care and the creation of Isapres (private health plans) exemplify this orientation. The regime's public spending cuts and targeting of resources solely to areas of extreme need were also applied to the area of health care. This sector suffered drastic spending cuts, with negative effects on the quality and coverage of public health services (Oyarzo 1991).

The regime's focus on maternal and child care and on extremely poor groups was accompanied by spending cuts in all other areas of the system, leading to a general deterioration in health care. Deficiencies in infrastructure and equipment worsened under the military government. Spending decreased steadily: between 1974 and 1987, contributions to the sector fell by 40%. The decentralization of the system was initiated, and decisions concerning the provision and financing of health care were transferred to the private sector.

The public health system lost high-income contributors, who opted out in favor of private Isapres. The drop in state financial support and the lower revenues collected through user fees forced a rise in the rate of mandatory contributions, which increased from 4% to 6% in 1982, with a readjustment in 1985 to the current value of 7%. The quality of health care received by the majority of the population deteriorated considerably (Schkolnik and Bonnefoy 1994).

The health care system was decentralized into 27 Health Services, and the transfer of outpatient care — government health clinics and primary care centers — to municipalities was undertaken between 1981 and 1985.

Decentralization led to deficiencies in coordination between primary, secondary, and tertiary levels of health care, a problem which persists today. The primary level was separated from the other two, which remained under the direction of the general health system. Hospital care continued to be administered by regional Health Services, and the National Health System (SNS) was replaced by the National System of Health Services (SNSS). The regional services did not undertake any major administrative changes, since they were subject to the Ministry of Health in financial matters, while fixed staffing hampered the possibility of changes in other areas. Decentralization mainly involved the deconcentration of administrative procedures. The Services and hospitals were not granted any significant degree of autonomy in decisions related to financial resources or personnel. The administrative changes had no net impact on efficiency or service, while hospital care suffered due to the cuts in spending.

Further changes occurred with respect to financing. The National Health Fund (Fonasa) was created to channel financial resources to public sector health institutions. Mechanisms were introduced for the allocation of resources based on services rendered: the Invoice for Services Rendered (FAP) for the Health Services, and the Municipal Invoice for Services Rendered (Fapem) for the municipalities. These mechanisms did not serve their intended purpose of improving the efficiency of health care. In fact, they contributed to further diminishing the quality of care, since they encouraged increases in the quantity, but not the quality, of treatments. Curative treatment was emphasized over preventive health care, and unnecessary examinations multiplied (Schkolnik and Bonnefoy). Since more treatments were invoiced than the Ministry of Health could reimburse, a limit was imposed on municipalities, based on previous levels of service. This contradicted the logic of the Fapem system and served to widen the differences in health care between needy and wealthy municipalities, since further treatment could be financed by the latter after the limit was reached. Furthermore, the values of treatments and limits were not adjusted for inflation, so that the gap between public and private health care increased.

The result of all of these measures was a serious lack of equity in health care. High-income patients enjoyed quality health care, while the public system, which served more than two-thirds of the population, suffered from a reduced budget, obsolete equipment and infrastructure, low salaries, and the loss of labor rights for its professional and non-professional personnel. Due to the grave deficiencies in the quality of public health, manifested in decaying infrastructure, long waits for treatment and a lack of resources, among other problems, the state health care system entered a period of crisis.

Health Care in the 1990s

By the early 1990s, the situation in the health care system had become critical, mainly due to the lack of investment. Therefore, one of the new government's priorities was to increase the resources allocated to the sector and to improve deficiencies in human resources as well as the low salaries of the sector's personnel.

The tax reform of 1990 brought in additional resources for the government; some of these funds were allocated for hospital infrastructure and primary care supplies, services, and personnel. Ongoing increases in allocated resources have brought about a gradual reversal of the health care deficit inherited from the military government. The sector's budget nearly doubled between 1990 and 1996, allowing improvements in equipment and infrastructure for hospitals and primary care centers, along with a gradual turnaround in the depressed salary levels for health care personnel.

Labor regulations have been modified or are being modified, including changes linking salaries to performance. New legislation has improved health workers' wages. A bill is being debated in Congress that would modify Law No. 15,076 to the benefit of health care professionals (including doctors, dentists, pharmacologists and biochemists). In addition, the Primary Care Statute was created for employees of primary care facilities.

Investments in the sector have expanded, and various measures designed to improve resource management have been carried out since 1994. Management commitments have been created, tying the granting of resources to the fulfillment of certain obligations. A public sector reform initiative has also been designed, aimed at modernizing the National Health Fund (Fonasa) and linking the sector's actions more closely to the objectives of equity, decentralization, participation, and user satisfaction.

In order to overcome the health sector's budgetary inertia and to promote more effective management, new forms of financing have been designed for hospitals and primary care facilities. A per-capita payment system was established for primary care centers, and a mixed system of diagnosis-based payment (PAD) and payment for services rendered (PPP) was implemented in hospitals. These mechanisms were also a response to criticisms of the FAP and Fapem. The per-capita system is a payment mechanism for basic health services granted to each primary care center according to the number of people registered at the center. This sum is indexed to the poverty rate in each municipality, its location (urban or rural), and the fulfillment of its management commitments. The PAD-PPP financing system links payments to a concrete medical result: the patient's final prognosis. Thus, resources are granted to hospitals according to demand, the effectiveness of diagnoses and outcomes, and the fulfillment of management commitments (Lenz 1995).

Increased resources and improvements in administration have gradually lessened the problem of access to care. The Primary Care Emergency Services (Sapus) were created, offering expanded office hours for primary care. Additionally, programs have been implemented to reduce hospital waiting lists and to permit appointments at primary care centers to be made over the telephone. Similarly, a number of steps have been taken to improve the quality of care. These include the admission of fathers to delivery rooms; the establishment of specific rights for hospitalized children; the extension of visiting hours;

and programs to improve the quality of information and treatment provided by health care workers to patients and their families. Although these programs have been successful, their coverage and effectiveness must be expanded further, since problems still persist.

User participation was strengthened through the creation of Development Councils and the "Health with the People" program. The former are evaluative bodies, composed of hospital or primary care center staff and representatives from community organizations, which examine health care management (Ministry Secretary General of Government 1996). The "Health with the People" program provides financial and technical support to community health care organizations. Both programs have continually expanded their coverage throughout the country.

The targeting of health care programs has improved, especially toward women and the elderly. Furthermore, equity budgets (which allocate a greater share of resources according to medical risks, the complexity of services, and cost differentials in remote areas) have been implemented to correct imbalances in the public health care system.

With respect to the private sector, the Isapres Law has been modified in areas such as the use of surplus resources, cases of exclusions and shortages, and collective agreements. The Isapres' capital and guarantee requirements were also increased, and the oversight activities of the Superintendency of Isapres were expanded. These reforms were aimed at improving equity in the private system, but coverage failures continue, mainly among the elderly and patients suffering from catastrophic illnesses. Moreover, the equity gap between the high-quality private health care system and the low-quality public system has continued without substantive change.

According to the 1996 Casen survey, nearly 68% of the population was enrolled in the public health care system in 1990, while 15.1% belonged to the Isapre system. By 1996, the Isapre system had increased its coverage to 24.6%, while the public system served 60% of the population. Membership in Isapres increases as income levels rise; practically all of the country's neediest citizens receive care from the public sector (public coverage is 84% in the first quintile and 71% in the second quintile). The state also serves the majority of children under the age of six and adults over the age of 60, in addition to providing care for catastrophic diseases. This results in the overloading of the public health care system, since it serves the sectors with the greatest health care needs and the lowest ability to provide co-payments for services rendered. The Isapres, in contrast, tend to care for the richest sectors of the population and for healthy young adults. They incur lower costs and, therefore, earn higher profits. In addition, the public system is burdened by middle and lower-middle class Isapre members who do not receive sufficient coverage through their private plans and turn to public hospitals, generating costs that are assumed by the state. The state also grants various subsidies to the Isapres, through preventative programs (vaccinations, information campaigns, etc.) and a worker subsidy of 2%. It should also be mentioned that the Superintendency of Isapres does not possess sufficient powers to effectively oversee these organizations.

Conclusions

Despite the shortcomings of its public health care system, Chile currently enjoys quite favorable health indicators. Annual infant mortality (11.2 per 1,000 live births in 1994, the lowest in the country's history) and life expectancy rates are on par with those of fully-industrialized countries (as shown in the UNDP's 1996 Human Development Report).

These positive indicators are explained by environmental conditions (such as the high coverage of water and sewer systems), skilled health workers, and successful preventative campaigns (anti-cholera programs, vaccinations), among other factors.

Since 1990, primary care centers and hospital infrastructure and equipment have been significantly improved. However, problems in quality and access (lines, waiting lists, treatment deficiencies) have not yet been completely solved.

The Ministry of Health is currently initiating a reform of Fonasa which will include provisions for a "Beneficiary Contract" between patients and the Ministry of Health, identifying users' rights and responsibilities. The reform also adds redistributive elements to Fonasa's operations and eliminates the 2% subsidy for Isapres.

Despite the successes mentioned above, public opinion surveys show a high degree of dissatisfaction among users of both the public and private systems. The same surveys reveal that health care is considered to be one of the country's main problems. Deficiencies identified in the health care system include limited access, incomplete coverage, inadequate quality of care, and imbalances in information, efficiency, and equity.

The private health care system exhibits numerous deficiencies as well. Among these is the fact that when enrolling in Isapres, users lack the necessary information to decide which plan is best for them. Since there is no unified fee structure for the Isapres' services, comparing their health care plans — of which there are many — becomes practically impossible. Additionally, significant gaps in coverage affect Isapre members, especially the elderly, sufferers from catastrophic diseases, and members with short-term contracts. The Isapres' lack of transparency is also a problem area.

The public sector provides service to the majority of the population and does not discriminate among users. It takes on the costs of providing care to groups which require greater resources and provide little or no returns. Thus, their financial burden is greater than that shouldered by the Isapres. The public sector continues to be the country's mainstay in health care, and thus its deficiencies have repercussions for the majority of the population.

Overall user evaluation of the quality of medical care provided by the public sector has been positive. The main problems identified involve access to care. Examples of these problems of access, especially for the lower and lower-middle classes, include waiting lists for hospital treatment; long lines at primary care center appointment desks; shortages of specialists, especially at the primary level; and the referral system, which often delays care. Public management must gain a new orientation toward the goal of user satisfaction. This will mean not only expanding services and increasing the quality of care, but also improving the relationship between health workers and patients, as well as devising mechanisms that expand users' freedom of choice. Inefficiencies in clinic administration affect the quality of care and result in the under-utilization of resources such as infrastructure and medical equipment.

Aside from the coverage and quality problems mentioned above, the current system institutionalizes, in practice, a health care ceiling for the poorest strata of society. Equity will result from lifting the public sector to levels of sustained excellence, not from institutionalizing deficiencies that effectively limit the right to health care.

The decentralization process has advanced slowly and with serious inefficiencies at the local level. Problem areas have included administrative weaknesses within the municipalities, difficulties in adjusting to new financing methods, and the lack of funding in poor municipalities. The municipalization of health care has produced serious inequalities between municipalities with greater resources and those with fewer resources, which often have a larger population to serve as well.

Since 1990, various entities, from the Health Services to hospitals, have been decentralized, so that they can manage their own human and financial resources (within the framework of established budgets), as well as a large part of their investments (Ministry Secretary General of the Government 1997). Nonetheless, health care services and hospitals are still far from achieving management and decision-making autonomy, since authority still rests on a centralized structure.

Meanwhile, the health care system is divided into two tiers — public and private — with practically no coordination or complementation between the two. There is no consensus as to the direction that health care reforms should take. The debate over the modernization and reform of the health care system is hampered by technical, ideological, ethical, political, and cultural considerations. The challenge will be to find solutions to the problems of coverage, equity, and efficiency which can win support from diverse forces in society. This is especially difficult due to the strongly-held views on health care issues expressed by groups such as the Medical Association, the Isapre Association, and the political opposition.

Reforming both the public and private health care systems is a vital task, not only to improve access, quality, and equity, but also to meet the population's changing health care needs. The outcome may be a mixed health care system, in which the private and public sectors compete with and complement each other. In the creation of such a system, Chile must address issues such as the state's role in financing; the relationship between resources, efficiency, and equity; human resource policies; competitiveness in health care; decentralization; and greater administrative autonomy.

HOUSING AND URBAN DEVELOPMENT POLICIES

Changes in Housing and Urban Development under the Military Regime
Soon after taking power, the military government transformed the state's role in the housing sector. State action was reduced to the granting of subsidies and the selection of beneficiaries (through the use of the CAS form). The concept of the subsidiary role of the state was applied, opening the way for the privatization of activities that the public sector had previously performed.

The private sector began to participate to a significant extent in decisions regarding the design, location, quantity, financing, standards, and costs of housing for the various socioeconomic classes. The government modified the subsidy system to stimulate private sector participation. Public aid was channeled through demand-side subsidies, and a more prominent financing role was granted to real estate companies and the capital market. The government eliminated the National Savings and Loan System (Sinap), and its function of offering mortgage loans to middle-class home buyers was transferred to private financial institutions (Mideplan 1996).

At the same time, overall public spending on housing was reduced. Between 1953 and 1973, public investments in this sector were some 2.6% of GDP, while between 1974 and 1989 they fell to 2%. By the end of the military regime in 1989, government expenditures on housing stood at only half of their 1974 level (Schkolnik and Bonnefoy 1994). The housing shortage had already increased noticeably by the mid-1970s, affecting both middle- and low-income families.

Beginning in the 1980s, the military government changed its initial policy of inactivity, taking on an active role in the housing sector by strongly subsidizing the construction of public housing projects. Several new programs were created during this period, including the Unified General Subsidy, the Special Public Housing Construction Subsidy (PEV), the Rural Subsidy, and the Settlers' Subsidy, which were designed to facilitate middle-class access to housing.[9]

Other programs, targeted toward impoverished areas, involved the construction of public housing units and the "cleanup" of shantytowns, channeling city development, and regularizing land ownership. The "basic living unit" program was the largest housing program. It provided homes built to minimum construction standards, with floor space varying between 30 and 36 square meters, on plots of land ranging from 60 to 100 square meters. These basic units had a maximum cost of 190 UF* and were subject to a 75% government subsidy. The shantytown "cleanup" programs included relocation operations and were complemented by the Ministry of the Interior's Neighborhood Improvement Program, which financed the construction of lots with sanitary service connections.

The public housing projects constructed under the military regime were located primarily on the outskirts of cities. New public housing units were not built in municipalities with high concentrations of middle- and upper-class residents, or even in poor city neighborhoods. This method of extending the peripheries of urban areas was inefficient, since it sprawled over formerly agricultural land, while at the same time leading to the abandonment of some city neighborhoods with significant existing infrastructure. At the same time, the policy of eradicating squatter camps from middle- and upper-class municipalities and relocating marginal populations to the urban periphery resulted in cities with high levels of socioeconomic and spatial segregation, characterized by geographical divisions between the wealthy and the poor.

Many ordinances that had regulated land use in residential areas were repealed by the military regime. For example, housing project planners were no longer required to set aside land for the construction of facilities and infrastructure; the management of water and sewer networks and facilities was privatized; and the problem of rainwater was left unresolved, leading to flooding during rainy seasons. Many new housing units lacked sufficient infrastructure, community facilities, green areas, roads, social service networks, or transportation links, all of which affected — and continues to affect — the quality of life for the poorest members of society.

The military regime eliminated a series of urban zoning regulations in 1979, giving the market a free hand in the determination of urban expansion areas, housing density, infrastructural investments, the location of services and activities, and the composition of residential, mixed, and industrial zones. The results of this free-market zoning policy were so clearly negative that in 1985 the state resumed its regulatory role. Yet many of the effects

---

9   These programs each have different subsidy levels. The General Unified Subsidy is for the purchase of
     houses priced between 400 UF and 2,000 UF* [*Unidad de Fomento*, a monetary unit indexed to inflation].
     The amount of the subsidy is inversely proportional to the price of the house, varying between 80 and 150
     UF. The PEV benefits public or private groups and organizations seeking quarters that are more expensive
     (between 220 UF and 260 UF) than basic housing units. This subsidy has a limit of 60 UF. The Rural
     Subsidy is applicable to houses priced up to 260 UF, and the subsidy limit is 150 UF, or 75% of the house's
     value. The limit of the Settlers' Subsidy is 300 UF, or 90% of the house's value. The "basic housing unit"
     has a maximum price of 190 UF, and the subsidy limit is 75% of the price of the house.

were irreversible. The lack of planning for the requirements of growth, the failure to invest in land improvements, the negative side effects of uncontrolled expansion, and unrestrained urban land speculation elevated the cost of city housing and thus of public housing programs. These effects were felt most by the neediest groups in society, since in addition to the increase in housing costs, they were affected by increases in the costs of transportation and services that often went along with the new housing projects.

In addition, the military regime's housing policies resulted in an unprecedented housing shortage, affecting close to 40% of households by 1989, mostly low-income families. That year, nearly one million families were forced to live with relatives as *allegados*, lacking a home of their own (Mideplan 1996; Raczynski and Cominetti 1994). By the end of this period, the housing shortage, urban problems, and the mortgage portfolio crisis, which affected families with mortgage debts, had reached critical levels. Their resolution depended largely upon increasing the sector's resources and targeting governmental efforts toward the most affected groups.

Housing and Urban Development Policies in the 1990s
Since 1990, the democratic governments have continued the housing subsidy program as well as the housing initiatives implemented during the military government. The housing access plan sets forth a specific state subsidy for middle- and low-income households. Subsidies are greater for the neediest strata of the population and are reduced as one moves up the income scale. Prior savings accumulated by families continue to be evaluated as a prerequisite for housing applications (Etchegaray et al. 1997).

The main objective of housing policy since 1990 has been to reduce the housing shortage and to expand the coverage of housing programs. Another goal has been to improve the quality of life in Chile's cities. New urban development programs have made significant investments in green areas, public facilities, community infrastructure, and so forth. Thus, low-income housing projects have been complemented by measures to improve living conditions for their residents.

The state regained its leading role in the area of urban regulation, combining the public sector's planning and regulatory capacity with the involvement of private actors and community organizations in city development. Cities were encouraged to develop regulatory plans; the Santiago Master Plan was set forth to channel and regulate the capital city's expansion.

The private sector continued to be progressively incorporated into housing construction and financing, in order to increase both coverage and quality. The state continued to regulate and direct the sector's policies, aiming at increased equity and an improved distribution of resources.

One of the first challenges during this period was the easing of the housing shortage, which had been growing at an explosive rate. One of the prerequisites for achieving this goal was to increase the resources available for housing programs. However, the 1990 budget reduced funding for housing by 14%, and the resources the sector received had been almost fully allocated, since investments in housing are made biennially (Mideplan 1991). Nonetheless, the new resources brought in through the 1990 tax reform allowed the targets for the construction of housing and urban facilities to be increased.

The government attempted to stimulate an increase in housing construction, targeting resources toward the neediest strata of the population, without disregarding the middle classes, and emphasizing the zones suffering from the greatest shortages. Total investment was increased, and new criteria were applied to resource allocation, including provisions for greater regional decision-making power. New programs were designed and implemented, and new methods for applicant selection and housing designation were applied.

A wider range of offers from the financial sector made it easier for families to save for the purchase of a house. The government's goal was to develop a competitive market in this area, broadening the spectrum of possibilities for the financing of housing purchases. Savings and mortgage options were offered by institutional investors, financial brokers, banks and financing companies, as well as by brokers from mortgage companies.

New programs were designed to improve access to housing for low-income families. The "progressive housing," aimed at extremely poor residents, is one of these. To limit the family's initial expense, the house is built in two stages. At the completion of the second stage, the housing unit has a size similar to that of the basic unit, but the overall cost to the beneficiary is lower. This program requires the active participation of beneficiaries in the construction of the housing unit.

A second new effort is the "housing construction, expansion, and improvement" program. This program is similar to the second stage of the progressive housing program. It is designed to provide substantial housing improvements for beneficiaries living in unacceptably substandard quarters. This program is complemented by the "housing improvement" program, designed for poor homeowners wishing to expand or repair their homes.

The "rural shantytown" program was created to provide housing and basic sanitation services to the rural poor. This program has lowered the basic costs of infrastructure development (including drains, potable water, and electricity connections) and has provided a badly-needed increase in housing program coverage for rural areas. The selection process for rural subsidies has also been refined.

The "free-choice basic housing" program is an innovative new system with the objective of creating a secondary market for public housing. It permits the purchase and sale of subsidized housing without the loss of the subsidy. The creation of this program required legislative modifications. Under the new law, subsidies are directed at families and not houses. This measure opens the possibility of using subsidies for both new and second-hand homes, as well as allowing beneficiaries to participate in determining the location, construction, and style of their homes.

The application criteria for some existing programs were also modified. Related applicants were permitted to make group applications, and more favorable conditions were created for female heads of households, the elderly, and disabled individuals. However, prior savings continue to be the main factor in the granting of subsidies, a situation which serves to restrict housing access for the poorest citizens. Subsidies for middle- and high-income home buyers were reduced. However, a new subsidy was created, aimed primarily at middle-income households, which provides incentives for urban renewal and the re-population of downtown areas.

Basic housing standards were upgraded, with an increase in floor space to 42 square meters, as well as the requirement that projects include paved streets, green areas, and land set-asides for community facilities. These changes increased the value of the basic houses from 190 UF to 223 UF. This measure was accompanied by an increase in the Housing and Urban Development Service (Serviu) credit and a reduction in the level of subsidies (Mideplan 1996). In addition, the weight of applicants' savings in the selection process was reduced. The basic housing program continued to be the largest and most widely-used housing program for the non-indigent poor.

In the General Unified Subsidy program, the overall amount of subsidies was reduced, while new subsidies were established to encourage urban renewal. The leasing system is part of this program; it grants subsidies to renters who make a commitment to buy.

The Special Public Housing Construction Subsidy (PEV), which enabled organized groups of workers from public and private institutions to select housing priced higher than the basic housing unit (between 220 UF and 260 UF), was modified and transformed into the Special Workers Program (PET). This program grants subsidies and also supplements employee savings with contributions from their employers.

Conclusions

One of the most successful aspects of housing policies during the 1990s has been the ongoing expansion in home construction. During the 1990-94 period, an average of 90,000 housing units were constructed annually, which rises to 100,000 when private activities are included.[10] Since 1994, this figure has expanded to an annual average of more than 100,000 units, enabling the country to reduce the previous housing shortage of some 30,000 to 40,000 homes, as well as to halt the upward trend in the number of *allegados*.

Another noteworthy factor is the increased targeting of housing programs. In 1989, approximately half of all government housing resources (53%) were aimed at middle-income groups, while the other half (45%) went to low-income households. In 1996, however, the state concentrated nearly all of its efforts (80%) on low-income households (Minvu 1997). This more effective targeting was accompanied by greater program diversification, offering more options to needy families. These changes are still insufficient, however. Marginalized social groups still have inadequate access to housing, and the effectiveness of programs designed for them, such as progressive housing, has been questioned, since these programs require prior savings — without access to credit — as well as beneficiary participation in the construction process.

The Chile Barrio program stands out due to its innovative design and its focus on overcoming the social and economic marginalization of residents in poor areas throughout the country. This program uses decentralized management techniques to coordinate the efforts of the government, the private sector, and community organizations in order to improve living conditions in poor areas.

In 1997, the scandal concerning public housing units built by the Copeva company[11] led to public questioning of the success of the housing policies in place since 1990. The main criticism of the housing programs was that they placed their highest priority on the number of units built and neglected the quality of the homes' construction. One of the

---

10 Approximately 43,000 homes were built annually between 1973 and 1989.

11 During a storm in the winter of 1997, the basic housing units built by the Copeva company, which were put up for bid by the Housing and Urban Development Service (Serviu), under the Housing Ministry (Minvu), began to leak and showed evidence of other severe construction deficiencies, forcing the inhabitants to vacate them. The situation was particularly serious in the areas of El Volcán and San José I and II, leading to vigorous public protests in those areas. A dispute arose as to who was responsible for this failure: Minvu, for not establishing adequate technical specifications, or Copeva, for using low-quality construction methods and materials. The conflict ended up in the courts, and the Housing Minister resigned from his post.

results of the Copeva crisis was the acknowledgment of serious deficiencies in technical standards as well as in oversight and inspection of construction activities. By the end of 1997, the first modifications to the public housing programs had been made. More stringent regulations were enforced in areas such as rain gutters, drain pipes, outdoor drains and roofs for outdoor stairwells, and passageways. The new government policies reaffirmed the need to toughen specifications and standards and to improve the oversight of construction projects, in order to raise the quality of public housing.

In the area of urban development, spending has tripled since 1985, and a high priority has been placed on programs to improve streets, sidewalks, and water and sewer infrastructure and facilities. New programs encouraging community participation (such as the Participatory Paving Program and Community Facilities Construction) have achieved positive results, combining support from the community, the local government and the Ministry of Housing to help solve urban problems.

One of the main challenges in this area is the accelerating rate of urbanization, which has created larger real and potential housing markets, but has also produced serious adverse effects such as pollution, traffic congestion, shortages of infrastructure and basic services in certain city areas, and a general decrease in the quality of city life.

Numerous initiatives have been undertaken to channel the haphazard development of large cities. These efforts include the creation of regulatory plans for large cities, in particular for Santiago; the establishment of incentives for renewal of downtown areas; the creation of sub-centers as an alternative to the city center; and the search for mechanisms to coordinate institutional actions, transcending traditional sectorial divisions. A debate is in progress between those who believe that urban development can be successfully regulated and those who argue that the expansion of cities is inevitable and that the authorities must anticipate the phenomenon of urban sprawl and take the appropriate measures. Another topic of discussion is a proposal to establish metropolitan governments to regulate the development of large cities; this idea is opposed by those who favor endowing local mayors with greater powers.

It is clear that improvements in city management are necessary. Reversing the decline in the quality of life in urban areas is an urgent challenge. Large sectors of the population suffer from serious shortages of housing and urban facilities, degraded environmental quality, and a lack of recreational and sports facilities. In addition to launching massive construction programs, it will be necessary to confront the problem of the unrestrained growth of urban areas. Unrestricted growth adversely affects infrastructural costs, the feasibility of medium-term housing policies, and especially the quality of city life, due to accessibility problems, traffic congestion, pollution, and the rising costs of urban activities.

SOCIAL SECURITY

Changes in Social Security during the Military Regime
The main achievements of the pension system before 1973 were its expanded coverage and the relatively generous benefits it provided. However, significant weaknesses in the system were recognized, including inconsistencies and inequalities in benefits and access requirements. The same contribution would earn different returns according to the *caja de previsión* [institutional pension fund] an individual was affiliated with, a situation which favored organized workers. There were also financing problems; the *cajas'* deficits had to

be made up by the state, taking resources away from health care and housing. Finally, the administration and efficiency of the system were viewed as less than optimal.

This state-run social security system continued to be implemented until 1981. In that year, Decree Law No. 3,500 created the individual capitalization system, in which social security benefits are determined by the savings deposited into beneficiaries' accounts. This individualized model replaced the pay-as-you-go system based on intergenerational solidarity. The administration and management of the pension funds was placed in the hands of corporations designated as Pension Fund Administrators (AFPs), whose creation was stipulated by the above-mentioned law. Thus, the pension system was privatized at a stroke. The AFPs, in addition to administering their members' funds, charge commissions for the maintenance of social security accounts. The majority of the assets from the existing *cajas de previsión* were transferred to these accounts; only the Armed Forces retained their own pension system.

This model became mandatory for all salaried workers entering the social security system beginning in May 1981. A monthly contribution of 10% of taxable income was established. The AFPs grant pensions according to a worker's accumulated social security savings, plus the returns on the AFP's investments. Under this system, accumulated pension resources cannot be used for other state purposes such as housing or health care (Raczinsky and Cominetti 1994).

The new system established the immediate readjustability of pensions, which are expressed in UF, and it created different types of payout plans (life annuities, programmed retirement payments, or lump-sum payments with differential life annuities). The system does not restrict the transfer of members from one AFP to another, although it does establish commissions for account administration. A Superintendency for AFPs was created and charged with regulating the system in order to provide stability and to protect AFP members (Mideplan 1996).

The Social Security Normalization Institute (INP) was created to replace the *cajas de previsión*. Its purpose was to administer public funds for the payment of pensions, allowances, and other benefits for workers remaining in the old system. The state's obligation to guarantee a minimum pension to AFP members was also established.

The state further financed a "recognition bond" for people who switched to the AFPs. The transitional costs of changing the social security system resulted in an increase in government spending in this area between 1985 and 1989. Social security accounted for 41.2% of social spending in 1985, while by 1989 its share had increased to 49.9%. Spending on social security continued to be significant under the democratic governments. In 1995, nearly half of social spending went to social security, demonstrating the importance of state support to the system. As a result of this reform, a large proportion of social spending resources were earmarked for social security, at the expense of investments in other areas.

Another effect of the social security reform was that pension and health contributions were separated. Payroll contributions for health care were collected by Fonasa, the new organism in charge of financing public health care, or by the individual health care plans (Isapres).

With increasing numbers of members and relatively few pension payouts, the AFP system rapidly accumulated funds between 1981 and 1989. This buildup had a strong impact on national savings, and investment alternatives were expanded.

During that decade, the system's coverage decreased. Between 1974 and 1975, social security coverage reached 65%, while during the period from 1983 to 1989 it was 53%. This reduction was due to the effects of the economic recession on employment during the 1980s. The fall in contributions during 1982 and 1983 was counterbalanced by the creation of the Family Subsidy (SUF) and social aid pensions. The pensions granted under these plans were meager, but they covered a significant percentage of the population that was unemployed or not part of the formal labor market (Raczinsky and Cominetti 1994).

Individuals not affiliated with the private social security system suffered reductions in their pensions. Those who received subsidies through the social safety net (the SUF and social aid pensions) saw progressive decreases in their benefits due to cuts in social spending. Regular retirement pensions also decreased, since a readjustment of 10.6% over the 1985 level was due but not enacted. The result of these measures was a general impoverishment of the country's elderly population.

Social Security in the 1990s

Since 1990, the democratic governments have maintained the established system and have focused their attention on improving the regulation of the substantial funds accumulated in the individual capitalization accounts. Pensions have been increased in real terms, through a readjustment viewed as a "payback" of the decreases imposed by the military government. Resources allocated for social security benefit payments increased by 50% in real terms between 1990 and 1997 (Ministry Secretary General of the Presidency 1997).

In December 1990, minimum pensions were readjusted by 10.6% and social aid pensions by 20% over the Consumer Price Index. The 10.6% adjustment outstanding for the remaining types of pensions was subsequently implemented. In 1994, revenues from a gasoline and tobacco tax helped finance a 10% increase in all retirement pensions of less than 100,000 pesos (Mideplan 1996).

As overall social spending increased, monetary subsidies were raised, and benefits for target groups. Family allowances were inversely linked to the income of the beneficiaries. Coverage was expanded, and a winter supplement for social aid pensioners over 65 was created. The targeting of general pensions was also improved through the increases and readjustments granted after 1990. For example, the lowest income quintile of the population received a 100% pension increase (Mideplan 1996). In spite of these benefits, non-working Chileans, including some of the neediest members of society, remain disenfranchised by the social security system.

Diverse measures have been implemented to modernize the administration of the Social Security Normalization Institute (INP), to improve customer service, and to coordinate the work of various institutions to raise the quantity and quality of services offered.

Support for the social security system claims a significant proportion of the national budget. In 1990, social security consumed 52.4% of all social spending. This percentage was reduced to 45.8% by 1995 (Mideplan 1996). The high percentage of state spending on social security results from the fact that the state pays for the pensions of those who cannot afford a minimum pension plan or who are not covered by social security, as well as the fact that public resources are used to finance retirement benefits for the Armed Forces. Further elements in this equation are the debts inherited from the old pay-as-you-go system, including the recognition bond and pensions for retirees who did not switch to the AFP system.

Among the main challenges for the social security system are the need to broaden coverage, as well as to ensure that the AFP system can finance minimum pensions. The majority of people not covered by any type of social security are independent workers, such as the self-employed. The number of salaried workers enrolled in social security varies significantly according to income quintile. In the poorest quintiles (I and II), 47.6% and 38.4% of salaried workers, respectively, fall outside the social security system. In the middle quintiles, this rate falls to 35.7% (III) and 30% (IV). In the top income quintile, the proportion is 28.7% (Uribe-Echeverría 1996).

Improving these figures, and increasing the proportion of employers and independent workers making social security contributions, remains a challenge. Other areas for concern include administrative costs; the profitability of the pension funds; worker participation in fund management; the concentration of investments in certain sectors; and the close relations between AFP administrators and the business world.

Conclusions

The social security funds administered by the AFPs have given an important boost to the country's internal savings rate. The AFP system has become well-established and now represents one of the country's main institutional investors. The management of the social security funds' portfolios has taken on increasing importance in expanding pension capital and returns. The drop in AFP returns in 1995 highlighted the lack of diversification in the sector's investments, which were concentrated in the energy and telecommunications fields. As a result, priority was placed on projects that developed new investment alternatives, both abroad (with the creation of International Investment Funds) and locally (with investments in infrastructure and mining).

The AFP-based social security system has produced satisfactory results; the pensions paid today are substantially higher than those paid by the old *cajas de previsión*. Using figures from December 1994, old-age pensions under the new system are greater by 42%, disability pensions by 61%, and survivor's benefits by 41%. Only payments to orphans were greater under the old system (13%). It should be noted that the pensions granted by the AFPs through December 1994 were financed in part by the recognition bonds, which to date have yielded 4% annually (Fuentes 1995).

The success of the pension funds is due in part to the high average yields achieved on investments of the funds in social security accounts. However, the sustainability of the system when it is called upon to finance benefits for the majority of the non-working population remains a point of debate. This will depend upon the average rate of contribution throughout each individual's working life, as well as long-term levels of real annual investment yields (Elter 1993).

POLICIES PROMOTING EQUAL OPPORTUNITY
AND TARGETING VULNERABLE GROUPS

Beginning in 1990, policies were initiated to promote social integration among the country's most underprivileged groups (those disproportionately affected by poverty or discrimination). The target populations for these policies were women, children, youth, the elderly, ethnic minorities, and disabled persons (Mideplan-UNICEF 1993). Numerous institutions were created to promote equal opportunities for groups subject to discrimination, including the National Youth Institute, National Women's Service, National Indigenous Peoples Association, and the National Disabilities Fund.

The assumption behind these actions is that poverty is not brought about simply by a shortage of basic necessities, but also by the social vulnerability or discrimination experienced by certain groups or communities. These negative factors restrict the full exercise of these people's rights as citizens as well as their integration into society.

Policies directed toward a specific group, whether a physical community or a social group with certain characteristics, are not aimed solely at individuals living in extreme poverty, but rather at all of the group's members (as with Sernam's Equal Opportunity Plan, designed to eliminate gender discrimination). Nonetheless, the characteristics of a particular group may be combined with existing conditions of poverty in order to create narrowly-targeted policies and programs, such as Sernam's Program for Female Heads of Households (Racsynski 1995).

The institutions created for each disadvantaged group seek to coordinate and complement the policies and programs carried out by other organizations which affect their target group. The objective is to overcome the traditionally segmented and sector-based view of public action, in order to address the needs of a particular group or locality on a more comprehensive scale. Efforts in this direction have been undertaken throughout the 1990s. The results have included the institutionalization of coordination measures through the various Inter-Ministerial Committees, which seek to harmonize policies on topics such as rural poverty, productive development, domestic violence, etc. Initiatives such as the National Program for the Elimination of Poverty, which focuses the actions and investments of various government agencies upon the country's neediest municipalities, have also been instituted.

The creation of the Fund for Social Investment and Solidarity (Fosis) was a fundamental step forward in the country's efforts to eliminate poverty. Fosis' main function is the financing of projects that benefit needy and marginalized groups, particularly microenterprises, impoverished rural inhabitants, and disadvantaged youth. The projects are carried out by third parties, include a strong emphasis on investment in human resources, and utilize decentralized and participatory management systems.

A preliminary examination of needy and vulnerable groups reveals that children are the group most seriously affected by poverty. Child poverty rates declined from 52% in 1990 to 33.4% in 1996, with the total number of needy children falling by one-third, from 1,913,000 in 1990 to 1,332,000 in 1996. However, these rates continue to be very high, reflecting inequalities in health and education that must be corrected (Mideplan 1997c). There is no entity specializing in policies aimed at children, although the Ministry of Planning and Cooperation (Mideplan) coordinates the group of initiatives comprising the National Childhood Plan.

Poverty rates among youth decreased from 37.8% in 1990 to 22% in 1996, with the number of needy young people dropping from about 1,300,000 to some 790,000. Unemployment is one of the main problems for this group. Figures from the 1996 Casen survey show that 10% of young people between the ages of 15 and 29 are unemployed, almost double the national unemployment rate. Furthermore, education and employment gaps between high- and low-income sectors persist. In the neediest quintile, 16.3% of young people are neither part of the educational system nor participating in paid activities. In the wealthiest quintile, the figure is 4.9% (Mideplan 1997d).

The National Youth Institute was created to formulate and coordinate policies and initiatives aimed at the comprehensive economic, cultural, and social integration of young people. The *Projoven* program was also initiated, providing job training, education, and personal development programs for young people. Various other organizations offer youth-oriented programs, such as the job-training courses held by the National Training and Employment Service (Sence) and Fosis.

Poverty among the elderly is not only a current policy problem, but also a pressing issue for the future, due to the general aging of the population. In 1992, 9.8% of Chile's total population was 60 years of age and over. This age group will reach 16% of the total population (more than three million people) by the year 2025. The growing proportion of elderly people must be addressed through preemptive policies, especially in the areas of health care and social security, that take the aging of the population into account and address the issue of the quality of life in old age. There is no specialized institution or comprehensive program for this segment of the population; however, the National Elderly Commission has been created to help generate proposals on issues affecting the elderly. Existing policies are mainly directed toward improving the income of elderly persons, primarily through increases in pensions. Resources have also been allocated for the establishment of retirement homes, and special health and housing programs for the elderly have been created to complement the services provided by Fosis.

Women's participation in the labor market has been increasing, but under discriminatory conditions. Problems include unequal job access and income, the inappropriate division of household responsibilities, insufficient child care support and the lack of flexible working hours. Poverty is especially prevalent among female heads of households. In 1990, 33% of female heads of households lived in poverty. By 1996, this ratio had fallen to one in five (19.3%) (Mideplan 1997b). Various programs have been created in an attempt to prevent the feminization of poverty. One notable initiative among these is the Program for Female Heads of Households with Limited Resources, implemented by the National Women's Service (Sernam), which focuses broad, inter-sectorial attention upon this group. Progress toward equal opportunity will require specific policies aimed at women. Sernam has implemented an Equal Opportunities Plan in coordination with other institutions. It has also created the Women's Rights Information Center, as well as job training programs and workshops on specific topics (such as teenage pregnancy, domestic violence, and the problems of seasonal workers).

The number of rural poor continues to decrease, but advancing against the remaining, entrenched pockets of poverty is becoming increasingly difficult. Poverty is also deeply entrenched in cities, where it is exacerbated by urban problems such as crime, transportation difficulties, long commuting distances, infrastructural deficiencies, the poor quality of services, and the lack of recreational opportunities.

An Indigenous Law was passed in 1993 to improve opportunities for Chile's indigenous population. The National Commission for Indigenous Development (Conadi) was also created. Conadi is responsible for formulating indigenous policy in Chile.[12] It allocates public resources to subsidize the purchase of land and water rights, as well as for the financing of productive and cultural projects.

The National Disability Council, created in 1994, has set the guidelines for a National Disability Policy. Its aims are to promote research and prevention programs related to disabilities and to support the rehabilitation and social integration of people with disabilities.

---

12 Conadi is headquartered in Temuco and includes South and North Sub-Directorates, based in Temuco and Iquique, respectively.

In the same year, a law was passed addressing the social integration of people with disabilities (Law 19,284). This legislation provided for the creation of an insolvency fund, the National Disability Fund (Fonadis).

Other state entities, such as the Corporation for the Promotion of Production and the National Farming and Fishing Development Institute, have developed support programs for microenterprises, small-scale mining and fishing operations, and small agricultural and urban entrepreneurs.

The National Program for the Eradication of Poverty was founded in 1994. The Special Municipalities Program of this organization has formulated a plan for the territorial targeting of social spending.

The first conclusion that can be derived from these equal opportunity initiatives is that a more heterogeneous social policy is now being forged, a policy seeking to eliminate the discrimination that hinders the full integration of certain groups into society. At the same time, social programs aimed at vulnerable and needy Chileans have improved their targeting criteria and moved away from a direct subsidy approach. This shift should lead to expanded opportunities for these groups over the medium and long term.

Second, it is clear from the figures presented here that innovative new policies are still needed to address the problem of extreme poverty, particularly in rural areas. The concentration of poverty among women, children, and youth demonstrates the need to create additional programs or to strengthen existing efforts affecting these groups.

A third conclusion is that the heterogeneous nature of poverty — both in its composition and geographical location — requires the continuation of socially and territorially targeted programs. The implementation of equal opportunity policies and programs will require both an overall increase in resources and a more extensive decentralization of these resources. Municipalities must play a more active role in these initiatives. The successful pilot programs launched between 1990 and 1994, which affect very small percentages of the target groups, should be expanded (García and Schkolnik 1995).

IV. Challenges for Social Policy

The combination of increased social spending and Chile's sustained economic growth over the last seven years has led to significant advances in the fight against poverty. However, the remaining pockets of extreme poverty depend more upon structural factors and are more difficult to eliminate. Specific policies must be directed toward this "hardcore" poverty, which cannot be eliminated through economic growth alone. This is a fundamental prerequisite for the promotion of social and economic opportunities for all of our country's inhabitants.

These programs must be both expanded and decentralized, since the diversity of the households living in poverty calls for increasingly specialized solutions. More resources must be allocated to such programs, and the management and financing capacities of the municipalities must be improved.

Since 1990, social policy has been diversified, with the aim of integrating economically disadvantaged groups into the country's development process. The government has increasingly sought improved compatibility between social and economic policies. Continued progress in harmonizing these areas is necessary in order to improve opportunities for society's neediest groups, as well as to ensure sustainable, long-term economic growth.

To improve the level of results achieved by the state's social policies, several policy areas must be subjected to thorough revision and reform. Such a transformation has already been undertaken in education. However, in the areas of health care, social security, and housing, no consensus exists about the desired direction of this change, nor about the processes and policies needed for its implementation. The quality and equity of public services, especially in education and health care, must be enhanced. Nationwide indicators in both sectors show that Chile has achieved adequate coverage of services, but serious imbalances emerge when the indicators are broken down by gender, age, class, or geographical area. This is a widely-recognized phenomenon, and the challenge lies in reaching a consensus as to the specific measures which will remedy the situation.

The state has gradually lessened its participation in the providing of services and has transferred these activities to third parties (the private sector, non-governmental organizations, and the community). This requires a strengthening of the state's regulatory and oversight role, to ensure that the population enjoys equal access to quality services. This is especially important since the Casen surveys show substantial inequities in education, health, and housing services for the country's most impoverished groups. The state must also retain a central role in the definition, design, and evaluation of policies and programs.

Community participation in social programs must be intensified for various reasons. One is that beneficiaries are able to contribute their efforts, skills, and abilities in order to raise the quality of the results. Microenterprises can contribute to economic development; social housing beneficiaries can participate in home construction and improvement; and communities can become involved in the resolution of specific problems. Highly successful initiatives have been undertaken in all of these areas; these include Minvu's Participatory Paving Program, Fosis' *Entre Todos* program, and numerous economic development partnerships.

A second benefit of participatory mechanisms is that they broaden the range of input and feedback about specific projects, allowing them to be fine-tuned for greater effectiveness.

A third reason for user participation is that it gives people an opportunity to question the government's actions, obliging the authorities to provide clear explanations about the objectives of their activities.

The decentralization process must become more efficient. The advantages of decentralization in the area of social policy are numerous; for example, decentralized systems allow more accurate diagnoses of problems as well as the formulation of differentiated and highly-targeted policies.

Current hindrances to the decentralization process must be overcome. These include the contradiction between the rigid administrative procedures of the central government and the need for flexible programs; political clientelism; deficiencies in the municipalities' technical and financial capacities; and the absence of cross-sector coordination. Issues such as economies of scale and the outsourcing of services must also be taken into account.

Increasing efficiency and equity in the use of public resources is a further challenge. Although the conflict between rising social demands and limited resources will surely continue, this dilemma may be partially resolved through greater efficiency in social spending. This clearly calls for more effective evaluation of social programs. A monitoring system for public investment projects has been developed, along with pilot evaluations of social and economic programs.

Performance and management indicators have been devised for public entities, and government spending is monitored. These mechanisms, however, do not necessarily assess the quality and impact of social programs. Most programs are not evaluated, and if they are, auditors focus on coverage and expenditures, but not on the program's actual impact on beneficiaries or its comparative returns to society. The state must find ways to ensure that its social investments produce real improvements in the population's quality of life.

Targeting is viewed by some experts as the only mechanism for achieving greater effectiveness and efficiency in social policies. Although targeting is useful in directing spending towards impoverished groups, it is a limited tool for resolving general problems of social policy. For example, deficiencies in areas such as health care and education, which affect a majority of the population, cannot be resolved through targeting, but require more complex solutions addressing all of the issues involved (management, decentralization, institutional autonomy, resource allocation, etc.). Environmental and urban management problems also cannot be solved through targeting.

Targeted social aid programs do not take into account beneficiaries' social networks, community organizations and initiatives, or their potential achievements. The concept of poverty as set forth by proponents of targeting emphasizes what individuals lack and does not consider their potential for improving their situation. Targeted social programs are palliative; while they may increase the incomes of people who urgently need such help, they do not provide the opportunity to escape permanently from poverty. One suggestion has been to link targeted social aid policies with policies promoting opportunity (as was done with the extension of the SUF to youth up to age 18).

If targeting is viewed as the only strategy for increasing efficiency, universal social programs should be reduced or even eliminated. This was the dominant logic under the military regime. However, the democratic governments have worked to achieve a balance among different types of social policies, transcending the arguments favoring targeted, selective, or universal programs. Thus, the spectrum of current social policy includes universal programs (health, education), targeted programs (the social safety net), selective programs (aimed at specific vulnerable groups or localities) and selective targeted programs (focused on groups which are both vulnerable and impoverished).

Today, policies are selected according to the target population's characteristics and the type of problem to be solved, not according to rigid ideological tenets. Other criteria within this flexible system include the conditions under which social services will be provided, as well as the feasibility of reaching program objectives with the resources available. Indicators such as the quality of service and management are especially valued, underscoring the need for mechanisms to evaluate policies and programs.

The goal of integrating social action does not mean attempting to solve a greater number of problems; rather, it refers to the coordination of different policies and programs to achieve a specific goal. Comprehensive social programs seek solutions to the diverse problems of a particular group or locality. This is more effectively achieved through coordinated and inter-sectorial efforts than through targeted programs.

Today, there is debate about whether the modernization of social management requires additional resources, or whether it is sufficient simply to improve the efficiency of social spending. Yet there are other issues as well. Improving management will also require increases in coordinated and inter-sectorial policies, particularly for programs aimed at specific groups or localities. In addition, if the management of social policies is to be improved, the effectiveness of these policies must be evaluated in some manner. This can only be achieved through the development of measurement techniques linking social policies with real improvements in the quality of life for Chileans, especially those in greatest need.

BIBLIOGRAPHICAL REFERENCES

Beyer, H. 1997. "Distribución del ingreso: antecedentes para la discusión." *Estudios Públicos* 65. Santiago: Centro de Estudios Públicos.

Concertación de Partidos por la Democracia. 1989. "Programa de Gobierno." Santiago.

———. 1994. "Un gobierno para los nuevos tiempos." Program for the second Concertación administration. Santiago.

Cox, C. 1994. "Las políticas de los años noventa para el sistema escolar." Santiago: Cepal.

Durston, J. 1994. In *Diario Financiero*, December 30.

Elter, D. 1993. "El sistema previsional privado: elementos para un diagnóstico de la situación actual." Working Document 54. Santiago: Pries.

Etchegaray, A., et al. 1997. "Las reformas sociales en acción: vivienda." *Serie Políticas Sociales* 20, LC/L.1057. Santiago: Cepal.

Fuentes R. 1995. "Evolución y resultados del sistema." In: S. Baeza and F. Margozzini, eds. *Quince años después: una mirada al sistema privado de pensiones.* Santiago: Centro de Estudios Públicos.

García, A. and M. Schkolnik. 1995. "Superación de la pobreza: balance y propuestas." In: C. Pizarro, D. Raczynski, and J. Vial, eds. *Políticas económicas y sociales en el Chile democrático.* Santiago: Cieplan-UNICEF.

Gemines Consultores. 1995. "Determinantes de la reducción de la pobreza entre 1987 y 1992." *Informe Gemines* 187, July.

Göske, J. and A. Traub. 1996. "La empresa de menor tamaño: ¿objeto o sujeto de la política de fomento?" Santiago: Fundación Friedrich Ebert.

Hardy, C. 1997a. "Las políticas sociales en Chile." In: *Chile 96. Análisis y opiniones.* Santiago: Flacso.

———. 1997b. "Gasto social para la igualdad de oportunidades." Santiago: Fundación Chile XXI.

Larrañaga, O. 1994. "Pobreza, crecimiento y desigualdad: Chile 1987–92." Research Series I–77. Ilades/Georgetown University.

Lenz, R. 1995. *Cuadernos de Economía* 32(95), April.

Mac-Clure, O. and R. Urmeneta. 1995. "Exclusión social en Chile." ILO.

Martínez, G. 1995. "Crecimiento con equidad: La política económica de los Presidentes Aylwin y Frei 1990–1995." Presentation to the semi-nar "La experiencia chilena: Desarrollo con equidad." El Salvador, April.

Mideplan (Ministry for Planning and Cooperation). 1991. "Un proceso de integración al desarrollo nacional: Informe social 1990/91." Santiago, August.

———. 1996. "Balance de seis años de las políticas sociales: 1990–1996." Santiago, August.

———. 1997a. "Pobreza y distribución del ingreso en Chile, 1996." Resultados de la Encuesta Casen. *La Época* newspaper, July 27.

———. 1997b. "Situación de la mujer en Chile, 1996." Resultados de la Encuesta Casen 1996. *La Época* newspaper, August 17.

———. 1997c. "La situación de la infancia en Chile, 1996." Resultados de la Encuesta Casen 1996. *La Época* newspaper, September 7.

———. 1997d. "Situación de los jóvenes en Chile 1996." Resultados de la Encuesta Casen 1996. *La Época* newspaper, September 28.

———. 1997e. "Situación del empleo en Chile, 1996." Resultados de la Encuesta Casen 1996. *La Época* newspaper, October.

———. 1997f. "Situación de la educación en Chile, 1996." Resultados de la Encuesta Casen 1996. *La Época* newspaper, November 9.

Mideplan-UNICEF. 1993. "La impresión de las cifras: Niños, mujeres, jóvenes y adultos mayores." Santiago: August.

Mineduc (Ministry of Education). 1996. "La reforma en marcha. Jornada completa diurna para todos." Santiago: Mineduc.

Ministerio Secretaría General de Gobierno (Ministry of the Secretary General of the Government). 1996. *Zona Pública* 6. Santiago.

———. 1997. *Zona Pública* 21. Santiago.

Ministerio Secretaría General de la Presidencia (Ministry of the Secretary General of the Presidency). 1997. "Más oportunidades para la gente. Las transformaciones del período 1990–1997 para el Chile del 2000." Santiago, October.

Minvu (Ministry of Housing and Urban Development). 1997. Presentation of the Minister before the Investigative Commission of the Chamber of Deputies, September 2.

Oyarzo, C. 1991. "Análisis crítico de las transformaciones financieras del sector salud en la década de los 80 y propuesta de una reforma." In: J. Jiménez de la Jara, ed. *Sistemas de salud en transición a la democracia.*

Pérez, L. 1994. "Focalización y programa de vivienda básica: postulación a través de grupos."

Cuaderno de Trabajo 42. Santiago: Cordillera.

Raczynski, D. 1995. "Focalización de programas sociales." In: C. Pizarro, D. Raczynski, and J. Vial, eds. *Políticas económicas y sociales en el Chile democrático*. Santiago: Cieplan-UNICEF.

————and R. Cominetti. 1994. "La política social en Chile: Panorama de sus reformas." *Serie Reformas de Política Pública 19*. Santiago: Cepal.

Schkolnik, M. and J. Bonnefoy. 1994. "Una propuesta de tipología de las políticas sociales en Chile." UNICEF, July.

Uribe-Echeverría, V. 1996. "La exclusión social de los grupos pobres." Report prepared for Cepal. Santiago: Catholic University of Chile.

Vergara, P. 1990. "Políticas hacia la extrema pobreza en Chile. 1973–1988." Santiago: Flacso.

————. 1993. "Ruptura y continuidad en la política social." Doc. 44, April. Santiago: Flacso.

The New Challenge:
Quality and Equity in Education

Isidora Mena
Cristian Belleï

Introduction[1]

The modernization of educational institutions in the 1990s has brought about a significant cultural shift. At the heart of this shift lies an unprecedented surge in knowledge and learning which has reached all corners of the globe through technology. The generation and use of this knowledge and learning has become vital to countries seeking to develop, to organizations looking to maintain leadership positions in their respective sectors, and to individuals who want to lead successful personal and civic lives.

For these reasons, the educational system has become central to modern societies and therefore is an institution which governments, businesses, and families constantly seek to improve. Indeed, educational reform is a hot topic in every region of the world.

The proposals designed by the United Nations' Economic Commission for Latin America and the Caribbean (ECLAC) and the United Nations' Education, Science, and Culture Committee (UNESCO) coherently outline the program for "a new style in education reform" for the region. This model has two primary objectives: to develop human resources to better utilize science and technology, with the aim of making the region's countries more competitive; and to make individuals capable of grasping "modern citizenship," in which citizens are able to function in a society which is democratic, technologically sophisticated, and based on information and communication.

In general terms, three periods in the development of Chile's educational system can be identified. The initial period was marked by the challenge of creating a system in which all students were covered and which could absorb new students. The second was concerned with modernizing administration, optimizing the use of financial resources, and decentralizing the organizational structure. In the 1990s, the third stage has been marked by the attempt to ensure that all students, independent of their socioeconomic position, get the most out of their education. In this last stage, the quality-equity[2] issue has become

---

1   We would like to thank Ivan Núñez for his valuable commentary.
2   In this paper, equity refers to equal opportunity in education.

essential. Moving to the third stage does not imply that the other stages have been success-fully completed. Quite often the later stages add to or complicate the issues dealt with in the earlier stages.

In Chile, satisfying the demands of educational reform in the early 1990s implied three challenges: fulfilling the goals of the early stages (such as total coverage and reten-tion) even while focusing on the issues of the later stages; replenishing deficits that result-ed from educational deterioration during the military government; and perfecting the decentralization plan, which focused on quality-equity issues, beginning in the 1980s.

The fundamental goal of education policy in the 1990s has been to improve the quali-ty of individual student's experiences and to distribute these experiences more equitably. The motto "High Quality Education For All Students" synthesizes the Concertación's[3] education policy. With this focus on quality education, government policy seeks to improve the system's structure, management, and use of resources.

With this in mind, the reform program is distinguished by its focus on the schools themselves. The reform's central aim is to direct resources to the exact "contact point," where students actually learn. This focus on learning reflects the novelty and, ultimately, the strength of the educational reform. However, it also makes it highly complex. The edu-cational reform does not depend on the dictates of policy makers, but rather on a diverse group of committed citizens and groups.

The thesis of this article is to provide a perspective on the new challenges that have arisen out of the educational reform carried out by the Concertación administrations from 1990 to 1996 and its quality-equity premise. We seek to critically analyze the reform's advances and limitations.

The first section of this essay examines what has been called "the heart of education reform": the various Improvement Programs designed and implemented by the Ministry of Education aimed at improving the quality of students' learning experiences and the way they are distributed. Because the reform was carried out "in the classrooms," we need to analyze these lines of action, the challenges they represent, and their impact on the educa-tional framework. We begin by focusing this analysis on the specific programs that formed the core of the reform package. These programs led to new educational concepts and improved use of educational resources, which had been insufficient. The historical and political context of the early 1990s, along with the urgent need to reform education, influenced the decision to center education policy on specific programs rather than on structural adjustment.

The second section covers the most important dimensions of the institutional context of elementary education: financial resources, the faculty and administrators, and the administrative system. This section examines the changes that occurred in these areas and how they created new challenges, and it concludes with a discussion on the tension between public and private alternatives in education and how they determine educational changes. The central question is: ideological symbols in the complex choice between the state or the market aside, how far advanced is Chile in configuring an educational system that efficiently combines public and private elements to form a better system?

---

3   The Concertación is Chile's center-left governing coalition.

This study will have achieved its stated goals if it communicates the complexity of the pertinent issues while acknowledging the advancements that have been made, even as it challenges readers to creatively tackle unresolved problems.

I. The Heart of Education Reform: Quality-Equity Improvement Programs

Educational reform has focused since the early 1990s on learning in the classroom. Reform strategy has taken shape through *quality and equity improvement programs* (known as MECEs). These programs rely on innovative initiatives to improve general education for all students. The MECE programs exist for different schooling levels, such as pre-school, elementary school, and secondary school, as well as rural education. Total investment in the MECEs is more than 500 million dollars.[4]

The MECE programs are implemented and overseen by the Ministry of Education, which will be cited hereinafter as Mineduc. Mineduc is responsible for evaluating MECE programs and setting education policy in general.

The task undertaken by the Concertación governments to improve education while providing equal access to all has brought with it significant challenges. On one hand, the reforms sought to distribute resources for education more evenly throughout the society. On a deeper level, they sought to change Chile's student and learning culture.

Improving *quality* in schools required a paradigm shift because notions of what and how students learn were being changed; the very nature of what schools were teaching was called into question. Educators argued that modern society requires people to do more than accumulate an existing body of knowledge. They said that students need to have sufficient cognitive skills to apply ways of learning and thinking to a constantly changing world. People, they said, also need to be educated in social ethics and to value other individuals. These aims became the focus of the educational reform.

The *quality of the learning experience* improves when students forge a relationship to knowledge itself so they can apply it to their present and future lives.

On the other hand, distributing educational opportunities *more equally* means leveling the playing field so that all students, regardless of their sociopolitical background or living conditions, have the same opportunities. This objective meant introducing complex changes into the educational system.

Once the obstacles to educational access are lifted, equity in the classroom is achieved by ensuring that each student receives an education tailored to his/her special needs. This kind of policy can generate different learning experiences among individual students but ensures that all students have equal access to education.

The reform program is based on transforming the triangular relation between teachers, students, and knowledge itself. To make this happen, an overhaul of school policy and administrative policy was necessary, both within individual schools and throughout the system in general.

---

4 For an overview of global education policies in the1990s, see Cox (1994 and 1997). For a comparative analysis of educational reform in Latin America, see Braslavsky (1996).

A cultural shift such as this is an even greater challenge considering the poverty that affects Chile and specifically its educational system. As a country in the midst of its modernization process, Chile in the 1990s faces three sets of challenges in this regard:

- *Poor country challenges:* which make covering all Chilean children in the educational system difficult. Impoverished Chilean children have little time to study, have few learning resources like books or tapes and they may be under-nourished. These challenges include low teacher salaries.
- *Administrative modernization challenges:* which due to historical or cultural circumstances produce inefficient and bloated bureaucracies. In addition, the decentralization program of the 1980s was inadequate in generating skills in local bureaucracies.
- *Cultural transformation challenges:* which are at the heart of education itself and are particularly cumbersome for Latin American countries which tend to be conservative. Education reform addressing cultural issues requires that teachers and students themselves no longer focus entirely on learning about their own culture.

These challenges were posed starkly before Chile in the early 1990s. At times, achieving one set of goals means sacrificing others: overcoming poverty, for instance, makes teaching computer skills more difficult.

The educational reform programs begun in 1990 have had a tremendous effect, opening up a number of new doors in education while creating new problems. We will examine some of these now.

1. PRESCHOOL EDUCATION

Although the number of preschool children covered by the education system rose notably in the 1980s, only 20% of children under the age of six were attending preschool in the early 1990s. Most of those who were not covered were between ages four and six (in preschools called *jardines infantiles*) and came from poor urban areas or isolated rural areas.[5]

For preschoolers, much of their education has a social "child care" aspect: the children receive basic nutritional elements, protection, and, to a lesser degree, some language stimulation. These "day-care schools" were characterized by poor infrastructure, unprofessional teachers, and insufficient teaching materials. In general, the level of education was profoundly unsatisfactory, especially in light of the fact that young students have tremendous learning capabilities.

General Description of the Reform

Much of the evidence in this area shows that investment in preschool education has the best effect on the poorest children and families. Getting children who come from the poorest homes into preschools becomes increasingly critical as the number of children in extreme situations grows and more women enter the work force. Despite these facts, preschool reform is not favored by all experts. Critics question its impact on families, the job market, communities, and the functioning of the educational system itself.

To answer the critics, the 1990s preschool education reform has a number of alternative options to the educational needs of very young children (Hermosilla 1996, 1997). The

---

5   Only 12% of the children surveyed came from rural areas.

FIGURE 1

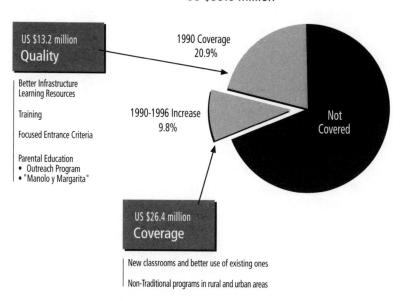

Preschool Quality and Equity Improvement Program
US $39.6 million

US $13.2 million
Quality

Better Infrastructure
Learning Resources

Training

Focused Entrance Criteria

Parental Education
• Outreach Program
• "Manolo y Margarita"

1990 Coverage
20.9%

1990-1996 Increase
9.8%

Not
Covered

US $26.4 million
Coverage

New classrooms and better use of existing ones

Non-Traditional programs in rural and urban areas

reform supported the existing preschools dependent on the National Board of Preschools (Junji) and the Integra Foundation, as well as programs that were being administered by non-governmental organizations. In this way, the reform sought to promote different programs, from traditional to newer such as one in which mothers get materials and tutoring for their children from Mineduc or programs run by community tutors.[6]

The MECE-preschool reform program has had wide-ranging effects. First, it has put preschool education on the political agenda,[7] increasing the national budget for this type of schooling. On a political level, the program has also demonstrated that educational reform that strengthens ties between communities and schools, and provides alternative options, can be popular. Secondly, it has improved the network of communication between different levels of schooling. Last, the MECE program has been able to improve learning conditions for individual preschoolers and increase the sources directed towards them.

MECE's primary strategy is to focus on covering students in specific rural and urban-poor areas. Approximately two-thirds of MECE's preschool budget was used for

---

6   Preschool reform has been administered by a number of groups and through various financing schemes. Mineduc, through the MECE program, utilized US$39.6 million (or 16.3% of MECE- Elementary Schools' total budget) over a period of six years. This figure does not represent a significant percentage of money spent on overall preschool spending. Among 5- and 6-year-old children (who make up 80% of the preschool population), growth in coverage achieved through domestic financing shows 35,000 new students in Junji since 1996, 25,000 in Integra, while MECE has recruited only 18,000 new students.

7   Preschool education is not mandatory in Chile and, as such, does not receive the benefits that the elementary school system receives. Junaeb, for example, does not provide nutritional meals to preschoolers. Junji and Integra do provide nutritional meals for their students.

this purpose. The final third was used to improve the quality of existing educational opportunities. This program required a concerted effort by the traditional players in the system — preschools, Junji and Integra — and the assistance of private institutions such as the Center for Educational Investigation and Development and the Interdisciplinary Center for Educational Development.

In terms of promoting coverage, the plan of action was: (1) to optimize the use of existing programs in poor areas and diversify the areas in which they were offered (schools and Integra); (2) to set up non-traditional programs in order to increase coverage, with the focus on rural and urban-poor sectors; and (3)to improve educational infrastructure.

Improving the quality of education was achieved through a multi-faceted action plan which included: (1) hiring more employees with professional backgrounds in child care and community service; (2) improving resources and educational tools available to children at their schools; (3) hiring professionals to help schools reach out to their communities, either through programs aimed at parents or through public campaigns; and (4) improving the connection between preschool and elementary education.

Diagnostic Evaluation of the Reform

Diversity
The preschool reform is in many ways distinctive because it combines a number of strategies including non-traditional ones. A number of programs have been implemented to improve schools' ability to coordinate the different groups —students, parents, teachers, and the community they serve. Today there is a significant track record in terms of programs that have been implemented. (They are no longer just pilot programs as they were in the early 1990s.) This track record can serve as an example for other program coordinators. The experiences of the rural communities are especially important here.

Community Framework
Another important aspect of the reform is how communities have been drawn into the educational system in an effort to familiarize schools with students' backgrounds and to make communities more involved in the learning process. The ability of parents to continue their child's education at home, among other things, makes a child's school experience more positive and plays a role in the student's ability to function better in society overall. Indeed, evaluations have demonstrated that the programs have generated networks of support within the community for preschool education.

Bringing together schools with families and communities represents a concerted effort to use policy to secure a much needed cultural change. In Chile, the relationship between parents and children and between schools and children tends to be authoritarian, highly controlling, and often quite aggressive. To break with this pattern while children are young could have significant ramifications as they grow and learn. Such programs as *Manolo y Margarita aprenden con sus padres* (Manolo and Margarita Learn with their Parents), which combines texts and audiovisual materials, and *Conozca a su hijo* (Learn About your Child), which targets poorer Chileans, are examples of how families can give their children a better educational grounding.

TABLE 1

PRESCHOOL COVERAGE BY INCOME QUINTILE, 1990-96

Quintile	1990	1992	1994	1996	Percentual Change 1990-96
I	16.9	19.8	21.1	22.3	32.0
II	17.5	22.1	22.7	26.8	53.1
III	20.4	23.9	27.7	30.0	47.1
IV	27.2	27.9	33.4	36.8	35.3
V	32.4	44.6	46.0	48.4	49.4
Total	20.9	24.8	26.9	29.8	42.6

Source: Ministry of Planning and Cooperation, Casen Survey 1990-1996.

Decentralizing Effort and Evaluation

Coordinating different actors and institutions, both at the national and regional levels, has been an important subject in preschool education. The National Commission on Preschool Education was created precisely to bring together the different groups active in this area in an effort to coordinate their actions (even though the regulatory framework for each differs widely).[8] This venture has greatly facilitated problem-detection and problem-solving throughout the system. For example, a framework now exists for transforming administrational organizations from pyramid-like structures to more regional, decentralized ones.

Few public programs have made evaluation a central part of their overall strategy. There are evaluations for implementation, time series, and impact statements. These studies are frequently conducted by third-party groups like the Center for Children's and Women's Studies (Ceanim) and the Center for Social Development Studies (Cedep). These evaluations give planners more information for redesigning programs, improving efficiency, and focusing on specific areas. In general, they play an important role in improving education policy.

Impact on Results

The number of children covered by the preschool system has risen in all regions, up from 20.9% in 1990 to 29.8% in 1996. While the figures show improvement, the biggest jumps were made among those in the lower-secondary class (quintile II), not those in the lowest economic segment (quintile I) (see Graph 1).

Similarly, both Junji and Integra have increased their hours, closing at 7 p.m. instead of 5 p.m., to care for children of parents who work. The 3,000 children at Junji

---

8   Junji, which is state-funded, functions autonomously, except on matters related to curriculum formation. Integra depends directly on the offices of the First Lady and the respective wives of regional authorities. It only consults with Mineduc on curriculum issues and coverage strategies. Mineduc does not have a supervisory role, as it does in other areas of the educational system.

and the 6,574 children at Integra using these extra hours represent small fractions of their total clientele.[9]

Reform planners have achieved significant goals in terms of carrying out their plan of action. They have hired professional personnel, trained supervisors and professors, improved material resources in the schools, and generated public image campaigns over the radio and television.

According to studies, these improvements have led to cognitive skill advancements in students, as well as increased student motivation and higher overall skills by the end of the first year. In addition, they have identified variables that have a positive impact on students from different backgrounds.

The results of an evaluation carried out by Cedep state that "the preschool services we studied show improved adaptation in all children. The number of children with cognitive deficits fell slightly. Overall, the opportunities and resources do not exist to achieve levels of cognitive development comparable with normal distribution."

Despite the unquestionable advances, there are still a number of challenges. The first is to increase coverage in poor and rural areas through measures ranging from legal action (following through on preschool laws that have not been enforced and writing laws to make preschool mandatory) to new financial schemes for funding education. One ultimate goal is to offer a diverse set of schooling alternatives for preschoolers, ranging from schools that just care for children to ones that actually teach specialized types of students. Reaching this goal of diversification should occur on the local as well as the national level.

The second remaining challenge is defining an institutional policy for preschools. The third is creating a system for the continued improvement of teaching.

There are also specific challenges for the different age groups of children who comprise the preschool system. For infant to 2-year-olds, the challenge is to find strategies that look beyond the traditional Junji program or that of the earliest preschools. For 2- to 4-year-olds, who are the biggest group in the system, the challenge lies in increasing coverage (77% of the population is not covered, according to a 1996 Casen study). For 5- to 6-year-olds, the challenge is passing a mandatory attendance law. Preschool is not part of mandatory schooling, but 90% of Chilean children attend in one form or another. Ensuring that the most vulnerable children attend preschool and are not pulled out is another issue that deserves attention.

Addressing these issues will help the political basis of the reform — equal opportunity in education — gain popularity.

2. ELEMENTARY EDUCATION

The enormous expansion in elementary education in Chile in the second half of the 20th century has allowed the country to overcome the coverage crunch. Although certain segments of the population still have problems gaining access to elementary education,[10] it is safe to say in general terms that elementary education in Chile is universal.

---

9   Junji has 92,000 children, ages 0 through 5, in total. Integra has 45,000 children, ages 0 through 6.
10   Ten percent of children in rural zones, which tend to be isolated geographically and have poor education systems, do not complete elementary school.

The expansion in coverage was achieved without increasing the amount of money invested into the system. The consequence however was a deterioration in the quality of education, reflected in the short school day.[11] This deterioration was the result of a drop in infrastructure investments and lack of teaching materials and supplies.

Indicators in tests like those given by the Education Quality Measurement System (Simce) reflect this backsliding. When the first Concertación government took office, the average number of objectives achieved by municipal schools for the fourth and eighth grades barely reached 50%; it was less than 60% in private schools which received public financing. The level of inequality among schools serving different socioeconomic segments of the population was significant, considering that private schools (with only private financing) achieved more than 70% of their objectives.

The main reason for the deterioration in education quality was the widespread decline of teaching conditions, which hit the poorest sectors the hardest. For example, the textbooks students received in first grade were loaned to them and had to be shared until fifth grade. Furthermore, these conditions limited library resources and the availability of teaching materials. Moreover, teaching methods and the curriculum in the elementary school system were profoundly inadequate, mainly because they were not pertinent to the conditions of poor students.

FIGURE 2

ELEMENTARY SCHOOL QUALITY AND EQUITY IMPROVEMENT PROGRAMS
US $180 Million

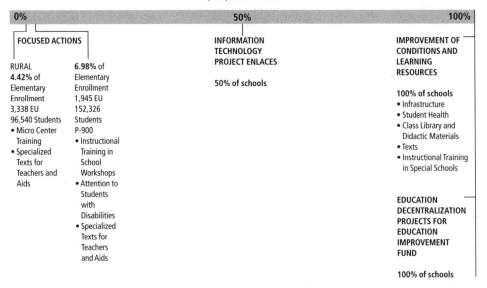

100% Coverage
10,000 Educational Units (EU)
2,180,000 Students

0%	50%	100%

FOCUSED ACTIONS

RURAL
4.42% of
Elementary
Enrollment
3,338 EU
96,540 Students
• Micro Center
Training
• Specialized
Texts for
Teachers and
Aids

6.98% of
Elementary
Enrollment
1,945 EU
152,326
Students
P-900
• Instructional
Training in
School
Workshops
• Attention to
Students
with
Disabilities
• Specialized
Texts for
Teachers
and Aids

**INFORMATION
TECHNOLOGY
PROJECT ENLACES**

50% of schools

**IMPROVEMENT OF
CONDITIONS AND
LEARNING
RESOURCES**

100% of schools
• Infrastructure
• Student Health
• Class Library and
Didactic Materials
• Texts
• Instructional Training
in Special Schools

**EDUCATION
DECENTRALIZATION
PROJECTS FOR
EDUCATION
IMPROVEMENT
FUND**

100% of schools

---

11   While the average number of school hours per year for children in developed countries is 1,200, it was only 830 in 1980 and 1,000 in the mid-1990s. The average in poorer countries is currently 865.

A plan of action drawn up by the major academic institutions in Chile at the end of the 1980s outlined areas for improvement in elementary education: quality, in terms of distribution of resources and teaching methodology; and equity, in terms of focusing on bolstering the poorest sectors. Even unconventional ideas were recommended to solve the situation. Eventually, elementary schools became known for their innovative reforms, a characteristic that Chilean education had been known for in the past.

General Description of the Reform

One of the first moves by the new Concertación government was to implement an education "emergency plan." The mainstay of the plan was the 900 Schools or P-900, which would later serve as the design framework for the MECE system. The P-900, which was financed by the Chilean government as well as the Swedish and Danish governments, was an all-out commitment to improve education in the worst 10% of schools in the country (there were 969 schools in this category). The program confronted a variety of needs in these schools, including resource distribution, faculty organization, and help for the most at-risk students.

In 1991, a US$243 million plan called the Quality-Equity Improvement Plan (MECE) was approved for the years 1992-1997. Of this total investment, US$180 million, or 70%, was invested in elementary education (Mineduc 1993). Drawing on the experience of the P-900 and various school studies, the MECE programs relied on various tactics including: direct support in the schools; targeted programming in the most vulnerable sectors; and indirect actions to promote school autonomy. In general, the MECE program had the following features at its core:

a) Thirty-seven percent of the total investment went to improving the level of learning resources and conditions. These included classroom book collections, school manuals, textbooks (which became the property of the students), didactic material, improvements in school infrastructure and health services, and teacher services.

b) Nine percent of the investment went directly to the most vulnerable sectors: rural, multi-grade schools (one room schoolhouses); one-, two-, and three-teacher establishments (just over 7 million dollars; and schools for the handicapped, which received almost US$2 million for specialized programming. Since 1994, the P-900 program has been incorporated in the MECE plan for elementary schools.

c) Ten percent of the investment went to information technology, which consisted of linking 50% of Chile's schools to a national communications network linked via e-mail and the Internet. Implementation of computer systems and software was also part of the strategy. Nine percent of the investment went to the education decentralization plan, implemented with financing from Projects for Education Improvement (PME) and designed by the individual communities.

Diagnostic Evaluation of the Reform

Improvement in Resources and Conditions

INFRASTRUCTURE

Public investment in this area has quadrupled since 1990. Through 1994, repairs were completed in more than 22% of Chile's schools. However, the lack of infrastructure investment

TABLE 2

INVESTMENT IN TEACHING AND LEARNING RESOURCES

	Program Investment (in dollars)
Texts	23,661,000
Didactic Materials	3,516,000
Class Libraries	2,991,000

Source: Elementary Quality-Equity Improvement Program, Ministry of Education.

in the years preceding this reform set schools so far back that there are still weaknesses in this area.

STUDENT HEALTH

Junaeb, the National Commission on Student Aid and Scholarships, has greatly improved its ability to deliver health services to students. Professors in grades one through six learned to diagnose learning disabilities in their students. These children get help in clinics where they are treated with medication, special glasses, or earphones. Through 1995, 233,739 children in grades one through four received such treatment. This figure surpassed the program's original goal. These improvements relied on a bold administrative system which integrated the skills of various groups, and decentralized boards and evaluation teams.

TEXTS AND DIDACTIC MATERIAL

By 1995, reformers had achieved their goal of installing a classroom book collection in every first grade class in subsidized schools (in fact, they surpassed their original goal by 10,000 libraries). Each library consists of a set of 35 to 60 books. Educators expect the libraries in grades five though eight to be completed by 1997. In addition, this reform provided dictionaries and significant didactic material to schools. Finally, the reform delivered textbooks to 100% of students. These books, contrary to in past years, became the property of each student. This shift clearly improved students' ability to learn and eased the burden on teachers.[12]

INFORMATION TECHNOLOGY (PROJECT ENLACES)

All educators recognize the importance of information systems in modern learning. However, implementing a full communications network is an enormous challenge, as it requires more than just building "computer rooms." Recognizing that information technology is a vehicle

---

12 Between 1988 and 1990, the government investedUS$1.6 million annually in textbooks. Between 1990 and 1996, the average annual amount spent on textbooks was US$4.7 million. That provided three textbooks for students in grades one through four and five textbooks for students in five through eight. Experts continually cite availability of textbooks and length of the school day as factors that most affect student learning.

TABLE 3

ADVANCES IN SIMCE FOURTH-GRADER AVERAGES
(in Spanish and Mathematics)
IN P-900 SCHOOLS

Quintile	1988	1990	1992	1994	1996
Free Schools	54.70	58.98	66.37	67.74	67.93
P-900	43.15 *	52.11	60.91	61.62	64.34
Difference	11.62	6.87	5.46	6.12	3.59

*Refers to the poorest 10% of schools in the system (objective Program population).

for growth and access to a global world, MECE's objective was to install a national computer network that would unite — before the year 2000 — 50% of Chile's schools.[13]

The project was coordinated out of the Ninth Region (southern Chile) through the Universidad de la Fontera. The program gave every school an adequate computer system, including hardware, software, and technical support in running the system. Seven technology centers, operated in conjunction with various universities throughout the country were organized to implement the program, each in its own region. They were particularly valuable in providing technological assistance and know-how. Through 1996, 500 institutions were included on the new computer network. The goal is to reach 1,500 by the end of 1997.

The communications network is supported by a software system called La Plaza that contains educational programs and allows for friendly communication between teachers and students in different schools.

Support Programs in Vulnerable Sectors
HELP FOR THE POOREST SCHOOLS (P-900)
This support program, targeting the country's poorest schools, was budgeted between 1990 and 1996 with US$16.8 million and sustained by the governments of Chile and other nations.

The institutions eligible for P-900 funding participated in elementary reform programs like other schools but because of their special condition they received special help, which included:

• Strategies to improve Spanish and Math skills. These included teacher workshops supervised by Mineduc to acquaint educators with new teaching methods. In these workshops, they worked with materials specially designed for their interactions with students.

• Learning workshops called TAPs, which were basically tutoring sessions for the most disadvantaged children. The sessions were conducted by local teenagers. Special materials were also provided for these teenagers and their pupils. Evaluative studies show that

---

13 The success and popularity of this program caused the government to promise to expand its goal, pledging that the national computer network would reach all the secondary schools in Chile as well as 50% of elementary schools. The total investment was US$120 million.

children who attended these sessions bridged the gap in cognitive skills with those who did not in four years.

- As something of a footnote to the P-900 program, a pilot program to improve management within a few individual schools was set up. This pilot has created a number of new strategies for improving school administration. It has also generated ideas for improving ties between schools, local communities, local governments, and local boards of education.

The reform's impact on teaching methods was studied by external organizations like the CDE and UNESCO. These groups underscored: the higher standards teachers had for their students (studies show the direct relationship between teacher expectations and student performance); renewed respect among the teachers for the different learning styles and needs of the students; and the development of more interactive and flexible teaching methodologies in areas such as problem solving, creating incentives to participate in class, and using the library. Moreover, professors demonstrated an improved ability to critique their own work (Gajardo 1994).

In terms of student performance, Simce reported important advances in scores in all sectors.

RURAL REFORM (MECE-RURAL)

Rural schools, which comprise 20% of all elementary schools, have traditionally been subject to the same policies as urban schools. The MECE-Rural program was the first attempt by the government to design a special policy for rural establishments. This program worked with multi-grade schools which tended to be in the worst conditions. Approximately 5% of elementary schools are multi-grade.

The MECE-Rural school reform was designed especially for such schools even though they also benefited from general elementary school reforms. The MECE-Rural plan was based on various lines of action:

- Workshops in local centers for teachers who work in isolated areas. These workshops were an opportunity for teachers to share their experiences, learn about other styles and methods, and develop new curriculum. In this sense, the workshops dealt with both theoretical and practical issues. These meeting were also used by professors to develop Education Improvement Projects (PMEs) for their respective schools. In total, 591 PMEs have been created at the 506 microcenters in Chile.
- Developing study books and texts that suit rural students. These students were also allowed to participate in the process of updating the texts.

TABLE 4

TOTAL SELECTED EDUCATION REFORM PROJECTS

	1992	1993	1994	1995	1996	92/96
Elementary Education	436	738	739	736	672	3,321
Special Education	39	69	52	58	48	266
Rural Micro Centers	–	–	104	140	347	591
Total	475	807	895	934	1,067	4,178

The rural reform is regarded as an example of good policy throughout Chile and Latin America in general for its coherence, focus, and professionalism.

LEARNING DISABILITY AND SPECIAL EDUCATION REFORM

This program, set in special education schools, used new studies and techniques to educate 2,482 teachers and 1,087 principals on how to develop programs for the learning disabled. Furthermore, the Feurstein enrichment program for special education was implemented as a pilot program in 46 schools. It trained 77 professors to teach the learning disabled.

Thorough investigation into these programs has provided valuable critiques that can be applied to future reforms for special education. These programs have served as a model for reform in other areas of the education system, especially teacher training.

Decentralization

EDUCATION REFORM PROJECTS (PME)

The Education Reform Projects (PMEs), in which the central government encourages innovative reform through decentralized policies, have become a model throughout Latin America. The MECE-Elementary reform was founded on this notion that decentralization increases efficiency and that those closest to a specific learning situation are best able to alter it.

Under the guidelines of the program, schools present their initiatives for improving education in annual competitive bids. These bids determine who receives funding for their proposals. With weight given to those schools who serve disadvantaged children and schools, projects are selected on the basis of quality. A school that obtains an award, or PME, receives funds proportional to its size (between US$2,700 and US$8,000) as well as a "teaching packet" (worth an additional US$1,500). The "teaching packet" includes a television, a VCR, educational videos, recorders, microscopes, telescopes, etc.

The government's ability to offer financial incentives to disadvantaged schools has made this program special and a cornerstone of decentralized education.

The PMEs capitalize on professors' positions in the classroom and thus their ability to develop and endorse reforms. It gave teachers and administrators flexibility. Above all, the reform encouraged collective action, as projects were developed and implemented through a consensus between professors, administrators, and sometimes students.

The effect a PME program has in schools is directly proportional to its ability to meld into the schools' curriculum and mission. Defining that mission has been the responsibility of teachers and administrators and when they have done their job well, i.e. create consensus and evaluate programs, the PMEs have been successful.

Curriculum Reform

Elementary school curriculum was altered by a new approach to learning. After consulting with professionals and carrying out studies, the government implemented the Fundamental Objectives and Minimum Requirements Plan (OFCM) for elementary schools in January 1996. The plan defined the new areas of study, improved the organizational framework for learning, and established overarching thematic subjects for students. It relied on an inclusive, consensual framework to meet the requirements of all involved. The ultimate goal of this reform was to create minimum curricular requirements for all of Chile's schools. For example, teams of specialists would frequently develop proposals for

---

TABLE 5

RESULTS OF THE EDUCATION QUALITY MEASUREMENT SYSTEM (SIMCE) EXAM
1990-1996

FOURTH YEAR
(National averages based on percent correct responses on the SIMCE examination)

	1990	1992	1994	1996
Mathematics	60.1	67.3	69.3	71.2
Spanish	61.2	68.0	67.4	71.8

EIGHTH YEAR
(National averages based on percent correct responses on the SIMCE exam)

	1991	1993	1995
Mathematics	51.63	56.27	58.21
Spanish	55.08	58.89	59.24
History	–	56.73	59.64
Science	–	54.55	58.87

FOURTH YEAR: Comparison between the top and bottom 10% of SIMCE achievements
(National averages based on percent correct responses in mathematics and Spanish)

	1990	1992	1994	1996
Top 10% of Schools	78.22	85.48	84.78	86.7
Bottom 10% of Schools	40.17	46.29	48.79	53.6
Difference	38.05	39.19	35.99	33.1

EIGHTH YEAR: Comparison between the top and bottom 10% of SIMCE achievements
(National averages based on percent correct responses in mathematics and Spanish)

	1991	1993	1995
Top 10% of Schools	74.4	78.9	79.4
Bottom 10% of Schools	33.2	37.7	38.9
Difference	41.2	41.3	40.5

curriculum reform which would then be revised and critiqued by other groups and institutions through public forums. This inclusive strategy gave the reform legitimacy with a broad cross-section of the educational community and, ultimately, the whole society.

Beginning this year, the new curriculum designs were implemented by elementary schools across the country. These reforms were carried out under the auspices of the Education Law (LOCE), which sets the guidelines for education policy for local and state government, by granting individual schools the right to develop their own curriculums.

(Mineduc provides curriculum designs for those schools who do not develop their own in-house.) To improve curriculum implementation, universities have started workshops for teachers to acquaint them with the new material.

School Hours
One radical change in Chilean education is the move to increase the number of school hours by 200 a year. Schools with financial flexibility have already implemented such changes, and the subject is popular with private school reformers. The extra 200 hours per year would boost the total to 1,200, much closer to figures in more developed countries. For now, those schools that have not had to invest in infrastructure improvements or expansions to handle the larger schooling load have been able to increase their hours. These schools tend to be small and have fewer students. Experts agree this issue will remain an important subject of conversation so long as funds are available for implementing such change on a large scale. Financing, however, is not the only challenge. Using the extra school hours to increase learning is also an important topic of discussion. More hours in school ultimately means creating legal measures and incentives to take classroom advantage of the extra time.

Impact on Learning Test Results
According to the national Simce test, the government achieved its goal of increasing average student scores by five percentage points in the basic areas of study. In addition, the traditional gap between the worst schools and regions and the best was slightly reduced.

Results for students in grades 1-4 actually beat the average by jumping 9.2 percentage points in math and 6.2 percentage points in Spanish. In grades 4-8, students only outdid the average in math with a 6.58 percentage increase. Their Spanish scores only rose by 4.16%.

The goal of creating more equity between the bottom and top Simce scorers was not fully achieved, especially in grades 4-8, although there was some improvement. The fact that grade 1-4 students made greater strides than their counterparts in grades 5-8 was expected because many of the new reform programs targeted that group.

The graph shows that general learning is improving, but the reforms and increased budgets have not done much to narrow the gap between the best and worst students. With this in mind, more programs focused squarely on the most disadvantaged students, i.e. those who received the worst scores, are needed to bring equity to Chile's elementary school system.

3. SECONDARY SCHOOL

Evaluation, Emergency Measures, and Long-Term Strategies (1990-1994)
At the outset of the first Concertación government, there was no overarching measure of evaluation for Chile's secondary schools, although experts did share some common concerns. First, they agreed that Chile's secondary school program lacked identity. That is, it lacked focus and a mission. Second, they said its purpose was basically irrelevant because of its poor reputation and the low value its degree held in the economy. Moreover, this was the schooling period when many poor Chileans dropped out. Third, experts believed the schools were not connected to society as a whole because their curriculum inadequately

dealt with larger issues. Last, they argued that Chile's secondary schools reflected the enormous inequality of the system as a whole. The unequal distribution of resources disproportionately affected the poor. Taken together, these four points formed a line of criticism which came to be called "the crisis in secondary schools," (Cariola and Cox 1991).

Despite the problems, the government decided not to significantly reform secondary schools for two reasons: it had not gathered enough information to attack specific problems, and its priority was improving conditions in elementary schools. It did however develop a two-point program for secondary schools that combined improved technical resources at schools with a foundation of knowledge on which to build a future reform program.

The technology improvement plan was created at the behest of low-income families and because it led to employment opportunities[14] (an issue in light of high unemployment rates among recent graduates). The technology program reinforced a concept central to previous secondary school reforms in that study material and curriculums should be closely linked to the workplace. Years later, when a better system for evaluating secondary schools was developed, this concept was called into question when the link between technology and the workplace was rethought.

One component of the MECE-Elementary plan that carried over to secondary schools was the effort to perfect an evaluation framework that would allow experts to assess progress in the secondary school system. The ultimate goal was to acquire a sufficiently broad basis of knowledge on which to carry out a full-fledged reform. As part of this

---

FIGURE 3

Strategy and Components of the Secondary Quality-Equity Improvement Program

Definition of a New Curricular Framework (Curriculum and Evaluation)

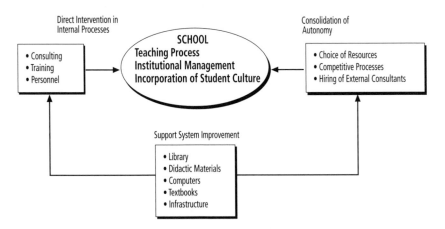

---

14 For a detailed analysis of the program, see Belleï (1996).

MECE program, the following were developed: 13 studies — dedicated to various areas like curriculum, teaching methods, evaluation frameworks, administration, and student recruitment — conducted by Chile's most prestigious study centers; a new "town-hall" dialogue, organized by Mineduc, which united 30,000 people from 2,000 groups to discuss educational reform; and a series of surveys designed to test new programs on school communities. These two years of research, overseen by Mineduc, not only served to collect a wealth of information on secondary schools but also to create an important precedent for public policy in education.

The word *anachronism* best described the general state of secondary education in Chile. In short, its orientation, organization, and curriculum were based on a past that no longer reflected reality. Both society in general, which has changed its relationship with development, institutions, and information, and the students, who are more diverse than before, made Chile's style of education outdated. This gap between secondary school practices and reality manifested itself in various problems. The government was aware of this and accepted the fact that only a major reform to secondary schools would resolve the core of the matter. It was generally agreed that any major reform would have to tackle structural issues such as administration, curriculum, and linkages with society, and be accompanied by important legal and political shifts. Implementing a series of smaller reforms in advance, experts said, would help secondary schools improve their internal workings and their ability to evaluate themselves. Such mini-reforms would ultimately carve out a fertile ground for full-scale reform in secondary schools.

MECE-Secondary School Program (1995-2000)[15]
While the MECE-Secondary School Program defines a series of proactive steps, it is better observed by considering the subjects it does not broach. They include: coverage (neither attracting new students nor lowering the drop-out rate); adult education; teacher training; and school financing.

The current central idea of the program is to strengthen the fundamental processes that occur, or should occur, within the school themselves. The plan is focused on the *teaching process* which includes teacher-student relations and the development of general activities and resources. Its central principle is incorporating the issues and trends that matter to the students into schooling itself. The plan encourages self-thinking and self-critique among students as a basis for increasing equal educational opportunities.

The program also seeks to redefine the substance of secondary schooling; this area especially will be redefined in coming years. The MECE-Secondary School program includes a branch focusing on developing a new Fundamental Objectives and Minimum Requirements (OFCM) system for core curriculum.[16] These new objectives and requirements

---

15 This section describes the MECE-Secondary School Program and its implementation into the school system, as well as outlining some basis for evaluation. External evaluations of the MECE-Secondary School Program were not available for inclusion in this analysis.

16 In June 1997, Mineduc introduced its OFCM proposal for secondary schools and called for a national debate on it. In March 1998, the revised proposals were sent to the High Council on Education for approval, which was granted in April. This act paved the way for new study and reform programs to be applied in 1999. In addition, a national system for evaluating secondary schools was developed in conjunction with the new programs.

will be established throughout the country as mandated by LOCE. The new additions seek to renovate the secondary school curriculum by making it more accessible to young people. In the spirit of reconnecting students with their education, the new curriculum was developed by teams of experts, teachers, and, for the first time, students.

Moreover, observers agree that secondary schools would also benefit from longer school days.[17] Additional hours could especially help poorer students who lack the family structure to complement their education. In coming years, Chilean secondary schools will undoubtedly recover the standards for longer days that once guided these schools.

It seems clear, however, that both areas of reform — curriculum and length of the school day — will only be successful if the MECE-Secondary School programs function well at the student level. In other words, the conditions for revising the curriculum and expanding the school day must be derived from a higher level of student learning and achievement.

To reach these goals, three reform mechanisms are necessary (see Figure 3): improving the material resources that are integral to the learning process; attempting *direct* actions to carry out the reforms; and attempting *indirect* actions to give schools more autonomy in running and reforming their programs.

Material Resources
The reform plan stipulates that the minimum for improving this area involves: various infrastructure improvements (including furniture); an endowment for all schools to provide high-quality books to be housed in academic libraries (including subscriptions to magazines and newspapers); modern teaching materials; textbooks, with an eye to newer curriculum, for every student and professor (for the first time all secondary school students will have their own textbooks); and new computer technology (including software and technical support) to teach students how to learn through computers. Schools will also receive a national computer linkup, Enlaces, and Internet capabilities.

Direct Actions
First, the installation of Professional Work Groups (GPT) in every school has helped speed the education reform. These groups are designed to help professors revise and evaluate their own work, make their lesson plans more flexible to meet the changing needs of their students and create a dynamic foundation for improving teaching methodology, evaluation, and design.

Second, the proposal to modernize the administration of individual schools calls for setting up an Institutional Administration Team in every school that promotes the participation of members of the school community, especially professors and students, in decision-making. It also calls for an Institutional Education Project to centralize projects and initiatives within the school and to develop institutional policies.

Last, observers agree that schools would benefit from the development of an Optional Extra Curricular Program (ACLE). ACLE would be comprised of a series of workshops in various areas, such as the environment, communications, art, and sports. Students would attend

---

17 In 1997, 198 secondary schools implemented the Complete School Day plan (longer hours). These 198 schools represent 15% of all schools in the country, and comprise 13% of all secondary school students.

TABLE 6

SECONDARY QUALITY-EQUITY IMPROVEMENT
PROGRAM FINANCIAL RESOURCES

	Resource Type–Total Program Cost (in millions of dollars)	Total Cost per School (in millions of pesos)
Textbooks	25.0	8.0
Library Books	26.3	8.4
Didactic Material	9.3	3.0
Technology	29.2	9.3
Infrastructure (Improvement)*	26.9	8.6
Infrastructure (Equipment)	22.0	7.0
PME Projects and External Consulting	27.3	8.7
Direct Training and Support **	40.5	12.9
Total	206.5	65.9

*   Only includes municipal schools

** Includes seminar and workshop attendance and training; discussion materials and direct support of program activities; Ministry of Education coordination, consulting, and supervision; costs of the elaboration of the new secondary education curricular framework.

Source: Secondary Quality-Equity Improvement Program, Ministry of Education.

these sessions on a voluntary basis and help guide and direct them, along with teacher mentors. These workshops have three objectives: (1) keep children occupied in their free time in educational and creative ways. In doing so, communities can take advantage of school facilities when classes are not scheduled; (2) build school spirit by giving students a way of identifying themselves with their school; and (3) provide educational lessons about citizenship and responsibility that may ultimately increase their motivation to learn inside the classroom.

The strategy that underlies these proposals relies on participation (seminars, exchange programs), technical support from supervisors at Mineduc, and work materials, especially for self-teaching (videos, guides).

Indirect Action

The reform proposes a number of indirect actions to make schools more autonomous and better able to capitalize on their specific strengths. These mechanisms are activated from within the schools themselves and focus on the use of financial, material, and human resources.

First, the reform grants book catalogs, teaching materials (developed through strict public bidding processes), and a sum of resources, allocated according to the size of the student body, with which professors can draw up a list of materials they need. Through this system, 80% of books and almost all teaching materials are financed. Accordingly, each school can build its own library or resource center according to the needs of its students. Moreover, efficiency can be maximized when students themselves help decide what materials the school needs.

Second, the plan calls for a fund for projects — similar to the MECE-Elementary Plan — to which all schools have access. Through this program, teachers should design

Education Improvement Projects (PMEs) to improve their teaching capacity. This would aid in providing educational answers to the growing question of how to serve an increasingly diverse group of students.

Last, in order to satisfy teachers and enrich learning experiences, teams of teachers can hire external consulting teams through the Directory of Technical Assistance, which is comprised of 260 Chilean institutions. These institutions are usually universities. (To a lesser extent, think-tanks, institutions, and private companies also provide technical assistance.)

The Current Situation

The MECE-Secondary School Program provides universal coverage at 1,300 establishments. The different reform strategies are implemented in a variety of ways depending on the school — all at once, in order, or at the discretion of the individual institution. Because these mechanisms are being implemented at varying paces, one secondary school may not resemble its counterpart. Although no impact studies have been completed, it seems in general that the fruits of the MECE-Secondary School Program are beginning to appear.

All of the country's secondary schools have received the first part of their library and have defined which titles will appear in the second part (end of 1997); have received the basic equipment in the technology packet; and have requested the first half of their teaching materials. All of the textbooks on language and math have been distributed for first- and second-year students. In addition, 461 schools (a little more than a third of the total) have been incorporated into the Enlaces computer-based information program. This year all municipal schools (more than 500) will be brought into the reform program and receive infrastructure investment. The review of 392 PME-Secondary School selections has begun and 770 schools now have resources and information to contract outside technical assistance.

Despite the absence of impact studies, it seems that efforts by Professional Work Groups (GPT) have begun in almost all of Chile's secondary schools as has the construction of student space for the Optional Extracurricular Program. The deployment of these programs has demonstrated that schools are experimenting with their general organizational structure and administration. The strategy for building libraries seems to have been converted into a multi-faceted Learning Resource Center Plan.

Two categories of principal problems have emerged in the area of secondary school reform. First, the quality of the implementation and operation of these programs is entirely dependent on a school's internal functioning. For instance, the amount of time students have to work on new projects is directly related to their schedule and the amount of support they receive from teachers. Many of the new projects rely on teacher-student dialogue which may or may not exist. Furthermore, school principals may be resistant to change. Second, schools receive different components of the reform plan at different times, thereby losing the ability to participate in complementary development programs. The schools also may compete for students. In other cases, the reform grant is not sufficient to rouse interest in solving the school's problems. Finally, in many cases the reform produces a "rigidization" of action in which specific strategies and ideas are sought at all costs. When this occurs, the notion of flexibility at the heart of the reform is lost.

Despite the difficulties and the challenges that lie ahead, it seems that the MECE-Secondary School reform has helped secondary schools emerge from an extended period of crisis in which expectations were eroded and perspectives were skewed.

4. CRITICAL ANALYSIS OF PROGRAMS AS EDUCATION REFORM

With so many strategies for reforming education, it is useful to analyze the top programs and consider their implementation and utility, their strengths and weaknesses, and their origin. More than just an impact statement, this critical analysis of program strategy and function is meant to identify which mechanisms need to be improved.

Teaching and Teaching Methodology

Evaluations
One of the notable achievements of the 1990s in Chilean education is the development of a systematic manner of gathering and evaluating information. This assessment system is frequently carried out by independent academic institutions, whose early work during the military government laid the groundwork for the boom of the 1990s. The major programs of the decade, like the P-900 and the MECE-Elementary plan, were founded on evaluation and information gathering. In secondary schools, major reforms were put off precisely because of the dearth of information on which to base new programs.

At every level of schooling, these analyses and studies take different tacks to find ways to maximize resources, work patterns, and competitive advantages. They offer specific and pertinent ideas and arguments for new programs. Moreover, because the studies are often performed by different groups working together, they can create consensus on educational reform.

Teaching Objectives
In general terms, the improvements that have been made in teaching objectives and strategies have had a direct effect on the quality of students' education. These improvements have transformed the role of teachers, giving them better didactic resources, more autonomy, and greater motivation.

This new teaching system has become widely accepted, partly because there was general agreement that old concepts needed to be reformed. More importantly, this system has given the Ministry of Education a new sense of legitimacy, especially in the area of teaching methodology and technique. The Ministry has achieved widely-accepted common ground in this area. It is safe to say that this common ground has laid the foundation for a significant shift in the philosophy of education in Chile.

Design of a School Reform
At every level, the MECE program demanded that schools adjust to the idea of implementing reforms and new programs. In terms of strategy, a number of methods were used: they included direct intervention, decentralized action, autonomous actions by the schools themselves, use of incentives and competitions, and outsourced consulting and assistance. The design of the MECE-Secondary School Program — three years after the MECE programs for Preschool and Elementary school — drew on previous experiences to create an implementation strategy that combined new assistance mechanisms, greater resources, and more autonomy for schools.

Remaining Challenges in Teaching Concepts
Despite the general acceptance of these ideas, it is still a challenge to incorporate the individual changes of every new program into a larger system that represents a true shift in the teaching paradigm. This is important because without the paradigm shift, individual programming changes will lose value. To ensure this does not occur, more information about successful programs and achievements is needed. In addition, exchanges of ideas and personnel will allow teachers to see new perspectives and share concrete models that will help solidify educational reforms.

Reform Acceptance
Due to the fact that these reforms grant professors and administrators a key role in the reform process, their willingness to accept the goals and strategies of the reforms is central to their success. However, it is not possible to measure this level of acceptance now because sufficient information on the subject has not been compiled.
It does seem, however, that when new programs arrive in the hands of teachers, either directly or through other means (through education reform representatives or self-explanatory directions and guidelines), they are understood and generally well-liked. It seems that few professors oppose or attempt to subvert the new reforms.

Weaknesses in Coordination and Administration
A number of weaknesses exist in the coordination of the reforms, mostly because teachers are unfamiliar with the new programs' administrative or legal foundations. Furthermore, the bureaucratic committees that may design the reforms have little contact with the schools. These problems have made program implementation difficult in some areas. They have also slowed timetables for reforms and in some cases created friction between schools and bureaucracies.

Weaknesses in Objectives for Student Management
The necessity to refocus the learning experience on teaching rather than management has led to a shortage of proposals on administering students and general organization. Experience has shown that the schools that have successfully implemented administrative reform have strong principals. When these leaders do not exist, however, the lack of coordination from the top of the school structure weakens reform programs and teacher motivation.
The natural friction between the teachers and the administration tends to keep this issue off the reform agenda. Initiatives dealing with these issues frequently fall apart and are often forgotten.

Weaknesses in Relying on External Actors in School Reform
In some cases, the choice of external players to participate in or assist with reforms has dogged new programs and hampered their success. For example, the programs fail to take into account that schools report to two very different organizations (their financial backers, administratively; and Mineduc, in terms of teaching and oversight) and provide no coordination mechanisms to address this difference. The technical supervisors who implement reform programs at a given school are frequently unaware of the school's financial situation. This issue has been fundamental in an ongoing conflict that has arisen over teacher salaries and hours. Additionally, coordination regarding the reforms between

schools and families/communities has been poor, except in preschools and grades 1-4 in elementary schools.

The real challenge lies in defining what type of links between schools and external actors — such as families, municipalities, Mineduc, and local communities — are most suitable. Better communication about the roles and responsibilities of the different groups and the schools themselves is also needed.

Weaknesses in Program Coordination

Coordinating the use of various reform programs is essential to their success. Part of the problem is the lack of coordination in the different aspects of the programs themselves. In general, the void in implementation standards means that programs compete for students and resources, provoking a sense of unevenness. The programs sometimes compete for teachers as well. In addition, local bureaucracies and school boards begin implementing programs before prioritizing and coordinating them. This has weakened a number of programs.

Another coordination conflict stems from the gap between prevailing student culture and the orientation of the programs. These differences are frequently built-in to the respective sides and are thus difficult to modify. They can have a serious effect on the success of new programs. This "student culture" gap widens when one considers that the reform programs often try to change student culture. This is one of the great paradoxes of the education reform: it seeks to develop new student culture by using current student culture as the building block.

Communication Challenges

Public policy in the 1990s has been founded on the notion that education has an important effect on society and the economy overall, but much less has been said about the impact those two areas have on education. If we accept that education is part of the cultural fabric of a society, then attempting to reform schools, to the extent Chile has reformed, implies altering that fabric to achieve some type of cultural change.

Part of the education reform has mandated schools to work more closely with their local communities and other outside groups. To really achieve a cultural shift, however, more is required. Drawing a broader link between schools and communities, making school reforms more visible, stating the legitimacy of school reforms in public, incorporating families, and informing politicians and business leaders are necessary steps in this direction. Ultimately, a society that understands and supports the reforms will make them more successful.

This implies improving the public relations and communications aspects of schools so they can publicize relevant experiences and efforts.

Challenges to "Open Design"

The process of incremental reform is only possible if it is accompanied by an "open design" policy; that is, maintaining flexibility and adaptability in regards to the implementation of new programs and their contexts. In effect, the most successful programs are accompanied by an "open design" policy. It is one of the great strengths of current education reform policy.

To continue building on this policy, mechanisms to encourage and handle constant program redesign are necessary throughout the school system. These mechanisms are at present insufficient in the Ministry of Education and in many schools. What is desired is a system of evaluation and alignment that sets a significant goal (cultural shifts in education, teaching social values, etc.) and attempts to reach it with or without its original parameters and timetables.

The illusion constructed by official plans hides the real nature of how changes can be made in productive ways during the course of the program. It seems that certain in-house changes have had greater effects than would initially appear and in some cases have provided the basis for major changes that will lead the next generation of reforms.

There is also a significant amount of experimentation in the area of teaching methodology which needs to be reviewed to judge its appropriateness.

Remaining Challenges for a "Program Strategy"

It was common knowledge in the early 1990s that Chile's education sector faced three challenges: shifting the cultural paradigm to realize the goals of quality and equity; providing better coverage and resources to Chile's youth; and modernizing and decentralizing administrative bodies, a goal which has still not been fully attained. The best education strategy is one that combines these three concerns with a focus on teaching. With this goal as the utmost concern, the resources to change schools' administration styles can be generated.

In practice, teaching concerns still do not guide education policy or financial/administrative efforts within the schools. This problem coincides with a growing sentiment of discontent among teachers and principals who sometimes feel that decisions on reforms are not made collectively. The programs themselves do not provide mechanisms to overcome these obstacles. This situation will undoubtedly increase tensions over the next few years, adding to pressure for new solutions.

The Grand Challenge of Equity in Education

The reform programs are formulated on the concept of equity in education: providing more resources where there are shortages. This principle is applied throughout the education system. "Achieving quality education for all" has been the guiding philosophy. In this way, the reform programs represent the best that education policy has to offer.

All the programs strive to incorporate this principle. The P-900, the MECE-Rural program and the preschool programs are particularly focused, through the use of new methods, on helping the most vulnerable sectors. The PME and MECE-secondary school bids, while not specifically devoted to the poorest students, consider these groups by granting awards to the schools in worst condition.

However, much work still needs to be done to make the Chilean school system a level playing field: (1) financial resources for programs targeted to the poorest sectors account for a relatively small percentage of the total educational reform budget when one considers the severity of the problems these sectors face; (2) some reform strategies are insufficient to overcome shortages. In particular, the P-900 program has revealed a "hardcore poverty" in education that shows a chronic inability to improve. In this sense the PME appears to be appropriate for schools with a minimum level of resources but not for every school; and (3) in the poorest sectors, the fundamental equity problem — access to education — has not been resolved.[18]

The main obstacle to improving the poorest schools, aside from their inability to use new resources in positive ways, is that the reform programs clash with the existing cultural trends of the students and the schools themselves. In poor areas, teachers and principals face the challenge of developing an attitude for learning among students that makes students open to another type of school culture.

The overall concepts of quality and equity are implicit in Mineduc's programs and are the crux of the MECE programs. However, more radical measures are required to ensure that they are integrated into education policy.

This discussion of equality and equity requires asking more complex, theoretical questions:

• What other segments of society need to take action so that investments in education, which are regarded now as a matter of social policy, are more effective? In the education policy of the 1990s, two occasionally antithical concepts guide government policy: the State perceives education as a public policy designed to improve the country's human capital, but its involvement in education is also regarded as a type of social policy used to narrow the gap between rich and poor. At the heart of the tension between the two aims is the need to integrate the concept of education more deeply within the range of social policy, and not just as a means of increasing economic activity.[19]
• How do reformers ensure that they attack different problems in diverse ways? The success of reform is based on the notion that reformers are capable of generating appropriate responses to every situation. Bad results do not always stem from the same source, and merely equating poverty and low results is overly simplistic. Every school has a different ability to use the resources it possesses. As such, studies on resource shortages and the like can be problematic when used as criteria for designing reform programs.

These questions once again reveal the urgent need for a systematic framework for making evaluations, not just for general sectors, but rather for areas that have been neglected. This subject takes on greater importance when one considers that more advantaged schools are better prepared to capitalize on reforms while the lack of resources tends to chronically marginalize poorer schools.

Creating such an evaluation system is reliant, like everything else, on the most basic assumption: that more resources can successfully narrow the gap between poor and rich schools and make schooling more egalitarian. As was mentioned above, the amount of investment in equity in education is still insufficient.

---

18 According to the 1996 Casen study, the difference in preschool coverage between the fifth and first socioeconomic quintiles is 26%; in secondary education, it is 22%. In 1994, the preschool rate of coverage in urban areas was twice that of rural areas; in secondary education it was over 30%. Reformers have not resolved this problem of equity and, based on their programming plans, are not prepared to do so.
19 See I. Núñez, "Politica social en educacion: equidad, calidad, cualidad" in the *Revista de Trabajo Social* (Santiago) 68.

TABLE 7

MINISTRY OF EDUCATION EXPENSES, 1982-1997

Year	Ministry of Education Expense (millions of 1997 pesos)	Ministry of Education Expense Index (1982 base=100)	Monthly Student Subsidy (in 1997 pesos)	Subsidy Index (1982 base=100)
1982	646,542	100	11,582	100
1983	599,666	93	9,955	86
1984	583,726	90	9,351	81
1985	583,148	90	8,784	76
1986	530,378	82	9,827	85
1987	487,771	75	9,226	80
1988	504,710	78	9,329	81
1989	492,615	76	9,345	81
1990	469,688	73	8,874	77
1991	511,120	79	9,159	79
1992	578,827	90	10,016	87
1993	646,871	100	10,904	94
1994	702,094	109	12,145	105
1995	810,308	125	14,346	124
1996	925,529	143	15,936	138
1997	1,032,262	160	17,214	149

Source: Ministry of Education, Planning and Budget Division 1997.

II. Reform Politics

1. FINANCING

Increasing Resources

At the outset of the first Concertación government, resource shortages were acute and were felt in every sector of the education system: student subsidies were insufficient; teacher salaries were very low; investments in infrastructure were stagnant; and funds for improving education policy were almost non-existent. The 1980s was the decade of the systematic collapse of education resources. Chile's economic recession (1982-1983) and lack of attention to education did not help matters. The economic growth of the late 1980s did not improve the situation. In 1990, government expenditures on education had been reduced by more than a quarter from their 1982 levels, even as enrollment figures rose (especially in secondary schools).[20]

The Concertación governments have reversed this trend and have significantly increased financing for education. The financial resources allocated to education in 1997 more than double those for 1990.

---

20 In the case of elementary education, for example, coverage rose from 95% to 98% in spite of the fact that 100,000 less students enrolled during the decade.

TABLE 8

PUBLIC RESOURCES ALLOTTED TO EDUCATION

Year	As Percentage of Total Public Spending	As Percentage of GNP
1987	13.7	3.2
1988	13.2	2.8
1989	13.1	2.6
1990	13.2	2.5
1991	13.4	2.6
1992	13.7	2.7
1993	13.8	2.8
1994	14.2	2.8
1995	14.9	2.8

Source: Budget Administration (1997) Estadística de las finanzas públicas, Ministry of Housing, Santiago, Chile.

However, despite this significant increase, the proportion of funds which education receives from the government is still insufficient. It is lower than that of comparable countries and far from levels in developed nations.

Graph 2 shows that the Concertación governments have allocated increasing funds to education as a share of the national budget. The total increase has been two percentage points over 10 years, which is more than any other social sector and comparable only to the increase in infrastructure. But when considered in light of its percentage of GDP — a mere 3.1% — it becomes clear that education needs more fiscal attention. In fact, as a percentage of GDP, education in 1997 has not recovered the levels of a decade ago (which were already a percentage point lower than earlier levels). Comparable countries have an average of 3.7% of total GDP for education, while in developed countries the figure stands at over 5% (National Commission for the Modernization of Education, 1995).

It is clear that the volume of resources schools require can not be met by the State. Keeping in mind the government's pledge to continue increasing investment in education, consensus exists that more private funds are necessary. There are a number of avenues through which private institutions can contribute to education. The most important ones are the Education Donation Law and Shared Financing Law, both from 1993.

The donation law provides a system of tax incentives to companies who contribute money. Its effect has been limited, however, and it is not utilized often. It is only commonplace for schools that rely on corporations for funding. Municipal schools in particular have failed to benefit from the law.[21] In 1996, approximately 170 institutions received some form of private donations totaling US$8 million (10% of this total was obtained through shared financing). Among the principle causes for the under-utilization of the law are poor information distribution about the project, complex legal technicalities, the fact that it operated not through the school system but rather through a "parallel" system (Regional

---

21 Of the private resources earmarked for education in1996, 44% go to schools reliant on corporate financing, 43% go to public schools, and only 13% go to municipal schools.

TABLE 9

SHARED FINANCING: TOTAL RESOURCES COLLECTED BY YEAR
(in millions of dollars)

1994	1995	1996	Total 1994-96
35	55	80	170

Source: Fortalecimiento Institucional, Ministerio de Educación

Cooperation and Planning Offices) and the inferior nature of programs administered by municipal and school officials.

On the other hand, the shared financing system has enjoyed rapid and widespread success. The system authorizes schools which receive state funds (except municipal elementary schools) to charge parents a monthly rate. In 1996, almost 25% of all students attended school under the co-payment plan. The system generated US$150 million in its first three years.[22]

The shared financing system has significantly increased school resources, but has also had some negative side-effects such as reinforcing social segregation and segmentation among students. In spite of its clear ability to generate much-needed financing, the system's divisive nature, especially since educational reform is meant to create opportunity for all students, has called its legitimacy into question.

Clearly, both laws have had ambiguous results, especially in terms of exacerbating inequalities in the system (perhaps because they were designed with financial criteria, not educational reform, in mind).

Taken together, however, the prospects for public and private financing in the medium term seem to be improving. The government, through its Finance Ministry, has defined education as its "top priority" (1994) and established 7% of GDP as the national investment goal. Later, the National Commission for Modernizing Education set the target at 8% of GDP for the year 2002.[23]

Use of Financial Resources
Educational reform has been concerned with boosting school financing. While much work is still needed, this has dramatically improved the depleted state of school funding which the Concertación governments inherited. Subsidies for students, after regaining previous values, have risen 50% above initial levels. The quality-equity programs (P-900, MECE-Elementary, and MECE-Secondary School) have received almost US$500 million, invested over the decade. Investments in infrastructure have risen four-fold from US$22 million in 1990 to US$88 million in 1996, in 1996 dollars. Teacher salaries have also spiraled 80% in real terms.

---

22 It is worth making a comparison to emphasize the importance of these resources: in 1996, shared financing brought in US$80 million. The total expenditure in that year for the MECE-Elementary and MECE-Secondary School programs was US$66 million.

23 In 1994, the Commission estimated that 4.5% of GDP would go toward education. Other estimations put the figure closer to 6%.

In general, school subsidies have risen. However, these gains are not spread equally through the entire system. They have gone to areas which the government is eager to promote, such as special education and adult education, and to secondary school technical programs, where operating costs need to be met. In other areas, the government has raised the minimum amount for rural schools and has perfected its internal system of calculating grants.

The government has focused on paying *back debt*, on the one hand, and on strategic *future investments*, on the other. On both sides, a minimum acceptable threshold has been established. As a result, certain groups have withheld their acquiescence to agreements on certain issues until a satisfactory minimum floor on financial issues is met. This occurs with financial backers in the case of subsidies and with teachers on salary issues. The entire term of the first Concertación administration was spent recovering the previous value of student subsidies. Meanwhile, salary increments for teachers are preceded by the announcement that the increase is "better but not enough."

The above, along with communication difficulties among the various groups, explain some of the difficulty in converting the reform's priority (expressed as bolstered financial resources) into a political successful political reality (in terms of labor unions and vows of support for the reform).

Remaining Tasks

With regard to school financing, one central issue remains unresolved: finding mechanisms to distribute public resources to schools.

The per-student educational subsidy is one of the most important legacies of Chile's dictatorship because it was the cornerstone of the "education market" in the country. Later, academics discredited these subsidies as a means of improving the quality of education through competition. They said families were not choosing programs on the basis of quality and that the system provoked distortions in the learning process. They also noted that these subsidies made administration more difficult for some schools (see Espinola, 1989; or Cox and Courard 1996). Fifteen years of such subsidies have revealed that their primary goals — efficiency and quality — have not been fully met. Of the two, only efficiency has been partly achieved. Few people still believe that orthodox neo-liberalism can generate quality education.

The Concertación maintained the subsidies for students because the government thought they were a good source of financing and that they increased efficiency in educational investments. In practical terms, subsidy supporters say such financial aid helps to cover the operating costs of different types of educational programs (technical, professional, humanistic, scientific, urban, and rural) while offering incentives for programs that are not profitable from a market standpoint, such as programs for rural areas, low-density areas and extreme poverty. Such a reality however would create a highly unbalanced subsidy system, based solely on the plans of clients and available market options.

Furthermore, the government has recognized the intrinsic limitations of subsidies in making sustained improvements in reform programs because their market orientation leads them away from the reform's goals of quality improvement and equal opportunity. These goals require large pools of financial assistance guided by good policy, not market profits or political games.

Unfortunately, no significant alternatives to subsidies are on the horizon despite the fact that many groups reject them. Some liberal (associated by no means exclusively with

MUNICIPAL SECTOR TEACHERS' SALARIES (30 HOUR WORK WEEK)
(in 1996 pesos)

Year	Average Monthly Salary (Teacher employed 20 years)	Accumulated Real Increase with Respect to 1990 (percentages)
1990	141,674	–
1991	150,671	6.35
1992	173,438	22.42
1993	191,962	35.50
1994	218,741	54.40
1995	241,240	70.28
1996	256,997	81.40

Source: Ministry of Education, *La Reforma en marcha*, Santiago, Chile (no date)

the political right) propose channeling all public resources for education into subsidy increases. The government proposes complementing the subsidy system with other means of financing.

The challenge in this area is identifying funding mechanisms that are geared toward improving quality in education rather than merely providing services and that reorient public officials' ability to allocate and channel funds for education.

2. TEACHERS

The definition of teachers labor' terms and social function is by no means simple or agreed upon. In recent times, the subject of teachers roles, qualifications, and identities have been a subject of discussion.

- The tradition of *state educators* assigns teachers the role of public servant. Under that definition, they operate under the guidelines of the government and local bureaucracies. They also enjoy certain benefits such as job stability.
- Through the course of the labor struggle in Chile, teachers have been defined as *workers in education* (as "intellectual workers"). This designation was intended to align them with the working class and labor groups. This process was reinforced by the period of "proletariatization" which teachers endured during the military regime.
- In the 1980s, the forces of decentralization and privatization made teaching a private labor market, equating teachers with other types of workers. This stripped teachers of their special status within the job market and provoked a sort of identity crisis.
- The ensuing academic debate has not resolved these identity questions, and there are still different definitions of what teachers do and who they are.

The Concertación has defined a proposal to "professionalize" teachers but it has not been fully developed. The government has not delved into the complexities of the philosophy or history of teaching, and it has stopped short of developing a meaningful concept of Chilean educators.

The central role teachers play in reforming education obliges the government to resolve these issues. The first step in doing this is redefining teachers' roles and unifying their interests with reforms.

Taken together, the political policies directed at improving teachers' working conditions implemented over the last decade can be divided into three groups: (1) material improvements and intellectual enrichment; (2) higher salaries; and (3) the elaboration of a legal statute regulating teaching.

Material Improvements and Intellectual Enrichment

Each of the Education Improvement Programs introduced mechanisms to improve teaching conditions. They provided teachers with better teaching materials, such as computers and textbooks. With schools deciding autonomously how to use their funds, more money is now being allocated to the teaching process. In addition, new resources are being devoted to the intellectual enrichment of teachers themselves. These resources include manuals, self-teaching materials, and technical assistance.

The instructors have been slow to acknowledge these gains despite the fact that thousands of them have benefited. There are two possible explanations for this phenomenon.

The first is that the government reform has offended teachers by emphasizing students at their expense. In its public presentation of reform strategies, the government omitted improving teaching resources. It has played up the reforms that *improve education*, not those that *improve the learning process*. For teachers, it is difficult to see how the reforms will improve their skills or develop their careers. Some see the reform as a mandate coming from above that demands obedience from teachers.

The second explanation is that the teachers' unions have not shown great foresight with respect to the reform and the government, which the union regards as a failure in defining teachers' roles and objectives. The unions have not developed an adequate framework for discussing the new changes that are sweeping through education. In some ways, this refusal to acclimate to the new trends has excluded them from active participation in the reform process. This situation is being played out in the schools themselves with thousands of teachers taking sides on issues in which the unions are not well-versed.

Salaries

At the end of the military regime, two problems plagued the discussion over teacher salaries. First, there was the chronic deterioration of salaries which was a product of lowered subsidies. Salaries reached very low levels, approximately US$300 per month in real terms. Second, the salary scale was varied because the job market had been deregulated and different employers attached different values to teaching.[24] Through 1991's Law 19,070, which became known as the "Teachers Statute," the government tried to correct both problems. The law created a salary structure that provided benefits based on a number of special categories, such as experience, performance, working conditions (rural

---

24 The average hourly wage for elementary school teachers in municipal schools and private ones varied between US$4.90 andUS$3.68. In the private schools, salaries ranged from US$8.21 to US$1.27 per hour. (Mineduc 1997)

areas, isolated areas, social marginalization), and responsibilities.[25] It also established teachers' right to a basic minimum salary (expressed in an hourly wage backed by law).

Through successive increases in the minimum salary[26] and the establishment of a minimum total salary (benefits included) if the benefits do not exceed a certain amount — common among young professors in under-subsidized school zones — the two Concertación governments have significantly lifted teachers' salaries.

The government and the Teachers' Board have negotiated every salary increase. Up until now, three concepts have been used in making the increases, although the government and the board have not seen eye-to-eye on them. The first, what is known as "basic dignity" has been used to elevate the minimum salary. The government favors these increases because they have an ethical component and they attract younger teachers. A great symbolic step in this regard was taken in 1998 when the government decided to make new teachers' income equal to that of first-year public servants. Although the Teachers' Board has often trumpeted this concept, recently they have come to realize that as a tool this approach is ineffective in securing grassroots support within the organization (primarily because it affects a very limited number of teachers who hold even more meager lobbying power). As the minimum national salary continues to rise, the concept of "minimum income" is doomed to disappear or become part of the minimum salary.

The second concept guiding these increases, known as "public servant," is oriented toward associating salaries with a number of personal or labor conditions considered valuable. These valued conditions are the entitlements and benefits noted earlier. This package of benefits is highly valued by teachers' unions. Accordingly, it is the least valued by the government which is trying to weed traditional bureaucratic entitlements out of the education sector (like all public sectors).

The third concept, known as "modern administration," is associated with rewarding teachers (either individually or collectively) for the achievements their students make. The government favors this idea. The teachers' unions have reacted stubbornly to this practice in spite of the landmark 1994 agreement they reached with the government to create the National System for Evaluating Subsidized Schools (SNED). SNED, which has had a big impact in this area, was created via Law 19,410 in 1995. It was applied for a two-year period for the first time in 1996, offering bonuses for excellence to teachers who work in the top 25 percentile schools (2,274 schools that employ 30,600 teachers).

This new system has laid the foundation for future strategies based on similar concerns. It has also provided criteria, specific rewards for excellence, for designing such strategies.

However, more work is needed to define the instances when salary negotiation is appropriate and which players should be involved. In simple terms, the issue is whether the government (the Finance Ministry) will continue playing the role of "employer" and

---

25 These categories are only significant for the municipal sector. Professors who are contracted by private schools which receive subsidies from the State have the right to the category benefits dealing with job conditions. They also receive the right to collective bargaining (which does not exist in the municipal sector). They often ask their employers to provide a package similar to category one.

26 This figure represents the base of any teacher's total salary with the extra "category-based" money determined as a proportion of it. In this way, compensation for experience can be 100% of the minimum salary; job performance, 40%; degree of difficulty, 30%; and administrative responsibility, 20%.

the Teachers' Board will continue acting as the "union representative" for the teachers. At stake are serious issues involving policy, economics, and traditions in education.

For its part, the government has wavered on its role in this area, validating a centralized scheme for negotiations while arguing in public forums and in other labor disputes that it would decentralize its operations.

Labor Statute

The "privatization" of the teachers' job market during the military government, which by law made teachers the employees of municipal and private schools, caused them to lose long-held economic benefits and labor rights. In essence, it also caused a collective identity crisis by undermining some of the criteria on which their identity had been built. The results of the new trends — job insecurity, loss of protection from employers, and lowered social status — gave the teachers more than enough ammunition to fight the changes.

The first Concertación government acknowledged their demands and in 1991 set up a special body of law to regulate the labor market: the Teachers' Statute. The legislation gave teachers more financial stability by setting up a salary scheme of minimum wages and benefits. It also guaranteed teachers' professional enrichment and career development.

The government was divided in its stance on the statute. Some thought it was ill-advised to give teachers such special, open-ended rights. In the end, the ethical component of the statute and the need for teachers' participation in implementing reforms carried the day for the law's proponents in government. The Teachers' Board however opposed the regulation saying it was insufficient, and above all because the board distrusted the government's pledge to raise wages immediately.

Since then, the statute has been modified. Municipalities (the principal employers affected) and the political opposition lamented how rigid the market for teachers had become. The statute, they said, had tied employers' hands and was blocking the sector from modernizing. Unions, after initial opposition, embraced the statute as a historic step toward job security and stability.

But to assuage employers, the government tried in 1995 through Law 19,410 to make the statute more flexible in terms of human resources. The modifications they introduced included: limiting the term of school principals and that of the Municipal Education Director to five years, lifting some guarantees on teachers' contracts, and, through the Annual Municipal Education Development Plan (Padem), hiring teachers according to yearly budgets.

Chile is still trying to find a middle ground in the job market for teachers that satisfies administrative responsibilities and is good for student education. The Concertación has clearly strengthened the teachers' hand in recent years. However, the professors still harbor negative feelings toward the government for failing to do enough to help them. The explication for these negative feelings despite government attempts to improve teachers' working conditions can be found in the relationship that has been formed by the three major groups in this debate: the government itself, the Teachers' Board, and the municipalities.

The teachers feel disillusioned with the government on salary issues. They have criticized the government's lack of communication with the teachers and their misreading of teacher culture in policy-making. Meanwhile, the teachers in general are divided on the stance of the Teachers' Board. This division stems from the distance teachers perceive between the board's stance and the classroom reality in which teachers work. Last, the teachers blame Mineduc for persistent problems with employers relating to legal issues. The teachers feel as if the authorities in general have abandoned them to the cruelties of the unregulated marketplace.

The challenge Mineduc faces is to unify the teachers around a coherent program. It needs to strive to make improvements in the politics of teaching rather than just in teaching itself.

3. ADMINISTRATION

The most controversial change in Chile's educational system implemented during the military regime was the transfer of control of public schools from the Ministry of Education to the various municipalities. Opponents of this shift, many of whom were teachers, had three central complaints: (1) that the transfer was arbitrary, drastic, and "violent"; (2) that the municipalities, because they were poorly run and undemocratic, were not suitable school administrators; and (3) that transferring power to the municipalities was an intermediary step towards privatizing the whole public school system.[27]

This shift took place in a global context of decentralization in education in which international experts were arguing that decentralized schools were more efficient and produced better results. They argued that more autonomous schools could adjust more easily to changing social trends and thereby make education more pertinent to the lives of students.

When democracy was restored in Chile, many members of the education community, especially many teachers, hoped the new government would undo the changes made by the military and assert greater central control. Without going that far, the Concertación struck a middle ground. It valued the decentralized plan because it was more efficient and helped schools reach out to their respective communities. At the same time, it recognized that it had to play a larger role in education after years of deregulation which had left the system partially weakened.

In taking the middle ground, the government tried to improve municipal administration. In this sense, it has taken a larger view of decentralization, not just in terms of how it functions but also how it affects education in general.

---

27 This proposed change never came to fruition. For economic reasons, the conversion of public schools to private ones never occurred on a large scale (a minority of public professional schools — around 70 — were turned over to companies). Interestingly though, the municipal sector has been losing students since 1980 while private, subsidized schools have gained students. While no new municipal schools were built, 1,200 new private schools were. In effect, the school system was being "privatized" in that more and more students were attending private school.

	Fiscal/Municipal Sector			Subsidized Private Sector		
Year	Schools	Students	Percentages of Total Enrollment	Schools	Students	Percentages of Total Enrollment
1980	6,370	2,260,524	79	1,627	401,898	14
1996	6,536	1,828,022	56	2,996	1,079,924	33

Municipal Administration

Municipalities have been plagued for years by a lack of financing, political patronage, and a shortage of long-term strategies. The added responsibility of running schools has aggravated these chronic problems which in turn have negatively affected schools.[28] These issues have caused motivation problems among teachers and reignited old conflicts. Teachers' mistrust of the municipalities has risen, and they complain of an "absence" of municipal leadership.

Considering that school resources, both financial and human, are subject to the relative wealth of the municipality, these problems are particularly acute in poor communities. In some small municipalities there are not enough resources to carve out an educational administration team from other areas.

Three proposals have been utilized to improve municipal administration. The first is to make the municipal governments more democratic in composition and more receptive to community participation. The second is to develop pilot programs and specialized studies in the field of educational administration.

The third and most important improvement came in 1995 with the creation of the Annual Municipal Education Development Plan (Padem), which applied to every municipality in the country. This plan outlined ways of increasing financial resources for local governments and involved them in some long-term growth strategies. Although the law that guides the plan instructs municipalities to create programs for schools in its community, its main focus is forcing municipal governments to conserve financial and human resources for education. This has provoked friction between schools and the municipal governments because it has created the sensation in the schools that cutbacks and fiscal conservancy (especially in the area of contracts for technical teachers) are necessary. This sensation does not always result in action, which leaves both sides frustrated.

In-School Administration

In many schools, conditions of stiff hierarchy, bureaucracy, and overworked administrators are commonplace. These problems tend to impede efforts to improve school administration and ultimately affect the ability of educational reform programs to function.

The different administration improvement plans contemplate raising the expectations for internal management. The programs, which sometimes do not fall under the heading of "administration improvement," ask teachers and administrators to form teams, improve the efficient use of resources, and consult external groups and agencies. All of these programs strive to make school administrations more autonomous. Indeed, new government laws authorize and provide incentives for municipal governments to hand over resources for education received from the Ministry of Education, as well as resources generated within the schools, to the individual establishments themselves.

However, in practice, the municipalities have been reluctant to turn over administrative duties to schools. The establishments, in turn, have been hesitant to implement the shift in the teaching paradigm. In fact, it would appear that the most important factor in

---

28 In some cases, the municipalities have failed to carry out basic responsibilities such as paying teachers and honoring contracts.

determining the viability, quality, and sustainability of these improvement processes is the quality of the institutional context. That relationship is not always circumscribed to the school but tends to involve school owners and the regional and local divisions of the Mineduc itself.

Ministry of Education

The biggest challenge for the Ministry of Education, even in a world of decentralized education, was to regain a position of leadership within the system. Its goal was at the very least to use the Regional Education Departments, which made up the Ministry's supervision network, to act as a consultant on education to the schools and municipalities.[29] The Ministry placed the highest priority on doing this in poorer areas where academic achievement was low. This attitude shift was significant because in the 1980s schools did not receive counseling or support from either municipal governments or the Ministry itself.

A number of innovations to improve the regional departments of the Ministry (including the Regional Secretariats) were carried out. In addition, the Ministry created a fund for schools to finance their own reform initiatives.

The abilities and administrative capacities of the Regional Education Departments vary from office to office and have not been the focus of major reform. In many cases, these departments are bloated bureaucracies and provide poor advice and technical information to schools. The Ministry itself suffers to a lesser extent from similar problems, those characteristic of any large public agency. These include duplication of functions, lack of coordination, and rigid structures.

In general, improvements in Ministry administration at its different levels have not occurred even in reforming education or in meeting the government's pledges. With all the attention on targeting education policy "in the classroom," modernizing administration within the various state organizations has fallen by the wayside.

The following factors will continue to be central to the success of state administration in education: (1) human communications, working practices, and forms of using authority; (2) facilitating resources to schools, promoting reforms, and honoring pledges to teachers; and (3) capable support systems for technical assistance, improved information network, and quicker project approval. Studies have shown, however, that reforms dealing with these factors have only marginal effects.

The Pending Debate

There has not been an adequate, informed debate in Chile concerning the administration of schools that are decentralized, yet successful and legitimate. Filling the void left by this lack of discussion are various counter-proposals, with implicit and explicit motives, and a sensation that the current system is reaching a crisis.

Conservative groups — associated with the political opposition, although not exclusively — push to continue centralizing schools through privatizations. The municipalities, despite some exceptions, generally demonstrate disinterest in running schools and

---

29 The most concrete aspect of this shift was to give the heads of the Regional Education Departments the authority to install the various reform programs throughout the rest of the system. This meant that they would act as advisors and consultants on the various projects.

clamor for more state support and intervention. Teachers and their political allies reject municipal control, even though they have not offered an alternative plan. The government has not taken a firm stance on the issue, opting to favor an eclectic group of principles around loose support for decentralization. The government, to teachers, has come off looking timid and uncreative.[30]

The decentralization plan created over 15 years ago has not proved to be temporary, as was intended. As a system, its legitimacy is still being questioned and its future is by no means certain. The search for viable alternatives is still underway.

4. THE FINAL DISCUSSION: THE PUBLIC/PRIVATE RELATIONSHIP IN CHILEAN EDUCATION

Within the global context, the educational system implemented by the military government in the last decade (officially called "modernization") in effect turned over education to market forces. The pillar of this transformation was subsidizing the demand for education as a means of financing the schools themselves. The schools would compete to win "clients" and the state mandated that the schools would be paid after they performed their services. In this fashion, families were to shop around for the best offers to suit their needs. In doing so, the families effectively regulated the whole system. Schools offering the best services at the lowest costs would be able to develop and make a name for themselves in the market.

Within this system, the various reform programs were implemented. The decentralized nature of the system sought to grant more autonomy to schools, to increase competition among them, and pave the road for total privatization (this of course has not yet occurred). In effect, the line between private and public schools was blurred. The system for compiling information about the schools (Simce) was meant to inform families about the best offers. The absence of regulations in the use of resources would permit new administrative strategies (thus the liberalization of the market for teachers). Finally, the LOCE programs made curriculum requirements more flexible, providing parents with different options, i.e. diversified offers, in choosing a school.

There are three fundamental limitations in the military regime's educational system:

(a) Competition between schools may increase the efficient use of resources but it does not make the learning process, or the quality of education, any more effective. This occurs to a large extent because of the nature of consumer culture in Chile. Many families lack the perspective to make rational consumer decisions and the criteria to evaluate the services received. Some families find it hard to distinguish between offers. The lack of public control over the service — sometimes none at all — does not help matters.

(b) The system does not recognize the principal public services that education provides. The central ones are:

   • equity: in Chile, the market system is slanted against the poorest students and

---

30 The Concertación's support in principle of the military government's decentralization plan angered many of their traditional political allies, especially teachers and unions. The government has not organized a capable communications network to smooth over these issues with these groups.

communities[31] and disregards the state's duty to provide equal access to education.

- national competitiveness: considering that education is a key to economic development, the low quality of teaching the system provides, and its inability to servic the needs of the best students is a detriment to national competitiveness in the global context.

(c) The system lacks the institutional administrative basis to provide a good education and opportunities for development. In all three tiers of education — schools, municipalities, and the Ministry of Education — administrative conditions and capacities are extremely precarious. The decentralization plan was carried out without training for the administrators to give them the skills they need to function in the new system. In some divisions, whole areas of education are neglected while in others they are duplicated.

Assuming that the structural reforms of the 1980s — making the use of resources more efficient, decentralizing the administrative structure — are continued, the Concertación's current stance on education seems to combine old and new strategies. In general, the government proposes a school system that combines:
- market instruments
- a strong role for the state, in terms of reform and control
- decentralized administrative organization

This system strives to safeguard educational norms from the mechanical operation of market forces. It also tries to maintain the essential public service components of education. The Concertación's position will face a bigger challenge in the future as it deals with increasingly complicated issues related to education, such as economic development and changing cultural attitudes. Traditional pillars of education are also being weakened, complicating the picture.

In general, since the recuperation of democracy, the results of the Concertación's efforts in education can be categorized as significant advances, important problems, and unresolved issues.

Advances

The Concertación has been successful in repositioning education as a top social issue. The government has taken a principled stand on improving education and that has attracted the attention of actors in civil society, who have taken greater interest in education.

Government Commitment

The increased and sustained financing that the government has provided to schools has demonstrated its serious interest in improving education. Without alienating private

---

31   There are many reasons for this: (a) private schools (which are generally better than their municipal peers) are not interested in serving students from poor areas. This disinterest is the basis for a type of geographical discrimination, especially in rural and low-density zones, because only municipal schools operate there. It also represents a type of academic discrimination as poor students never receive the opportunities provided in the private schools; and (b) the financial resources of the municipalities are also skewed, with the poorest municipalities providing the least money to education in their own communities.

financiers (whose contributions it needs), the government has promised to increase education funding in coming years. It has also set for itself the goal of quality education available for all. In this regard, it has developed programs that have shifted the nature of education reform from coverage to quality. The programs themselves are powerful signals that government is committed to changing the system. Behind these developments is the government's desire to regain legitimacy as the top player in Chilean education.

The Ministry of Education has shown it is capable of designing quality programs which combine various mechanisms: (1) to allow the Ministry to intervene in the system; (2) to make schools more autonomous; and (3) to connect schools with other actors inside and outside the educational system, such as universities, academic centers, social groups, and businesses, all of whom can play important roles.

Civil Society Involvement

The government, in making education a political priority over the last decade, has positioned school reform in the larger national debate over civil issues. The government's commitment has maintained a coherent direction that has resulted in a long-term consensus on reforming education.[32] The creation of the National Commission on Modernizing Education has been a significant achievement in this regard.

The school system, and the private establishments in particular, have increasingly shut themselves off from general society. In fact, their key players perceive this distancing as normal and desirable, in part due to a culture in which responsibility for education must be "delegated" to specialized agencies and appropriate authorities. The most important efforts made to overcome this culture and transform the relationship are: financial support to families; increased participation among non-school groups in reforming curricula; empowering universities and academic institutions to be more involved in teacher training and to help Mineduc design and evaluate its policies; and create community education networks to make innovative recommendations.

Problems

There are a number of problems that have been addressed by reforms but have shown little improvement. Foremost among them is equal opportunity for education.

While some advances have been made, inadequate designs, limited resources, and the intrinsic complexities of the problem have slowed progress. In general terms, addressing this problem runs contrary to some of the society's most basic cultural and societal assumptions. Furthermore, existing inequalities have deviled even the most well-intentioned programs aimed at creating equity. Last, current configurations in education, from teaching methodology to study habits to curricula, have an intrinsic bias against the poor.

Some successes in this area confirm the effectiveness of public sector support for equal opportunity in education. More creative and widespread attempts at reform, administrative changes in the poorest schools, incentives for new programs, and investments in poor schools appear to be necessary.

---

32 This consensus exists on fundamental education issues, like teaching improvements and curricular changes, rather than on "contextual issues" like administration, school control, and labor laws. In general, the progress made in creating agreement on the first group of issues has come at the expense of the latter group.

Another problem is the dearth of mechanisms the government has to guarantee quality education. Despite the features of a decentralized, market-dependent system, the government should have important powers of evaluation, as well as supervision and enforcement.

The system of evaluating educational quality has logistical problems in terms of how and what it measures. (It needs to anticipate curriculum and teaching changes better.) But more importantly, its focus should be expanded beyond just achievements by schools and students to cover the entire system, including issues of curriculum, teaching, and administration.

With respect to evaluating professional personnel in education, there have been few advances but many heated debates. The National System for Evaluating Subsidized Schools (SNED) is a positive step towards improving the methodology with which schools are evaluated. However, it is utilized to evaluate professionals in schools and therefore renders the system outlined by the Teachers' Statute limited and, sometimes, irrelevant.

Moreover, an important issue is how the information gathered in the evaluations is to be used. Clearly, the initial definition of "consumer information" fails to consider any considerations beyond private, personal interests. Nonetheless, other uses of the data can also be made in the public interest: to evaluate programs, detect problem areas, and target investments.

The government's systems for monitoring and evaluating are also flawed because they do not reflect the realities of the new educational context. Bureaucratic and out-dated practices are still used. In addition, the number of skilled professionals to conduct studies has fallen off, causing distortions throughout the system and hindering all kinds of efforts from compiling information to making recommendations for new reforms.

Last, as discussed above, the administrative cogs at this level of government are in need of modernization. Mineduc, while showing signs of improvement in its administration, has lost ground in its regional and local offices. This lack of sound management has spread throughout the system, crippling municipalities and schools themselves.

Unresolved Issues

There are still a number of decisions to be made in order to secure the educational system we have (and want), although consensus on them does not currently exist. It is not that these issues have been ignored, but rather that they are still mired in ambiguity because no proper solutions or agreements on them have been reached.

What is the minimum that the state should demand of educational-service provider institutions? How should that be done? In effect, the legal system establishes certain minimum requirements on schools in order to grant them official recognition and for them to receive state subsidies.[33] However, the oversight mechanisms are limited and minimally enforced. This is not only because it is difficult to overcome a tradition of lip service to regulations, but also because it is unclear what should be enforced and what should not. In the confusion, the state's requirements of school operators who receive public funding suffer. There are many examples to be found in an array of areas: the huge number of classroom hours

---

33 For official recognition: have a financial backer who holds at least a high school diploma, follow plans and programs submitted to and approved by Mineduc, have appropriate staff, operate in an appropriate facility, and have basic equipment. For subsidies: be officially recognized, have a student/classroom ratio within the standards, provide education at the level stated, and be up-to-date in the payment of staff salaries and social security benefit payments. This clearly establishes a minimum — but entirely insufficient — floor.

wasted each year, facilities with severe infrastructure problems (health, safety, and livability), administrative problems with the staff (lack of contracts and unpaid social security taxes), and discrimination among students (expulsions and arbitrary selections). It is clearly insufficient that the State limit its role to "paying for services rendered" since that position is based on a concept of education as a private good. The collective good is above that (manifested in the enormous sums of public resources allocated to these service providers each year) and as such is entitled to more stringent requirements and more effective enforcement by government officials.

Who should finance public education? The sectors that oppose municipal control (an odd coalition of those who want to privatize the system and those who want to return control to the government) seem to forget the precarious situation in which the system has operated. This may be because the approach was always thought of as a stepping stone to a totally private system. It is as if the critics berated the municipal system without ever giving it the organizational and technical infrastructure it needed to thrive. In fact, municipal management has some comparative advantages in light of the other options. However, it would be foolish to close the doors to other financial alternatives, which, in order to be successful, would have to promote participation and community involvement. This kind of alternative would have to be based on the concept that education is an inalienable social right, necessary for social development, and not merely a set of traditional policies that need to be conserved.

What is the right financial mechanism for funding education? Despite criticism, subsidies continue to be the leading form of financing education. There are good reasons for this, but we have to consider their advantages and disadvantages. At this time, subsidies are only used to finance students' presence in classroom. But subsidies that consider the quality of education, as well as place value on the care and results of students in different socioeconomic levels, could be a valuable development.

Complementary improvements that can improve financing include: providing more funding for school projects; perfecting the incentives system for teachers and ultimately for investors; focusing reform programs on priority groups; and avoiding creating incentives for private investment that reinforce current tendencies to invest in certain areas at the expense of others.

BIBLIOGRAPHICAL REFERENCES

Belleï, C. 1996. "Equidad social y expansión de la educación media técnico-profesional." *Proposiciones* 27: *Chile: modernidades y pobrezas*. Santiago: Ediciones SUR.

Braslavsky, C. 1996. "Las actuales reformas educativas en América Latina: cuatro actores, tres lógicas y ocho tensiones," (Mimeo).

Cariola L. and C. Cox. 1991. "La educación de los jóvenes: crisis de la relevancia y calidad de la educación media." In: I. Mena y S. Rittershausen, eds. *La juventud y la enseñanza media: una crisis por resolver*. Santiago: CPU.

Cedep. 1997. "Evaluación del impacto de la educación parvularia sobre niños." Informe final. Santiago (Mimeo).

Comisión Nacional para la Modernización de la Educación. 1995. *Los desafíos de la educación chilena frente al siglo XXI*. Santiago: Ed. Universitaria.

Cox, C. 1994. "Las políticas de los años noventa para el sistema escolar." Serie *Políticas Sociales* 3. Santiago: ECLAC.

_____. 1997. *La reforma de la educación chilena: contexto, contenidos, implementación*. Colección de Estudios Cieplan. Santiago: Cieplan.

Cox, C. and H. Courard. 1996. "El Estado, el mercado y la educación en los 90." In: *Educación en Chile: un desafío de calidad*. Santiago: Enersis.

Espínola, V. 1989. "Los resultados del modelo económico en la enseñanza básica: la demanda tiene la palabra." In: J. E. García Huidobro, ed. *Escuela, calidad e igualdad. Los desafíos para educar en democracia*. Santiago: CIDE.

_____. 1996. "Revisión de 15 años de política educacional en Chile: ajustes en función de la equidad." Documento de Trabajo ECLAC. Santiago: ECLAC.

Gajardo, M., ed. 1994. "Cooperación internacional y desarrollo de la Educación." Santiago: AGCI.

Hermosilla, B. 1996. "Políticas para la educación parvularia 1990–96." Santiago: Mineduc (Mimeo).

_____. 1997. "La educación parvularia en el marco de la reforma educacional." Santiago: Mineduc (Mimeo).

Mineduc (Ministerio de Educación). 1993a. *Educación de calidad para todos. Políticas educacionales y culturales*. Santiago de Chile.

_____. 1993b. *Programa de Mejoramiento de la Calidad y Equidad de la Educación Básica*. Santiago de Chile.

Núñez, I. 1995. "Gobierno, municipalidades y profesorado: dificultades para un consenso." In: *Viabilidad económica e institucional de la reforma educativa en Chile*. Serie Políticas Sociales 11. Santiago: ECLAC.

Union Organization and Labor Relations

Guillermo Campero

T his article examines the development of Chile's labor movement during the period from 1990 to 1997. The first section describes how union leaders have viewed the transition to democracy as well as their role in the process. The second section outlines the strategies followed by Chilean unions during the democratic transition. The third section examines the current state of labor relations in Chile and around the world, the principal challenges faced by unions today, and their prospects for the future.

I. Labor's Perception of the Transition to Democracy

Labor's strategy in the political process initiated in 1990 was directed toward two main goals. First, the labor movement hoped to play a central role in the new democratic landscape. Second, it aimed to restore the pro-labor policies which Chilean workers had enjoyed in the period before the military takeover. Fundamentally, Chilean unions hoped to recover the ground they had lost under the military regime.

Playing an Active Role
The labor movement in Chile had won broad social support and legitimacy through its participation in the efforts to restore democracy. It justifiably sought an active role in Chilean society during the 1990s.

During the military government, Chilean unions had fought the regime's restrictions on workers' rights. They were also influential in defending general social rights. The labor movement's efforts were broadly directed toward the restoration of democracy. Two labor groups formed in 1975, the Group of Ten and the National Labor Board, coordinated labor leaders' efforts on wider social and democratic issues. In 1980, these two groups were joined under the leadership of the National Workers' Command. The Command was instrumental in the 1983 social uprising, which helped initiate the process leading to the end of the regime in 1990. The Command mustered support for the "No" vote in the 1988 national plebiscite on the military government's rule and urged workers to turn out in 1989 for Chile's first democratic election in 20 years. During these years of change, the Command was a prominent member of the Democratic Alliance, the precursor of the current center-left governing coalition, the Concertación.

When democracy was restored, the leaders of Chile's labor movement enjoyed sufficient influence and legitimacy to press for union-friendly policies and socially-oriented legislation.

Restoring Organized Labor

Drawing upon the social capital earned in their struggle against the regime, labor leaders sought to reinstate the institutions and standards in effect before the military government took control. These leaders argued that the military government's 1979 Labor Plan was "illegitimate in origin," because it had never been approved democratically, nor had it been recognized by the unions themselves. The Labor Plan, which rested upon neo-liberal economic theories, was viewed as fundamentally contrary to union interests.

Through this argument and others, labor sought to regain lost ground. This was the central strategy pursued by organized labor between 1990 and 1997, and it will undoubtedly continue to influence labor activity in the future.

II. Labor Policies and Strategies under the Concertación Governments

1. 1990-1993

The labor movement had two priorities when the military government relinquished control in 1989. The first was to assure its place in the Concertación coalition led by presidential candidate Patricio Aylwin. The second was to develop a coherent identity as well as a set of institutional policies, through the development of the Central Workers' Board (CUT). The CUT gathered together the majority of Chile's union organizations under one banner. From a historical standpoint, the CUT viewed itself as a continuation of the Central Workers' Association, which had been disbanded by the military government in 1973.

Policy Debates in 1989 and Early 1990

Changes and Continuity
The debate over changing or maintaining existing labor laws began in 1989, when Concertación candidate Patricio Aylwin, who would become Chile's president in 1990, began to develop his platform. Chile's labor unions demanded representation in Aylwin's future government, and once they had won this commitment, they set out to incorporate labor concerns into the larger Concertación platform. This was accomplished through the Concertación's Policy Commission, which worked closely with the CUT to design labor policy.

Differences with regard to labor policy quickly surfaced during meetings between the two groups. Both agreed upon the need for reforms, recognizing the existing laws as undemocratic. The CUT, however, argued for the restoration of the labor policies in force before the military government. The Policy Commission disagreed, maintaining that labor policy should focus on current conditions rather than the revival of past policies.

The Policy Commission's argument was based on the recognition that Chile's socioeconomic situation had changed considerably since the military takeover in 1973. According to the Commission, the labor and economic policies of the late 1960s, based on a closed economy, import substitution, and an active governmental role in the economy, were no longer appropriate. They argued that Chile's new, open economy and growing economic competitiveness demanded new and innovative labor policies. With rising salaries and falling unemployment in the new economy, and with the government taking on a limited role in industry, the country's entire economic infrastructure had changed.

The Policy Commission's labor plan called for the introduction of new labor policies within the existing economic model, in order to provide workers with better access to the job market and a greater share of the benefits of growth. It was unclear whether the Concertación was advocating the new economic system itself or merely labor's role within it.

These issues led to heated debate within the labor movement. Traditional union members had serious reservations about the military regime's neo-liberal economic model, and thus about the Concertación's proposals. While this conflict peaked in the early 1990s, it has continued to provoke debate up to the present.

In spite of the discord produced, this conflict was productive, since it generated much-needed dialogue in this area. Eventually, the unions agreed that reflection on the need for change was a positive step. Meanwhile, the Policy Commission realized that the CUT's concerns were legitimate and that gradual changes were necessary to assuage their fears.

Limited Consensus: The First Labor Agenda

The Policy Commission outlined a number of labor proposals, which were recognized by both sides as requiring further revision. However, many of the issues surrounding these proposals have not been resolved to date.

The agenda of labor proposals covered nine areas:

- Regarding *individual workers*, proposals included reforming the regulations on contract termination, eliminating firing without explanation and extending the limit for severance pay to five years. Financial sanctions would be imposed on employers in cases of improper job dismissal, as determined by the courts. The reforms would also eliminate dismissals based on "non-labor" factors, a policy which had been implemented by the military. The Commission also proposed new types of formal work contracts, such as seasonal contracts, to help protect workers.
- In the area of *collective bargaining*, proposals included modifying the Collective Bargaining Agreement to grant inter-company unions the right to negotiate with companies with less than 50 employees. Workers on temporary contracts would also gain the right to union representation. The Commission proposed to eliminate various prohibitions on subjects for collective bargaining, as well as abolishing the 60-day limit on strikes and the use of replacement workers. Finally, it proposed official recognition of the Local Union Federation, offering legal privileges to its leaders and granting public employees the right to unionize.
- With respect to *social benefits*, proposals included creating a regulatory system to enforce transparency in the private sector, monitoring conflicts of interest between workers and companies, and improving union coverage. In addition, the reforms sought to improve the system of minimum pensions and family benefits.
- Proposals regarding *oversight* included expanding the resources of the Workers' Board.
- The Commission proposed to modernize the workings of the *labor courts*.

- To expand *job training*, the Commission proposed to design special programs for unemployed youth.
- In the area of *minimum wages*, plans were made to develop mechanisms linking salaries to inflation and to make other adjustments reflecting economic growth.
- Proposals to promote the *recuperation of workers' rights* included legislation to exonerate workers who had been blacklisted for political reasons, as well as the reimbursement of unions for assets expropriated by the military government.
- Finally, in the area of *social dialogue*, the Commission proposed to promote inter-sectorial communication.

This agenda represented the labor policy goals of the first Concertación government, which won the support of unions on most issues. However, consensus was not achieved about the mechanisms with which to achieve these goals. Underlying this debate was the unions' continuing perception that the government's measures were insufficient, and that the goal of recovering past achievements remained out of reach. Many union leaders argued that more radical policies and mechanisms were necessary in order to achieve a more favorable balance of power between unions and employers.

Both groups agreed that a more profound discussion of labor policy was needed. It became clear to the unions that finding consensus on these issues was of the utmost importance. The unions came to recognize the need to deal directly with the other leading participants in the debate, including the government and, above all, the business community.

After Patricio Aylwin was elected president in December 1989, these issues surged to the forefront of the discussion within the labor movement. The unions agreed to join what would become known as the "social alliance," in order to represent their cause and to focus public attention on the needs of labor.

The Social Alliance: Building Consensus on Labor Issues

The need to achieve consensus on labor issues posed two complex problems for labor leaders. First, it obliged them to accept the business community as a suitable negotiating partner, although memories of companies' support for anti-labor measures under the military government were still painfully fresh. Second, they had to come to terms with the fact that some long-held tenets of the labor movement would have to be altered in order to accommodate Chile's new social and economic developments.

With the encouragement of the new government, labor came to accept the search for consensus as a necessary component of the political and social environment during the transition to democracy. Thus, despite their reservations, the unions agreed to support the social alliance called for by the Aylwin administration. This was a significant step, demonstrating labor's willingness to contribute to the prevailing "vision for Chile," above and beyond its own narrow interests.

Nevertheless, the government's call for dialogue still faced significant obstacles. Business groups, who formed an important part of the opposition to the new Concertación government, held a different vision of labor policy in Chile. In their view, the labor legislation established in the late 1970s by the military government (the 1979 Labor Plan) had been effective in promoting economic growth and creating jobs. Thus, their tendency from the outset was to refuse to consider major changes in labor policy.

Meanwhile, despite the fact that the union leadership had agreed on the need for consensus, some trade unionists, especially within the CUT, were reluctant to give up ground. They believed that radical measures were necessary, and that dialogue and discussion might not be the best manner in which to achieve them. Some factions within the new government also shared this position.

The official government standpoint was that all groups shared the responsibility to contribute to socioeconomic stability, and thereby to ensure a successful transition from military rule to democracy. Labor policy was seen as a key factor in achieving this stability, precisely because it was so controversial.

After much debate, the business community, through the Trade and Production Board (CPC), headed at that time by Manuel Feliu, agreed to discuss labor policy with unions and the government.

National Accords

In April 1990, the government called upon the major labor and business organizations in Chile, namely the CUT and the CPC, to develop a document outlining their positions on labor reform. The goal was to find areas of consensus between the two groups which might serve as a foundation for progress on labor policy.

The Tripartite National Framework accord of May 1990 was the result of this effort. Although the trade unions, through the CUT, continued to criticize the neo-liberal economic model, they demonstrated their willingness to remain receptive to the viewpoints of the government and the business community. The trade unions' overriding goal was to make progress in labor policy, with an emphasis on the social equity issues associated with economic growth.

The accord was a first for Chile. Its value lay in the willingness of all groups involved — the unions, the government, and business — to come to the same negotiating table and work towards consensus. This search for consensus contributed to the smooth transition to democracy which the government had pledged to bring about.

Concessions were made by all sides in the formulation of this pact. The accord was above all "a pact of understanding." Although the parties continued to negotiate on specific substantive issues, the road to dialogue had at least been opened.

The trade unions, in particular, modified their positions as a gesture of goodwill. They justified these concessions in the name of the transition to democracy and the need to give ground to achieve consensus. Their biggest shifts were in recognizing the value of the private sector in economic development, as well as acknowledging the necessity to take the requirements of an open and competitive economy into account when formulating social and labor policy. At the same time, however, they argued that these facts called for stronger pro-labor policies, in order to protect workers during economic adjustments and transformations, to give them a greater voice within companies and a greater share of the profits, to improve the balance of power between companies and unions, and to allow workers to reap more of the benefits of economic growth.

Businesses argued for a more cooperative approach to labor relations. They endorsed better enforcement of labor laws, the recognition of unions as representatives of workers, and improved access to employment opportunities.

The national accord between workers, businesses, and the government also paved the way for a minimum wage increase in 1990-1991 and outlined issues for future discussion. Although full agreement was not achieved on all issues, this process created a framework for further tripartite dialogue. This spirit influenced Congressional passage of the accord and its implementation by the Ministry of Labor as the basis of the government's labor policy.

Three more accords were signed, in 1991, 1992, and 1993. The central issue in each was the adjustment of the minimum wage to keep up with overall salary increases. Other important issues remained unaddressed, and many of the proposals made during negotiations did not come to fruition. However, the accords set forth valuable guidelines for labor policy in relation to economic growth and stability. Moreover, these negotiations continued in the consensual spirit that had marked earlier sessions. Although conflicts among the parties continued, the opportunity for dialogue was retained.

Unions, led by the CUT, maintained their willingness to participate in the new social alliance of the early 1990s, in spite of internal tensions regarding this strategy. Some trade unions criticized the CUT, accusing it of giving too much ground on labor issues and claiming that companies were not fully complying with the provisions of the 1990 accord. Meanwhile, the reform proposals sent by the government to Congress in compliance with the inter-sectorial accords continued to meet with criticism from various business organizations.

The CUT itself was deeply ambivalent. Its leaders were pleased at the legislative advances that had been made, but they still viewed many measures as insufficient. At times, they seemed to doubt that negotiations with business groups could lead to meaningful progress. The CUT complained that it was making more concessions than the other two parties.

Labor analysts at the time tended to agree with the CUT's reasoning, yet they pointed to the CUT's poor job of acknowledging and publicizing its achievements. In their view, the CUT's defensive and pessimistic stance tended to obscure its positive record in establishing itself as the leading voice of labor and in bringing labor issues to the forefront of the country's agenda.

Nevertheless, the CUT leadership maintained its commitment to the social alliance throughout the period from 1990 to 1994, viewing it as a necessary contribution to the consolidation of democracy.

Sectorial Accords

The national pacts approved by Congress paved the way for smaller, yet significant, accords on various aspects of labor policy. The most important of these were the four agreements concluded between 1990 and 1993, which raised public sector salaries and improved working conditions and career opportunities for government employees. The CUT consistently participated in the negotiations for these accords. Among the most significant accomplishments arising from this process was the passage of a law granting public workers the right to unionize. Groundbreaking accords were also put into place for port workers and coal miners.

Other Agreements

The CUT and the government agreed to create a National Tripartite Council in order to advise the Labor Ministry on policy questions in the area of vocational and professional training. In the area of oversight, a broad, tripartite program was created to publicize labor regulations and to promote compliance with them. The CUT and the government also agreed to establish a National Union Training Fund to finance training programs organized by labor organizations.

Union Expansion

During this period, union leaders sought to strengthen their organizations and increase their membership. The new climate of political freedom contributed to their efforts, allowing them to achieve substantial gains between 1990 and 1993, when the number of unions in Chile rose by 38%. Union membership rose 26% over the same period, expanding to 20% of Chile's salaried work force, up from 16% in 1989.

Two particular characteristics of this increase in unionized workers reflected the changes in the foundation of Chile's union movement. While the manufacturing and mining sectors — historic leaders in Chile's labor movement — showed significant gains in union membership, the largest advances, in relative terms, were seen in transportation, construction, and trade. In addition, the average number of members per union fell to some 60 workers, down from the historical average of 90. This reflected changes in the composition of the country's labor force, due to the increasing popularity of measures such as outsourcing and subcontracting.

Meanwhile, some of the economic forces at the leading edge of Chile's economy, such as the export branches of the forestry, agriculture, and fisheries industries, with their highly seasonal work patterns, responded poorly to attempts at union organizing. A trend toward dispersal of unions was observed, with the creation of many small organizations, as well as an inherent instability, derived from the greater job mobility of service sector workers.

Above all, it became clear that the traditional foundation of the union movement — large, stable unions in the manufacturing and mining sectors — was shifting. Labor leaders began to recognize that they faced new challenges which would require new solutions.

The Overall Balance, 1990-1993

Union Strategies During the Transition to Democracy

The observation that best sums up the position of the labor movement as a whole between 1990 and 1993 is that it was pulled in two different directions as it attempted to find its place within the country's transition to democracy. On the one hand, it was determined to be involved in this process as a representative of the interests of labor. On the other hand, its decision to cooperate forced it to face the fact that the country's new economic conditions precluded a return to pre-1973 labor policies.

Ultimately, the political decision to participate in the new social alliance prevailed over the reservations expressed by some labor leaders. However, tensions continued within the labor movement, exacerbated by the attitudes expressed by the business community. These tensions fueled the consistently pessimistic outlook held by labor, as mentioned above, as well as the recurring complaint that its gains were insufficient. This pessimistic stance affected labor's public image, weakening its claim to be a significant player in the democratic transition and emboldening its critics.

Structural Shifts and Changes in the Labor Force

The labor movement found it difficult to expand union membership in emerging industries, underscoring the realization that it would be nearly impossible to recover the labor order of pre-1973 Chile.

The political parties traditionally aligned with the labor movement focused less attention on workers' needs, as the new socioeconomic order gave rise to new political priorities.

Thus, the labor movement became something of a political orphan. The gap between unions and their traditional political allies diminished the labor movement's ability to push its agenda through Congress. At the same time, the appointment of many talented labor activists to government posts weakened union ranks and affected labor's capacity to come up with innovative proposals.

These factors help explain labor's reactive, rather than proactive, stance in negotiations. This phenomenon was further exacerbated by the assertive manner in which business leaders staked out their positions. In addition, the business community's position was strengthened by the prevailing neo-liberal outlook, while labor's stance, linked to the discredited economic theories of the 1940s-1970s, was weakened. In the new international economic climate, unions were viewed as cumbersome and unproductive. Neo-liberal thinking emphasized individual action and spurned collective measures such as union organization and negotiation. The economic currents of the 1990s shook the labor movement to its core, forcing it to adapt to prevailing notions.

While both the unions and the government criticized orthodox neo-liberalism, they disagreed significantly about how a revised version of this economic model would affect labor. These differences remained a sticking point in negotiations between the two sides. Thus, the period from 1990 to 1993 was a time of complex challenges for Chile's labor movement. The new social dialogue promoted by the government opened up new prospects for the labor unions, yet by agreeing to participate in it, they also agreed to play by its rules, thus limiting their range of action. The prevailing preoccupation with the country's stability further complicated labor's agenda. Meanwhile, the new economic model led businesses and the government to take different approaches to labor issues. While labor leaders were able to attain significant achievements, they were plagued by doubts about their strategy and their role in Chilean society. These concerns continued to affect the actions taken by labor between 1994 and 1997.

2. 1994-1997

Labor Redefines Its Strategy

The labor movement's position at the inauguration of the second democratic administration in 1994 differed from that of the first period in two essential ways. First, it had begun to view the strategy of seeking consensus with business and government more critically. In addition, it had begun to lift the restrictions it had imposed upon its own activities during the first phase of the transition, which it now considered complete. The unions did not completely abandon the hope of reaching agreements; however, they began to distance themselves from the government's position and to become more antagonistic toward the business community. They also became more assertive in bringing issues to the nation's attention which had not been resolved under the first democratic administration.

New Policies and Relations

The government, like the unions, hoped to move forward on labor issues and implement the unfinished reforms from the 1990-1993 agenda. The administration focused its strategy on six areas: improving hiring mechanisms in the public and private sectors; modernizing the labor courts; expanding oversight of labor-related matters such as working conditions and pension fund administration; expanding collective bargaining rights and coverage in the public and private sectors; improving the social security system; and establishing mechanisms to safeguard workers' opportunities for mobility in the labor market.

As it embarked upon this reform effort, the government called upon unions and businesses to come together in the collective spirit that had guided previous negotiations. The business sector, however, refused to cooperate, claiming that earlier negotiations had fulfilled their purpose and that there was no need to make them a permanent institution. In short, the negotiations had gone far enough, and the business community was unwilling to consider any further concessions in labor policy.

Although the unions agreed with the government about the need for further reforms, their own reservations, coupled with the hostile reaction from business, led them to publicly reject further collective negotiations on labor policy. Thus, the formulation of labor policy in 1994 became more difficult than it had been in 1990, as both unions and businesses took more autonomous positions and resisted cooperation with the government.

Thus, the annual tripartite negotiations between the government, the unions, and the business community were suspended for 1994. Talks were confined to a limited number of bilateral negotiations on smaller issues. The unions became increasingly reluctant to negotiate with either of the other two parties. However, the three sides continued to work together on the Economic Development Forum, which was created by the new government. The administration proceeded with its strategy for labor policy, often crossing swords with the business sector, which opposed many of its proposals.

In spite of this opposition, the government managed to gain Congressional approval for a number of its proposals. These included improving the Labor Courts; granting new budgetary powers to the Labor Administration; and reforming the Training and Employment Statute. The Chamber of Deputies approved a bill to expand collective bargaining rights and other union prerogatives, but it was blocked by the Senate after strong protests from the business community. A mixed Congressional commission was appointed to decide the bill's fate in 1998. A proposal for a Retired Workers' Protection System was also presented to Congress, to be considered in 1998.

Labor's Strategy
In contrast to the 1990-1993 period, labor's strategy in the mid-1990s focused on presenting original proposals in the areas of worker rights and collective bargaining. The unions thereby staked out positions which were clearly distinguished from those of the government and of other voices in the social policy debate.

The unions argued that they needed a stronger institutional framework and greater recognition to compete in the new marketplace. The government responded that it agreed with the unions' goals, but that many of the mechanisms that the workers had proposed were unrealistic. The unions protested that the government's proposals were insufficient. The business community claimed that both sides' proposals were unnecessary, reiterating its position that labor reform had been successfully completed by the first Concertación government.

Despite these disagreements, the three sides continued to cooperate in the Economic Development Forum. Here, progress was made in the government's efforts to create the Retired Workers' Protection System, as well as in bringing labor and business closer together on some issues.

The three groups' dialogue within the Forum helped make the discussion of the bills before Congress more cordial. Subjects debated in Congress ranged from the changing labor market to the technological challenges of the new economy. The contributions of the unions to these debates demonstrated that they were rethinking many of their long-held beliefs in order to adapt to the new economic climate. This adaptation process, however, was hindered by business leaders' express hostility against unions. Many businesses continued anti-labor practices, despite their pledges to the contrary during tripartite negotiations. These broken promises hardened labor's position, causing union leaders to question the benefits of modifying their outlook.

While the Forum opened up new areas of agreement between the unions and the government, internal divisions were becoming evident within the labor movement. Traditionalist or "hardline" union members resisted their leaders' search for a new vision of labor compatible with the new economy. Although almost all union leaders agreed that new ideas were necessary, this internal division hindered the formulation of new proposals. The conflict within the labor movement reduced its influence upon the content of the union rights and collective bargaining bills before Congress. The bills eventually approved by the Chamber of Deputies reflected the administration's positions. This led to a feeling of isolation among the unions. Furthermore, it weakened their image as a major player in the formulation of labor policy.

The unions' autonomous and increasingly combative strategy during this period thus does not appear to have been successful, at least up to the present time. While this stance is an understandable one, considering the labor movement's political and historical situation, it has produced poor results for a number of reasons, which it is useful to examine briefly here.

The Need for a Conceptual Framework

Political strategies such as those followed by the unions from 1994 to the present require an underlying conceptual framework, in order to keep them in line with changing economic, social, and technological trends. To achieve success, the labor movement needed to develop policies as practical and popular as those set forth by the government and the business community. In spite of the perceived legitimacy of the unions and their goals, the policies proposed by labor suffered from the lack of a sound conceptual framework.

The Importance of a Negotiating Platform

Another reason that labor's proposals floundered was that its negotiating strategy was ineffective. The unions could have achieved more effective results by putting together a broader base of support in Congress, cultivating ties with political parties or carrying out mass public awareness campaigns. However, the unions' negotiating style during this period was hampered by internal divisions in the labor movement. Even the idea of negotiation divided the leadership ranks of the CUT, and a serious rift appeared in 1996 during internal elections. The CUT's leadership ranks are undergoing a gradual recomposition process, which is still underway at the present time. This transformation process has affected the overall unity of the CUT, as well as its status as a leading player in the national debate over labor policy.

The Results of Labor's Efforts from 1994 to 1997

The period from 1994 to 1997 was filled with complex challenges for Chile's labor unions. These challenges arose from various forces that pulled the labor movement in different

directions. Unions wanted to maintain their traditional role as a power player in national politics, even as they took a more autonomous stance in their relationship with the
government and increased their antagonism against the business community. Many of
labor's difficulties have arisen from its need to adjust to structural changes in the country's economic system. The unions' view of the new economy has been more defensive
than proactive, and their attempts to devise an effective strategy for the future have been
hampered by internal disagreements. The unions have turned their back on the tripartite negotiation mechanisms, without opening alternate channels of communication
with government and business leaders. To date, they have failed to satisfactorily resolve
the ideological debate about their role in Chilean society. Finally, they have lacked innovative leadership capable of identifying and successfully meeting the challenges they
continue to face.

III. Labor Today: A Long-Term Vision

Up to this point, we have reviewed the strategies pursued by Chile's labor movement
between 1990 and 1997. To complement this review, a deeper analysis of the problems of
organized labor is necessary. The years we have analyzed have brought such far-reaching
transformations in Chilean life that these domestic changes might be viewed as the sole
determinants of the country's changing labor trends. This would be an error. Without
downplaying the effects of developments in Chile and the increasingly defensive and isolated standpoint of Chilean unions, it is important to analyze the Chilean labor movement
within a context of global change. Broader phenomena are at work here, affecting many
developing countries as they, like Chile, experience profound change in their models for
national development.

1. THE NEW ORIENTATION OF SOCIO-ECONOMIC DEVELOPMENT
AND ITS IMPACT UPON TRADITIONAL UNION ACTIVITY

The main thesis of this section is that the current challenges faced by the Chilean labor
movement arise from its attempt to integrate itself into the new society taking shape in
Chile, as a result of structural changes to the economic, social, and institutional order.
These changes go far beyond short-term policy battles such as those undertaken by the
Chilean unions in the early 1990s. They pose long-term challenges that address the very
nature of labor's role in the economy and society of the future.

   The demands of this new order require unions to shift their focus from their historical social foundation to new industries in the trade, service, and export sectors.
Unions must also recognize that employment in the new economic order is more transitory than before, as subcontracting and specialization take on increasing importance. The new order has led to a questioning of unions' traditional role. As their historical "model" for action begins to fade, unions throughout the world must
undertake a search for innovative new concepts and strategies. This climate of change
has also generated tensions and uncertainties, which explain in part the labor movement's current predicament.

2. TENSIONS ACCOMPANYING THE TRANSFORMATION
   OF THE HISTORICAL MODEL OF UNION ACTIVITY

Every transformation produces tension and conflict, as people attempt to adjust to a new situation. Labor has been called upon to adjust to a rapidly-changing, technologically-based economy. The Chilean labor movement has not only faced the challenge of finding new forms of representation; it has been forced to adjust to transformations in politics, the economy, and society itself.

Unlike intellectuals and even politicians, social movements require a great deal of time and effort to adjust to a new social, political, and cultural environment. In order to identify, evaluate, and adopt new orientations and forms of action, they must undertake an arduous process of internal reflection. In this process, attention must be paid to group members' attitudes toward the changes in progress, as well as to the new risks and opportunities arising from these changes. Social movements, and the labor movement in particular, are representative in nature; they are required to faithfully reflect the perceptions of their members. For this reason, they often undergo phases of acute internal tension when faced with far-reaching change.

Some analysts of the situation have maintained that these conflicts over current change signal a terminal crisis in the labor movement. They predict that unions will eventually disappear from the new societies now taking shape around the world.

In my opinion, these diagnoses are wrong, because they do not take long-term trends into account. It is true that the new economic climate in Chile and the world has weakened union recruitment and collective bargaining, seemingly demonstrating the loss of unions' decisive role in socio-political decisionmaking. However, in my view, these new conditions are merely generating challenges, not crises.

As in the historical period when the industrial economy replaced a more informal one, profound changes are occurring today in the organization of human labor, the operation of job markets, the use of technology, and the role of labor leaders and unions. Drastic adjustments may be required in order to realign the labor movement with new economic conditions.

These economic changes present new challenges to labor, as well as other social movements, but they do not eliminate the need for these movements entirely. To believe this would be to accept the idea that society has been totally absorbed by the market, or by the State, and that it has completely lost its capacity for collective action. Such a hypothesis, in my view, has no historical or sociological foundation.

Instead, I believe that we are in a period of transformation between the old type of collective union activity and a new kind of labor movement that is flexible enough to adjust to new economic conditions. The birth of this new movement will be a difficult one, requiring profound cultural transformations. This explains the sense of uncertainty felt by so many today. For the same reason, the policies of the past often seem more comfortable to union members and leaders. This is an understandable response to the transformations which are shaking the foundations of their movement's social history.

However, there is no basis upon which to claim, as some analysts do, that workers now prefer individual action to collective action. Nor have any other forms of representation arisen within the new working environment as an alternative to unions.

In fact, the labor movement has continued to survive in spite of ferocious attacks from orthodox neo-liberal theorists, who view unions as obstacles to the free operation of the market. This is not a trivial victory. In weathering these attacks, labor unions have demonstrated their historical, sociological, and political viability. The labor union as an institution, although weakened and divided in many parts of the world, is still on its feet, and it is working toward its own transformation. Recent events in Europe, South Korea, and in Chile itself have demonstrated that labor unions remain active participants in the global socio-economic debate.

Unions are irreplaceable contributors to the search for a new consensus in the workplace. Without collective representation of workers' interests, this consensus will be lost, in spite of neo-liberal technocrats' beliefs to the contrary.

Chilean unions are no exception to this. Their crisis manifests certain unique local characteristics, including issues of leadership and management. Yet to be fully understood, it must be placed in the context of global change discussed above.

IV. Outlook for the Construction of a New Labor Model

New trends are emerging among leaders of organized labor in many parts of the world. In Chile, many of these strategies are still in undeveloped form. We emphasize these emerging lines of thought because they are an appropriate basis from which to analyze the future of Chile's labor movement. These trends can be grouped into five main areas.

1. Unions are launching a debate as to how to transform their strategy while maintaining their identity as a social movement representing workers as a group. This debate focuses on new definitions of workers' situations and interests. Unions seek to maintain their historical function as representatives of a social group, in spite of new conditions.

    The very idea of representing a social group runs counter to an intellectual tenet of neo-liberalism and post-modernism: that modern society is based upon individuals and not upon group interests. To refute this line of thinking, unions must adjust to new economic and political realities while finding ways to maintain their historic role as the collective representatives of workers.

    The continued legitimacy of labor unions as representatives of a social category is vital to modern society, as a check on economic and state power. While the political system strives to give a voice to all constituents in order to construct a pluralistic society, the labor movement does the same with workers.

2. Especially among younger union leaders, there is a growing tendency to combine the objectives of economic growth and social progress into an overarching vision for labor. Unions have traditionally focused on promoting the fair distribution of the fruits of development. This vision, however, tends to downplay other economic goals such as growth and the individual accumulation of capital.

    Labor's historically one-dimensional vision of a more equitable distribution of existing wealth has its counterpart in neo-liberal theory's one-dimensional view that only economic growth can produce progress. More recently, however, labor has been outlining a multi-dimensional vision, combining the goals of economic growth with those of more equitable distribution. Thus, economic growth is viewed as providing expanded job opportunities and higher standards of living for workers.

This multi-dimensional vision is reflected in the new policy approach beginning to emerge within the labor movement. In the past, labor legislation was often regarded as the "social" counterweight to economic policy. The new labor vision seeks to integrate the policies of growth with those of labor, recognizing that both aim at expanded opportunities and the fair distribution of those opportunities.

3. The traditional assumption that unions can reach any policy goal through expanded size and increased political power is being questioned. While these aims are still sought, unions are beginning to recognize that some economic imperatives, such as controlling inflation and maintaining the link between income and productivity, represent restrictions on policy which cannot be removed through the exercise of political will.

    In addition, the idea of competing and antagonistic forces in the workplace is being replaced by one of consensus among the participants in the modern economy: workers, employers, consumers, and political representatives at various levels. Political will must be channeled into a negotiation process to ensure that the policies decided upon are sustainable.

4. It appears that a new culture is arising within companies, affecting relations between workers and management. The 1997 Economic Development Forum seminars, designed to showcase companies with innovative workplace cultures, revealed that businesses are reorganizing work patterns to accommodate new technologies and a changing marketplace.

    In fact, individual companies often stand on the front line of changes which are later recognized as global phenomena. Union leaders are coming to recognize that the innovative collective agreements and management techniques pioneered within specific working environments can serve as starting points for debate on the sectorial or national level on subjects such as worker flexibility and deregulation.

5. Unions are increasingly concerned with developing new methods of representation for their constituents, in accordance with new economic, technological, and social trends.

    This subject has received particular emphasis in recent years at events sponsored by organizations such as the Ebert Foundation, devoted to rethinking the structure of union representation. One of the most important developments in this area has been the democratization of the selection of union leaders. As the union leadership crisis in Chile demonstrates, it is increasingly important for unions to choose capable leaders who represent the new categories of workers — and their demands — in the changing marketplace.

    In addition, there has been much discussion about decentralizing union federations and syndicates, in order to allow local groups to take on more initiative and to interact with local public authorities. At this level, there are also greater opportunities for cooperation and coordination among unaffiliated unions, representing workers in the public and private sectors or in different lines of work. Local unions may combine their efforts on issues related to the job market, worker training, social benefits, and other areas. Thus, union solidarity — a major goal of the labor movement — may find new opportunities for expression.

Another important subject of debate is the protection of the interests of workers hired under the new types of contracts which are increasingly popular in today's economy. Unions must recognize the new characteristics and needs of workers hired for seasonal, future, temporary, freelance, or subcontracted work. Representing these workers' interests poses a particular challenge, since companies using these types of contracts tend to strongly resist union involvement.

In general, today's labor movement seeks to decentralize and diversify the structure of union organizations, while maintaining their traditional divisions into local, sectorial, and national levels.

All of these levels must be redesigned, in keeping with the new tasks they face. Yet perhaps the most important challenge is that of creating a stable institutional structure capable of coordinating local and sectorial actions — especially collective bargaining efforts — as well as formulating innovative proposals for the country as a whole. Thus, the national level may provide strategies to be implemented by a more decentralized and diversified organization. As technological and economic changes continue to advance, they will incorporate an increasing number of innovations arising within particular companies and industries. Careful observation of these innovations will permit the labor movement to develop new policies, to identify the needs of emerging categories of workers, and to represent Chilean workers more effectively within a changing society.

Urban Action:
Collective Efforts at the Grassroots Level

Gustavo Rayo
*Gonzalo de la Maza**

Introduction

T he purpose of this essay is to describe and interpret the changes that have taken place in the various forms of collective action in Chile's large, poor, urban centers during the 1990s. We will attempt to describe community group patterns and the meaning assigned by the groups themselves to their activity, as well as the link between those groups and the State.

Our focus has been on the community as a space for social integration. We have excluded from our analysis the work environment, which is dealt with in a different chapter of this book. However, the opinions and life stories of the people described in these pages are frank in saying that their weak ties to the rest of Chilean society are directly linked to their lack of opportunities in the workplace. Their vision of country and community, as well as their perception of political institutions, is often bitter. The distribution of wealth and opportunities in their lives is widely perceived as disheartening.

In our observations, we have concentrated on the community of Peñalolén and interviews with members of the area's community organizations. The area was selected because of its rapid transformation in social composition and land use. Time constraints prevented us from conducting fieldwork in a second community. Thus, our choice of a case study format limited the scope of reference to Peñalolén.

We have attempted to give this study the truthfulness of the direct accounts given by its protagonists, of their life experiences, and of their vision of the country. The cases analyzed here were, for the most part, selected from the lists of projects funded by the *Fondo de Solidaridad e Inversion Social* (FOSIS) from 1990 to the present. Other organizations surfaced through contacts with politicians or through municipal professionals, as is the case of San Joaquín. While examining grassroots economic organizations, we focused our attention on the evolution experienced by the community kitchens of the 1980s, which became food service companies in the 1990s.

The study is made up of three parts. The first gives the context of the changes observed in urban associative patterns. In our opinion, three types of variables should be

---

* We would like to thank sociologist Daniela Vicherat M., a researcher with the project Chile 90, for her valuable assistance with this study.

highlighted: first, how the "social" sphere, as an arena for public action, has changed due to the reforms implemented in the preceding decade; second, the changes in the social stratification of communities; and, finally, the new areas targeted by the State's social policies, represented primarily by biddable projects.

This first part is supported by our own investigations and those of other authors, as well as by our original inductive exercise. The second part is composed of a review of the motivations and expectations of the urban players and constitutes a direct study of six cases characteristic of the diversity of urban organizations. This review was based on semi-structured interviews held at collective meetings with leaders and members of the organizations studied.

Finally, a third part explores the forms of action employed by urban grassroots organizations today in the Metropolitan Region. We focus in particular upon their strategies for obtaining resources, their networks and intermediation systems, their sources of leadership, and their links to the formal political sector. The review of FOSIS project databases allowed us to identify and classify those organizations with a seemingly higher level of activism in the Metropolitan Region, as well as the most common focal points of projects presented by community organizations.

However, it is important to caution the reader regarding the scope of this study. Our purpose was to learn more about organized action, without attempting to draw conclusions about the relative importance of its manifestations. Similarly, the review of the organizations and the themes of the projects presented by these organizations to FOSIS or other municipal funds is grounded in the methodological assumption that the development and presentation of projects to those sources of financing imply some degree of organizational sustainability among the proposing associations.

I. The New Background of the Social Contract

The form taken on by collective urban action throughout the 1990s has been affected by three different types of fundamental variables. The first is related to the revolution in the "social sphere" at the beginning of the 1980s, as a result of which the link between the State and civil society that had prevailed throughout most of this century was radically altered. The second type of variable includes physical and social modifications in the urban setting, expressed in new ways of organizing urban space. Finally, in our analysis we have considered the change in the collective perception of politics and how this perception is expressed in the grassroots organizations examined in this study.

THE STATE AND SOCIAL MODERNIZATION

The "social modernization" project of the late 1970s and early 1980s took shape through a series of measures carried out by the State in the spirit of neo-liberalism. Among them were the privatization of the social security system; the "municipalization" of the health and educational systems; the promotion of an economy lacking in social factors; the legal introduction of private universities; the labor plan; and the reform of the professional schools. The intended transformation of the relationships between State and civil society reflected in these measures may be separated into four key ideas, whose impact can still be felt, despite the political and institutional progress made during the current decade.[1]

First, the "social modernization" project sought a de-politicization of civil society, concurrent with a de-socialization of the political system. In other words, it sought to use reforms to disassociate the political system from the demands of the different social sectors and, simultaneously, to imbue the political system and Chilean society with the concept of a universal technical rationality capable of managing State resources. Within this paradigm, only the economic sciences would be able to ensure such rationality.

The implantation of the first of these key ideas was effected through two mechanisms: on one hand, the State's partial or total withdrawal from the principal areas of social action; and, on the other hand, neutralization of the pressure groups and severing of their contact with the political party system.

Second, the "social modernization" project sought to substantially modify the cultural-economic orientation of individuals and social groups. The collective action orientation, so strongly a part of the *Estado Compromiso* (Committed State) before 1973, disappeared and gave way to the apparent primacy or sovereignty of the consumer. Since then — in keeping with Talcot Parsons' dichotomy — it appears that individual orientation toward action has prevailed, particularly in the satisfaction of basic needs: individual and family savings, private initiative, and the individual definition of priorities, as well as individual ways of resolving problems.

The people behind the reform counted on this greater individual rationality to translate into an observable weakening of social interest in participating in the public sphere. In other words, the economic rationality was expected to bring about the de-politicization of individual and collective attitudes and behavior within Chilean society.

Third, the "social modernization" project of the early 1980s sought to create positive feedback about the market system from an ideological point of view (support and legitimization) as well as from a material one. The case of the privatization of social security is paradigmatic. The replacement of the pay-as-you-go system with that of individual capitalization will have as its principal consequence, from this point of view, the forced introduction of the individual into the logic of private accumulation. In a certain manner, this model supposes that the individual feels solidarity with the performance of companies and the investments made by their pension fund administrators. From a material point of view, it is evident that the enormous transfer of resources to the productive system, associated with the potential for retirement savings for the Chilean labor force, should act as an extraordinary reinforcement for the market economy and private investment.

Finally, "social modernization" implied a redefinition of the state's priorities of social action. The government was compelled to make a basic contribution to counterbalancing the deficiencies of the market, concentrating its action on groups living in extreme poverty. Thus the State's social intervention in the 1980s was defined within the limits of subsidiary action: the state intervenes solely because these groups are not in a position to satisfy their basic needs for themselves.

---

[1] The creators of the new order which emerged from the authoritarian experience hoped to set pre-established limits for political reforms as a final step in perfecting the economic and social reforms which preceded them. G. Rayo (1987) closely examines these concepts.

It is paradoxical that the new social pattern which took shape in that global project of "modernization" is perceived today at the grassroots level as a fact associated with the return to democracy, precisely because during the difficult years of the previous decade a collective orientation toward action still prevailed among the poor, more than within any other social group. Moreover, the collective bond was formed around a shared community, which could be subjected to ongoing siege and harassment.

While it is true that since the reinstatement of democracy, social policies have been enriched and made more extensive; social expenditures have increased; innovative organizations focusing on specific subjects (women, youth, indigenous peoples) have been created; and regional territories have been further empowered; there has been no alteration of the underlying stimulus that would encourage citizens to renew old patterns of collective or community action.

Chile's economic dynamism, complemented by active social policies, has brought an improvement in income for the population, particularly in the Metropolitan Region. However, when judgments about society are expressed, the gap is enormous between the figures which speak of increased social expenditures, decreased unemployment and fewer households in poverty on the one hand, and on the other, the perceptions of the residents of poor communities in relation to their daily lives, their expectations for the future and their role in the construction of the nation.

Municipal Changes

A second aspect that must be considered in the development of the forms of collective action at the urban grassroots level is the changing face of local administration. Municipalities, which represent one of the areas of greatest administrative change over the last 15 years, are undoubtedly the political-administrative sphere with the greatest meaning in relation to the development of collective action, especially among grassroots organizations.

Under authoritarian rule, the administration of educational establishments and primary health services was transferred from the national government to the municipalities. Simultaneously, reforms to the internal administration of the State were begun, which increased the number of municipalities through the subdivision or regrouping of those already in existence. This process carried significant costs in terms of the fracturing of communities and the weakening of spatial links or social integration in the municipalities. During that period, massive *"erradicaciones"* (forced movement of people from one geographic area to another in the name of slum clearance) took place that brought about the social homogenization of the city landscape. All too frequently, the new municipalities were staffed with less-than-inspired personnel from the central government.

The community and functional organizations in rural as well as urban areas, especially during the second half of the 1980s, became a preferred arena for manipulation by the mayors appointed by the political powers. The local governments and administrative structure created by the military regime gave the county-based Development Councils (Codeco) decision-making power in the approval of municipal plans, programs, and budgets. The participation of the community entities in these counsels was one of the justifications for the mayors' special power to modify the boundaries of existing neighborhood groups and appoint their leaders.[2]

The democratization of local administration in the early 1990s through new municipal legislation modified the selection of local authorities and led to a new vitalization of democratic culture in local management. In this process, the contribution of professionals emerging from the non-governmental world has been decisive, since many of them had gained vast experience in social and political work during the authoritarian years. However, the renovation of the administrative structures has been quite slow, and substantial changes to the basic management structure have been lacking.

Thus, the municipalities present an extremely heterogeneous picture as to their resources, the problems they face, and their capacity for action.[3] In general, poor municipalities have serious problems in maintaining significant social programs, not only because of their structural financial restrictions, but also because of the deficits caused by the dismal financial status of the services transferred during the past decade, a situation which has begun to be reversed only during the last few years. Thus, the municipalities in general, and particularly in poor communities, have seen their role limited to that of an organizer of social demands, albeit based almost entirely on sectorial decisions.[4]

Several municipalities have implemented participatory systems in order to allocate their budget for social investment, based on the model of the *Fondos de Desarrollo Vecinal* [Neighborhood Development Funds]. While the amounts involved are not significant, these funds have helped make grassroots organizations, such as neighborhood committees, more dynamic. In fact, this represents practically the only source of external funding for their community actions. In the following section we will expand on this point.

Social Investment Projects

Various governmental agencies, and increasingly the municipalities as well, allocate their funds through public bidding processes, in which local organizations compete for funding through proposals. In this way, initiatives have been undertaken such as the paving of small streets, the installation of public lighting, and the creation of parks. These social investment projects, beyond their material accomplishments, serve as a point of interaction and dialogue between the State and grassroots community organizations.

The principal stimulus mechanism for community participation used by the municipalities is the County Plan of Action (PLAC). It consists of an annual call issued to the

---

2 The guidelines in this area were very clear: "Before modifying the boundaries of a neighborhood committee, a study must be conducted as to the historic origins of the neighborhood, neighborhoods, or low-income sectors which make up these territorial units, taking into account the administration they were created under and whom they favored. Similarly, the socio-political composition of the residents must be studied, seeking to facilitate the control and predominance of moderate sectors that support the government." National Plan for Civic Action, presentation by the director of Organizaciones Sociales, Mr. Alberto Cardemil, before the VIII Congreso Nacional de Alcaldes, July 1986.

3 "The hierarchical scale in the municipal setting goes far beyond the levels of inequality seen in Chilean society itself; the three richest municipalities in Chile — Santiago, Las Condes, and Vitacura — have budgets that are 300 times higher than those of the majority of the country's municipalities," (Sepúlveda 1997).

4 Sepúlveda (1997:64-67). The same author calculates that while municipal transfers increased from 23.5% of the municipality's total budget to 35% between 1985/89 and 1994, social investment decreased from 21.6% to 13.4% during the same period.

neighborhood organizations (traditional Neighborhood Committees and newer community organizations) to present projects to the municipality. The organizations examine local problems, propose projects agreed upon within the organization and present them for financing by the municipality. The municipality assigns a certain amount of resources per neighborhood unit, and this amount is divided among the entities presenting projects.

The bidding system as a method for assigning resources in various spheres of social and cultural action is perhaps the most characteristic aspect of the social policy of the post-authoritarian period. Under this system, the state transfers responsibility to civil society for the co-design of government programs. Public agencies define a general policy of economic, social, or cultural integration, while participating institutions — public or private, universities or municipalities, or community organizations themselves — each contribute a specific vision, according to the particular needs of each place or situation.

In almost one-third of the investments made by FOSIS, the project is the result of a training and promotion process which has been preceded by the participation of the community itself in diagnosing the problems affecting it, prioritizing of those problems, and proposing possible alternatives for action. A handful of other projects are the outcome of open bids presented by community organizations that have not necessarily participated in previous training processes.

Thus, it is the people themselves who define a hypothesis for a cause of poverty (a causal link) as well as a hypothesis for overcoming it. In conceiving a project within certain budgetary limits, the group or organized community increases the project's chances of success while making the best use of available resources (see Rayo and Cordoba 1994; and for a comparative Latin American vision, Rayo 1996).

In general, the format of specific projects allows for the undertaking of multiple initiatives which are relatively easy for grassroots organizations to implement. This makes possible a highly participatory and decentralized process for generating initiatives for the improvement of the quality of life. Thus, the term "project" has come to be extensively incorporated in the language and organizational practice of the urban low-income world, although opponents of this system can still be found in this setting.

II. Motivations and Expectations Associated with Collective Action

The motivations and expectations of the various groups interviewed center on three focal points: the attempt to end urban exclusion and segregation; social contact and improved quality of life; and the creation of a safer environment for children and youth. It is very probable that the same motivations and expectations would have been expressed by similar groups two or three decades ago. However, in this new historical environment, there is a markedly different interpretation of these subjects among group members.

As the information collected through the semi-structured interviews has been processed and put in writing, we have tried to reconstruct as truthfully as possible the environments in which the protagonists have lived and formed their judgments. These are firsthand accounts by community leaders at group sessions. We have included interviews with *Grupo Solidario del Comité de Vecinos de Villa El Parral, Colectivo de Mujeres Malhuén, Vecinos Solidarios de Villa Cousiño II, Campamento Esperanza Andina, Comunidad Terapéutica de Peñalolén,* and *Coordinadora de Rock de San Joaquín.* All of them, with the exception of the last group, are from Peñalolén.

1. A SPACE IN MY CITY: BEYOND EXCLUSION AND SEGREGATION

One of the most significant themes emerging from a review of the projects presented to FOSIS or other funds created for grassroots community organizations is that of urban segregation and exclusion.

The Dynamics of Urban Segregation

It is useful to differentiate among three principal dimensions of urban social segregation, as they have been manifested in Santiago in the past few years:[5]

a) *Economic segregation,* or inequality of income within areas of the city. Economic segregation is expressed in Santiago as an increasing differentiation in the quality of life among different neighborhoods and sections of the city.

b) *Geographic segregation,* or physical isolation of various social groups. Isolation can occur in two different ways: through the geographic scale of the segregation (the great size of socially homogeneous areas creates greater segregation) or by the frequency of interactions (travel) between the zone of residence and other zones within the city. The best urban services and equipment are territorially associated with the ability to pay for them. If segregation is reduced, sectors with fewer resources can have access to such services and equipment. The appearance of new satellite shopping areas and malls in different sectors of Santiago may be reducing the scale of segregation, at least in terms of access to these opportunities and equipment.

c) *Subjective social segregation,* or the perception of living only among peers and being separated from others.

It is interesting to observe the perceptions of the residents of Peñalolén in relation to the diversification of the community, as a result of the introduction of middle-class housing developments and higher-income settlements. The leaders interviewed point out a series of advances in their community which have come about to a certain extent as a result of the increased purchasing and consumer power of the community. However, they perceive a clear division between themselves and the new inhabitants ("from the canal down and from the canal up"). This is due to the way the middle-class housing developments are structured and the fact that the homeless have had to move far from the community. The poor residents feel that the "rich" have taken land that was theirs (in a social sense, not in terms of property ownership). Only in one of the cases considered in the fieldwork was a positive value placed on the diversification of the community as a factor of integration: among those other "new inhabitants" of Peñalolén, the residents of the Esperanza Andina encampment.

---

5   This point includes contributions from Francisco Sabatini of the Catholic University's Institute for Urban Studies.

Above and Below the Canal

The community of Peñalolén has experienced extraordinary growth in real estate development, followed by an exponential rise in land prices. Thus, a substantive change has occurred within just a few years in a community previously having a population living in extreme poverty, due primarily to the construction of large middle- and upper-middle-class housing developments in the area. Perhaps one of the most interesting challenges and opportunities for Peñalolén's inhabitants and authorities is the creation of a community that incorporates both worlds, transforming the San Carlos canal from a natural frontier into a point of contact for different social groups.

As with Villa Parral, which we will discuss later on, Peñalolén has received an influx of poor families from other communities in Santiago during the last 10-15 years. Today, however, as a result of the tremendous increase in land values, poorer residents have begun to emigrate toward other communities in greater Santiago, including Puente Alto.

In each of the interviews, we set out to gather the poor inhabitants' perceptions about this modification of their community. Here is a comment from a member of the *Colectivo Mujeres Malhuén*:

> "I believe that Peñalolén is divided in two by the canal. From the canal up I believe it is the upper class, because of the huge houses, and from the canal down it is us, the marginal people. For the people in the housing committees this thing has been bad, because, for example, while the land could be for the people from right here, they are being sent to other communities, communities that are very far away for school, work, like Quilicura, La Pintana... it's like, the rich people are taking from us the land that should have been for us... they tell the committee that there is no land here, because they are selling the land very, very expensive. In the paper you find beautiful houses that I didn't even imagine were here in the community and there they do have land... so this thing is painful... some years ago people were brought here from other communities and they don't give priority to the people from this community, where they already have family roots, schools, friends, work, organizations. So, it's beginning all over again somewhere else.
>
> And that's also an uprooting of people because, for example here in this community, in the sector where we're doing the workshops, the people don't identify with this community, they don't like it because they were brought from other communities. There are no roots, they don't care at all about the municipality, they haven't even registered at the neighborhood committee or for voting, because they don't identify with this community..."

CASE 1: ESPERANZA ANDINA ENCAMPMENT

On the night of July 18, 1992, 13 committees of *allegados* (otherwise homeless families who live with relatives), comprising a total of several hundred families, began a movement toward Peñalolén Alto, at the foothills of the Andes. Many of them brought little more than the accoutrements necessary to set up shacks and tents.

> "There was an immense coming and going of people on the night of the 18th. So all of this movement alerted the police, who came three times that night to ask

me: "Mrs. Olga, did you know there are rumors of a *toma* [land occupation], and is it true?" And I said: "No captain, I don't think so, because I would know and we've been in a meeting all afternoon and nothing's happened," and we had a ton of people behind us ... that's how I fooled him all night. But in the morning they came at about six o'clock, and we had figured out a lot of strategies, I went out towards the Municipality and others somewhere else, to fool people. If they saw me at the Municipality they weren't going to think it was going to be a *toma*."

This operation was planned by José Luis and Olga, longtime partners. Olga had already solved her housing problem in 1990. In fact, after personal effort and several mobilizations carried out by the housing committees of the area, they won the project of Lo Hermida Alto which provided housing for 422 families. However, many others were waiting in different parts of the community. They had concluded the first half of the progressive housing program when both José Luis and Olga realized that they could not leave aside the other members of the "common family."

When we interviewed Olga, this encampment struck us as being very different from the Las Canchas Camp, just a few blocks from Esperanza Andina. It was well-kept and clean, with painted and dignified houses. The progressive housing program that Olga took part in had an influence over the people that followed. Still, from the previous account, we could deduce that the leadership of José Luis and Olga at the "takeover" and in the collective life that followed had impregnated the encampment, and their influence could be felt.

Olga not only left her mark on the Esperanza Andina camp. She also maintains relations with different women's committees of Lo Hermida and San Luis, although her main activity today revolves around the day care center she opened, as well as an organization dedicated to working with area youth, in which she plays an important role.

Olga defines herself politically as left-wing. She campaigned for the Peñalolén city council in 1992 as a left-wing independent. Her experience of the last few years has shown her, as she states, that people were left prisoners of the past. "Under the dictatorship, we all fought with just one aim: to rid ourselves of the regime." Then came the calm: "People were left very affected and marked by their suffering and everything they struggled against. So they don't want to fight anymore. Unless we begin to save the young people."

It does not seem an easy matter. Even the young people that have approached the organization dedicated to them seem not to believe in anything, says Olga. "It's hard for them to believe in people, in the system... they don't have faith. They always have something to object to. So there's no way to latch onto the young people." She is convinced, though, that the key is education. Her activity in the day care center expresses her conviction. "But we won't achieve much," she maintains, "if we can't turn around the attitude of the young people."

"Because it seems to me that children don't have any incentive to study, there are no child psychologists that work with you in the schools, to motivate the child. He may be very good at school things, but if the child is not motivated... if the child has other ideas? So it's good that in all schools there should be child psychologists, and that the government should have offices that make sure that no child goes without education, not one. Because the foundation of a human being, of the individual, is study, without study . . . because not many people have the chance to study, that's what happens. Assault, robberies, juvenile delinquency..."

In the political area, Olga thinks the return to democracy created excessive expectations among the people:

"... that everything would be better, that there would be better laws, that there would be justice about the disappeared persons, that there would be social justice, so that extreme poverty wouldn't be so extreme, and I have seen that there is one side of Chile that is doing that, it is the Jaguar, but the other side of Chile, the Chile that we the poor have, goes on being about the same, no more."

The Chilean society that she imagines is one where it would be possible to share more. Now, there are those who have a lot and others with little or nothing. Her ideal is a "common middle class":

"That will never be, it's a dream. That we would all be the same. There will always be more rich people than middle class, but there shouldn't be poor people. Why would a person want to be born into tremendous poverty? We should all be middle class. And for that we need what we were talking about before: education."

Her vision of Peñalolén illustrates to some degree the possibility of a community that better shares its progress:
"I believe that Peñalolén has advanced somewhat, has progressed. A little more has been shared. And when I say share, I'm saying share in housing. The topic of housing has very much marked me. So I see ... if here we have land, why can't we share? And people with more money and with public housing share the land together, so that it isn't just a community of rich or a community of poor, like they have La Pintana, for example."

CASE 2 : NEIGHBORHOOD COMMITTEE # 31 OF VILLA EL PARRAL

The Neighborhood Committee of Villa El Parral is the result of a long history of housing action which does not greatly differ from that of many other communities in our capital. It retains an inheritance of social mobilization as well as State actions in housing matters. Various political contacts have allowed its members to establish a "space of their own," perceived as a direct result of the effort made over the years. When we requested their opinions on the national situation, it appeared as a negative backdrop against which the inspiring story of Villa El Parral unfolds.

Making a Space of One's Own
The group at Villa El Parral and its longest-serving leaders come from land *tomas* in San Miguel, in an area belonging to the current community of San Joaquín. In 1974, they created the Aurora de Chile encampment when they were not able to obtain housing due to insufficient savings. They remained there for seven years. An agreement between Mayor

Juan C. Bull and the Municipality of Ñuñoa eventually gave them access to housing at El Parral, in what is today Villa Cousiño.

El Parral was an area near Avenida Grecia, surrounded by empty land and scarce work opportunities. The arrival of the new inhabitants in municipal trucks angered the inhabitants of Lo Hermida, who had counted on the assignment of the newly-built houses to their own homeless families. The reception by the combative population of Lo Hermida was violent. The newly-arrived were forced to create protective forces to defend themselves. The links with María Angelica Cristi, then the first Mayor of Peñalolén, date back to that time. In addition to the terrible reception on the part of the neighbors, this move had distanced the people from their work sources, which made the first years very difficult.

Later on, in the warmth of the community kitchens of the 1980s, trust was re-established between the two groups of neighbors. Sergio Ampuero, a Lo Hermida leader, helped usher in this new phase in the relationship. The two leaders in El Parral (Cristina Huincales and Rebeca) became coordinators of the community kitchens in Peñalolén Alto and Bajo, with a total of 16 kitchens. Their principal source of support was the Vicariate of Solidarity.

The neighborhood organizations were subject to leadership appointed by the military authorities. In the case of Villa El Parral, its last leader, Adriana Galleguillos, remained for seven years as head of the organization. The deceased Congresswoman Laura Rodríguez and her colleagues in the Humanist Party were recognized as the principal source of support for the current directors in the democratization of the neighborhood structure, as well as in the organization of housing committees among the new homeless families.

In the early 1990s, the neighborhood organization faced a crisis, apparently due to personal conflicts among its leaders. The community center remained closed, and the level of activity was low, until the reappearance of Cristina and Rebeca, whose principal motivation was to end the indifference reflected so prominently in the abandonment of the community center. Elections for new leaders were planned, attracting 16 candidates and 162 voting members. The previous administration did not provide a copy of registered members, so people had to enroll again.

Currently, the number of members is over 426 people among some 800 families inhabiting the area. It is also estimated that within the Villa there are still approximately 400 people without homes, mostly offspring and close relatives of the original inhabitants.

The Neighborhood Organization

The neighborhood organization operates on the basis of block or sub-sector directors, which make up the Board of Directors' information and communication network. There are 36 people in total, including the wife of Manuel (vice-president) who holds the position of general director on the Board. The community center is by far the greatest center of activity. It is open every day from 7 p.m. until midnight or later.

The work of the directors mainly involves issuing residency certificates and carrying out various administrative tasks at the municipality, including requests for visits by the community social worker. Emergency actions also commonly begin at the center, especially responses to the illness or death of particularly poor neighbors. In the case of El Parral, this gave rise to the Grupo Solidario, an organization composed mostly of young people. That committee undertakes preventive measures to combat emergency situations or severe poverty among the neighbors. Its president, Solange, is a young woman who has just graduated from a technical/professional high school (as a secretary) and is working as an intern for the municipality.

There are four athletic clubs in the Villa, each including some 80 people: men and women, youth and adults. A significant part of the Villa's social activity revolves around fundraising among its members. However, states Manuel, the sports associations, comprised of several clubs each, absorb a great deal of the resources, and thus it is difficult to assign money to other community activities.

There are also "mothers' groups" for women. Although the women of the Villa have not been very keen on using the community center, they are gradually beginning to participate, as are the young people. The Grupo Solidario, along with Cristina, is now working on a project for an "ecology group" called "The Three Trees." Finally, there is a senior citizens' group, supported by a FOSIS project, since many elderly people live alone and in extreme poverty. The purpose of the project is to attend to their needs and at the same time create opportunities for conversation and recreation.

With the onset of democracy, the *Centros de Accion de la Vivienda* (Housing Action Centers, CEAVI) were formed. Laura Rodriguez created a leadership school to support these, along with Cristina and Rebeca. CEAVI leaders are tasked with doing the necessary paperwork at the municipality offices and the Housing Service (Serviu), and ensuring that the municipality registers members with the CAS (government-sponsored subsidy program). They also promote various activities to supplement the funds of families that for one reason or another fall behind in the savings plan required to obtain housing.

Strategies and Spaces for Action

Last April the Villa organized an anniversary week to celebrate its 13th year. The activity focused on choosing a queen, with points awarded for the social activities that candidates' teams were able to accomplish: cleaning and decorating the center and other community spaces; obtaining books for the center library; donating clothing to the Grupo Solidario, and obtaining notebooks and pencils for the directors.

The closing festivities, which attracted prominent radio personalities, were funded by equal contributions from the municipality and the neighbors (for amplifier rental, stage setup, etc.). The jury was composed of representatives from the municipality (Community Development and Public Relations divisions) and neighborhood leaders.

Two weeks later, the Grupo Solidario organized a "mini-telethon" to raise funds for a terminal patient and care for other ill and unemployed people of the Villa. They were able to collect almost 25,000 pesos.

The women leaders interviewed (Cecilia, Rebeca, and Solange) show extensive knowledge of the various public institutions that administer social programs in the country. Among the organizations they have dealt with, or have been anxious to work with, are FOSIS, the sports agency (Digeder), the fund for the disabled (Fonadis), the women's service (Sernam), the women's education and development agency (Prodemu), and the National Institute for Youth (INJ).[6]

---

6 It is highly probable that these women will, with very little effort, achieve what repeated inter-Ministerial coordination efforts have unsuccessfully sought to do: harmonize investments and programs in one territory.

The community center is the principal focal point for social activity. Built of concrete in an open-air style, the building is in excellent condition. Its walls are peppered with posters brought from the municipality by Solange, promoting activities sponsored by various government programs (on such topics as domestic violence, senior citizens, and the opportunity to learn skills in the military). People come to the center quite eagerly. While we were there, about 15 people of different ages were present, for very different reasons. All of them were welcomed by the leaders, whose authority over the place was manifest.

At the same time, 8-10 young men played ball on a small stretch of barren land located between the center and local homes. They were the same young men who the previous Saturday had told us very clearly where Cristina lived and where we could find her at that moment. Cristina explained that those boys and young men, along with many others, had participated in activities that had once been organized with university students from the Catholic University and U. Diego Portales. These activities, years ago, had been one of the community's first learning experiences about seeking professional support. Cristina, Rebeca, and Manuel, on separate occasions, asked us to make the necessary contacts so that this type of university activity could occur once again.

The Community Center hosts many activities. Aerobics classes (sponsored by Digeder) are held three nights a week. The participants, a total of 70 housewives, attend in two different schedules and pay 200 pesos toward the instructor's transportation expenses and a mirror for the class. There are also two training courses on catering and hair styling (Prodemu); these take place in the early afternoon and attract mainly housewives. A young musician, Jorge Perez, a friend of city council member Nibaldo Mora, offers guitar classes which 10 young people attend regularly. The senior citizens' program also functions regularly at the center. For a small contribution, the use of the center is offered to all organizations. Says Cristina: "The idea of the center was to bring children and young people closer to their elders. In the grandfathers' meetings you can always see young people along with them. Young people are always helping to advertise our activities."

The contributions paid by users help to cover electricity and water expenses. Protestant church groups have also asked to use the center and will soon begin some activities there. The center also allowed a woman and her family who were forced to abandon shared living quarters to take shelter there. She has been "hired" to watch the center.

The athletic facility, located on an avenue on the south side of the Villa, is another activities center used by area organizations, thanks to efforts by the leaders and the new mayor (Carlos Alarcon). There the Grupo Solidario will hold its next activity, "The Great Mexican Show." The Grupo Solidario and the Neighborhood Committee's plan of activities for the next few months includes a get-together for area mothers, a contest for the most outstanding neighbors (which the delegates must choose), and the celebration of Father's Day and Children's Day.

The Catholic Church and its congregations "have shut themselves in around their own activities," states Rebeca. "The days when they supported us with *Comprando Juntos* (a bulk buying co-op) seem so far away."

A Long List of Remaining Items

We asked our interviewees at Villa El Parral, as well as those of the other groups, to give their opinion on two recurring issues in politics and the media: *modernization* and *growth with equity*. This group's answers typify our consistent findings among other leaders.

When we mention the first term, a list of new operations and developments in the area over the past few years spontaneously emerges: the government bank, supermarkets (Agas, Extra, Monserrat, Ekono, Homecenter), police and detectives, fire crews (two companies), clinics (two), public emergency medical service (SAPU), a sports store, the Municipal Library, a Notary Public, the Civil Registry, the post office, and an increase in local petty crime.

However, when we first talked about the concept of "growth with equity," none of our interviewees understood it. After some explicit references to reports in the media, they had much to say. The tone of their opinions changed markedly. They no longer had the same proud and optimistic attitude so characteristic of the accounts of their community experiences. The magic of their collective self-reference was broken. The complaints emerged against a society which they perceive and define as extremely unjust: a minimum wage which does not allow them to satisfy their fundamental needs in a dignified way, along with a long list of issues on which they consider themselves to be neglected and unjustly treated. It is worthwhile to attempt to sum up some of the especially relevant issues.

Rebeca, who works as an aide in a private state-subsidized school, earns the minimum wage. Before this, she was employed as a housekeeper. There she experienced scorn and insolence, even from the children of her employers. She, and the rest of the women associated with this organization, are convinced that their concern and effort to provide a professional education for their sons and daughters will mark the difference between their lives and their children's:

"Everything I do is meant to keep my daughters from falling into doing the same thing ... I already have three children who are professionals: of the girls, one is a teacher, the other is a clothing designer and works at Ripley; the third is an electrical technician."

Rebeca's two youngest daughters and a niece have approached our conversation. The three are beautiful and full of vitality. Rebeca goes on:

"It is incredible, there is our compensation, our children, all the children of this community, how beautiful they are! And healthy. I sometimes find that the children of rich people are ugly and pale, without grace.

They pay me minimum wage, and by check on top of that. It's a joke, they are making fun of us. When I go to the bank and see the checks that other people cash, I don't even feel like counting the money. I feel ashamed to do it. It's 54,000 pesos, after all the deductions. That money is just enough for 15 days. At the supermarket I see so many people who buy so much. I have to concentrate on two or three things, and on the cheapest products possible. Meanwhile, the supermarkets throw away a lot of products. That's cruel. That induces the poor to steal. Many women and children go to the supermarket and under their clothes they take out socks and diapers. What causes shoplifting? The low wages."

Manuel says the same of his work in recycling:

"In the garbage cans of the rich, one finds food that I don't eat only because of dignity, but it's good for my dogs. Appliances, new diapers. The abuse is tremendous. Democracy has not meant democracy for the poor. It's true that today we are not scared like before; we express ourselves freely. During the dictatorship the police dumped out our community kitchen supplies, sometimes with all the children's milk. Democracy has allowed us to have a voice and to vote, freedom of action. The paper scavenger's right to work was recognized. Our complaints are heard. But we expected more and better jobs. The rich get richer every day. In Chile there should be greater control of the abuse by companies and the rich."

"For the poor," concludes Solange, "modernization is only a fantasy."

2. SOCIAL CONTACT AND IMPROVED QUALITY OF LIFE: WOMEN'S ASPIRATIONS

The aspiration for social contact and increased quality of life represents perhaps the central nucleus of the initiatives of the low-income population, especially for those receiving support from organizations such as FOSIS or the municipality.

In general, the projects in which neighborhood organizations participate are driven by various factors. On the one hand is the daily struggle by the established neighbors to improve living conditions in their local setting, in a context of scarce resources and few development programs. In fact, the success of programs based on cooperative payment for services, such as participatory paving projects and progressive housing, is due largely to the willingness of many inhabitants to invest their own efforts to bring about the benefits to which they aspire. On the other hand, the tradition of actions planned and carried out for the common good is quite strong, supporting organizational life in many places and addressing a great number of different issues.

In all the cases we have seen during the course of this study, it is women who are the protagonists, representing a focal point around which the interests of the community and women's aspirations come together.

CASE 3: VECINOS SOLIDARIOS DE PEÑALOLÉN

Some time ago, "Bottom" and "Teacher" were staging a show on a set made of wooden boards held between two truck tires to collect funds among the neighbors of Villa Cousiño 2, to help a boy with hearing problems. In the audience was Virginia Eissman, a young mother with four children and a grand-daughter, who had arrived six years earlier when the Villa opened its doors.

On that occasion, Virginia realized that it was quite possible to repeat this type of initiative, with some adjustments. For that purpose she prepared, with the help of a non-government organization, a project to present to FOSIS' local initiatives program. Its specific purpose was to obtain decorations and sound equipment to improve community presentations. Her group became established as a producer of arts and recreation events to the benefit of the community. Hugo Romero, her husband, is the second director of the organization and a full-time laborer at an aluminum factory.

The group currently has 24 members, for the most part young people, including several couples.

Hugo and Virginia's principal motivation for their work is their desire to create a barrier against drugs in their sector. While drug use is a critical problem in many places in Peñalolén, this is not the case in Villa Cousiño 2. However, states Virginia, "our children, the ones that got here very young, begin to socialize with the young men of the nearby villas that come here. And children begin just by copying others, and also because their parents do not take care of them. But if you don't want a child to turn out like that, you have to support him."

These community events have not only included the work of professional artists, but have principally presented talent from the Villa itself. This has had a positive influence on the group's finances and therefore in the number of family emergencies they have been able to assist with. Last Christmas they joined with the Municipality of Peñalolén to finance a wheelchair for a sick boy. They have also assisted other poor families in buying diapers and medicine, paying for funerals, etc. They keep a detailed record of the organization's revenue and expenditures.

The presentations have extended to the neighboring sectors of Población Santa Julia, Villa El Parral, and Aquelarre. An Evangelical pastor has requested that the group visit La Florida. They have also worked with youth groups from the Jesus Servidor parish. The only things they have absolutely refused to do are lend out their equipment and support political campaigns.

The group's orientation is fundamentally that of a self-help group in relation to various unmet needs. This is a traditional association pattern in the grassroots world, which in the past was normally supported by the local church. Today they receive support from organizations like FOSIS. The self-help activities play a supplemental role in facing problems in daily life that are not covered by state services and can not be covered individually by income or loans, as is the case in middle-class sectors.

The Grupo de Vecinos Solidarios is not interested in working with other groups to pool their initiatives. They prefer to work alone and mistrust some of their would-be allies. We can observe here a functional behavior of the "small investment" type of project, for which support can be obtained from the municipality and from the public sector in general. In those systems, pooling efforts does not provide any special advantage, but it does bring many difficulties and a much slower decision-making process.

CASE 4: COLECTIVO DE MUJERES MALHUÉN

This 18-year-old group originated at a day care center of the Fundación Missio, where a group of mothers took on the challenge of facing collectively the problems that affect their gender. Workshops on personal development, sexuality, and other subjects followed. There were also opportunities for folkloric expression. Later on, like many others in the area, the group was forced to organize a community kitchen which brought together some 30 housewives. The Vicariates of Solidarity and La Morada, among other institutions, contributed to the organization's development. Since the re-institution of democracy, Sernam and the *Facultad Latinoamericana de Ciencias Sociales* (Flacso) have provided technical and training support to the group.

The majority of its leaders are women with long experience in various grassroots organizations, including human rights, youth, neighborhood, and housing groups. Today, their activities revolve around some of the most important issues directly affecting women, and they have also dedicated themselves to the development of particular interests, such as Tarot reading groups and expressive dance workshops. In their first line of work, the Colectivo Malhuén carries out training programs for women in various neighborhood units, using resources obtained from two projects selected for funding by FOSIS. One of them is focused on preventing early pregnancy in adolescent women and the other on the prevention of domestic violence.

National and Community Vision
As with the rest of the people interviewed, we asked the members of the Colectivo Malhuén to react to commonly-heard concepts or phrases in the current political debate. In general, responses heard from the other groups were echoed here.

In relation to the impact of the return to democracy on their lives, doubts immediately appeared as to its true scope: "It meant working more in peace...although in the past we did it anyway, but in a more undercover way." However, they add, the lack of opportunities continues, especially among women: "We continue to feel left out."

"I believe that on a more global level, what happens is that the grassroots sectors don't feel that their demands, their most basic needs, are considered. Like in the more day to day things, which are the things we feel the most... When there are elections and candidates present themselves with tremendous platforms, and what you hear from the young people is that they "don't care at all," you don't just hear it from them anymore, but from adults too, because in the end it's feeling that you are being taken for granted in the problems that you have: electricity, water, pavement... Then, if you don't have positive experiences in relation to these concrete necessities, the other thing comes, which also comes together with all the atomization of the movements at a grassroots level also, the thing about retribution..."

Participation in the municipality is perceived as discriminatory:

"Politicians show up for elections and then they are in their offices behind closed doors and to be able to get to see them and demonstrate your needs you have to have very good contacts... except for the organizations which have the same political tendencies as they do, but not even always then. For example, in the City Council meetings you can't speak unless you are invited to talk on a specific problem, but in general one does not have the right to an opinion or vote. So, what are we going to go there for?...not even for the 8th of March, when we could have something to say; not even for the county zoning code, there is no participation."

Once again, modernity and quality are associated with education. For these women of the Colectivo Malhuén, the great challenge for the country lies in improving the quality of education.

"Children go to school and sit in a classroom four or five hours and don't have infrastructure to do any other kind of activity, not even cultural activities; or developing their artistic capabilities, that doesn't exist here. I believe that this is what education should be worried about, educating a whole person, not just teaching them to read and write. That to me would mean modernity, that is, advancing in that sense... that children can go and develop all their abilities at a school; but we don't have that here, we don't have that."

The concept of a modern school and quality education is defined in the following terms by our interviewees:

"In the community there are schools with complete education all day, but this doesn't mean anything more. There are no schools with gymnasiums, showers, laboratories, or things where they can do other types of things. I feel that education is just teaching children just to read and write, and there is no more beyond that...In the community there are one or two schools which offer technical education, but the kids come out of there and they have no place to work ...he young women go back to their houses to play their historic roles of raising children. Some get married, others just keep raising children just like that, and there is no place to work...the young men the same: they come out with their profession and can't find work. In that sense the community is also not concerned with creating industry or creating sources of work for the young people ... In that sense, education has not advanced at all; on the contrary, it has suffered a setback."

"This country has lost a sense of the common good," state our interviewees. "We have locked ourselves in our own homes in front of our TVs. We don't worry about the neighbor, if he's all right or not; nor about much going on around us." "In the past," they add, "we shared more and we could spend whole days together. Now individualism reigns."

"I believe that, besides losing solidarity, we have lost transparency in our work, which in turn gives you credibility and allows us to believe in others. Sometimes today it's difficult to look at someone's work and look at the person and believe him...Also being able to believe in something and work for one's ideals, respecting what the other does, what the other thinks. But that has been lost, the ability to believe in something has been lost."

3. THE RIGHT TO BE DIFFERENT

These cases highlight how closely people are tied to their communities, along with the persistent will of some to organize to improve them and make them more livable. But these orientations do not cover the whole range of community organizations. There are others, among which youth groups are emblematic, that are structured around the expectations and motivations linked to self-expression and the recognition and legitimization of differences. These are not about aspects associated with a particular place, as seen with initiatives developed by adults which have "conquered" a space or have developed a life in a place and plan to remain there. The young do not have this sense of belonging, since their life histories are very short. They do not find it, either, in places that do not offer space for them in the community centers, nor in the streets and squares watched suspiciously by neighbors and the police. They also do not associate their plans for the future with the local space they inhabit. Most probably, the achievement of their goals will take them far away.

What strongly arises among young people is the need to express themselves in their own manner, speak their own language, and be heard and recognized. They perceive their proposals and even their conduct to be different from those predominant in their local communities. Thus, self-expression, recognition, and the legitimacy of differences become the focal points of young people's motivations and expectations.

The two previous factors produce an orientation that is "outward" and "toward change," something that in the sociology of action would be conceptualized as an orientation toward social movements. Perhaps the concept cannot be applied exactly to the situation of the organized youth of these communities, but in any case it contrasts with the localism and "inward" orientation of the initiatives we have previously analyzed.

CASE 5: COORDINADORA DE ROCK DE SAN JOAQUÍN

Young people between 18 and 28 years old are the protagonists of an associative experience which is not infrequent in the Metropolitan Region. Their prime motivation is music. Their first priority was to find a place to practice and listen to heavy metal music. They know that they are different, and that they are rejected for this difference. The creation of the Coordinadora de Rock, and the space contributed to them by the Municipality of San Joaquín, now opens up the opportunity to practice not just at the homes of some of the more tolerant families, but in bigger spaces with room for an audience.

The purpose of the organization was to break out of their isolation, reverse their social image, find a place and a way to say things, and open the possibility for social change. To live in marginality or choose social integration seems to be a dilemma they are still grappling with, perhaps because their marginality has become the key to an integrating proposal. At least, this seems to be the interpretation of some government agencies, such as the National Institute for Youth, FOSIS, and the Municipality of San Joaquín, who have supported and funded initiatives of this group and others like it.

Thus, the neo-Nazi image associated with their dark clothing and shaved heads does not imply a loss of societal reference. As we will soon see, their group strategy is aimed at contributing to the development of their true image. This is perhaps one of the few cases collected in this investigation in which a reference to a kind of social movement is expressly made, uniting the principles of identity and opposition with an overall vision of our society.

The contributions of this "marginal" group have been especially valued by the municipal authorities, in particular on subjects such as drug prevention among youth. After obtaining the appropriate permits, the group is now awaiting approval for a 5-million-peso grant to buy equipment and other necessities which will allow them to perform "concerts against drugs" in various San Joaquín neighborhoods.

The use of institutional resources by this group has a meaning and a purpose. It allows them to be what they are: young people who like music and who are also trying to express through their physical appearance the discontent of those who started out in life with disadvantages.

> "As for the nonconformity... it is rebellion more than anything; rebellion, when you go beyond the limits society sets and you are different from them, and the musical part influences me very much. I also look from the outside, when I began with this I looked from outside, I looked at the groups from outside, rock, heavy metal... it's as if we had a separate system... the Coordinadora was formed here in San Joaquín, well, the Coordinadora of Conchalí north zone came first. My idea is to launch the Coordinadora south zone and eventually join forces with the other Coordinadora. This thing is going to be made big, from San Bernardo to La Pintana and from Prat or from Alameda that way, that is our idea... Support from important groups is key: there are the Miserables, the Criminales, and all those groups, the groups which are now at the top, they all want to create the Coordinadora north zone, south zone, and at the same time that it be one, that it be the Black Sheep or the Black Wasp movement. I'm interested in making the bands succeed and getting rid of the idea that the longhairs are bad, they're crazy, they're drug addicts... maybe now that things are more open and people understand a little more... I went the way of showing that it's not like that, of showing that we are kids just like other kids and that maybe there are problems about succeeding in life and that maybe music can be a good release for that and at the same time not to get into other things like drugs, bad things... There are more bands coming that can do better things for this, for everything that surrounds us. So if we can, why not help those others that are coming from the other side?"

Their urban experiences seem caught up in their own and others' prejudices that often end in fist fights. Not only do they experience mistrust and beatings from the forces of law and order, but also from neighborhood gangs, or simply from neighbors, who, agitated by their shrill music, shower their practice house with stones.

> "What happened recently and was on the news... some guy in a van threw some garbage out the window. This punk was walking by. He was a punk, with shaved head and dyed hair. He took the bag of trash and threw it back at a van where there were three guys from the prison police dressed in street clothes. The guys got out of the van and beat him up, they had him for about half an hour in the van, they arrested him. Why? Because he was punk, he was somebody with a different haircut. The guy is a freshman journalism student. I think he is a good person. He spoke on the news and I think that he speaks a lot better than the three guards do; I mean his education."

The local community emerges as a natural space for the activity of youth organizations. It is there that barriers against citizen participation by youth can begin to be broken down, barriers which exist even between them and the rest of the local population.

A good example is a group of rappers from Villa Francia, which recorded a tape through a project presented to the Fundación Ideas. The recording of the cassette has allowed them to hold local shows and perform their art with great acceptance. They have even been asked to appear at the same school they were earlier expelled from for behavioral problems. In this and other experiences, we see that developing a task that affects the community allows marginal groups to project a positive image, which caps and partially modifies the pre-existing negative image. It does not involve abandoning their own practices or customs, nor does it erase the negative image held of them among some sectors of the community; it simply complements these with a socially accepted element and activates a process of dialogue and the removal of barriers. Certainly, this process is bolstered by changes in self-image among the groups, which opens up opportunities for a different role in their community.

CASE 6 : COMUNIDAD TERAPEUTICA DE PEÑALOLÉN

On one of the streets of the center of Peñalolén Alto (Población Nueva Palena) is the pizzeria "Tallarin Gordo," where approximately 35 schizophrenic patients from the *Comunidad Terapeutica de Peñalolén* are doing internships. Their age ranges from 18 to 50 years old.

The leaders of this job training program are relatives of the patients. The association was born some 10 years ago, in a small room in the parish of San Roque, with the only capital investment being love. "The young people were painting on the floor," comments Teresa, one of the longest-serving members, and today treasurer of the organization, although her child already "graduated," rehabilitated, a few years back.

The task they have imposed on themselves is that of finding jobs for their relatives and thus contributing to their integration into society and the labor force. They also set out to improve and enlarge the facilities of the community's halfway house. For this purpose, they developed and presented two projects for FOSIS funding. They have received technical support from the program *Trabajo para un Hermano*, the San Roque parish, and the pizzeria "Tallarin Gordo" of Peñalolén.

Bernardita Miranda, one of the key leaders of the group, explains the purpose of the program:

> "Our relatives, in many cases, were the skeleton in the family's closet, something which had to be hidden. Sometimes as a way of protecting them from ridicule, and even from the aggression of others. Sometimes because they embarrassed the family. Finally, they were no more than little animals. Our decision was to fight for their dignity. The success of this job project at the pizzeria came because the neighborhood began to recognize and value them, and to accept their differences. It has been a beautiful and marvelous experience. There has been a change; the objectives have gone far beyond what we had thought. The change in their quality of life, it's because they feel important, they feel more like people, they have their own values, now they recognize their own values . . . it's what they deserve, of course."

While a great number of the patients belong to families from the area, and the leaders of the group are all from Peñalolén, families living in different counties of the west zone of Santiago, and even in Las Condes, participate as well.

In the Metropolitan Region, we find 354 community organizations acting as partners to the health services. More than half of the organizations in the directory for the Metropolitan Region are active in prevention, recuperation, and/or rehabilitation on a local scale (support groups for chronic patients, disabled persons, persons under stress, and recovering alcoholics). Thirty percent are linked to initiatives to promote health in local communities, among which are the senior citizens' clubs, health committees, and the community health monitors.[7]

In the following section, we will discuss further the action of these groups and the way in which their motivations translate into associative models and strategies for action.

III. Strategies and Spheres of Action

Our fieldwork was partly oriented towards investigating the strategic approaches used by grassroots community organizations as well as their preferred spheres of action. We will present, first, some general data about the associations existing in the Metropolitan Region and particularly in Peñalolén, based on the rich array of information offered by the FOSIS databases and project bank. Second, we will comment on four aspects that, in light of this study, appear decisive for what we might call the "sustainable presence" of the community organizations of the urban grassroots world. They are: legal recognition of the organizations by the public authorities; access to public funding; the control of physical spaces; and effective leadership. Finally, we will examine the type of relationship established by community organizations with political institutions.

SPHERES OF ACTION IN THE METROPOLITAN REGION

In spite of all the time that has passed and the country's drastic economic and social changes, the Neighborhood Committee continues to be the principal form of community grouping in urban as well as rural areas. During the last few years there has been a multiplication of these in smaller territorial spaces, as a result of new legislation which allows their creation with a smaller number of members. The reasons for this have included urban expansion and higher density; the lack of sufficient leaders and organizational resources to maintain the traditional structure; and, certainly, the political strategies of the various partisan formations in community spaces. However, beyond regulatory considerations, what can readily be established is that this multiplication of associations tends to break the territorial, organizational unity of the neighborhood units.

According to the most recent figures for the Metropolitan Region, there are more than 2,438 Neighborhood Committees.[8] Information as to the number of members is only available for 1,003 of these; their total is 318,385, giving an average of 317.4 members per organization. The mothers' groups in the Metropolitan Region number 1,032, and membership information is only available for 32.1% of these (331 organizations) with a total of 10,113 members, indicating an average of 30.6 members in each mothers' group.

---

7   See *Directorio de Organizaciones de Salud Region Metropolitana*, Ministerio de Salud, and Division de Organizaciones Sociales del Ministerio Secretaria General de Gobierno.

8   The data were obtained through the Department of Information of the Ministerio Secretaria General de Gobierno (Information Office). The total for the Metropolitan Region is probably much greater, since no figures are included for several of its important counties.

In Peñalolén, there are 156 Neighborhood Committees, with up-to-date membership information available for only 22.4%, far below the regional average of 41.0%. The average number of members per organization, based on the available information, is 392.1.

In contrast, Peñalolén's mothers' groups keep much more up-to-date records, with information on 61.5% of the cases.[9] The number of mothers' groups is 26, and 16 of them have up-to-date information on their members, representing a total of 347 women with an average of 21.7 people per organization.

The athletic clubs in the Metropolitan Region number 1,383. Those with up-to-date membership information number 557, with a total of 47,366 members, resulting in an average of 85 people per organization. In Peñalolén, the athletic clubs total 122 with approximately 78.9 members on average. Here, the number of clubs is far beyond the regional average per community. This is consistent with the statements of the majority of local observers, who maintain that the area's athletic clubs have an outstanding capacity to attract participants from different age groups, including a substantial number of women.

FOSIS, through the more than 20,000 projects it has received and evaluated, has recorded an interesting sample of the topics focused upon by civil society during the 1990s. This universe includes those projects selected by FOSIS as well as those that, since they were not selected, have not gone through the filter of relevance exercised by the regional or local authorities. Of the projects, approximately 20% stem from various urban and rural community organizations, which are possibly those with the greatest levels of protagonism in their respective social spaces.

These FOSIS projects represent initiatives that can be carried out with very limited budgets, and whose development includes contributions not only from the participants themselves, but also from third parties, especially in the financing of ongoing costs. These limitations determine the range of possible investments. However, in spite of the enormous associative energy demonstrated by several hundred organizations all over the country, some of the testimony collected harshly judges the insufficiency of the State's efforts to change the current order of things.

Relative Participation of Community Organizations in Biddable Social Investment Funds

When examining the projects presented to FOSIS since it began its operation, we find that, in the case of the Metropolitan Region, only 13.5% represent initiatives by community organizations. It is important to mention, however, that 338 projects (8.4%) are recorded without information in relation to their executors, and because of their subjects as well as the level of investment involved, it is highly probable that a significant number of them come from grassroots community organizations.

The Neighborhood Committees are responsible for more than 50% of the projects proposed by community organizations in the Metropolitan Region. Thus, they continue to represent the principal organizational structure in the urban grassroots world, largely because of their legal recognition with the public authorities on the local and national levels. However, they are far from being an urban phenomenon; in rural regions, we find relative participation to be even higher than that found in the Metropolitan Region.

---

9   The key here is former mayor and current Congresswoman M.A. Cristi.

TABLE 1

PARTICIPATION IN THE FOSIS PROJECT DATABASE BY VARIOUS ASSOCIATION TYPES FROM THE METROPOLITAN AREA, 1990-97

Type of Organization	Number of Projects	Percentage
Sports Clubs	52	9.6
Independent Workers' Unions	44	8.1
Work Groups	42	7.7
Neighborhood Organizations	273	50.2
Youth Organizations	30	5.5
Local Development Committees	89	16.4
Mothers' Groups	10	1.8
Church Groups	4	0.7
Total Social Organization Projects	544	100.0
Metropolitan Area Projects	4,031	

Source: Figure taken from the FOSIS database.

TABLE 2

PARTICIPATION IN THE FOSIS PROJECT DATABASE BY VARIOUS ASSOCIATION TYPES FROM THE PEÑALOLÉN NEIGHBORHOOD, 1990-97

Type of Organization	Number of Projects
Sports Clubs	6
Independent Workers' Unions	0
Work Groups	4
Neighborhood Organizations	6
Youth Organizations	2
Local Development Committees	0
Mothers' Centers	0
Father/Head of Household Centers	2
Women's Groups	4
Labor Workshops	2
Church Groups	0
Human Rights Commission	1
Total Social Organization Projects	27
Peñalolén Projects	128

Source: Figures taken from the FOSIS database.

The local development committees or coordinators, units conceived by FOSIS itself, have the second highest representation among biddable projects (16.4%). These committees are in all likelihood the most temporary organizations in the sample, since they are created solely to encourage the community to devise social investment projects. In fact, for

TABLE 3

NEIGHBORHOOD ORGANIZATION THEMES AND PROJECTS, METROPOLITAN AREA, 1990-97

Theme	Description	Number of Projects	Percent of All Neighborhoods
Quality of Life	Athletic Fields and Locker Rooms	23	
	Housing Improvement	8	
	Pedestrian Walkways	6	
	Plazas and Green Belts	16	
	Playgrounds	13	
	Environmental Health	3	
	Drug Prevention	7	
	Fire Prevention	10	
	Subtotal	86	35.0
Basic Services	Street Lighting	18	
	Potable Water, Public Restrooms, Drainage, and Sewers	12	
	Subtotal	30	12.2
Generation of Income	Work Training	7	
	Subtotal	7	2.8
Communication and Expression	Libraries	8	
	Cultural Activities	2	
	Social Centers	82	
	Youth	7	
	Children	21	
	Senior Citizens	2	
	Women	1	
	Subtotal	123	50.0
Other	Not Classified		
	Total Neighborhood Organization Projects	246	100.0

Source: Figures taken from the FOSIS database.

the most part they have been no more than an instrumental resource of the Neighborhood Committees, to associate themselves with other organizations such as athletic clubs and mothers' groups.

The mothers' groups show a low rate of participation in project proposals. In the Metropolitan Region, they present only 1.8% of total projects to FOSIS. The athletic clubs represent a significantly greater proportion than the rest of the traditional organizations. These are, without a doubt, the leading form of association among the youth groups, enjoying nearly twice the participation of any other youth organizations in the conception and presentation of projects. Cooperative links are also more frequent among athletic clubs.

In the community of Peñalolén, the grassroots community organizations were the originators of 21.1% of the projects presented to FOSIS throughout its history. This is a significantly higher rate than that seen among similar organizations in the Metropolitan

Region as a whole. In Peñalolén, the Neighborhood Committees and athletic clubs exhibit similar rates of participation in the presentation of projects. The independent workers' unions as well as the mothers' groups have presented no projects, whereas the collectives or women's groups and cultural associations emerge as significant protagonists in this county. Also completely absent are the parish groups or other church entities, which exhibited high levels of social action in Peñalolén in the past. This is a tendency seen throughout the Metropolitan Region.

Priority Topics Among Projects
Proposed by Community Organizations[10]
The topics associated with social investment have been classified into four groups: quality of life, basic services, fundraising, and communication and expression.

Among the topics of greatest frequency, 56.9% of the projects relate to the area of *social contact, communication, and expression*. They are generally aimed at constructing, restoring, or improving community centers, the preferred meeting place of the urban and rural poor. Within this same group, it is important to note the number of projects oriented toward the recreation and care of the neighborhood's children. On the other hand, projects specifically oriented toward area youth are only one-third of the latter.[11]

Among the projects presented to FOSIS by Neighborhood Committees in the Metropolitan Region, topics related to *providing basic services* only amount to 12.2% of all the projects proposed by these institutions. On the other hand, the array of projects aimed at the creation of *meeting, social contact, and communication facilities* reaches 50% of this same total, always with the absolute priority of the construction or improvement of the community centers. Finally, those projects related to *improvem
ent of the quality of life* reach 32% of the total, covering areas such as athletic fields, fire prevention, parks, drug prevention programs, projects oriented toward children, etc.

CHANGES IN ASSOCIATIVE PATTERNS

Probably one of the most revealing aspects of the new relationship between neighborhood organizations and political power is the party de-affiliation of local leaders. In the case of Peñalolén, it is instructive to note what has happened with the Christian Democratic Party. In the mid-1960s, the *Programa de Promoción Popular*, among its other effects, facilitated the emergence of a generation of prominent Christian Democratic leaders in the low-income sectors of Peñalolén, as in the majority of counties across the country (some later became Congressional candidates). In the 1990s, despite the fact that two community

---

10 A survey conducted by the Programa de Economia del Trabajo (PET) in 1993 in various low-income communities of Santiago, among them Lo Hermida of Peñalolén, ranked people's problems and priorities with regard to the development of the neighborhoods. That study concluded that citizen safety stood at the first rank of priority, with 27.8% of weighted references (priorities of 1, 2, or 3), at a time when this topic earned the same priority in all public opinion surveys in Santiago. The two topics that followed, in order of importance, were street paving (18%) and improvement of health centers (13.6%). This is one of the few opinion studies on this topic focused on low-income sectors, and 73.8% of its sample was made up of women. See Urmeneta (1994).

11 See the examination of youth issues and self-managed projects by youth in Gonzalo de la Maza and Carlos Ochsenius, "Evaluación del Programa Jóvenes y Ciudadanía, de la Fundación IDEAS," (Santiago, 1997).

organizations are led by Christian Democratic representatives, among leaders of functional organizations in Peñalolén, there are practically no members of that party.

All of the organizations interviewed cultivate political relations on the municipal and
parliamentary levels, while with varying intensity and approaches.[12] Municipalities,
meanwhile, have established policies of liaison and resource allocation that do not especially favor the traditional Neighborhood Committees; any functioning organization is
considered a valid intermediary, as long as it has legal recognition.

A close link can immediately be discerned between improvements in living conditions — housing, electricity, water and sewer systems — and a lower associative intensity
within the Neighborhood Committees. In the opinion of local leaders, the community
organizations, and especially the Neighborhood Committees, have been weakened by the
evolution toward better conditions in the poor urban environment. The organizations
which have succeeded in overcoming this growth crisis are those which have been able to
diversify their themes and proposals.

A third aspect which should be mentioned is the relative weakening of the mothers'
groups. These continue to follow an associative pattern exhibited throughout their history, principally oriented toward training workshops. They continue to be a nuclear and
atomized organization, although some of their second-degree associations enjoyed
moments of splendor in the past, such as the Union of Peñalolén Mothers' Groups.
However, they still exist as a preferred point of contact for women of the community.
According to the testimony of an experienced leader, they represent a space where women
can seek training in the hope of generating additional income for their family group, and at
the same time escape from their household routine for a while in order to unite in "collective catharsis" with their peers. Out of the mothers' groups, many other forms of association have arisen, both women's organizations and functional ones (such as buying co-ops).
We will develop this subject a bit further in the sections that follow.

Instrumental Relations with Politics

It is common among members of grassroots community organizations to hold a strongly
critical opinion of the functioning of political institutions. Institutionalized politics are
perceived to occur "over there," in another place, with other subjects as protagonists.
Frustration is manifested in relation to the hopes placed on democracy (as opposed to dictatorship).[13] A negative opinion of politicians is a constant in the various public opinion
polls. However, community leaders and organized groups make some allusions to the
expectation of a more direct participation in political issues, as well as a feeling that others
are preferred instead.

The demand for profound changes in the situation of the sectors the organizations
wish to represent may take the form of nostalgia for state action, radical socio-ethical criticism, desperation, or even cynicism. In all cases, it is a confession of powerlessness, since it

---

12 In almost all of the cases, any political or party link is either absent or is denied; however, in nearly all of
   them, these did exist in the past, and local political observers and operators have no trouble identifying the
   political affiliations of the majority of the leaders we interviewed.

13 "Tremendous mistrust exists among community leaders, without distinction. This extends to several sectors: the national government, Congress, and the municipalities, among others. Political activity is seen as
   a field that is foreign to the reality of poverty and the poor, centered on satisfying the interests of those who
   are involved in it," Consejo Nacional de Superación de la Pobreza (1996:38).

is recognized that these changes will not take place. As Tomas Moulian states, "politics sees itself faced with a double restriction which conspires to asphyxiate it. The first restriction is the absence of a cultural space for the transforming ideologies, which are still tainted by the stigma of irrationality they have not been able to overcome. The second is the trend toward technification which emanates from hegemonic neo-liberalism and which separates politics from the representatives as well as from the common citizens, unless it is about local issues where the underlying aims are not questioned . . . " (Moulian 1997: 60).

A cynical position is held by Chilean society, a symptom of the degradation of the institutions. Here we can not help but evoke the warning of Bengoa (1996: 103): "'Public lies' murder collective memory, but the truth, in contrast, allows the re-establishment of the order which has been shattered."

> "We are opposed to all of those things that are known as the system, we use their own methods to work against them... We are realists. Yes, that is what happens, we have grown up with a realist mentality. A politician easily controls a young person. Because this has a history: young people who fought for vindication years ago, they used young people and where were the young people left? Why are there so many drug addicts and all that? . . . It's not that we are resentful either, on the contrary, we all work, study. Still we are in the system, we have to adapt to it, even if we disagree; we have to adapt all the same, any way we can."
>
> "Nowadays I don't think we can say that politics helps the people... that's what I read and what caught my attention and I thought that it was kind of crazy that they pay them on top of it all and that in Congress they do nothing. . . politics can be done in different ways; it's not just doing party politics, but a politics let's say about everything that's happening daily, in other words, politics we do without wanting to, social politics. I think that it is a joke. If I had the chance to speak to a parliamentary representative I would tell him. I haven't had the chance to be with Mrs. Cristi, because we are going to tell her, she's the closest one we have here in the Villa."
>
> *(Grupo Solidario Villa El Parral)*

> "Besides being a candidate for city council at that time. . . the community organizations of Lo Hermida or Peñalolén chose me to represent them as an independent candidate, knowing we would not win. Electoral law does not anticipate the election of an independent. It would have to be a landslide of votes in order to win. We knew we wouldn't, but that gave us the option of covering up the land takeover, covering up all the work of the toma. They saw groups, in meetings, it was the work of the campaign to everybody; that is, to everybody that didn't know, but we were organizing the land occupation then."
>
> *(Interview with Olga, Esperanza Andina)*

The leaders cultivate relations with all the city council members, independent of their political inclinations. A neighborhood leader states that he has to maintain relations with all of them. Each one commits to something. About their relationship with Congresswoman M.A. Cristi, they confess:

"I would say more than anything else because of necessity. For the need to obtain perhaps some gains, for the well-being of our Villa and the well-being of our people, but we are not politically linked to her, no. Because I have talked to her, Berta also, about leaders and projects launched by ourselves or by our people... that is, we are taking advantage . . . We are taking the example from them as politicians. They take advantage from us as people, as residents, as the population. When they need votes, they promise the moon and the stars. They convince the people, and after they get what they want, they forget. We are doing exactly what they do."

(Grupo de Jóvenes Solidarios Villa El Parral)

For her part, Olga, as leader of the Esperanza Andina camp, defines her relationship to the parties as "bittersweet":

"Because we are from the left, we do not have a political party. But we consider ourselves from the left because we are . . . because it's our class, because we are poor, because we are from the poor neighborhoods, the *pobla*, we are the people, the *pobla*. So we consider ourselves from the left because we have leftist ideas, but the political parties from the left or the right have left a lot to be desired in the community. Like sometimes a little better, then a little struggle, because we never let ourselves be manipulated, by any political party, even if it is from the left. Although I appreciate very much the people from the left, we have never let ourselves be manipulated by anyone. At the beginning of the *toma* we were in contact with the Communist Party, with Gladys Marín, we were with Mireya Baltra, but when we first did the *toma*, a day came ... That day of the *toma* all the political parties were there to say to the government "well, no, don't kick the people out of here." Then, they came to suggest that now that the *toma* had been done, why not give them control of the organization of the camp. And our own people from the left, we were supposed to put them out in the street. How could they even suggest that, these are grassroots organizations, not political parties... that is, you can't ask anybody for a favor if they plan to collect the bill ... no, we are not here for that. We don't work to hand over our effort to the political parties. Never. Because people would stop believing in us..."

Low-intensity Associative Organizations and Networks

The organizations studied here are, in all cases, small nuclei with low-intensity participation. In the case of the active Neighborhood Committee # 31 of Villa El Parral, for example, the number of homeowning families is approximately 800, while it is estimated that approximately 400 additional families or nuclei are sheltered by these families. However, the number of actual members is 426 people, that is, just 18% of the potential members (two adults per family). Furthermore, the number of voters in the last Neighborhood Committee elections was 162; that is, 38% of registered members and only 6.8% of potential members.

The grassroots organizations of the 1990s, contrary to the pattern of the previous decade, have opted for an autonomous and atomized way of working, where each organization focuses its activity upon its own environment and needs. There is some mistrust in relation to "the others," as well as the fear of being used in various ways. As we will soon show, the impulse toward broad social movements seems completely non-existent.

There are relationships established among organizations, however, for the shared use of equipment and physical spaces for recreation activities, for example. Visiting a range of organizations in different areas of the county, we found repeated references to the same names and groups.

Protagonism of Women

In almost all cases, except for those of the Neighborhood Committee of the Población la Faena and the Coordinadora de Rock of San Joaquín, our main interviewees were women. Only occasionally could we find a lone male figure, playing more of a companion role to the women's protagonism. This is the case of Virginia's humble but well-read partner, who, disenchanted with trade unionism, chose to help her in her neighborhood project.

The community space, with the sole exception of the athletic clubs, is definitely the domain of women, a fact which is interpreted in different ways:

> "I believe that women keep their values at all times. I think that social values are more concentrated in women. Women are more organized, women have been in good times or bad times, always organized, although less than before, but in the same way ... Because they began at that time, 10 years ago. Women began to value themselves ... men have just let themselves be, the rest of the people have just let themselves be, they have become demoralized."
>
> *(Interview with Olga, Esperanza Andina)*

> "Women as the transmitters of roles, as teachers, as educators, have a great effect on what future society will be like, future generations ... One knows one's situation, how things are happening, and one has to have an opinion."
>
> *(Colectivo de Mujeres Malhuén)*

> "In these cases it is always the mother that has the responsibility. That is the reason why you will always see few men, whether it's the father or brother or any male relative, because his woman, mother, sister, always women, they always take the responsibility ... in illnesses especially, it is women who bring people into this world and women have to bear it. It's what happens with this illness, with what we know."
>
> *(Comunidad Terapeutica)*

Formalization and Economic Rationalization of Social Assistance Organizations

We will next examine a set of organizations different from the previous ones, whose spheres of action are located in various counties of the Metropolitan Region. These are the old community kitchens, now turned into service companies. Here, women are also the protagonists, but they are oriented toward finding their place in the job market. These organizations may have their own particular characteristics, but they clearly exemplify the tensions involved in the changes of the last decade, especially the ways in which they have affected the forms of collective action developed by grassroots sectors.

SCENARIO 7: FROM COMMUNITY KITCHENS TO SERVICE COMPANIES

Community kitchens (*ollas comunes*) emerged in the 1980s as an initiative by women residents to cope with the critical unemployment and hunger of that period. In many cases, they accompanied land *tomas* and legal and illegal strikes. These groups would gather economic resources, materials, and food, along with their willingness to cook collectively, and thus contribute to filling the community's nutritional needs.

The community kitchens became an opportunity for participation and identity, and at the same time for the development of new women community leaders, many of whom have come to be among the principal creators of the community organizations of the 1990s. They enjoyed the support of the Catholic Church through the Vicariate of Solidarity and those of their areas, which in turn channeled international aid to these community organizations. Thus at the beginning of democratic rule there were approximately 190 community kitchens in the Metropolitan Region.

The conversion of the community kitchens began as a way of adapting them to the democratic setting. Their principal objective was to achieve economic autonomy, closing the chapter of dependence on international help and Chilean churches. The option chosen to achieve this goal involved an unusual link with some government agencies.[14] In fact, the national scholarship and assistance board (Junaeb) formalized an agreement with the community kitchen coordinators contracting for the supply of 20,000 daily meals for its school nutrition program (PAE). The community kitchens' national leadership served as the central coordination point for the project, and the sector coordinators were put in charge of overseeing the implementation in the counties.

The idea of the conversion was to combine the concept of solidarity (inherent to the organization) with entrepreneurial ideas, retaining the kitchens' internal efficiency as far as possible, as well as its systems for decision-making and equal participation by the members. The kitchens would become local companies that would contribute to the development of their areas and which would be recognized in community life, under a sectoral community kitchen coordination unit. In order to reach these goals, the kitchens were supported technically and financially by FOSIS through a non-government agency (*Programas de Acción con Mujeres*, Prosam) which had assisted them in the earlier period.

The first concessionaire company emerged from the coordination unit "La Pincoya," which brought together eight kitchens and began to serve primary school D-149. After the signing of the relevant agreements and the formalization of the organization as a limited corporation, the enormous success of the experience motivated La Pincoya to participate in a public bid to take over all the PAE catering in the entire county. In 1994, the organization went from serving just one school to providing meals for 11 schools and eight day care centers.

A similar experience occurred with "Pudahuel Norte," which already serviced four schools in 1993. Between 1993 and 1994, PAE concessions were assigned to six more

---

14 In 1990, Novib, a Dutch assistance agency, contributed support toward the conversion of the community kitchens, supporting the work of the National Command. The Food and Nutritional Services Support Agency (Prosan), created later, assisted the community kitchens in acquiring self-management techniques in addition to their focus on community service, allowing them to broaden their services to Junaeb. Economic support was thus accompanied by technical consulting.

coordination units, bringing the challenge of broadening their coverage in the number of meals served as well as the number of women workers.

In order to carry out new functions, the coordination units incorporated themselves as limited partnerships. Out of the 20 existing coordination units emerged eight food service companies, concessionaires of the Junaeb, supported by a total of 58 grassroots organizations. The number of educational establishments served rose to 53, generating a total of six million pesos in profits.

The development of this initiative brought positive consequences for the schools (in the improved quality of the food and a better relationship with the children), as well as for the organizations themselves, whose members now enjoyed a formal, paid job. However, during the conversion, substantial changes occurred in the dynamics of the organizations. Only a small group participated in the businesses, since these had to be profitable. The women who formed the companies are decisively split: some are the "bosses" (the legal partners) while the others are the "employees" (the food handlers). The operation of the businesses accentuated the differences between the women in order to ensure productivity, the fulfillment of obligations, the ongoing development of the company, etc. Within the internal structure, the women who were leaders took strongly hierarchical roles, which did not allow for greater levels of participation. Among them, the position of the woman responsible for finances acquired the most power (more even than that of the supervisor).

Thus, the community kitchens turned into small and homogenous work groups, which for the most part had charismatic and authoritative leadership, and therefore very limited participatory opportunities within an authoritarian, paternalistic, and trustworthy organizational culture. On the other hand, an informal and flexible operational structure was developed, with implicit rules for its worker members.

The historic leaders personified an entrepreneurial sense of risk, direction, and even ownership of the service companies. The concentration of information at the managerial level also contributed to the weakening of the self-management idea among the women who prepared the food.

In relation to the distribution of profits, while the original idea was to distribute a percentage to remaining community kitchens to purchase groceries, this occurred only the first two years. After that time, the share of the profits was increased for the service teams, and that of the kitchens was reduced, as they simultaneously decreased in number. After a lengthy debate it was decided that a percentage of the profits would be divided among the partners and the rest would be utilized to finance wage improvements for the workers, and also to create a social fund for activities of the women of the company.

Once the root cause for the organization of the community kitchens had disappeared, the running of the companies became complex, putting an end to the intention of democratic management and shared ownership. The legal structure adopted by the companies was used as an argument by the leaders to claim its ownership, and the premise of equality of conditions and shared ownership was used by the workers to justify their lack of discipline.

Currently there are a number of relatively well-established companies. For example, in Cerro Navia and Huechuraba, approximately 50 people work in each company, serving about 15 schools each. They depend, however, on the "quota" from the Junaeb, since they suffer from a lack of working capital, high labor costs, and the inability to achieve economies of scale.

The State has taken an active role in reserving a small quota of the "market" for the small concessionaires, such as these service companies. However, it "negotiates" that space with the bigger concessionaires, who hope the state will end this "charity" given to the women. Yet it has not followed the local small business logic, since it has also granted them concessions in communities different from those of their origin, creating "competition" expressed in sharp conflicts among the women. The State has confirmed the quality of the service —which is much better than that of the big companies — but not the quality of the companies themselves. These operate highly "informally," with much more relaxed procedures for contracts, retirement funds, salaries, etc., than those of the larger catering firms.

The companies have been gradually changing their work force, although employees are still predominantly relatives of the women partners, some of whom also played important roles in the community kitchens. The "businesswomen" continue to hold leadership positions within their communities, often chairing Neighborhood Committees, with a degree of influence which is increased by their new economic roles. At the same time, some of the companies also carry out social activities in the neighborhood and in conjunction with the municipality.

The self-image of the leaders, today partners in a business, is that of great effort, great success, and in some cases, great social responsibility. On the other hand, those who obtained jobs this way (the women food handlers) consider the contrast with those who took a managerial role to be unfair, although this division of labor may be more economically efficient. A large group of women was left by the wayside in this process, without being absorbed by an organization, within a trend of de-activation and atomization of individual groups.

While the collective action represented by the community kitchens in the low-income neighborhoods of Santiago has not completely disappeared, the conversion supported by State and non-governmental agencies has been difficult for the women involved, a phenomenon also seen in other organizations, such as labor workshops. Small and medium-sized companies have appeared which are kept afloat in conditions of high economic exploitation and self-exploitation of their participants. A great deal of the community logic that inspired the groups internally has been lost, although in some cases, local activity has been instituted which contains elements of community development. A "family" spirit runs through all of the stages of the process: it was present at the creation of a local space through the *toma* of lands; it was key in the emergence of the community kitchens; and today it is at the foundation of the service companies. Finally, the State has become an economic player in providing partially-protected market conditions, but it has not picked up on the local, community, or gender experiences analyzed here.[15]

---

15 Sources: Prosam; interview with partners of Empresa de Servicios de Quilicura, Mrs. Ruth Gálvez, and Lutgarda González; and the debate surrounding the doctoral dissertation of Benedetta Calandra, "From low-income economic organization to food service company: a case study," (University of Rome III, Santiago, July 8, 1997).

3. STRATEGIC ORIENTATIONS AMONG ORGANIZATIONS

The leading groups interviewed agree that grassroots community organizations require certain basic institutional, material, and human resources to develop and thrive. Among the absolute requirements are legal recognition; access to public funding and the possibility of generating income; and the availability of physical space and effective leadership.

The Right to Exist

Legal recognition by public powers remains a decisive factor for any type of associations which aspires to some degree of organizational sustainability. This is especially true given that recognition is the first step in gaining access to public programs and funding sources, among local[16] as well as national agencies. It is no coincidence that the community leaders interviewed demonstrate extensive knowledge of the opportunities offered by the State through its various participatory programs. There is widespread familiarity with institutions such as FOSIS, Digeder, Prodemu, and Fonadis, among others. The publicizing of these programs by the municipality and other social communication mechanisms have undoubtedly contributed to this.

Legal recognition is also the recognition of a social function, and that is how it is understood by the leaders of the Comunidad Terapeutica de Peñalolén:

> "The other day I went to a convention and I was surprised to find out that our organizations, because of the fact that all its leaders are all volunteers, are tertiary organizations; and I asked why and they said that we were the most important thing in the world. And if you start thinking, if it is in a county, if you go step by step, we are the base of sustainability for a municipality, us, the tertiary organizations as you call them . . . Because if weren't for us, the government would not acknowledge this, the health authorities would not acknowledge this, and it's sort of like lighting a wick, and the wick goes until it gets to something like a firecracker. So, I think it's time the government took us seriously, like real organizations... we are the driving force of a new political structure of the country, because we, in the end tell the government 'this is what's happening,' because they see what's at the top, they see what their ministers, what their aides show them, so we from down here below say: 'you know what, there is also this.'"

Even those organizations most removed from public formalities, such as the Coordinadora de Rock de San Joaquín, have not been able to elude this step and have had to accept it:

> "Now as a Coordinadora, with the official stamp of approval, we are going to demand a letter: 'You committed on such-and-such a date to fix this thing' and with the letter we are going to go and they are going to have to fix it. Whatever activity there is, we are going to be there. It's that simple."

---

16 Several municipalities have implemented participatory systems for the allocation of their social budgets (originating in the experience of the Fondos de Desarrollo Vecinal). While the amounts are not considerable, they have nonetheless added to the dynamism of organizations such as the Neighborhood Committees.

The Coordinadora de Rock recognizes the flexibility of the Youth Office of their county, and although it thinks that even for this office things aren't easy at the municipality, it applies for funding for local projects through them.

"They also have to fight against red tape to get sponsorships or get us resources, not only money but also places to play, or whatever. We are against what they call the 'system,' but we operate within the system, we use its own things to work against it."

This is the situation and the attitude of many youth groups that seek projection and stability in their work, with more specific demands than those of other groups, involving institutional resources and support (places to play, funding, transportation, etc.). The extreme weakness of the local institutional networks in channeling the interests and activities of young people is manifest among these groups. The great majority of groups proposing projects supported by the Fundación Ideas, for example, showed difficulties in obtaining other contributions, even over the short term, from other institutions and local organizations. The shortage of municipal youth programs, the lack of support from educational institutions, the refusal of Neighborhood Committees to let youth groups use the community centers, and the absence of alternative organizations or institutions to the municipality in some counties, are all factors affecting young people's integration into the community. The impact of small projects in this area is greatly reduced if there is no explicit provision for the sustainability of the initiatives in the future.[17]

An aspect especially highlighted by youth leaders in their relationship with local institutions is the absence or shortage of initiatives and municipal offices oriented toward young people. Links to the municipality are valued, but it is considered to be an institution that is inhospitable to young people, which does not have programs for them and which tends to exploit their groups for political purposes. For example, after the end of the project by the Coordinadora de Rock de Conchalí, the organization lost the right to use the municipal facility, which was interpreted by its leaders as a change in the political needs of the Mayor, after his re-election.

Fundraising

As the previously cited youth experiences demonstrate, legal recognition of an associative entity is the prerequisite for a flow of resources and the public help necessary for the development of the group's activities. In some situations, however, this support has only been the initial step in a strategy aimed at the generation of independent revenue and the reduction of dependency on the State, to the extent possible.

A case of successful fundraising is that of the Colectivo de Mujeres Malhuén, which has accomplished this on the basis of their increasing experience and skill in adolescent training. The beginning was not easy, since the potential customers for their services, the educational institutions, were hesitant due to the group's lack of professional accreditation.

---

17 These observations emerge from an analysis of fifteen projects selected in the Concurso de Iniciativas Juveniles, "Contigo Igual," of the Fundación Ideas, for the Metropolitan and Eighth regions. This contest allowed for three areas of action: civil rights, labor rights and sexuality (G. De la Maza and C. Ochsenius, op. cit.).

However, as the women tell, "later, when they began to see us work, they realized that it was a necessary and well-done job, especially because of the enthusiasm and motivation that the students showed."

> "The Colectivo uses the money from the project as a salary, an incentive for the monitors, and for materials. But they also, as an organization, have maintenance expenses, which they finance with parties and folklore shows."

The Coordinadora de Rock de San Joaquín follows a similar logic in explaining the use of the funds they may obtain through the project presented to the municipality:

> "To buy implements, equipment, and then we're going to put on shows against drug use in all of the counties. There we're going to show the groups we have for now and we're going to go out on the street with everything. We're preparing it, because there are people who are seeing the social impact this should have, and there are people who see more the musical part; so, there are brains thinking on both sides, but we all work together. I go for the music side, by far, but there are also people who see the social part, and we're connecting all this and we want to be a part of it."

Availability of Physical Space

A second key aspect for the development and sustainability of organizations is obtaining a physical space in which to function. This is demonstrated by the enormous frequency of projects presented by all sorts of organizations seeking to build and improve community centers.

A well-used community center, as demonstrated by the Neighborhood Committee of Villa El Parral and the Grupo Solidario, encourages cross-generational interaction, a basic factor in the ongoing renewal of leadership in community organizations as well as in the diversification of topics and initiatives. In this sense, Villa El Parral and the Población La Faena are located on opposite poles. In the first center, the scene is one of youth activities, library spaces, training courses, game and tarot room, gymnasium, party room, kitchen, and meeting room, with the walls giving colorful accounts of public and private life. At La Faena, a center which triples the other in size, only emptiness reigns.

Due to the strategic importance of this subject, it lies at the heart of many organizational tensions. It is the conflict between Virginia Eissman, director of the project Vecinos Solidarios de Villa Cousiño 2, and the president of her sector's Neighborhood Committee. Eissman is already preparing her campaign for Committee president, because she believes it necessary to "take back the center for the children and the young people... so that they don't have to be out in the street and can get together and do their homework, listen to music, and have a space. The president opens it up once a month for her meetings and lends it out for Digeder activities."

It is also part of the conflict which pits the Coordinadora de Rock against "the rest of the world":

> "We need more space for more bands. We have no space for the bands that we already have...you see there is a school...an entire school with classrooms that aren't being used, the rooms there are closed...and why don't they give us that

space? For example, for the Coordinadora de Rock, with three or four practice rooms you can have three or four bands practicing at the same time...that's why I'm telling you, the space is very badly distributed."

Effective Leadership

The modern concept of leadership in social psychology has a variable character, especially in relation to the attributes that groups demand of their leaders (Hollander 1971). In the case of grassroots community organizations, possession of the right kind of leadership has been decisive for their sustainability.

At least three factors can be identified which are associated with recognized leadership: *competence*, defined as the person's contribution toward reaching the objectives of the group; *identification* with the group and its aspirations, especially in taking charge of its internal dynamics and its internal communication and participation processes; and finally, the person's *adaptability* to changing demands or situations.

The fragility of leadership represents perhaps the greatest weakness in the majority of the cases examined here, perhaps with the exception of the Grupo Solidario of Villa El Parral and its leader, Cristina.

The demands on leadership in the organizations considered in this investigation are clear:

> "If people get along like this, well, the ideal would be that there is no leader. We would all be doing well and going forward, but it's not always like that. I think that we have leaders for all kinds of things; not leaders by force, but leaders in opinion, of a different kind; that is, maybe a person who is really responsible can be a leader... that is, in anything, that they feel identified with those people, in their way of thinking, in their way of doing things."
>
> *(Coordinadora de Rock San Joaquín)*

> "They understand us, they help us and all those things...We can't say that they are political leaders, because they are not, but they have leadership power in our eyes ... We are like the delegation of all of them, we follow them...but not political leaders, because we don't look at politics, we look at unity; and if we look at politics, there is always disagreement. So that would mean disunity and we here want unity."
>
> *(Grupo Jóvenes Solidarios Villa El Parral)*

The leader appears as the one who articulates the others' needs and helps them to be recognized. He or she is the person who represents the idea of "us." Thus, the leadership profile projected by Jose Luis through Olga in the Esperanza Andina camp is notable:[18]

> "Well, José Luis later got disillusioned with the political parties and began only with the social arena, and he organizes things. No matter how hard it might be,

---

18 The parallel with the worker leadership profile proposed by L.E. Recabarren is equally notable.

he gets things done. And people believe in him very much, because he's convincing also, with the people, because he achieves things. He says 'let's do this,' and off they go to do it... Those who take other paths are less successful. So people follow him a lot because of that. Because he knows perfectly well what he has to do.

"When I started to work with the *Comités de Allegados*, it was very difficult for me to get in...well, I got very much into the position that we are *allegados* and we have to solve the problem. But I didn't get into the position that the family that joined my organization was now part of my family. Like I would have to know what was happening to a family, if there was a sick child, I would at least have to ask how the child was. If there was a problem the husband had, I would have to deal with it...deal with it as if it were our problem in order to solve it. If people had leaks where they were renting, we would have to fix it. You never get involved in such things. But José Luis does. The families become his family. And it took him a while to make me understand. He would tell me: 'Listen, the *allegados* of this county that we have organized, they are our family. So we have to know what happening with them. What's happening. How they are. What's up with their children.' And I admire him a lot; besides, he's my partner. Sure, I had gotten into women's issues, but to know things were the way they were, I never felt it deeply, seeing that a baby doesn't have diapers, asking what diapers the baby was getting... José Luis notices even those things. Even that kind of thing José Luis checks. That's why he organized the health committee, the hygiene committees, to know what was going on. One delegate from each block to know what was happening with those families."

In this testimony, one can take as satisfied two of the three factors associated with the recognition of leadership: "competence," since Olga and José Luis were capable of successfully carrying out the *toma* and organizing the life that followed; "group identification," since in their paternalistic management, with great proximity and authority, they knew how to combine and read the challenges and changes of the group, as though it were a large extended family. But perhaps their greatest weakness, which explains their estrangement from several groups, was their lacking ability to adapt to new situations, which demanded greater flexibility in negotiating with the outside world. The group senses the risk of a dead-end in confrontation.

"Young people had to begin, new people, people that really were from the camp, because we weren't from the camp and we said because of the people, no more, and the package was ready and suddenly they lost the whole package, it got ruined ... We trained them, we organized all the mobilizations, we set the rules. So it's like we retired and they were left without a father. So they didn't have confidence in the new leaders...and that was what ruined the camp somewhat. The lack of trust in the other leaders... So that provokes, and it provoked, unfortunately, rejection from the new leaders toward us. People made a lot of comparisons, so that created a rejection, a rivalry."

Another interesting aspect of leadership emerges from the comparison between the Grupo Solidario de Villa El Parral and the Villa Cousiño 2 group. From the beginning, while in the first case the group was visible, and each one of its various protagonists acted naturally, in the second only the leaders were visible. Virginia Eissman, director of the latter organization, clearly had a high level of competence, shown in her strength and conviction, while her greatest weakness was her mistrust and aggressiveness. "While it's true that the organization would not die if I weren't here," she states, "they would probably not have enough push, because where I go to get something, I always get it, because I fight for my people, since they are neglected."

With Virginia it was difficult to imagine adaptability in dealing with young people, and thus it was hard to visualize an identification with the organization. In reality, in spite of the 24 declared members, the organization consisted of herself and her plans for the neighborhood.

The most effective[19] leadership from an organizational point of view is that of Cristina Huincales of the Grupo Solidario de Villa El Parral, who broadly satisfies group demands for competence and the ability to consider collective goals. In addition, her mediation skills, the result of extensive experience in church groups and political parties, among other organizations, has allowed her to provide the organization with stability in spite of change. Her contacts with Mayor Alarcón, of National Renewal, are as fluid as those she once forged with the deceased Humanist Party Congresswoman, Laura Rodríguez, or with Claudio Orrego, Christian Democratic city councilman from Peñalolén.

Finally, perhaps one of her greatest merits has been her notable capacity to identify with the organization, in spite of the diversity of its members. The key has been her ability to interpret the needs of each member and to devise adequate forms of communication to deal with internal conflicts, such as drug addiction among some of the young people. In other words, she was able to make each member a protagonist in the recovery of those young people, and thus they became protagonists in overcoming a crisis for the group as a whole.

CASE 8: NEIGHBORHOOD COMMITTEE #10 OF POBLACIÓN LA FAENA

A fundamental feature of effective leadership is the capacity for mediation, which identifies the leader as the group's representative in external relations with other groups or with higher authorities. We attempt to present the way in which this important social function of community leadership has evolved through one last case study, that of the Neighborhood Committee of the Población La Faena, and in particular of Rubén Lizama, its president.

An old, abandoned building, solid but open and cold, houses Neighborhood Committee #10 of the Población La Faena. Its story goes back 30 years, to a *toma* at La Faena farm. That time seems so long ago, states Rubén:

> "They called our area 'dog land' because it had an image of crime and violence, but that was never really true. Our priorities then were urbanization, electrification, and the paving of our streets; also, being able to get public transportation closer to us, for which we staged sit-ins on buses, as a form of putting pressure on the authorities. That was the hour of glory of the Neighborhood

---

19 We have defined effectiveness in leadership as the process of influence by which the leader obtains the voluntary support of the group in securing the group's goals.

Committees. Little by little different housing programs followed. La Faena is a succession of housing programs and policies of different governments, and it still is that way."

However, the neighborhood organization is dying today, states Rubén, because of legislation that has allowed smaller neighborhood organizations to multiply, each with a lower number of members. In his judgment, this has led to the loss of an overall vision of the community's problems.

Rubén is an important political operator in the county of Peñalolén, but no less than Eliana, his rival and comrade, who not only vies for control of the Neighborhood Committee with him through a parallel organization, but also competes for political alignments in the internal elections of the Christian Democratic Party (PDC), as well as in the elections for city council members and Congressional representatives.

The only one of our interviewees who speaks proudly of a long-standing party membership, Rubén attempts to play the role of a traditional mediator, in which the community leader serves as a transmission mechanism between his organization and the municipality, as well as with local members of Congress.

For members of Congress or candidates for higher office, legitimacy is grounded upon a knowledge of the community agenda, as detailed as possible, at a reasonable cost. This normally includes names, addresses, and religious and economic information on a significant number of potential voters, as well as other information relevant to the leader's level of influence.

In contrast, a local leader's legitimacy among his or her following lies in his close and personal dealings with members of Congress. The difficulty Rubén has encountered, like many other community leaders of past years, is that these political representatives have increasingly fewer tools available to them to solve community issues. And in an environment in which every action has been commercialized, it is evident that such leaders are no longer willing to pay the price for these transactions.

> "People don't want to have anything to do with politicians, because after the elections they forget what was done, they forget about the residents. Besides, people stop participating in organizations because that takes time, which makes it possible that they will lose their jobs and therefore also lose money."
>
> *(Junta de Vecinos # 10, La Faena)*

Rubén's role, however, is deeply appreciated not only within the political party, but also in the municipality. In this case, he says, some have the responsibility of transcending their narrow party interests. "We are a sort of unpaid municipal employee." This constitutes his principal letter of recommendation among his fellow members. It is a point of view which coincides with that of the leaders of the Colectivo Malhuén, who are also neighborhood leaders:

> "The role of the directors of the Neighborhood Committees is to be the *unpaid employees of the municipality*, because they bring the information from the municipality to the residents, but few of the problems of the residents get to the municipality through the directors ... There isn't much representation in that, but that is the responsibility of

the municipality. Many of the problems of the residents here are not respected there, not even if you're a director ... We are supposed to bring the problems of the residents to the municipality and they must solve them. *The Neighborhood Committee can't solve the problems; it's only a mediator with the municipality*, but at the municipality everything gets filed and forgotten ... "

In a previous era, Rubén's status in the community was closely linked to his relatively easy access to Housing and Urbanization ministry authorities, thanks to his Congressional ties. Today this is a much more remote possibility, and his sphere of action and "know-how" is limited to the municipality.

Conclusions

This essay did not seek to make categorical statements about tendencies among community organizations, but rather to infer projections based on various specific cases, not necessarily representative of the full complexity and breadth of the chosen topic. However, the regularities found, principally among the statements of community leaders, allow us to formulate some indications of the current trends in organized social action in urban low-income settings. Many of these trends also suggest ideas for the formulation of public policies toward this segment of society.

Community Organizations in the 1990s
In the low-income counties of Santiago, such as Peñalolén, there is a multiplicity of associative initiatives, mainly focused on the community management of basic services which are not adequately provided by the State and which cannot be purchased with the meager income of area households. These associations normally originate among small groups pursuing objectives of equally limited scope which are of direct interest to the members or their immediate community. In contrast to what was seen during the previous decade, these organizations are heterogeneous in their orientation and structure; they are not interrelated, nor do they maintain active ties to larger endeavors, whether political or regional.

In analyzing the forms of collective action in the urban low-income world over the last few years, it is impossible to ignore the effect of the new approaches to social policy conceived with the return of democracy to our country. In fact, our study serves to confirm the central role which the Chilean State continues to play in the formation of community organizations.

One of the merits of allowing participants to formulate social investment projects to be financed with public resources lies in establishing a link between the State and community organizations, both in the definition of local priorities and the determination of the type of action to be taken by public agencies. In the interplay of forces, the State exercises its influence in the definition of associative patterns.

A second set of conclusions is related to the decline of the generalized social movement as a driving force behind community organizations at the local level. Observing the community associations existing in an urban community like Peñalolén, we find numerous small organizations — small both in their number of members and the scope of their action. Their principal concern is rooted in *doing* something, and not in *representing* anything. With the exceptions of the leadership of Esperanza Andina and the Coordinadora de Rock de San Joaquín, none of the organizations seek to represent increasingly large territorial spaces; they are more interested in constructing networks focusing on specific topics. Thus, autonomy and greater effectiveness seem to coincide.

The physical distance between places of work and residence, increased occupational segregation, and the intensity of the work schedule have certainly contributed to greater difficulties in the development of common interests and organizations in low-income communities. Meanwhile, contact with public powers is facilitated by private contacts, even though this is no longer a family tie as was characteristic of the social assistance policy under the authoritarian regime, but a group association.

A markedly widespread phenomenon in grassroots community organizations is women's leadership, a situation which does not differ to that observed in previous decades. The community kitchen, an organization with community origins which became "sectorized" with relative success in the 1990s, illustrates an exceptional case of transformation and conversion of the strong women's leadership born in the 1980s.

However, despite the role of women in community action, within this new environment of greater organizational competitiveness, the traditional mothers' groups seem to have lost their past activism. These organizations' share in the formulation of projects is marginal, probably due to their historically receptive behavior in relation to the goods and services of the State.

While the State has established opportunities for links to all sorts of community organizations, the Neighborhood Committees continue to be the principal actors and organizational interlocutors in poor urban neighborhoods and rural areas. The loss of credibility suffered by these organizations during the period of political-military control seems to have been overcome, and they have reasserted themselves in the nation's communities as the principal link with public officials on a local scale.

Athletic clubs, another traditional organization of the urban low-income world, continue to be an important vehicle for community activity and identity. They are, at the same time, the institutions which can best achieve a cross-generation link. In fact, neighborhood organizations have only rarely been able to spur social contact between adults and youth.

Other youth manifestations, such as the heavy metal bands, have shown significant development in various areas of the city. They are the closest to the concept of a social movement in the urban world, where traditional political formations have virtually disappeared. The rebellious creativity of the world of low-income youth has found in this urban poetry a language that is highly effective when it comes to constructing identity and unmasking the "senselessness" of today's world.

Spheres of Action: Motivations and Expectations

On the basis of the projects examined and the interviews conducted, we have been able to deduce and conclude that people in the communities studied form associations mainly focused on the following topics:

- The search for a space to live in that is one's own, and the resolution of matters of common interest, principally the providing of basic services
- Social contact and the forging of interpersonal bonds, clearly demonstrated by the importance of the community centers and athletic facilities

- Improvement in the quality of life, within which the key issue is the construction of a safer environment for children and area youth. A multitude of preventive initiatives in relation to drug abuse, crime, family violence, and so forth are related to this.
- Youth form groups principally for the purpose of spending time together and pursuing recreational and cultural interests. Their search for spaces of their own emerges as an objective in itself, remaining as an unsatisfied need.

The social segregation of the city represents, whether explicitly or implicitly, one of the most frequent issues raised among members of the community groups studied. Underlying this is the perception of the deliberate segregation of counties, which has isolated poor people from the upper- and middle-class areas of the city.

The action of the Población Esperanza Andina in Peñalolén is not merely the exercise of their right to housing, but also of the right to remain in the place where they have lived for years. It is, at least in the eyes of its leaders, a rejection of the physical exclusion they perceive to be associated with government housing programs. For the residents of Esperanza Andina, amid the growing social diversity of Peñalolén, there are concrete expectations of progress, which they feel are much less likely to be reached in other counties of the metropolitan periphery, which contain only *poor people eradicated from the rest of the city*.

As the *toma* at Esperanza Andina shows, however, there are still ways to break out of the social order that escape the channels envisioned by the State. This is analogous to how prices arise in slum clearance camps. Departing residents, and those who replace them in their self-constructed housing, pay prices that turn out to be surprisingly close to the amount of accumulated savings required by the State for access to new basic housing.

The experiences collected here include interesting signs of new forms of protagonism in society. We have been able to discover, for example, new opportunities for action, which until now have been monopolized by the professions and public or private bureaucracies and mainly closed to community participation. The experience of the Comunidad Terapeutica de Peñalolén suggests new public policy proposals in this area, related to the social definition of mental illnesses and the options for their treatment. Similarly, the Colectivo de Mujeres Malhuén represents a notable example of the achievements of a self-improvement project forged over the years with the help of various non-government organizations.

The experience of solidarity among one's nearest neighbors, the creation of spaces for social contact and self-expression, improvements to the quality of community life — these are some of the specific motivations behind the community initiatives we have identified and reviewed. All of them would seem to be fundamental for the creation of a safer and more welcoming community space, one which acts as a shield to protect social relationships against degradation.

Visions of Community, County and Country

Despite the enormous growth in social spending; the new focus on active intervention; the new topics introduced into the public agenda; and the attractiveness of their presentation, the perception of stagnation persists among the people. The technification of social topics; the disappearance of emblematic public figures capable of personifying government effort; the rupture of paternalistic links; the communicational fragmentation of our social condition; and the diluting of the government's message in the media are hypotheses still to be explored in explaining this apparent cognitive or affective dissonance between society and the State.

The orientation of urban community organizations toward "the solving of concrete problems" does not necessarily mean that ideology has disappeared from their discourse. On the contrary, there is an underlying sense of accusation surrounding the concepts of *exclusion* and *injustice*. Viewing the modernization of the country, all agree that it has been inequitable. They perceive an increase in expectations for improvement, associated with democracy. Yet this improvement occurs far from them (or "on the other side of the canal"). Within their vision of society and country, the poorest groups' limited expectations of social mobility emerge quite clearly, even across the generations. Given their difficulties in accessing quality education and good jobs, they do not see promising possibilities for social integration. However, they invariably see improvement in the quality of education and access to higher levels of professional training as the key to a different future for their children.

Two external figures receive most of the scorn of the group leaders: politicians and businessmen. The first, they maintain, make promises and do not deliver; they exploit and manipulate the community's interests in order to achieve their own aims. The second group "holds the handle of the frying pan" in society: they always find a way to profit, and they pay excessively low salaries. They are not seen as generating opportunities.

The community associations' vision of the municipality appears to be centered on the Mayor and his/her management, considered effective if the incumbent maintains a direct presence in the community and shows an ability to find resources to solve problems. The representative dimension of the Mayor's office or the municipal bodies does not clearly appear.

The role of the municipality is extended to the community organizations, which appear as "miniature municipalities," facilitators, and organizers of municipal action on a neighborhood scale, but with unpaid personnel and without feedback to the municipality or participation in its decisions. Residents tend to demand solutions from neighborhood leaders, but they do not commit to participating in the organization themselves. Specific problems give rise to new committees, organized by street or sector, which on occasion become parallel neighborhood organizations.

Among the principal non-material capital of the urban community organizations is the presence of dynamic and responsible leaders, in most cases with vast organizational experience forged during the 1980s, as well as political links that allow them to "reach" politicians and negotiate support for their specific demands. The organizations enjoy technical support through the assistance of non-governmental agencies which have granted them access to limited amounts of resources through project bids.

Three judgments can be discerned from the leaders' views of their organizational action and the setting in which it occurs: a highly positive evaluation of the action they carry out along with their group; a negative perception of the low-income community setting and the willingness of the neighbors to mobilize; and a severe criticism of the country's current situation. In their projects, the groups tend to focus on issues related to improvement of the quality of life, social contact, and self-expression, although at the same time that they express increasing doubt as to their capacity to have an effect on society.

The sustainability of the organizations examined in this paper has depended on achieving legal recognition by public officials, obtaining physical space, and electing effective and assertive leaders. This associative pattern is repeated in all of the organizations interviewed, even in those that define themselves as being opposed to or outside the system.

The legitimization of leadership within the organizations is associated with responsibility, honesty, and loyalty to the group, as well as the leaders' effectiveness in achieving the instrumental goals of the organization. Moreover, in all of the cases analyzed, the affective link, or the leaders' ability to facilitate communication within the organization, is revealed as one of the leading requirements of internal leadership.

Political ties and liaison abilities are losing relevance. The majority of the leaders interviewed have extensive knowledge of public agencies and the bureaucratic buttons to push to gain access to the municipality. Independent of their political roots, they cultivate relationships with those who have decision-making power at the local level, or those who can influence decisions. Thus, a clearly instrumental link has been established with those forms of political mediation that are within reach, while the affective links with the national political order have been obviously weakened. The groups view politics as something external and instrumental. With politicians, one negotiates in order to gain advantages for the community.

This last affirmation is perhaps one of the most worrisome conclusions of this study, since it demonstrates a substantial weakening of the legitimacy of democratic political institutions. The conclusion that emerges from the accounts, time and time again, is that a symbolic void has formed between the activity of the community groups and the political management of State powers.

We live in a society with a serious deficit of social integration, the result of an unfortunate combination of great expectations for personal and family improvement -- a product of our country's political and economic progress in the 1990s — and the perception of tremendous social differences in opportunity. Yet this troublesome picture should not become a justification for pessimism. On the contrary, the message should be one of an environment rife with challenges for the people and their political institutions, as they seek to strengthen the meaning of citizenship in the dawn of the new millennium.

BIBLIOGRAPHICAL REFERENCES

Bengoa, J. 1996. *La comunidad perdida. Ensayos sobre identidad y cultura: los desafíos de la modernización en Chile.* Santiago: Ediciones SUR.

Calandra, B. 1997. "De organización económica popular a empresa alimentaria: un estudio de caso." Doctoral Dissertation. University of Rome III.

Consejo Nacional de Superación de la Pobreza. 1996. *La pobreza en Chile. Un desafío de equidad e integración social.* Santiago: Consejo Nacional de Superación de la Pobreza.

Hollander, E. 1971. *Principios y métodos de psicología social.* Madrid: Amorrortu.

Moulian, T. 1997. *Chile actual. Anatomía de un mito.* Santiago: ARCIS/LOM.

PROSAM s/f. "De la olla común a la empresa de servicios. Un camino de integración social." Santiago: Prosam.

Rayo G. 1987. "La politique sociale sous le régime autoritaire chilien: l'expérience néo-libérale." Doctoral Dissertation. Institut d'Etudes Politiques, Université des Sciences Sociales de Grenoble.

———. 1996. "El aporte de los Fondos de Inversión a la política social de los Estados." Santiago: FOSIS.

Rayo G. and J. Córdoba. 1994. "Fosis: un nuevo concepto de política social." FOSIS Working Document. Santiago: FOSIS.

Sepúlveda, L. 1997. "Espacio local y transformaciones del sistema municipal." *Persona y Sociedad*, vol. 11, no. 1, April.

Urmeneta, R. 1994. "Opiniones de los pobladores respecto de las políticas sociales." PET Working Document no. 101. Santiago: PET.

Between Modernization and Equality:
Women, Domestic Life, and the Family

Teresa Valdés

Introduction

In 1990, after the restoration of democracy in Chile, many in the country sought to extend the democratic transition to all aspects of national life. This process was based, above all, on respect for the rights of all Chileans. At the same time, the government began the political and economic re-integration of our country into international life, along with the successful decentralization of governmental functions.

From the perspective of the topic we deal with here — women, domestic life, and the family — it is interesting to note that this democratic reconstruction process, which began in 1990, coincided with a new phase of modernization. The repercussions of this modernization process have been felt especially strongly in the areas of culture and domestic life. Many things have changed in both the private and public spheres, as well as in intimate and social relations (Giddens 1990; 1995).

The combination of Chile's re-integration into the international community, the release of pent-up pressure from the struggle against the dictatorship, and the beginning of the construction of the long-hoped-for democratic order created a new cultural atmosphere. New practices, meanings, proposals, and models arose on both a social and personal level. Yet the transition to democracy also created new uncertainties, arising from the greater freedom of action that was now possible. All of this coincided with a historical moment that witnessed the collapse of the ideological framework of collectivist thinking, along with the rise of an economic model accentuating individualism and competition while downplaying feelings of community and solidarity.

Some of the changes we are seeing in Chilean society have long-standing structural roots. However, there are also new developments which differ from earlier trends. For example, the changing position of women in society is clearly rooted in 19th-century industrialization, the idealistic principles of the French Revolution, and broad democratic ideals. Yet the expression of these changes during the last 30 years, and especially in this decade, has been unique. Drastic changes in the public, political, economic, social, and cultural spheres threaten traditional structures, particularly the gender-based division of labor and the subordination of women in the family. Today, women are recognized as full citizens entitled to rights, not just responsibilities.

These developments have occurred at a time when, all over the world, the expansion of markets has led to greater female participation in the labor force. In Chile, the economic and social crises of the 1970s and 1980s, the country's structural adjustments, and the successful establishment of a neo-liberal economic model have placed women in a strategic position to help improve living conditions among impoverished and marginalized groups. In fact, it is women's participation in paid activities which has allowed increasing numbers of these families to satisfy their basic needs and to rise out of extreme poverty.[1]

While this process has forced a certain rearranging of the tasks socially assigned to men and women, it has not automatically brought about an improvement of women's position in society. Women retain the responsibility for children, and they are subject to a double work shift, with clear negative effects on their mental and physical health as well as their opportunities for personal development. An immediate shift to a model of equality between men and women has not taken place. The characteristic patterns of subordination of the last few centuries cannot easily be changed, especially since women's work within the family has historically been of great social and economic importance.

Cultural globalization calls these patterns into question. Many parts of the Northern Hemisphere, in particular the Scandinavian countries, exhibit notable levels of female participation in all aspects of social life, accompanied by widespread male participation in activities reserved, until recently, for women. More democratic models for couples and the family have emerged.

Chile's social and cultural opening process is not unique in the world. However, its impact is greater here, since 17 years of dictatorship had turned back the clock in this area.[2] Under the military regime, the most conservative social forces were strengthened; these continue to control the media as well as some circles of the Catholic Church. However, Chile's current opening process is taking place in society itself, beyond the grasp of these critics.

Another important issue closely related to globalization is the growing concern — deepened under the dictatorship — for human rights such as equality, equal opportunity, and full citizenship.[3] In the new cultural atmosphere of democracy, these rights have acquired new meanings and have raised concrete expectations among the population, heightened by the abovementioned emphasis on the individual. This concern for rights has helped spur new demands for improvement in living conditions, new kinds of conflict between men and women, and rising cross-generational tension within families.

However, as the emphasis on collective feelings and actions has dissipated, new and complex problems have emerged. The isolating effect of entrenched poverty is deepened. As State action is reduced to remedial efforts, as "solidarity" has lost its force and been replaced by telethons and "Christian charity" in its more traditional forms,[4] no counterweight to the effects of the current economic model has yet made itself felt.

What we are witnessing, then, is a dynamic process, with new situations and ideas meeting with resistance from a traditional, conservative culture. Many conservatives do

---

1   This is shown by the Casen surveys of 1992, 1994, and 1996. By 1996, only 23.2% of the population and 19.7% of households were below the poverty line, and only 4.9% were truly indigent, taking total household income into consideration (Mideplan 1997).

2   Note, for example, Pinochet's speech in relation to women and the family, as well as the ideological discipline promoted by the Women's Secretariat and CEMA-Chile. See Lechner and Levy (1984).

3   The specific human rights of women are also recognized.

4   The loss of interest in "politics" should not come as a surprise, since politics are unable to address people's needs. This situation is exacerbated by the elements of government persisting from the authoritarian legacy.

not accept that the country's present stage of development requires women's participation in the work force; nor do they recognize the implications of this fact. We have witnessed the politicization of matters that were once considered private, with laws against domestic violence, institutionalized sexual education for children and adolescents, and the elimination of distinctions between legitimate and illegitimate offspring. The changes in our society can also be observed when, for example, the concept of gender becomes threatening to some people, or a marriage law is proposed that includes provisions for divorce.

These transformations have brought tremendous challenges for Chilean families, and especially for women. Men have adjusted to changes in domestic life at varying speeds, with professional and middle-class men being the most flexible. Meanwhile, democratic ideals are slowly permeating private life, leading to more equal relationships between the genders and generations, along with the rejection of authoritarianism.[5]

This phase of modernization — as it has been described — is manifested by Chilean men and women through the formation and dissolution of couples, as well as through political demands for changes in public policy. This is the drama currently unfolding in our country, one we would like to reflect in these pages.

Concretely, this paper attempts to present a snapshot of women's advances during Chile's modernization process, their action in organized groups, and the hoped-for benefits that the democratic transition has not yet produced for them. As players on the social stage, women are promoting a far-reaching change in culture, and particularly in relationships between the sexes, on both the intimate and formal levels.

We will also present a view of Chilean families and the current changes they are facing. Because of the cultural role of the "pillar of the family" traditionally assigned to women, the changes experienced by women naturally affect families, just as the economic and social transformations affecting the family have influenced women's situations.[6]

I. Women's Changing Roles: Advances, Resistance, and New Challenges

Chile's modernization process over the last few decades has had a broad and profound impact on the lives of Chilean women. It has altered their position in society and led to the questioning of the traditional gender-based division of labor, particularly within the family, but also in society as a whole. It has given rise to new female identities, both individual and collective. These new identities have not displaced motherhood from its central position in the life of the majority of women, yet new elements and expectations have been added to this role as well.

The changes experienced by women have met with strong resistance in conservative political and ecclesiastical circles. These groups defend women's traditional role as wife and mother in the domestic sphere. At the same time, they consider the democratic ideals which underlie the changes to be a threat to the current order, since they call for changes in

---

5   See Valdés, Gysling, and Benavente (forthcoming), and Valdés, Olavarría et al. (pending research results).
6   In keeping with the aims of this paper, we will emphasize data showing trends and evolution over time in the analysis which follows. We include the latest information possible for each indicator.

the relationships between men and women, the organization of everyday life, and public responsibilities for the raising of children.

The current economic and social environment is fragmented; women throughout the country are experiencing these changes at different rates and with different intensities. Undoubtedly, Santiago and the country's other large cities have been fertile ground for change, especially among middle-class, professional groups. Yet today the ideals of modernity are being extended to new social groups, many of them affected by economic modernization, in rural as well as urban areas. The demands of the economic system, the increased desire for consumer goods, and visions of alternative courses of action have spread throughout society and have put increasing pressure on women.

In this chapter, we will examine the most important changes taking place in our country, their impact on the lives of women and their families, the tensions they create, and the new challenges they raise.

Chilean women have enjoyed rising levels of education,
yet socialization and cultural practices reduce their opportunities.

In recent decades, Chile's female population as a whole has attained considerably higher levels of education.[7] In 1982, 55% of women over five years of age had fewer than seven years of schooling; this percentage decreased to 43.5% by 1992. At the other end of the spectrum, only 4.8% had 13 or more years of schooling in 1982, while by 1992, this figure had reached 10.7%. Illiteracy has been reduced considerably, to approximately 6% of the

TABLE 1

AVERAGE AMOUNT OF SCHOOLING FOR PERSONS
15 YEARS OF AGE, BY SEX AND AGE GROUP
(School Years)

Age Group	Female	Male
15 - 19	10.0	9.7
20 - 24	11.6	11.4
25 - 29	11.1	11.1
30 - 34	10.6	10.6
35 - 39	9.9	10.4
40 - 44	9.6	9.9
45 - 49	8.5	9.3
50 - 54	7.7	8.5
55 - 59	6.9	7.4
60 - 64	6.4	7.1
65 & over	5.6	6.1
Total	9.3	9.6

SOURCE: Ministry of Planning and Cooperation, 1996 Casen Survey.

---

7   This section utilizes information from Valdés and Gomáriz (1994).

female population aged 15 or older. Male and female enrollment in primary education is nearly equal; it is similar in secondary education and in higher education as well, if one includes professional institutes and technical training centers as well as universities. These improved educational levels among women have undoubtedly provided them with better chances to enter the labor market.

The most recent data derive from the 1996 National Socioeconomic Characterization Survey (Casen). According to these figures, females aged 15 or above have an average of 9.3 years of schooling. This is very close to the 9.6 years completed by men (see Table 1). Up to 35 years of age, the amount of schooling is practically the same for both sexes, with about 10.6 years of average study. The highest average, for both sexes, is exhibited between the ages of 25 and 29.

The average figures shown in Table 1 conceal important distinctions, however. In fact, advances in education vary significantly among different segments of society. Educational opportunities are strongly influenced by the availability of family resources, since public education has suffered a significant drop in funding and quality, and higher education is costly.

Thus, for example, illiteracy rates are higher in rural areas (around 17%, in contrast to 6% in urban zones). The transfer of the control of schools to municipalities, which lack the economic or technical resources to guarantee their quality, has led to the deterioration of public education and transformed it into "education for the poor," channeling its graduates into ill-paid jobs. Many private, subsidized schools are no better, although they provide students and their families with more social prestige.

Likewise, the shortage of schools in many communities creates obstacles for young women. The time and expense involved in traveling to school in another community, combined with the obligation of helping their mothers with domestic chores, prevent many female students from completing their studies.

In spite of the significant contributions to education made by the democratic governments of the 1990s, this situation has yet to be turned around. Even the new regulation obliging schools to allow pregnant students to continue their studies has not kept these young women from dropping out. Many schools, even among the subsidized institutions, ignore the rule and expel pregnant students, thus limiting their prospects for the future. Teenage mothers who stay in primary or high schools generally do so only for the first year. Raising a child makes it practically impossible for them to complete their education. The generational reproduction of poverty,[8] as well as the concentration of poverty in the female population, are closely linked to women's difficulties in completing their secondary education and thus obtaining the necessary skills to secure a good job.

Ministry of Education statistics show high levels of educational attendance and performance among female students, but this does not always translate into the opportunity for higher education. In middle-class families with male and female children, the women are frequently encouraged to pursue technical training and the men a university career. This is reflected in the enrollment statistics of technical training centers, professional

---

8   The generational reproduction of poverty is exemplified by a female head of household with little education, who will probably live in poverty, even if she works; her children will have difficulties in completing their education and will continue among the ranks of the poor, especially her female children, who may leave their studies in order to take care of domestic tasks and permit their mother to work. They will reproduce the cycle by repeating their mother's experience.

institutes and universities. In 1990, women represented 41% of total university enrollment, 51.1% of total professional institute enrollment, and 47.9% of total technical training center enrollment. In spite of accumulated evidence, many families still assume that
only their sons will be called upon to be heads of households, and that if a daughter mar-
ries, her income will only serve to complement that of her husband.[9]

Common socialization patterns in families do not offer varied opportunities to girls,
but instead pass along traditional views of womanhood. In fact, besides being exposed to
the models represented by mother and father and the division of tasks between the two,
girls continue to be discriminated against through the requirement that they, and not the
male children, carry out domestic tasks, as well as through restrictions on their autonomy
and mobility, but not those of the male children. Rarely are female children encouraged to
undertake activities not fitting the traditional model. Thus, they learn subordination within the family and internalize the differentiation of tasks and opportunities according to
gender (Alaclay and Milicic 1995).

School texts continue to perpetuate the traditional stereotypes of male and female
behavior, even within the newer programs implemented in the last few years. Added to
this so-called "hidden curriculum" are typical classroom practices, which tend to promote
and recognize the contributions of boys and inhibit the development of independent projects and assertive behavior among girls (Edwards, Calvo et al. 1988). The belief that girls
have innate abilities in the humanities but not in mathematics is expressed in differing levels of attention given to girls, translating into a reduction of opportunities for women's
technical and scientific studies.

Like school textbooks, the media daily present to girls and adolescent women the
models offered to them by society, mirroring a social organization with a traditional division of labor. Furthermore, commercial advertising makes extensive use of sexism, highlighting only those female attributes which are believed to contribute to selling their products.[10] Physical stereotypes of beauty, derived from those of the Northern Hemisphere, are
predominant, putting severe pressure on young girls' expectations. The labor market takes
pains to exclude those who do not fit the desired pattern, including height as well as skin,
eye, and hair color.[11]

Enrollment statistics from professional and technical institutes as well as universities
show a strong segmentation by gender. Predominantly "male" and "female" activities and
majors can be identified. Those women who choose majors considered "male" often face
tremendous pressure from family and society, accompanied by warnings about "losing
their femininity," being unable to find a husband, or facing marital conflicts because of
their higher income.

Most of the time, women seek professional training in specialties that are an extension of their traditional roles: social service, teaching, nursing, preschool education,

9   Some improvement is observed in the years that followed. In 1996, women represented 44.34% of total
    undergraduate enrollment at the 25 universities belonging to the Consejo de Rectores (Consejo de Rectores
    de Universidades Chilenas 1997).
10 The number of associations between female figures and automobiles, cigarettes, beer, etc. is surprising.
    Furthermore, it appears that to the advertisers, only women are interested in new technology for the
    home, and only they will use it.
11 Eating disorders such as anorexia and bulimia are on the rise among girls, due to the pressure of these
    models; unattainable ideals lead girls to reject themselves and fear rejection by others.

design and fashion, hairstyling, etc. These professions command lower salaries in the job market and enjoy less prestige. This ensures that differences in income between men and women are maintained, along with an inferior quality of life in homes where women are the principal providers.

However, some advances can be observed. Historically male majors such as psychology, journalism, and engineering now have a large number of women in their ranks, although women still account for less than 20% of engineering majors. The current educational reform, designed to improve the quality of education through the lengthening of the school day, may have a positive impact on young women's primary and secondary education. However, as we will see in the following section, higher levels of education do not ensure better integration into the job market, nor do they guarantee equal income. There is still much to be done to achieve fairness and equal opportunity for Chilean women.

Chilean women have joined the job market and have gradually increased
their numbers in traditionally male occupations, yet working conditions and
salaries are still unsatisfactory in many cases.

Chilean women entered the job market comparatively early, and their organization in unions was also early in historical terms (Salazar 1985). The beginning of the 20th century saw activism by many organized groups of women workers, who fought for an eight-hour work day, better working conditions, and other advances (Salinas 1987). This work force participation is invisible in official histories, although it reached significant levels, according to figures from the 1950s.[12] Women's presence in the labor market is not a recent phenomenon. What is novel is its current range and intensity, the extension of women's working years, and the accompanying modifications seen in childbearing, the family, and the relationship between motherhood and work, as well as the meaning work holds for women.

In the 1970s, the economic and social paradigm imposed by the military dictatorship led to drastic reductions in the size of the State, economic shock treatments, and persecution of political and social leaders and activists. Not only did these measures have a strong impact on the male work force, but thousands of women were also forced to seek alternative sources of income in order to be "good mothers" and feed their families at any cost. Community workshops and so-called "grassroots economic organizations" were created to help families face drastic reductions in income as well as the State's withdrawal of services (Valdés and Weinstein 1993; Hardy 1987).

These phenomena became common across much of Latin America, especially during the 1980s, when external debt crises, inflation, and the demands of international financial organizations put pressure on other societies similar to that faced by Chilean women. Yet the so-called "lost decade" did not lead to total despair in poor households, thanks mainly to the monetary contributions of women. Since no new sources of income existed in the formal economy, the necessity to survive propelled women and entire families to invent new activities and to produce goods and services that could be traded in the market. The "informal" sector of the economy, in which women were heavily represented, expanded as companies externalized various activities in order to reduce costs. Family survival strategies placed many women in a new situation of economic responsibility. This translated into greater

---

12 In 1950, the rate of female participation in the workforce, according to Celade, reached 28.91%. See Valdés and Gomáriz (1992b).

TABLE 2

CHANGE IN FEMALE WORKFORCE PARTICIPATION IN
GREATER SANTIAGO, BY AGE GROUP, 1960-1994
(Percentage Rates)

Year	Age					
	15-19	20-24	25-29	30-54	55-59	TOTAL
1960	17.2	35.2	32.9	31.1	12.2	26.4
1965	21.5	36.4	38.0	31.0	12.0	27.9
1970	12.0	43.4	39.9	36.8	13.6	30.2
1975	15.5	43.6	40.1	33.4	10.9	28.4
1980	10.9	41.4	46.4	36.7	9.2	29.7
1985	11.1	41.1	46.9	39.6	11.0	31.8
1990	9.2	41.0	47.0	46.1	10.2	33.6
1994	13.9	44.2	54.5	48.8	13.1	38.2

SOURCE: University of Chile, "Employment & Unemployment Survey: Greater Santiago [Encuesta de ocupación y desocupación. Gran Santiago]," June of every year. In Sernam, Equal Opportunities for Working Women [Igualdad de oportunidades para la mujer en el trabajo] (Santiago: Sernam, 1996).

female participation in the labor force, which increased 83% between 1970 and 1990. The corresponding rise in male participation was only 57.9% (Valdés and Gomáriz 1992b).

Economic improvements brought about by the modernization of agriculture, the development of exports, etc., have created expanding opportunities for women to enter the work force. Although they remain concentrated in the informal sector and in service jobs such as domestic help, their economic contribution is essential in many homes, since salaries in general remain low.

In spite of sparse statistics on female employment — particularly in rural areas, where it is more difficult to distinguish between production for home use and production for the market — and the powerful cultural images which have led women not to acknowledge that they generate income, the figures for Chile indicate a participation rate of 34.2% for 1995, which increased to 35.5% in 1996.[13] Table 2 shows the evolution of women's work force participation in Santiago, which reached 38.2% in 1994. The figures also show its distribution among different age groups, highlighting women's continuation in the labor market during their reproductive years. The highest work force participation by women is seen between the ages of 25 and 29, and it remains high until the age of 54.

In addition, the results of a recent study designed to measure the true rate of women's work force participation should be noted. The study found that 30% of women declaring themselves to be "non-working" nevertheless admitted, when questioned further, that they had done some type of paid work in the last 12 months, or that they were doing so at the moment (Henriquéz and Pérez 1995). Therefore, the economic participation of women is higher than the figures presented indicate.

---

13   INE, *Encuesta Nacional de Empleo* [National Employment Survey], trimester April-June 1995; and Mideplan, *Encuesta Casen 96*, Santiago, 1997.

The rise in female participation in the labor force is a two-edged sword. On the one hand, for many women, work brings the possibility of supporting their household or contributing to its support, as well as opportunities for autonomy and personal development. On the other hand, the conditions under which women enter the work force are still seriously unequal. This situation was worsened, for example, when labor regulations were made more flexible. Although this has spurred job creation, it has also led to more unfavorable working conditions for women. While activities such as domestic labor or seasonal work in the fruit and fishing industries provide numerous women with employment opportunities, they are often carried out under unacceptable conditions. Long workdays, unpredictable schedules, and a lack of benefits are typical of these jobs, as are unhealthy environments — because of the use of agricultural chemicals, for example — with severe consequences for the women workers' physical, mental, and reproductive health.

Chilean women tend to remain in the job market during their reproductive years, not even leaving their jobs when their children are young. This points to a continued need for income and professional development, and it translates into ongoing tension between work and family responsibilities. The introduction of women into the work force and public life has not brought a redistribution of domestic and childrearing tasks within the home. Only in middle- and upper-class households can women rely upon domestic help in order to remain in the labor market. The result is that these groups are less aware of the need for change, while low-income women bear the heaviest burdens.

The tension between work and family arises not only from the double work shift, as women come home after a day of work to domestic chores, but also because motherhood itself becomes a barrier to finding and keeping a job. Women are punished for motherhood by health care organizations, as revealed by required pregnancy tests, higher rates charged to women of reproductive age, and the rewards offered to women who promise not to have children.

The highly segmented labor market underscores the inequality of women's job opportunities. Women are mainly to be found in the areas of personal services and domestic help. They are scarce among managers, outweighed by men among the self-employed, but numerous among those who work, unpaid, in the household. A significant percentage of working women are professionals and technicians, but among these, nurses and teachers predominate, while men are the majority among architects and engineers. Almost all domestic employees are women, doing a job considered by society to have practically no value. Despite the improvements introduced by the Concertación governments, labor legislation still does not protect mothers. Many women work part-time, washing clothes or cleaning and cooking, without any kind of pension or health benefits, and with very low incomes.[14]

The data available for Santiago (1980-95) show a high concentration of males among employers, managers, independent workers, and laborers. These figures are very stable. The greatest concentration of women is currently found in the "non-supervisory worker" category, with a percentage of 43.2%. Women make up only 14% of employers and 25% of independent workers.[15]

---

14   Added to this today are the growing numbers of Ecuadorian, Peruvian, and Bolivian women who take jobs as domestic helpers in Chile. Without a home of their own, they are vulnerable to even greater abuse.

15   University of Chile, "Encuesta de Ocupación y Desocupación. Gran Santiago" [Employment and Unemployment Survey: Greater Santiago], undertaken in June of each year. In Sernam (1996).

TABLE 3

CHANGE IN FEMALE WORKFORCE PARTICIPATION IN GREATER SANTIAGO
BY FAMILY PER CAPITA INCOME QUINTILE, 1960-1994
(Percentage Rates)

Year	1ST Quintile	2nd Quintile	3rd Quintile	4th Quintile	5th Quintile	TOTAL
1960	22.6	23.8	28.0	30.0	34.3	26.4
1965	19.2	23.6	27.0	32.1	38.7	27.9
1970	21.8	27.5	29.8	33.3	39.5	30.9
1975	24.7	24.1	25.9	31.2	37.5	28.4
1980	22.7	24.6	30.8	32.1	39.9	29.7
1985	23.7	27.6	29.7	37.6	41.0	31.8
1990	20.4	26.8	37.0	41.5	44.7	33.6
1994	19.5	35.6	41.3	47.2	47.4	38.2

SOURCE: University of Chile, "Employment & Unemployment Survey: Greater Santiago [Encuesta de ocupación y desocupación. Gran Santiago]," June of every year. In Sernam, Equal Opportunities for Working Women [Igualdad de oportunidades para la mujer en el trabajo] (Santiago: Sernam, 1996).

Significant distinctions can be seen in female work force participation if family income levels are considered. In fact, the poorer the women, the less they participate in the labor market. The figures for Santiago between 1960 and 1994 (see Table 3) as well as the results of the 1996 Casen survey (see Table 4) reveal this fact. In other words, while financial need and instability are obviously greater among poor women, it appears more difficult or less attractive for them to join the paid work force.

For 1994, in Santiago we find a range from 19.5% in the poorest (first) quintile to 47.4% in the fifth quintile. This differentiation has increased since 1960. In 1994, the economic participation of first-quintile women is even less than it was in 1960, while it has risen considerably in the fifth quintile.

The 1996 Casen survey reveals a female participation rate of only 22.1% in urban areas for the first income quintile, compared to 52.8% for the wealthiest quintile. Worse still is the situation of women in rural areas. In the poorest homes, the participation rate reaches only 12.4%, while in the fifth quintile it rises to 34.9%.

The figures in Table 4 express women's difficulties, in both urban and rural settings, in combining productive tasks with the reproductive ones imposed on them by the social organization of family life, as well as the low quality of the jobs to which they have access. The income they could earn does not compensate for poor working conditions and the difficulty of making adequate child care arrangements. The recent educational reform lengthening the school day from the third grade onward may help improve this situation for women with children in that age group.[16]

---

16 This reform, since it does not include younger children, may have the perverse effect of promoting the withdrawal from school of older daughters so that they may take care of their younger siblings.

TABLE 4

PARTICIPATION RATE ACCORDING TO INCOME QUINTILE
BY AREA OF RESIDENCE AND SEX, 1996
(Percentages)

Area of Residence	Income Quintile					
and Sex	I	II	III	IV	V	TOTAL
Urban						
Female	22.1	30.0	37.0	45.0	52.8	**38.2**
Male	72.2	74.9	74.0	74.9	75.7	**74.5**
Total	44.7	51.0	54.6	59.4	64.1	**55.4**
Rural						
Female	12.4	21.5	27.5	31.3	34.9	**20.1**
Male	71.4	76.1	77.4	80.4	83.6	**75.4**
Total	41.7	49.9	55.5	58.8	62.6	**49.1**

* Excluding live-in domestic servants.

SOURCE: Ministry of Planning & Cooperation, 1996 Casen Survey.

Many women who wish to take part in paid activities cannot find a place in the labor market. Unemployment is higher among women, especially young women. This is true even among previously-employed women with a higher average educational level than comparable male populations. Among the many barriers faced by women seeking a job are the aesthetic stereotypes demanded by the market.[17]

The incorporation of women into the work force has also had a great impact on women's identities and expectations. Studies reveal that while motherhood continues to be at the center of many women's identity, the proportion of women at all levels of society who seek to escape from the domestic routine, to continue their professional development, or to undertake personal endeavors beyond motherhood is increasing. Some mothers work for personal development reasons, viewing work as equally important or more important than motherhood. Others work because of the need for sociability and because they feel that motherhood and work should be compatible. Still others work merely for necessity, since motherhood is their main focus, and they would rather remain at home while their children are young (Gysling and Benavente 1996; Valdés, Gysling, and Benavente, forthcoming).

However, remaining exclusively at home has been demonstrated to have negative effects on women's mental health, and hundreds of depressed women are being advised to find activities outside the home (Isis Internacional 1990). Many women of the upper-middle and upper classes who are not economically active fill their lives with other activities.

---

17 References to a "good appearance," the requiring of photographs, and stated age limits in newspaper job advertisements are an indication of this situation.

Their husbands encourage them to study, involve themselves in creative projects, etc. Generally, they have help for domestic tasks and child care.

Women are the principal organizers of the family's day-to-day consumption, and commercial advertising is directed principally toward them. This has raised women's expectations for acquiring goods, encouraging them to carry out informal or occasional activities to earn money. These activities allow them to raise the quality of life for their families.[18]

As mentioned above, in our country, women who work retain family responsibilities, and this is reflected in their forms of participation in the labor market. Thus, they tend to prefer shorter workdays, and they are often willing to accept temporary work or to work at home, so that they can integrate their activities with family responsibilities. Sometimes they pass domestic tasks to an older daughter, who may end up abandoning her education in order to care for younger siblings, with obvious consequences for her own development.

At the same time, the market implicitly assumes that women take time and energy from their work to care for their families, considering them to be less suitable for certain jobs. This is reflected in their lesser relative participation in better-paid professions and those which involve high levels of responsibility. Some business groups claim that female labor carries higher costs, but this turns out to be false in light of empirical evidence, since costs which could affect employers are either absorbed by the State or passed on to the workers themselves in the form of lower salaries (Todaro 1996).

This combination of factors produces the wide gap between the wages of men and women. Women's lower income can be understood as a penalization by the market for family activities (Pardo 1996). Including all employed people in the country, women in 1990 earned 50.8% of the male income level.[19] The figures for the following years show some improvement, although great differences remain depending on the occupational group: the higher the qualifications required, the greater the difference in salary. Among managers, executives, and technicians, the difference is greater than among blue-collar workers.

Table 5 shows the evolution of salary differences by occupation between 1960 and 1994 in Santiago. The proportion has improved among blue-collar workers, supervisory and non-supervisory white-collar workers, while it has worsened among employers. Higher levels of education lead to income improvement, but they do not automatically translate into greater parity: executive women earn 65% of what men earn in the same category. Salary discrimination is extending into new areas, such as professional careers and specializations (within the company itself or through graduate degrees).[20] Independent women workers face different problems. Here, income differences tend to be related to the availability of capital, access to loans and similar factors, which are also unequally distributed by gender.

The 1996 Casen survey shows how the difference in women's average monthly income increases by quintile, varying from 70.3% of men's income for the first quintile to 54.2% for the fifth quintile. The tendency toward greater differences at higher educational levels remains. With this, the commonsense idea that a higher level of education is

---

18 Credit card use reaches surprising figures. It would be interesting to investigate the percentage of credit card spending accounted for by women.

19 INE, *Encuesta de Empleo* [Employment Survey], October-December 1990, Santiago.

20 The study by Hola and Todaro (1992) provides very valuable data in this area.

TABLE 5

CHANGE IN FEMALE EMPLOYMENT INCOME IN RELATION TO MALE EMPLOYMENT INCOME IN THE GREATER SANTIAGO ARE, BY OCCUPATION : 1960-1994
(Percentages)

Year	Female Employers	Female Executives	Female Non-Executives	Independent Female Workers	Female Laborers
1960	87.0	41.0	57.0	50.0	68.0
1965	60.0	44.0	63.0	44.0	74.0
1970	80.0	44.0	64.0	42.0	74.0
1975	58.0	42.0	73.0	64.0	79.0
1980	54.0	51.0	73.0	61.0	86.0
1985	55.0	69.0	84.0	78.0	81.0
1990	57.0	62.0	90.0	88.0	82.0
1994	56.0	65.0	85.0	88.0	84.0

SOURCE: University of Chile, "Employment & Unemployment Survey: Greater Santiago [Encuesta de ocupación y desocupación. Gran Santiago]," June of every year. In Sernam, Equal Opportunities for Working Women [Igualdad de oportunidades para la mujer en el trabajo] (Santiago: Sernam, 1996).

enough to secure a better place in the job market and a better income is refuted. In fact, along with the job segmentation which values male professions over female ones, the impact of motherhood on a woman's professional career must be added. Remaining in one job, women will have to interrupt their professional career with every pregnancy, delaying or adversely affecting their access to positions of greater responsibility. They will also find it more difficult to participate in training activities held outside their work schedule or requiring travel.

Despite these unfavorable conditions, women's work has a great impact on the economic situation and quality of life of their families, especially among the poor. Cepal studies have demonstrated that if women did not work, poor households in Chile would have increased from 27% to 38% in 1992. If all wives worked, this figure would have been only 19% (Cepal 1995). This is linked to the fact that women usually spend their total earnings to improve living conditions for their family group.

The lower economic participation of poor women, due to their child care responsibilities and the low-quality jobs available to them, seriously impairs their chances to aid their families. Thus, there is a pressing need to formulate programs and policies to help provide satisfactory job opportunities to poor women. This includes more effective action in support of child care — support which must be granted to both mothers and fathers — as well as better regulation of labor conditions.

In the area of social security, women face severe discrimination from the Pension Funds (AFPs), the National Social Security Institute (INP), and the health insurance companies. In the case of health insurance, women must pay higher premiums because of their risk of pregnancy. Pension funds do not always consider women's full remunerations when calculating percentages for retirement savings, a problem which especially affects domestic help. In general, women face serious disadvantages in securing adequate

TABLE 6

**AVERAGE MONTHLY EMPLOYMENT INCOME
BY SEX AND INCOME QUINTILE* : 1996**
(In November, 1996 pesos)

Income Quintile	Female	Male	Female Income as a Percentage of Male's
I	48,490	68,950	70.3
II	68,549	106,546	64.3
III	91,994	142,555	64.5
IV	136,492	220,267	62.0
V	383,920	707,804	54.2
Total	178,971	254,415	70.3

* Live-in domestic servants are excluded from this income level analysis.
SOURCE: Ministry of Planning & Cooperation, 1996 Casen Survey.

retirement or pension income. With the AFPs, they also find themselves at a disadvantage with respect to almost all of the variables affecting the accumulation of retirement savings (Elter 1996).

This leaves many categories of women in insecure retirement situations, above all those who completely lack social security benefits. Women's life expectancy is higher than men's, and it is rising, leaving an increasing number of women to face poverty and homelessness in old age, or to be economically dependent on relatives. The pensions granted to widows, which represent only half of the husband's retirement pension — reduced under the military dictatorship and not yet at a "decent" value, in spite of efforts made by the Concertación governments — leave women especially vulnerable at a time when their medical expenses tend to rise.

*Women's public presence and participation is increasing only slowly,
despite their significant social contributions.*
The modernization process has served to increase women's contributions to society. Added to the historic contributions they have made in community life, childrearing and the transmission of customs, values, and beliefs are the goods and services they now produce, their artistic creations, and their social and political activities.

However, despite the country's return to democracy and the commitments made in government platforms and election campaigns, there has been a notable deficit of female leaders among political representatives and decision-makers. The high levels of women's contributions described here are hardly reflected.

The presence of women in government positions has been limited by the fact that the Concertación parties did not present women candidates. However, President Frei has expressed a clear commitment to remedy this situation, naming the highest number of women to politically-appointed posts that the country has ever seen, in the ministries as well as sub-secretariats, public services, and other offices. The number of women diplomats has also increased. Comparable advances have not occurred in regional and provincial governments, however.

TABLE 7

WOMEN IN CONGRESS, 1965-2002
(Totals & Percentages)

Year	House of Representatives			Senate		
	Total	Women	%	Total	Women	%
1965-69	147	12	8.2	45	2	4.4
1969-73	150	9	6.0	50	1	2.0
1973	150	14	9.3	50	1	2.0
1990-94	120	7	5.8	36	2	5.6
1994-98	120	9	7.5	36	2	5.6
1998-2002	120	12	10.0	36	2	5.6

NOTE: Designated Senators are not included for figures after 1990.

SOURCE: Electoral Service.

There is a disturbingly low female presence in Chile's Congress, compared to that seen in other countries of the region. While the current vice president of the Senate is a woman, female representation in the Chamber of Deputies only reached 10% in the last elections, with 12 women among the 120 deputies. In the Senate, there are only two women among the 36 elected positions (5.6%).

This lack of female representation undoubtedly affects the quality of legislation. Throughout Latin America, women members of Congress have brought the day-to-day problems of men, women, and families onto the public agenda. The Chamber of Deputies' Family Committee, which facilitates the development of bills of great interest to Chilean citizens, was created through the efforts of women deputies. However, the Senate does not possess a similar committee; this is one reason why bills approved by the Chamber of Deputies have often become stalled in the Senate.

In general, the political parties have done little to increase the numbers of women in representative positions. Despite the enthusiasm of their supporters, the campaigns of women candidates for municipal and parliamentary elections have been rather lackluster, although some improvements were seen in the last elections. The extra-parliamentary Left and the Humanist Party proposed the greatest number of women candidates in the 1997 elections. The neglect of female candidates by the leading parties has resulted in a low percentage of women mayors, council members, senators and deputies.

In addition, the binomial electoral system tends to accentuate the problems faced by women candidates. Because of the importance of gaining a majority, the political parties are forced to field candidates with a high probability of being elected, that is, people who are already prominent and well-known. The low visibility of women in society makes their position more difficult. When the parties do select female candidates, they favor women having a family relationship with a recognized politician, or those with visible public positions. The fact that there is no public financing for electoral campaigns also decreases the motivation of potential female candidates. Because of the socio-cultural context described in this paper, women have fewer resources available to them with which to finance a campaign, as well as fewer contacts to provide donations.

A growing number of female party members has come to the realization that action is needed to spur their parties to create effective opportunities for women, in internal decision-making as well as in the proposal of female candidates for election.

The Party for Democracy (PPD) and the Socialist Party (PS) established internal quota systems for women — 20% for Board positions — in the early 1990s. In 1996, measures favoring women were implemented by the PS and the Christian Democrats. The last General Congress of the PS, which has a National Vice-Presidency for Women, agreed to progressively increase the proportion of women in order to reach gender equality by the year 2000. Thus in 1997 and 1998, a standard of 70/30% in favor of women will be applied in party elections, changing to 60/40% in the 1999-2000 elections. The Christian Democrats, for their part, approved a motion prohibiting the holding of more than 80% of party positions by a single gender.

Most of the political parties currently have at least one woman serving on their directive boards, whether as vice-president, political commission member, or central directive board member. This represents an advance for women in the political parties. However, only the Communist Party has a woman president. In any case, since 52% of voters are women, parties of all political orientations draw closer to women at election time, addressing their problems and offering solutions, and thus creating opportunities for participation, communication, and negotiation.

Following the positive examples of some Northern countries, as well as a closer neighbor — Argentina — a group of 10 male and female deputies recently presented a bill which would establish mandatory internal democracy within the political parties, as well as an obligatory proportion of male and female candidates in elections for representative office. In both cases, no more than 60% of positions could be held by either sex. While this proposal is still awaiting discussion, its approval could significantly increase women's representation in elective positions, and therefore deepen the democratic character of Congress, the municipal councils, and the parties themselves.

Meanwhile, it is not easy for women to rise to influential positions in political parties. The parties' inner operations are strictly male, in their organizational form as well as in their culture. Historically, women have served the coffee, been good secretaries, and helped organize the men's campaigns and mobilizations. The limitations placed on women by the organization of the family and the distribution of domestic tasks are not taken into account. Women make up high percentages of party members, but they can hardly have an active political life if they must care for their family aside from pursuing their own professional activities. Also, women have historically been socialized to prefer domestic roles and have been discouraged from pursuing a career in public service.

The general absence of concern about female participation which can be noted among male political figures does not contribute to improving this situation. Male politicians' concerns with respect to women are centered on the issues of sexuality, divorce, and abortion, and their main consideration is how these phenomena will affect the nuclear family.

In the judicial branch, a marked stratification by gender can be seen. Female presence is high in first-instance courts (some 46% of judges at this level in 1992), low in appeals courts (19.1%, including lawyers, an all-male group in 1992), and zero on the Supreme Court. However, recently, for the first time in history, a woman — Raquel Camposano — was named to the five-member group for the designation of ministerial candidates (Valdés and Gomáriz 1992b). The paucity of women in Chile's judicial branch stands in contrast with the situation of other countries in the region. The reform of Chile's legal system, which is currently underway, promises changes, but it appears that these will be slow in coming.

While social movements such as labor unions found themselves displaced from the spotlight during the democratic transition, labor leaders have come up with some interesting new ideas during the last few years. Although male leaders could not accept the election of a woman to the presidency of the Central Workers' Board (CUT), even though she had obtained a majority of votes, an overall increase of women in leadership positions is evident. A special commission dedicated to women's problems in the workplace has also been created. The National Association of Federal Companies (ANEF) and many other public sector employee associations have active female leaders. In the organized groups of AFP workers, women leaders have demonstrated strength, leadership ability, and an activist spirit.

Although systematic information is lacking in this area, partial studies reveal a large female presence in community or neighborhood organizations, with women holding a high percentage of leadership positions. The community crises during the 1997 winter storms led to the emergence of numerous women leaders. A recent leadership training program carried out by the Prodemu Women's School, aimed at women leaders from grassroots organizations all over the country, brought together 6,182 leaders representing 3,133 organizations, from 287 townships stretching from Arica to Punta Arenas, in 246 meetings. These figures indicate the breadth of female leadership in community organizations in low-income areas, which is not matched in social activities at other levels of society (Escuela de la Mujer-Prodemu 1997).

In the recent elections for the University of Chile Students' Federation, a woman leader with a history of participation in the student movement was chosen as president. Other university federations have also selected women leaders in the recent past. Women are gradually emerging from their traditional positions as secretaries and organizers of social events.

However, this progress has been painfully slow. This is why the complaint was heard on International Women's Day in 1997 that "democracy still owes a debt to women."

Groundbreaking policies have been directed
toward women since the restoration of democracy.
Besides the return of democracy itself, a definitive advance for women has been the creation of the National Women's Service (Sernam).[21] Originating from proposals made by women members of the Concertación coalition, it also made use of the suggestions of the 10 "Nations United for Women" (1975-85). The new organization focused on implementing the International Convention on the Elimination of All Forms of Discrimination Against Women, which the Chilean government had ratified in late 1989.

---

21 Created through Law 19,023, which came into effect in January 1991.

Sernam's work has led to the formulation of specific plans and programs on a national, regional, and municipal level. Among the most notable of these are:

- the network of Women's Rights Information Centers, which have helped thousands of women in all regions of the country to recognize their rights and find out where to turn for help with their problems
- the Program for Women Heads of Household, implemented in many municipalities with government assistance, which seeks to solve the employment difficulties of low-income women and to assist them in other areas (mental health, child care, legal aid, and skills training)
- the Teenage Pregnancy Prevention Program, which has undertaken various projects as well as research on this subject
- the Roundtables on Sexuality and Emotion (Jocas)
- the Child Care Program for Seasonal Women Workers, which has helped provide adequate child care arrangements for working mothers, thanks to contributions from municipalities and private companies in various regions
- the Family Violence Prevention Program, which has trained male and female public servants and police personnel throughout the country, as well as women in various communities, in an effort to prevent and treat this serious problem. The approval of the Family Violence Law has opened the way for prosecution of instances of this crime and has set up mechanisms to coordinate the offices responsible for dealing with it.

Sernam's mission also requires it to undertake activities within the government itself. The organization has conducted numerous training and awareness programs for public officials, in order to promote the incorporation of gender perspectives into the planning, execution, and evaluation of government programs.

Significant legislative reforms have also been developed by Sernam and presented to Congress; some have been approved, some are still being discussed, and others are still in the proposal stage. Among them are:

- a constitutional reform which explicitly establishes the equality of men and women before the law, presented and initially rejected during President Aylwin's government, and currently approved by the Chamber of Deputies and pending in the Senate
- the establishment of a compensation fund for domestic workers (Law 19,010)
- various modifications to the individual work contract which are beneficial to women (Law 19,250)
- the recognition of shared property in civil marriage law, as well as the modification of several texts harmful to women in the Civil and Penal Codes, such as the sections on adultery (Law 19,335)
- the penalization of family violence and child abuse (Law 19,325)
- the bill eliminating the distinction between legitimate and illegitimate offspring (still pending in the Senate)
- the bill to penalize sexual harassment in the workplace
- the proposal to modify the Municipal Organic Law to guarantee equal opportunities and gender equality in municipal operations

Meanwhile, various ministries have created programs specifically aimed at improving the condition of women. The Education Ministry's Women's Program has undertaken initiatives to eliminate sexism from school texts, to retain pregnant adolescents in the school system, and to incorporate the principle of equal opportunity into the new curricula. The Roundtables on Sexuality and Emotion (Jocas), also coordinated by this program, have received much attention. They have allowed students to ask the questions that are on their minds and to gain an adequate understanding of these vital areas, in a participatory forum within the school community.

The Ministry of Health modified the old Maternal Health Program, transforming it into the Women's Health Program. The objective of the new program is to cover all stages of women's lives, not just their reproductive years. This ministry has also participated in several inter-ministry commissions, coordinating actions that benefit women such as the prevention of teenage pregnancy and family violence.

Specific measures have been undertaken to incorporate women into the Technology Transfer Program in rural areas, through the National Institute for Agricultural Development (Indap). This is a critical sector of the economy, where the country's integration into international markets has had a dramatic impact. Thousands of families risk losing their sources of income if they are not able to sell their products in the new marketplace.

The Ministry of Labor has created an Equal Opportunity Commission to examine problems in the labor force. Similarly, the Labor Directive has carried out joint activities with Sernam in order to oversee and regulate women's working conditions.

The National Employment Training Service (Sence) has included women in numerous courses over the last few years, as well as in the Young Chile program. Likewise, the Social Investment and Solidarity Fund has gradually incorporated an awareness of women's needs into its programs directed toward small entrepreneurs and community organizations.

At the end of the Aylwin administration, Sernam developed the Equal Opportunity Plan for Women 1994-2000, which was incorporated into the President Frei's government platform. This is currently Sernam's principal working tool, providing the orientation for all of its policies. The plan calls for Sernam to carry out studies and spur project development on the regional and national level. Various public policy priorities are established by the plan. The Secretary General of the Presidency has made a commitment to work toward the implementation of this plan in all of Chile's ministries and government institutions. In fact, the Ministry of National Assets has already implemented such a policy, internally as well as in its relationship with the public. In 1997, the Rural Women's Equality plan was approved, with the help of women's organizations, expressing the government's commitment to assist rural women.

During the last few years, the municipalities, as intermediaries for Sernam initiatives, have developed an increasing number of programs directed toward women. Today, numerous municipalities have established offices or programs for women, which coordinate the programs promoted by Sernam. These measures are highly diverse in nature, but all testify to the increasing institutionalization of public policies for women.

The Chilean government has been represented at numerous international events dedicated to improving the situation of women. Sernam attended the Sixth Latin American Regional Conference for Women, held in Mar del Plata in 1994, as well as the Fourth World Conference for Women, which took place in Beijing in 1995. Chile's delegation, consisting of professionals from the various ministries involved in women's issues, contributed actively to the debate to construct a Platform for Action.

In November 1997, Chile presided over the Seventh Latin American Regional Conference on the Integration of Women in Development, which took place in Santiago. This conference was attended by representatives of many of the governments of the region, and it produced the "Santiago Consensus," in which the attending countries reaffirmed their will to enact the agreements of the 1995 Beijing World Conference.

The Prodemu Women's School, presided over by Chile's First Lady, has created a series of programs dedicated to improving the personal and family lives of low-income women. In accordance with the government's aims of eliminating poverty and achieving equal opportunity, it seeks to strengthen leadership in community organizations and to provide skills training to help women enter the labor market. It also offers recreational, artistic, and sports activities.

A new awareness of women's development spreads through Chile's culture,
new identities are strengthened, and models for women's lives are discussed and disputed.
The activities, demands, and dreams of all segments of society unfold upon a stage of culture. Many institutions are involved, including the family, the educational system, the art world, the media, and so forth. Culture also plays a part in interpersonal communication, through the establishment of "common knowledge." Within culture, individual and collective identities are established.

An important change in the 1990s has been the increasing visibility of women's concerns in the overall culture. A kind of opening can be perceived, which is still in a fragmented and even contradictory stage, but which is increasing society's awareness of the situations and concerns of women throughout the country. Among these concerns are advancing in study and work; the right to sexual pleasure beyond reproduction; the diversity of family situations and arrangements; the question to have or not to have children; the problem of male chauvinism and the subordination of women; and so forth.

In fact, the existence of a chauvinist organization of private and public life and the need to advance toward equality is already part of our culture's common knowledge. Likewise, topics which were once cloistered in women's institutions and organizations, such as domestic violence and teenage pregnancy, are now publicly recognized and addressed. Additional topics on the agenda formulated by the women's movement of the 1980s, as well as by Sernam programs, are gradually taking on relevance.

However, it is here that a heated debate opens up, one which easily takes on an ideological coloration. Conservative elements use the media under their control to try to stop women's advance. These debates cut across political lines. The creation of Sernam awakened numerous suspicions, reflected in the subsequent parliamentary debate and in the conservative media. In 1995, Sernam's participation in the U.N. Fourth World Conference on Women led to renewed debate and confrontation between the Chamber of Deputies, which fully approved the report of the Sernam Minister, and the Senate, which supported a statement, backed by senators from all political orientations, rejecting the concept of gender and recognizing only one kind of family.

In 1996, the Jocas program led to another vigorous dispute; this time, the wills of the majority of both male and female students, as well as those of the parents and guardians who value the program, clearly prevailed. Meanwhile, Catholic schools are resisting the regulation allowing pregnant students to complete their education. In 1997, despite a standing boycott on the discussion of a bill addressing divorce and remarriage, the Chamber of Deputies approved it, and it is currently awaiting consideration by the Senate.

The idea of family and the subordinate role of women which is central in many conservative circles makes it difficult to introduce a perspective of equality and women's rights. Yet research of feminist origin has shown that the subordination of women in the family causes conflicts and perpetuates relationships of unequal power.

The concentration of the media in the hands of conservative groups allows the frequent reiteration of these groups' messages, giving the impression that the majority of Chileans hold the same opinions. However, public opinion polls, as well as the concrete practices of the population, have repeatedly contradicted this idea, revealing, for example, sexual experience at an increasingly younger age, along with the prevalence of premarital sex and the use of contraceptives. Young Chileans today are expressing new identities, new personal plans, and a desire for greater freedom and autonomy. Similarly, the development of more equal relationships among young people, who recognize the need to share not only the economic burden, but also child care and domestic responsibilities, foretells further changes in the future.

The alternative roles and lifestyles presented by television, especially on cable channels, have brought about a change in perspective for women in general, both young and old. While traditional television programs rarely contradict women's old-fashioned roles, movies and some conversation and youth programs have begun to encourage women to venture into new undertakings, seek more equal relationships, and insist upon equal rights.

Nevertheless, the democratic ideals of fairness and equal opportunity are still controversial. The debates mentioned above reveal that these concepts have not yet fully permeated our society, in spite of the declarations occasionally made by political and ideological leaders in favor of women, especially on Mother's Day. The change toward a more democratic balance between the genders is sought only by certain segments of society. The same applies to respect and tolerance for the diversity of women's identities and plans for their lives.

However, courses on gender issues, gender studies programs, and some gender-focused graduate programs have been appearing at both private and public universities.

And despite all of these advances, barriers, and tensions, women of all generations continue to live their lives, attempting as best they can to shape their own destinies and the future of their families and communities.

II. Women as Social Protagonists

The organization of a segment of the female population to fight for women's interests has venerable historical roots. In Chile, women's associations are more than 100 years old, and their contributions to social and charitable work, culture, and the more than 50-year struggle for civil and political rights are especially noteworthy. During the 1970s, women's social movements were reborn throughout Latin America, arising from different sources, but all strongly committed to democracy, human rights, and women's rights.

At the beginning of the democratic transition, Chile enjoyed a significant women's movement, more diverse and widespread than ever before in its history. Hundreds of women's groups and social and political associations, as well as numerous non-governmental organizations (NGOs) were distributed all over the country. This movement, emerging from the struggle for democracy and human rights, formulated proposals for change in society, culture, and the balance of power in relationships between the genders.

The ideals of these groups were symbolized by the slogan "Democracy in the nation and in the home," a phrase which would later be repeated throughout Latin America. During the final phases of the dictatorship, human rights organizations, low-income women, professionals, feminists, union leaders, rural women, and female political party members were brought together by "Memch '83" and "Mujeres por la Vida" [Women for Life], as well as a series of similar events throughout the country. In 1986, a large number of women participated in the Civil Assembly and in the "Chilean Demand," through the umbrella group "Pliego de las Mujeres."[22]

During the 1980s, the women's movement was recognized not only as fighting for its specific interests, but also for the general interests of society. This was underlined by its work for the "No" vote in the 1988 plebiscite, as well as through its formulation of a political platform for women. In 1988, the feminist movement published a list of "Women's Claims upon Democracy," and various institutions began to circulate the United Nations Convention on the Elimination of All Forms of Discrimination Against Women as a basis for the new government's policies.

Professionals from non-governmental organizations (NGOs) and other institutions created the National Concertación of Women for Democracy, while other women, through the Coordination of Women's Social Organizations, carried out the "I'm a woman…I have rights" campaign, with help from organizations in Santiago and other regions of the country (1991 Coordination of Women's Social Organizations). The former elaborated an agenda of policies and measures to be added to the Concertación coalition's platform, including as the creation of institutions to formulate and implement public policy to advance women and to promote change in the relationship between the genders. The latter developed a series of demands and proposals for the new democracy. Close ties between the broader social movement and women's political groups allowed the women's proposals to be included, at least in their central aspects, in the Concertación's platform (Montecino and Rossetti 1990).

The Concertación also publicly raised the issue of discrimination against women and included actions, policies, and programs to combat this problem among its priorities. The country's reintegration into international cultural currents brought more emphasis on gender equality as well as democratic values. The slogan "democracy in the nation and in the home" not only reflected the intention of the women's movement, but also a broader democratizing impulse.

However, this pattern was not repeated within the political parties, which had recovered their role as mediators between the State and civil society after years of persecution and exclusion. The parties included few women in their lists of candidates for Congress and executive appointment in President Aylwin's administration, a fact which was reflected in the composition of the legislature and the ministerial cabinet.

With the onset of the democratic transition, the women's movement was institutionalized in various NGOs and became highly professional. It addressed a great variety of topics, seeking to formulate specific public policies to improve the situation of women and modify the imbalance of power. In 1991, there were 159 NGOs involving women all over the country, 44 of them with an academic component. Dozens of women leaders emerging

22 See, among others, Kirkwood (1986); Palestro (1991); Valdés and Gomáriz (1992a); Valdés and Weinstein (1993); and Frohmann and Valdés (1993).

TABLE 8

WOMEN'S SOCIAL ORGANIZATIONS, 1991
(Absolute Numbers)

Type of Organization	Grassroots Organization	Members	Second-Degree Organization
Legally Permitted Mothers' Centers	4,243	93,346	13
Working Class Economic Organizations	575	7,668	48
Metropolitan Area Settlers' Organizations	1,968	17,415	51
Rest of the Country	1,986	24,229	3
Peasant Organizations	1,542	27,432	–
Women's Collectives & Groups	182	nd	–
Union Organizations	12	nd	–
Guild Organizations	17	nd	–
Volunteer Groups	32	35,938	–
Integra & Prodemu	2	3,730	–
Members			
Total	10,541	209,758	115

SOURCE: T. Valdés and E. Gomáriz, Mujeres latinoamericanas en cifras. Chile (Santiago: Flacso, Women's Institute, 1992).

from the ranks of these organizations later joined the government and helped to carry out the movement's program on the national and regional levels (Frohmann and Valdés 1993).

According to a 1991 study, women's social organizations, including their most diverse variants, numbered in the thousands at that time, with a total membership of over 200,000 (see Table 8). The objective of many of these organizations was to contribute to the improvement of women's lives. Many had established inter-group coordination bodies, in order to harmonize their efforts and focus their action on specific issues. The above-mentioned study notes 159 second-degree organizations. In addition, women's centers had multiplied, as well as small women's institutions and meeting places where women could pursue their own interests, particularly in low-income urban areas.

Since the 1970s, organized Chilean women have pursued an internationally-inspired action strategy which led them to undertake reflections and discussions with organizations all over Latin America. Chilean delegations have taken part in the Latin American Women's Meetings which have been held periodically since 1982. Numerous international networks for organized action have been created, including the Women's Health Network (1984), the Low-Income Women's Education Network (Repem 1988), and the Latin American and Caribbean Network Against Domestic and Sexual Violence (1990). These networks have promoted specific legislative goals, achieving widely-recognized public policy advances in favor of women. They have also established commemorative days to heighten visibility of women's problems. The Women's Health Network institutionalized the Day of Action for Women's Health (May 28), carrying out annual campaigns with a different theme each year. The anti-violence network instituted the Day of Non-Violence Against Women (November 25). These commemorative days are recognized by women all over the region, and today Latin American governments themselves carry out activities on these dates.

However, in the 1990s, just as institutional opportunities were opened up to it, the Chilean women's movement seemed to lose its vigor and visibility, both of which are necessary to push through its proposals for change. The NGOs, perhaps the movement's most visible players and those who have made leading contributions to the dissemination of information and the formulation of policy proposals, have suffered significant financial difficulties as a result of the withdrawal of international aid from the country and the scarcity of domestic funding. State contracts for the implementation of social programs can hardly substitute for the previous conditions under which these organizations carried out their efforts, and these contracts also create a situation of dependency which limits the formulation of criticism and alternative proposals. The grassroots organizations that previously acted in concert with the NGOs became largely isolated as the social network of the 1980s disintegrated. Coordination among groups almost completely disappeared, with only the day-to-day problems of their own communities left as an incitement to action.

This phenomenon has been explained in various ways. Some see its roots in the contractual nature of the transition to democracy, which depended upon the actions of a select group of specialized political actors who could guarantee a minimum consensus for negotiation, displacing social forces from the political arena. Others see it as characteristic of late 20th-century market democracies, which exalt individualism, relegating social solidarity to a secondary position. Another explanation points to movement leaders' exhaustion after the struggle against the dictatorship; they may have viewed the democratic restoration as a "calmer" period, during which they could turn their attention back to their personal lives. Low motivation among women activists may also derive from frustration at the lack of participation characterizing our "democracy of spectators." Finally, the leadership of the women's movement may have been siphoned off through the State's "co-opting" of prominent women leaders, who seized opportunities for action where only exclusion and inequality had reigned in the past.

Regardless of the explanations of the future of the women's movement — some more optimistic than others — it is clear that Chile has lacked a mobilized and vociferous women's movement in recent years. The national networks have been an exception: the Women and Work Network (1988), the National Network Against Sexual and Domestic Violence (1990), and the Open Forum for Sexual and Reproductive Health (1992), which bring together NGOs, professionals, and community organizations, have maintained their dynamism and their creativity in formulating new proposals.

Most women's organizations and NGOs have applauded the establishment of Sernam, appreciating the fact that, for the first time, the Chilean government publicly recognized female inequality and created an institution to help remedy the situation. The existence of a public body seeking to promote equal opportunity between men and women has been seen as a victory.

Nevertheless, the relationship between Sernam and non-governmental women's groups has begun to change. At the beginning of the democratic transition, many women's movement leaders and women legislators from the Concertación parties stood together in a tacit agreement to support the actions of the government. Today, however, as some organized groups seek to revive the women's movement and assert grassroots influence over gender policies, the former unconditional alliance is becoming more of a dialogue. Since 1995, women's groups and NGOs have begun to signal their independence from Sernam, as well as discomfort with the role it has assigned them. Sernam is seen as overemphasizing technical consulting and the role of program executors. For the latter, Sernam contracts individual consultants, not recognizing the harm thereby done to NGOs and other institutions with experience in the field, at a time when they are trying to develop a more independent and energetic stance.

During the past two years, Sernam has shown its willingness to create opportunities for participation, organizing forums such as the Program for Women Heads of Household and the Regional Parliaments, as well as roundtables for the discussion of equal opportunity measures on a sectorial or local basis (such as the Rural Roundtable and the Women's Leadership Council of the Metropolitan Region). It has even established an internal commission focusing on participation. In 1997, Sernam organized several meetings with NGOs, and it has also participated in activities organized by the NGOs themselves.

In spite of the abovementioned difficulties, a gradual reorganization of the remaining women's organizations and NGOs has been taking place since 1993, and has become even more dynamic since 1996. This can be seen in the discussion process initiated by the Chile Initiative Group, made up of several NGOs participating in the Beijing conference. A group of NGOs also worked together to formulate an assessment of the condition of women to be presented to the Latin American and Caribbean Regional Conference (Mar del Plata 1994), and also to serve as the basis for an NGO Forum held immediately before the Fourth World Conference on Women. This effort led to the creation of working groups in Chile's 13 regions, with regional meetings and specific regional assessments of the condition of women. Later, a definitive text was hammered out at a national meeting in Santiago. This text was influential at Mar del Plata as well as at the NGO Forum in China.

After the conference, the group Iniciativa Chile published a synthesis of the approved platform to assist women's groups in their efforts. The meeting "Beijing: a year later" (1996) was a landmark event, bringing together hundreds of women from all walks of life,[23] in a forum generated by civil society for civil society. Proposals from many groups were raised in an Open Council, allowing participants to appreciate the wide range of problems affecting and uniting women. The agendas for action in 12 of the 13 regions were also debated, in order to broaden their content and to establish regional, sectorial, and national priorities. This meeting illustrates the new political force gathering among organized women today, as they attempt to gain a more influential voice in public policy.

During 1997, the women's movement determined a series of priorities to guide their dialogue with the authorities. The underlying aim was to ensure the government's adherence to the tenets of the Beijing Platform. Meetings among sectorial and regional representatives produced an agenda for the National Follow-up Forum for the Beijing Agreements. After a series of conversations with ministers and other officials, the first forum session was held on September 23. The subject matter was the Agreement's provisions on "women in the exercise of power and decision-making processes." In this session, which took place in the Ariztia palace, the government made several formal, signed commitments:

• to strengthen the representation and participation of women in community and labor organizations, political parties, and positions with decision-making power in various State bodies

---

23 Participants included regional activists, women labor leaders, rural and indigenous women, young women, representatives of health groups, HIV-positive activists, representatives of Christian groups, members of political organizations, and others.

- to ensure that the debate over electoral reform will include measures to eliminate discrimination against women
- to promote women's participation as citizens through various measures
- to include the concept of equal opportunity in plans for the modernization of public institutions

At the same time, conversations were begun with the presidents and vice-presidents of the Concertación parties, in order to introduce the women's movement agenda into the parties' internal debates and to gain their support on legislative issues.

With the help of Sernam and other government institutions, annual activities were also initiated to focus on issues of concern to women. The most important of these are International Women's Day, the International Day of Action for Women's Health, and the International Day Against Domestic and Sexual Violence.

The steps taken during 1997 constitute advances for the women's movement. However, maintaining this progress depends on the continued recognition of organized women as a force in society, as well as the fulfillment of the agreements made with various parties.

In spite of the difficulties encountered in the new environment of the democratic transition, it is evident that organized women and their movements are a driving force behind changes in society that affect women. The pace of the change process will depend on their political and organizational abilities.

However, it must be remembered that the women who are fighting for improvements in women's lives and for changes in gender relations face numerous impediments. They, too, are subject to the workplace, educational, cultural, and family difficulties noted above. Additionally, they are operating within an economic system which does not take responsibility for the rearing of the next generation, as well as a political system which does not recognize social groups as mediators between the State and the citizens.

III. Chilean Families in the 1990s

As we have implied, the modernization process — in its economic, productive, institutional, and other aspects — has strongly affected families, in their structure as well as in their internal dynamics. Women, with the special responsibility for childrearing tasks which society has placed on them, feel the pressure of changes which affect their reproductive role, along with the other pressures of modernization.

Opinion polls carried out in the last few years reveal the continuing importance of the family for many people, regardless of sex or age group. The family is valued as a source of affection, protection, and support.

Proposals for the construction of couples and family relations on a more equal basis have emerged from the ideals of modernization. A move in this direction can increasingly be seen among young couples, mainly in middle-class and professional circles. At the same time, new demands are being made of romantic love and one's partner. The gender-based division of labor is being questioned, and new models of fatherhood are being explored. Finally, separation is being legitimized as a possible response to serious conflicts between partners.

Chilean families are increasingly heterogeneous.

Following Elizabeth Jelin (1994), we understand the family unit as a social organization; it is a microcosm of productive, reproductive, and distributive relationships, with an internal power structure. This small organization is composed of people of different sexes and ages bound by family, alliance, and affinity relationships, whose aim is extended coexistence. They undertake the social reproduction of their members: biological or more precisely bio-social reproduction, replacement of the work force, primary socialization of children and youth, and, in general, activities aimed at cultural and symbolic reproduction (Reca, Tijoux, Crovetto et al. 1996). The family implants ideological and affective components which support its continuation and reproduction.

However, there are structural foundations for conflict and struggle within the family unit. We believe that along with collective tasks and motivations, family members also have their own personal needs and interests, deriving from their individual positions in the productive and reproductive processes, internally as well as externally (Jelin 1994). The family is subject to variations in composition, as a result of the actions of its own members as well as its economic and social integration.

Because of the family's key role in social reproduction, any action or relationship occurring within it affects society as well as individuals. In this sense, the family is an intermediate entity between individuals and society, and because of this, it becomes an object of concern and public policy attention. Society has also transformed the family into an institution regulated by legal norms.

In a subjective sense, we understand the family as the space in which we obtain affection and caring. There, one "discovers the meaning of life." The family represents "the founding structure of human sociability," with "physiological and existential functions which are added in an essential way to its reproductive functions," (Bernales 1995).

The modernization process has introduced new dynamics into families, such as the predominance of voluntary and love-based marriages or cohabitation, although at times partners may marry in order to escape a difficult situation in the home of origin, or because of an unplanned pregnancy. Other trends influenced by modernization include marrying at a later age; earlier initiation of sexual activity; greater premarital sexual experience; the increased incorporation of women into the labor market, with an emphasis, in many cases, on personal development; more marked life cycle stages, with prolonged adolescence and difficulties in becoming independent; and changes in relationships between the genders. The process of "individualization" mentioned earlier reveals growing individual needs within the family, as its members demand more satisfaction out of life.

In the course of this process, diverse family forms and situations, also called "family types," have arisen. While these diverse environments carry out the same bio-social, economic, cultural and social functions as other families, they involve differing resources and dynamics (Reca 1992).

Serious methodological challenges impede the study of the heterogeneous and multidimensional nature of the Chilean family. In general, available data are obtained from surveys and polls based on the concept of "households"; that is, groups of people living under the same roof and having a common nutritional budget. These household entities do not necessarily coincide with true family groups.

The association of the family with a "domestic unit" or "household" — including all of the members who share a residence and contribute their skills and resources to childrearing

TABLE 9

HOUSEHOLD AND FAMILY TYPES, 1992
(Absolute & Percentual Figures)

Type Household/Family	Number of Households	Number with Primary Economically Active Women	% of Total Number of Households w/ Primary Economically Active Women	%
Single Person	267,271	38,890	1.2	8.1
Nuclear Family, Working Woman	276,533	276,535	8.4	8.4
Nuclear Family, Unemployed Woman	1,093,538	-	-	33.2
Nuclear Family, Without Children	252,107	101,233	3.1	7.7
Single Parent Nuclear Family	288,407	62,546	1.9	8.8
Extended Family, Working Woman	95,072	95,072	2.9	2.9
Extended Family, Unemployed Woman	444,999	-	-	13.5
Extended, Single Parent Family	237,534	57,386	1.8	7.2
Composite Family	137,727	34,632	1.1	4.2
Non-Nuclear Household	199,865	38,072	1.2	6.0
Total	3,293,053	704,602	21.6	100.0

SOURCE: Sernam-PET Study, National Sample of the 1992 Population and Housing Census, INE. In: Sernam, "Familias y hogares en situaciones críticas en Chile según Censo 1992", Documento de Trabajo 46 ["Chilean Families and Households in Critical Situations, According to the 1992 Census", Working Paper 46] (Santiago: Sernam 1996).

and daily life — allows the establishment of an operational concept of family. Thus, it permits the detection of overall developments within countries as well as the measurement of changes over time. Yet it omits a series of key dimensions in the composition of the family. By reducing its definition to a common roof and budget, it does not give an account of the economic relations existing beyond the home.[24] Likewise, it excludes affective bonds, which play a substantial role in the development of the family unit. Additionally, significant misinformation, exacerbated by cultural factors, occurs in the case of unmarried couples and female heads of household, for example. However, this is the data available to us, and we must work with it.

The surveys indicate the heterogeneous nature of Chilean homes, uncovering a multiplicity of family situations. The basic types observed are one-person, nuclear, extended, composite, and non-family homes.[25] Between 1970 and 1992, we see a notable increase in nuclear homes and a decrease in composite and extended homes. The predominant type is the nuclear home. There has also been an increase in one-person homes, especially in urban areas. We can foresee the continued growth of this type of unit in the future, based

24 It also fails to recognize the situation of one-person households lacking autonomous income, such as those of young people or the elderly, which are supported economically by third parties, generally relatives.

25 A one-person home is composed of only one person. A nuclear home is composed of one or both members of a couple and their unmarried offspring. An extended home includes one or both members of a couple, their unmarried offspring and other relatives. A composite home includes one or both members of a couple, their unmarried offspring, as well as other relatives and non-relatives. A non-family home results when two or more people who are not relatives share living quarters.

on the aging of the population, and, to a lesser extent, on the increased tendency among young people to establish autonomous households, independent of the coupling process. This tendency is a recent one and is mainly seen among middle- and upper-class groups, due to the economic restrictions faced by lower-income youth.

Distinguishing whether one or both members of a married couple is present in these basic types of families leads to a further differentiation: between homes with one parent and those with two. According to the 1992 census, there were 558,996 one-parent homes, including both nuclear and extended types, of which 83.9% were headed by women (469,199 homes).

It is a recognized fact that households headed by women have been steadily increasing in Chile. However, official statistics tend to distort this phenomenon, due to cultural factors leading men to be identified as heads of household, even if their income is not the family's main source of support. Women tend to name themselves as heads of household only if they alone are responsible for the family. According to the 1992 census, 25.3% of all Chilean homes were headed by a woman (Valenzuela 1995).

If we consider the activity or inactivity of the household's central woman figure (wife, partner, or head of household), the diversity of family situations increases even further. Data from 1992 show that the central woman figure was employed in a significant percentage of nuclear and extended homes. These households' situation is clearly quite different from that of homes in which the leading woman is not employed, especially those with children (see Table 9). These figures indicate ongoing change in the traditional cultural pattern restricting women to domestic activities.

Interestingly, however, when we compare employed principal female figures to the total of employed women, it becomes clear that most women who work are not the heads of their households, but hold other positions in the home, such as daughters or other relatives. Similarly, numerous female heads of household are not employed.

Table 10 shows that the category "domestic activity," that is, non-employed, includes a significant percentage of the heads of household of one-parent families (27.3%) and extended families (23.5%). In other words, the economic arrangements of those families must include contributions from other family members.

Another contributing factor to the diversity of family situations is the so-called "family cycle." This cycle divides family life into periods or stages, based upon the presence of children in the home and the age of the oldest child, since children's needs and demands at various stages clearly affect the dynamics and operation of the family.[26]

When this "family cycle" dimension is added to the above analysis, the figures begin to reveal the survival arrangements made by various types of families. For example, almost 60% of extended one-parent families — which have a high proportion of non-employed, widowed women as household heads — have children older than 25, while 18.6% have children between 19 and 24 years old. An analysis of the relationships within extended-family homes shows that in middle-class groups, the head of household often brings his or

---

26 Seven stages can be distinguished in the family life cycle: young couple or family without children; couple or family whose oldest child is of preschool age (0-5 years old); couple or family whose oldest child is school-aged (6-13 years old); couple or family whose oldest child is an adolescent (13-18 years old); couple or family whose oldest child is 19 years or older; older couple or family without children living at home; and widow or widower (Informe Comisión Nacional de la Familia [Report of the National Commission on the Family], Santiago, 1994).

TABLE 10

HOUSEHOLD OR FAMILY TYPES ACCORDING TO
SOCIOECONOMIC INSERTION OF THE HOUSEHOLD HEAD
(Percentages)

Socioeconomic Insertion	HOUSEHOLD / FAMILY TYPE										TOTAL
	Single	Nuclear, Working Woman	Nuclear, Unemployed Woman	Nuclear, No Kids	Nuclear, Single Parent	Extended, Working Woman	Extended, Unemployed Woman	Extended, Single Parent	Composite	Non Nuclear	
	%	%	%	%	%	%	%	%	%	%	#
Employers	5.0	17.0	33.7	10.0	4.2	5.8	11.3	3.3	5.5	4.2	139,202
Professional and Technical Positions	7.0	20.9	29.5	8.1	7.0	6.2	7.5	3.5	4.4	5.9	305,108
Service Employees	6.8	14.4	34.4	6.9	8.0	4.8	9.8	4.7	4.5	5.7	441,816
Qualified Primary Workers	6.9	4.0	49.7	6.5	2.5	1.5	18.5	2.2	4.6	3.6	302,330
Qualified Secondary Workers	4.9	8.6	48.7	6.6	4.9	3.0	15.5	2.7	3.0	3.0	411,537
Qualified Tertiary Workers	4.2	10.8	48.4	6.8	2.1	3.7	16.4	1.3	3.6	2.7	262,636
Workers not Qualified	7.7	8.4	37.2	6.1	10.5	3.0	12.6	6.3	3.3	4.9	349,190
Domestic Chores / Activities	8.6	0.1	14.4	2.8	27.3	0.1	8.3	23.5	5.4	9.5	385,004
Retired	15.1	1.3	15.1	14.0	8.6	1.0	19.1	11.9	4.3	9.6	500,754
Other	12.9	4.9	28.1	9.1	7.0	1.5	15.4	4.9	4.4	11.8	153,977
Total	8.2	8.3	32.9	7.7	8.8	2.9	13.5	7.3	4.3	6.1	3,251,554

SOURCE: Inés Reca, et al., "Las familias de Chile según el último Censo de Población de 1992," Documento de Trabajo 44 ["Chilean Families According to the 1992 Population Census," Working Paper 44] (Santiago: Sernam 1996).

her parents into the home to live. Among low-income families, women heads of household tend to shelter other family members as a survival arrangement (Reca et al. 1996b). Thus, the needs and arrangements of extended families differ according to their socio-economic status.

Aside from the information provided by the Population Census and analyzed above, there exists another type of family: the so-called "blended," "reconstructed," or "simultaneous" family. This family type is the result of a union to which one or both partners bring a child from a previous union. These families are created after the death of a partner or the dissolution of a previous relationship. Their members may belong to more than one family simultaneously: the original and that resulting from the new union.

Although available information is scarce, this type of family appears to be a growing phenomenon in our country. According to the Civil and Identification Registry, approximately one thousand cases of bigamy occur each year. Some remarriages also take place abroad, due to the partners' inability to obtain a divorce and to remarry in Chile. No figures are available for separated couples living with new partners. People with annulled marriages who marry other partners comprise approximately 2% of the total number of marriages each year. Most of these are men marrying women with no previous marriage.

TABLE 11

NUMBER OF CONJUGAL UNIONS OR STABLE COMMON LAW UNIONS, BY AGE
(Percentages)

| | | | Age | | |
# of Unions	18-24 Years	25-34 Years	35-54 Years	55 Years & Total	Total
One	97.1	95.0	88.3	88.6	90.8
Two or More	2.9	5.0	11.7	1.4	9.2

SOURCE: National Family Commission, 1994 Household Survey [Encuesta de Hogares].

TABLE 12

NUMBER OF STABLE COUPLE UNIONS, BY SEX AND SOCIOECONOMIC GROUP
(Percentages)

| | Sex | | | Socioeconomic Group | | |
# Unions	Total	Men	Women	High	Middle	Low
One	86.0	85.9	86.4	92.8	86.2	84.6
Two or more	14.0	14.1	13.6	7.2	13.8	15.4

SOURCE: CEP, *Estudio Social y de Opinión Pública* [Social Study and Public Opinion] (Santiago, March 1993)

The proportion of Chileans who have had more than one marriage or long-term cohabitational relationship has been estimated at between 9% and 14%. Similarly, among households composed of a couple with children, 10.8% include children from a previous relationship of one of the partners (Muñoz and Reyes 1997).

These second or third unions are more common in people over 35. They also vary among different social groups, with a higher rate of incidence at lower socioeconomic levels, as a 1993 study reveals.

Reflecting the cultural changes discussed by this paper, these blended families are generally accepted as a reality in society, as a survey by the National Commission on the Family reveals. In fact, 72.8% of the people interviewed "agreed" or "strongly agreed" with the statement "when love ends, each member of the couple has the right to a new life with someone else." The level of agreement increases as the age of the person interviewed decreases, and decreases as the person's position on the social scale decreases (National Commission on the Family Report 1994).

Families are formed in different ways.
Families arise in different ways, but most begin with the union of a man and a woman. In Chile, these unions are generally undertaken through the free will of the partners and are formalized through legal marriage. The marriage rate (annual number of legal marriages) has remained stable, although a marked increase has been seen in the age of the partners at marriage. In 1982, men married at an average age of 24.8, and women at 22.8 years. By 1997,

TABLE 13

CHANGE IN CHILDBIRTH, BY MOTHER'S CIVIL STATUS AND AGE GROUP : 1982-1995*
(Absolute and Percentual Figures)

	1982	1986	1990	1992	1993	1995
Births	256,503	259,347	292,146	279,098	275,916	265,932
Illegitimate	76,821	83,246	100,138	102,739	104,997	107,641
Illegitimate Births (percentages)	30.0	32.1	34.3	36.8	38.1	40.5
10 - 14 years	73.5	82.6	83.0	85.7	84.2	90.1
15 - 19 years	49.5	55.5	60.6	66.8	68.0	70.7
20 - 24 years	31.6	34.4	37.2	41.4	43.6	46.8
25 - 29 years	22.2	24.1	25.0	26.6	27.7	29.7
30 - 34 years	22.1	23.9	26.2	26.4	26.8	28.0
35 - 39 years	24.7	26.2	29.7	31.5	31.6	31.8
40 - 44 years	27.4	29.2	32.1	35.2	36.4	38.4
45 - 49 years	25.5	23.8	31.0	35.2	34.6	34.4
50 and older	18.7	–	36.4	41.7	41.0	20.0

* Up until 1981, figures correspond to a mother's civil status. After the 1992 census, information corresponds to the legitimacy or illegitimacy of a child.

SOURCE: INE, *Anuario de Demografía* 1982-95 [Demographic Yearbook, 1982-95] (Santiago: INE).

these figures had increased to 27.06 years for men and 25.96 years for women. The postponement of marriage is related to changes brought by modernization, as well as the difficulties faced by low-income young people in establishing an independent family, as reflected in the high rates of youth unemployment.

Among the unions formed each year, some are not the result of the free choice of the partners; instead, they are the product of a situation which forces the union. Such situations may include the desire for "freedom" from an oppressive family, the need to escape an abusive situation (as when a young woman is sexually molested at home), or an unexpected pregnancy.

In fact, numerous one-parent families, consisting of a mother and child alone, arise as a result of teenage or unwed pregnancy. These new families frequently remain in the parental home of the mother, unable to establish a new household for economic reasons. This is especially the case with adolescent mothers who have not completed their education and do not form a lasting relationship with the child's father.

National statistics show a high percentage of births among women younger than 20, within a decreasing total number of births in the country. In 1995, there were 38,885 births to women under 20, representing 14.6% of all births. These births do not all result in single motherhood; in some cases the young parents later marry or live together, and many of these births simply represent early childbearing by married or cohabiting women. However, the figures reflect a considerable increase in the number of children born outside marriage, especially in the younger age groups (see Table 13).

Teenage pregnancy is a complex issue, influenced by personal, cultural, and social factors. Many teenage mothers are faced with a change in their lifestyle for which they are not prepared.[27] In addition, they are forced into a more vulnerable economic situation. Comparative studies clearly demonstrate the relationship between poverty and early pregnancy. Pregnancies also tend to recur in much greater proportion among those adolescents who do not return to school or work after having a child. The young mother's opportunities depend greatly on the help she receives from her partner or family. Research has indicated that the earnings of these young mothers remain inferior to those of others in their age bracket for the rest of their lives.

Births outside of legal marriage increased to 40% of all births by 1995, with very high percentages among mothers younger than 20 (90% among girls aged 10 to 14, and 70% for those aged 15 to 19). This points to a change in society, with adolescent pregnancies less likely to result in marriage. The high percentage of births outside marriage also appears to reflect the formation of new families by separated persons who cannot obtain a divorce or legally remarry.

Poverty, along with the restricted employment opportunities faced by young people, has a negative effect on the formation of households. Where urban life is expensive and stable sources of income are rare, many couples tend to delay the formation of independent households and remain in the homes of their parents. Often, this kind of couple or family is not reflected in official statistics.

Within the total population, the marital status of women shows different patterns than that of men. Fewer women than men are in the never-married category, but women make up a greater proportion of the separated and widowed. These differences result from women's higher life expectancies, their tendency to marry at a younger age, and the fact that widowed or separated men more frequently establish new unions (Valdés and Gomáriz 1993).

Families have fewer children and are generally decreasing in size.
The number of people per household has decreased during the last few decades, although not dramatically. In 1982, the average family size in Chile was 4.4 persons, falling to 4 members in 1992. Rural families continue to be bigger than urban ones. In addition, low-income households are larger than those of other income groups. The smallest families are found among the middle class. These differences express two phenomena: the voluntary limitation of pregnancies as well as the economic restrictions forcing low-income families to gather more people under one roof as a survival mechanism.

The reduction in family size is undoubtedly related to the overall drop in the fertility rate. This has been due in part to increased access to modern birth control methods, but it is principally explained by the establishment of an ideal family pattern which includes a reduced number of children. As various studies have shown, this ideal model has permeated all levels of Chilean society with a notable homogenizing force, in light of the deep social and economic differences within our country. Nevertheless, significant differences in fertility rates by area of residence and social group can be seen. The overall rural fertility rate was twice the urban rate between 1985 and 1990, with 4.4 children per woman in

---

27 One indicator of this situation is the higher infant mortality rate among illegitimate children of adolescent mothers. These children also exhibit higher rates of malnourishment as they grow (Valdés, Gysling, and Benavente 1994).

rural areas, versus 2.2 in cities. Indigenous groups in the Ninth Region showed an overall average of 3.9 children per woman during the same period (Valdés and Gomáriz 1993).

Recent studies show how the desired family size has decreased: adult and adolescent women from both rural and urban areas place the number of children they would like to have at two or three.[28] This number is in proportion with the actual fertility rate. However, many women, especially those in poor areas, tend to have more children than they desire, since modern birth control methods have not reached the entire population. Unequal access to birth control has led to an unsatisfied demand in the area of reproductive rights, and thus to demographic inequality (United Nations, Cepal/Celade 1993). Surveys and studies have shown that the majority of the population wishes to determine their own reproductive conduct freely, but that a significant proportion of this majority cannot do so, due to inadequate information and material resources. "Demographic inequality" refers to the fact that this unsatisfied demand is greater among low-income groups, increasing the socio-economic inequality they already suffer. This inequality is expressed through higher pregnancy rates among poor women, along with lower life expectancy and higher infant and maternal mortality rates.

The State has played a significant role in the reduction of family size. Family planning programs have had an impact, although its extent has not been specifically studied. State actions have also contributed to establishing the cultural ideal of small families mentioned above. Family size among recipients of government aid has been affected by the size of social housing, the amount of assistance to poor families, and the cost of education and health services. In addition, images of smaller families are presented in school texts, as well as in the media. These images portray a certain quality of life associated with a small family.

The prices of goods and services, the organization of female labor, and the cost of health care and education have strongly influenced Chilean women to have fewer children. The strength of this cultural pattern is so great that women manage to have fewer children in spite of the inadequate coverage of family planning programs. This fact points to the importance of other birth control practices, including abortion.

At the same time, this model has affected the traditional ideal of motherhood among Chilean women. Motherhood continues to be highly valued in Chile, but the status of mother is attained, of course, after the birth of the first child. It is not surprising that young women view having a child as an opportunity to gain social recognition, to have "something of their own," or to fill a deficit of affection in their lives.

Thus, the drop in Chile's fertility rate has come about as a result of numerous cultural, economic, political, and social changes. Much remains to be studied in this area.

Smaller households also reflect the aging of the population, as the proportion of adults and elderly people rises. Traditionally, elderly Chileans have lived in three-generation households, with the nuclear family of one of their children. Increasingly, however, elderly couples and widowed senior citizens are maintaining independent households. Senior care facilities have also become more common.

---

28 See APROFA-CERC, "Encuesta de Fecundidad Región Metropolitana, Chile. Informe Preliminar. 1989" (Santiago, 1990), and "Encuesta de Fecundidad VI y X Región. Chile. 1990." Unpublished report. See also Valenzuela et al. (1989).

TABLE 14

HEADS OF HOUSEHOLD, BY POVERTY LEVEL AND SEX : 1990-1996
(Percentages)

Age and Sex of Head	Indigent	Poor Non-Indigent	Total Poor	Total Non-Poor	Total
1990					
Female	11.9	21.1	33.0	67.0	100.0
Male	10.3	23.1	33.4	66.6	100.0
Total	10.6	22.7	33.3	66.7	100.0
1992					
Female	8.0	18.9	26.9	73.1	100.0
Male	7.0	21.0	28.0	72.0	100.0
Total	7.2	20.5	27.7	72.3	100.0
1994					
Female	7.5	15.7	23.2	76.8	100.0
Male	5.8	17.4	23.2	76.8	100.0
Total	6.2	17.0	23.2	76.8	100.0
1996					
Female	5.5	13.8	19.3	80.7	100.0
Male	4.7	15.1	19.8	80.2	100.0

SOURCE: Ministry of Planning and Cooperation, 1990, 1992, 1994 & 1996 Casen Surveys (Santiago: Ministry of Planning and Cooperation).

Many Chileans continue to live in poverty,
aided by family members and mutual support networks.
As mentioned above, 34.5% of Chilean households were below the poverty line at the beginning of the decade, with 11.6% living in truly indigent conditions. Then, as now, rural poverty tended to be more extreme than urban poverty, although poor Chileans were becoming increasingly concentrated in cities. Under the military regime, a shrinking labor market, falling wages, and reduced social expenditures contributed to a declining standard of living for broad segments of the population.

The first democratic administration quickly implemented programs and policies dedicated to relieving poverty. As the country's economic progress continued, poverty levels systematically declined, dropping to 19.7% of households (3.3 million people) by 1996. Extreme poverty or indigence has been reduced to 4.9% of households. However, eliminating rural poverty has proved more difficult; here, poverty affects 30.6% of the population, versus 21.8% in urban areas (Mideplan, Encuesta Casen 1996).

Similarly, entrenched or "hardcore" pockets of poverty remain, which are proving extremely difficult to eradicate. Some of these impoverished groups have been marginalized for generations, such as families living in remote areas of the country, as well as some families headed by women. The association between poverty and female-headed households is well-known. Households headed by women have a higher poverty rate than other households; this tendency has persisted from 1990 up to the present (see Table 14).

TABLE 15

HEADS OF SECONDARY NUCLEAR FAMILIES, BY POVERTY LEVEL AND SEX : 1990-1996
(Percentages)

Sex of Head	Indigent	Poor Non-Indigent	Total Poor	Total Non-Poor	Total
1990					
Female	15.9	28.6	44.5	55.5	100.0
Male	6.3	23.6	29.9	70.1	100.0
Total	11.3	26.2	37.5	62.5	100.0
1992					
Female	9.4	25.2	34.6	65.4	100.0
Male	4.8	22.0	26.8	73.2	100.0
Total	7.3	23.8	31.1	68.9	100.0
1994					
Female	9.5	23.4	32.9	67.1	100.0
Male	4.6	17.8	22.4	77.6	100.0
Total	7.3	21.0	28.3	71.7	100.0
1996					
Female	5.3	20.0	25.3	74.7	100.0
Male	3.4	14.9	18.3	81.7	100.0
Total	4.4	17.6	22.0	78.0	100.0

* Excludes live-in domestic servants.

SOURCE: Ministry of Planning and Cooperation, 1990, 1992, 1994 & 1996 Casen Surveys (Santiago: Ministry of Planning).

Numerous households today include secondary family nuclei. These may include the children of the heads of household who form their own families but continue to live in the parental home; other relatives of the heads of the household who have their own dependents; or unrelated persons, with or without their own dependents (Irarrazabal and Pardo 1994). Many of these households are formed because the families within them are not able to live independently, for financial or other reasons. Poverty levels among secondary nuclei follow the same general pattern as those of principal families, with a considerably higher poverty rate among homes headed by women (20% are below the poverty line, versus 14.9% of homes headed by men).

Households and family nuclei headed by women present higher levels of social vulnerability. This vulnerability results from persisting discrimination against women in education, training, hiring, and salary levels. Thus, households that depend on the income of women are at a disadvantage. Numerous factors work together to perpetuate poverty in these homes, giving rise to the so-called "feminization of poverty."

Families also show varying levels of dependency, which is defined as the number of people supported by each working member of the family. A study by Ines Reca concluded that a family's situation is critical if every working member must support more than three people (besides himself or herself), or if all members of the family are dependent, young, or non-working. In 1992, 34.3% of Chilean households were in this category. Among people living alone, 51.1% did not receive income from work. The great majority of these are

TABLE 16

DISTRIBUTION OF HOUSEHOLD MONETARY INCOME [a/],
BY PER CAPITA INCOME DECILE* : 1992-1996
(Absolute and Percentual Figures)

Decile	1992	1994	1996
1	1.7	1.5	1.4
2	2.9	2.8	2.7
3	3.8	3.6	3.6
4	4.7	4.6	4.6
5	5.6	5.6	5.5
6	6.6	6.4	6.4
7	8.0	8.1	8.1
8	10.4	10.5	11.0
9	14.7	15.3	15.4
10	41.6	41.6	41.8
Total	100.0	100.0	100.0

Number of Households   3,366,413   3,536,774   3,587,641

a/ Total monetary income, not including imputed rent.

* Corresponds to distribution by national per capita income decile.

SOURCE: Ministry of Planning and Cooperation, 1990, 1992, 1994 & 1996 Casen Surveys
(Santiago: Ministry of Planning).

senior citizens who depend on a pension, survivor's benefits, or aid from relatives. Following these homes in critical dependency levels were extended families with a non-employed woman as head of household (43.2%) and nuclear one-parent families (38.3%) (Reca et al. 1996b).

The Casen survey data for 1994 showed the following average dependency rates: in an impoverished household, the average working person supports 5.6 people; in a moderately poor household, each worker supports 3.7 people; and in a non-poor home, each worker supports 2.4 people (Hardy 1997). Nuclear families including an employed woman exhibit a markedly reduced level of dependency.

When the stages of the family cycle are considered along with dependency, the problems faced by many families become more evident. According to 1992 census information, 32.6% of households with children suffered from a critical level of dependency. This percentage rises to 50.7% among households with only one parent and children younger than six years old. It is 49.9% for those with children between 6 and 13 years old. Once again, the vulnerability of families headed by women is obvious.

In this analysis of the situation of Chilean families, it is also necessary to consider the country's current economic development model and its impact on income distribution. The figures clearly show that the gap between rich and poor households has widened. Thus, the poorest homes receive a negligible share of national income, as shown in Table 16. On a country-wide level, in 1996, the poorest tenth received 1.4% of national income, while the richest tenth garnered 41.8%, giving a ratio of 1 to 29.9. These data show a worsening of the situation since 1992, when the richest tenth was 24.4 times wealthier than the poorest. In rural areas, the distribution was slightly more equalized. Here, the poorest tenth received 2.35% of overall income, while the richest tenth took in 38.16%, giving a ratio of 1 to 16.2.

It is no surprise that poverty influences family behavior patterns. Family networks and support systems are vital in poor households' struggle for survival. Studies have shown that the most impoverished neighborhoods tend to establish inter-family assistance networks providing informal aid. Women generally play a central role in this process. These networks provide mutual support mechanisms, community information flows, and in general, all of the processes commonly known as "survival strategies."[29] The importance of these strategies increases when public social services are absent or inadequate.

Family ties are also very important for the adaptation of rural migrants to an urban setting. In fact, networks of relatives may be the only source of support relied upon by newcomers, who may be reluctant to seek official help for their day-to-day problems. The importance of informal networks is demonstrated by a study indicating that a lack of support from relatives, friends, or neighbors is associated with poverty, although it does not serve to explain it (National Counsel on Poverty 1996).

The State influences family life with legislative and policy changes.
State policies strongly influence the organization of the family. As a social institution, the family has been regulated by all societies and cultures. Chile's Civil Code (1855), inherited from Napoleon, places a strong shield around the family, only regulating the effects of marriage and parent-child relationships. It emphasizes inheritance rights to the exclusion of other aspects. Thus, this body of law has not facilitated the incorporation of economic, social, and cultural changes into family life, especially those derived from modernization and the situation of women today. Divorce is conceded only as a physical separation of the partners, without dissolving the marital tie or permitting either spouse to marry again. The code very clearly establishes the authority of men over women and children.

Only during the last decade (in 1989 and 1994) has the law been altered to remove the provisions most damaging to women. Several controversial areas have still not been resolved, such as the lack of recognition for divorce and the differentiation between legitimate and illegitimate offspring. These legal issues continue to affect the lives of countless families on a daily basis.

Aside from this legislation, the State affects families through social policies and the resources assigned to social programs: employment programs, training, housing, the educational and health care systems, agricultural credits, and so forth. An impact also results from the absence of policies; for example, the lack of a health program directed toward the family. Families' needs for health care, education, housing, training, and in the case of poor families, subsistence itself, can be met by the State in various ways. The characteristics of these programs contribute to shaping families' behavior, in a reproductive sense as well as in their plans for the future. State actions may determine the opportunities open to members of a family, the quality of life they can aspire to, their possibility of social mobility,

---

29 It should be mentioned that at all levels of society, relatives play a signiflcant role in support for childrearing tasks. Among low-income groups, these networks have an even greater impact.

and so forth. To date, there have been very few evaluations of the concrete impact of various policies on the lives of Chilean families.

The country's 17 years of military dictatorship took a heavy toll on the family. Persecution, repression, executions, "disappearances," State terrorism, exile, unemployment, and impoverishment afflicted countless families. The regime exposed the Chilean family to problems it had not faced in decades.

President Aylwin created the National Commission on the Family in 1992 in recognition of various "distorting factors" faced by Chilean families, as well as the multiplicity of family situations. Composed of people from different walks of life, with different activities, beliefs, political positions, and ideologies, the Commission's aim is to "truthfully assess the situation of the Chilean family ... analyze its principal problems, their causes, and possible solutions ... [and] suggest appropriate policies and legal reforms to strengthen the Chilean family."[30]

This commission was created during the period of preparation for the International Year of the Family (1994). Sernam prepared a report on these activities. After a year of intense work, this report was presented to the president. It suggested numerous legal reforms, some of which were introduced in Congress, with varying degrees of success. Among the reforms approved were:

- Law 19,250 (9/30/93), which modifies the Work Code to provide, among other changes, for male workers' right to one day of leave in case of the birth or death of a child, as well as the death of the spouse; grants paternity leave under certain circumstances; and obligates fathers, under certain conditions, to assume responsibility for the health care of a child with a serious illness
- the Domestic Violence Law (19,325, 8/27/94), which identifies the crime of domestic violence and establishes procedures for dealing with it
- Law 19,335 (9/12/94) which establishes standards for joint property and modifies the Civil Code, Penal Code, Penal Procedural Code, and other laws, eliminating previous provisions discriminatory to women
- Law 19,505 (7/14/97), which grants male workers special leave to care for an ill child

In addition, the approved educational reform, which lengthens the school day for children from third grade onward, will undoubtedly have an impact on family life, aside from its benefits for the students themselves.

Several bills approved by the Chamber of Deputies are now before the Senate. Among these are the expansion of rights for working mothers who breastfeed their children; new regulations for the visitation rights of non-custodial parents; the new civil marriage law (which includes provisions for divorce); a law which would eliminate pregnancy tests as a condition of employment for women; and the filiation law (equality of offspring before the law). Other bills have been approved by the Family Committee of the Chamber of Deputies and are awaiting discussion on the floor.

The creation of a legislative committee in the Chamber of Deputies specializing in family issues has allowed more expedient discussion of bills aimed at helping families. Unfortunately, the Senate does not possess a similar committee. This hinders the processing

---

30 Speech by President Patricio Aylwin, on the creation of the National Commission on the Family through Supreme Decree #162 (July 9, 1992).

of bills on family issues considerably; they often languish for years awaiting discussion in committee or on the Senate floor.

In the early 1990s, Sernam instituted a Program for Female Heads of Household, which benefits the entire family group, although it is directed toward women. President Frei has placed a high priority on research related to the family and the development of policies to strengthen it. Many of the studies and assessments referred to in this paper were undertaken as a result of this new focus. Aside from the legal reforms being discussed in Congress, a proposal has been formulated for a child care system to help working mothers and fathers. Another new bill aims at protecting mothers who work as domestic employees.

The wives of both Concertación Presidents have helped promote actions that benefit low-income families. Thanks to the Family Foundation, created in 1990, Family Centers have been created in several regions of the country. These centers offer education, training, recreational activities, and opportunities for social contact.

Chile's efforts at legal reform have the potential to help solve some very difficult problems for the country's families, as well as to uphold the principles of equality and fairness. The creation of Family Courts may lead to the development of new laws to support families. The need for Chilean society to pay more attention to childbearing and childrearing issues will also become more evident.

Thus, as the government becomes more aware of the effects of its actions on family life throughout Chilean society, it will be able to support the nation's families more effectively through government programs and public policies.

IV. Everyday Life in the Family

Family life today, as never before, is torn by problems, insecurities, conflicts, tensions, and even ruptures. Each family member, caught within a rigid hierarchical structure, finds it increasingly difficult to bear the growing demands of the work and social environments, along with the demands of other family members. As the modernization process has accelerated, it has led to contradictions between the social messages to the family and community, on the one hand, and the market mechanisms used to assign resources on the other. Social and cultural changes have not kept up with economic modernization, resulting in a growing gap in society's ability to comprehend and adapt to these transformations.

The classic dream of the family, in which education ensures good jobs and rising social status for the children, has been shattered, and no alternative is visible. The middle and lower classes are most strongly affected, since the State policies which had favored them a few decades ago have now changed direction. An increase in insecurity can therefore be observed among middle- and lower-class families.[31]

Furthermore, changes in the position of women in society, especially related to their participation in the labor market, have created tensions in family life. While partners grapple with the difficulty of resolving conflicts in a non-authoritarian manner, crises and separations among couples have increased.

---

31 Bengoa and Valdés (1997) have undertaken an excellent study on this subject. We have used some of their concepts in this section.

Many families find it difficult to plan their lives
and to imagine a better future for their children.

The changes in the economy, social programs, and education and health services, along with the emergence of new threats such as violence, delinquency, and drug addiction, have thrown a great number of families into a new state of vulnerability, especially among the middle and lower classes. This vulnerability creates feelings of deep insecurity and affects these families' daily lives, their hopes for social mobility, and their plans for the future. The fabric of social integration is being torn for many families throughout the country, for various reasons. The problems include those of coal miners, seasonal women workers, farmers in drought-stricken areas, the Mapuche families of Lumaco, and even of families forced to face the alcoholism or drug addiction of a child or the teenage pregnancy of a daughter.

Changes in the labor market, job insecurity, and the insufficiency of family income to satisfy the needs of the group weigh heavily on many families. The use of credit cards and other consumer credit can mask the imbalance between income and consumption for a while, but over the long term, the options become increasingly painful.

During the years of dictatorship, many Chileans lived in desperation, feeling that it was useless to attempt any changes. Since the country's return to democracy, many people find themselves experiencing a similar feeling without being able to identify the exact cause. In low-income neighborhoods in Santiago, hundreds of young people who cannot find work become addicted to drugs and involved in small-scale trafficking; they are arrested and frequently beaten by the police. Their parents, many of whom are social leaders with a history of participation in community work, find these developments incomprehensible and do not know how to react.

The problems and tensions experienced by many families lead both men and women to question their identities and the meaning of their lives, as well as their ability to achieve their goals.

Hierarchical family relationships produce conflict and division.

Following E. Jelin, we understand that "the family is a paradoxical space: it is a place of affection and intimacy, but also a favored setting for violence." The latter fact tends to be concealed by most witnesses, either to save face or because they fear revenge. The family home is a place of both love and violence, a sphere of private life into which State action does not penetrate; it is unable even to defend the human rights of family members (Jelin 1994).

Historically, as reflected in our legal system, marriage has created a hierarchical social organization, in which the woman and children are subject to the authority of the father, to whom they owe obedience and respect.[32] Thus, the family has been a vehicle for the reproduction of this social hierarchy and the unequal relationships within it.

The isolation in which many young women live, their inability to visualize any other alternative except marriage, and their difficulties in establishing a plan for their own lives have molded female identity, centering it on the traditional roles of mother and housewife, and furthering the reproduction of this phenomenon (Valdés 1988).

---

32 The civil code, in effect since 1855, which required obedience to the husband and forced the wife to follow him wherever he established his residence, was not reformed until 1989.

Recent improvements in women's educational levels, their integration into working life, and their increasing levels of social and political participation have revolutionized this situation. Yet these changes have not produced corresponding modifications in family life, such as the breakdown of traditional roles and the redistribution of power and responsibilities between marriage partners. It remains an unquestioned expectation, mainly among men, that women will continue to play their traditional role within the family.

These conditions also produce violence, which is a type of learned conduct used in an attempt to solve conflicts rooted in the inequalities between men and women in the sexual hierarchy. Violence also serves to confirm the male's identity through his dominance of women. Male power is manifested in various ways, including physical and sexual violence, which comes to be considered "natural," (Jelin 1994).

The high incidence of domestic violence, directed principally against women, is indicative of the tension and maladjustment in couples' changing relationships. Women's integration into the labor market and the fact that they can earn independent income have often sharpened these tensions. The situation worsens when men are unable to recognize alternative models for identity beyond those of being protectors and providers for their families. The expectation that women — and children — will submit to paternal authority is still strong. Legislation does not provide an effective mechanism for the modification of these behavior patterns.

Studies undertaken in Chile reveal a high percentage of women who acknowledge having experienced domestic violence, whether physical, psychological, or sexual. A study carried out in the Metropolitan Region shows that more than one-fourth of women who live with a partner — whether legally married or not — have suffered physical violence, and a third have experienced psychological abuse (Larraín et al. 1992). This violence cuts across all social levels, although its pattern varies, with psychological abuse being more common among middle- and upper-class couples.

Abuse causes women to limit their actions and robs them of their freedom of expression. They fear violence from the very person who, according to the law, is required to respect and protect them. This appears even more paradoxical among unmarried couples, since affection is presumed to be the principal motivation of the union.

Intimacy and sexual relationships are a particularly difficult subject for research. Studies reveal that sexual activity is begun at an earlier age, and that premarital sexual relations have become a frequent practice.[33] However, this does not necessarily mean that more equal relationships are being constructed, or that sexuality has become more enjoyable.

Within sexual relationships, women's needs and desires are often subordinated to those of their partners. As this becomes a habit, it affects women's self-esteem and harms the quality of the relationship. The hierarchical character of these relationships is the basis of numerous conflicts. Even worse, the notion that women must fulfill their so-called "marital duties" has come to be a cultural assumption, reinforced by civil norms and also by religious teachings. Refusal on the woman's part may bring about "punishment" — in other words, abuse by the male — without any other means of resolving the conflict even being considered.

---

33 See, among others, Valenzuela et al. (1989); Rojo (1991); Gysling and Benavente (1996); Gysling, Benavente, and Olavarría (1997); and Rossetti (1997).

Because of this situation, many women cannot completely control their reproductive lives, although responsibility for this area is assigned exclusively to them.[34] Unwanted pregnancies are a common result of this problem, which is worse among lower-income groups, since the daily lives of women in these communities are more marked by subordination.[35]

The limited access of many women to effective birth control methods restricts their control over their own reproductive lives even further and gives rise to numerous abortions. In fact, the rate of induced abortions in Chile is estimated to be the highest in the region. According to rigorously-conducted studies in Chile, one out of every three pregnancies results in induced abortion, with all of the risks and consequences implied by this fact (Valdés and Faundez 1997).

Many crises, separations, and definitive breaks between couples are an expression of the difficulties faced by people today, as they seek to satisfy their needs and expectations within a structured hierarchy which subordinates women, or as they recognize the impossibility of carrying out the roles imposed by culture on men and women.

In the absence of a divorce law in Chile allowing new legal unions after separation, informal unions are common, although they are not acknowledged in surveys and census reports. The available data reveals serious misinformation, since declarations of marital status are influenced by the cultural pressure to deny separations and cohabitation. The "annulment" of marriages has been used by wealthier couples to achieve a sort of "divorce by common agreement." This figure has not shown a significant increase in recent years. Better indicators may be found in the incidence of childbirth outside marriage mentioned above, as well as the growing number of legal cases involving child custody and alimony payments.

Any public legal aid office can give an account of the conflicts faced by low-income families today. In fact, the principal issues addressed by these offices fall under the area of family law: child support, visitation rights, custody, domestic violence, and paternity suits. Similarly, child support disputes are the leading type of cases presented at family courts. As a recent study shows, 68,154 civil suits were introduced on behalf of minors in 1991. Of these, 48.3% of these were related to child support, followed by custody and visitation rights. By 1994, the number of suits had increased to 73,640. In other words, these courts spend much of their time dealing with the consequences of marital breakdowns. The majority of these cases concern legitimate children, making it even more difficult to protect the interests of children born outside marriage (Provoste 1996).

Cross-generational relations within the family have also been changing. Over the past few decades, children have become more independent and their development more autonomous. At the same time, parental authority has been weakened. Rising educational attainment has meant more years of dependence on parents, but also a growing generation gap. In rural areas and small towns, there is also a tendency for young people to migrate to the cities, separating early from the parental family. All of this leads to cross-generational confrontations, with young people demanding economic resources and autonomy, and parents expecting their children to contribute to meeting the family's needs. This situation is exacerbated in households headed by women.

---

34 The "responsible parenthood" activities of the Women's Health Program do not include males. Also, male sterilization is not generally considered as an option if the couple decides not to have any more children, and female sterilization is not accessible to many who would choose it.

35 See Valdés (1988); Gysling and Benavente (1996); Valdés, Gysling, and Benavente (forthcoming).

TABLE 17

NUMBER OF MARRIAGES REALIZED AND NUMBER OF DECLARED ANNULMENTS, 1970-1993
(Absolute and Percentual Figures)

Year	Number of Marriages	Number of Annulments	% Annulments Compared to Marriages
1970	71,631	1,511	2.1
1980	86,001	3,072	3.6
1981	90,564	3,474	3.8
1982	80,115	3,090	3.9
1988	103,484	5,152	5.0
1991	91,732	5,852	6.4
1992	89,370	6,006	6.7
1993	92,821	6,405	6.9

SOURCE: National Statistics Institute, *Compendio Estadístico*, [Statistical Compendium] 1970 to 1995 (Santiago: INE).

Thus, young people today are affected by crosscurrents of autonomy and dependence, while parents are frustrated by their shrinking sphere of influence in the upbringing of their children. These phenomena have consequences for young people's plans for their lives, as well as for the daily interactions of the family group.

The limited economic resources of young people often lead to forced dependency. If they leave the parental home to establish their own household, either alone or as a family nucleus, they face many difficulties. Although this problem is most serious among low-income families, it affects young people at all socioeconomic levels of our society.

At the same time, the ongoing reduction of parental control over the upbringing of their children has had consequences for both parties. The generation gap is expressed through the new expectations and values held by young people, which make it more difficult for them to discover their identities and find a place for themselves in society. The role models of their mothers and fathers are questioned, leaving a void which is not adequately filled by new social referents such as the high schools and the mass media. Increased rates of teenage pregnancies, youth violence, and juvenile suicide are some of the more drastic results of this confusion among the young.

Many parents find themselves in a weakened position, with impaired communicational and affective relations with their sons and daughters. On the one hand, children are a heavy economic burden, and on the other, parents have less influence over their children. The chain of culture passed on from generation to generation becomes damaged, reducing the importance of family ties in shaping identity. This tension can foster violent tendencies among young people and cause deep anxiety in adults.

Turning the prism around, we can observe that the mass media and peer groups have partially displaced the family in the socialization of young people and the creation of role models. Sometimes these influences introduce new cultural content, but most frequently they reproduce the traditional model. The consequences can be seen in the personal and professional plans of both men and women: these tend to perpetuate the gender-based segmentation of professional education and the labor market, with all of the problems that this implies.

V. Late 20th-Century Dilemmas

As we near the end of the 1990s, Chile faces a series of challenges posed by modernization and globalization. At the same time, the country is also working toward greater expression of democratic ideals in national life. The government's attempts to improve the current situation of women and families of all types reflect this effort.

The advances of modernization have been unequally distributed, in the social and cultural spheres as well as in economic results. The contradictions thus created have impeded progress toward the goals of fairness, equal opportunity, and participation which the governments of the Concertación have set for themselves.

Several serious dilemmas have emerged. First, because of the increasingly heterogeneous identities and social environments arising in our country, Chilean society must fully incorporate the ideal of tolerance into its social relations. This includes tolerance of different identities (ethnic, gender, generational, etc.) and of different social groups and their experiences. What is needed is nothing less than a broadening of the idea of citizenship, both individually and socially.

Second, we can observe new vulnerabilities among middle- and lower-income groups. These families risk new kinds of isolation, marginalization, and exclusion. The breakdown of social networks and protective systems, placed next to the complex requirements for survival in a modern society, has left many Chileans in a precarious position. The benefits of democracy and development remain invisible to these families.

Third, the changing position of women in society calls for the modification and redefinition of the roles and identities assigned to them. The tension between work and family responsibilities cannot remain a matter to be resolved individually by each woman or couple, but must be recognized as a challenge for society as a whole.

Fourth, our national culture must recognize the central importance of the right to intimacy and the exercise of healthy and gratifying sexuality. These very private matters affect the quality of life for men and women, the creation of families, and even the dynamics of society itself. The ideological debates of conservatism have become outdated. The practices of young Chilean men and women today do not permit the continued withholding of a complete recognition of their rights in this area. Inequalities in the area of human reproduction must be eliminated.

Finally, the country faces the challenge of constructing an effective social and political democracy which allows for full participation by all its members, including women.

Various social forces are called upon to provide answers to these dilemmas, including the government, political parties, the mass media, the business community, civil society, and women themselves. Each of these can make great contributions.

The government, guided by its ideals of democracy and fairness, is principally responsible for developing policies that promote change in culture and communications, that broaden citizenship, that produce more equal relations between the genders, and that help integrate all members of society into decision-making process and collective activities. Special efforts must be expended to achieve the social and economic integration of those who are now marginalized and excluded.

Policies related to women and the family are of particular importance. Scattered programs and activities are not the answer; we must revise all policies, both general and sectorial, to ensure that they promote equality between men and women as well as democratic relations within the family.

The business community can play a central role in addressing the new vulnerabilities in society, as well as the traditional roles assigned to men and women. They can promote a more equal distribution of tasks and privileges. Along with the mass media, they have the opportunity to help guide our country toward a more global, tolerant culture which recognizes the importance of all members of society.

The political parties must acknowledge the profound changes occurring in our society and make a commitment to promote the full integration of all social groups and classes into their activities. They must grasp the opportunity to promote women's participation in all aspects of political and social decision-making.

Women, united in collective action, have been and will continue to be the driving force behind changes that bring more democracy to our culture and the family, as well as to those that favor new gender identities and roles. Movements have also arisen to support a new kind of male role: one with a deeper emotional dimension and a new appreciation of the value of fatherhood. These courageous men can find an important ally in organized women, as they strive together to construct a culture that will carry all Chileans forward into the third millennium.

BIBLIOGRAPHICAL REFERENCES

Alcalay, L. and N. Milicic. 1995. "Qué aprenden las adolescentes sobre género en su sistema familiar?" In: A. Rodó and J. Valdés, eds. *Aproximaciones a la familia. Proposiciones* 26. Santiago: Ediciones SUR.

APROFA-CERC. 1990. "Encuesta de Fecundidad Región Metropolitana, Chile. Informe Preliminar. 1989." Santiago.

———. 1990. "Encuesta de Fecundidad VI y X Región. Chile." Unpublished report.

Bengoa, J. and J. Valdés. 1997. "Seguridad e inseguridad social en Chile de los 90. Un estudio de trayectorias de vida familiares e itinerarios sociales." Proyecto PNUD. Santiago. Unpublished report.

Bernales, S. 1995. "Las relaciones familiares en el Chile de los 90." In A. Rodó and J. Valdés, eds. *Aproximaciones a la familia. Proposiciones.* Santiago: Ediciones SUR.

CEDEM (Centro de Estudios para el Desarrollo de la Mujer). 1992. *Directorio Nacional de Servicios y Recursos para la Mujer.* Santiago.

CEP (Centro de Estudios Públicos). 1993. *Estudio Social y de Opinión Pública* 18. Santiago (March).

CEPAL 1995. *Panorama Social de América Latina 1995.* Santiago: Cepal.

Concertación de Partidos por la Democracia. 1989. *Programa de Gobierno.* Santiago.

Consejo de Rectores de Universidades Chilenas. 1997. *Anuario Estadístico 1996.* Santiago.

Consejo Nacional para la Superación de la Pobreza. 1996. "Encuesta sobre oportunidades y disponibilidades de los pobres." Preliminary results. Santiago.

Coordinación de Organizaciones Sociales de Mujeres. 1991. *Soy mujer... Tengo derechos.* Santiago: Flacso-Sepade.

Edgard, D. and H. Glezer. 1994. "La familia y la intimidad: las 'carreras' familiares y la reconstrucción de la vida privada." *Revista Internacional de Ciencias Sociales* 139. UNESCO.

Edwards, V., C. Calvo, et al. 1988. *El liceo por dentro. Estudio etnográfico sobre prácticas de trabajo en educación media.* Santiago: PIIE.

Elter, D. 1996. "La situación de la mujer en el nuevo sistema previsional chileno." In: Sernam. *Igualdad de oportunidades para la mujer en el trabajo.* Santiago: Sernam.

Escuela de la Mujer-Prodemu. 1997. "Encuentros regionales de dirigentas y líderes de organizaciones sociales y funcionales de escasos recursos." Santiago.

Frohmann, A. and T. Valdés. 1993. " 'Democracy in the Country and in the Home': The Women's Movement in Chile." Documento de Trabajo. Serie Estudios Sociales 55. Santiago: Flacso.

Fundación de la Familia. 1996. *Semillas de cambio. El desarrollo social se inicia en familia.* Santiago: Fundación de la Familia.

Giddens, A. 1990. *The Consequences of Modernity.* Stanford, CA: Stanford University Press.

———. 1995. *La transformación de la intimidad. Sexualidad, amor y erotismo en las sociedades modernas.* Madrid: Cátedra.

Grupo Iniciativa ONG-Chile. 1997. *Foro Nacional para el Seguimiento de los Acuerdos de Beijing. Acta de la Primera Sesión.* Santiago.

Gysling, J. and M. C. Benavente. 1996. "Trabajo, sexualidad y poder." Documento de Trabajo. Nueva Serie. Santiago: Flacso.

Gysling, J., M. C. Benavente, and J. Olavarría. 1997. "Sexualidad en jóvenes universitarios." Documento de Trabajo. Nueva Serie. Santiago: Flacso.

Hardy, C. 1987. *Organizarse para vivir. Pobreza urbana y organización popular.* Santiago: PET.

———. 1997. *La reforma social pendiente.* Santiago: Chile 21/Flacso.

Henríquez, H. and E. Pérez. 1995. "La subestimación de la participación femenina en las actividades económicas: Encuesta suplementaria a mujeres inactivas." Santiago: Sernam-PET.

Hola, E. and R. Todaro. 1992. *Los mecanismo del poder: hombres y mujeres en la empresa moderna.* Santiago: CEM.

INE (Instituto Nacional de Estadísticas). 1970–1996. *Anuario de Demografía.* Santiago: INE.

———. 1970, 1982, 1992. *Censo de Población.* Santiago: INE.

———. 1990. *Encuesta de Empleo.* Santiago: INE, octubre-diciembre.

———. 1995. *Encuesta Nacional de Empleo.* Santiago: INE, trimester April-June.

———. 1994. *Mujeres de Chile: Radiografía en Números.* Santiago: INE.

Instituto de la Mujer. 1993. *¿Cómo les ha ido a las mujeres chilenas en la democracia? Balance y propuestas mirando al 2000*. Santiago: Instituto de la Mujer.

———. 1997. *Veredas por cruzar. 10 años*. Santiago: Instituto de la Mujer.

Irarrázabal, I. and J. P. Valenzuela. 1992. "La ilegitimidad en Chile. ¿Hacia un cambio en la formación de la familia?" Documentos de Trabajo 188. Santiago: CEP.

Irarrázabal, I. and L. Pardo. 1994. "Jefatura familiar femenina, estructura del hogar y pobreza". In: M. E. Valenzuela, S. Venegas and C. Andrade. *De mujer sola a jefa de hogar. Género, pobreza y políticas públicas*. Santiago: Sernam.

ISIS Internacional. 1990. *El malestar silenciado. La otra salud mental*. Ediciones de las Mujeres 14. Santiago: ISIS Internacional.

———. 1994. *Familias siglo XXI*. Santiago: ISIS Internacional.

Jelin, E. 1994. "Las familias en América Latina." En: ISIS Internacional. *Familias siglo XXI*, Ediciones de las Mujeres 20. Santiago: ISIS Internacional.

Larraín, S. et al. 1992. *Violencia intrafamiliar y la situación de la mujer en Chile*. Santiago: Sernam-OPS.

Lechner, N. and S. Levy. 1984. "Notas sobre la Vida Cotidiana III: el disciplinamiento de la mujer." *Materiales de Discusión* 57. Santiago: Flacso.

Mideplan (Ministry for Planning and Cooperation). 1997. "Situación de la mujer en Chile, 1996." Results of the National Socioeconomic Characterization Survey (Casen) 1996. Santiago.

Montecino, S. and J. Rossetti. 1990. *Tramas para un nuevo destino. Propuestas de la Concertación de Mujeres por la Democracia*. Santiago.

Muñoz, M. and C. Reyes. 1997. *Una mirada al interior de la familia*. Santiago: Ediciones Universidad Católica de Chile.

Palestro, S. 1991. "Mujeres en Movimiento. 1973–1989." Documento de Trabajo. Serie Estudios Sociales 14. Santiago: Flacso.

Pardo, L. 1996. "La mujer en las decisiones económicas: un desafío pendiente." In: Sernam. *Igualdad de Oportunidades para la Mujer en el Trabajo*. Santiago: Sernam.

Provoste, P. 1996. "La pensión de alimentos: desigualdad y ruptura en le familia." Documento de Trabajo. Santiago: Instituto de la Mujer.

Ramírez, V. 1995. *Cambios en la familia y en los roles de la mujer. América Latina y el Caribe*. Santiago: Cepal/Celade.

Reca, I. 1992. "Modo de vida en familias obreras y de trabajadores intelectuales." In: VVAA. *Sistemas políticos, poder y sociedad*. Caracas: ALAS/CEA/ED, Nueva Sociedad.

Reca, I. et al. 1996a. "Las familias de Chile según el último Censo de Población de 1992." Documento de Trabajo 44. Santiago: Sernam.

———. 1996b. "Familias y hogares en situaciones críticas en Chile según Censo 1992." Documento de Trabajo 46. Santiago: Sernam, Área Familia.

———. 1996. "Familias vulnerables. Caracterización de sus principales necesidades." Final report. Santiago: Sernam.

Rivera, D. and A. Meschi. 1995. "Los rematrimonios o familias simultáneas: una oportunidad de redefinición de las relaciones afectivas y sociales." In: A. Rodó and J. Valdés, eds. *Aproximaciones a la familia*. *Proposiciones* 26. Santiago: Ediciones SUR.

Rojo, C. 1991. *Conocimientos, actitudes y comportamiento sexual de jóvenes rurales. VII Región*. Santiago: Corsaps.

Rosetti, J. 1997. *Sexualidad adolescente: Un desafío para la sociedad chilena*. Santiago: Biblioteca Nacional, Centro de Investigaciones Diego Barros Arana.

Salazar, G. 1985. *Peones, labradores y proletarios*. Santiago: Ediciones SUR.

Salinas, C. 1987. *La mujer proletaria*. Concepción: Ediciones LAR.

Sernam (National Women's Service). 1993. *Informe Comisión Nacional de la Familia*. Santiago: Sernam.

———. 1995. *Plan de Igualdad para las Mujeres 1994–1999*. Santiago: Sernam.

———. 1996. *Igualdad de oportunidades para la mujer en el trabajo*. Santiago: Sernam.

———. 1997. *Hagamos un compromiso de futuro. Propuestas en torno a la mujer para el nuevo Parlamento*. Santiago: Sernam.

Todaro, R. 1996. "Los costos laborales del trabajo de la mujer." *Igualdad de oportunidades para la mujer en el trabajo*. Santiago: Sernam.

United Nations, Cepal [ECLAC]/Celade. 1993. *Población, equidad y transformación productiva*. Santiago.

Valdés, T. 1988. *Venid, benditas de mi Padre. Las pobladoras, sus rutinas y sus sueños*. Santiago: Flacso.

Valdés, T. and A. Faúndez. 1997. *Diagnóstico de salud reproductiva en Chile*. Foro Abierto de Salud y Derechos Reproductivos. Santiago.

Valdés, T. and E. Gomáriz, coords. 1991. "Mujeres latinoamericanas en cifras. Avances de Investigación Chile. Serie Estudios Sociales VII. Participación Sociopolítica." Documento de Trabajo. Santiago: Flacso.

————. 1992a. "Mujeres latinoamericanas en cifras. Avances de Investigación Chile. Serie Estudios Sociales VIII. Organismos y Acción de Promoción de la Mujer." Documento de Trabajo. Santiago: Flacso.

————. 1992b. "Mujeres latinoamericanas en cifras. Chile. Avances de Investigación. III. Trabajo (empleo)." Documento de Trabajo. Serie Estudios Sociales 22. Santiago: Flacso.

————. 1993. *Mujeres latinoamericanas en cifras. Chile*. Instituto de la Mujer, Ministerio de Asuntos Sociales, España/Santiago: Flacso.

Valdés, T. and M. Weinstein. 1993. *Mujeres que sueñan. Las organizaciones de pobladoras en Chile: 1973–1989*. Santiago: Flacso.

————. 1997. "Corriendo y descorriendo tupidos velos". In: Flacso. *Chile 96. Análisis y opiniones*. Santiago: Flacso.

Valdés, T., J. Gysling, and M. C. Benavente. 1994. "Género y políticas de población en Chile." Report prepared for Sernam. Santiago: Flacso.

————. Forthcoming. "Las relaciones entre los géneros en la sexualidad y la reproducción: una mirada desde las mujeres." Research Report. Santiago: Flacso.

Valdés, T. et al. Findings of research in progress. "Construcción social de la masculinidad en Chile: crisis del modelo tradicional. Un estudio exploratorio." Santiago: Flacso.

Valenzuela, M. E. 1996. "El empleo femenino en el marco de la globalización de la economía." *Igualdad de oportunidades para la mujer en el trabajo*. Santiago: Sernam.

————. 1995. "Hogares con jefatura femenina: una realidad invisible". In: A. Rodó and J. Valdés, eds. *Aproximaciones a la familia. Proposiciones 26*. Santiago: Ediciones SUR.

Valenzuela, M. E., S. Venegas, and C. Andrade, eds. 1994. *De mujer sola a jefa de hogar. Género, pobreza y políticas públicas*. Santiago: Sernam.

Valenzuela, M. E. et al. 1989. *Encuesta sobre salud reproductiva en adultos jóvenes. Santiago 1988*. Santiago: Departamento de Salud Pública, División de Ciencias Médicas Occidente, Facultad de Medicina, U. de Chile.

Culture

Changes in Public Opinion

Jorge Manzi
Carlos Catalán

Introduction

T his paper is an effort to synthesize and integrate the information accumulated in recent years from public opinion surveys, both quantitative and qualitative. The overall purpose of this effort has been to extract data or background material from various sources, in order to identify stable or systematic trends in public opinion over the last few years.

1. THE QUANTITATIVE SOURCES

This paper synthesizes some of the tendencies emerging from the principal public-opinion surveys periodically carried out in Chile over the last several years. Various regular public-opinion surveys have been undertaken recently, whereas in previous decades such information was scarce. This means that comparisons indicating trends over time are now possible, at least for a certain set of questions. Nonetheless, the spectrum over which we can establish such reliable comparisons is limited.[1] This is because many of these surveys were instituted very recently, lasted for only a short time, or focused on different themes each time they were taken.

This article is grounded in the reports published by the companies carrying out the surveys. It is important to note that the majority of the published results are marginal totals based on the entire survey sample, or on a cross-referencing of the answers with the sample's stratification variables rather than raw data. It is relatively uncommon for these reports to cross-reference the responses to two questions, and more complex calculations are even less common. Naturally, a deeper analysis, enabling us to identify the core issues in public opinion, requires the complementary analyses to be undertaken using the original databases. This is the only way to overcome the analytical limitations of the published results. Unfortunately, access to these key databases is restricted.

---

[1] For the comparisons to possess a high degree of accuracy and validity, certain conditions must be present, including: equivalency of question content (both in how they are phrased and the response choices offered); consistency in the contextual location of the question, within the framework of the survey; and stability in the methodological conditions of the survey (sampling technique, margin of error, etc.). As it is difficult to find cases in which all these criteria are fulfilled (even in data produced by the same polling agency), we have attempted to single out comparisons that meet at least some of these conditions.

This study has also incorporated, as a frame of reference, a public-opinion survey known as the *Latinobarómetro*, carried out in several Latin American countries. This poll commenced in 1995, and consequently a time series that would enable us to compare Chile's relative tendencies with those of other countries in the region is not available. Nonetheless, the comparison of our current domestic public opinion with that of Latin America in general does shed some light on the peculiarities or specifics of our domestic political culture as compared to that of the region.

Finally, it is important to note that the nature of the information produced by public-opinion studies is subject to a set of limitations that must be considered when interpreting the data as a reflection of a country's political culture. It is a well-known fact that the answers provided by this type of survey tend to reflect whatever is foremost on society's agenda at the time when the survey is conducted. Typically, the responses obtained in opinion polls are strongly affected by the issues receiving considerable exposure in the media during the period immediately preceding the poll.[2] For the same reason, the surveys constitute a very limited snapshot, temporally speaking. Issues that gain notoriety in the public eye generally tend to maintain high visibility for periods of less than two weeks. In addition, survey responses are subject to a variety of potential biases, of which only a small fraction can be counterbalanced by the people designing the questionnaires.[3]

Despite the aforementioned limitations, it is possible, to an extent, to establish fairly steady trends (over the period analyzed) for some indicators and topics evaluated in opinion polls. It is therefore also possible to presume that these tendencies correspond to more lasting phenomena and, consequently, serve to identify aspects or dynamics that are relatively well-consolidated in Chilean political culture.

2. THE QUALITATIVE SOURCES

One source of information used in this essay is a series of qualitative public-opinion studies about the country's situation during the last three years.[4]

The samples in qualitative surveys are not parametrically or statistically representative of the general population. Consequently, these techniques do not allow us to make inferences about the public opinion tendencies prevalent among the general population. Still, such surveys do enable us to identify meaningful and significant categories, patterns, and perceptions that arise as members of the general public attempt to evaluate the country's situation.

Thus, qualitative studies provide valuable material that complements the information gathered in public-opinion polls, providing a richer and more complex understanding of the thoughts and feelings of Chileans' in the 1990s.

---

2   Studies in this area (Iyengar and Kinder 1987) reveal that the main effects of the media on public opinion include priming (the tendency to repeat the issues and concepts of greatest visibility at the time of polling) and accessibility (the willingness to consider the issues or problems noted by the survey taker).

3   The biases of acquiescence and social desirability are relatively easy to control; however, aspects like contextual effects (the relative position of the question), sequencing effects, the informational value of the response alternatives, the use of open-ended versus closed-ended questions, the use of response scales with different numbers of alternatives, etc., are more difficult to manage and control.

4   The qualitative studies used in this report form part of the Observatorio Social study program, carried out by Consultora Cruz y Souza between 1995 and 1997. These studies used 250 focus groups distributed throughout the country.

This essay is predominantly descriptive and focuses more on the trends emerging from qualitative surveys and polls than on the interpretations drawn from them. The information analyzed has been organized into four chapters: (1) perceptions of the country and its economy; (2) perceptions of the country's main problems; (3) perceptions and evaluations of political activity; and (4) psycho-social considerations.

3. METHODOLOGICAL ASPECTS

As previously indicated, this study is based on the main public-opinion polls using time series sampling techniques. The following describes the sources of information employed, identifying their principal methodological aspects.

Estudio Nacional de Opinión Pública [National Public Opinion Study] by the *Centro de Estudios Públicos (CEP)*. This study, conceived as a barometer of issues relating to the political and economic spheres, has been carried out since December 1986. It utilizes a standard set of questions, as well as additional questions on special topics, for each survey. Since 1993, the survey has used a nationwide sample, with a multi-step procedure.[5] The approximate sample size is 1,500 people above the age of 18, with a margin of error of 3% and an accuracy of 95%.

Barómetro CERC. This is a public-opinion poll carried out since 1988, which studies the perceptions and evaluations of people over 18 in the areas of the economy, society, and politics. The survey uses a stable set of questions, to which it adds special barometric questions that vary with each taking. The sample includes 1,240 people in 29 cities with more than 40,000 inhabitants, representing 67% of the country's total population. The sampling system is three-phased, meaning that the respondents are obtained via a non-probabilistic procedure (using quotas based on census data). If the sample were probabilistic, it would have a margin of error of 2.3% and an accuracy of 95%.

Los Chilenos y la Democracia: La opinión pública 1991-1994 [Chileans and Democracy: Public Opinion 1991-1994], by Participa (CERC was in charge of the actual polling). This study was carried out annually from 1991 to 1994 by Manuel Antonio Garretón, Marta Lagos, and Roberto Méndez. It focused principally on perceptions, attitudes, and evaluations pertaining to democracy. The sample, containing about 1,500 persons aged 18 and above, was obtained in nine urban centers containing 49% of the country's total population. The sampling procedure was multi-phased, providing a margin of error of 3.5% and a confidence level of 95%.

Estudio de Opinión Pública DESUC-COPESA. This survey was begun in 1995 to research the perceptions of adults over 18 on diverse topics: politics, the economy, society, education, the family, and other psycho-social issues. The sample group exceeds 2,000 subjects and comes from the seven largest urban centers (Antofagasta, Valparaíso, Viña del Mar, Greater Santiago, Concepción, Talcahuano, and Temuco). Altogether, this group represents 56.8% of the country's urban population. The sampling procedure is multi-phased, with an approximate margin of error of 2.5% and a confidence level of 95%.

---

5   Before 1993, the survey used a multi-phase sample of 13 cities, representing 65% of the country's urban population.

Latinobarómetro of the *Corporación de Estudios de Opinión Pública Latinoamericana*. This study evaluates opinions on politics, economics, and international relations in a group of 17 Latin American countries, plus Spain. The application of this barometer began in 1995 with eight countries. For the majority of the survey countries, the sample is probabilistic (in some cases by quota), and covers 1,000 to 1,500 respondents. For the majority of the sample, the margin of error is 2.8% and the confidence level is 95%.

I. Overall Perception of the Country and Its Economy

Opinion surveys indicate that the majority of the nation perceives the country and its economy, overall, in a positive light. Nonetheless, several indicators suggest that public opinion has taken an increasingly critical posture with respect to the country's performance in general and the economy in particular. The CEP survey includes a question about the progress, stagnation, or decline of the nation as a whole (see Figure 1). This shows that the majority of the population continues to hold an optimistic perception of the country's progress, although this proportion has recently declined substantially. We see that the reduction in optimism is not due so much to an increase in the most negative viewpoint (that the country is in decline), but rather that a growing number of people believe the country is stagnating.

To understand the significance of Chileans' image of progress in our country as compared to the Latin American context in general, we can turn to a question in *Latinobarómetro* that is very similar to the one by CEP. The 1996 results show that Chile has the second highest level of optimism (51%) among the countries surveyed, after Peru (58%).

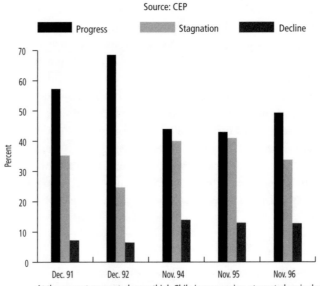

FIGURE 1

PERCEPTION OF NATIONAL PROGRESS

Source: CEP

■ Progress   ▨ Stagnation   ▨ Decline

At the present moment, do you think Chile is progressing, stagnated, or in decline

FIGURE 2

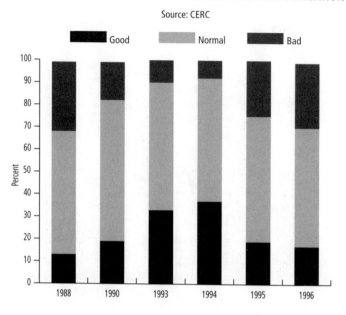

EVALUATION OF THE COUNTRY'S GENERAL ECONOMIC SITUATION

Source: CERC

Latin America's average in this area is 26%, while that of Spain is 45%. That is to say, Chileans possess, in this respect, markedly more optimistic perceptions than those prevalent throughout the region.

The perception about the present state of the economy shows a trajectory similar to that observed with the perception of the country in general. This is not surprising, since these evaluations tend to be related. In fact, the majority of people tend to judge the general status of the country on the basis of their opinion of the state of the economy. The CERC data series, which is synthesized in Figure 2, indicates that after a period of sustained growth in optimism, 1994 marks the start of a negative tendency. The graph reveals that the percentage of Chileans evaluating the performance of the economy as "average" remains relatively constant. The changes in tendency occur, therefore, in the polar categories. We see that, at present, there is a lesser percentage of Chileans falling into the positive pole than the negative when evaluating the state of the economy.

The relatively negative evaluation that Chileans give to the country's current economic situation nevertheless constitutes the most favorable evaluation among all the nations considered in the *Latinobarómetro*. In fact, the percentages of Chileans who say the current economic situation is good (15%) and who say it is bad (34%) compare very favorably with the respective percentages for all of Latin America (7% and 57%, respectively).

In contrast to their perception of the current state of the economy, we see that Chileans maintain high expectations with respect to its *future performance*. In this area we find that, throughout the period considered, the favorable expectations exceed the pessimistic ones (see Figure 3). Negative expectations have consistently remained below 20%. Still, as in the case of the current performance of the economy, we see a marked decline over the course of this decade in the percentage of people who are optimistic about

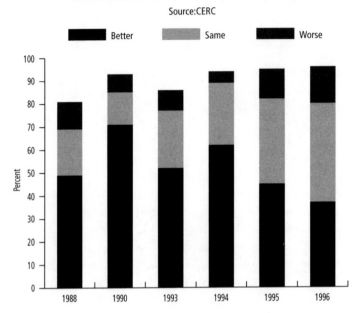

FIGURE 3

EVALUATION OF THE COUNTRY'S ECONOMIC FUTURE

Source:CERC

the future of the economy. This decrease has in turn led to an increase in the number of people who think the future of the economy will be similar to the present. The number of respondents in this category presently exceeds the number who think the future will be better. Again, the data from the *Latinobarómetro* reveal Chile to be among the countries with the highest levels of optimism, and it is at the same time the country with the lowest proportion of inhabitants with negative expectations for the future of the economy.

In summary, in their overall perceptions of the country's situation, Chileans continue to evaluate the present and future favorably. However, this perception is on a downward trajectory. This translates into a growing percentage of people who believe the state of the economy (and of the country) is tending to remain the same.

Naturally, this fact allows for various interpretations. One negative interpretation is that the people expect the future situation of the country to be exactly the same as it is now. Another possibility is that the people have internalized in their expectations the factor of economic growth, which has been positive over all these years. In this case, maintaining the status quo would mean the country would continue to grow in the same manner it recently demonstrated. The latter interpretation is reasonable, given that the predominant messages heard by Chileans are that the economy is stable, that there will be no dramatic fluctuations, and that future growth rates are to be equivalent to those we have experienced over the last decade. However, it is a fact that the country has left behind the times of easy economic achievements, which also opens the door to reasonable doubts about the nation's capacity to successfully confront the current phase of economic growth.

It is important to note the composition of the group of survey respondents who perceive this increased stagnation. According to the CERC poll (1996), people whose incomes are insufficient to meet their needs and people above age 61 have the most negative views of the present state of the economy. These are also the groups with the greatest representation among respondents reporting a negative perception of the future economic situation. Thus, while 52% of those who feel their incomes are sufficient to cover their necessities believe the economy will improve, only 26% of those who possess insufficient resources have the same opinion. Likewise, 43% of respondents aged 18 to 25 believe the future economy will be better, while only 29% of those older than 61 agree.[6]

The CEP survey also confirms that the variables of income and age correlate with opinions about the present and future economic situation. The poll further indicates that people's political opinions affect this evaluation; in particular, those who define themselves as moderates tend to be more optimistic than those on the right or the left. This tendency has accentuated slightly during the present decade.

Despite the trend toward a less optimistic vision of the future, Chileans maintain a strong sense of rootedness or identification with their country. In 1995, the Desuc survey asked people whether they would emigrate to another country where their income would be double its current amount (an offer that should certainly be attractive for a public that, in the majority, feels dissatisfied with its current income level). Only 21.3% declared themselves willing to emigrate immediately, while twice that amount, 42.6%, said they would remain in Chile. Surprisingly, these proportions were highly similar among all three socioeconomic groups surveyed.

1. THE RELATION BETWEEN PERSONAL ECONOMIC SITUATION AND THE NATIONAL ECONOMY

The CERC (1996) poll undertakes a more detailed comparison of perceptions of the national economy and the respondents' personal economic situation. In March 1996, personal economic situation receives a better evaluation than the national economic situation. The personal situation is good for 25% of those surveyed, while the national situation is good for only 17%. Although both evaluations exhibit a similar trajectory, we can see that only in the past two years have evaluations of personal economic situation manifested a clear superiority.

The fact that people perceive their own current economic situation more favorably than the country's general economic state represents a logical distortion. The country's overall economic situation, after all, is merely the aggregate of the economic status of each member of the population. This distortion, aside from being characteristic of self-evaluations by people with positive self-esteem, may reveal the existence of growing feelings of autonomy among people, in relation to their surrounding environment. If this trend becomes further established, it would mark a shift away from the predisposition to attribute responsibility for personal outcomes to the external environment (e.g., the government). This predisposition has been a characteristic of our country's traditional political culture.

Nevertheless, the asymmetry between evaluations of one's personal situation and that of the collective varies significantly according to the socioeconomic position of the individual. Socioeconomically speaking, the most privileged classes perceive that their

---

6   We must note that the latter difference is valid only for the measurements in March of 1995 and 1996, since from 1991-1994 the differences were not significant.

FIGURE 4

CHANGES IN PERCEPTION OF
PERSONAL & NATIONAL ECONOMIC SITUATIONS (1989-1996)
(Only "good" and "very good" answers)

Source: CERC 1996

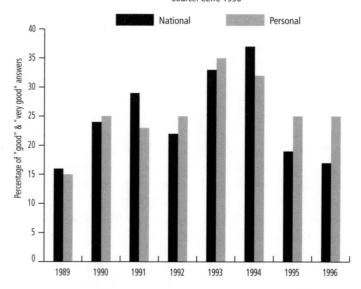

personal comfort is well above the national average (a difference of 30 percentage points, with 66% of well-off respondents and 36% of the rest of the population responding affirmatively). In contrast, the perception of those who believe they have "difficulties," from a socioeconomic standpoint, stands at two points below the nation's average (8% and 10%, respectively). The large socioeconomic differences indicated by these perceptions have manifested themselves similarly throughout the decade. Nevertheless, the fact is striking that the poor do not have a more markedly negative perception of their personal situation, relative to the national economy. This result would suggest that, even within this income group, people hold interpretations of their personal condition that are compatible with optimistic expectations for the future.

2. INSIGHTS FROM QUALITATIVE STUDIES

Value and Importance Assigned to the Economy

Qualitative studies are eloquent in establishing the importance of the economy in the formation of opinions. It is not only the issue that generates the greatest interest, but also the issue that plays the most decisive role in the perception and evaluation of the country. In other words, the vision of our national situation is based in large measure upon judgments about the economy.

Furthermore, it is interesting to note the complex nature of the opinions people form about the national economic situation. People depend on a series of variables, including income, consumption, employment, prices, indebtedness, investment, and the integration and internationalization of the economy. Economic opinions tend to crystallize preponderantly around two issues: economic growth and poverty.

An Ambivalent Judgment

We can deduce from qualitative studies that, currently, Chileans largely share a similar vision of their economic situation. In evaluating the changes undergone by the country in recent years, the majority of the population recognizes economic growth and progress on the one hand, and poverty and inequality on the other (although different people have different points of emphasis).

Generally speaking, people express their opinions about the country's economic situation in both positive and negative terms, exhibiting moderated and mixed opinions, founded on daily experience and an ample amount of information.

Likewise, as evidenced in the quantitative polls, polar opinions about the economic situation — visions that are totally positive or totally negative — are in the minority.

Given the above factors, we can argue that this shared vision of the economic reality, despite differences in emphasis, is a relatively new phenomenon. Until the start of the 1990s, various studies and opinion polls indicated that the majority of the population held polar visions of the economic process, and that only one sector of society acknowledged the country's economic growth.

The Variant of Positive Opinion

The moderated positive point of view is held by the upper class and some middle-class groups, particularly liberal professionals, business people, and entrepreneurs. Its focal point is the perception that the country is experiencing considerable growth and economic progress.

This vision, while acknowledging the persistence of conditions of poverty and inequality, counterbalances them with a series of perceived extenuating factors. Among these, members of this group habitually cite progress in the eradication of poverty, the gradual nature of this process, the fundamental role of growth in fulfilling this objective, and the need for individual effort in order to overcome poverty. In addition, they emphasize the cultural determinants of the phenomenon, insinuating in some cases that some poverty is inevitable and "natural" in all societies. In summary, these people recognize that the benefits of growth have not reached everyone, but they are not particularly emphatic in criticizing this situation. Rather, they tend to favor economic growth as the only recourse for enabling the country to overcome, in the long term, its present inequalities.

In addition, the groups that offer this positive evaluation largely take a macroeconomic perspective, which clearly values the economy's integration and internationalization processes, along with the growth in both domestic and foreign investment.

Likewise, this viewpoint tends to identify the free market system and private enterprise as the two great factors which have made the country's current progress and growth possible. This lends an ideological element to the positive position.

Finally, this group presents a good level of economic knowledge, which translates into adequate skills in the handling of information, statistics, and the technical language of economics.

The Variant of Negative Opinion

The variant of moderated negative opinion prevails among the lower class and a significant part of the middle class. Basically, this view includes a dominant perception that the country still exhibits disproportionately high levels of poverty and inequality in light of the growth and development achieved in recent years.

We must make clear that this variant of opinion acknowledges the country's growth and progress. This constitutes a relatively new phenomenon, since until a short time ago, these income sectors tended not to recognize this progress. Nevertheless, the recognition of this growth has not changed these groups' overall opinion of the country's economic situation, since they perceive this greater progress and growth as benefiting only the most privileged social minority. In other words, in their perception, the "poverty and inequality" component carries more weight than the "growth and macroeconomic stability" component. As a consequence, their final evaluation is negative. This interpretation allows us to suppose that those who express a negative opinion of the country's economy are not denying its macroeconomic achievements, but rather manifesting their dissatisfaction with the distributive results of the growth achieved.

Another factor that influences this group's development of a negative judgment is its perception about consumption and indebtedness. These people tend to perceive increased access to all sorts of consumer goods as one of the positive elements of the current economic situation, but they object to the high level of debt brought about by this greater consumption. This objection is further accentuated by their belief that their own income level is low and the job climate is unstable.

Adherents to this variant are distinguished by the fact that they form their perceptions and evaluations on the basis of their personal and family situations and experiences, focusing on factors such as income, prices, employment, and indebtedness.

For this group, macroeconomic variables tend to play a secondary and more distant role, compared to their daily economic experiences. Nevertheless, the most recent studies find broader acceptance of some macroeconomic processes. Examples of these are the country's economic integration and internationalization, which in the early 1990s were considered threatening.

The negative group tends to evaluate the persistence of poverty in two different ways. On the one hand, the perception exists that the country's current growth may make the eradication of poverty possible. Yet, on the other hand, some believe that the dynamic of the economic system, along with the political programs of the nation's decision makers, are driving the country in the opposite direction from this objective.

Finally, the groups expressing a negative vision call for a more active government role in economic matters. These sectors perceive the government's current policy as having little relevance for the neediest social groups. As for business interests, the negative group accepts their central role in the development of the country, but criticizes their lack of social sensitivity.

Changes in the Economic Culture

It is interesting to note that qualitative studies not only reveal changes in perceptions of the country's economic situation, but also shifts in the economic culture of the population. One of the most significant changes has been seen in the value placed on work and personal effort, as well as education, as decisive factors for development and for both individual and collective success. This perception is particularly accentuated among the upper and upper-middle classes, but also in some lower-and lower-middle-class groups. For the latter, this is especially true among those who work independently in some manner.

Likewise, there have been important modifications in the way people assess the historical factors that have influenced economic transformations. One of these is the relatively

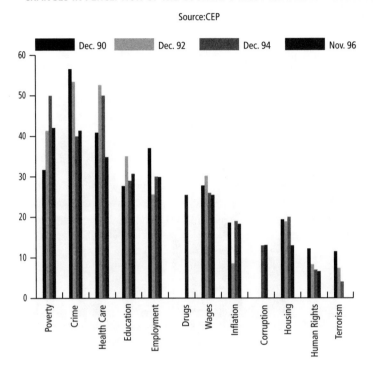

FIGURE 5

CHANGES IN PERCEPTION OF THE COUNTRY'S MOST IMPORTANT PROBLEMS

Source:CEP

widespread consensus that these transformations, regardless of the judgment they deserve, originated with the military government. The other consideration is the perception that the Concertación governments have not, in economic matters, diverged from the policies initiated during the military regime.

II. Perception of the Country's Most Important Problems

1. GENERAL TENDENCIES

A traditional subject for opinion polls is the identification of the most important problems facing society. This indicator tends to vary substantially from survey to survey, depending on the visibility or public notoriety of particular issues or problems during the preceding period. Consequently, this measurement tends to exhibit sudden rises and falls in the prioritization of problems.

Within this volatility, however, we can see a significant decline, since the beginning of the decade, in the relative importance occupied by the issue of crime (see Figure 5). At the same time, we find that public concern for the problem of poverty has tended to grow. Other traditional issues, such as economic problems (inflation, employment, and wage levels), demonstrate a certain instability in different measurements. In addition, leading social problems (health care, education, and housing) exhibit somewhat erratic trajectories, with a certain downward tendency in the concern for housing. Citizen concern for

FIGURE 5A

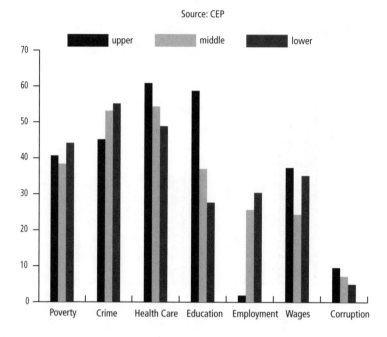

**SOCIO-ECONOMIC COMPARISON OF PERCEPTIONS
OF THE COUNTRY'S MOST IMPORTANT PROBLEMS IN 1992**

Source: CEP

FIGURE 5B

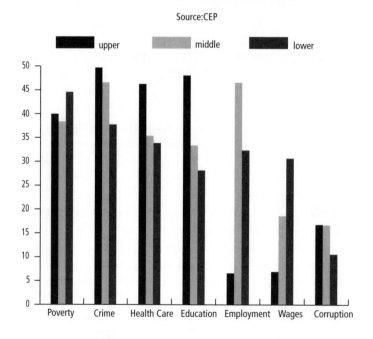

**SOCIO-ECONOMIC COMPARISON OF PERCEPTIONS OF THE COUNTRY'S
MOST IMPORTANT PROBLEMS IN 1996**

Source:CEP

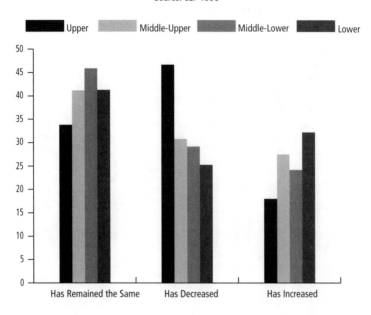

FIGURE 5C

**PERCEPTION OF CHILEAN POVERTY OVER THE LAST 5 YEARS
BY SOCIO-ECONOMIC STRATIFICATION INDEX**

Source: CEP 1996

Upper   Middle-Upper   Middle-Lower   Lower

human rights, one of the key problems of the democratic transition, has remained in a consistently secondary position throughout this decade, and has even shown a tendency toward declining importance. Finally, the table shows that at least two problems have emerged as new preoccupations during this decade: drug addiction and corruption. In contrast, the issue of terrorism has tended to disappear as a citizen concern.

We note with interest that the perceptions of the country's most pressing problems among various socioeconomic groups do not differ as much as one might suppose, given the great differences in their living conditions. In fact, poverty, crime, and health care appear among the top three concerns of all social groups. Particularly noteworthy in this respect is the social consensus about the importance of poverty. Still, there are some significant differences, as we can see in the comparative profile of problems for 1992 and 1996, shown in Figures 5a and 5b. On the one hand, we find that preoccupation with economic issues (employment and wages) tends to be most heavily concentrated among less-privileged groups. On the other hand, the main problems of a social nature (health care and education) tend to gain importance as we move up the social scale. These results seem paradoxical, particularly in the case of health care. To explain them, we must consider the fact that the question upon which this analysis in based requires the respondents to rank the problems. Most probably, the poor assign relatively greater importance to problems of an economic and distributive nature.

In the variable context of national problems that we have presented, public interest in the issue of poverty stands out in particular. This is because the objective data on this issue show a trajectory opposite to that of public opinion. During this decade, the number of

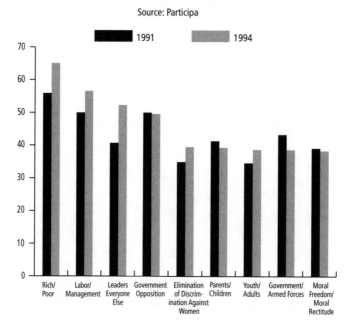

FIGURE 6

PERCEPTION OF PRINCIPAL CONFLICTS IN CHILE

Source: Participa

1991   1994

poor people has seen a sustained decline, and yet public opinion shows itself increasingly concerned about this matter. In fact, a CEP survey from 1996 shows that the majority of the population does not recognize significant progress in the elimination of poverty; 42% believe the problem has remained the same over the last five years, while another 27% believe poverty has increased during the same period. Interestingly, the various socioeconomic groups do not exhibit great differences in the proportion of people believing the problem has remained unchanged. Nevertheless, the percentage of upper-class people who believe poverty has decreased is notably higher. By contrast, the percentage of people who believe the problem has worsened tends to increase slightly as we go down the social scale (see Figure 5c).

The most reasonable explanation for this tremendous preoccupation with the issue of poverty, given that the statistics reveal a significant reduction in the problem, is the one provided by the notion of relative deprivation. The confluence of high economic expectations and income distribution problems make this explanation plausible. This would indicate a growing dissatisfaction with the speed at which economic progress is reaching the least privileged sectors of society. Also supporting this interpretation is the fact that a large proportion of the population (40%) perceives that economic growth is brought about by the efforts of the workers, and almost three-quarters (72%) believe that economic development benefits a minority.[7] The results of qualitative studies on this issue, revealing a change in the meaning of poverty from "lack of resources" to "inequality," reaffirm this interpretation.

---

7   *Barómetro* CERC, 1996.

Complementing this picture of the country's principal problems are the perceptions held by the citizenry about the principal conflicts existing in society. The Participa survey reveals that citizens perceive the main conflicts to be of a distributive and social nature, which reaffirms the importance of the issue of poverty. As shown in Figure 6, in both 1991 and 1994, the public emphasized conflicts between rich and poor, as well as conflicts between labor and management. In both cases, we see an upward tendency in the relative importance of these conflicts. By contrast, conflicts of a political nature are perceived as the least important. We should also note the low importance assigned by public opinion to the conflict between the government and the Armed Forces, which, by 1994, appears as one of the least significant conflicts.

2. INSIGHTS FROM QUALITATIVE STUDIES

Evaluation of the Social Situation

On the basis of the information provided by qualitative opinion polls, we can establish that the country's social situation continues to be a source of interest and concern for the majority of persons, particularly those of the lower strata and a significant part of the middle class. Social issues permeate these groups' vision of the economic situation and represent a determining factor in their evaluation of the country's position.

In general, their perception of social concerns tends to revolve around the "poverty/inequality" relationship, with the great majority believing that Chile still exhibits high indices of poverty. This is perceived as one of the country's most negative characteristics and one needing to be remedied.

Nonetheless, this widely-shared vision contains different variations or shades, basically conditioned upon the greater or lesser degree to which people directly experience the phenomenon. Thus, the lower class and the section of the middle class who consider themselves to be close to poverty tend to express a more critical and negative view on the subject, with greater detail and emotional force. The upper class and the upper portion of the middle class, however, have a more distant and generic viewpoint.

Perception of the Factors Associated with Poverty

Nevertheless, these groups coincide considerably in associating poverty with a series of economic conditions. All of them recognize that, fundamentally, poverty has to do with an insufficient income level that does not cover the basic necessities of a significant percentage of the population. The lower-class sectors also link other elements with poverty, such as the lack of employment opportunities, an unprotected and unstable job situation, and the growing indebtedness affecting lower-income groups.

Another factor associated with poverty is unequal access to certain basic services. The first of these is health care, which is universally considered to be of poor quality and insufficient in coverage. Likewise, unequal access to quality education is considered, with ever-increasing emphasis, to be one of the factors that prevents people from rising out of poverty.

With regard to housing and urban facilities, complaints of a lack of access have decreased. Negative judgments about the poor quality and limited supply of housing have increased, however. These have been inspired particularly by the notorious quality problems of government-subsidized housing, which became especially evident last winter.

Finally, the lower-income sectors in particular associate the phenomenon of poverty with a perceived lack of protection and safety, related to a justice system viewed as deficient, along with worsening problems of crime and drug addiction. Although it is believed that these phenomena threaten the entire population, lower-class groups feel especially defenseless against them.

We must emphasize that the latter two factors — a sense of discrimination and lack of access with regard to justice, and a lack of protection and safety in the face of crime and drugs — are the ones that are beginning to prevail in the notion and in the experience of what it means to be poor. In other words, we see a steady increase in the number of expressions that identify "being poor" not so much with living in a deficient home or having difficulty obtaining health care and education, but rather as the situation of living in a "bad neighborhood" rife with crime and drugs.

It is interesting to note that the widely-held concern regarding the issue of poverty also tends to spread into the spheres of culture and values. As discussed above, we see greater sensitivity toward, and a growing demand for, greater equality of opportunity, along with sharp criticism of injustice and unsafe communities. At the same time, however, there is criticism of an accentuated individualism and a lack of solidarity that respondents believe are beginning to prevail in our society. In particular, low-income groups judge very severely what they qualify as the "selfishness" and indifference of the upper and middle classes with regard to the fate of the poorest members of society.

Populists especially object to the image generally held of the poor among upper- and middle-class sectors, an image they believe to be reinforced by the media. Lower-class people say that this image stigmatizes them by associating them with drugs, crime, and unfavorable situations in general.

Perception of the Causes of Poverty

Opinions about the causes of poverty appear to be more divided. While the upper class has a more generic and abstract point of view, the lower class manifests a more concrete and detailed vision.

In general, the upper class and part of the middle class tend to identify three causes of poverty. The first is the country's still-insufficient level of development. The second is the lower level of education, culture, and (according to the upper class) effort exhibited by the poor, which keep them from improving their condition. Finally, this sector believes that a certain amount of poverty is inevitable and forms part of the "natural" order of society.

Lower-class people identify quite different causes of poverty. First and foremost, they attribute it to the insufficient will to eradicate it on the part of those who wield economic power in society. They blame the business community in particular, saying that it is only concerned with personal gain and not with general social well-being. Overall, the lower class considers the greatest determinant of poverty to be the nature of the economic and social system, which does not provide equality of opportunity and has an operational logic that is difficult to modify. These sectors also acknowledge the lack of education and culture, along with the need for a more rigorous work ethic, as causes of poverty, demonstrating evidence of self-criticism.

Perceptions of the War on Poverty

Nor do the classes coincide in their evaluation of advances in the war on poverty. There are those who believe these advances have been significant and have resulted both from the increased growth the country has experienced in recent years and from the application of effective policies. Others, in contrast, deny the existence of such progress or consider it quite insufficient. They attribute this situation to the absence of genuine and effective will on the part of the government to overcome the problem. These sectors manifest a clear disenchantment with the Concertación governments, since their hopes of substantially improving their living conditions have been frustrated.

Consequently, we find among the lower class a favorable disposition toward greater state activism in the areas of health care, education, housing, and, in general, providing greater protection to the population. However, these groups also tend to favor equality of opportunity, as a stimulus to effort and participation, over direct government assistance.

Finally, there are again two distinct opinions with regard to people's expectations of overcoming poverty. The first expresses emphatic confidence that the country will be able to eradicate poverty through economic growth. This position, which is prevalent among the upper and middle classes, places great importance on education and personal effort, so that the poor can lift themselves out of this condition on their own. The second position, which is widely shared among the lower class, shows a high degree of skepticism about the possibility of overcoming poverty merely through economic growth. Proponents of this view call for a more active government role in guaranteeing a satisfactory level of opportunities. Nevertheless, this group also emphasizes the importance of individual effort and initiative in order to take advantage of these opportunities.

III. Perception and Evaluation of Political Activity

It is an established fact that political activity currently attracts limited interest in the majority of countries. In response to a question on the subject ("How interested are you in politics?"), only 7% of Latin Americans said they were very interested. Eighteen percent said they were somewhat interested, and 73% said they had little or no interest in politics. The pattern in the majority of countries is strikingly similar on this point. Nevertheless, it is noteworthy that Chile is among the countries where the lowest interest in politics is observed. The trajectory uncovered by opinion surveys in our country is clear: following a rise in political interest after the country returned to democracy, citizens have exhibited a sustained decline in political interest (see Figure 7).

Quantitative studies of public opinion do not directly indicate whether this lack of interest is the consequence of an outright rejection of politics, or simply indicative of the lesser importance of such activity in people's daily lives. There are certainly indicators for both attitudes, but a more definitive answer requires complementary investigative efforts. Information from qualitative studies, which is described at the end of this section, confirms a growing tendency in public opinion to develop markedly negative representations and evaluations with regard to politics. In fact, at present people emit negative responses about politics almost automatically. However, they tend to moderate their opinions when they have the opportunity to go into more detail about the

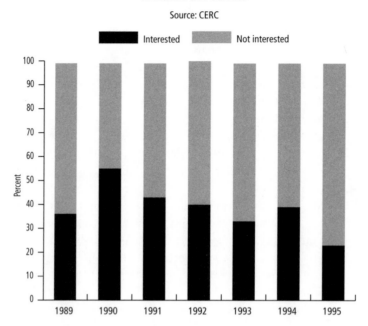

FIGURE 7

INTEREST IN POLITICS

Source: CERC

issue. Consequently, quantitative studies, which generally tend to gather the simplest and most automatic responses, will probably produce more adverse results in this area than qualitative studies. In the first part of this section, we concentrate on noting some of the important tendencies observed in public-opinion polls relating to politics and political institutions.

One way to approach the problem of understanding the withdrawal of citizens from politics is to find out whether the rejection is specific to this type of activity or represents a more generalized tendency toward the progressive loss of confidence in all institutions. The available data reveal that a combination of the two is occurring; that is, citizens possess an increasingly negative vision of institutions in general, but at the same time, the loss of confidence is particularly accentuated for political institutions. The Participa survey analyzed citizens' perceptions about the effectiveness of various institutions in solving problems. The results, summarized in Figure 8, reveal that all the institutions analyzed are suffering an erosion of public trust. Some institutions, like the Church and the police, nonetheless maintain very high levels of confidence. The most significant percentages of decline in confidence levels between 1991 and 1994 are seen with Congress and the political parties. It is interesting to note that at the start of the democratic period these institutions were very positively perceived, with Congress enjoying a level of confidence close to that of the Church. In 1994, however, Congress placed near the bottom. Of all the institutions considered in the survey, political parties were perceived as the institutions least capable of solving problems.

Despite this negative trend for political institutions, Chileans currently possess greater confidence in such institutions than do citizens of other nations, according to 1996 *Latinobarómetro* figures. The confidence Chileans place in their Congress puts them first

FIGURE 8

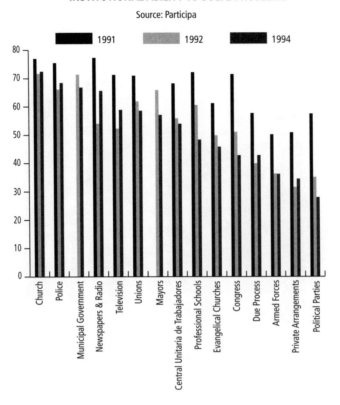

INSTITUTIONAL ABILITY TO SOLVE PROBLEMS

Source: Participa

■ 1991   ▨ 1992   ▧ 1994

TABLE 1

CONFIDENCE IN INSTITUTIONS : CHILE AND LATIN AMERICA IN GENERAL

Institution	% Confidence Chilean Sample	Chile's Relative Position	% Confidence All of Latin America
Government	51%	1	28%
Police	48%	1	29%
Congress	44%	1	27%
Due Process	36%	5	33%
Political Parties	28%	4	20%

SOURCE: Latinobarómetro (1996)

among Latin American countries, while their confidence in political parties puts them in fourth place. In the same survey, we find that Chileans' confidence in their government is also the highest among Latin American nations. Interestingly, in contrast to Latin America in general, Chileans generally manifest high levels of confidence in the performance of their institutions, as indicated in Figure 8.

FIGURE 9

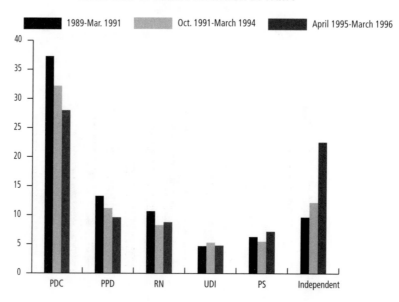

EVOLUTION OF VOTING INTENTION BY PARTY

1989-Mar. 1991   Oct. 1991-March 1994   April 1995-March 1996

1. PARTY MEMBERSHIP AND IDEOLOGICAL SELF-DEFINITION

Party membership in Chile has shown itself to be a relatively stable variable in the country's political culture. Figure 9, constructed by averaging voting intention by party for three periods of the democratic transition, shows a fairly stable distribution. Nonetheless, two trends emerge from these data. The first is the progressive erosion of support for the Christian Democratic Party (PDC), which shows a decline in membership of around 10 percentage points. The second is the significant growth in the group of people defining themselves as independents, which at present amount to nearly a quarter of those surveyed. The most notable rise in independents has occurred in the last period, a result of the lost membership of the majority of parties, but of the PDC in particular. The only party achieving modest growth in the last period considered was the Socialist Party.

As a complement to this phenomenon, ideological self-definition exhibits a trajectory equivalent to that observed in party membership. As Figure 10 indicates, the center[8] of the ideological spectrum has declined in relative importance, identification with it having fallen 10 percentage points from its position at the start of the democratic period. At the same time, the number of respondents declaring they have no defined political position have been rising since 1992. The greatest relative stability is shown on the right of the ideological spectrum, where fluctuations since 1991 have been minimal. By contrast, the left has displayed significant shifts, although all of them have occurred in the upper range of the

---

8   In this analysis, we have condensed the answers from a 5-point scale into a 3-point one, placing the center-right and right in one category, and the center-left and left into another.

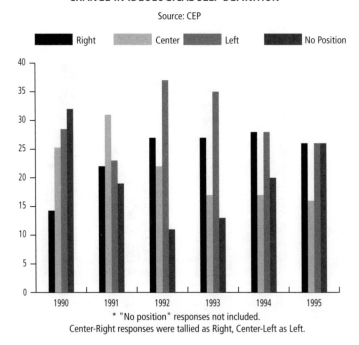

FIGURE 10

CHANGE IN IDEOLOGICAL SELF-DEFINITION

Source: CEP

Right   Center   Left   No Position

* "No position" responses not included.
Center-Right responses were tallied as Right, Center-Left as Left.

ideological self-definition scale. At the close of the period considered, we find a tie between those who define themselves as independents, on the right or on the left, with the centrists falling into fourth place.

In summary, the evolution of the period shows a steady increase in those who define themselves as independents or as being uncommitted to any of the existing political parties or positions. Apparently, this growth has occurred through the erosion of the political center. Simultaneously, the degree of party membership on the right has been rather stable, which could be linked to its position as the opposition bloc throughout the period considered. This fact may be interpreted to show that adherents of the right are more hardline than the sector supporting the Concertación governments, which has shown great instability. In the case of the left, membership has exhibited ups and downs, and among moderates, membership has steadily declined.

2. THE IMAGE OF POLITICS AND POLITICAL PARTIES

In the context previously described, it comes as no surprise that citizens' image of politics has experienced a progressive deterioration. Opinion polls reveal considerable growth in the level of political cynicism during the democratic transition. Figure 11, based on the results of the CERC survey, shows that at the beginning of the democratic period the most commonly expressed belief was that all the political parties are necessary for democracy to exist. Five years later, this belief is still held by a majority of citizens, but the number is lower. Meanwhile, increasing numbers of respondents have agreed with various statements expressing political cynicism during this period. Currently, more than 80% of the

FIGURE 11

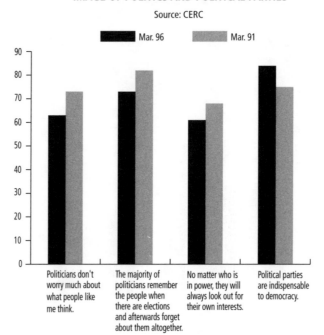

IMAGE OF POLITICS AND POLITICAL PARTIES
Source: CERC

FIGURE 12

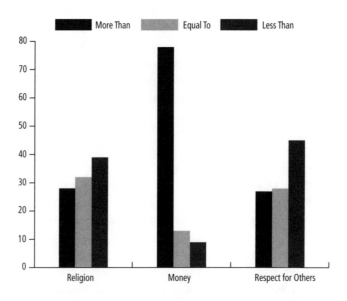

WHAT CHILEANS VALUE ABOVE ALL ELSE?
(percentages)

1995 FLACSO Survey

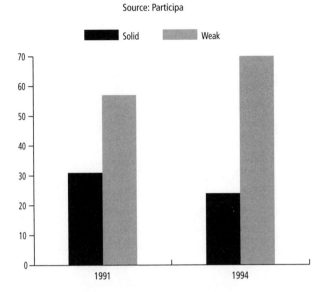

FIGURE 13

APPRAISAL OF THE SOLIDIFICATION OF DEMOCRACY

Source: Participa

population maintain that politicians only think of them during campaigns, and 75% of Chileans agree with the statement that politicians do not care very much about what the people think.

The distancing of citizens from politics also manifests itself in the low frequency of political exchanges between people in their daily lives. In response to the question "How often do you discuss politics in your home?" the Desuc survey of 1995 found that two-thirds of respondents practically never do (36.5% said they never speak of politics, and 33.9% said they almost never do). In comparison, less than 10% say they discuss politics often. There were significant socioeconomic differences on this issue, however. As seen in Figure 12, the frequency of political dialogue decreases substantially as we descend the social scale. The table indicates that while 55% of upper-class people discuss politics at least sometimes, only 20% of lower-class people do. The absence of political conversations in the home not only reduces the effectiveness of the family as an agent of political socialization, but also opens up serious questions about citizens' abilities to process the political information they receive. The lack of opportunities to discuss politics may ultimately lead to high volatility in political attitudes and behavior. The most recent parliamentary elections have been a clear example of this tendency.

3. EVALUATIONS OF DEMOCRACY

The political attitudes described above are indicative of a certain disenchantment with the democratic transition on the part of the population. A series of surveys carried out by Participa between 1991 and 1994 give evidence of this phenomenon. The public does not feel that democracy has solidified during the transition; on the contrary, the percentage of Chileans who believe their democracy is weak has increased, as shown in Figure 13. In the same series of surveys, we find that, despite the ostensible economic achievements of the democratic period, the proportion of Chileans who think our democracy has many problems yet to be resolved remains at around 70%. This figure must be compared with the 9% of Chileans who, in 1991 and 1994, agreed with the statement, "Our democracy is fine as it is."

Moreover, the percentage of Chileans expressing satisfaction with their democracy is declining, while the percentage of those expressing dissatisfaction is on the rise. This paints a picture of growing frustration with the results of the democratic restoration. This frustration may be a strictly political phenomenon, or it may be an evaluation of Chilean democracy based on the personal results experienced by people and families during the transition. The Participa reports do not include data that would allow us to answer this question. They do, however, present results that are consistent with both lines of argument.

Between 1991 and 1994, the percentage of Chileans believing that the current democracy had improved the country's situation, relative to the final years of the military regime, decreased (47% agreed with this statement in 1991, while only 32% agreed in 1994). Likewise, the percentage of Chileans believing that their personal situation had improved during the democratic period, relative to the final authoritarian years, also decreased (33% in 1991, 21% in 1994). In both cases, the majority of Chileans maintain that the country's situation, as well as their own, has remained the same as it was during the final stage of the military regime. This may explain why Chile, among all Latin American countries, emerges as the country with the lowest percentage of its population willing to take a strong stance in defense of democracy, according to *Latinobarómetro*. (Chile's willingness to defend democracy is 53%, while for Latin America as a whole it is 72%.) It is interesting to note that Chileans' relative degree of satisfaction with their democracy is not that low. In fact, the percentage of Chileans who say they are satisfied in this area is equivalent to the Latin American average. Consequently, we cannot interpret the low willingness to defend democracy as a direct consequence of dissatisfaction with it. There are other issues involved here that must be explored in the future.

4. INSIGHTS FROM QUALITATIVE STUDIES

Evaluation of the Political Situation

Qualitative opinion studies eloquently confirm the accentuated disinterest in politics exhibited by the great majority of people. This translates into a reduced motivation to participate in political activities, as well as a lack of attention to political events. The evidence indicates that not only do people pay little attention to the news and to political debates, but they also believe that the media grant too much importance to such topics. Likewise, people admit that they rarely talk about or debate political issues with family members, friends, or co-workers. These phenomena are expressed in a lack of information about political actors and events, which is particularly acute among the lower class.

In general, the lack of interest in politics is closely linked with a negative evaluation of it and, above all, the perception of politics as having lost social value and prestige. It is therefore symptomatic that very few people declare that they participate in politics or spontaneously acknowledge their ideological affiliation or party membership. It is also meaningful that the first assessment people make of politics is habitually very critical, even though their judgments later become more moderated and complex.

We can argue that the majority of the population shares a common orientation toward politics. This orientation shows ambivalent features when we integrate the two large variables of democracy and political activity, which are perceived and evaluated in different manners.

Evaluation of Political Activity

In general, people coincide considerably in identifying "politics" exclusively with the actions carried out by the parties, legislators, and politicians. Thus, people do not necessarily conceive the work of the administration as politics, and when they do so, they include only administration actions that appear expressly linked with Congress and the political parties, excluding the independent performance of the executive branch.

Further, the notion that political activity is essentially connected with obtaining power, and not with service in the public interest, is very widespread. This perception is especially accentuated among the lower class, because members of this group typically consider politics part of a broader chain of power, which includes the business world, the military, and the media.

In close connection with the above, the great majority of people perceive politicians as an elite profiting from influence and privileges which are considered unjust and illegitimate. For example, the high salaries and expense allowances of legislators are cited. Many people take this view to the extreme, associating politics in general with dishonest practices and corruption.

Viewed in these terms, politics appears as an activity that is far removed from the interests of the people, and one that is fundamentally irrelevant and of little social significance, since it neither influences nor changes people's lives. Similarly, the opinion is widespread that politics is a self-referential and self-centered activity. Strictly speaking, people believe that the issues that occupy and preoccupy politicians have sense and meaning for them alone.

Equally widespread is the belief that politics is an inefficient process, having little to do with concrete achievements. People identify it as a sphere where talking and debating, rather than doing and working, reign supreme. Among the lower class in particular, there is a sense that politicians are driven more by an urge to make promises than a desire to fulfill those promises.

Qualitative studies also confirm this negative perception of politics. We see this in the fact that public figures who elicit approving comments or judgments, and who are perceived as highly effective, are mostly people who are not associated with party politics. Rather, they are people who manage a particular department of the central government, who work in municipal government, or who have concrete responsibilities for work and performance.

In addition, one of the greatest criticisms directed at political activity is that it represents a forum for argument, confrontation, and conflict. Such conduct is generally perceived as impeding the success of initiatives that promote the common good, since the people value a strong component of consensus in public action. There is also a prevailing opinion, particularly among the upper class, that politicians are clinging to traditional and obsolete methods, and that they are poorly prepared to face the challenges of the present and the future.

Finally, the qualitative data, like the quantitative surveys, clearly indicate that the lack of interest in politics and critical appraisal of it have expanded and intensified since the start of the decade.

Evaluation of Democracy

People make a much different assessment of democracy. In many cases, democracy is even perceived as dissociated from the connotations of party politics.

In general, positive evaluations of democracy tend to focus on political and civil liberties, especially the freedoms of expression and the press. People also value free elections and representative voting, but they are developing a certain skepticism about the possibility of electing genuine representatives.

In any case, the broad consensus is that the transition from the military regime to the democratic system was positive, and that it was a prerequisite and component of the more extensive process of modernizing the country. This positive evaluation, however, does not extend to other institutions of the political system, such as Congress and the political parties. These results apparently contradict those obtained in quantitative studies, which depict, as shown above, the image of a weak, unconsolidated democracy that does not engender strong feelings of support. Nevertheless, we can see that the opinions gathered in qualitative studies address aspects of democracy not focused upon in the quantitative studies.

The quantitative studies have been driven by an interest in evaluating democracy in terms of its results. Within that context, attitudes toward democracy are inevitably linked to general evaluations of the direction of the country. Qualitative studies, in contrast, have focused more on establishing the meanings that people assign to democracy. In this case, people express distinctly positive associations, particularly in the realm of civil liberties, where the contrast with the authoritarian regime is evident. The quantitative and qualitative studies have thus pointed toward different evaluative dimensions, so it is not altogether surprising that the results are not in accordance. At the same time, however, this indicates that democracy is not perceived as uniformly positive, leading us to conclude that the task of legitimizing the system in the eyes of the citizenry is still incomplete.

Within the generally positive assessment of democracy obtained in qualitative studies, we can identify some variations or shades of opinion. For example, the upper class and the business community manifest an affinity with the military regime, and their positive evaluation of democracy is of a more instrumental nature. They value democracy only to the extent that it is a source of stability and consensus which helps promote growth and economic development. In some cases, democracy is even viewed as a necessary evil that, despite its inertia and inefficiency, must be tolerated to preserve social harmony and peace.

Lower-class respondents, by contrast, associate democracy more strongly with the value of freedom, due to their more direct experiences with the restriction of liberties and human rights violations under the military regime. In spite of their positive evaluation of democracy, we can also identify elements of disenchantment (and in some cases, more radical expressions of frustration), insofar as lower-class people perceive that the change in system has not improved their socioeconomic situation. However, this disenchantment tends to fade from view if the debate focuses exclusively on the question of liberties.

In general terms, it is widely believed that democracy and the political situation are relatively stable, since there are no impending conflicts or serious threats. But there is also a strong perception that Chilean democracy may still be vulnerable, in light of the persistence of *de facto* powers, particularly the military. This situation generates an ambivalent perception among those holding these opinions. On the one hand, people criticize the weakness of civil society, but on the other, they approve of restrained conduct that does not create tension or introduce elements of crisis or instability into the system.

We should note that the people's criticisms of, and lack of interest in, political activity does not suggest that the value they place on democracy lacks conviction or is diluted. Feelings of nostalgia for the authoritarian regime are marginal and insignificant, as people emphatically express their opposition to returning to such a system.

Furthermore, this criticism and dissatisfaction with politics tends to mellow during election periods. With the act of voting, people acknowledge differences and choose particular options, and in so doing they recognize the possibility of redirecting and improving political activity.

Finally, it should be noted that people's positive disposition toward politics gains strength and increases when politicians take up issues that interest the people and, above all, when leaders within the national and municipal governments commit themselves to action.

IV. Psycho-Social Aspects

Although the majority of public-opinion polls have focused on political and economic issues, some enable us to recognize tendencies with regard to matters of a psycho-social nature. One of these is interpersonal trust, the level of which correlates positively to the level of democratic development. The available data, based on the CERC barometer, indicate that this characteristic has remained very stable since before the return to democracy, aligned near the pole of distrust (see Figure 14). This suggests that mistrust is a deeper element of the cultural character of our society.

FIGURE 14

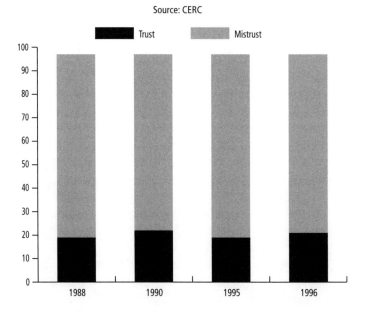

EVOLUTION OF INTERPERSONAL TRUST

Source: CERC

It is interesting that the degree of distrust citizens express with regard to their peers is equal to or even greater than the distrust they show towards the majority of the institutions of the political system. At the moment, it is difficult to establish the nature of the causal relationship between interpersonal trust and trust in institutions. We might suppose that part of the interpersonal distrust derives from citizens' experiences with the institutions of society. It is more plausible, however, that interpersonal trust (or the lack thereof) is the result of direct social relations, and that this trust or distrust is then projected onto social institutions as a whole. We are clearly faced here with a central challenge in the formation of our citizenry, since an environment of interpersonal and institutional mistrust and suspicion promotes social conflict and reduces a society's overall efficiency. Interpersonal mistrust is a characteristic trait of all Latin American societies, but Chile finds itself among the least trusting countries, according to the data from *Latinobarómetro*.

1. SOCIAL VALUES

We do not possess sufficient longitudinal information to establish the evolution of values over time. Nevertheless, given the importance of this issue and the existence of comparative international information provided by the CERC survey, we will summarize some of the relevant aspects that emerge from these international comparisons.

Figure 15 indicates that of the four values analyzed, the one appearing strongest among Chileans is solidarity. More than two-thirds of the citizens of our country believe

FIGURE 15

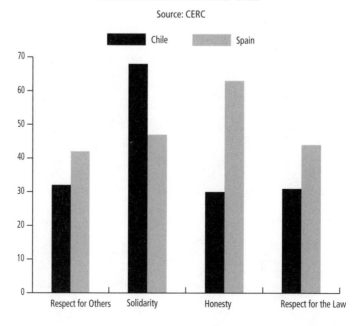

SOCIAL VALUES IN SPAIN & CHILE

Source: CERC

we exhibit solidarity, which is consistent with the sociocentric orientation of our culture.[9] This self-definition is also probably a conscious reflection of our society's demonstrated capacity to react positively to adverse situations (like earthquakes or floods) or to social welfare campaigns (like the Telethon). It is nonetheless notable that less than half of those surveyed believe that integrity and respect for others and for the law are values characteristic of Chileans. Respect for others is a fundamental value in social and political relations. It is possible that a lack of respect for others is the flip side of the lack of interpersonal trust, with the aggravating factor that a lack of respect is a direct precursor to conflict. Perhaps even more worrisome is the low percentage of survey respondents who consider integrity very characteristic or moderately characteristic of Chileans. Only 30% of respondents affirm this trait, which compares very unfavorably to the 63% of Spaniards who do so. Integrity is one of the basic dimensions of social perception and is what enables us to form relationships based on trust. At the same time, our low perception of integrity among ourselves can make us especially inclined to suspect the motives of others in their public behavior. This may be one of the reasons Chileans appear to be so willing to impute the existence of widespread corruption to their country, even though its actual level here is very low on an international scale.

FIGURE 16

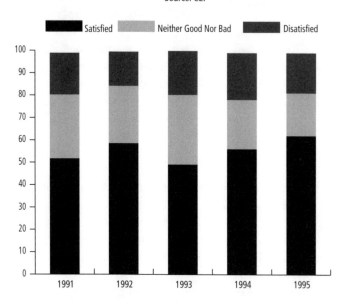

**EVOLUTION OF GENERAL SATISFACTION
WITH ONE'S PERSONAL LIFE**

Source: CEP

---

9   In contrast with the results reported in Figure 14, the Desuc survey of 1995 reported results that would indicate a low level of solidarity. Nevertheless, the question was different than that used in the CERC poll. The latter poll asked to what extent Chileans exhibited solidarity, while the Desuc poll pitted solidarity (trying to help others) against individualism (concern only with oneself). In this survey, 71.4% of respondents said that people are individualistic most of the time. We must also note that the Desuc survey does not specifically refer to Chileans, as does the CERC barometer.

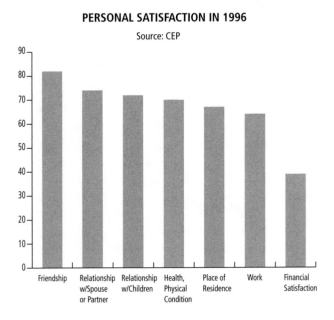

FIGURE 17

PERSONAL SATISFACTION IN 1996

Source: CEP

Figure 15 shows that Chileans perceive themselves as lacking respect for the law. Here again, we compare unfavorably with Spain. In the aforementioned context of mistrust and low integrity, this result should not be surprising. Respect for the law is a foundation of the rule of law, and constitutes a guarantee of the social contract between citizens and their leaders. Lack of respect for the law is also a cause of social inefficiency, as it obligates a nation to devise and maintain costly control mechanisms. These mechanisms may even be necessary to enforce laws that are obviously beneficial for society and that have the support of a majority of the population. (It is sufficient here to note the example of the laws and regulations designed to minimize urban pollution.)

2. CITIZENS' PERSONAL SATISFACTION

It is appropriate to ask how generally satisfied or dissatisfied the inhabitants of our country are with their lives. Beyond their assessments of our country's development, its economy, and the attitudes of their peers, we must inquire: how satisfied are Chileans with their lives? CEP has carried out a series of measurements on this subject that reveal a notably stable prevalence of positive evaluations. As shown in Figure 16, more than half of Chileans feel satisfied with their lives, and this tendency has risen slightly over the last few years. In contrast, only 20% of our compatriots feel dissatisfied.

Upon investigating the specific factors that might contribute to this overall feeling of satisfaction, the CEP survey of 1995 reveals that the most satisfying aspects of Chileans' lives are their personal relationships with their friends, spouses, and children (see Figure 17). Further, the majority of Chileans also have positive feelings about their health, their jobs, and even where they live. At least 64% of Chileans say they feel satisfied or very satisfied with the six aforementioned aspects of their lives. On the other hand, Chilean's personal financial situations are their greatest source of frustration. Only 39% say they are satisfied in this respect. Nevertheless, the same CEP poll finds that only 16% of Chileans express pessimistic expectations about their financial future. That is, in spite of the strongly negative sentiments Chileans express about their current financial situation, their future expectations are positive in the majority, as we indicated in the section on perceptions of the economy.

3. INSIGHTS FROM QUALITATIVE STUDIES

Evaluation of the Value Situation
Two characteristics appear to define the trends in opinions about value-related matters. The first is the high degree of clarity in people's judgments when they refer in detail to the ethical guidelines governing their personal, family, social, and work relations. The second is a consciousness that Chilean society is experiencing a process of rapid change that affects the framework of values governing citizens' public and private conduct.

The results of the qualitative studies indicate that people generally group their perceptions of value changes into two large areas, each with its own logic and each visualized in a different way. The first is associated with the new socioeconomic reality that has taken shape in this country over the past few years. The second area, in contrast, involves matters belonging to the private sphere; in particular, questions relating to romantic relationships and orientations of sexual morality.

Value Perceptions Related to the Socioeconomic Realm
A rather widespread and intense sense of unease tends to prevail with regard to the effects of economic transformation upon values and interpersonal relations. There is much criticism of a set of phenomena that people believe have been on the rise in our society in recent years. Among these are cited consumerism, individualism, obsession with work, workaholic-type behavior, and the excessive importance placed on money and material gain.

All these conducts and attitudes are perceived as signs of a breakdown of values in Chilean society, or at least part of it, resulting in an excessive emphasis of certain material aspects of life. To be exact, what people object to is not so much these attitudes in and of themselves, but rather their overblown value in modern life. This is the case, for example, with the excessive focus on work, and especially with consumerism. People do not oppose the desire to acquire material goods or the greater ease with which they can be acquired; on the contrary, they value this greater access. Instead, they object to the fact that these aspirations supersede other goals and objectives that they consider to be more important.

The criticisms especially center on the way in which these behaviors and orientations interfere with the quality of personal relationships, especially family life. Thus, survey respondents mention, first, the negative effects on the family of the excessive attention people give to their jobs. The growing frequency with which women are entering the work force, the search for second jobs, the lengthening of the work day, and frequent episodes of work-related stress, among other phenomena, are perceived as threats that weaken and erode family communication and harmony.

People feel that this work-oriented focus both promotes and feeds off of the exaggerated inclination toward consumerism and the compulsion to place material goods over human values. Young people, for example, criticize the excessive pressure to choose careers that guarantee wealth and comfort over those that offer a vocation and personal satisfaction.

All of the above leads the majority of people to develop a negative and critical perception of this specific value area, to the point that they believe the country is undergoing an appreciable decline in this respect.

When it comes to interpreting the causes of this phenomenon, people's opinions do not coincide. In general, upper-class people believe that value reorientations and breakdowns are the result of Chilean society's unpreparedness or lack of moral fortitude as it attempts to assimilate its accelerated transformation process. The middle and lower classes, along with the young, attribute a large part of the responsibility for this decline to Chile's reigning socioeconomic model. They especially blame new work demands, which impede people from acting in harmony with their values, as well as the influence of the media. Above all, they charge advertising with promoting behavior foreign to the people's traditional standards.

It is no surprise, therefore, that these two groups' expectations about the future of this problem are also dissimilar. Upper-class people trust that Chilean society will, after a necessary learning period, understand how to confront the realities of modern life. The middle and lower classes, however, are much more skeptical, since they believe the country's distortion of values is inherent to the market economic system.

Value Perceptions Related to the Private Realm

In contrast to the socioeconomic sphere, the value changes in the private sphere are in the majority considered to be positive and to be an expression of the necessary and healthy modernization of Chilean society.

Far from seeing the new moral guidelines as signs of relaxation or permissiveness, what people generally perceive is a new sensitivity toward complex problems and situations that require an open and flexible approach. The prevailing conviction is that in matters as personal as the relationship of a couple and sexual conduct, it is not necessary to impose rigid and authoritarian precepts. Instead, individual freedom and responsibility should be respected. Thus, the former custom of interfering in issues of private morality is harshly criticized as being excessively repressive.

The new sensitivity with regard to issues of the personal and private sphere does not imply an absence of values in this area. The people retain the values of family, stable partners, and emotional commitment. What we are seeing is the development of a greater tolerance for people facing difficulties in these areas and for the problems that tend to occur in these aspects of life.

A specific example is that the majority of people are now in favor of a divorce law, since they believe it would offer a solution for the problems of many couples and would not violate the fundamental values of family and marriage.[10]

---

10 In line with qualitative studies, the Desuc survey of 1996 found that 84% of people considered marriage to be a lifelong commitment, while just 14% considered it an obsolete institution. This reaffirms the value marriage continues to have in our society. At the same time, the survey found qualified majority support for the legalization of divorce. Of the respondents, 15.4% were definitely opposed to such a law, while 38.2% said divorce should be legal. The most popular alternative, however, chosen by 46.4% of respondents, was that divorce should be authorized only in certain cases.

Likewise, there is a tendency to accept premarital sexual relations,[11] without disregarding the adherence to and appreciation for the values of emotional commitment and marriage. In addition, a large majority of people also show great understanding toward cases of adolescent pregnancy, arguing that a more harsh and rigid reaction to the situation would expose a young woman to much more serious problems, like abortion or a break in family relations.

Another significant fact in this area is the widespread opinion, even among professed Catholics, that the Church is not responding adequately to the dilemmas of private morality that arise in modern society. For example, people repeatedly cite Catholic high schools' discriminatory tendency to deny admission to children with separated parents.

Finally, there is a predominant feeling, especially among young people, that the culture and the media exercise a great deal of censorship, above all in matters of sexuality. Without denying the fact that children should not be exposed to inappropriate content, the imposition of canons of censorship is widely considered a restriction and a violation of freedom of thought.

Conclusions

Considering the trends that have been described in this chapter, based on both qualitative and quantitative public-opinion studies, one of the most striking factors is the relative homogeneity of the opinions gathered. This is an unprecedented situation in our country's political culture. Chile, especially in political matters, has traditionally been thought of as a nation wracked with great conflicts and dissent, to the extent that it has been said many times that there could be two countries or societies within our nation. The studies summarized here still reveal differences based on people's social position, gender, age, and place of residence. However, these differences emerge in the context of a relative consensus regarding problems, needs, aspirations and evaluations in the social, economic, and political spheres.

Among the main trends detected in the various sections of this chapter, one of the most pronounced tendencies is the ongoing decline in positive assessments of our country and its economy. All of the indicators (including the current and future situation, personally and collectively) display a similar profile. The bright side of this phenomenon is the moderation of the perhaps excessive expectations cherished at the start of the decade. Nevertheless, the danger involved in this trend is that pessimism may take hold, leading to negative reactions at any sign of faltering in the economy. Since perceptions of the economy largely determine the public's judgments about the country's situation, it is imperative that we pay attention to developments in this respect. In the new economic culture that has been establishing itself during this decade, we see a clear departure from the fatalism often observed in economic attitudes in the past. This is reflected especially in the fact that the majority of the population believes the future economic situation (both personally and collectively) will be better than the current one.

---

11 On this matter, the Desuc poll of 1995 found that 20% of those surveyed placed premarital sexual relations in the most negative category ("they are always wrong"), and 25% placed them in the most permissive category ("they are not wrong"). Another 37% said they are sometimes wrong, and 15% said they are almost always wrong.

There is a broad social consensus that poverty is a growing concern, despite the statistics that show an objective decrease in poverty indices. Qualitative studies in particular show a change in the prevailing concept of poverty, with the notion of inequality generally coming to displace the definition of "lacking resources." This change suggests that the population pays express attention to the rate at which the benefits of our economic progress reach different sectors of our society. This reaffirms the need to place special emphasis on economic and social policies that have a direct effect on resource distribution, especially in those areas where sensitivity to inequality is strongest (education, housing, and health care).

Citizens' attitudes toward politics have evolved steadily, without showing signs of slowing, toward a state of severe withdrawal from political activity. The people do not trust politicians or political institutions, and they display a growing political cynicism. At the same time, citizens are progressively moving further away from allegiance to political parties, indicated by the systematic rise of self-declared independents. The most significant erosion of political support is occurring in the center.

The ultimate risk posed by this development is the discrediting of democracy as a political system. Although Chileans value democracy, they are among the Latin American nations with the lowest percentage of their population willing to fight for democracy. This situation imposes a stark challenge. The country must reconstruct a positive, interdependent link between citizens and the political class, one that legitimizes political activity. Chile also must reconnect the people with the mechanisms and institutions dealing with the issues that affect our overall social welfare. It is worrisome that our country's education system almost entirely lacks formal procedures to instruct students in fundamental civic duties.

In summary, we can establish that our country's public opinion has assimilated many of the changes that have occurred during this decade in the economic, social, and political spheres. There are, nonetheless, clear signs of concern, withdrawal, and frustration that testify to the emergence of a public opinion that is not content to merely hold on to what we have already achieved. There are many new demands, but the most sensitive issue, now and in the future, is that of distributing the economic and social benefits produced by our country's progress.

Modernization and Concentration:
The Media in Chile

Flavio Cortés

Introduction

T he media in Chile and their transformation in recent years, like all social phenomena, may be analyzed using multiple conceptual approaches. In the following pages, we have chosen to provide a primarily descriptive view of the developments occurring in this area. This choice is based on the nature of the work in which this article appears, as well as the absence to date of a timely analysis that explores and synthesizes the major transformations in progress.

The data reveal that political, economic, and socio-cultural changes, as well as technological ones, have taken place in Chile's national media industry. These dimensions, which can be distinguished analytically within each medium, reflect the far-reaching transformations taking place on the national and international levels.

In political terms, the media changes have been shaped by the democratic transition process and the particular form that it took: a transition established from the top down, with the peculiarity of a lengthy, one-year interim between the electoral defeat of the authoritarian government and the inauguration of the new administration. This interim permitted the establishment of an institutional framework preserving a particular type of media structure.

It cannot be said that this structure, and the actors and institutions comprising it, emerged solely as a result of market forces. On the contrary, the authoritarian government clearly designed it with a bias toward the politically conservative media. Examples include the transfer of the company El Mercurio S.A.P.'s debt with the government bank to private banking institutions, under extremely favorable conditions; the arrangement in which the newspaper *La Tercera* eliminated its debt to the state television channel (TVN) in exchange for advertising space; the military junta's passage, in the eleventh hour of the authoritarian administration (September 30, 1989), of the law creating the National Television Council (*Consejo Nacional de Televisión* or CNTV); the establishment in the same law of the possibility of selling television frequencies to the private sector; and the sale of frequencies 9 and 4, which belonged to TVN. In addition, at the end of the last decade, powerful multi-media groups formed that were linked to entrepreneurs with conservative cultural and political backgrounds.

A second political aspect of the media is the clear decline in public interest advocacy journalism, as well as in political journalism in general. As a result, a significant number of

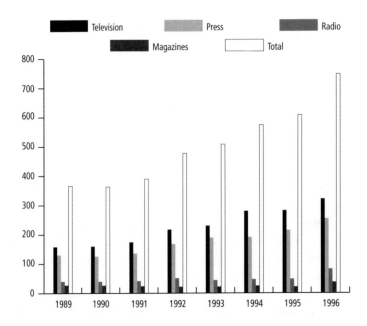

ADVERTISING INVESTMENT IN CHILE
TOTAL AND SELECT MEDIA 1989-1996

(in millions of 1995 dollars)

the publications dedicated to these issues, aimed at moderate and leftist audiences, have disappeared in the 1990s. The rare attempts during this period to provide alternative news sources capable of competing successfully with already-established media have been largely fruitless. Alternatives to the existing media outlets have not received the necessary financial backing and commercial support to become established and expand their operations.

Second, media changes have been brought about by economic, financial, and market processes. The Chilean media are part of a cultural industry that has contributed to fortifying market forces within the country during the 1990s. Spending on advertising in Chile has more than doubled, rising 104.5%, from US$365.7 million in 1989 to US$747.8 million in 1996. The greatest advances were seen in 1992 and 1996, when growth rates over the preceding years were 23.3 and 22.8, respectively. By contrast, 1990 showed a decline of 0.8%.

Television advertising has maintained a growth rate very closely tied to that of print advertising. In 1996, television advertising accounted for 43% of total advertising, or US$321.6 million. With the exception of 1994, its proportion has remained relatively constant throughout the period. While TV advertising increased 103.5%, print media advertising rose 95.3%, reaching US$254.3 million in 1996.

Radio broadcasting has displayed a different pattern. Up to 1995, radio advertising had exhibited growth of only 20.7%. Nonetheless, as the result of an extraordinary leap of 70.7% in 1995, radio advertising demonstrates an overall growth rate similar to that of TV and print. Considerably lower growth is seen in magazine advertising over the same period, with a rate of 37.4%, representing revenues of US$37.4 million.

TABLE 1

NUMBER OF TELEVISIONS, RADIOS, NEWSPAPERS, AND NEWSPAPER CIRCULATION FOR SELECTED COUNTRIES (1994)

	Country newspaper circulation per per 1,000 inhabitants	Estimated newspaper circulation (in millions)	Televisions per 1,000 inhabitants	Number of newspapers	Estimated number of televisions (in millions)	Estimated number of radios (in millions)
Argentina	138	4.7	187	219	7.5	23.0
Brazil	45	7.2	317	209	33.2	62.5
Chile*	100	1.4	32	211	3.0	4.8
Colombia	64	2.2	46	118	4.1	6.1
Spain	104	4.1	148	402	15.9	12.3
Mexico	113	10.4	309	163	15.0	23.5
Industrialized Society Average	286	28.9	355	601	64.0	136.2

* Approximate figures for Chile; the INE's Media and Culture Survey doesn't take into account all media. According to this study, the number of newspapers is 48.

SOURCE: Unesco, *Statistical Yearbook*, 1997.

The extent of the media expansion in Chile is evident in the fact that advertising investment rose from 0.79% of GDP in 1990 to 0.92% in 1995. These magnitudes notwithstanding, it is essential to note that the national media market, when compared to other Latin American markets, is extremely small. It is just one-third the size of Argentina's market, and barely a tenth of Brazil's. (Chile's market is much greater than that of Peru, however, which amounts to about US$250 million.) This small size severely limits the application of economies of scale to media products, and the resulting high costs impede national production. This limitation is related not only to the country's size, but also to its level of development. As Table 1 shows, compared to the highly industrialized nations, our country possesses just one-third the number of television sets per 1,000 inhabitants. Newspaper circulation shows roughly the same proportion.

In absolute terms, the contrast between Chile and the large Latin American markets is considerable. Yet this small-market phenomenon is not limited to our country or even our region. In the worldwide market, the United States has unrivaled dominance in the culture industry, owing to the size of its domestic market, among other factors. Demonstrating this distinction is the fact that the United States has 1,300 theaters for any cinematic release, compared to 450 in Germany, 350 in France, and less than 200 in any other highly industrialized country. Likewise, people in the United States watch television an average of 240 minutes per day, more than in other countries with similar levels of development (*The Economist*, Nov. 29, 1997).

In spite of the limitations of the Chilean market, it is clear that domestic competition has increased substantially in recent years. Previously, the ratings battle in the television market was waged between just two companies. Today, the market exhibits falling ratings, greater instability, and increased openness. In the case of radio, competing broadcasters have multiplied. Even in as well-established a market as the print media, a recent shake-up has taken place. This was the result of *La Tercera*'s makeover and the emergence of competition in afternoon newspapers with the introduction of *La Hora* by the Consorcio Periodístico de Chile, S.A. (Copesa).

This rising competition, however, has gone hand in hand with the concentration of media property. Thus, in reality, what we are witnessing is the diversification of outlets possessed by the large media groups. Such concentration of ownership undoubtedly provides for a degree of influence over the formation of public opinion. The incursion of particular businesses or social groups into the realm of media is not always, as one might suppose, motivated by commerce or politics. The profusion of Protestant religious broadcasts is an unprecedented phenomenon in our country, and it is noteworthy for both the financial strength they have demonstrated and their rate of expansion.[1]

Socio-cultural changes in the media are closely tied to their unquestionable social relevance in the modern world. Television is the most influential medium, since it not only communicates, but also generates new forms of social interaction. The prominent role of TV in our time has redefined daily domestic life, people's lifestyles, and the various forms of entertainment and information. It also provides mass access to an audio-visual logic that displaces simple oral or written language, as well as facilitates the emergence of a cultural industry based on entertainment and advertising.[2]

Television viewing as an activity varies both socio-economically and seasonally. The peak viewing period in Chile extends from March to October, with its highest point in July. From October to February, average daily viewing is less than two hours. Workdays are the highest viewing days of the week, with Monday being the top ratings day. This pattern is the inverse of newspaper reading habits.

This frequency distribution generally applies to all socio-economic groups, although there is an inversely proportional relation between socio-economic level and television viewing. Thus, on workdays members of the lower class (stratum D) watch at least two hours of TV per day every month of the year, and they exceed that amount during at least eight months. Viewing by this group peaks during May, when its members watch three hours of TV per day. By contrast, the highest-income groups do not watch more than an hour and a half of TV per day during any month.

These high rates of TV viewing rest materially on the fact that, based on 1996 statistics, in the country's urban areas there are an average of 1.89 television sets per home (2.77 in high-income homes, 2.04 in middle-class homes, and 1.59 among the lower class) (CNTV 1996a). Altogether, 97% of Chilean homes possess a television.

The elderly and children view the most television, with the latter reaching an annual average broadcast TV exposure of 1.41 hours per day (CNTV 1996b), without accounting for cable TV (CATV) viewing. This viewing frequency correlates with the high value that the general public assigns to TV. The public assigns television an average value of 5.4 on a scale of 1 to 7, with little difference between broadcast and cable television (the former receiving a rating of 5.3 and the latter a rating of 5.4) (CNTV 1996c).

---

1   A good example is Radio Portales, bought by the Misión Poder Pentecostal, directed by Pastor Fernando Chaparro.

2   In a study in the late 1980s, watching television was the second most common family activity (Céneca-Flacso 1988), and in a 1997 study, 32.4% of people indicated that watching TV was their primary free-time activity, compared to 12.7% of respondents who predominantly listen to music (Adimark 1997).

Applying classical socio-demographic distinctions, we can determine that the upper class and youth are the groups most attracted to cable television. The upper-income bracket assigns broadcast television a grade of 4.7, compared to the grade of 5.5 given by the lower class. Nonetheless, there is practically no difference in how these two economic groups rate CATV. Meanwhile, young people give cable a rating of 5.8, compared to the mean rating of 5.3 given by all other ages. Analyzing the data by sex, we see that men view broadcast TV less favorably than CATV, while women value both types of TV equally.

The cultural value afforded TV is directly related to the socio-economic level of the population. For the majority (51.8%) of lower-class individuals, TV is a positive contributor to the creation of moral values. An even higher percentage, 58.4%, believes TV helps unite the family. In general, as we advance up the socio-economic scale, there is a more critical assessment of TV and the education it provides. Among the highest-income sectors, only some 20% of people agree with the lower-class assessment mentioned above.

People appreciate TV because they consider it informative, entertaining, relaxing, and, in the case of certain programs, educational (CNTV 1996c). As an information medium, TV is rated as the preferred source for news about what is happening in Chile and around the world. Of the respondents to the National Television Survey carried out in 1996, 80.1% named TV their top choice as a source of information. Compared to the other media, respondents said they perceived TV as the most accurate, informative, objective, and entertaining medium (CNTV 1996a).

The particular appeal of radio, on the other hand, is based on its affirmation of daily and family life, as well as its social role as a forum for public and private expression. Thanks to the expansion of the medium's network of broadcasters and its flexibility and dynamism in adopting new formats and types of programming, radio functions as an avenue of expression and recreation for an increasingly broad and heterogeneous public. Changes in lifestyles have allowed the formation of a more direct relationship between broadcaster and listener. Radio stations offer easily-understood language, effective geographical and physical proximity, and a capacity for fine segmentation with respect to the public's differing socio-cultural attributes, especially among FM stations. This provides a wide range of opportunities for the audience to interact on the public stage, establishing anonymous and intimate ties with each other and with third parties.

Radio also plays an important role in formulating public opinion. It offers a public space with ample room for debate on the issues of daily life. The medium presents itself as an area free of censorship, where it is possible to raise a question without face-to-face confrontation, and where a seemingly private, almost intimate atmosphere can be created between the broadcaster and listener.

With regard to magazines and newspapers, the changes have been much subtler. In the face of a growing diversification of interests, these media have had to confront an increasingly fragmented audience. In the case of newspapers, this has required the presentation of various themes within the same package. Among magazines, it has resulted in the proliferation of new, more niche-oriented publications.

For print media, this decade has meant confronting the demands of a more pluralistic and heterogeneous social structure than that of the 1980s. In response, and supported by technological modernization, each medium has diversified its content, for example by adding new sections and weekly supplements to its traditional structure. These additions are no longer designed to satisfy a specific target audience, but rather multiple audiences.

Print media has been forced to assume a more dynamic format to transmit different types of information and messages, complicating the structure of each publication.

The focus on multiple audiences within one publication may lead to seeming contradictions. This possibility is elevated by the gradual emergence, in some periodicals, of a more interpretive style of journalism. Thus a single newspaper, reporting freely and in depth within differing contexts, might present various interpretations of the same issue. All this is made possible by the expansion of political freedom in Chile.

Distinct audiences, along with emerging themes that open up new market niches, multiply the styles and targeting efforts of each medium. In the magazine market, political and opinion publications have become scarcer, and those that remain have notably altered their styles. This displacement is giving way to a distinct thematic segmentation, in response to the fragmentation of the public and the diversification of communication systems. The rise of these market characteristics has been accompanied by the increasing sophistication of the media, in line with the population's rising income and consumption levels. Thus, a new elitism can be observed in media offerings, regarding the audiences targeted and the issues discussed.

The local media aim to satisfy certain information, entertainment, and education needs among the populace, and at the same time they are capable of stimulating public debate about issues of specific interest. Provincial newspapers and radio stations represent vital sources of communication and connectivity in the daily life of the local population.

Finally, in the area of technology, the main innovations have taken place in television. The rapid spread of the video cassette recorder, the massive market presence of cable television, and the introduction of electronic ratings systems, together with the use of satellites in signal transmission, have redefined the way we produce and view television. Print media too have undergone a considerable technological overhaul, as seen in the use of computers for design, editing, and printing. Nonetheless, the impact of these changes on the reader is less evident than the effect of television's changes on viewers. In radio, new technologies have led to cost reductions and higher-fidelity transmission, leading numerous stations to move over to the FM band. Also, some pioneering radio stations have begun to use digital technologies in editing programs, although audiences are surely unaware of the difference.

The technological advances in the television industry are reflected in today's programming styles and the type of programs receiving high ratings. As we discuss in greater detail below, one result of these technological changes has been an increased focus on local programming with which domestic viewers can identify.

I. Changes in Print Media

In the late 1980s, the national media, particularly the main conglomerates, faced a set of dilemmas. The country was entering a transition from a political situation which had remained stable for a long time to a phase that threatened to be marked by conflict. During the authoritarian period, the leading media groups had identified closely with the military regime. It was now clear to these companies that they would have to make adjustments to their editorial philosophies and even to their commercial operations. The large media chains shared with big business a mistrust of the Concertación government, and they felt that they must move quickly to avoid being left in a potentially uncomfortable financial position.

Yet while the print media have undergone significant transformations in response to political changes, they have not come close to exhausting the possibilities offered by the country's concurrent economic and technological progress. The period that began in 1990 has been a time of massive change. In a context of increasing competition, politics must be seen as one of the multiple factors affecting the large newspapers' commercial fortunes. This should not, of course, obscure the fact that the leading media conglomerates play a clear, though not always explicit, role in the formation of public opinion.

Our intention in this chapter is simply to highlight the major milestones in the transformation of the print media in Chile. To that end, we will present an analysis of the leading newspapers, classified by media group, with the aforementioned analytical focus in mind.

1. THE POWER OF *EL MERCURIO*

Toward the end of the military government, the El Mercurio media group was having serious financial problems. Its estimated debt at the time was 14 billion pesos, 60% of which was controlled by the government bank (*Banco del Estado*). Confronted with the imminent end of the military regime, El Mercurio S.A.P. transferred its debt to the private sector with the assistance of the bank's president at the time, Álvaro Bardón.[3] These difficulties notwithstanding, the media consortium's investments provided the basis for a technological modernization that complemented its solid role as a shaper of public opinion. Thus, at the end of the 1980s, El Mercurio continued to be the most powerful media force in the country, consisting of a network of 13 regional newspapers,[4] plus the morning newspaper *Las Últimas Noticias* and the afternoon paper *La Segunda*, aimed at informing the political elite.

The aforementioned 13 regional newspapers comprise 31.7% of the country's 41 existing regional papers. Adding Santiago newspapers, the total number rises to 48, of which El Mercurio possesses one-third, or 16 papers (SECC 1995).

After the financial crisis of the 1980s, the group strengthened economically during the first Concertación government and maintained its power as a key reference point for public opinion. In 1992, it was able to increase its advertising revenues by 30% over the preceding year, and in 1993 it added color printing to its format. In an atmosphere of dynamic progress and competition, *El Mercurio* reached an agreement with the women's magazine *Paula* in November 1992 to provide the magazine free each month to the newspaper's subscribers. *Paula* thus increased its circulation to 42,000, and the newspaper improved its competitiveness among the middle and upper classes.[5]

---

3 Some estimates claim that the treasury lost 12 million dollars in this transaction.

4 This network includes *La Estrella* of Arica, *La Estrella* of Iquique, *El Mercurio* of Calama, *La Prensa* of Tocopilla, *La Estrella del Norte* of Antofagasta, *La Estrella del Loa* in Calama, and *El Mercurio* of Antofagasta, all newspapers belonging to Empresa Periodística El Norte S.A. The newspapers *El Mercurio* of Santiago and *La Estrella* of Valparaíso are managed by Empresa El Mercurio S.A.P. *El Diario Austral* of Temuco, *El Diario Austral* of Valdivia, *El Diario Austral* of Osorno, and *El Llanquihue* of Puerto Montt belong to Empresa Periodística Araucanía S.A. (SECC 1995).

5 In 1992, 47.7% of its readers were middle-class and 45.3 % were upper-class; in 1995 the proportions were 54% and 41%, respectively. This indicates that the newspaper had made significant headway among the middle class, thereby threatening *La Tercera* (BBDO 1995).

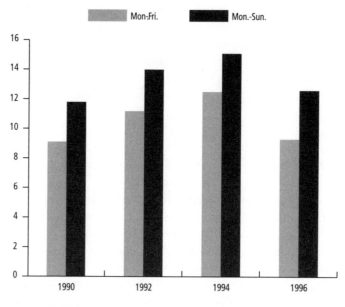

FIGURE 2

EL MERCURIO READERSHIP LEVELS
MONDAY-FRIDAY • MONDAY-SUNDAY

Source: Search Marketing

During the same year, *El Mercurio* began to publish a monthly supplement on various topics and started overhauling its thematic supplements, which were directed toward specific audiences (Sports, Countryside, *Ya* magazine, Twenty-first Century, Weekend, TV Weekend, Contact Zone, Home and Decoration, Sunday Magazine and Book Review). Some of these supplements have exhibited a progressive specialization. *Siglo XXI* (Twenty-first Century), for example, has moved from a general science orientation to an exclusive focus on computer-related issues. *Revista del Domingo* (Sunday Magazine) underwent a similar change, moving from a general magazine format to one specializing in travel narratives and tourism information.

Furthermore, *El Mercurio* utilized these supplements to present a variety of ideological/cultural orientations that did not necessarily represent its own editorial directives. The newspaper has become a forum for a widening range of opinions and values, enabling it and its advertisers to gain access to specific market niches. Thus the publication can shift from the highly critical viewpoints predominant in *Zona de Contacto* (Contact Zone, created by a group of young journalists assembled by Alberto Fuguet in late 1992), to the more conservative positions in the Sunday Section D reports, directed toward readers of the ABC1 stratum who are interested in daily political events.

With these adaptive changes, the newspaper has managed to reconcile its political identity with the pressures of the market, which has meant targeting specific audiences, composed of people who are experiencing the cultural changes that accompany modernization. As shows, readership has generally remained stable during the indicated time period, tending to increase until 1994 and then falling back to the level exhibited at the start of the decade. This drop cannot be attributed exclusively to the behavior of *El Mercurio* readers, but rather correlates to a general decline in readership levels throughout the country. Nonetheless, it is important to note the difference between weekday and weekend levels of that newspaper's readership. The three-point difference, with Saturdays and Sundays exhibiting the greater readership, is the highest of any newspaper in the country.

The newspapers *Las Últimas Noticias* and *La Segunda* have also undergone modifications. In mid-1993, the traditional newspaper *Las Últimas Noticias*[6] separated itself administratively, financially, and journalistically from its parent company and formed its own corporation. The paper thereby changed its headquarters, and its staff terminated their contractual relationship with El Mercurio company, although it continues to use the latter's printing presses.

La Segunda improved its graphic quality and increased its size, while maintaining its well-defined profile as an afternoon newspaper aimed at readers interested in the public sphere and particularly in political events. Sixty percent of its readership is middle-class and 32% upper-class. In addition, this afternoon daily has moved toward a more complex journalistic approach, whereas in past decades it had exhibited a rather sensationalist editorial policy. It enriched its thematic variety, both in factual reporting and commentary on the cultural world. Although *La Segunda*'s market position was not at all threatened until the end of the indicated period, the newspaper carried out various advertising campaigns intended to strengthen its image as an agile and dynamic news-seeker. As of mid-1997, the only effort to establish an afternoon paper with an editorial philosophy distinct from that of *La Segunda* was unsuccessful.[7] Thus, until the end of 1997, when competitor *La Hora* was introduced, *La Segunda* was able to retain an undisputed position in its niche.

2. COPESA'S PURSUIT OF THE EMERGING MIDDLE CLASS

El Consorcio Periodístico de Chile S.A. (Copesa)[8] began to develop in the 1980s, when it acquired a 35% share of the newspaper *La Tercera* from the Picó Cañas family. That newspaper was dominant among middle-class readers, as it still is today. In November 1998, the Picó Cañas family founded the newspaper *La Cuarta*,[9] taking advantage of the lack of media focusing on the public represented by the C3 and D strata; that is, they established a consortium directed toward the lower-middle and lower socio-economic groups.

La Tercera and *La Cuarta* enjoyed quite solid positions in the market, illustrated by the fact that *La Cuarta* had absolutely no competition for its target readers and that *La Tercera* outpaced *Las Últimas Noticias* during the 1980s and continued to do so in the 1990s (Figure 3). Still, by the end of the military government, *La Tercera* was indebted to the State, owing

---

6   This newspaper is aimed at the lower-middle class, bridging the gap between *La Tercera* and *La Cuarta*. Fifty-four percent of its readers are middle class and 43% lower class. This situation could change with the hiring of Andrés Benítez, former supplements editor of *El Mercurio*, who became editor of the newspaper on December 1, 1997.

7   The publishing company Sopel was formed for this purpose, assembling directors of the defunct magazine *Apsi*. However, the project never came to fruition due to financial problems.

8   Formed by Juan Carlos Latorre Díaz, Álvaro Saieh, Carlos Abumohor, Alberto Kassis, and Sergio de Castro.

9   Three out of four *La Cuarta* readers belong to the lower class, and the remaining portion belong to the middle class.

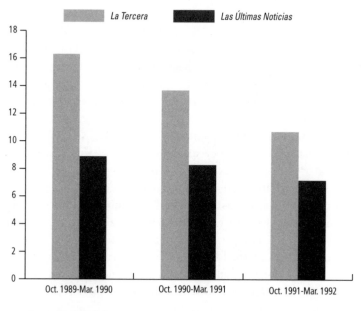

FIGURE 3

READERSHIP: *LA TERCERA* VS. *LAS ÚLTIMAS NOTICIAS*

Source : Search Marketing

the *Banco del Estado* 374 million pesos. This debt was expunged when the newspaper agreed to provide the government TV channel (TVN) with advertising space in exchange.

In 1990, the Picó Cañas family sold its shares of *La Tercera* and *La Cuarta* to the Copesa business group. Copesa drew up an aggressive market penetration strategy that entailed the incorporation of diversified media outlets. In the early 1990s, it acquired the magazine *Qué Pasa*, a share of the television station *La Red*, and joint control of the newspaper *La Época*. The aim of this expansion, as indicated by one of the partners, Juan Carlos Latorre, was purely commercial: competition obliges businesses "to diversify to survive," (*Revista de Publicidad* 76, July/August 1992).

Like *El Mercurio*, *La Tercera* captures a segmented public via its supplements (including subjects such as sports, the business world, women's interests, a TV guide, the home, and entertainment), which during the first half of the 1990s were aimed at the C2 stratum of the population. This focus clearly coincides with the profile of its readers; in 1995, 68% of them belonged to the middle class, 24% to the lower class, and only 9% to the upper class (BBDO 1995).

Seeking to retain its position as the newspaper with the highest national circulation, *La Tercera* set the objective of reaching the emerging middle class. This translated into a reformulation of the newspaper, beginning in September 1994. *La Tercera* altered its design, structure, and content, incorporating more photographs and computer graphics and dividing the paper into five well-defined sections: news, business, sports, Greater Santiago, and Tercer Tiempo (culture and entertainment). In September 1995, further changes were made to the Sunday edition, adding contributions from a cluster of prominent

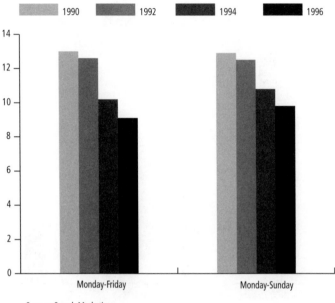

FIGURE 4

LA TERCERA READERSHIP LEVELS
MONDAY-FRIDAY • MONDAY-SUNDAY

1990 1992 1994 1996

Source : Search Marketing

journalists (Fernando Villegas, Patricia Politzer, and María Eugenia Oyarzún, among others) to its special reports supplement. This reformulation process continued in 1996, when the newspaper once again redesigned its supplements.

Nevertheless, the downward trend in readership continued despite these modifications, as indicated in Figure 4. To confront this situation, Copesa hired Fernando Paulsen as editor of the newspaper in early 1997. Paulsen's objective was to bring a more flexible and inquisitive journalistic spirit to the paper, with "new informative approaches, new informational fronts, and changes in journalistic processes," (*Medios & Publicidad* 25, March/April 1997). The newspaper's style was to become more modern, open, pluralistic, and competitive. With that, *La Tercera* distanced itself from its historical ties with the most authoritarian elements of the Chilean political spectrum. The changing composition of its reporting staff further confirms this shift in direction. Certainly, this transformation can be analyzed in terms other than political ones, since it accompanied an effort to attract a segment of the population which is actively improving its socio-economic status, modifying its attitudes and values, and becoming more critical in the process.

Since November 1997, Copesa has also published a new p.m. daily intended to compete with *La Segunda*. The newspaper, called *La Hora* and also edited by Fernando Paulsen, presents a clean and simple layout style and is oriented toward a reading public similar to that of its competitor: middle- to upper-middle-class readers interested in politics. In contrast to *La Segunda*, *La Hora* thus far has emphasized more straight news and investigative reports, while paying less attention to social affairs.

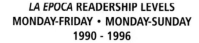

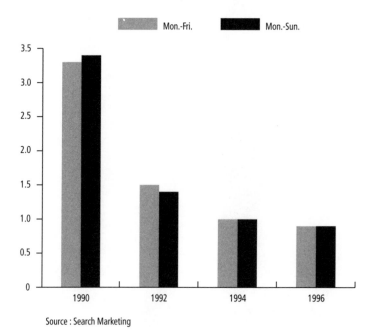

FIGURE 5

**LA EPOCA READERSHIP LEVELS
MONDAY-FRIDAY • MONDAY-SUNDAY
1990 - 1996**

Source : Search Marketing

3. LA ÉPOCA: AN ATTEMPT TO BREAK UP MEDIA HEGEMONY

In 1987, a group linked to the Christian Democratic Party founded the newspaper *La Época* in an attempt to produce a serious and modern alternative medium, following European models such as *Le Monde* in France and *El País* in Spain. Much more than journalistic ambition stood behind this project: the intention was to create a cultural enterprise that could wrest away some of *El Mercurio*'s influence as a shaper of public opinion among the country's elite upper class.[10] A team of journalists was assembled, headed by Emilio Filippi. Despite its high aspirations, the project exhibited weaknesses from the beginning. When the media company was formed, its founders were unable to raise the US$8 million necessary to launch the newspaper.

The founding partners collected only half that sum, making up the difference through outside credit. Simply to service these loans, the newspaper would have to rise to a sales level of 70,000 copies per day within the space of one year. Contrary to the owners' expectations — and despite the fact that this watershed political period was a favorable one for new periodicals — *La Época* did not meet sales projections. During its first year, the newspaper's top sales levels reached only half of the target figure.

10 In fact, *La Época* has been read predominantly by the middle class (65%), with a more modest upper-class readership (27%).

Paradoxically for *La Época*, the inauguration of the democratic government created more obstacles than advantages. The new government's communications policy involved a hands-off approach, so that the periodicals politically close to the administration did not enjoy any particular support. To this was added the predominantly political tone of the newspaper (expressed in the importance accorded to political issues and the subject of human rights), and its image as a supporter of the administration at a time when the public was becoming increasingly disinterested in politics. The end result was a sharp decline in sales between 1990 and 1992 (see Figure 5).

Poor financial management further aggravated the situation. By 1991, *La Época*'s debts had climbed to nearly 3.3 billion pesos. The newspaper responded by re-launching the paper in the middle of that year with much fanfare, but without significant changes in either the style of the publication or its financial situation. *La Época* then began negotiations with Copesa to ensure its survival as a company and to avoid bankruptcy. In April 1992, *La Época* reached a preventive legal agreement with its creditors[11] and signed contracts agreeing that Copesa would take charge of the printing, distribution and marketing of the newspaper. In January 1993, Ascanio Cavallo replaced Emilio Filippi as editor. These changes inaugurated a new phase in which two separate companies were formed.[12] These companies made up the board of directors of Inversiones Publicitarias S.A., which took charge of the newspaper's day-to-day operations.

Copesa's reason for expanding to incorporate *La Época* was clearly commercial: the conglomerate thereby acquired a medium directed toward the upper-middle and upper classes, which until that time it did not possess. This enabled it to compete on that level with *El Mercurio*.

As a result of its new corporate structure, on May 12, 1993, the newspaper inaugurated a new style, consisting of layout changes, the newspaper's division into two sections, a strengthened emphasis on cultural and economic issues, and the expansion of its Friday and Sunday supplements. This renovation had a healthy effect on the newspaper's ability to attract advertising, which rose 29.3% between January and November of that year. Nonetheless, as indicated in Figure 5, the overhaul had no effect on readership which, from 1991 on, shows a clear downward tendency. Even the improvement of the supplements did not manage to raise weekend readership.

Despite the involvement of a powerful business group in the newspaper, *La Época* did not receive the massive injection of capital needed to turn its situation around. Nor were its changes in format extensive enough to bring about a rebound in readership. Under Cavallo, *La Época* continued its already-familiar history of ups and downs. Consequently, by mid-1994 the multimedia business conglomerate had already decided to sell its share of the newspaper. Ownership was renegotiated in September 1995, with Copesa retaining a minority share of 20%, while Radio Chilena corporation acquired the remaining 80%.

---

11   Banco del Estado (689 million pesos), Comunicaciones y Desarrollo S.A. (468 million pesos), Banco Sudamericano (151 million), Codesa Cesionario Banque Pariente (144 million), and Banco de Santiago (109 million), as well as other private individual creditors.

12   The companies were Nuevo Amanecer S.A. and Nueva Imagen S.A., the first composed primarily of professionals and entrepreneurs linked to the Christian Democrats (such as Fernando Molina, Alberto Coddou, and Luis Ajenjo) and the second made up of Copesa executives (including Juan C. Latorre, Álvaro Saieh, and Carlos Abumohor).

Ascanio Cavallo left his post as editor, and Mario Fernández was chosen to replace him. Fernández would later resign to become Undersecretary of War. The newspaper proceeded with an administrative reshuffling, while at the same time lowering costs, as a product of its association with the radio station. As a result, *La Época* has recently rebounded in circulation, settling at a level of about 10,000 copies a day, after having fallen to half that amount in the preceding period. The publication is nonetheless far from having stabilized.

A few other newspapers with specialized outlooks should be mentioned here. Tremendous difficulties have been faced by periodicals closely associated with militant political positions. *Fortín Mapocho* disappeared at the start of the decade, and *El Siglo* was forced to convert to a weekly in order to stay in business. As a counterpart to this phenomenon, newspapers specializing in economic and financial topics, such as *Estrategia* and *El Diario*, have gained new strength. *Estrategia*, founded in 1978, has maintained a leadership position, currently ranking in third place among all media in the attraction of advertising dollars. *El Diario*, begun in 1988, underwent a change in image and content in July 1994, when the Ricardo Claro multimedia group bought a 42% stake in it.[13] *Estrategia* nonetheless remains the leader in this segment of the market.

4. ADVERTISING EXPENDITURES IN PRINT MEDIA

The distribution of advertising dollars in print media has been extraordinarily stable throughout the decade (see Table 2). In spite of this general stability, which is far more pronounced than in other media, several interesting shifts and other noteworthy phenomena have occurred.

TABLE 2

NEWSPAPER ADVERTISEMENT INVESTMENT, 1990-96
(in percentages)

Newspaper	1990	1992	1993	1994	1995	1996
El Mercurio	67.7	66.2	62.2	59.2	63.3	61.6
La Tercera	18.0	14.4	14.5	14.5	13.8	14.4
Estrategia	0.0	7.3	8.7	11.3	9.3	9.3
LUN	4.4	4.1	4.6	4.8	4.7	4.2
La Segunda	2.1	3.2	3.7	3.8	3.5	3.8
El Diario	0.0	-	2.0	2.3	1.4	2.0
La Nación	2.0	2.7	2.0	1.5	1.5	1.3
La Época	4.8	1.2	1.4	1.3	1.1	1.4
La Cuarta	1.0	0.8	0.9	1.2	1.4	2.1

Source: Megatime.

---

13 Through Ediciones Financieras S.A., Claro formed a professional team composed of Roberto Pulido, Roberto Undurraga, Mauricio Hoffman, Andrés Velasco, and Nicolás Vergara (*Apsi* 502, May 28, 1995).

El Mercurio has typically accounted for two-thirds of all advertising expenditures in print media. While this concentration has tended to decline slightly over the course of the decade, *El Mercurio* still receives 47% of total print media advertising dollars at present, thereby maintaining a significant distance from its nearest competitor.

La Tercera, which directly follows *El Mercurio,* has also shown tremendous stability in its ability to attract advertising. With the exception of the 1990-92 period, its variations have never exceeded one percentage point. The same trend is seen with *Las Últimas Noticias*, although at 4% of advertising dollars it is in a much lower category. *La Segunda* and *La Cuarta* are on the rise and have nearly doubled their share of total advertising revenue. *La Época* and *La Nación* are suffering a downward trend, although in both cases their share of advertising is very low. The more dramatic fall has been that of *La Época*, which at the start of the decade had an advertising share of some 5%, but in the following years fell to about 1%, further worsening in 1995.

5. THE DIFFICULTIES OF MEASURING NEWSPAPER READERSHIP

In 1987, the National Advertisers' Association (ANDA) and the Chilean Association of Advertising Agencies (ACHAP) called for bids to carry out a study of readership levels for Santiago newspapers and those of six other cities, and to analyze reader profiles (such as readership tendency as related to property ownership). The winning bid was presented by Search Marketing, and the company began to provide information on readership levels. Search obtained this information with survey samples of 7,560 in each application (1,080 interviews for each day of the week). The interviews were carried out in homes among persons above age 15, who were asked what they had read the previous day. Limitations of this study included the frequency of the reports; the difficulty of capturing particular segments of the sample; an analysis by medium which was too general and did not specify sections of the newspapers; the lack of sorting by geographical sectors within Santiago; and insufficient data about general and specific reading habits. Search Marketing has acknowledged the validity of the criticism, but has stated that, at the time the bidding was carried out in 1987, the information gathered was believed to be sufficient.

Given the difficulty of adequately defining the segmentation of the different reading publics, ANDA and ACHAP called for a new bidding process in early 1995.[14] The goal was to determine readers' socio-demographic profile, and according to José Medina, president of ANDA's Market Studies Committee, to "link the data on the reader profile for a particular newspaper, for a particular section of the medium, with reading habits as related to buying habits" (*ANDA* 46, April 1995). This initiative received financing from the media consortia El Mercurio and Copesa, and the winner of the bid was the same company that had won the previous bidding: Search Marketing.[15] The first of these studies, which would enable the analysts to pin down reader profiles for Santiago newspapers, used a sample of

---

14 This bidding process had the full backing of the powerful ANDA, but the support of industry representative ACHAP, judging by the tenor of the comments of then-president Julián Morrison, was not so evident. (*Mercado & Publicidad* 14, May/June 1995).

15 In general, media market studies carried out in Chile receive 80% of their finances from the media and 20% from advertising agencies. Individual advertisers do not finance these studies, as they feel that their agencies' commissions cover these costs.

TABLE 3

EXTENT OF NEWSPAPER READERSHIP

Newspaper	DESUC April-May 1996	SEARCH April-June 1996	DESUC April-May 1996	SEARCH April-June 1996
	Monday to Friday		Monday to Sunday	
El Mercurio	11.1	16.3	25.4	36.7
La Tercera	21.0	19.2	28.6	26.1
LUN	11.7	11.4	16.5	17.1
La Época	2.3	2.3	2.6	3.0
La Cuarta	15.5	13.8	19.3	17.0
La Segunda	3.7	4.2	n/a	n/a
La Nación	1.1	1.3	1.4	1.4
Estrategia	3.1	1.7	n/a	n/a
El Diario	0.4	0.5	n/a	n/a

4,360 subjects between April and June 1996. The study used a weekly-reminder methodology via telephone calls to the upper-middle and upper-class sectors and personal interviews for the C3 and D strata (*ANDA* 58, Oct. 1996).

Immediately after Search released the results, Copesa questioned them, saying the study did not control for the "image bias"; that is, a reader's tendency to claim he or she reads a certain newspaper in order to present a more socially prestigious image. This factor, according to Copesa, affected the middle class in particular, slanting the results in favor of *El Mercurio* at the expense of Copesa's publications. The conglomerate later withdrew its support of the study and continued its market analysis with the help of the Sociological Research Department (Desuc) of the Catholic University of Chile.

Table 3 compares and contrasts the studies carried out by Search (supported predominantly by *El Mercurio*) and those carried out by Desuc (contracted by Copesa), over highly similar time periods. The studies vary greatly in their assessment of readership, from Monday through Sunday, of the two main newspapers of the conglomerates in question.

If we focus on these two newspapers and analyze the disparities between the studies on the basis of socio-economic level (see Table 4), we make a suggestive discovery: the greatest differences for *El Mercurio* readership are concentrated in the ABC1 stratum (20% difference) and in the C2 stratum (more than 10% difference). The difference becomes extremely pronounced when we look at *El Mercurio*'s readership from Monday to Sunday in the C2 stratum, which is practically twice as large in the Search study than in Desuc's. There are differences among the other groups as well, but they are much less significant.

The extreme differences noted call for a detailed study that goes beyond the framework of the aforementioned research. Unfortunately, there is currently no entity capable of carrying out this type of analysis while providing guarantees to all involved.

In addition to the efforts already cited, since 1988 the Marketing and Research Department of the BBDO advertising agency has analyzed sales and market share for newspapers and magazines. The analysis surveys 128 newsstands in areas of Providencia, Apoquindo, downtown Santiago, Estación Central, Irarrázaval, Independencia,

TABLE 4

COMPARISON OF EXTENT OF READERSHIP: EL MERCURIO AND LA TERCERA

Newspaper	DESUC	Search	DESUC	Search	DESUC	Search	DESUC	Search
				Monday to Friday				
	ABC1	ABC1	C2	C2	C3	C3	D	D
El Mercurio	38.5	59.7	16.7	28.5	3.3	8.0	4.3	2.9
La Tercera	13.3	13.3	29.3	21.3	21.0	25.0	14.1	15.6
				Monday to Sunday				
El Mercurio	79.1	89.9	37.3	67.7	16.5	27.8	7.1	10.1
La Tercera	33.0	16.6	39.3	28.4	29.2	33.8	20.4	22.0

Source: DESUC and Search.

Recoleta, and Gran Avenida. The limitations of this study include its focus on circulation and not readership, along with the tendency of the sample composition to skew the information collected.

All of these difficulties point to the need for our country to establish a Circulation Verification Institute (IVC), as found in other nations. Such an agency, established as an objective and neutral third party, would enable us to gather rigorously accurate information about the print media market. Without such an institution, this market will continue to lack basic transparency about its most elemental characteristics.

II. Magazines: A Segmented Market

The magazine market in Chile is characterized by low readership levels, compared to those found in most countries with literacy rates similar to our own. In addition, the market is quite fragmented, a characteristic which became more accentuated after 1988. The medium is segmented with respect to the types of magazines that exist, as well as to the particular audiences they address, in accordance with readers' personal interests and buying power.

1. OWNERSHIP STRUCTURE AND ADVERTISING EXPENDITURES

Changes in Magazine Advertisement Investment

Between 1980 and 1990, spending for magazine advertising, as a share of total media advertising expenditures, increased 1.15 percentage points, rising from 6.1% in 1980 to 7.25% in 1990 (*ANDA* 14, Sept. 1991). By 1997, however, this share had fallen to 4.99%, almost two-and-a-half points below its 1989 level. Over the first five years of the 1990s, investment in this medium had dropped 18%. Growth for the 1990-96 period reached 42% only because of a spectacular recovery of 73.3% in 1996 (see Figure 6). We are as yet unable

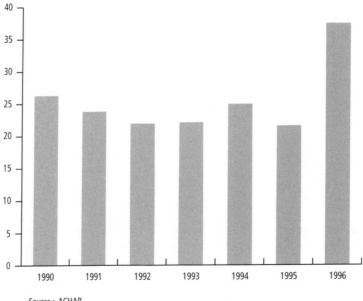

FIGURE 6

MAGAZINE ADVERTISEMENT INVESTMENT 1990-1996
(in millions of 1995 dollars)

Source : ACHAP

to find an explanation for the surprising dynamism exhibited in 1996. In any case, these figures show that the magazine market has grown at half the pace of the strongest media sectors.

It is surprising that advertising in this medium exhibits such a stark decline while the other media markets are growing. Nevertheless, it can be explained in part by the grave financial problems faced by many of the country's magazines, especially the so-called opinion (or political) publications, which have mainly been pushed out of the market. Another factor is the high concentration of advertising expenditures among a few periodicals. In 1990, half of this investment went to the market's top six magazines (*Cosas, Caras, Paula, Qué Pasa, Vanidades,* and *Hoy*). Six years later, with a higher overall number of magazines being published, that share had continued to rise, reaching 67%.

In addition to this advertising concentration, the magazine market is segmented, with a bias toward upper- and middle-class groups. An illustration of this phenomenon can be found in Figure 7, which indicates that all of the top-selling magazines in Chile attract at least 80% of their readership from these income groups, and in four out of five the proportion is 90%.

This situation translates into a clear segmentation of the target audience and the type of advertising purchased within this medium. Thus, while magazines cannot compete with radio, television, or newspapers in the coverage of their audience,[16] when it comes to

---

16 This refers to magazines' current readership share within the potential audience, composed of all those who have ever read a magazine, without necessarily having purchased it. This readership share generally hovers around 30% of the population.

FIGURE 7

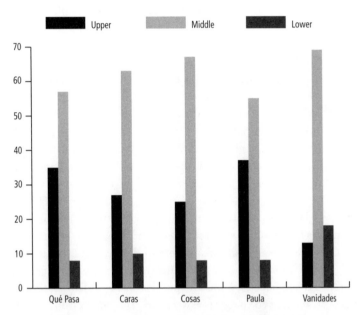

PRIMARY MAGAZINE READER PROFILE BY SOCIO-ECONOMIC LEVEL
(in percentages)

Source: Search Marketing, "Panorama de los Medios en Chile." BBDO, December 1995

carving out niche markets, they are quite viable and efficient (*ANDA* 42, Oct. 1994). This is especially true if we consider that the messages they transmit to the reader are more enduring, accessible, and sophisticated than those of other media. The profitability of magazines, therefore, does not rest primarily upon mass distribution, but rather on the use of targeted advertising. Success in this medium is determined not so much by the number of copies sold but by the ability to maintain a certain harmony between the magazine's editorial approach and the advertising it contains.

Publishing Groups

Large business conglomerates exist in the magazine market. Analyzed by investment share, the five most important are Editorial Televisa, Editorial Tiempo Presente, Editora de Publicaciones S.A., Holanda Comunicaciones, and Consorcio Periodístico de Chile. Ranked by magazine circulation per conglomerate, the leading ones are Editorial Televisa, Holanda Comunicaciones, Editora de Publicaciones S.A., Editorial San Luis, and Tiempo Presente.

The Editorial Televisa group (Editorial Andina until 1994) is majority-owned by the Azcárraga-Laviada family of Mexico. This group has developed its business with a strategy of market globalization. Its strength is in segmenting editorial content according to the characteristics of each market where its publications have a presence.

In Chile, this group controls the magazines *Vanidades*, *Caras*, *Cosmopolitan*, *Ideas*, *Marie-Claire*, *TV y Novelas*, *Condorito*, *PC Magazine*, *Nintendo*, *Geomundo*, *Mecánica Popular*, and *Conozca Más*, as well as the children's magazines *Barbie* and *Disney*. It also distributes

Tú, Buen Hogar, Harper's Bazaar, Men's Health, and, since November 1997, the Spanish edition of *National Geographic.*

The consortium's editorial policy for the magazines *Caras* and *TV y Novelas* is to keep the publications independent and restrict its intervention to distribution and marketing matters. Editorial Televisa controls 40% of advertising pages published, and *Caras* magazine enjoys the highest advertising revenue in the Chilean market. *Vanidades* and *TV y Novela,* however, account for 82% of the publisher's total investments (*Mercado & Publicidad* 22, Sept./Oct. 1996).

Editorial Tiempo Presente has Mónica Comandari as editor, Cristián Plaetner-Moller as general manager, and Mario Balmaceda as operations manager. It publishes the magazines *Cosas* and *Casas* in Chile, and *Cosas* in Peru and Ecuador.

Editora de Publicaciones S.A. (Epsa Comunicaciones) belongs to Roberto Edwards, Rubén Caro, Roberto Yáñez, and Germán Frick. It publishes the magazines belonging to the Paula Comunicaciones Group: that is, *Paula, Paula Práctica,* and *Proyectos Especiales.*

The Holanda Comunicaciones Group, owned by Juan Ignacio Oto, publishes the magazines *Miss 17, Video Grama, Cine Grama, Publimark,* and *TV Grama.* This group also owns Sociedad Ercilla Ltda., whose partners are Juan Ignacio Oto and Manuel Cruzat. They publish *Ercilla* (since its reintroduction in 1994), *Vea,* and *Deporte Total.*

Aside from these powerful groups, others in the market include: Editorial Hernán Garfias S.A., which publishes the magazines *Diseño, Casa Diseño,* and *Mercado & Publicidad;* Editorial San Lucas, which buys publishing rights from Editorial García Ferrer in Argentina and publishes the magazines *Ser Padres Hoy* and *Muy Interesante;* and the EDITAS Group, which publishes specialized magazines such as *Cocina, Vinos del Gourmand, Automóvil Club,* and *Buena Onda.* Finally, *Gráficas Deportivas* belongs to a company which is 40% controlled by the magazine's publisher in Spain, with the other 60% distributed among various businesspeople linked to the Chilean national sports scene. This group also publishes the magazine *Don Balón.*

2. WHAT DO PEOPLE READ?

Readership Levels

On average, magazine readership as a percentage of the population hovers around 29.5%. This figure has tended to increase since 1990, when it was only 25%. Table 5 shows the ratings of the leading magazines, grouped by category. In the area of news or opinion magazines, *Qué Pasa* maintains a comfortable lead, having doubled its readership in the period shown. In second place is *Ercilla,* which, despite disappearing from the market for a prolonged period, has succeeded in regaining the readership level it possessed in 1990. The magazine *Hoy* has experienced a rather sharp decline, although this slide has apparently come to a halt in the last year. In the category of women's magazines, the clear leader is *Paula,* which doubled its readership from 1990 to 1996; however, it peaked in the middle of the period with 4.8 points and has since declined. Following is *Vanidades,* with a behavior similar to that of *Paula.* The third segment consists of society magazines, which achieve the highest readership. Here, *Cosas* has been the most widely read. The sustained climb of *Caras* is nonetheless noteworthy, as it has risen from 1.3 to 4.5%. *Muy Interesante* leads the science-related magazines, with a readership of 2.3%. Youth and children's magazines draw a significantly lower percentage of readers. Entertainment magazines, on the other hand, display

TABLE 5

MAGAZINE READERSHIP*
(total population)

Type	Magazine	SeptDec. 1990	SeptDec. 1991	SeptDec. 1992	SeptDec. 1993	SeptDec. 1994	July-Dec. 1995	July-Dec. 1996
Opinion	Qué Pasa	1.4	1.6	2.1	2.3	2.9	3.0	3.2
	Ercilla	1.0				1.1	1.4	1.0
	Hoy	1.1	1.2	0.8	0.5	0.6	0.5	0.5
Women	Paula	1.7	2.3	2.6	4.8	4.4	4.4	3.4
	Vanidades	1.7	2.1	1.9	2.8	2.8	3.1	1.9
Society	Cosas	4.4	5.5	5.4	6.3	5.3	6.8	6.1
	Caras	1.3	2.5	2.2	3.5	3.5	4.1	4.5
Scientific	Muy Interesante	1.9	2.5	1.4	2.2	2.1	2.2	2.3
	Conozca Más	0.2	0.4	0.5	1.0	1.0	1.1	0.9
	Geomundo	0.1	0.4	0.1	0.2	0.2	0.2	0.1
Youth	Miss 17	1.3	1.1	1.3	1.5	1.3	0.7	0.7
	Rock&Pop				0.0	1.5	1.5	0.6
Entertainment	Vea	1.5					3.0	4.1
	TV y Novelas					2.4	2.3	2.2
	TV Grama	2.0	1.7	1.6	2.0	2.1	2.7	2.1
	Video-Cinegrama	0.4	0.1	0.2	0.2	0.1	0.1	0.1
Others	Condorito	0.9	0.4	0.7	1.1	0.5	0.8	0.5
	Reader's Digest	1.2	1.2	1.3	1.0	0.7	1.7	2.1
TOTAL AVERAGE		25.0	28.7	27.1	33.1	29.9	33.0	29.8

Source: Search Marketing, 1996.

* Random sampling of magazines.

high readership. *Vea* reigns in this category, with 4.1%, followed by *TV y Novelas* and *TV Grama*. All of these enjoy very stable readership levels. Finally, the publication *Selecciones del Reader's Digest* has a respectable audience, with 2.1% of mentions in the most recent survey.

Each of these magazine categories has undergone a process of market segmentation, pursuing specific niches of the reading population on the basis of socio-demographic variables (age, sex, income level, education) and cultural characteristics, which are identified with specific lifestyles.

Types of Magazines
An analysis of each magazine genre is presented in Table 5, using the publications currently receiving the greatest share of advertising revenue in each genre as examples.

Opinion Magazines
It is noteworthy that of all commentary or opinion magazines existing during the 1980s and early 1990s, the only ones remaining in the market are *Qué Pasa, Ercilla,* and *Hoy.* In a later

section of this chapter, we examine the structure and character of these magazines more closely. *Qué Pasa*, a weekly with a circulation of 25,000, is directed primarily toward middle- and upper-class men (although the percentage of women readers has already risen to 41%), with its highest concentration among readers aged 35 to 44 with some college education. The magazines *Hoy* and *Ercilla* have the same profile and almost the same circulation (24,000 copies).

Women's Magazines

The magazine *Paula*, belonging to the Paula Communications Group, reached an agreement at the end of 1992 for distribution to the *El Mercurio* Readers' Club, thus joining the EPSA Communications Group. This enabled *Paula* to expand its circulation to a captive market of readers, reaching a specific market niche with 80,000 copies a month (*Mercado & Publicidad* 23, 1996). With this, *Paula* moved to establish itself among the audience of young women ages 20 to 24, of the upper and middle classes and with college degrees.

Vanidades, which has been published for more than 35 years, is aimed largely at the mature women's market (ages 45 and above) among the middle and upper classes. It sells approximately 23,000 bi-weekly copies (*Mercado & Publicidad* 22, 1996) and leads in the lower-middle class market, (followed by *Paula* and *Cosas*). The magazine is based in Miami, with six society pages incorporated in Chile.

The problem faced by women's magazines in general stems from the competition represented by women's supplements in newspapers, as these have recently shown drastic improvement in the quality of their content and printing, becoming true weekly magazines.[17]

Society Magazines

Cosas is a bi-weekly publication with an approximate circulation of 32,000 copies, directed primarily at upper-class women (of the ABC1 and C2 strata) between ages 25 and 44, having a high school diploma and some college. The bi-weekly *Caras* has the same profile, with an approximate circulation of 22,000. The publication is characterized by its approach to political news, which combines a journalistic touch with magazine glamour. It sells some 18,000 copies every two weeks.

Scientific Magazines

Muy Interesante is currently the leading mass-distribution publication in this category, with a monthly circulation of 40,000 copies. Published by Editorial San Luis, it also deals with scientific and technological developments, including supplements on specific topics in some issues. It began monthly publication in August 1987. The magazine *Conozca Más*, published by Editorial Andina, is a monthly with a circulation of 22,000, which also deals with scientific and technological subjects.

---

17 Entertainment and sports magazines face the same problem, although the factor of printing quality has been less significant. Newspaper supplements offer weekly entertainment reviews, offering commentary on events and people. The increased social importance of soccer and, to a lesser extent, tennis, has led to daily newspaper inserts on these sports.

Youth Magazines

Miss 17 magazine emerged in 1989 under the direction of Holanda Comunicaciones. It is a bi-weekly with an approximate circulation of 30,000, directed toward upper-middle-class adolescent girls between the ages of 15 and 18.

One of the most successful magazine debuts was that of *Rock&Pop* in 1993, which targets the youth market and has a circulation of 24,000. At first, *Rock&Pop* reached only the upper class, taking over the spot previously occupied by the magazine *Tú*. It later made significant headway among the middle class as well. The publication's marketing strategy involved an energetic subscription drive, through which it acquired extensive readership and became an attractive product for advertisers. However, since the departure of editor Iván Valenzuela, the magazine has demonstrated a certain lack of focus which has resulted in readership losses.

Entertainment Magazines

Vea, the most enduring magazine in the entertainment category, appeared in 1939 as a continuation of *Crack*. After remaining in the market for more than 50 years, it suspended publication from October 1991 to December 1992, starting again in 1993. It is a bi-weekly with a circulation of 55,000, aimed primarily at female high school graduates between the ages of 25 and 34. *Vea* nonetheless has a significant male readership.

The magazine *TV y Novelas*, debuted at the time of the Viña del Mar Festival in 1994, has an average bi-weekly circulation of 54,000. Its target audience is predominantly adolescent and female, and its readership is distributed equally among the various socio-economic categories. The other major publication in this category, *TV Grama*, is a weekly with a circulation of 50,000. It is the leading TV programming schedule magazine, and it is read primarily by lower-class, adolescent females. Both publications have advertising exchange agreements with television stations, arising from the obvious interrelation between the two media types.

3. WHO READS WHAT?

Of the 10 magazines with the largest readership in 1996, two are in the society genre (*Cosas* and *Caras*), three cover the world of entertainment (*TV Grama*, *Vea* and *TV y Novelas*), two are women's magazines (*Paula* and *Vanidades*), and one is a news magazine (*Qué Pasa*). The remaining publications are *Selecciones del Reader's Digest* and the weekly *Datoaviso*.

The upper-income group prefers *Paula* and the two society magazines (*Cosas* and *Caras*), followed by the weekly *Qué Pasa*. In the middle-income group, society magazines head the list, followed by *Paula* and *Vanidades*. After these come the entertainment magazines (*Vea* and *TV Grama*), which did not appear among the top preferences of the aforementioned income group. Among the lower class, entertainment magazines (*TV Grama*, *TV y Novelas* and *Vea*) lead the ranking, followed by *Cosas* and *Paula*. Other significant entries are the sports magazine *Don Balón* and the humor magazine *Condorito*. In short, the upper-income group prefers society and informative reading. This trend continues into the middle-income group, which also adds entertainment publications. Lower-income groups tend to read television, society, sports, and humor magazines.

In analyzing reading habits by gender, we find that men have rather heterogeneous preferences. Among the five magazines most read by men, there are two society magazines

(*Cosas* and *Caras*), one sports magazine (*Don Balón*), a newsmagazine (*Qué Pasa*), and one miscellaneous: *Selecciones del Reader's Digest*. Among women, there is a greater thematic concentration, with society and women's magazines (*Paula* and *Vanidades*) being top preferences, followed by entertainment magazines (*TV Grama*, *Vea*, and *TV y Novelas*). Of the 10 magazines most read by women, not one weekly news magazine is on the list. For men, by contrast, two of the top 10 publications are weekly news magazines.

Among younger readers, aged 15 to 19, the most-read magazines are entertainment publications (*TV Grama* and *TV y Novelas*), followed by sports magazine *Don Balón* and youth publication *Rock&Pop*. Following these are society and women's magazines (*Paula*), with *Miss 17* closing out the list.

As we advance to higher age brackets, readership of entertainment and sports magazines declines, and we begin to see a greater prevalence of news magazines. In the 44-and-above age group, such publications have a 20% share of the top 10. Nevertheless, in all age groups except adolescents, society magazines and *Paula* occupy the top spots.

Executives' and professionals' magazine reading habits tend toward informative periodicals in the economic, political, and scientific spheres (*Qué Pasa*, *América Economía*, *Gestión*, *Muy Interesante*, *Time*, etc.), and a high percentage of "other" category publications. The latter indicates that the interests and preferences of members of this reading group are highly segmented (Search Marketing 1995).

The preferences of the population as a whole during this decade have been exhibited in the dominance of society magazines (*Cosas*, *Caras*, and *Paula*)[18] over informational publications. In 1991, news magazines held respectable positions in the readership ranking, but many of them later disappeared from the market. In that year, middle-class men and women preferred the magazines *Análisis* and *Apsi*. However, by 1996 the only news magazine remaining popular among readers was *Qué Pasa*, aimed primarily at the middle and upper classes (Search Marketing 1996).

4. THE CHANGING OPINION MAGAZINE MARKET

The development of opinion magazines during this period may be characterized as a progressive decline, as politics became less associated with people's daily concerns. Under these circumstances, these types of magazines had to alter their profile, curbing or eliminating more militant journalism and downplaying issues such as human rights. Their slow rate of adjustment and their failure to recognize the changes taking place in civic society led to rapidly falling sales of these magazines, since they depended more on socio-political trends than on advertising. As a result, magazines like *Cauce*, *Análisis*, and *Apsi* disappeared from the market. The following paragraphs present a summary of the opinion magazine market from the late 1980s to the present.

Sociedad Editora La República, linked to Masonic and Radical circles, published the bi-weekly *Cauce* beginning in November 1983. This was one of the first victims of the attrition in this category, closing in December 1989. Throughout its six years of existence, it generally maintained a 45-page layout. It had no advertising at the start, but by 1984 had acquired four pages, increasing to its maximum of six by 1989. *Cauce*'s controversial

---

18 Although *Paula* is a magazine directed primarily at female readers, its editorial approach attracts a broader audience.

image, which cost it two six-month suspensions in 1985 and 1986, was abandoned in 1989 for a more theoretical and intellectual leftist line. This change nonetheless failed to prevent its demise at the onset of the democratic transition.

The magazine *Análisis*, sponsored by the Christian Humanist Academy and linked to the moderate left, came into being in 1977 and continued until 1993. In 1990, it began to undergo a series of modifications, reducing its focus on national politics and placing a greater emphasis on literary and cultural issues. *Análisis* in those years remained critical of the democratic government, mainly for failing to support the media which had opposed the military regime.

At the start of 1992, the magazine instituted improvements in printing quality and expanded its advertising space, yet it was unable to reverse its financial situation, and it closed down in 1993. In addition to the magazine's financial difficulties at that time, its editor Francisco Martorell was mired in a conflict over the censorship of his book *Impunidad diplomática*.

Apsi was the most enduring political magazine of the time. It was launched in July 1976 and closed in September 1995. *Apsi* (Agencia Publicitaria y de Servicios Informativos) emerged as a sort of analytical summary of international political events, in the style of an "information service." In mid-1979, it incorporated national analysis, maintaining the same format. It gradually began to delve into the political issues typically addressed by political magazines in the 1980s. It took on a stance of clear opposition to the military regime, aligning itself with the moderate left and constantly questioning the moral, political, and legal legitimacy of the government.

Starting in 1992, it became less confrontational in character and granted more space to cultural and social issues. Nevertheless, *Apsi* was forced to ceased publication in September 1995. The main causes of its failure were its lack of financial support and its unsatisfactory adaptation to the new environment in Chile.

The magazine *Hoy* was founded in June 1977, with Emilio Filippi as editor and Abraham Santibáñez as assistant editor. It did not take an editorial approach of strong opposition to the military regime, and in fact it provided a platform for many government figures and those ideologically linked to the regime. However, it gradually began to establish a point of view distinct from the official government line, taking an analytical approach toward political and economic issues. The publication had approximately 64 pages, with a significant portion (nine to 22 pages) devoted to advertising. The magazine's leading departments included national news, culture, the economy, and society.

By 1985, *Hoy* still exhibited its original structure, but with Hernán Millas as writing director it had taken on an unmistakable image as a moderate opponent of the regime. Thus it focused on political and human rights issues, while continuing to strongly emphasize national news, art, and culture. Toward the end of the 1980s, Abraham Santibáñez took over as editor-in-chief and Hernán Millas as assistant editor. The magazine retained its earlier characteristics, while adding discussions of ecological issues and the importance of natural resources, as well as increased coverage of cultural and entertainment topics.

In 1990, *Hoy*, edited by Marcelo Rozas, continued with almost the same formal structure as before, but allowing more space for political opinion interviews. The magazine upgraded its paper quality and began to highlight economic and business issues, along with the culinary arts, health, fitness, and other lifestyle topics. In 1996, with Ascanio Cavallo as editor, it adopted a more pared-down, dynamic, and flexible approach to news, incorporating sections like "Los Tiempos de Hoy," and fortifying its economy and special reports sections, without neglecting the traditional importance of the cultural section.

In the 1980s, *Ercilla* was the country's longest-standing magazine, having existed without interruption since 1934. During that decade it was edited first by Joaquín Villarino and later by Manfredo Mayol. Under this leadership, the magazine expressed a rather traditional rightist viewpoint. It had 66 pages, of which 36% were advertisements.

As part of its sales effort in the late 1980s, the magazine awarded books as subscription premiums, including anthologies of history and international literature or thematic encyclopedias. Despite this effort, *Ercilla* faced a financial crisis in 1991, mainly attributable to a reduction in government advertising, according to then-editor Alejandro Molina. This crisis forced the magazine to discontinue publication.

Three years later, in March 1994, the magazine reappeared with a new publisher, Holanda Comunicaciones, and with Juan Ignacio Oto as editor. Although *Ercilla* retained the basic principles of its traditional editorial philosophy, it began to place more emphasis on current economic, scientific, and social issues than on politics, where it distanced itself from its previous conservative positions.

The most successful case of image overhaul in this category is that of *Qué Pasa*. Begun in 1971 under the direction of Editorial Portada S.A., the magazine offered a politically conservative alternative during that decade, with Gonzalo Vial as editor and an editorial board including Jaime Guzmán, Diego Ibáñez, and Jaime Martínez. During the 1980s, Roberto Pulido took over as editor. Graphic quality improved substantially, and advertising increased to a high of 15 pages. Around the middle of the decade, the publication reduced its total number of pages and lowered its printing quality. Yet by the end of the 1980s, *Qué Pasa* managed to reverse this slide.

In February 1990, Copesa bought *Qué Pasa*, retaining Roberto Pulido as editor. With 47 total pages and six of advertising, it focused its attention on political, economic, cultural, and social issues. The new format also included a different approach to political issues: the magazine shed its ideological slant and began to focus on the anecdotal or "human interest" aspect of the political game.

In August 1990, Cristián Bofill became managing editor of the magazine. For Bofill, success in transforming *Qué Pasa* from a "magazine in the political trenches to one of pure information" depended on responding to the public's new demands by broadening the spectrum of issues addressed, to include business, international news, science, and technology. At the same time, the periodical took on a watchdog role in the political arena, monitoring the government's promises and performance. With a team of young journalists "uninfected," as the editor put it, by the political vices of 1980s journalism in Chile, the magazine established a more critical posture, oriented toward "an elite audience of the country's influential people, who need to be informed."[19]

Thus, the magazine began to present politics as a social game, a drama of simulation and disguise. Business and economics, likewise, were analyzed as the interplay of powerful figures. In both areas, the magazine's essence consisted of looking behind stylish appearances to reveal the status games played for social recognition and influence. *Qué Pasa* thus

19 Interview with Cristián Bofill, editor of *Qué Pasa*, in the magazine *Mercado & Publicidad* 20 (May-June 1996), p. 45.

redefined the position of advocacy magazines, taking a suspicious view of political activity during a cultural transition in which such an attitude enjoyed undeniable social acceptance.

Since the mid-1990s, the magazine has consistently sought to put official versions of events to the test, as well as to broaden its potential audience among women and younger people by linking political issues to news of daily life in society. Its primary competition is not the other opinion magazines (against which it has a significant lead as the weekly with the highest readership and advertising revenue since 1991), but rather with *El Mercurio*. This competition has led *Qué Pasa* to redesign itself and to incorporate culture and society sections, probably as a reaction to *El Mercurio*'s restructuring of its Weekend supplement.

5. CURRENT CHALLENGES

The magazine market has experienced significant changes over the last few years. As we have seen above, these changes have been brought about by cultural modifications causing public issues, especially political ones, to lessen in importance among the people who buy and read magazines. Also evident is the powerful impact of rising disposable income among middle- and upper-income groups, which include the highest proportions of magazine readers. Publications have reacted by updating their designs, content, and editorial approaches, resulting in the proliferation of media directed toward highly sophisticated consumers.

There has not been a corresponding progression in knowledge about this market. Magazines, like newspapers, lack an independent circulation certification system, although some in the field have expressed interest in rectifying this situation. Consequently, the accuracy of the available circulation figures may be seriously questioned. Clearly, more complex data collection techniques can be devised, making it possible to dig deep enough into the profile of the magazine reader to discern specific habits and preferences within each category.

III. Radio in Chile: Public and Private Voices

1. RADIO, A MASS MEDIUM

Radio broadcasting is one of the most widely distributed and accessible types of media. Since its origin in 1922, radio has generally functioned as a rapid, effective, reliable, and pluralistic instrument for transmitting information of interest to the people. It has taken on a democratic role by providing a forum for diverse expressions of information, opinions, and entertainment by and for the people, enabling the creation of an effective link between the public and private worlds.

The cost reduction brought about by the advent of transistors made access to radio virtually universal by the 1970s. In Chile today, 97% of the population listens to radio, and 84% of people do so daily (Desuc-Archi 1996).

In the 1980s, under the authoritarian regime, various radio broadcasters provided a forum for dissidents and other critics of the government. The radio stations Chilena, Cooperativa, and Santiago (one linked to the Catholic Church, the others to the Christian Democrats), played a key role in the country as pluralistic and democratic media, providing an informational alternative to the official version of events (SECC 1996).

After the passing of that time of intense public and political debate, the strength of radio in this decade, perhaps more so than other media, has been its rapid and effective adaptation to the changing needs of its audience. At a time when people's identification with social and subcultural groups is being re-established, radio addresses the demand for the banal and familiar, for the private and compartmentalized, providing one of the few links existing today between the public sphere and private expression. Through radio, those who speak and those who listen are momentarily participants on a common stage, where their own experiences, opinions, and visions of daily life mingle with those of others. In fact, it can be said that talk radio programs constitute the "ultimate public forum,"[20] allowing for fully democratic participation. Radio is capable of creating an atmosphere of intimacy and connection between broadcaster and listener, appearing as a trustworthy and credible source of information. Finally, radio can easily vary its format according to the interests and tastes of the public.[21]

2. RADIO'S ECONOMIC DEVELOPMENT

Radio advertising expenditures, in absolute terms, have grown consistently since the 1980s. Taking that decade into account (see Table 6), spending has more than doubled. During the last half of the 1980s, however, growth was 59.2%, compared to 36.3% in the first five years of the 1990s. This slowdown in radio advertising growth is also illustrated in its declining share of the country's total advertising expenditures. In the 1980s, radio's share stood at around 10%, and since then it has declined steadily, with an especially pronounced slide over the last few years. Advertising expenditures in this medium peaked in 1990, only to fall to 3.1% of the total by 1995.

TABLE 6

RADIO ADVERTISING PARTICIPATION AND EXPENDITURES
1985-95

	1985	1986	1987	1988	1989	1990	1991	1992	1993	1994	1995
Registered Investment (millions of dollars)	22.8	26.2	28.5	30.9	36.3	35.8	37.8	46.3	40.0	42.5	48.8
Percentage of Total Investments	10.0	10.6	10.8	0.8	10.9	11.0	10.8	10.7	8.7	8.2	7.9

Source: ACHAP.

---

20 Ruth Mayard, adjunct professor at the University of Montclair, New Jersey, is cited here in the magazine *Archi* 17, March 1997.
21 Radio has clearly adapted to the needs of each era. In the 1980s, it exercised the role of the most reliable information source available. In the 1990s, it served as a forum for debate and a source of human companionship, as with the programs designed for rush hour drivers in Santiago.

Further, these advertising dollars are generally concentrated among a limited number of broadcasters, especially the large Santiago radio chains, while local and regional transmitters face severe financial difficulties. In fact, in 1995, the bulk of advertising income was concentrated among just 9.4% of the country's radio stations. This trend has worsened due to the absence of audience measurement instruments in local and regional markets; advertisers are reluctant to pay for commercials if they do not know the reach or impact of radio stations within the community. Due to these problems, along with the growing numbers of competing FM stations, many broadcasters have been obligated to sell airtime at certain hours, particularly to Protestant churches and to commercial promoters of alternative medical treatments. Under these circumstances, many stations have lost the capacity to offer a consistent style of programming and to establish a readily identifiable image among their listeners.

Small local radio broadcasters thus have serious difficulties in competing with large chains. The reluctance of large businesses to advertise with them leads to great financial insecurity (SECC 1996). To this must be added the decline in overall AM radio advertising, as growing numbers of listeners switch to the FM band. FM has enjoyed strong growth due to its low installation and operating costs, along with the high fidelity and sound quality it offers.

3. THE STRUCTURE OF THE RADIO MARKET

Technical Characteristics of National Radio

The broadcasting spectrum in our country is mostly composed of stations with a local radius; that is, with no more than 1 kW of power. Of the 864 broadcasters active throughout the country, 87.6% are at this power level, which clearly limits their audiences to the specific locality of transmission. Nearly 90% of the country's FM stations and 80% of its AM stations are located in the provinces (SECC 1995).

The high number of stations in operation has led to a full dial in several locations around the country. This is the case in Concepción, Iquique, Valparaíso, San Antonio, Chillán, Quillota, and five of the Santiago municipalities. However, in 1992, the Undersecretary of Telecommunications cut the broadcasting spectrum from 800 to 400 MHz — half of the requirement under international norms — to make room for new stations (SECC 1995). Therefore, in addition to financial problems, the radio industry faces technical problems derived from this saturation.

TABLE 7

RADIO STATIONS BY TYPE AND STRENGTH OF TRANSMISSION (1995)

Power Range	Total	FM	AM
0 - 250	226	16	210
251 - 1,000	453	96	357
1,001 - 5,000	17	15	2
5,001 - 10,000	87	43	44
10,001 - 50,000	7	7	-
50,001 - 100,000	2	2	-

Source: National Statistics Institute, 1995.

Various Forms of Ownership and the Large Radio Chains

Radio broadcasting in Chile is based on 543 broadcasting concessions awarded to individuals and corporations, upon which the country's 864 radio stations depend (Archi 1997). The broad range of business structures exhibited by broadcasting companies can be broken down into three general levels:

- A large number of small companies with limited, local, community, or regional reach, like Radio El Faro of La Serena, Radio Estrella del Mar of Chiloé, or Radio La Voz on the Osorno coast. In the majority of cases, these stations have 1 kW of output, which allows them to satisfactorily reach the population living near their point of transmission. Accordingly, these stations orient their programming toward a highly local audience, offering an ongoing forum for communications such as personal messages, community service announcements, local news, and so forth.
- Regional media groups located outside Santiago, which have tended to acquire other media properties. This is the case with Sociedad Bío-Bío Comunicaciones, owned by Nibaldo Mosciatti, which covers a large part of the country's southern region and whose FM station in Santiago began broadcasting in mid-1997. This concession, awarded at the end of 1995, filled the last opening on the Santiago dial.
- A handful of companies that are organizationally, financially, and technically solid and have formed national chains, thanks to the acquisition of regional media. Examples of this group are Radio Chilena S.A., which has broadcasters throughout the country, and Radio Finísima S.A., which emerged in La Serena in 1986 and soon began a progressive expansion to the northern and southern parts of the country, establishing itself in Santiago in early 1994.

It is important to note that radio chains can be organized in different ways. The most common type uses a powerful transmission system with booster antennas around the country. These chains exhibit the most centralized programming. Taking the opposite approach, some chains purchase or establish a string of local stations with customized programming.

The origin of the radio chains traces back to the economic boom of the early 1980s. At that time, two large radio companies were established: Radio Portales, belonging to the Vial-BHC group, and Radio Minería, belonging to the Matte and Cruzat-Larraín organizations.

Among Chile's leading radio chains today are:

- La Compañía Chilena de Comunicaciones S.A., owner of the radio stations Cooperativa AM and FM, Rock&Pop FM, and Corazón FM. Its top executive is Luis Ajenjo.
- La Sociedad de Comunicaciones S.A., owned, directed, and managed by Uros Domic, Jorge Saint-Jean, and Teresa Aránguiz. The group owns Nina FM and Metropolitana AM. Under the company name Recreo S.A., it also owns the station Recreo AM (Fifth Region), as well as the Sintonía FM and Cien AM stations, under the name Radio Publicidad S.A.
- La Sociedad Radio Concierto Ltda., owned by Julián García-Reyes Anguita, parent company of the stations Concierto FM, Horizonte FM, and Futuro FM. The company's general manager is Carlos Parker McPherson.
- Pudahuel FM Satellite Network, owned by Blaya y Vega S.A. since 1994. Its owners are Joaquín Blaya and Jaime Vega, who serve as general manager and operations manager, respectively.
- Radio Chilena AM, owned by La Compañía Radio Chilena S.A., which belongs to the Archbishopric of Santiago. It also owns Aurora FM under the name Sociedad Publicitaria

Aurora Ltda. Thanks to the growth of Radio Aurora, the company was able to expand, acquiring the Talca and Concepción units of Radio Nacional.
• The Mosciatti chain, a property of the Mosciatti group, started up in Concepción and Temuco in 1966. It has a presence in Santiago, Los Ángeles, Concepción, Temuco, Lonquimay, Osorno, Puerto Montt, Ancud, and Castro. It has also received approval for concessions in Arica, Antofagasta, Reñaca, San Antonio, Rancagua, Curicó, Talca, and Punta Arenas, where broadcasts are scheduled to begin during 1998.

While these chains have formed, the solitary state radio network has experienced an opposite trend. In May 1992, Radio Nacional began a restructuring process with the sale of its provincial affiliates, with the exception of the Arica and Punta Arenas stations (for national defense reasons). The state company needed to eliminate a mature debt of 1.2 billion pesos held with the Treasury (SECC 1994).

4. SHIFTS IN LISTENERS

In the infancy of radio broadcasting, AM stations clearly predominated. During the 1960s and 1970s, 87% of radio stations still transmitted in AM. As Figure 8 shows, this trend was not decisively reversed in Chile until 1990.

FIGURE 8

AM - FM RADIO STATIONS
(1960 -1996)

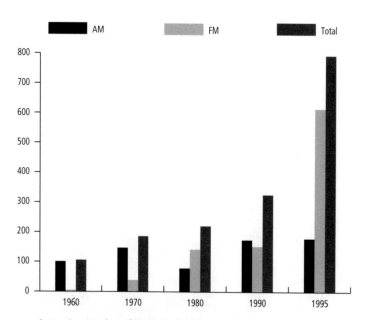

Source : Superintendency of Electric, Gas, and Telecommunication
Services (1960-1970). Subsecretariat of Telecommunications (1980).
National Statistics Institute (1990-1996).

FIGURE 9

AVERAGE AM-FM LISTENING AUDIENCE
TOTAL POPULATION 1988-1996
(in percentages)

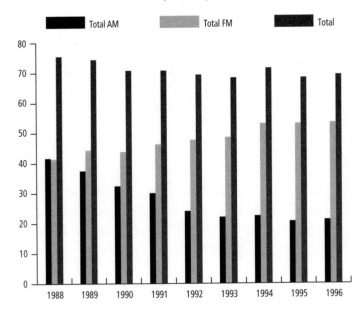

SOURCE: Search Marketing. 1996 is included with an estimated annual average.

FIGURE 10

PROGRAM PREFERENCES BY SEX
(in percentages)

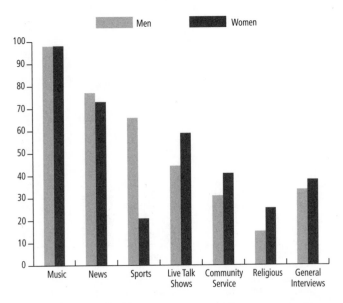

SOURCE: Desuc - Archi, 1996.

From that point on, AM radio has generally remained stable at 179 stations, while FM experienced a dramatic leap from 152 stations in 1990 to 614 five years later, an increase of more than 300%. By 1996, the number of FM stations had grown to 685.

Yet it has not been only the number of stations and their transmission characteristics that have changed. Beginning in 1990, the country experienced an overall decrease in radio listeners. This was mainly attributable to the extremely sharp decline of AM radio stations, which have lost half of their audience since 1988, falling from 42% of listeners that year to 21% in 1996 (see Figure 9). The rise of FM stations did not fully compensate for this decline, as the latter's listening audience climbed less than 15% during the same period.

This shift of listeners from one band to the other is seen across the various socio-economic levels. At the start the FM band was preferred by the upper class; consequently, the change has been much more accentuated among the middle and lower classes, particularly among women and listeners under the age of 24.

The audience shift to the FM band at first occurred exclusively in the area of musical programming, while AM broadcasters maintained their predominance in news and sports (SECC 1996). Later, however, Chile's FM stations themselves changed their format. In its early days, FM tended to broadcast classical and orchestral music. In the 1970s, stations broadcasting youth-oriented music in English began to appear, thus establishing FM as the preferred band of the middle and upper classes. By the late 1980s, the FM band had become relatively saturated with upper-echelon formats. It then began a growing appropriation of styles traditionally associated with AM stations: live interviews, romantic Latin music, news, talk shows, and even advice programs.

5. RADIO PREFERENCES

Radio listening habits vary according to socio-demographic variables (see Figure 10). Men and women prefer music and news programming almost equally. While sports programs appeal mainly to men, a large percentage of the female audience listens to live interviews, talk shows, community service programs, and religious programs.

There is no significant socio-economic distinction in preferences for musical programs. News programs, however, have more listeners among the middle and lower classes, by a difference of about 10 points. A similar trend occurs with sports programs, but with a sharper difference of 15 points. This tendency is also seen with live reporting, interviews in general, and community service programs. For religious programs, the size of the audience is inversely proportional to the socioeconomic level of the listeners.

In general terms, radio listening in Chile is seasonal, increasing in the summer months and declining in the winter (the inverse of television viewing habits). In addition, radio listeners tune in more often on weekdays. Radio listening habits are also clearly related to the amount of time available for this activity, which explains the higher rates among senior citizens, homemakers, and youth.

Despite this fact, the group of listeners tuning into the radio every day (more than 80% of the population) cuts across the variables of age, sex, socio-economic level, and education, and in general does not vary more than 4% on the basis of these factors.

The population segment most listening to radio is youth aged 15 to 24, with 87.2% tuning in, followed by women, with 86%. Furthermore, 85.9% of middle-class Chileans with an average level of education listen to the radio, a relatively higher level than that of other

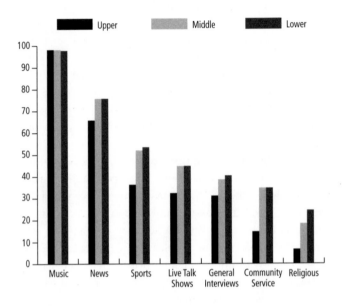

FIGURE 11

PROGRAMMING PREFERENCES BY SOCIO-ECONOMIC GROUP
(in percentages)

SOURCE: Desuc - Archi, 1996.

economic groups. Women tend to listen in the morning, from 9 a.m. to 1 p.m., while youths tune in during the evening and at night.

With regard to audience preferences for Santiago radio stations, we can observe a great variance in preferences for the AM band, shown in Table 8, along with a tremendous decrease in rating differences for the 10 main AM radio stations. The ratings difference between the first and last stations fell from 12% in 1990 to 4.2% in 1996.[22]

Within this trend, the AM station experiencing the largest decline was Radio Cooperativa, falling 8.4% over the six-year period. The other top 10 broadcasters also lost a proportion of their audience, with the exception of Radio Nacional, which rose 3.6% to share first place with Cooperativa. The only station demonstrating comparative stability is Radio Chilena. Three stations, Monumental, Cien, and Nuevo Mundo, have disappeared from the preferred list over the course of the decade. This overall ratings decline is linked to the general reduction in AM listeners, setting up a much more competitive stage than that which existed at the start of the decade. In 1990, the AM listening audience was 35.4% of the population, while six years later it had fallen to 21.5%.

On the FM dial, ratings variations have been less pronounced, but leading stations have tended to stand out more clearly from their less successful peers (see Table 9). The expanding listening audience for this band (from 42% in 1990 to 54.3% in 1996) has led to

22 This information was made available by Cecilia Navarro, manager of studies and media for Search Marketing.

TABLE 8

LISTENING AUDIENCES OF THE TOP TEN AM RADIO STATIONS IN SANTIAGO
Monday - Sunday*

Station	1990 Ranking	Rating	Station	1996 Ranking	Rating
Cooperativa	1	13.3	Cooperativa	1	4.9
Minería	2	5.9	Nacional	1	4.9
Portales	3	5.4	Chilena	3	3.5
Colo-Colo	4	3.9	Minería	4	3.2
Monumental	5	3.8	Portales	5	2.3
Chilena	6	3.6	Colo-Colo	6	1.9
Santiago	7	2.2	Agricultura	7	1.2
Cien	8	2.1	Armonía	8	0.9
Nuevo Mundo	9	1.4	Santiago	9	0.8
Nacional	10	1.3	Corporación	10	0.7

* Taken from the month of June each year.

Source: Search Marketing

TABLE 9

LISTENING AUDIENCES OF THE TOP TEN FM RADIO STATIONS IN SANTIAGO
Monday - Sunday*

Station	1990 Ranking	Rating	Station	1996 Ranking	Rating
Aurora	1	10.9	Rock&Pop	1	8.9
Carolina	2	10.8	Pudahuel	2	8.3
Pudahuel	3	8.0	Nina	3	7.4
Galaxia	4	4.7	Aurora	4	6.8
Concierto	5	4.5	Carolina	5	6.7
Tiempo	6	3.4	Romántica	6	6.5
Umbral	7	2.0	Zero	7	4.2
Sintonía	8	1.9	Concierto	8	3.2
Futuro	9	1.8	Universo	9	2.9
La Clave	10	1.7	San Cristóbal	10	2.4

* Taken from the month of June of each year.

Source: Search Marketing.

TABLE 10

TYPES OF FM RADIO, RATING, AND TARGET GROUPS, 1995

Radio Format	Adult Contemporary	Entertainment/ Latin Music	Progressive Jazz	Modern/ Youth	Orchestral/ Classical	Religious
	Horizonte	Aurora	Clasica	Rock&Pop	A. Bello	Armonía
	Infinita	Niña	Futuro	Carolina	Beethoven	
	Manquehue	Pudahuel		Concierto	El Conquistador	
	Universo	Romántica		La Ciudad	San Cristóbal	
	Finísima	Sintonía		Tiempo	U. de Chile	
		La Clave			U. de Santiago	
Diffusion	8.1	28.5	3.5	30.3	8.3	0.5
Upper Class	15.5	11.3	6.8	36.7	17.6	0.2
Middle Class	10.4	26.5	4.6	37.5	11.2	0.4
Lower Class	3.1	36.1	1.0	19.1	2.1	0.7
Men	7.8	19.0	5.4	33.7	9.7	0.5
Women	8.3	37.3	1.7	27.1	7.1	0.5
15 to 19 year-olds	7.6	18.2	2.3	93.2	0.8	0.3
20 to 24 year-olds	13.0	27.7	5.7	65.1	1.9	0.3
25 to 34 year-olds	11.5	36.0	5.5	30.5	4.5	0.7
35 to 44 year-olds	8.6	39.9	3.9	11.1	9.3	0.9
45 years and older	3.4	20.4	0.3	3.0	16.4	0.4

Source: Search Marketing, 1995. (Radio Zero and Radio Duna are not included in the Adult Contemporary format because they have only been on the air since October, 1995. Radio Viva and Radio Galaxia were excluded because they were shut down.)

an increase in the number of Santiago stations from 24 to 27, causing a minor slip in ratings for the most popular stations.

As a result of the massive changes in this band, 60% of the originally popular stations disappeared from the list by 1996. This indicates the high instability of the market. At the same time, as seen with the AM stations, the difference between FM stations has narrowed. In 1990 the distance between most and least popular stations was 9.2%, while in 1996 it was 7.5%. The stations' efforts to adapt to changing listener preferences is illustrated here in the successful debut of Rock&Pop and the recovery of Radio Nina. The latter, thanks to a change in programming (to tropical music), has moved to third place. Pudahuel has maintained its listening audience, while Aurora and Carolina, the first and second place stations at the start of the decade, have fallen to fourth and fifth place, both slipping by 4.1%. Radio Concierto experienced a more moderate decline of 1.3 points, falling from fifth to eighth place.

Finally, a specific typology can be established for the listeners of each radio band. The typical AM audience is composed of "infrequent listeners," often men between 35 and 44 years old. AM listeners are more likely to belong to the lower class, with the exception of those aged 45 and older, who are distributed more evenly among the different social classes. On the other hand, FM listeners tend to be habitual radio users. The audience is primarily composed of women under 45 and youths between 15 and 24, from the middle and upper classes (SECC 1996).

Market Segmentation: Radio Formats

Among the FM broadcasters, the audiences are segmented by programming format (see Table 10).

That is, these stations seek out market niches or specific target audiences. Currently, six leading radio formats can be identified in Chile:

• The *modern/youth* style, with Radio Rock&Pop leading the overall ranking since its debut. The competition is now more balanced, due to the increasing number of stations switching to this format. It is aimed at young men and women aged 15 to 24, of all socio-economic groups. Its peak listening hours are evening and nighttime. Despite efforts to incorporate Chilean rock into the format, North American-style music continues to predominate.

• The *entertainment/Latin music* style, preferred by women aged 20 to 34 in the lower class, and women aged 35 to 44 in the middle class, primarily homemakers. Its programming includes various musical genres traditionally considered popular. Of all FM styles, this is perhaps the one most influenced by a typical AM format: music in Spanish, a live disc jockey offering companionable talk, and the opportunity to participate, along with community service segments. The leading stations in this genre are Aurora and Pudahuel, which achieve peak listening rates during the morning.

• The *contemporary adult* style, aimed at men and women aged 20 to 34, of the upper and upper-middle classes. The leaders in this format are Horizonte, Manquehue, and Universo.

• The *progressive jazz* style, addressing a target audience of upper-class men between the ages of 20 and 44. Examples here are the stations Classica and Futuro.

• The *orchestral/classic* style, with a listening audience mainly composed of upper and upper-middle class men aged 45 and above. These include the Beethoven, Andrés Bello, El Conquistador, San Cristóbal, and Universidad de Chile stations. This style and the previous one reflect FM's traditional slant toward a more elite audience.

• The *religious* format, recently started in the FM band with Radio Armonía, with a listening audience that remains quite small.

IV. The Dizzying Change in Chilean Television

There can be no doubt about the importance of an analysis of television. It exhibits both the greatest dynamism and communicative presence of all media. Television's audiovisual nature, the relationship it establishes with the television viewer, its mass distribution and the nature of its programming contribute to making it a powerful cultural influence. This power of television is so significant that some analysts see it as molding a new cultural relationship. In contrast with the detachment between the reader and the first-person singular author of the written word, television generates a participatory and immersive relationship, stirred by emotions and communitarian sentiment, and bringing with it a weakening of the subject, along with a de-objectification of the object. This complex and dialectical process gives rise to a society in which meaning "could be configured as a conflict (or game) of interpretations and not as a true and defined reality."[23] We thus have before us a phenomenological perspective that makes the television industry a hub of socio-cultural transformation.

1. STRUCTURAL CHANGES

The Institutional Framework

Chilean television emerged experimentally in 1958, but it took 12 years for the country to set the ground rules for its operation. Constitutional Law No. 17,377, of October 24, 1970, reserved television broadcasting rights for the State and the University of Chile, Catholic University of Chile, and Catholic University of Valparaíso. This legal text also defined television's objectives.[24] It created the company Televisión Nacional de Chile and instituted a National Television Council (CNTV) in order to "guide," "supervise," and "regulate" television.[25] A mixed financing system was created, including the income earned by each channel as well as funds from the national budget and those apportioned through special laws.

During the military regime, the CNTV's powers were expanded, and its appointments came to depend completely on the executive branch. Through most of the 1980s, there were no drastic changes to the Chilean public television system. Only toward the end of the military government, in September 1989, did the regime issue Law No. 18,838, revamping the CNTV and bringing about the most radical change in Chilean television since its introduction. The law ended exclusive State and university control over television stations' property and operations. With that, Chile established a commercial model for the operation of television channels, with no structural counterweight. In the words of Twitchel, television "is first a marketing medium and second an entertainment medium."[26]

A great capacity to influence values and attitudes has been attributed to television, for which reason all societies have subjected it to a system of public regulation. Our country was no exception. The aforementioned legislation established that CNTV was responsible for "ensuring the proper functioning"[27] of television services and could supervise and regulate them for that purpose.[28]

---

23 See Carlos Catalán's work (1997), in which he comments about the contribution of Vattimo.

24 The objectives are: "To communicate with and integrate the country; to disseminate knowledge about basic national problems and inspire all Chileans to participate in the great initiatives undertaken to solve them; to affirm national values, cultural and moral values, and respect for the rights and dignity of individuals and the family; to promote education and cultural development; to provide objective information and healthy entertainment; and to assist in the spiritual and intellectual training of children and youth."

25 CNTV is composed of 15 members: the Minister of Education, who presides over it, along with a representative of the President; three advisors elected by the Senate; another three elected by the Chamber of Deputies; two representatives of the Supreme Court; the deans of the University of Chile, Catholic University, and Catholic University of Valparaíso; the president of TVN; and a representative of TVN's workers.

26 Cited in Brunner and Catalán (1995).

27 The law defines proper functioning as "the continuous affirmation, through programming, of the dignity of individuals and the family, and of moral, national, cultural, and educational values, especially the moral and intellectual training of children and youth."

28 The Council, under this new legislation, was now composed of seven members: two designated by the President, of which one was nominated with the Senate's approval; a third designated by the Supreme Court; two by the leaders of the Armed Forces and Carabineros; and two by the deans of the state universities.

To fulfill its mandate of regulating and overseeing television services, CNTV issued general regulations prohibiting TV broadcasts containing scenes of "excessive violence, offensiveness, pornography, or the participation of children or adolescents in acts contrary to morality or proper behavior." The board had the power to impose sanctions in the form of warnings, fines, or suspensions, and even to terminate broadcasting rights. The law established a system of concessions to be awarded by CNTV, allowing private individuals or corporations to enter the television industry. These concessions could be sold or transferred and had no expiration date. Acquisition of concessions was conditioned only on the technical availability of frequencies. The regulations permitted the opening of Chilean television to foreign investors, without entry barriers. There were no safeguards to avoid the concentration of media ownership (Brunner and Catalán 1995).

During its first two years of existence, the Council — presided over by former military government minister Alfonso Márquez de la Plata — exercised an active disciplinary function.[29] Nevertheless, two and a half years after the original law came into effect, the democratic government approved Law No. 19,131, which significantly modified its predecessor. This law redefined the "proper functioning" of television broadcasting from an active role in constantly affirming a set of moral values to the more moderate definition of programming that manifests "ongoing respect for the country's moral and cultural values; for the dignity of individuals; for pluralism; for the protection of the family; for democracy; for environmental protection; and for the spiritual and intellectual education of children and youth within this value structure."[30]

The Council's powers were limited to preventing the distribution of films not approved by the Cinema Ratings Board; imposing time-of-day restrictions on broadcasts of films rated for adults 18 and above; setting requirements for up to 40% domestic productions; providing support (with government funds) for television broadcasting in regions where there was no commercial interest in providing such services;[31] and, of course, imposing sanctions ranging from warnings to the termination of broadcasting rights. A new aspect of this law was that the sanction process would now involve hearings, with an opportunity for the alleged offenders to dispute the charges. Finally, the new law allowed any private citizen to file a complaint with the Council against a program he or she considered a violation of "ongoing respect" for the established set of values.

With this new law, Chilean TV now possesses a tough regulatory system capable of imposing harsh sanctions and subjecting a wide range of the medium's activity to supervision. This system extends to cable television, in spite of the fact that this involves limited services subject to a private contract between the cable user and the operator. Despite the

---

29 CNTV sanctioned Channel 7 for "violating the dignity of women, morality, and proper behavior," (Sept. 1990), for excessive brutality (April 1991), for the "repeated transmission of scenes of violence," and for broadcasting expressions considered "denigrating toward our heroes and patriotic symbols," (Sept. 1991). Megavisión was reprimanded for broadcasting violent scenes and required to pay a fine of 150 UTMs (Sept. 28, 1992) for violating Article 1 of Law No. 19,131, as a result of the appearance of the owner of Megavisión, Ricardo Claro, on the program "A eso de... ." In the case of Channel 13, the station was reprimanded for showing drugged-up youths on a soap opera. Finally, CNTV sanctioned UCV-TV during this period for showing a music video it considered pornographic.

30 Brunner and Catalán (1995) present a detailed discussion of this difference.

31 In 1997, a contest sponsored by the Fund for Television Programs of High Cultural, National, or Regional Interest offered an amount of 78 million pesos.

extent of control established during José Joaquín Brunner's period as Council president, from 1992 to 1994,[32] it has been said that the crux of the new relationship between the regulatory body and the TV channels is self-regulation. The CNTV "must make the decision to intervene only as a last resort, when certain limits clearly established by law are transgressed." The Council has continued to carry out its disciplinary role to the present day, sparking sporadic controversies. Meanwhile, the body has also strengthened its role in analyzing programming and viewing habits.

The People Meter

The second key event in the transformation of Chilean television has been the incorporation of a new audience measurement technique. Until early in the current decade, this was done using a notebook system.[33] In March 1992, winning bidder Time-Ibope put in place a people meter valued at US$4.4 million.[34] The system was installed in a sample of 300 homes in Santiago, stratified into four target groups (ABC1, C2, C3, and D). The sample is changed every six months. This instrument provides information about a home's electrical connection, whether the existing television sets are on or off, what channel(s) they are tuned to, and the number and identity of the viewers. The information is delivered on line; channels can therefore instantaneously detect any changes in their audience.

The people meter presents limitations in both its technical and sampling characteristics. It is technically accurate with respect to the number of television sets turned on in a home, but not with respect to viewer behavior, since determining this depends on their direct cooperation. With regard to sampling characteristics, it would seem the system functions well only at the level of statistical aggregates. The small sample size (300 homes, at first) is insufficient to detect the behavior of population subgroups, such as those formed by dividing the population by two or three socio-demographic variables at once. Tracking such groups is sometimes necessary for channels with low ratings (*ANDA* 60, Dec. 1996).

When the people meter was introduced, it confirmed the downward trend in the ratings of individual channels. This trend is explained by the fact that there are now six and not just four channels sharing the viewing audience. Thus, while the most successful programs used to enjoy ratings of up to 65 points, today it is rare for any program to receive 45 points, and reaching 20 points is significant. Second, as the audience of the leading channels declines, the distance between them and the smaller channels narrows. The data also show that children watch more television than was indicated by the previous ratings system, and that a significant number of viewers no longer regularly watch news programs.

The people meter has led to the establishment of a much more transparent and dynamic television market, as well as one which operates on much shorter time scales.[35]

---

32 Brunner would later be replaced by Pilar Armanet.

33 This method used a registry with one page for each day of the week, with each day divided into 15-minute blocks from 7 a.m. to 3 a.m. (the following morning). A designated person in each surveyed family was responsible for registering each family member's TV viewing. The Time company, in charge of audience measurement, collected the registries weekly.

34 This method costs 10 times more than the previous one. Eighty percent of the cost is shared equally among participating channels, and 20% is covered by ACHAP. Currently, the channels pay 14 million pesos per month to obtain the people-meter ratings.

35 For example, advertising agencies' negotiations with TV stations are now undertaken monthly, rather than annually as in the past.

FIGURE 12

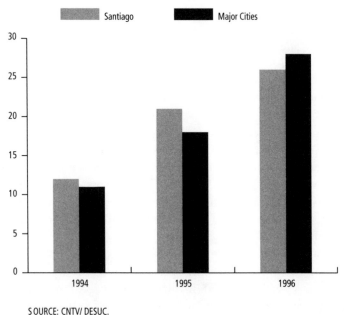

RATE OF CABLE TELEVISION EXPANSION
(1994 - 1996)

■ Santiago ■ Major Cities

SOURCE: CNTV/ DESUC.

The people meter has also contributed to redefining the logic of the television industry, by establishing a closer link between the audience's receptiveness to a program and the advertising dollars spent on it. The use of this ratings system thus affirms the advertising industry's influence in shaping the offerings on broadcast television.

The Expansion of the Television Market

The most recent of the major structural changes in television has been the expansion of its market through the introduction of cable television (CATV) and satellite TV.

The Explosive Growth of Cable and the Concentration of Ownership

The massive expansion of cable television in the last five years has been accompanied over the past two years by a significant concentration of CATV properties.

The first cable company in Chile, Intercom TV Cable (a subsidiary of Empresa Periodística El Mercurio S.A.P.), started up in Santiago in 1987 with a customer base of no more than 300 homes in wealthy neighborhoods. Four years later, the Argentinean company Metrópolis entered the market, covering the communities of Ñuñoa and La Reina, along with parts of Providencia and Las Condes. Other companies in the market in the early 1990s were Mundo Cable and TV Max, which by 1993 had been purchased by VTR Comunicaciones.

The truly explosive growth of cable television began in 1991. Previous to that year, the authorities had awarded two permits for the installation of cable services and three for microwave television services (CNTV 1994). Then, in 1991 alone, 46 cable permits and nine microwave television permits were authorized, and by June 1994, permits for limited-reception television had risen to 200, involving 75 companies. Of the total of 205 permits awarded up to mid-1994, 171 were actually in use at that time. This expansion vaulted Chile into fourth place in Latin America in the development of cable television, measured by numbers of subscribers, after Argentina, Mexico, and Brazil (*Producción & Distribución* 7, 1997).

In 1994, nearly three-quarters of cable subscribers were members of the upper class, and the rest were middle-class. One year later, a total of 487,578 homes subscribed to cable TV,[36] of which half were middle-class, giving an increase of 257.4% among that group. By contrast, upper-class subscribers only increased 2% during the same year, demonstrating that cable TV had already nearly saturated that stratum. According to the Desuc-CNTV television survey in 1996, total CATV subscribers had risen to 589,903. In reality, however, we can estimate that total nationwide access to cable television is approximately 755,000 households, or 23% of all homes, considering that some households access this service without subscribing (Marín 1997).

In conjunction with this huge expansion, CATV has also tended toward heavy concentration and internationalization of ownership. In 1995, just three companies controlled 95% of the market (CNTV 1994). VTR Cablexpress had an estimated total of 185,000 subscribing homes (38%), Metrópolis Intercom served 209,000 (43%), and United Holding International (UHI) had 80,000 (16.5%). The remaining 21 companies combined served only 12,000 homes.

Just one year later, the market was divided practically in two: Metrópolis Intercom controlled 43% and VTR Cablexpress (after a partnership agreement with UHI in the second half of 1996) had 55%. Over the course of two years, each of these large companies had undergone accelerated merger and concentration processes similar to those occurring in other Latin American countries.[37] According to Emilio Martinic (*Producción y Distribución* 7, June 1997), this did not occur as a consequence of competition over the same service areas, with certain companies achieving dominance through better-quality customer service. Instead, it was a manifestation of the financial capacities of the largest companies in the market.

The holding company VTR, owned by the Luksic group (with a 51% share) and Southwestern Bell (with the remainder), together with its subsidiaries VTR Telecable and VTR TVMax (microwave TV), bought 100% of the shares of Cablexpress[38] for about US$60 million, transforming itself into the country's largest limited-reception television company: VTR Cablexpress.

Further, in October 1995, the groups Cordillera Comunicaciones[39] and Invercom[40] merged to create Metrópolis Intercom, in a transaction with an estimated value of US$100 million. The new company was owned by Cordillera Comunicaciones (60%) and Invercom (40%).

---

36 C. Catalán (1995) provides a significantly lower figure (around 330,000).

37 Argentina, which has the most developed cable TV market in Latin America, with five million subscribers and a 50% penetration rate, has experienced an accelerated concentration process, in which three multi-operators (Multicanal, VCC, and VC) control almost half the market, in partnership with U.S. and Spanish companies. See *Producción y Distribución* 6, Florida, USA, June 6, 1997; and *Apertura* 12, Santiago, Dec. 1997.

38 Cablexpress was the property of Inversiones Penta, I.M. Trust, Teleducto, and executives of Sonda.

39 Cordillera Comunicaciones was owned 50% by Cristalerías Chile and 50% by Bresnan International Partners (a North American company 80%-owned by TeleCommunications Inc., the largest cable company in the world).

40 80% of Invercom belonged to CTC and the rest to El Mercurio S.A.P.

As has been the case in many parts of the world, the sport of soccer played a powerful role in this chain of mergers. The first company to utilize the sport as a resource was Cablexpress, which in 1994 obtained the rights to transmit the professional soccer league tournament for three years, through its winning bid of US$16 million. This provided the company with an exclusive marketing tool in its search for subscribers. VTR purchased Cablexpress in large part for that reason.

Facing a rival with exclusive rights for three years of national professional soccer, Metrópolis-Intercom attempted to stage a tournament involving the universities and other club teams. As the sport's regulations made this impossible, the company then acquired exclusive broadcasting rights for the Libertadores Cup. The two competitors thus achieved a tie, in addition to their nearly equal market share, so they agreed in 1997 to broadcast the two tournaments jointly.

Finally, we must stress that aside from these processes of market and ownership concentration, the eruption of cable television brought about a radical change in the television market. It signified a huge extension of total television broadcasting time, which at the end of 1995 passed the mark of one million hours of transmission annually. At the same time, the total number of channels reaching the country rose to 148, twice the 1994 figure. Channels received in the provinces, however, fell to an average of 54.8.[41] Within this astounding volume of broadcasting (2,700 hours per day), 67% of programs were specialized shows such as music videos, movies, sports, etc. In 1994, broadcast television transmitted 44,000 hours, rising to 49,000 two years later. During the same period, CATV went from 454,714 hours to 1,204,856. Together, broadcast and cable TV offered the impressive sum of 3,435 daily hours of transmission.

As CNTV discovered in an analysis in late 1995, advertising on cable television had fallen to 9% of total programming time, and just under half of that advertising time consisted of commercials presented by the cable operators themselves.

The vigorous entry of telecommunications and telephone companies into the cable television market should also be noted. Their presence, no doubt, anticipates the possible expansion of multimedia services and the pairing of domestic companies with large international conglomerates (Catalán 1995).

The Appearance of Satellite Television

The consequences of the rapid and massive expansion of cable television in Chile are still unfolding, and no systematic methodology has yet been implemented for measuring the viewing habits of cable audiences. Meanwhile, the television spectrum in Chile has expanded yet again with the introduction of satellite television. In March 1997, VTR Galaxy Chile[42] began selling its Direct TV service, allowing for direct downloading, via a Galaxy II-R satellite, of programming scheduled by the operating company in Miami. For Chile, the programming provides 60 movie channels alone and another 30 devoted to music (*Mercado & Publicidad* 25, 1997). The main advantages of the new medium include

---

41 The range extended from the 90 signals received in the Metropolitan Region to 17 in the Eleventh Region.

42 VTR Galaxy Chile is comprised of VTR Comunicaciones and Galaxy Latin America. The latter is made up of Hughes Electronics, a satellite manufacturer and the leading satellite television company in the United States; Cisneros Organization of Venezuela (ODC), the main Venezuelan TV company and one of the largest in the Spanish-speaking world; MVS Multivisión of Mexico, the largest pay-TV operator in Mexico; and Televisão Abril, a Brazilian media conglomerate.

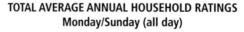

FIGURE 13

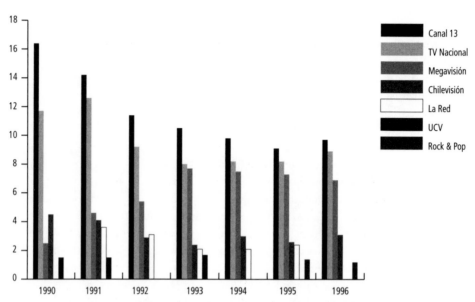

TOTAL AVERAGE ANNUAL HOUSEHOLD RATINGS
Monday/Sunday (all day)

Canal 13
TV Nacional
Megavisión
Chilevisión
La Red
UCV
Rock & Pop

the sharp quality of the image and sound; the option of blocking unwanted channels; its coverage of areas not served by cable; and the pay-per-view option, which offers recently-released films and other features. However, the system is expensive (about US$439 to purchase a satellite dish with a diameter of approximately 60 cm.), which for the moment restricts its use to high-income households. The fixed cost of renting the decoding apparatus is US$12 per month, and the costliest programming package is US$61.

For the moment, the operator itself regulates the new media, which by mid-1997 had about 2,500 subscribers. Using the decoder it rents to its subscribers, the company blocks signals that it deems to be in violation of Chilean law.

2. CHANGES IN RATINGS, PREFERENCES, AND PROGRAMMING

Changes in Ratings

At the start of the decade, the ratings situation was very clear, showing three distinct preference levels.[43] Channel 13 was first, with an average home viewing rating of above 16 points. Channel 7 was second with nearly 12 points, and third place and beyond were occupied by the smallest channels, none of which received more than five points. The first break in this order occurred in 1991, when the Catholic channel fell two points and TVN

---

43 The 1992 data stem from audience measurements made by the people meter from August to December. La Red began broadcasting in 1991 and in March 1996 terminated its subscription to the people meter. Channel 5 UCV-TV has participated intermittently in the study; it did not take part in 1992 and has not taken part again since 1994. The channel Rock&Pop began broadcasting in August 1995; therefore, its rating for that year represents its average from August to December.

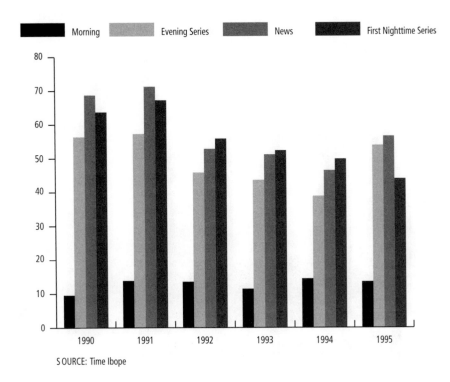

FIGURE 14

HOUSEHOLD RATINGS BY PROGRAMMING BLOCK
Monday-Friday (1990 - 1995)

Legend: Morning | Evening Series | News | First Nighttime Series

SOURCE: Time Ibope

gained one, leaving the distance between them at about two points. This difference remained stable from then on, while Megavisión gained almost one point.

This shift established a category composed of these three channels, ranging from 7 to 10 rating points. UC-TV has always maintained first place, but it experienced a sustained ratings decline from 11.4 points to 9.1 points between 1992 and 1995. TVN, meanwhile, has generally remained stable at around eight points. Megavisión suffered a minor slip of less than a point during this period. With regard to the lower-rated channels, Chilevisión suffered a sustained drop during the first three years of the six-year period analyzed, hitting its low point of 2.4% in 1993 before recovering slightly. La Red has experienced declining ratings from the start, from which it rebounded slightly in 1996.

The primacy of Channel 13 is also seen in the fact that six of its programs were among the 10 highest-rated in 1995. Channel 7 had three and Megavisión only one.

Analyzing the type of broadcasts that Channel 13 managed to place among the top 10 for 1995, we find that prime-time variety shows accounted for 58.9%, followed by movies, with 24.2%, and soccer games, with 15.9%.

The most-viewed program categories in 1995 were, in order of importance: news (8.2%), sporting events (7.7%), entertainment (6.8%), drama (6.7%), children's (3.8%), and cultural (2.5%). Expanding the scope to the decade, news programs share the highest ratings with prime-time offerings, closely followed by soap operas (see Figure 14). The

FIGURE 15

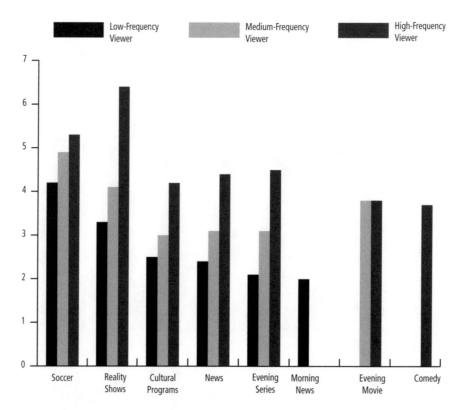

PREFERRED PROGRAMS BY TYPE OF VIEWER
(rating points)

data show a clear and consistent decline for the first nightly time slot, as well as a close association between evening soap operas and news. The 1992 ratings fall can be explained by the introduction of the people meter, but from then on, all the channels lost ratings for their evening soap operas and news programs, a trend which was not reversed until 1995.

Cable television has not adopted the use of the people meter, and consequently the only data available on viewing habits comes from the notebook system implemented by the company Search Marketing. These measurements indicate that, from Monday to Friday, cable television has a greater audience than broadcast television only during the 3 p.m. to 7 p.m. time slot, and again after 10 p.m., although at this hour overall ratings are down.

By contrast, on Sundays the CATV audience is greater than that of broadcast television throughout the day, with the exception of the news hour. CATV audiences are greatest for movies, series, children's shows, and music programs. Analyzed by age group, the two population segments showing the highest cable ratings are children aged 5 to 10 and young adults from 25 to 34.

Viewing Habits and Preferences
Despite the ratings and program rankings detailed above in a study by Desuc and CNTV (CNTV 1996a), television viewers stated that they prefer news programs by a large margin,

followed by movies, cultural programs, sports, soap operas, and real-life stories. It is paradoxical that the programs exhibiting the highest weekly ratings, such as prime-time variety shows, do not exceed 2.8% among the shows first mentioned in order of preference. This disparity may result from the influence of the social acceptance factor upon the survey subjects' responses.

Television viewers can be classified as low-, medium-, or high-frequency, on the basis of the time spent watching daily. We group them into viewing levels of one hour to 89 minutes per day, 90 minutes to two hours, and two hours or more:[44]

- Low-frequency viewers are typically men and women under age 44 in the ABC1 stratum, as well as men under 44 in the C2 stratum.
- Medium-frequency viewers include women under 44 in the C2 stratum and men over 45; males and females of the lower-middle class and between ages 5 and 24; lower-class men ages 15 to 44; and upper-class males above the age of 45.
- High-frequency TV viewers include lower-class women of all age groups, women 45 and above in all social strata, and men in the same age group in the lower-middle and lower classes.

As the graph indicates, the types of viewers preferring soccer and real-life programs coincide. Among high-frequency viewers, the top four preferences are soccer, reality programs, evening series, and the evening news. Comedy programs also make a strong showing. The low-frequency viewers prefer the news, followed by cultural programs. The medium-frequency group again chooses soccer and reality programs, with evening movies as their third preference, and the evening news and evening series equally preferred. In summary, there are several types of high-rated programs which cross socio-economic barriers: soccer games, reality shows, news programs, and television series.

New Programming Styles

An analysis of long-term developments in Chilean broadcast television must include a discussion of the programs offered by the various channels. There has been a gradual transformation in the "menu" of television offerings, along with variations in the programmatic profile of each television station.

During the 1980s, prime time programming was dominated by pre-packaged material from foreign countries. In the present decade, this tendency has begun to decline, with domestically produced variety-show programs taking on a more prominent role. In 1982, the proportion of domestic programs on broadcast TV was 39%. By last year this proportion had risen to 56%. During the peak hours of the heaviest viewing months, 63% of programs were produced in Chile and had domestic content (Marín 1997). This change occurred as a result of the arrival and expansion of CATV, which compelled broadcast television to offer programs of local and national interest, since the broadcast stations could not possibly compete with the variety of international programming offered by CATV.

This effort to bring programming closer to the people has been extremely successful. A clear case is that of Channel 13. The channel had transmitted only "packaged" programs

---

44 This classification and the data utilized are taken from the study *Tipología del consumidor de televisión señal libre*, from the Media Department of Northcote, Ogilvy, & Mather (1997), based on information provided by TIME Media.

during prime-time at the start of the decade, but by 1997 it had shifted to presenting a domestic variety format. Channel 7's main innovation has been in making use of the morning time slot, which until recently had gone unused by the large channels. That slot now accounts for approximately one-sixth of total programming. A second interesting change is the use of the second nightly time slot (beginning at 11 or 11:30 p.m.) for broadcasting cultural programs, which attract a considerable audience. Both channels, over the course of the decade, have noticeably increased the time dedicated to news programs, by about 5%. In the case of Megavisión, its programming of soap operas in the first and second nighttime slots has met with singular success.

Channel 11 is somewhat unstable in its programming. During the present decade, it has doubled its programming of movies, series, and soap operas, while decreasing its miscellaneous programs. La Red, meanwhile, exhibits extreme variability. In 1992, for example, children's programs predominated on the channel, but two years later they had disappeared from its schedule. On Channel 5 UCV-TV, however, children's programs are the most common feature, accounting for between 30% and 60% of programming.

We can conclude from this brief summary of broadcast television programming that, paradoxically, there is considerable stability at the two extremes of the television spectrum. Television viewing is organized on the basis of program offerings; therefore, the extreme variability of the small channels impedes the development of an identifiable programming style. Low ratings lead to further modifications, creating a kind of vicious circle.

Another factor we must consider is the large channels' low level of programming innovation. The programming day is divided into clearly established blocks,[45] which exhibit very little variation.

Two highly significant programming types for Chilean TV should be mentioned in particular:

• Soap operas, by their nature, have become valuable marketing instruments for the channels. Since they remain on the air for a long period of time, they can generate a stable audience and have a rollover effect in favor of the nightly news programs that follow them. In fact, it has been calculated that in 1993 some 50% of the rating points achieved by major newscasts were directly linked to the ratings enjoyed by the soap operas preceding them.

• Soccer has emerged in the 1990s as a singular force for capturing audiences. In September 1994, the winning bid to the National Professional Soccer Association (ANFP) for the rights to transmit soccer games for a period of three years amounted to US$23 million.

3. NEW CHALLENGES

Digital Television

Among the new communications technologies being developed in the world, one that will have a decisive effect on television is the movement from analog to digital transmissions.

---

45 These are the morning, the afternoon (divided into soap operas, movies, and children's programs), the evening series, and finally the nighttime block, divided into first and second night time slots. The first slot includes variety/talk shows (*estelares*) while the second slot generally offers movies.

Digital information is transmitted in binary code, the same technology used by computers, compact discs, and modern telephone systems, allowing the signals to be highly compressed.[46] Thus, on the same portion of the radio spectrum required today for a single analog signal, five or six digital TV signals can be transmitted. These signals can even transmit high-definition channels, although none presently exist.

Digital signals will be grouped in a type of band known as multiplex. The holders of concessions for these bands will be able to use them flexibly, grouping signals to transmit high-definition programs, or using just part of the band to transmit analog signals.

The bandwidth gained through the compression of the transmission signal will also allow traditional channels to broadcast paid services and thus to acquire a source of funding other than advertising. At the same time, this technology opens the door for interactivity between the audience and the television station, which in the future may allow viewers to design their own programming. Finally, it offers a spectacular expansion of the television spectrum, with the consequent fragmentation of viewing audiences.

The Future of Broadcast Television

Chile faces the dilemma of determining the future of broadcast television. While it is highly valued by the masses, it does not enjoy the favor of the political or cultural elite, and it generates a higher degree of criticism in upper-income, better-educated circles.

In a closed Senate hearing on July 4 of last year, television was characterized as offensive, vulgar, and violent. It was criticized for its failure to uphold constructive values (*Mercado & Publicidad* 22, 1996). The senators blamed this situation on the frenzied battle for ratings. In the same hearing, some senators criticized the National Television Council for playing a restricted, formal role, rather than actively encouraging the promotion of cultural values on TV. Yet the legal and institutional structure for Chilean TV does not provide any incentive for non-commercial activity. In a mostly symbolic act, Law No. 19,131 (Article 13) provides for a fund to support the creation of cultural programs. However, in the 1998 national budget, less than one million dollars is earmarked for this fund, or 0.3% of Chilean television's advertising revenue for the same period.

The law creating the company Televisión Nacional de Chile does not establish a specific public interest to be preserved. The alternative implied by the critics of Chilean TV is the use of market financing methods to finance programs which are not particularly marketable. This suggestion does not stand up to analysis. The market, as distinct from the State, cannot be asked to do anything other than aim to satisfy large groups of consumers.

---

46 This has generated competition among telephone, computer, and radio broadcasting companies. In the United States, Microsoft, Compaq, and Intel have united to present a digital TV proposal, based on a progressive search system that is not interlinked like current systems. Progressive search involves the sequential transmission of blocks of pixels, and it is compatible with the technologies for radio broadcasting, cable, computers, and telecommunications. For this reason, the FCC approved the proposal of the Great Alliance (composed of AT&T, David Sarnoff Research Center, General Instrument, MIT, Philips North America, Thomson Consumer Electronics, and Zenith Electronics) to adopt it. Television broadcasters will be assigned an additional band of the spectrum, equivalent to that already provided for analog transmission, through which they will be able to transmit some four lower-resolution channels (SDTV, standard definition television), alternating with digital television for particular programs or on a certain schedule. See *Producción & Distribución* 6 (June 1997).

Thus, the improvement of the general quality of television programming, along with the future of broadcast TV itself, remain open questions.

Marketing, Programmatic Differentiation, and Audience Measurement

Finally, we should take note of three current issues for Chilean television: marketing capabilities, programmatic differentiation, and advances in audience measurement techniques.

- The tough competition in the television market has resulted in increased production costs. This is especially true for the leading broadcast television channels, which must provide programming with local content to satisfy their audiences. Domestic shows, which have helped stem the loss of viewers to cable television or video rentals, have mainly consisted of evening series and prime-time variety shows aired during the first nightly time slot. However, both types of productions are expensive; dramas, for example, cost more than US$4 million annually.[47] So far, these domestic productions have generally remained within the local market (*Mercado & Publicidad* 7, 1994). However, rising international sales of Chilean television series[48] indicate that networks are turning this situation around.
- Another important area is the differentiation of content and services (*Mercado & Publicidad* 23, 1996). Up to now, the large CATV companies have followed a more financial than commercial strategy. Their mergers have not occurred for competitive reasons, but because of their financial capacity to acquire companies already in the market. It has been said that CATV cannot be understood merely as a technology capable of providing more and more channels. Instead, "a profound understanding of the audience, its viewing habits, and its attitude toward the television and the quality of service are indispensable in any attempt to change the programming structure and introduce new services. Multi-operators must undertake these efforts soon," (*Producción & Distribución* 7, 1997). Differentiation in service quality and the specific programming packages offered seems to be the path of the future for a television system which currently exhibits a high level of uniformity.
- Finally, although the Chilean television market involves US$300 million in domestic transactions, the only available source of information about these exchanges consists of a sample of 340 homes (connected to the people meter), all located within the nation's capital. Audience measurement techniques must be broadened and deepened, providing better information about highly specific factors in the domestic market which the current methods cannot detect. The system's limitations do not only concern the representativeness of the sample; there is also a shortage of sufficiently complex diagnostic techniques. It is both possible and desirable to move beyond the current measurement instruments, in order to better understand an industry of great social and cultural, as well as economic, importance.

---

47 Each one of the approximately 100 installments making up a domestic television series costs more than eight million pesos.

48 For example, TVN's sale of the series Sucupira to Televisión Azteca in April 1997, and its sale of the five most successful Chilean soap operas since 1994 to SiTV of Ecuador, (*Producción & Distribución* 6, 1997).

Conclusions

The foundations of the Chilean media system were laid out well before the current decade. It can therefore legitimately be said that "the change in political system has not brought about the collapse of the communications system constituted during the preceding period, nor the inauguration of a new framework for the field," (Tironi and Sunkel 1993).

The principle of private ownership in the media had been strengthened long before the start of the political transition, at a time when opponents of the military regime were hindered in their attempts to establish strong and influential media outlets. The expansion and privatization of the media came to depend upon private investments, in the areas of transmission (coaxial cable, fiber optics, satellites), production (computerization of work processes, the use of digital technology), and audience measurement (where the people meter led to new television marketing strategies).

Just as vital was the competitive logic of market mechanisms which led to the formation of large corporate multimedia groups, linked to prominent parent companies. The 1990s witnessed increasing concentration of ownership in various media sectors. Among newspapers, ownership accumulated within two large consortia: the traditional Edwards group and the emerging Corporación Periodística S.A. (Copesa). In the magazine market, the Mexican publishing company Televisa rose to a position of notable predominance. In television, an exceptional transformation was witnessed with the appearance of private stations among the free-to-air broadcast stations. The Claro group, with Megavisión, has become particularly strong in this medium.

In television, the cost of creating competitive programming has steadily risen over the course of the decade, imposing an effective barrier to market entry. It is no coincidence that all private television ventures since the beginning of the decade have suffered serious financial difficulties, and that the only successful case thus far has been Megavisión. This network was able to succeed because — in addition to the considerable financial support provided by its founding group — it found a foreign partner to provide the capital investment and television experience it needed to remain in the market. The search for such support has been an ongoing concern for stations such as Channel 11, which is attempting to overcome its weakened condition. Nevertheless, as proved by the association of La Red with Can West Global Communications Corp., as well as the difficulties experienced by Universidad de Chile channel during its first few years with Venevisión, partnership is not always an easy process and does not guarantee success. At the time of this writing (December 1997), La Red is pursuing this strategy again, in the hope that a partnership with Mexico's number-two chain, Televisión Azteca, will help improve its tenuous position in the Chilean television market.[49]

In cable television, a concentration process occurring between 1993 and 1995 ended with the formation of two business groups which now control practically the entire market. These are Metrópolis-Intercom, held by the Claro group (majority owner) and the multinational company Bresnam International; and VTR Cablexpress, majority-owned by the Luksic group.

---

49 In this strategic partnership, to be initiated in mid-December 1997, Televisión Azteca would acquire 75% of La Red's shares with an investment of 10.35 million dollars (*El Mercurio* Dec. 5, 1997).

Finally, in radio, two large chains dominate the market, as measured by the size of the listening audience: Radio Cooperativa and Radio Chilena. Here, however, in contrast to other media, there is a significant number of alternative outlets, giving the medium a more diversified ownership structure.

The center of gravity of Chile's media system is the television market. It receives the lion's share of investment, and it is where technological advances are most rapidly applied. Even more important, however, are television's socio-cultural effects. TV is a forum for expression, presenting images with which viewers can identify. It is a non-neutral forum, admittedly, since the true language of television is that of entertainment. This language permeates all TV programming and thus naturally "contaminates" the way a subject such as politics is presented to the public. If politics before the 1990s resembled a tragedy, its present post-ideological phase, thanks to television, runs the risk of appearing as a comedy, with a public image bearing little relation to its importance as a forum for collective decision making.

Another characteristic of this period has been the overall strengthening of the media market. Aside from the phenomena mentioned above, this rise has been based on a general increase in disposable income, resulting in greater demand for entertainment-related products. This is clearly demonstrated by the massive increase in color TV and VCR purchases, cable television subscriptions, and many other types of cultural consumption.

The Chilean media system has undergone diversification, segmentation, and fragmentation. It is clear that the process of audience fragmentation has increased with all media, while diversification and segmentation have been pursued as business strategies to capture specific market niches. The increasing segmentation of audiences, employed as a marketing tool, has given rise to the diverse styles and characteristics seen in the media. The risk remains, however, that the media may increasingly become mere receptacles for advertising rather than true vehicles for communication, losing the necessary balance between profitability and editorial mission.

Fragmentation has occurred as audiences have adapted to the emergence of new technologies and to the changes in programming offerings. Channel surfing, the way the younger generation watches TV, has arisen as a new phenomenon. Its effect upon television programming remains to be seen. Presently, during prime time, the channel-surfing factor has led to a certain sensationalism much more concerned with audience retention than with programming quality.

These changes in the national media system have taken place in an environment of increasingly globalized communications. The primary engine of this phenomenon is the dynamic North American cultural industry, which achieved dominance in the film world during the 1970s, overtaking European cinema. In the 1980s, the United States continued in the lead with the expansion of cable and video and reductions in the cost of communications satellites. To these capacities must be added the North American cultural industry's great economies of scale in its home market. All of the above has led to its predominance in the world market for mass culture.

Nevertheless, this process has been accompanied by a movement toward more local content. Along with international cultural products, the public increasingly appreciates domestically-produced programming. Thus Chile exhibits a hybrid of local and global media content that is certainly not unique to our society. Large multinational media groups are aware of this trend and have been investing in local companies. This provides opportunities for domestic firms, based on their knowledge of the tastes and preferences of the local culture. Consequently, we are not seeing, nor are we likely to see, the undisputed predominance of a global culture. Rather, we are witnessing the development of a complex dynamic in which domestic cultural production also plays a vital role.

Finally, we must note various remaining challenges. One is the media's rapidly accelerating technological progress, which compels us to confront its impact upon our country. We must ensure that the media satisfies the diverse interests of a broad and heterogeneous audience. Enriching the media with expressions of social diversity is a necessary step in the strengthening of our democracy. In an open, pluralistic, and democratic society, the communications media are an essential forum for citizen participation.

Yet since the mid-1980s, Chile's media have become increasingly privatized. A media structure based on private initiative is not necessarily pluralistic, if it is manifested in a heavy market concentration, and if broad sectors of society are hindered from expressing their communicational preferences. This contradicts the argument that freedom of expression automatically leads to broader choices for the people, therefore making media "more democratic."

Thus, we face the ongoing challenge to provide access to a multiplicity of forums for citizen expression, to satisfy demands for timely and accurate information, and to give all people — not just the country's elite — the opportunity to express their views. All this must be accomplished within a high-quality, diversified, pluralistic, and mass-audience communications system enmeshed in a complex relationship among the State, civil society, and the market.

Democracy needs well-informed citizens who can express themselves through the media. Obviously, this requires full freedom of expression, but it is also necessary to remember that the media play an irreplaceable role in the formation of a democratic citizenry. The media can uphold the virtues of pluralistic discussion, the competition of ideas, and responsible social critique. With their presentation of political activity, the media can contribute to the public's understanding of its legitimate and necessary role in society. This is the task that stands before our national media. The alternative — reducing political communication to a merely private matter — would make societal discourse utterly impossible. Extreme reduction in one sense or another implies a lack of democratic spirit.

Finally, to meet the challenges of accelerating change in the media, our country must strengthen professional training in related fields, as well as improving the instruments and technologies that can provide a better understanding of this complex sector. Too often, people are still denied access to vital information with the claim that it would affect the commercial interests of media enterprises. This damages the transparency of the market and impedes the investment process, ultimately affecting the quality of the media themselves.

The author would like to thank sociologist Daniela Vicherat for her valuable assistance with this work.

BIBLIOGRAPHICAL REFERENCES

Adimark. 1997. *La televisión abierta y su impacto en la sociedad.* Santiago.

ANDA magazine. 1990–1997. Santiago: Asociación Nacional de Avisadores.

Archi (Chilean Association of Radio Broadcasters). 1997. *Historia de la radio en Chile: 75 años de radiodifusión.* Santiago.

ARCHI magazine. 1997. Santiago: Asociación de Radiodifusores de Chile.

BBDO. 1995. *Panorama de los medios en Chile.* Santiago (December).

Brunner, J. and C. Catalán. 1995. *Televisión: libertad, mercado y moral.* Santiago: Edit. Los Andes.

Catalán, C. 1995. "Situación y proyecciones de la televisión por cable en Chile." Paper presented at the seminar "Televisión satelital y por cable en latinoamérica," organized by AIC Conferences. Santiago.

———. 1997. "Televisión y crisis del sujeto." *El Mercurio,* Santiago, July 27.

Céneca-Flacso. 1988. "Informe de consumo cultural." Santiago.

CNTV (National Television Council: Research, Oversight and Development Division). 1994. *Televisión por cable en Chile.* Santiago (December).

———. 1996a. *Encuesta Nacional de Televisión. Principales resultados.* Santiago.

———. 1996b. *Informa* 1. Santiago (September).

———. 1996c. *Informa* 2. Santiago (October).

DESUC/Archi. 1996. *Usos y costumbres en la audiencia de radio.* Santiago: Sociological Research Department, Universidad Católica de Chile/ Asociación de Radiodifusores de Chile.

Marín, C. 1997. "Nuevas tendencias de la televisión chilena: un escenario diferente para el debate sobre la identidad." Mimeo (April).

Mercado & Publicidad magazine. 1993–1997. Santiago.

Northcote, Ogilvy, & Mather. 1997. "Tipología del consumidor de televisión señal libre." Media Department.

Producción & Distribución magazine. 1997. Florida, USA.

Revista de Publicidad magazine. 1990–1993. Santiago.

Search Marketing. 1995. *Hábitos ejecutivos.* Santiago (November-December).

———. 1996. *Ranking general principales revistas por grupos objetivos.* October 1995-March 1996. Santiago.

SECC (Secretariat of Communication and Culture, Research Department, Ministry of the Secretary-General of the Government). 1994. *Tendencias y desarrollo de los medios en Chile 1990–1993.* Santiago (January).

———. 1995. "Estado y perspectivas de los medios de comunicación regionales." *Reseña de Medios* 31 (December).

———. 1996. "Las perspectivas de la radio en Chile." *Reseña de Medios* 32 (November).

Tironi, E. and G. Sunkel. 1993. "Modernización de las comunicaciones y democratización de la política: Los medios en la transición a la democracia en Chile." *Estudios Públicos* 52. Santiago: CEP.

Higher Education in Chile:
The Need for Regulation

Raúl Atria

Introduction

T hroughout 1997, growing concern has been voiced about deficiencies in Chile's policy framework for higher education. The shortcomings identified by institutions, the sector's key players (including faculty and students), and public opinion in general can be summarized into four basic areas: a lack of rationality in the system's structure and operations; ambiguity in its guiding principles; a lack of transparency; and confusion over the State's proper role in the system.

There is evidence that this concern is becoming a national issue, transcending the narrow circles of education officials and experts. This interest also cuts across ideological boundaries and is increasingly visible on the governmental agenda.

It is useful to review the evolution of Chile's system of higher education in the 1990s. The onset of the decade was marked by two highly significant events for the sector. The first was the transition to democracy and the swearing-in of the Concertación administration in 1990; the second was the enactment of Law 18,962 — known as the Constitutional Law on Education or LOCE — in the final days of the military government.[1] That legislation set the stage for activities by a range of players in the higher educational system, including the State. Due to space limitations, this paper will concentrate mainly on assessing and identifying current issues critical to policy progress in these areas. Specifically, emphasis will be placed on the formulation of a regulatory framework appropriate to the features the system has acquired. Additional note will be made of the changes needed to meet fundamental demands for equity and quality and to ensure that the new legislation is sustainable over the long term.

In reviewing the evolution of higher education in Chile, we must also address topics of enormous relevance in the current debate on public policy and the role of the State. The case of education is particularly noteworthy in several fundamental areas. One is the speed of behavioral change among key institutions (primarily universities) in response to government deregulation measures. In Chile's case, this occurred with the 1981 enactment of two key pieces of legislation, which deregulated the system in a veritable "big bang." A

---

[1] The Constitutional Law on Education (LOCE) was published on March 10, 1990, the final day the military government was in office. From 1988 through March 7, 1990, 35 universities and 57 professional institutes were created (Lemaitre, 1997).

second notable aspect involves the structural effects of deregulation and the rational responses of system participants within the new context. A third factor is the need to adjust the system as structural changes take hold, and as "putting the house in order" becomes a widespread aspiration among key figures in the field.

I. The Impact of Deregulation

Presidential Edicts 1 through 5 of 1981 sought to further the military government's goal of establishing an open, competitive, and academically high-quality university system. The legislation focused primarily on opening higher education to private sector initiatives, introducing an environment that, supporters maintained, would foster academic excellence through competition. From the regime's ideological perspective, one of the primary shortcomings of the previous system had been that it prohibited the creation of new private universities. With the arrival on the scene of new policy-makers in the early 1980s, the non-competitive funding regularly received by the eight existing universities began to be questioned.[2]

Since there was no market pressure within the sector, concern was expressed about the uniformity of the degrees granted and the lack of competition to enroll students, perceived as "consumers" of education. The eight "traditional" universities were viewed as a lobby which sought to secure increased funding commitments from the State without being held accountable for the results obtained with those resources. In keeping with these perceptions, the new university legislation of the 1980s sought primarily to open the system to competition and allow and facilitate the creation of new universities at the initiative of the private sector.

A central aspect in the newly opened, deregulated system was the implementation of oversight mechanisms to ensure correct application of the general curriculum in the private schools. There is no need to recount the specifics of this process, which fell into widespread disrepute. Basically, once the regulations implementing the first edict (known as DFL 1) were put into effect, it became evident that the oversight mechanisms were ill-conceived. Moreover, they were insufficient to enforce quality control in higher education in light of the expansion of the private universities created under the new legislation.

The 1981 legislation led to significant diversification of institutions, fostered opportunities for private universities, and paved the way for the creation of regional state-run schools.[3] The reform also introduced far-reaching changes to the system of public financing for higher education, reorienting it toward greater self-financing. This included a freeze on direct State contributions; a redistribution of available funds based on past data; the creation of indirect budgetary funding (AFI); the implementation of biddable funds; and authorization for tuition increases. Institutional diversification also brought about a significant weakening in quality control over the newly-expanded range of curricula.

---

2   The eight "traditional" universities are: University of Chile, Catholic University of Chile, Technical State University (currently the University of Santiago), Catholic University of Valparaíso, Universidad del Norte, Universidad Austral, University of Concepción, and Federico Santa María Technical University.

3   These regional universities were spun off from the regional branches of the University of Chile and the Technical State University.

Among the political players active in the transition to democracy in the early 1990s, two ideas began to emerge that, over the long term, would have a fundamental impact on higher education's position on the national agenda. First, higher education was not immediately relevant to the urgent demands and challenges faced by the government during the transition period. Second, the radical changes introduced in 1981 clearly needed time to mature so that they could be evaluated more effectively. The first outcome of this political and operational perspective was a set of recommendations formulated by the Presidential Committee appointed by President Aylwin to draft a policy proposal for higher education. That committee was unable to devise a comprehensive policy approach for the entire higher education sector. As a result, while the Aylwin administration did tinker with the system, it did not overhaul its policy in general.

During those years, two diverging approaches and sets of concerns emerged within the system. The public universities focused on recovering democratic legitimacy in the selection of university officials and revitalizing the academic community. Among the emerging private institutions, however, attention centered on constituting the Council on Higher Education (CSE) and developing the necessary criteria and procedures to undertake the unprecedented task of evaluating and accrediting these institutions based on their own institutional development plans (the LOCE assigned this task to the Council).

While the government's "tinkering" was somewhat effective in addressing immediate problems, the decision-making framework gradually deteriorated under this approach. Questions arose regarding the contradiction between the institutions' inevitable short-term outlook due to financial pressures (this was particularly true for public institutions but also affected the emerging private ones) and the long-term perspective required for the formulation of an effective academic strategy.

Another problem lay in the difficulties faced by the state-run universities operating in the new deregulated environment. While previous management controls had been appropriate for traditional State agencies, they became dysfunctional in a climate of competition in educational services such as teaching and research. A third problem area emerged from the nature of the funding mechanism, which emphasized low costs to the detriment of academic quality and relevance. Under this system, instituting new, low-cost majors became a perfectly rational strategy as a means of obtaining a continual flow of fresh capital.

Aside from the shortcomings stemming from the political framework, a problematic cultural shift also began to take place within the system. The new conception of the student as a customer — increasingly popular among management and administrators, as well as the academic and policy communities — lay at the heart of this issue. In this view, a student is, above all, a consumer of a good or service obtained through the payment of tuition. As consumers, students are expected to possess information about the comparative quality of the products they are purchasing, and they are assumed to be able to pay market rates for those products, either with their own resources or by going into debt, as any other consumer would. The consumer thus has no direct role in the management of the good or service and participates in that process only marginally, distantly, and anonymously by expressing his or her preferences in the marketplace.

This description provides an analytical framework that helps to explain certain patterns of behavior. It is clear, however, that the relationship between students and universities (or any other institution of higher learning) is not fully expressed by this analytical model. In fact, while the student can be perceived as a consumer, he or she is also a key player in the interactive process that emerges between faculty and students. Student participation is neither marginal nor distant nor anonymous.

To further complicate matters, the LOCE asked the Council on Higher Education to issue recommendations for the new universities and professional institutes. It is required to provide ongoing assessments of the development of these institutions in keeping with the accreditation regulations established by law.[4]

II. The Diversification of the System

Once the 1981 legislation was in place, higher education quickly took on certain features which are relatively well-established today and have gradually become seemingly irreversible as far as policy is concerned. Chile's system currently exhibits broad diversity with regard to:
• institutional differentiation, including universities, professional institutes (IP) and technical training centers (TTC)
• ownership (State or private)
• financing mechanisms (with or without direct budgetary funding)
• functional differentiation, including research-oriented universities, teaching-oriented universities, and other institutions
• geographic location
• level of complexity, from highly complex or multi-functional institutions to extremely simple ones
• size, ranging from institutions with some 20,000 students to several that serve less than 400
• historical origin, including institutions existing before 1980; universities spun off from state schools; universities derived from professional institutes; schools emerging out of private universities receiving budgetary support; and fully private institutions[5]

The aggregate figures for higher education in Chile in 1996 show that including universities, professional institutes, and technical training centers, there were a total of 262 institutions, with an undergraduate enrollment of 358,082 students and 3,905 courses of study (including all majors).

Table 1 shows a summary of the aggregate data for the system through 1996. As these figures show, a sizable portion of the system that evolved after 1980 is composed of the so-called "traditional" universities. This includes the eight schools already operating in 1980, plus their spin-offs, essentially created by granting autonomy to the provincial seats of the two largest state-run universities; that is, the University of Chile and the State Technical University (today the University of Santiago, USACH).

---

4   Law 18,962 (LOCE), in Section III, paragraph 2, describes the Council on Higher Education and the accreditation system.
5   It is somewhat odd that between 1990 and 1995, more universities with budgetary support were created than wholly private institutions.

TABLE 1

CHANGES IN THE CHILEAN SYSTEM OF HIGHER EDUCATION
(1980-1996)

Type of Institution	Number of Institutions		Undergraduate Enrollment		Number of Programs	Public Financing	Regulation
	1980	1996	1980	1996	1996		
Traditional Universities	8	25	118,978	167,282	1,417	Direct	Autonomous
		9.5%		46.7%	36.3%	Indirect Credits Scholarship	
Private Universities	0	42	0	77,212	429	Indirect Only	Autonomous (5)
		16%		21.6%	11%		Accreditation (29)
							Examination (8)
Private Professional Institutes	0	69	0	52,170	529	Indirect Only	Autonomous (5)
		26.3%		14.6%	13.5%		Accreditation (26)
							Examination (38)
Technical Training	0	126	0	61,418	1,530	Indirect Only	Supervision (109)
		48.1%		17.2%	39.2%		Accreditation (17)
Total	8	262	118,978	358,082	3,905		
		100%		100%	100%		

SOURCE: Ministry of Education, Higher Education Department.

The state-operated schools include these spin-offs and the so-called regional universities. Two universities also arose out of the two state-operated professional institutes: the Metropolitan Technological University (formerly the Professional Institute of Santiago, which in turn was an offshoot of the University of Chile) and the Universidad de Los Lagos, which has its roots in the Professional Institute of Osorno. The group currently includes 25 autonomous universities, coordinated by a body known as the Council of Presidents.

The traditional universities enjoy the unique privilege of direct State funding, provided through allocations in the national budget. These schools receive public funds through indirect budgetary contributions, loans, and scholarships. They account for 9.5% of Chile's institutions of higher learning. In 1980, enrollment at the "traditional" schools stood at 118,978 undergraduates. That figure rose to 167,282 by 1986, accounting for 46.7% of all enrolled students and a total of 1,417 courses of study that year.

A second extremely important group is the set of schools that emerged immediately following the deregulation of the system in 1981. These are the new or "emerging" private universities. By 1996, 42 such institutions existed in Chile, accounting for 16% of higher educational facilities, attracting an undergraduate enrollment of 77,212 students and offering 429 courses of study. These schools receive a limited amount of financial support from a meager allocation of indirect budgetary funding (AFI). The most important aspect of these institutions' diversity is their regulatory framework. In 1996, there were five autonomous private universities (four of which secured that autonomy via the accreditation process with the Council on Higher Education: University Central; University Diego Portales, University Mayor, and University Finis Terrae; while one, University Gabriela Mistral, was accredited via the non-CSE examination process). Twenty-nine were in the process of CSE-supervised accreditation, and eight, as with the case of the University Gabriela Mistral, chose the examination procedure while that option was still available (before the LOCE took effect in 1990).

The higher education system, as set forth in the LOCE, also includes the professional institutes and technical training centers. Following the privatization of INACAP in the early 1990s and the conversion of the two previously mentioned state-run professional institutes into universities, there were no public professional institutes left in Chile. Thus, higher vocational and professional education is fully in the hands of the private sector. The fact that the State has no presence at this level is clearly an interesting topic for public policy. There is no reason that this situation should continue indefinitely; in fact, it is nearly unprecedented internationally. Public financing for these institutes is limited to indirect budgetary contributions taken from the portion available to private universities. In 1996, there were 69 professional institutes (26.3% of the total institutions in the system) with 52,170 students and 529 courses of study. In terms of their regulatory status, five are autonomous, 26 are in the CSE accreditation system, and 38 opted for the examination system.

The technical training centers (TTCs) have always been private entities. Unlike the other two categories of institutions, however, they may be for-profit establishments. In 1996, the system had 126 TTCs (48.1% of all institutions), with 61,418 students and 1,530 courses of study. While they do not receive direct funding from the State, theoretically they are eligible for indirect funding. Nonetheless, since the distribution of AFI is based on the enrollment of students with the highest scores on the academic achievement test (PAA), in practice these centers receive no funding through this mechanism.

The TTCs are subject to the oversight of the Ministry of Education: 109 are under supervision and 17 are in the accreditation process. Particularly salient for public policy is the question of access to public funding, especially scholarships. The current system excludes these centers from such financing, even though they serve more than 60,000 students.

Thus, almost by default, the system has taken on a three-tiered institutional structure. Policies therefore must be designed and implemented that ensure *full institutional legitimacy and development at each level, without hidden incentives that encourage institutional transformations.* Such incentives may lead professional institutes, for example, to perceive themselves as potential universities or TTCs to see themselves as potential professional institutes. An upward transformation would mean that some students could perceive (or could be deluded by schools' marketing efforts into perceiving) that they are temporary, transitory occupants of the immediately "inferior" tier. Downward shifts might occur, for example, if universities offer vocational/technical courses of study that should more rightly form part of the curriculum offered by the institutes. A decisive factor in the consolidation and legitimacy of the three tiers will be the demarcation of areas of competency and a true specialization in the educational offering at each level.

TABLE 2

CHILE : A SELECTION OF HIGHER EDUCATION OFFERINGS
IN "TRADITIONAL" MAJORS, 1995

Majors (A)	Departments		Program Totals	Total Enrollment	Total Number of Professors
	Santiago	Regions			
Law	24	20	44	15,619	1,629
Journalism	21	15	36	6,662	919
Psychology	23	16	39	7,940	1,243
Commercial Engineering	52	21	73	17,086	2,117
Accounting (b)	36	48	78	10,482	1,715
Civil Engineering	5	9	14	1,997	248
Computer Engineering	25	36	61	7,552	1,007
Business Management	17	31	48	2,611	594

Source: Council on Higher Education, INDICES 1 and 2, 1996.

Notes: (a) Without differentiation between day and night schools.
(b) The Council on Higher Education has 12 accounting ("auditoría") classifications not included in this table.

III. The Quality Issue

The evolution of the system toward a high degree of diversification, along with the proliferation of institutions and programs, is causing increasingly widespread concern about the academic quality of higher education in Chile. For a factual framework of reference on current fields of study at these institutions, see the *Indices* publications put out annually since 1996 by the CSE. Based on this source and using the same categories utilized by the CSE, a revealing look at the current context of higher education in Chile can be obtained. Table 2 notes the nine "traditional" majors that are offered at the vast majority of the country's undergraduate establishments.

For example, take the 44 schools offering law degrees. The total enrollment in these programs is 15,619 students. This raises questions of quality, since with such a large quantity of programs, it is likely that a relatively high number are mediocre and some frankly deficient. The same question can be posed regarding the 73 schools offering business degrees, the 78 offering accounting programs, the 39 offering psychology, and in general, almost all of the remaining fields of study on the chart. The data are clear, especially since for certain majors the figures in the final two columns are underestimated because the institutions failed to provide complete information. With this data in hand, one can reasonably assume that the majors included in the table are reaching the saturation point for attracting new students. New majors have even more difficulty drawing enrollment. A still greater problem, however, is the saturation of the pool of qualified professors available in Chile to teach the requisite courses.

The truth is that Chile has a standard package of graduate majors: law, journalism, business, psychology, architecture, accounting, and various kinds of engineering (including so-called "implementation" engineering). This package, legally constituting the university program until the CSE was established, led to the proliferation of so-called "blackboard colleges" in Chile's higher educational system. This situation makes the question of quality a major regulatory issue.

Unlike the standard package, the case of bachelor's degrees is interesting because it represents a fairly innovative offering. There are currently bachelor's programs in the humanities and social sciences at several institutions, including Andrés Bello University (281 students enrolled in 1995), University of Santiago de Chile (186), Pontific Catholic University of Chile (304), University of Chile (337), and Universidad del Desarrollo, located in Concepción (26). In the two traditional universities, the bachelor's program serves as an entry point allowing students to follow a diversified curriculum before opting for a specific course of study.[6] Because of its very nature, the program cuts across the structure of schools within each university. The combination of scientific and liberal arts courses, when appropriate, is resolved through minors, as occurs in the cases of the University of Chile and USACH. Available information for Andrés Bello University in 1995 indicated that the program was closely linked to academic life within a given school.[7]

It appears that in general, these programs tend to emerge once the university is in a position to offer fairly well-established majors. This makes sense if the schools aim to diversify while at the same time ensuring continuity in their primary course offerings.

Finally, several other noteworthy phenomena emerge from the documentation provided by the institutions themselves,[8] as well as from the CSE's *Indices*. First, the number of hours worked by professors varies enormously (as shown by the *Indices'* average percentages) with the same course of study being taught by 4.2% and 46% of professor/days. Second, in general, the "traditional" universities systematically show higher percentages in this indicator. Finally, there does not appear to be a direct correlation between this factor and tuition; in other words, more expensive institutions do not necessarily offer higher percentages of professor/days. It can be suggested that professor/days are a good indication of the quality of instruction, and if this is the case, a higher price tag does not mean better quality in Chile's current system of higher education.

There appears to be little doubt about the historical professionalism of higher education in Chile. However, the proliferation of courses of studies and the maintenance of rigid systems in most cases (except for the potentially promising bachelor's programs, still in the test phase and limited as to their overall weight in the system) go against international trends. Undergraduate studies are too long, have an overly broad curriculum, and involve too many subjects and courses and not enough solid academic work, despite the added requirements for a "licentiate" degree.

In light of this diversification, a consensus has emerged among academicians and other observers that there is no longer a "model" university. This change has basic implications

---

6   This system is similar in concept to those institutions that allow students to study a range of topics for a period of time before "declaring" a major. The idea is novel in Chile, where traditionally students are accepted and locked into the university for specific programs of study, usually some five years in length. Students accepted into one major wishing to switch to another have historically had to go through the testing and application process again.

7   An additional program at the University of the Republic offers a bachelor's in social sciences as a preliminary course of study for law and journalism students.

8   It should be kept in mind that this information is provided voluntarily by the schools. This explains why there are gaps in the CSE's figures, since some institutions keep this data confidential.

for the formulation of policy and regulations and for the treatment of institutions which, in practice, represent a mixed bag of academic models and organizational formats.

The concrete expression of this heterogeneity in Chile is the — not always harmonious — coexistence of a variety of institutions, as noted earlier.[9] From a policy perspective, it seems important to underscore two aspects of this diversity. The first is found in the oversight mechanisms, which include *examination* (a throwback to the old system, as noted); *accreditation* via the Council on Higher Education; *non-binding coordination* through the Council of Presidents; and even the *complete deregulation* of private "autonomous" schools. The second aspect is the increasing concentration of universities in particular areas of specialization. For example, some institutions now describe themselves expressly as "teaching" schools, renouncing the classic trilogy of teaching, research, and extension services. Some call themselves "specialized" universities, rejecting the equally classic concept that universities are dedicated to a range of fields.

Despite its disorganized appearance, the system as a whole does possess an underlying rationality and some readily identifiable characteristics. These include: (1) progressive segmentation and limited intercommunication among groups at different types of institutions and among their respective clienteles; (2) marked stratification among institutions;[10] (3) an uneasy coexistence between regulated areas and those where regulation is simply not possible, due to the current legislation; (4) uncorrected distortions stemming from the use of indirect budgetary funding; (5) saturation in academic offerings, exacerbated by the repetition of outmoded courses of study as well as majors offered simply because of their short-term economic return; and (6) limited effective participation of student organizations, generating a misleading and inappropriate passivity among students regarding their school and their own education.

IV. Regulating for Quality

In outlining the key issues in the revived demand for regulation (and therefore the "reorganization" of the system), it is important to consider the different levels of autonomy enjoyed by the various institutions in the system. These lie on a continuum between full autonomy and complete dependency. At the full autonomy end of the spectrum, regulation is only possible based on voluntary agreements; at the other extreme, regulation is imposed from the outside.

In Chile's higher education system, the following institutions are autonomous:

---

9   A good source of empirical data supporting the analysis presented here can be found in the report on higher education published in 1993 by the Higher Education Forum, composed of the Latin American Faculty of Social Sciences (FLACSO), the University Promotion Corporation (CPU), and the Center for Public Studies (CEP), with support from the Ford Foundation. See specifically the article by Alfonso Muga, former Director of the Higher Education Division of the Ministry of Education, which provides a complete quantitative overview of higher education in Chile. Subsequent versions of the report, published in 1994, 1995, and 1996, make it possible to update the basic analysis conducted on the 1993 figures.

10 While this is not necessarily undesirable, it does tend to group the lesser-quality institutions together. The problem lies not in having a few schools that are "head and shoulders" above the rest, but in a plethora of poor-quality schools that can continue to exist at the bottom level of the institutional totem pole.

a) State universities; that is, those created by the State, such as the University of Chile and the University of Santiago (former State Tech), as well as those schools created by law or spun off from other state-run universities, all of which receive direct budgetary support
b) traditional private universities; that is, those acknowledged by the State as autonomous in the past, which are also eligible for direct budgetary contributions (Catholic University of Chile, Catholic University of Valparaíso, and Austral in Valdivia, among others)[11]
c) private universities approved during the examination period[12] established under Decree 1 of 1980 issued by the Ministry of Education (such as the Gabriela Mistral University); or those which began under the exam system but subsequently opted for and successfully completed the accreditation process (such as Diego Portales University, University Central, University Mayor, and University Finis Terrae).

The following institutions are not considered autonomous:
a) private universities that are still in the process of examination according to DFL 1
b) those private schools subject to accreditation which opted for that system prior to March 10, 1992,[13] or which opened their doors after that date.

The accreditation system under current legislation, discussed in greater depth below, is applicable solely to the *latter group* of institutions.

Under the CSE-guided accreditation system, the private universities, in order to commence instruction, must secure approval of their institutional proposal and courses of study. Once opened, the schools' institutional development and progress are carefully tracked. In addition, the schools must have sufficient human, instructional, economic, financial, and physical resources to provide the training required for students to earn a degree. Once these requirements have been met, universities are granted official recognition. The accreditation process continues until the school is declared to be fully autonomous. In other words, once the process is complete, the school is freed from any and all regulatory ties.

According to the LOCE (Articles 37, 39, 41, and 42), accreditation can be understood as "the process by which a new university is officially recognized by submitting its institutional proposal to the Council on Higher Education for periodic review during a period of no less than six and no more than 11 years, with the purpose, if approved, of certifying its full autonomy." If the proposal is rejected, the Ministry of Education must revoke official recognition and suspend the institution's legal status. In other words, for a period of up to 11 years, schools may attempt to qualify for full autonomy. Considering the number of private

11 This category involves institutions recognized at different times, but all prior to January 3, 1980, when Ministry of Education Decree (DFL) 1 was enacted.
12 An examination is given to the first five graduating classes, administered by a diversified committee composed of professors from the university being reviewed and from an "examining" school. The latter must be an autonomous institution, and in cases of disagreement, the opinions of its faculty members take precedence over those expressed by the faculty of the school under review.
13 Between March 1990 and March 10, 1992, schools could choose between the system established in DFL 1 of 1980, or the accreditation system established in the LOCE, according to Transitory Article 3 of the latter legislation.

TABLE 3

Examination and Accreditation Regulations in Chile

	Examination	Accreditation
Regulatory Institution	Examiners prior to 1980 (universities and professional institutes) or derivative institutions	Council on Higher Education (CSE)
Legal Framework	DFL 1/DFL 5 (1981)	LOCE (1990)
Goal	Assure product equality (students)	Public quality content Improvement of processes and products (*)
Evaluation Framework	Examination entity programs and culture (**)	Goals and purposes as defined byeach institution CSE evaluation criteria.
Focus of Evaluation	Specific programs geared toward student performance	Total institution: goals, programs, resources, plans, results.

Source: Lemaitre (1997)

(*)   Elements introduced by the CSE, not contained within the LOCE.

(**) An institution can have a variety of examiners.

universities that opened in 1990, we can expect to see a sharp increase in the number of fully autonomous schools by the beginning of the coming decade.

During the accreditation process, public officials exercise their powers of evaluation and review, and the schools are required to demonstrate that they comply satisfactorily with their proposal and curriculum. Schools under accreditation may offer courses of study outside the ones contained in their original proposal, and these offerings are also subject to evaluation. Table 3 provides a comparative overview of the examination and accreditation systems in place in Chile today for the non-autonomous private universities.

The composition of the Council on Higher Education is key to understanding fully its nature and role in the accreditation process. Fundamentally, the Council is *more a public entity than a State agency*. According to the LOCE, the Council shall be composed of the following individuals: the Minister of Education, who serves as Chairperson; three academicians appointed by the autonomous universities and professional institutes; three academicians appointed by the nation's scientific community (Academy of Sciences); one academician appointed by the Supreme Court; and one person appointed by the armed forces. The eight academic members are appointed by their home institutions. Nonetheless, they have tended to exhibit an independent rather than an institutional mind-set, much to the benefit of the system.

In the accreditation process, the CSE is empowered to:

• confirm the progress of institutional proposals in keeping with the rules of accreditation established in the LOCE

• establish selective examination systems for educational institutions subject to accreditation processes, in an effort to assess compliance with proposals and programs of study, as well as student performance

- declare certain majors (at universities undergoing accreditation) exempt from such testing, although not in the case of majors requiring a "licentiate" degree before the professional level[14]
- issue an annual progress report, conduct partial evaluations, formulate observations, establish time frames for corrections to be made, and require universities to furnish pertinent information
- recommend that the Ministry of Education apply penalties to institutions under accreditation when necessary
- extend the accreditation period for a new university up to five years following the minimum six-year term
- certify that a university has successfully completed its accreditation period, has attained full autonomy and is thus empowered to grant professional and academic degrees on an independent basis
- request that the Ministry of Education revoke official recognition and suspend an institution's legal status, should the school, in the Council's opinion, fail to comply with its institutional proposal
- set the fees charged by the Council for activities involved in the accreditation process, the minimum and maximum rates for which are established in article 38 of the LOCE

From a management perspective, it would be beneficial to establish a variety of regulatory structures based on the particular characteristics and requirements of each type of institution. However, the system appears to have reached a stage in which such regulation would be exceedingly complex (primarily because we lack substantive agreement about how to organize education at any level, whether secondary, vocational/technical, or higher). In any case, the best way to address curriculum problems is not to implement legalistic standards that define formal requirements for degrees. The more effective way is through a more substantive discussion that focuses on the nature of a student's education and the most feasible ways of evaluating his or her progress in light of the CSE's insights, as well as domestic and international experience.

V. Public Financing: Growth by Aggregation

The 1981 legislation created a radically different framework for the funding of higher education. Three new mechanisms were introduced, regulated by Decree 4 issued that year by the Ministry of Education. They are:

- Direct budgetary contributions (AFD in Spanish). These consist of public resources whose total amount is allocated each year in the national budget. The distribution of AFD among eligible schools (those existing in 1980 plus those spun off from the University of Chile, State Technical University, and Catholic University of Chile, all of

---

14 These professions are: attorney-at-law, architect, biochemist, dentist, engineer (agricultural, civil, business, and forestry), physician, veterinarian, pharmacist, psychologist, teacher (primary, secondary, and remedial), preschool teacher, and journalist (Law 8,962, Art. 52.3).

TABLE 4

USE OF FISCAL RESOURCES FOR HIGHER EDUCATION
SELECTED YEARS FROM 1981-1995
In millions of 1995 pesos

Year	Institutional Contributions	Student Aid	Research Development	Resources for Other Uses	Total
	(1)	(2)	(3)	(4)	
1981	147,553	0	0	0	147,553
1982	136,004	20,575	111	0	156,590
1983	100,190	26,994	68	0	127,252
1984	96,431	30,453	90	20	126,994
1985	85,997	27,370	117	19	113,503
1986	80,647	25,911	372	22	106,952
1987	75,751	24,172	193	16	100,132
1988	72,286	22,697	1,340	5,585	101,908
1989	68,814	16,211	1,917	7,739	94,681
1990	62,968	13,040	1,815	10,612	88,435
1991	70,052	20,231	4,651	4,924	99,858
1992	75,556	21,562	7,691	5,113	109,822
1993	80,096	23,946	12,937	6,317	123,296
1994	80,976	22,922	17,224	5,907	127,029
1995	82,418	24,309	14,458	4,912	126,097
1996	84,751	26,519	[9,755](5)	4,872	[125,897]

Sources: For the years 1981-1995, Basso and González, 1995 p.7. For 1995, Vice-Rectory of Economics and Business Management, U. of Chile.

Notes: (1) Comprised of the budgetary support of direct and indirect fiscal contributions (AFD and AFI).

(2) Comprised of Supplementary Support to the University Credit Solidarity Funds, Tariff Scholarships, and "Reparación" Scholarships. (Law 19.123)

(3) Comprised of Conicyt, Fondecyt and Fondef funds

(4) Refers to support arguments with the Catholic University of Chile, the Austral University, and the University of Chile.

(5) For 1996, information only available from the Development Fund (Fundef): M$9,755,225. Information not available for corresponding Conicyt figures.

which are represented on the Council of Presidents),[15] is based on historical criteria; that is, a percentage of the budgeted funds apportioned among the traditional universities at the time the law changed in 1981. The law calls for the gradual replacement of this direct contribution, equal at that time to 100% of the governmental funding of universities, by indirect budgetary contributions (up to 50%), in an effort to stimulate competition among the institutions.

---

15 Through 1992, two professional institutes continued to receive direct fiscal contributions. As of that year, those schools became universities (University de Los Lagos and Metropolitan Technological University). Thus, as of 1993, only the 25 universities represented on the Council of Presidents receive AFD.

TABLE 5

EVOLUTION OF INDIRECT FISCAL SUPPORT: 1982-1995
(In millions of pesos each year)

Year	Amount	Year	Amount
1982	1,656	1989	6,055
1983	2,010	1990	7,326
1984	2,054	1991	9,208
1985	2,395	1992	10,635
1986	2,730	1993	11,859
1987	3,087	1994	13,045
1988	3,793	1995	14,091

Source: Basso and González, 1995: p. 130

- Indirect fiscal contributions (AFI). These public funds are distributed among institutions based on the number of first-time Academic Aptitude Test (PAA) takers who score among the top 20,000 and enroll as freshmen in a major offered at a particular institution.[16]
- The elimination of free education at publicly-funded schools. This translated into the need to charge tuition reflecting the real cost of instruction and the private benefit obtained by students receiving university training. To offset the impact of these new fees on low-income students, a system of publicly-funded student loans to cover tuition costs was established.

The new financing policy established in 1981 was based upon two principles. First, a progressive reduction in the share of public funding allocated to higher education,[17] and second, strong pressure upon schools receiving AFD to secure independent sources of funding by competing in the marketplace to attract students as well as research, service, and outreach contracts. In addition, public policy on the financing of higher education since 1974 has significantly curtailed government funding through so-called "special legislation."

1. INSTITUTIONAL CONTRIBUTION OF PUBLIC FUNDS

Given the importance AFI has acquired as a funding mechanism, it is interesting to note some statistics related to its operation. In essence, AFI is a demand-side subsidy that rewards the schools best able to compete in "selling" their offer of majors to an elite group of students; that is, the top scorers on the PAA. As shown in Table 5, for the period 1982-

---

16 Subsequently, the number of top PAA scorers generating AFI was increased to 27,000, in order to expand the mechanism to a wider range of schools and raise the potential for AFI contributions to private institutions.

17 From 1965 though 1992, public spending on education as a percentage of GNP was as follows:

1965	1967	1969	1971	1973	1982	1984	1986	1988	1990	1992
0.99	1.08	1.11	1.28	2.11	1.28	1.04	0.80	0.64	0.52	0 . 5 4

The figures show a consistent downward trend during the military government (1973-1990). See Arriagada (1989) and Lehman (1993).

1995, State resources channeled to institutions of higher learning through AFI totaled over 89.8 billion pesos, with a clear upward trend in the yearly allocations.

Beginning in 1990, as a result of the expansion in the number of AFI-eligible scorers negotiated during the Aylwin administration, some emerging private universities began to receive funds through AFI. That year, these universities attracted 894 billion pesos of AFI. Henceforth, the trend has moved steadily upward, to the point that in 1995 these institutions received 1.78 billion pesos in AFI. All told, from 1990 through 1995, the country's private universities secured nearly 7.65 billion pesos through indirect budgetary contributions.

As one might suspect, the distribution of AFI among institutions is markedly unequal, since the top scorers tend to cluster in a limited number of institutions. The schools obtaining the greatest amounts of AFI are the University of Chile, Catholic University of Chile, University of Santiago, University of Concepción, and the Catholic University of Valparaíso. For the period 1982-1995, the total AFI figures received by these institution were, respectively, 15.95, 12.44, 10.16, 8.87, and 6.32 billion pesos. A further differentiating factor in AFI distribution comes in the form of a "bonus" paid to institutions based on the major in which the top scorers enroll for their freshman year. The areas of engineering and basic sciences generate bonus payments significantly larger than those of social sciences.

Finally, there appears to be a significant level of consensus among university officials that the current funding system for public universities is extremely weak in its generation of funds for investment. This area is in urgent need of a long-term policy which will allow corrective measures to be devised and implemented.

2. BIDDABLE FUNDS

Scientific and technological development are two areas in which a biddable fund mechanism has been extensively used to channel public sector resources to institutions of higher learning. Some of these resources reach institutions through research projects they sponsor and/or for which they provide operational capacity (infrastructure and services). In other cases, the resources reach the institutions through associations with private entities outside the educational system. In addition to support for research in science and technology, the Ministry of Education administers other biddable project-based funds, including the Institutional Development Fund, designed to finance academic infrastructural projects. The latter funds are available solely to educational establishments.

In 1982, the Ministry of Economics, Growth, and Reconstruction implemented a Science and Technology Program in an effort to encourage technological research among private Chilean companies in areas associated with the nation's commercial activities. The project sought to foster capabilities in research and development (R&D) at the corporate level as well as among technological institutes and research facilities. The program involves three project areas — Fontec, Fondef, and Fondecyt — that are funded by the IDB (a US$94 million loan) and the State (US$61 million) (Vergara 1995). Fontec and Fondef focus on applied research, development, and technological innovation related to production. Fondecyt seeks to foster world-class scientific research.

Fondecyt (the National Fund for Scientific and Technological Development) was created by a Ministry of Education Decree (DFL 33) published on October 27, 1981. It began operating in 1982, and throughout its 15-year history it has seen significant change in both the trends and volume of funding. In the process, it has become increasingly well-established as an institution.

While Fondecyt was established to fund scientific and technological research programs, its creators did not specify priority areas or disciplines. Thus, projects compete for funding on equal terms. The Fund has always been closely linked to the universities. In fact, the original idea was that the Fund would allow universities to fulfill their role, as mandated in the legislation in place at the time (DL 3541 of 1980 and DFL 1 of 1980), as institutions of higher education, research, thought, and culture designed to serve the country's needs and interests at the very highest of standards. Furthermore, it was initially hoped that the Fund would contribute to the development of doctoral dissertations as a prerequisite for the degree of Doctor of Philosophy (Ph.D.), since the legislation left such decisions in the hands of the universities.

Between 1982 and 1995, the universities represented on the Council of Presidents implemented 91% of the 4,871 projects awarded. The University of Chile and the Catholic University of Chile have clearly dominated the system, attaining 61% of funded projects (2,969). Approximately 9% have gone to non-university research centers, including independent academic centers, research institutions, state agencies, and private educational establishments (Santelices 1995). Data illustrating the Fund's progress can be found in a survey taken by Fondecyt in 1994 in which 756 researchers participated, among other sources (Manzi et al. 1994; Elgueta et al. 1995).

In 1991, CORFO created the National Committee for Technological and Productive Development Funding (Fontec) in order to promote, finance, and subsidize the implementation of R&D projects and the acquisition of infrastructure, as well as, in general, to encourage the development and sale of technological products by domestic companies. Fontec maintains three lines of funding open to private companies: technological innovation projects, infrastructure projects, and the contracting of scientific and technological services. The project innovation area includes a subsidy and an option for a supplementary loan. The subsidy is applied if the company chooses not to acquire the exclusive rights to the project results. Should the firm decide to retain the rights to its invention, 50% of the Fontec contribution must be reimbursed. The second area involves the funding of infrastructural projects and technology transfers. In the former case, loans for up to 80% of the total cost of the project are granted, with a subsidy of up to one-third the amount approved, as long as three or more firms are participating jointly. In the latter case, the project must be sponsored by at least five companies, and funding can reach up to 80% of the total, of which no more than 40% can be a subsidy. The cap on the latter type of funding is US$300,000. For scientific and technology projects, Fontec grants a loan that funds up to 80% of the total cost.[18]

From its initiation in 1991 through 1995, Fontec funded 368 projects involving a total cost of some US$46 million, of which the Fund contributed $24 million. Although Fontec targets private companies, its linkages with universities have been highly important. While this involvement may be somewhat overshadowed by this fund's emphasis on the private sector, it should be noted that 33 of the projects approved through July 1995 included six universities as participants,[19] either implementing projects jointly or providing infrastructure for them (Vergara 1995).

------

18 These credits include special conditions, such as interest at the average 3- to 12-month rate for deposits plus 1%; and payback periods of up to seven years after the end of the grace period (the maximum contract term for the project plus one year), with the total not exceeding 10 years.

19 The universities involved in Fontec projects were: University of Chile (13 projects), Catholic University (9), Catholic University of Valparaíso (9), University of Concepción (3), University Austral (3), and University of Bío-Bío (1).

3. RESOURCES FOR STUDENTS

The identification of support mechanisms for students is an area which must receive higher social and economic priority. In general, the State's responsibility to provide financial assistance to support the training of Chile's human capital should be expressed through policies that attain desirable results. Thus, funds should be granted to qualified students who lack the personal or family resources needed to obtain the schooling they need. Currently, three types of assistance are normally provided. *Scholarships* are grants of funds which students are not obligated to repay to the government. This aid is provided primarily to extremely disadvantaged students. *Government loans* require repayment at a rate of 5% of students' future incomes. These loans again target the neediest sectors. Finally, *student bank loans* in Chile are associated with the preferential line of credit established by CORFO for commercial banks. This mechanism targets middle-income students.

The current system of university loans in Chile[20] benefits only full-time students at establishments belonging to the Council of Presidents. The system has the following characteristics:
- It provides tuition assistance for students who clearly and credibly demonstrate their need.
- Repayment of this loan is not calculated on a purely financial basis, but is tied to 5% of the students' future earnings, thereby helping to prevent defaults bad loans due to unemployment.
- The methodology used to ascertain a students' repayment capacity[21] has been proven effective over the past five years.
- The repayment period of 12 to 15 years (nearly twice the time students spend earning their degrees) includes a grace period of two years so that students can gain secure employment.
- Opportunities for early payment are provided, as well as a system of 10 monthly payments per year over a 10-year period (and a waiver in filing annual tax statements).

In sum, the current system is based on the students' future earnings, not on the family's ability to pay (as has been the case in the past). For this system to be successful, sufficient funds must be made available to cover the demand for loans based on existing socioeconomic criteria. In support of this goal, we might consider creating a referential maximum tuition rate, since schools may otherwise have an incentive to raise tuition and hamper the system's operation. Similarly, since the government funds are allocated to institutions, and since there is no proper control on the creation of new majors, a negative incentive exists that encourages expansion in the supply of services, causing a subsequent rise in the number of beneficiaries of student aid.

Considering that all loans involve certain costs to be assumed by the beneficiary, it may be affirmed that student aid should not cover 100% nor fall below 20% of tuition, as is

---

20 The system is regulated by the provisions of Law 19,287, which in turn modifies Law 18,591, "Government Funding of University Loans."
21 Established by Education Decree 938 in December 1994.

the case today given the limited amount of funds available at universities (the current government loans or *Fondos de Crédito Solidario* are institution-based). This impedes efforts to achieve overall equity, since the socioeconomic situation of students at the most traditional schools, located in Santiago, and that of students in outlying regions or those attending spin-off schools may differ enormously.

Based on the experience obtained through the application of the current student financing mechanisms, and keeping in mind the State's fundamental role in this area — not only because of the unquestionable issues surrounding equity, but also considering the social return on the training of human resources — some ideas come to mind for a new system of student aid. A National Loan Fund for higher education might be established, aimed at a given number of students attaining a certain minimum score on the PAA plus a minimum grade point average in high school indicative of their academic skills.[22] The subsidized loans could be offered for training at institutions of proven quality, in areas of specialization the State seeks to promote due to their importance to national development. The institutions and majors accredited by the State to enroll the beneficiaries of this government-funded program would be reviewed periodically, with the results made available to the public.

In sum, in light of the characteristics and trends in the different public financing mechanisms for higher education in place since 1981, it is evident that without clarity in the criteria for establishing, modifying, or eliminating the current systems and financial instruments (once created, funding mechanisms tend to remain in place), little progress can be made. The situation appears to be widespread, affects all of the institutions in the system to a greater or lesser extent, including those private schools spawned by the 1980 legislation.[23] There is a considerable degree of consensus on the urgent need to clarify the State's responsibilities in the funding of higher education. Guidelines are needed for the use of the public goods present in the system, as well as for State support for qualified students who are unable to pay.

A wide-ranging debate is necessary over the funding mechanisms for higher education in place today. Measures to improve the system may include: tying the allocation of direct budgetary contributions to the attainment of certain goals (performance contracts); reducing (and potentially eliminating) indirect budgetary funding; substantially increasing post-graduate scholarships; reviewing resource allocation criteria with a view toward improving management capabilities; expanding resources and coverage for Fondecyt (perhaps aimed at priority areas such as regional universities or young researchers); renewing and expanding Fondef; and increasing the availability of university loans to ensure appropriate coverage while containing demand to prevent unchecked expansion.

---

22 In addition, it has been proposed that candidates be among the top 5% of their graduating class. This would help reduce discrepancies in academic performance between public and private secondary schools.

23 It is interesting to note that these institutions have suggested that while the sources of funding to which they have legal access "appear to be sufficient and sizable, they only permit private universities to engage in their institutional and educational projects in the field of teaching and provide some sporadic initiatives in the areas of academic and cultural outreach, as well as some timid research activities."
Corporation of Private Universities, "Estatuto patrimonial para las universidades sin aporte fiscal directo," p. 5, April 1995.

VI. Policy Options for Higher Education

1. CURRENT DISCUSSIONS ON SECTORIAL POLICY

A significant proportion of the issues involved in the higher education policy debate were touched upon in the Minister of Education's presentation to the nation's academic community during the period of student protests in 1997 (a series of events that contributed heavily to the current outlook on education).[24] The key points emerging from the Minister's presentation were: the equity challenge involved in offering equally-qualified students the opportunity to receive university, professional, or technical training; an excessively short-term management focus, impairing elements of the institutions' mission that "do not find an echo in the marketplace," such as basic research, basic science programs, humanities, and the arts; the virtually unrestricted growth of the system, which will eventually undermine the quality of educational offerings and consequently the role of higher education in Chile; and an inappropriate legal framework for state-run universities. The Minister called for revision of these universities' administrative systems and participatory mechanisms, as well as their relationship with national and regional development.

Another key component in the discussion of public policy for higher education is the proposed sweeping new legislation on state-run universities currently being reviewed by Congress (including the ideas expressed in the bill itself, as well as general guidelines contained in the corresponding Presidential Instructions). It is clear that the positions of those involved in the current discussion are still evolving. Thus, the present paper was written at a time of ongoing flux.[25] Nevertheless, qualitative changes of enormous import have already taken place, which will have a significant impact on the discussions in Congress and on future action by government officials.

The immediate effects include the fact that the topic of higher education has emerged from its status of "benevolent neglect" to stand at the very top of the domestic political agenda. Thus, it is not overly optimistic to expect that there *will* be a new policy on higher education. Although the catalyst for the debate has been the role of state universities, it is clear that the heart of the issue lies in the State's overall role in the system. In other words, conditions now appear favorable for a comprehensive reformulation of higher education policy that does not necessarily require changes to the current educational law (LOCE).

Second, the Ministry of Education has stated in no uncertain terms that "the challenge universities confront today is not only one of management, financing, and organization, but also one of concept, identity, and mission," (Arellano 1997). This means that, at long last, the idea has taken root that the crisis in these institutions is not one solely of modernization but also of modernity.

Third, the legally-mandated role of the government and the participation of internal university institutions in academic affairs have risen to the forefront of the debate. This

---

24 José Pablo Arellano, Minister of Education, "Políticas para la educación superior," document presented to the nation's academic community in Santiago, July 10, 1997.

25 The recurring sit-ins and the rapid expansion of the student movement in April/May of 1997 clearly captured the government's attention. After an initial reaction seeking to contain the issue by passing the conflicts back to school officials, the national government made a commitment to send a new bill on state-run universities to Congress. This bill went to the legislature in early July, 1997.

discussion alone has done much to revitalize the student movement's ability to attract members and inspire action.

Finally, it has become clear that the current dissatisfaction with the educational system can be found not only in Santiago but also in the provinces, where it has taken on considerable force. We can expect that the debate will become particularly vigorous with respect to public universities' relationship with regional development. In other words, the topic of regionalization and decentralization of higher education is increasingly salient.

2. TOWARD A NEW AGENDA

Some brief conclusions can be drawn from this discussion on the main impediments to the formulation of a national public policy on higher education. These problems are present in the attitudes of the players involved in the discussion, whether governmental officials, university officials, academicians, or the increasingly vocal and effective student organizations. As such, we can identify a very real, if occasionally obscured, agenda that clamors for the attention and the decisions that current conditions demand. That agenda includes:

- *The pressing need for equity.* Higher education policy must address the issue of equity, which involves a commitment by the country and its system of higher education to offer all those with sufficient academic merit the opportunity to pursue quality post-secondary studies at the university, professional, or technical level (Arellano 1997).

- *A long-term strategic vision.* Higher education policy must take on a longer-term vision. It must overcome the limitations of short-term management processes that compromise key elements of the institutional mission not reflected in marketplace considerations (such as basic research, basic science programs, the arts and humanities). Our nation's policy should actively promote strategic visions of higher education, science, and technology, aiming to develop national skills that will foster social integration and enhance our country's competitiveness (Atria 1995; Brunner 1997).[26]

- *The critical need for quality.* Higher education policy should focus on channeling the system's expansion so that academic programs can be properly evaluated and accredited, especially if the regulatory gap is not filled. If this is not done, the quality of the nation's educational offerings and thus the role of higher education overall will suffer immeasurably. Sustaining quality will require institutionalized and ongoing evaluation of schools and their programs, including the "autonomous" schools, by academic peers, public sector experts, and even private sector professionals in the case of certain courses of study (Brunner 1997; Lemaitre 1997).

- *Greater rationalization of funding institutions and activities.* The center of gravity should be shifted toward demand-sensitive public and private funding mechanisms. Government subsidies should be based on performance contracts and/or goals, solid results, biddable projects, competitive tenders, or formulas that better serve the public interest (Bernasconi 1994; Lavados 1995).

---

26 It is revealing to note that professional scientists and engineers in Latin America account for just 3% of the world total and a meager 1.3% of published authors in these fields. Of the global total of 400,000 patents granted by the end of the previous decade, Latin Americans received less than 3% (Brunner, 1997).

- *Increased flexibility for State-run universities.* Finally, identification of the development criteria common to all state-run institutions should be accompanied by recognition of the significant differences among them.[27] The legal framework should be adjusted to the needs of state-run schools.[28] This means revising not only academic management processes, but also the universities' systems of governance and participation as well as their relationship with national and regional development.

---

27 A modernization proposal for the state-run universities was presented in 1995 as a bill for Congressional debate. This effort sought to specify common elements but did not clearly address the problem of identifying factors inherent to the different types of state-run universities.

28 According to Brunner, "The traditional public universities seem to have lost their old sense of mission, and their role has also become more diluted and difficult to define. In comparison, a number of private institutions currently exist that are market-oriented and funded exclusively by the tuition paid by students or their families" (Brunner 1997).

BIBLIOGRAPHICAL REFERENCES

Arellano, José Pablo. 1997. "Políticas para la educación superior." Document presented to the nation's academic community in Santiago (July 10).

Arriagada, P. 1989. Financiamiento de la educación superior en Chile: 1960–1988. Santiago: Flacso.

Atria, R. 1995. "La transformación modernizante en la educación superior: un enfoque general." In: Atria R. et al. *Diálogos universitarios*. Santiago: Corporación de Promoción Universitaria (CPU).

Aria R. et al. 1995. *Diálogos universitarios*. Santiago: Corporación de Promoción Universitaria (CPU).

Basso, P. and E. González. 1996. "Fuentes y usos de los recursos fiscales para educación superior, 1981–1995." *Informe de la educación superior*. Santiago: Corporación de Promoción Universitaria (CPU).

Bernasconi, A. 1994. "La privatización de la educación superior chilena y la regulación a través del mercado." *Estudios sociales* 82. Santiago: Corporación de Promoción Universitaria (CPU).

Brunner, J. J. 1995. "Educación superior: Chile en el contexto internacional comparado". In: Atria R. et al. *Diálogos universitarios*. Santiago: Corporación de Promoción Universitaria (CPU).

―――. 1997. "La educación superior chilena como objeto de análisis y de políticas." *Estudios Sociales* 91. Santiago.

Brunner, J. J. and G. Briones. 1992. *Higher education in Chile: Effects of the 1980 Reform.* Santiago: Flacso, Education and Culture Series 29.

Corporación de Promoción Universitaria (CPU). 1996. *Informe de la educación superior*. Santiago: CPU.

―――. 1996. *Instrumentos gubernamentales para el desarrollo científico nacional*. Santiago: CPU.

―――. 1996. *Rol y destino de las universidades estatales*. Santiago: CPU.

―――. 1997. *Acreditación en Chile: La experiencia de un lustro*. Santiago: CPU.

Elgueta, C. M., M. E. Boisier, and A. Farcas. 1995. "Evolución del Fondo Nacional de Desarrollo Científico y Tecnológico (Fondecyt) 1982–1995." Santiago: Comisión Nacional de Investigación Científica y Tecnológica (Conicyt), Study Series 28.

Lavados, I. 1995. "Cambios y tendencias en la educación superior." In: Atria R. et al. *Diálogos universitarios*. Santiago: Corporación de Promoción Universitaria (CPU).

Lavados, J. 1996. "Rol y destino de las universidades estatales: una interrogante que recién comienza". In: CPU. *Rol y destino de las universidades estatales*. Santiago: Corporación de Promoción Universitaria (CPU).

Lehman, C. 1993. "Financiamiento de la educación superior en Chile: resultados del período 1982–1992." In: *Informe de la educación superior 1993*. Santiago: Foro de la educación superior.

Lemaitre, M. J. 1997. "La visión del Consejo Superior de Educación." In: CPU. *Acreditación en Chile: La experiencia de un lustro*. Santiago: Corporación de Promoción Universitaria (CPU).

Manzi, J., et al. 1995. "Evolución del Fondo Nacional de Desarrollo Científico y Tecnológico (Fondecyt) 1982–1995." Santiago: Comisión Nacional de Investigación Científica y Tecnológica (Conicyt), Study Series 28.

Santelices, B. 1996. "Fondecyt: Un análisis de su evolución (1982–1995). In: CPU. *Instrumentos gubernamentales para el desarrollo científico nacional*. Santiago: Corporación de Promoción Universitaria (CPU).

Vergara, J. 1996. "Comentarios finales." In: CPU. *Instrumentos gubernamentales para el desarrollo científico nacional*. Santiago: Corporación de Promoción Universitaria (CPU).

Religion and Culture

Cristián Parker

In the religious field, many things have changed in Chile since the time when several churches, mainly the Catholic Church, stood up decisively for human rights under the 17-year authoritarian military regime. These same churches, during the 1980s, played a very important role in generating the conditions for the country's return to democracy in 1990. Nevertheless, the changes in the religious field of Chilean society during these past eight years involve much more than Church-State relations. They encompass changes in the general mentality, influenced by diverse sociocultural and religious currents, regarding conflicts over morality and legislation about the freedom of religion in Chile. The dynamics of the Chilean religious field have moved far beyond the framework of the classic conflicts between Catholicism and laicism, and clericalism and anticlericalism, that characterized republican Chile before 1973.

To properly understand religious phenomena, at least two substantive elements must be considered. One arises from the specific nature of religion, defined by its content oriented toward transcendental subjects. The second rests in the fact that all religious manifestations form part of the social and cultural fabric of a particular society. Therefore, religious issues cannot be addressed without taking account of the cultural framework in which they are embedded.

An analysis of religion within the culture of Chile's post-authoritarian period (1990–97) must take note of the interaction of at least two general processes: the socio-political changes arising from democratization, and the cultural changes linked to globalization. Of course, these are broad cultural and political trends that began far earlier than the period analyzed here. Their impact on the cultural and religious fields during the 1990s has often been subtle and complex. Nevertheless, in spite of the limitations of a still-incomplete analysis such as the one presented here, it seems possible to identify certain fundamental tendencies in the trajectory of cultural and religious change. This analysis is important in order to identify the effect of these developments upon the role played by religion and the churches in the building of a democratic society.

The analysis of these matters from a sociological point of view is the central purpose of this article.[1] When speaking of religion, the first thing that comes to mind is the churches.

---

1   Although it is necessary to acknowledge the specific nature, depth, and complexity of the religious aspect of our societies, the author will approach this topic from a social science perspective, not a theological or ecclesiastical one.

Nevertheless, religion should not be confused with the Church, since the latter is only a small part of what religion entails. This is not a matter of simple semantic difference. Establishing this conceptual distinction will allow us to analyze with a fresh vision the relationship between religion and culture in Chile in recent years.

Religion can be understood as that part of culture that refers, fundamentally, to transcendental, extra-social understanding and legitimacy, beyond time and space. The practice of religion becomes a specific cultural field composed of a variety of elements, including beliefs, rituals, religious ethics, and religious institutions (churches and various religious groups).

All religions express a relationship with faith. Faith provides a belief, a relationship to certainties, and a source of solutions to the practical or existential problems encountered in the lives of men and women. Fundamentally, what all religions offer is meaning. Every religion, whether magical, mystical, or salvational, aims at recognizing a higher order that can plausibly resolve the eternal questions for a community of people: creation, life and death, good and evil, health and sickness, the beginning and the end of history, and so forth.

Among the set of beliefs that comprise a religion, one can discern transcendental and supernatural beings and realities, or sanctified or glorified historical ones, generally endowed with extraordinary powers and energy in their interactions with men and women: God, Jesus Christ, the Trinity, the Virgin, Mohammed, Moses, also Satan, the weküfes (from local Indian lore), Saint Barbara, Shangó, the Prophet Smith, Romualdito, Saint Sebastian, animitas (interceding souls), and so forth.

The relationship between man and this pantheon of supernatural beings –- whether cosmic, personalized, zoomorphic, or anthropomorphic –- is generally characterized by ritual practices: prayers, liturgy, pilgrimages, supplications, propitiatory rites, sacrificial rites, and an array of mystical, ascetic, or esoteric rituals and disciplines.

Religions also fulfill the function of setting norms for behavior, with their establishment of a certain religious ethic. This ethic may or may not involve a social component of morality. Highly-developed religions contain a strong component of ethical justification, along with highly detailed prescriptions and prohibitions. Religions involving magical, esoteric, or superstitious practices, however, have fewer ties to social mores.

Churches appear only as a specific manifestation of the organic institutionalization of a certain historical religion. The various elements that comprise institutionalized religions are displayed and developed within the religious field, which is that part of the social and symbolic space occupied by religious players, institutions, messages, symbols, practices, and morals in an ongoing and dynamic interaction (Bourdieu 1971). This religious field can be conceptually understood as part of the socio-cultural terrain of a society. Once it has acquired its own specificity due to its religious nature, it is also a product of the conflicts that make it dynamic, the terrain these conflicts manifest themselves in, and an active factor in those socio-symbolic conflicts (Maduro 1978).

Nonetheless, the degree of relative autonomy of social dynamics within the religious field must be made clear in each case. This is determined by the level of what has been called the secularization of society. It is true that the term "secularization" is very much debated today and runs the risk of intentional vagueness. Yet with regard to institutional secularization, at least, we can state that its advance leads to a greater probability that the religious dynamic will develop more autonomously, and that social unrest, for similar reasons, will be increased.

In fact, religion is one of the most significant manifestations, not only of civil society, but also of the very civilization in which each society develops. Therefore, religion is a core component of the culture of a nation and a people. Changes in religion are actually changes in the culture of a nation. Thus, religion serves as a excellent indicator of social change, which inevitably goes beyond strictly religious aspects.

With the historical arguments typical of a long life dedicated to investigating the history of civilizations, Fernand Braudel (1993:22) reminds us that religion is at the center of culture, in the heart of its past and its present, and that only Western civilization seems to have forgotten its Christian origins. Nevertheless, rather than the rupture between faith and culture brought about by rationalism, what must actually be studied today is the interrelationship between laicism, religion, and science in that alternatingly calm and tumultuous debate in which, despite outward appearances, so called "secularized" societies have been engaged.

Likewise, in modern societies it is not possible to meld the religious field with the other arenas of social life, whether economic, political, or cultural. Secularization should be understood more as a differentiation of fields of action in modern society, and therefore as a demarcation of the line between the churches and the modern State, rather than as a direct loss of religion's influence upon the minds of the people.

An analysis of the transformations witnessed and experienced by religion in Chile since the end of the military regime would require more space and a much more detailed and exhaustive treatment. Therefore, this analysis must remain partial and will focus mainly, although not exclusively, on certain aspects of the transformations of religious beliefs affected by globalization, as well as the responses of the churches, especially that of the Catholic Church, to the country's recent return to democracy.

I. Globalization and Pluralization of the Religious Field in Chile

1. GLOBALIZATION: A CHALLENGE TO RELIGION?

With Chile's reintegration into the international economy during the 1980s, the effects of the globalization process began to be felt with greater weight. This concept captures one of the core features of the social changes we are experiencing on the threshold of the third millennium. "Globalization" is an eclectic and polysemic term coined to refer to a complex process, including the spread of a new technological paradigm and changes in productive processes, financial flows, labor markets, organizational and procedural designs, education, information and communication systems, forms of urban and family life, consumption patterns, advertising and marketing, knowledge, values, and citizen preferences, and thus, ways of life for societies and individuals (Tomassini 1995). It is a set of changes which affects all areas of life in society and which, according to authors such as Robertson (1992), implies a growing awareness among members of society that we live in a global world. Changes that transform culture pose fundamental and meaningful questions about a relative "acceleration of historical time" in the transition from industrial to post-industrial society.

It is difficult to pinpoint the ways in which a long-term process such as globalization has affected culture and religion in Chile since 1990. However, as an interpretative hypothesis regarding the impact of globalization on specific cultures, four processes can be identified, at least in the Chilean case, that interact with the religious field (Parker 1997a) to generate a "post-religious" culture that is no longer secularist in nature.

First, globalization tends to introduce a "global culture" — a notion related to MacLuhan's widespread idea of the "global village" — emerging from the communication network made possible by technology. This global culture, with its universalizing effect and the homogeneity brought on by current techno-science, clearly opens enormous and unanticipated opportunities, yet it also poses serious challenges to local cultures and their identities and unique traditions.

This global culture, which is actually the culture of a global system, is not exempt from complex internal rifts and currents. It reinforces the universalist idea of certain global problems that can only be solved through an "ecumenical" approach. The strengthening of international organizations and an increasingly closely-knit network of international relations (bilateral, regional, and multilateral) are accompanied by a new role for religions on the world stage and serve as an incentive for ecumenical activity. The rise of a planetary consciousness of human rights, ecology, and the environment, for example, is accompanied by the efforts of religions to attain peace, justice, and understanding among nations and peoples.

However, when traditional religions are rooted in local and national cultures, and when they perceive themselves as the bearers of a tradition that is being challenged, they may exhibit different reactions. In some cases, a "back to the roots" movement is provoked, feeding fundamentalist and sectarian tendencies.

Second, globalization, at the end of the Cold War, has led to the formation of increasingly interlinked international capital, commercial, industrial, and financial markets, as a growing number of countries adopt a development model advocating an opening to the world. This leads to the spread of market-driven economic decisions, along with an accent on private initiative and competitive mechanisms. Some developing countries, Chile among them, have taken advantage of these changes to achieve steady economic growth, thanks to the contributions of their export industries.

From a cultural point of view, however, the booming markets vindicating the triumph of freedom are accompanied by the rise of individualism and a consumer-oriented society. Individuals and institutions — including religions and the churches — find themselves facing the challenges of a society tending increasingly toward materialistic behavior and the satisfaction of individual desires. The rising dominance of marketing and new patterns of socialization pose a threat to long-standing social traditions and the solidarity of the community.

While a consumer society in fact generates changes that affect religious thinking and practices, the churches tend to focus on condemning what they interpret to be the greedy materialism inherent to the new system.

Third, globalization itself is the result of the bewildering changes to society and culture brought about by the increasing pace of scientific and technological progress. The speed of change, along with the effects of urbanization and institutional modernization, combine with long-standing conflicts and contradictions in society to transform the psycho-social environment. Individuals feel they are caught up in circumstances that accelerate the rhythm of life, making it less manageable and increasing psycho-social perceptions of insecurity.

The spread of this new cultural "climate" of drastic and unpredictable change around the world opens the door to a questioning of life and existence, accompanied by the loss of the solid ideological and religious foundations that had previously kept society united. A wide range of possibilities opens up, offering different truths and values, multicultural standards — in short, diverse religious expressions. The "menu" of religions tends to expand in a cultural context of growing concerns about "meaninglessness" and rising uncertainty among members of society.

Fourth, from this globalization, a process that opens up hope for many and generates anguish in others, a culture centered on the present is emerging. It is resistant to the idea of absolute truths and to the classical approaches to society that emphasized structural foundations: the individual is vindicated by some and questioned by others. What seems certain is the advent of a new consciousness, one that has arisen as an additional cultural current alongside the previously existing ones. Some have described it as "postmodern," because it questions the rationalism of modern enlightened culture. It focuses on the here and now, flirts with nihilism and hedonism, and proclaims the fragmentation of individuals and realities. The social dynamic now becomes a mere contingency. Out of this arises a serious questioning of the "macro-legends," the theologies and ideologies of yesteryear. Yet a new consciousness also becomes evident: spiritual, aesthetic, relativist, and resistant to authoritarianism and the dogmatism of tradition. This leads to a questioning — implicitly or clearly anarchical — of institutions. These so-called "postmodern" currents may be manifested in various currents of religious and pseudo-religious spiritualism that tend to go beyond the framework of the established churches.

In fact, the globalization process has unleashed a set of changes that have undeniably affected religion, churches, and their evangelizing mission. Contrary to the notion that globalization is an entirely positive development — one that aids the world's religions in drawing spiritually and ethically closer in order to confront emerging world crises — this process also produces dialectical contradictions and conflict.

Globalization inspires inter-religious perspectives within a diversity of cultures, which converge upon similar viewpoints regarding peace, justice, and human dignity. At the same time, however — in reaction to the increased dominance of non-religiously inspired values or tendencies toward fragmentation — it provokes the accentuation of fundamentalist, millennial, and integrationist religious perspectives. These feed on the defiant vindication of local, ethnic, or individual identities which feel threatened by the very process of globalization.

The concept Enzo Pace (1995) has called the "Westernizing ethnocentric theory" — which conceives of globalization as a positive form of secularization — must be questioned, since it fails to consider the trend toward the syncretization of beliefs and their complex re-articulation in various forms. The theory also fails to take into account that religion is often among the forms of cultural resistance practiced by non-Western peoples against the modernization processes that threaten to uproot them from their traditions. It also neglects the growing complexity of the religious field, in which the tensions between clergy and laymen, between the official Church and grassroots religious experience, are no longer so clear-cut. Instead, they are buffeted by religious and cultural crosscurrents, as well as ethnic and class divisions, which cut across the religious field, filling it with vertical and horizontal tensions.

Faced with this situation, the churches must discover appropriate strategies to carry out their evangelizing mission in this emerging global environment. Furthermore, questions arise within society about the persistence, transformation, reformation and/or revitalization of the churches and religious currents, as they confront and are influenced by the transformations of globalization.

FIGURE 1

CATHOLICS IN CHILE
(1907-1992)
Percentage of total population

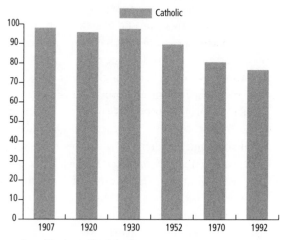

General Housing and Population Censuses

FIGURE 2

GROWTH OF EVANGELICAL CHRISTIANS
CHILE (1907-1992)
(per 1000 inhabitants)

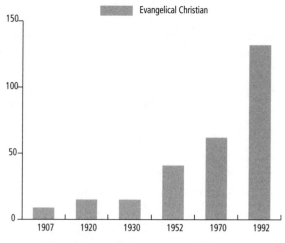

General Housing and Population Censuses

FIGURE 3

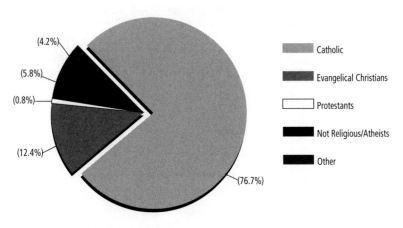

DECLARED RELIGION
NATIONAL POPULATION 14 YEARS AND OLDER
(percentages)

(4.2%)
(5.8%)
(0.8%)
(12.4%)
(76.7%)

Catholic

Evangelical Christians

Protestants

Not Religious/Atheists

Other

Source: 1992 Population Census

2. THE PLURALIZATION AND PERSISTENCE OF RELIGION

One phenomenon worthy of mention is the fact that within this globalizing environment, the trend toward increasing religious pluralism in Chile continues unabated and is in fact accelerating.

Let us remember that Chile has traditionally been a Christian country, where Catholicism has been the religion of the majority since the country gained independence in the early 19th century. Nevertheless, the tendency toward a plurality of religions in Chilean society is a long-standing one. In fact, Catholicism was never the sole religion. As can be seen in the accompanying figures, national census data during this century indicate a clear downward trend in the number of Catholics (see Figure 1) and an increase in the number of Protestant-Evangelical (see Figure 2) and other faiths.

This long-term tendency has been strengthened in recent years by globalization's effect of introducing new religious alternatives worldwide. Data from the most recent National Census, carried out in April 1992, indicate that although Catholicism is still the religion of the majority, increasing numbers of Chileans belong to a series of emerging religious alternatives. Figure 3 shows the religious affiliations declared by Chileans 14 years of age and older in the 1992 census.

If these census results are grouped by age, we can see that individuals in the older age groups maintain their traditional ties to Catholicism and religious beliefs in general. Within this group, a lower percentage profess agnosticism or atheism. Young people appear to be more open to diverse religious options, as well as to the secular influence of society that leads them to feel indifferent about religion. Religious pluralism is more accentuated among the younger generations (see Figure 4).

On the other hand, the rise of a powerful Protestant movement in Chile is one of the characteristic features of the contemporary religious landscape. Among these "Evangelicals,"

FIGURE 4

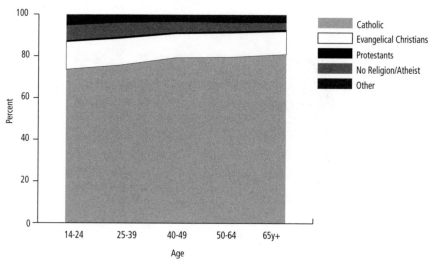

**DECLARED RELIGION
14 YEAR-OLDS AND OLDER**

Source: 1992 Population Census

as shown by the 1992 Census, it can be safely estimated that more than 85% belong to Pentecostal or Neo-Pentecostal churches and faiths. In fact, in the early 1980s, religious statistics for Latin America showed Chile and Guatemala to have the highest percentages of Evangelical church members among their national populations (Barret 1982). These figures may have changed in recent years, as Ecuador, Peru, and other countries have seen increases in Evangelical membership, but, in relative terms, Chile continues to be one of the most "Protestant" countries of Latin America.

As Figure 2 makes clear, the growth in the number of people professing an Evangelical faith in Chile has remained steady during this century. Considering that a very large percentage of the Evangelical or Protestant category is composed of those professing the Pentecostal faith, particularly after 1930, we can deduce that Pentecostalism today represents the country's second most prominent religion, following Catholicism. Its importance

TABLE 1

INCREASE IN THE NUMBER OF EVANGELICAL CHRISTIANS*
IN TWENTIETH CENTURY CHILE
(Percentages of Total Population)

YEAR	1907	1920	1930	1952	1970	1992
Evangelicals	0.97	1.46	1.50	4.1	6.22	13.2

* Includes Protestants, Evangelists and Orthodox.

Source: National Statistics Institute, Population Censuses.

FIGURE 5

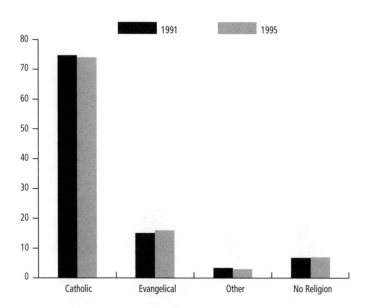

RELIGIOUS TENDENCIES
1991-1995
(percentages)

 1991   1995

Source: CEP National Public Opinion Statistics, 1995

is more pronounced among lower-income groups, in both urban and rural areas, as well as among indigenous populations (see Table 1).

Despite the long-term upward trend in Evangelical membership, the variations in people's professed religions do not appear to have been significantly affected by the democratization process. This has not been a factor in secularization, nor an outgrowth of an explosive increase in Evangelicals. Between 1991 and 1995, according to two surveys by the Center for Public Studies (CEP) using representative samples of the national population, the religions professed by Chileans have not varied substantially, as can be seen in Figure 5.

While the actions and influence of churches and religions in society have diminished considerably during the period of democratization, they are still of strikingly great importance. The relevance of the churches' position in civil society (including the Catholic Church, Evangelicals, and others) is seen in their outreach to broad and majority groups, such as families, women, young people, children, and the working classes. Within an environment of democratization and modernization, where growth with equity is a national goal and governmental campaigns against poverty are put into effect, the social work of these institutions and their significant position in national society are worthy of note (see Parker 1996a).

In general, the leading churches have a presence in Chilean public life. More specifically, the Catholic Church and some Pentecostal churches have achieved significant penetration at the grassroots level throughout the entire country. All have developed

FIGURE 6

**PRACTICING CATHOLICS AND EVANGELICALS
ATTEND MASS OR SERVICES AT LEAST ONCE A WEEK**
(percentages)

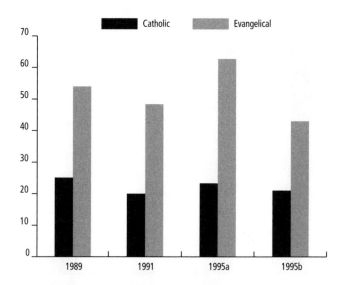

Source: 1989: CERC, Nacional; 1991: CEP-Adimark, Nacional;
1995a: MORI-Stgo; 1995b: CEP, Nacional

religious education programs. They work with families and maintain educational institutions. Because of this, the churches are key agents in the socialization process, promoting values of social integration and participation. It must be pointed out, however, that based on data from the previous census, (see Figure 4), the capacity of the churches, and particularly the Catholic Church, to socialize certain sectors of the country's youth in religious and moral values seems to have decreased.

Regarding the religious practices of the population, the figures for regular attendance at mass or services among both Catholics and Evangelicals are clear in confirming a consistent percentage with slight variations. Thus the proportion of practicing members fluctuates between 20% and 25% for Catholics and between 43% and 63% for Evangelicals. In general, these figures show a higher percentage of practicing members than those found in industrialized countries with a greater degree of secularization. They also clearly reveal much more active participation among Evangelicals than Catholics, measured according to the percentage taking part in official church rituals (see Figure 6).

Confirming the integrating role assigned by sociology to religion, the morality preached by established churches, in spite of its religious and theological overtones, is generally in harmony with the need for civic virtue. It is a moral framework that adapts individuals to their environment and offers opportunities for self-development, increased social participation, and promotion of the common good.

Within developing Latin American societies such as Chile, subjected to the intense pressures of modernization and globalization, the importance retained by the established churches is striking. Their power to bring people together and their deep roots in

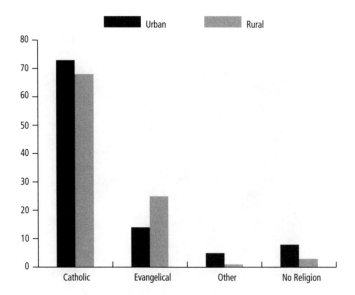

FIGURE 7

**1995 RELIGIOUS TENDENCIES
ACCORDING TO RURAL/URBAN DISTRIBUTION**
(percentages)

Source: CEP, National Public Opinion Statistics, 1995

the networks at the foundation of society, as well as the presence of their members in a high proportion of the country's households, give the established churches a much greater and more significant presence in civil society and in relation to the State than their peers in any country of Western Europe.

3. AN OVERVIEW OF CHILE'S MAJOR RELIGIONS

Aside from the presence of the established churches, the scope of observation must be broadened to include all of the religious expressions in Chile during this decade. Information gathered on an "inventory of churches" (Parker 1996a) from 1994 to 1995 allows us to provide a brief description of the most outstanding features of Chile's religious landscape.

First, despite the country's growing religious pluralism, Catholicism indisputably remains the leading religion, enjoying the broadest coverage and potential among the various segments of the national population. Catholicism is present in all social and geographic settings, but it is relatively more pronounced in urban areas than in rural ones. According to CEP studies for 1995, the proportion of Evangelicals in rural settings is 25%, but only 14% in urban areas (see Figure 7).

Second, the manifest expansion of Pentecostal churches in recent decades seems to have lifted them out of a position which had relegated them for many years to the sidelines and self-exclusion. Today they are opening up to a healthier interaction with society as a whole, vigorously led by the larger churches among them. In Troeltsch's words, they are

FIGURE 8

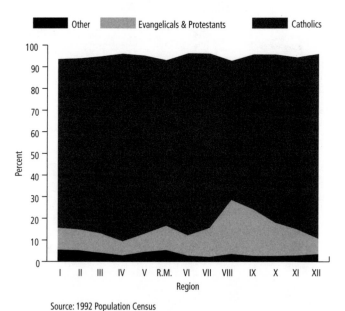

RELIGION BY REGION
CHILE 1992
(percentages)

■ Other   ■ Evangelicals & Protestants   ■ Catholics

Source: 1992 Population Census
*Atheists and those without religion are not included.

no longer sects, but are emerging as formalized churches. For the present author, the concept of "sect" is not a value judgment, but merely a description of groups who seek to revive primitive Christianity in a radical manner and thus find themselves in confrontation with the world.[2]

Continuing penetration by Pentecostal churches of working-class groups, rural inhabitants and the indigenous population, as well as in certain key areas of the country, especially from the Eighth Region (Biobío, Araucanía) to the Tenth Region (Los Lagos), may be expected in the coming century (see Figure 8). The higher incidence of Evangelical-Christian affiliation in the latter parts of the country can probably be explained by the fact that the Araucanía territory was incorporated into the nation at a very late date. For several centuries, the Mapuche lands remained a mission region, with a lower Catholic presence. From 1883 on, they have been considered mission territory by the Protestants and Evangelicals.

After the Catholic and Pentecostal churches are the traditional Protestant religions, as well as the Orthodox and Jewish communities. These are much smaller, being largely

---

2   The concept of "sect" originally proposed by Troeltsch described radical groups splintering off from the main church in search of a return to the original sources of Christianity, questioning the established churches and the sinning world. Today it has become an ideological phrase, used more for "witch hunts" than for serious analyses of the challenges posed by new religious phenomena to democratic society. For a critique of the misuse of the concept of "sect" in studies and discussions of new religious movements in Chile and Latin America, see Parker (1997a: 39).

confined to enclaves of immigrants and their descendants. They include mainly middle- and high-income groups with white-collar occupations. They retain a socio-religious prestige — probably reinforced by ties to their faiths on the international level — but their penetration into the population is more limited. Methodists and a branch of Lutherans, however, stand out with regard to their social actions and commitment, as well as their ecumenical outlook.

In fourth place are missionary churches and millennialist proselytizers, which have recently enjoyed considerable growth among the population. These include the Jehovah's Witnesses, the Mormons, and the Seventh-Day Adventists. In Latin America, these churches have usually been categorized as "new religious movements." In reality, however, they are an expression of a recent missionary penetration from abroad, mostly from North America.

The public presence of these diverse religious organizations is more attributable to their open and aggressive proselytizing style than to the number of believers they harbor (although this figure is not insignificant). Nevertheless, the degree of their penetration and influence, above all among middle-class groups and in outlying provinces, is remarkable in comparison with their meager resources. The Mormons are perhaps an exception here, since their resources, derived from support mechanisms in the United States, significantly exceed their relative success in recruiting new members (Acevedo 1990).

Nevertheless, it must be recognized that the growth of these churches and religious movements has been explosive over the last few years. The pace of expansion is gradually slowing, and communities such as the Adventists are increasingly achieving a more natural integration into social life, in many places generating a new type of religious ethos — neither Catholic nor Pentecostal — which promotes the integration and social mobility of these believers (González 1997).

Fifth, another prominent feature of the Chilean religious landscape involves latent tensions. In fact, within the dynamics characteristic of religious competition, we can discern a type of underground religious war among the different proselytizing churches and certain missionary churches, such as the Catholics and Baptists. Although the current trend is toward the surrender of discriminatory discourse among different groups to the influence of pluralism, the ecumenical impulse is still weak. It is less often put into practice, with the exception of certain institutions established by the churches themselves.

Churches such as the Jehovah's Witnesses, certain Pentecostal churches, Neo-Pentecostals, fundamentalist Evangelicals, and to a certain degree, the Mormons, seem to be less inclined to broad and benevolent community service. This is not the case with the Adventists, who demonstrate more openness in this area. Although the Adventists have millennialist characteristics, their public image is more moderate. For this reason, the Evangelical and mainline Protestant churches consider them closer to their own beliefs and do not subject them to extensive criticism.

Sixth, the role of the ecumenical organizations in social action is noteworthy, since they can achieve considerable coverage and are quite successful in mobilizing the population. Special attention should be paid to ecclesiastical or para-ecclesiastical organizations (whether individual, ecumenical, or inter-denominational) working in the social field or the area of human rights, such as the Fundación de Ayuda Social de Iglesias Cristianas (Fasic) [Foundation of Christian Churches for Social Assistance]. Others work directly with children, young people, and families, such as Feniprom, Hogar de Cristo [Home for

Christ], Fundación Programa de Menores [Foundation Youth Program], Visión Mundial [World Vision], and the Asociación Cristiana de Jóvenes [YMCA], among others.

The enormous educational efforts of all the churches are certainly no less relevant. There is practically no established church, whether Catholic, Orthodox, Protestant, or neo-Christian, without educational institutions at levels ranging from pre-school to university. It comes as no surprise that throughout this century, the Catholic Church has been a leading pillar of education in Chile and the main one in private education. In fact, seven Chilean universities, among them the influential Catholic University of Chile, are closely tied to the Catholic Church. The Church is also responsible for a sizable number of schools, especially private or subsidized secondary schools maintained by the local diocese or particular religious congregations. While the Catholic Church continues to be a strong force in education, Evangelical primary and secondary schools, and even universities, have been founded, although these may not yet be leading institutions.

4. NEW RELIGIOUS MOVEMENTS AND SYNCRETIC EXPRESSIONS

An important element in Chile's current religious panorama is the range of religious expressions not explicitly represented by the churches, although some of them are related to these institutions. These are the variety of beliefs, rituals, and practices of the so-called "folk religions," along with indigenous religions, the expanding expression of "New Age" spiritual sensitivities, and the new "post-religious" syncretism, also called new religious movements.

First and foremost is the increasing revitalization of indigenous religious practices. This refers not only to the revival of the rituals and beliefs of the Mapuche tribe (Marileo 1995; Salas 1996), the Aymara, Rapa-nui, and other groups, but also to their expression on a mass scale. Furthermore, they are being propagated among the younger generations, and their public expression is enjoying increasing legitimacy in Chilean society, which, despite its professions of tolerance, resists abandoning secular and ethnocentric prejudices. From this point of view, the mission work of various churches in indigenous communities appears somewhat contradictory. In fact, certain groups of Anglicans and Catholics are actively engaged in a mission of cultural indoctrination (not always welcomed by orthodox members within their own churches), while numerous Pentecostal groups have burst onto the scene with proselytizing practices that forcefully uproot the indigenous people from their cultural and religious context (Van Kessel y Guerrero 1987; Guerrero 1994).

Meanwhile, new religious expressions have gained ground over the past few decades within a generalized tendency toward the syncretization of beliefs. A multiplicity of cults, religious groups, and quasi-religious philosophies that do not fit the sociological category of "church" may be noted, although their prevalence and significance are relatively low. Sociology has termed these the "new religious movements" and noted their "sectarian" character. In Chile, these include:
• those with Christian or pseudo-Christian elements, such as Children or Sons of God or The Family, the Revolutionaries of Christ, and the Association for the Unification of World Christianity headed by Reverend Moon
• predominantly spiritual movements, such as spiritualism, theosophy, and Rosicrucianism
• those with Oriental and/or syncretic elements, including the International Association for Krishna Awareness, Divine Light Mission, Universal Baha'i Faith, etc. (Sanpedro 1986; Lagos 1987b; Santagada et al. 1991)

This religious pluralism and the breakup of the Catholic monopoly, especially among lower-income Chileans, is one of the country's most significant recent social developments. It gives evidence of an increasing pluralism of cultures and identities, which has been the object of some highly interesting studies.[3] It is thus not surprising that more attention is being paid to religious phenomena in Chile, even within academic circles previously eschewing the scientific study of this topic (Parker 1996c).

The central issue for the academic community, as well as for public opinion, is the visible growth of the "new religious movements" mentioned above (in common parlance often classified as "sects," with discriminatory overtones). Discussions of these groups in the media sometimes erroneously include the new Pentecostal and Evangelical churches, as well as the Mormons, Adventists, and Jehovah's Witnesses in this category of "sects." Current concerns regarding these religious groups — their ambiguous place in society, together with the fear they inspire in a culture seeking to defend its traditional order — lead to media treatment often characterized by a certain sensationalism.[4]

In Chile, furthermore, in contrast to neighboring countries,[5] no objective, scientific, and systematic studies of these new religious movements have undertaken. Research

FIGURE 9

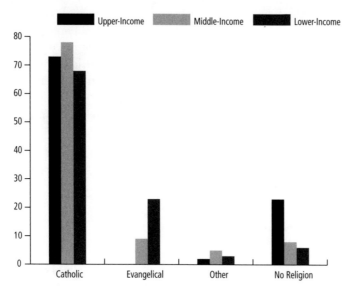

**RELIGIOUS TENDENCIES
ACCORDING TO SOCIOECONOMIC STRATA: 1995**
(percentages)

Source: CEP National Public Opinion Statistics, 1995.

---

3   Among studies in the current decade focusing on Pentecostalism and identity, the work of Canales, Palma, and Villela (1991) and Ossa (1992) has been especially prominent.
4   In Chile, we have observed the media's treatment of the group called "Children of God," also known as "The Family." For a study of the case in Argentina, see Frigerio (1992).
5   During the last few years in Argentina, Uruguay, and Brazil, empirical research on the new religious movements, new Afro-American cults, and new religious expressions has multiplied (Frigerio, ed. 1993).

FIGURE 10

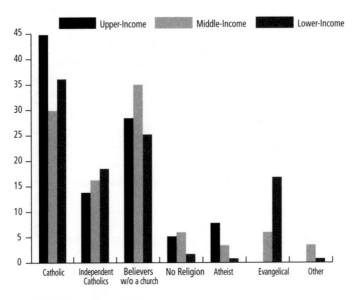

**RELIGIOUS TENDENCIES
ACCORDING TO SOCIOECONOMIC STRATA: 1996**
(percentages)

CERC-UAHC Matrimonial Research, 1996.

is needed on the growth of these new religious movements, their recruitment strategies, the implications of membership, and characteristics of their rituals and beliefs. Similarly, no studies currently exist on the new expressions of Oriental religions, or other new beliefs and pseudo-religious practices such as para-science, esotericism, and related phenomena among the population (beliefs and practices related to horoscopes, tarot cards, astrology, herbalism, spiritualism, folk medicine, etc.).

Thus, renewed efforts are necessary in order to analyze recent developments in the expressions of folk religion, since the phenomenon is widespread and more significant than one might expect in a country such as ours.

5. CHANGES IN FOLK RELIGION

The sociology of religion has come to acknowledge that formerly accepted theories of secularization, characterizing it as a mostly mechanical and linear process accompanying modernization as both a cause and consequence of the latter, are no longer valid for the analysis of the interrelationship between religion and globalization. It is true that a phenomenon congruent with classic secularization theories could be observed in Chile through the 1960s, but that situation has since changed enormously.

Religious affiliation data from the years just prior to the military regime (1969–73) strongly suggest a trend toward disaffiliation, coupled with a qualitative loss of influence by religion in Chilean society, fitting the definition of a secularization process in classical terminology (Smith 1982: 260–261). Yet under the authoritarian regime, this tendency in

Chilean society was reversed. All of the available data regarding religious affiliation and practices indicate that this trend toward non-belief, atheism, and religious indifference did not continue during the 1980s. In fact, during this period, religious variables increased slightly or varied around a steady average. For Catholics, for example, the number of baptisms per 100 live births increased between 1975 and 1988, while in 1991 it remained stable, with slight variations, at 66% (Parker 1996a: 51).

During the 1990s, however, it can no longer be affirmed that religious commitment is remaining constant, or that religion is on a clearly ascendant path. On the contrary, the situation today appears more differentiated and complex, with dissimilar patterns seen among the various groups and classes of Chilean society. High-income and high-status sectors today tend, according to a 1995 CEP survey, to be more Catholic, but at the same time this group shows high rates of indifference or atheism (responses of "no religion"). Middle-class groups mainly identify with Catholicism or with "other religions," possibly new religious movements. Among lower-income groups, however, a greater proportion of members of Evangelical churches is found, as well as a lesser relative proportion of Catholics and those who profess no religion (see Figure 10).

Research done in 1996 in Greater Santiago (Salinas et al. 1997), based on three random samples in neighborhoods of high, medium, and low socioeconomic status, yielded the responses displayed in Figure 10.

As we can see, the high-income sectors have the highest figures for Catholicism and atheism, and are the least Evangelical. The middle sectors include proportionately more "believers without a Church" and non-believers, whereas among the lower-income group there is a greater relative proportion of Evangelicals and "independent" Catholics. Among the upper and upper-middle classes, with their higher levels of schooling and exposure to an "enlightened" culture, higher levels of religious dissidence are exhibited. Among the working class, in contrast, a revitalization of Catholicism is seen, along with a surge in Pentecostalism, as we have noted.

In general, comments are made about the notable increase of Pentecostals among the working class, and there is certainly a trend in that direction. Most noteworthy of all, however, is not the quantitative indicator of religious revitalization, but the qualitative indicators. There is little doubt that, overall, the most significant indicator of the persistence of religion in an environment of globalization and socio-cultural change is the enormous influence still exercised by various forms of folk religion on the urban and rural masses. Nearly every available study corroborates this assertion.[6] The day-to-day experiences of Catholic and Evangelical missionaries, whose daily lives are deeply entwined with those of the people, even in the most distant areas of the country, confirm this as well.

Folk religion accompanies the various stages of people's lives, in the personal as well as the family and community spheres. Profound meaning is found in it, which is not offered by political ideologies, the State, or the advertising-filled media. Among the important milestones in religious life — aside from large and showy pilgrimages, ceremonies for the taking of religious vows, and devotions to the Virgin and the saints — are the two rituals of greatest significance for individuals: baptism and wakes, marking the beginning and the end of life. The numerous healing practices of traditional medicine must not be forgotten, as they are laden with religious connotations.

---

6   Mella et al., (1991); Irarrázaval (1994); Parker (1992a; 1992b; 1996b).

TABLE 2

RELIGIOUS AFFILIATIONS IN URBAN WORKING CLASS SECTORS
Research Study of the San Joaquín Neighborhood
(Metropolitan Area)

Category	Percent
Catholics	70.9
Believers Without a Church	15.4
Evangelicals	7.7
Atheists	5.1
Other Religion	0.9

Source: CERC - UAHC Study, 1996

Several pieces of research have shown that beliefs stemming from traditional religious folklore (Plath 1966) persist even within large, secularized cities, among educated populations with access to modern services and communications.[7] Clearly, the affirmation that folk religion fulfills a set of diverse functions is valid here, both in terms of the folk culture itself and society as a whole. Contrary to the analytical proposals of Marx and Weber, folk religion is not simply an instrument of domination, used for the domestication of the economically underprivileged masses. Depending on the particular historical circumstances, it can also be a factor in social protest (Houtart 1989). Of course, this protest is not always manifested as a social movement. It often remains closed within its symbolic-ritual function, nurturing a counterculture of life and faith that acts as a barrier to the meaninglessness and materialism of consumer society, making sense out of life beyond the daily struggle. Few are the cases where folk faith reinforces fatalism and contributes to the perpetuation of the vicious circle of poverty. In many cases, it offers practical reasoning that does not inhibit people's ability to search for solutions to their own problems.

Thus we are confronting an aspect of religion which is not modern, not secularized, and most paradoxically of all, reaffirmed by lower-income populations with high levels of schooling, urbanization and access to modern means of communication. The basis of the unique expression of meanings found in folk consciousness can be expressed with the term "hemidernal" (Parker 1996b: 115). It is a semantic and semiological combination in the working class symbolic field which, while pre-modern in certain aspects of

---

7   Through research in Santiago in 1987, 1990, and 1995, we were able to show that, although people universally resort to modern medicine when they are ill, they continue to believe in the "evil eye" as an illness mainly affecting small children, which is only treatable by a faith healer (*santiguadora*). Thus, the belief persists in a traditional "evil" and a magical-religious healing ritual. Faith in *animitas*, religious promises, and other traditional rituals can even be seen among the younger generation, although they are not heavily practicing believers. In the 1987 survey, 73% believed in the "evil eye." The percentage in 1990 was 60%, among a set of respondents with high levels of schooling (80% had completed the 7th grade). In 1995, 33% of working-class social leaders agreed with the statement that "the evil eye can be cast upon a baby," and an additional 36% responded "don't know"; that is, they did not deny the possibility. Some 47% of these leaders had attended secondary school, and 13% had completed studies beyond that level.

its representation of reality, is not anti-modern with regard to its integration into the economy and modern society. There is no "traditionalism" here that rejects advances in science or progress in general.

This statement makes it possible, perhaps, to understand how a modern debate over human rights can take place within a mentality exhibiting so many traditional characteristics. This was the case during the Chilean dictatorship. Thus we can understand how these characteristics can be compatible with a modern view of political democracy, the rule of law, and the responsibility for national development.

Folk religion manifests itself strongly in everyday life, where family, groups, and the community tend to gather. In public life, however, it is probable that the secularizing tendency — not in its classic definition, but with regard to the rationalization of beliefs and the decreasing visibility of religious factors — increased during the democratization process. This appears typical for a culture that is opening up to a plurality of options and emerging from the protective mantle of an authoritarian model.

A recent study (Parker 1997b) among leaders of urban working class sectors[8] in the township of San Joaquín shows the following distribution according to religion:

Those interviewed (with the exception of the atheists) unanimously accepted the dogmatic beliefs of established (Catholic and Protestant) churches regarding God, Jesus Christ, and the Bible. Nonetheless, they also confessed to believing in a broad range of supernatural beings.

Although more than 70% of those surveyed professed to be Catholics, a figure which coincides with census data, it can be seen that a certain type of non-institutionalized religious belief, gathered within our survey category of "believers without a church," has recently gained in force. The figures for this group here even surpass those of Evangelicals, contrary to previous trends. This new increase in "relative secularization," at the expense of the traditional religions dependent upon a particular church, seems to exhibit two tendencies:

a) On the one hand, a move is seen toward the rationalization of belief accompanied by a withdrawal from institutional membership — that is, a certain aversion to institutions or to established churches — rather than the abandonment of basic beliefs in the transcendental sphere. This is supported by the survey mentioned above (Parker 1997b): all those who calling themselves "believers without a church" still believe in God, and the great majority of them even admit to believing in Jesus Christ. To this category one should add the "independent Catholic" group, who also demonstrate an opposition to ecclesiastical institutionalization. There are also many Catholic believers who do not observe ecclesiastical prescriptions or official ritual practices. Thus, some 50% of the Catholics stated that they "hardly ever" or "never" attend Mass. They lean more toward "popular Catholicism," characterized by folk practices that are more or less autonomous from clerical control.

b) On the other hand, the trend toward relative secularization also carries with it an increase in non-institutionalized beliefs, of the "diffuse" New Age type. These include

---

8   This was a statistically representative sample of all the leaders of the Neighborhood Committees (*Juntas de Vecinos*) and Progress Committees (*Comités de Adelanto*) in the township of San Joaquín. These leaders are more highly educated than the members of their groups. Moreover, they are more exposed to modernizing culture due to their higher levels of social participation and greater civic and social awareness (Parker et al., 1997b).

a heterogeneous set of magical-mysterious beliefs, combined with esoteric and natur-
ist traditions, many influenced by Oriental religions, syncretically combined with
Christian, Gnostic, and indigenous traditions. In fact, these types of beliefs have an
influence that is far from negligible on the religious mentality studied here.

A cross-referencing of beliefs by educational level shows that higher educational levels
are associated with a greater trend toward the rationalization of beliefs, combined with a
dislike of institutions (producing, for example, the believer without a church). Conversely,
as educational levels decrease, greater adherence to established religions is seen.

The data from this and other research seem to indicate that religion coexists with a
belief in magic revitalized within a "New Age" context (the believers of this type were
those who in any case showed higher "belief" indexes). This type of belief, precisely
because it fits into a cultural pattern associated with the so-called "post-modern culture,"
heavily influenced by globalization processes, does not conflict with openness to modernity, change, and technology. It might, however, have reservations with regard to the pragmatism and rationalism of a consumer and technocratic culture.

If religious authorities do not fully understand these cultural changes, they may perceive them as a threat to their institutions and beliefs. As a result, as seems to have been the
case with some influential Catholic circles, as well as certain fundamentalist Evangelical
groups, a defensive reaction arises, closing itself off from all possibilities of social and cultural change. The opposite attitude, very much present in many church circles, consists of
sufficient openness to consider these changes, to analyze them, and to judge their positive
and negative qualities.

II. The Churches in the Democratization Period

The other set of transformations undergone by the religious field in Chile stems from the
Church-State relationship during the democratization process from 1990 to 1997. The
main points of analysis during this period are the strong stand of the Catholic hierarchy on
moral issues, as well as the efforts of the Evangelical churches to modify the country's legislation on religion.

A brief historical review is necessary to illustrate the context of the period analyzed.
One of the most decisive changes in Chilean culture in the last two decades has been the
growing acceptance among the nation's elite of the relevance of religion and the churches
in national public life. With the breakdown of secularizing ideologies such as Marxism in
the 1980s, laicism has lost strength, and ideas of tolerance have gained ground, both
among believers and non-believers. Much of this increased tolerance can be attributed to
the decisive contribution of ecumenical efforts — notably by several Protestant churches
and the Jewish community — to the struggle for human rights under the military regime.[9]
The Catholic Church also played an outstanding role in this task, and as the country began
its return to democracy from 1986 on, the Church provided vital support with its insistence on national reconciliation.

---

9   Lowden (1996), Gómez (1995), Meneses (1990), Correa (1986), Dooner (1989) Lagos (1988), Parker (1988a;
    1989).

The Catholic Church's efforts — we refer mainly to the work of its hierarchy — throughout the 1990s have mainly focused on support for the democratic system; an insistence on clearly establishing the Catholic doctrine on the moral aspects of social life; concern about poverty and inequality; and finally, its own significant internal changes. The latter have included a renewed emphasis on doctrine and the pastoral sphere, the rise of spiritual movements, and the reinforcement of internal discipline, along with the no less decisive factor of the appointment of conservative bishops driven by the Roman Curia.

The central public campaign of the Evangelical churches during this period has been their battle to obtain effective institutional recognition guaranteeing them true equality under the law.

1. THE CATHOLIC CHURCH AND THE DEMOCRATIC STATE

Huntington (1993:35) proposes that, on a simplified level, democratization involves three phases: the end of an authoritarian regime; the establishment of a democratic regime; and the consolidation of the democratic regime. These stages occur due to the confluence of a set of factors, some internal and others external. The so-called "third wave" of democratization, occurring in Chile since 1990, has been strengthened by the influence of Christianity, and especially by the new positions taken by the Catholic Church around the world.[10] These led it to oppose authoritarian regimes and support actions on behalf of democracy in various countries.

The Chilean Catholic Church in the 1980s was no exception. Without disregarding the contribution of other churches and religions such as Judaism, it should be emphasized that the Catholic hierarchy in Chile played an active and vital role in sustaining the momentum toward democratization within civil society, despite some internal circles which clearly supported the military regime.

Chile's religious landscape has changed during these last few decades. Public opinion took increasing note of religion as an issue, as civil society began to wake up from its lethargy in the 1980s and rise up against the continuation of the military government. In the struggle for democratization, the Church acted both as a forum for the regeneration of civil society, and as an institutional intercessor with the authoritarian State (Parker 1989). Meanwhile, the commitment of significant Evangelical sectors to the Pinochet regime attracted the attention of a professional sociologist (Lagos 1988), who suggested that Evangelicals constituted a "supplementary legitimization" for the regime, since Catholicism as a bloc no longer supported it.

The Church found itself in confrontation with the military regime because of its unconditional defense of human rights up to the last days of General Pinochet's presidency. A key moment occurred as a result of the court order to seize the medical records of the Vicariate of Solidarity, when Monsignor Valech refused to hand them over, stating that they were privileged information. He was supported by the Bishopric in this matter, which resulted in a serious conflict with the authorities. Furthermore, the regime blamed the

---

10 ". . . the surprising changes in the doctrine and activities of the Catholic Church manifested in the Second Vatican Council from 1963 to 1965 and the transformation of the national churches from defenders of the *status quo* to opponents of authoritarianism and proponents of social, economic, and political reforms," (Huntington 1993:45).

Church for its defeat in the plebiscite on October 5, 1988 (Bishopric Documents, March 1989, p. 122).

In 1989, after having welcomed and morally supported the constitutional reforms approved in a plebiscite,[11] and once Patricio Aylwin was elected as President of the Republic, the Catholic bishops issued a document which was the product of a broad consultation process. Certeza, coherencia y confianza [Certainty, Coherence and Confidence] (November 1989) set out their position with regard to the democratization period that was just beginning. They touched upon the main issues of concern to the Church for the transition period, in continuity with its work in the preceding years. These included social concerns, such as the dignity of humankind, poverty, work, politics, and solidarity in economic relations. Cultural and moral values were also addressed, including the crisis of modernity, youth and the family, consumerism, permissiveness, and secular positivism. Finally, they proposed certain demands linked to the rights of man:
• the right to life, which includes opposition to abortion
• the right to property — not only for the private sector, but expanded to include public property and the environment
• the renunciation of violence
• the search for truth and justice with respect to past human rights violations

In September 1990, Monsignor Oviedo, recently named as Archbishop of Santiago, issued a pastoral letter called "Los católicos y la política" [Catholics and Politics]. Therein he made general observations about the political challenges to Christians in the context of democratization. One affirmation appears particularly decisive: "The most mature democracies function where there is a certain minimum and basic consensus on cultural and ethical [values] that are above temporary majorities," ("Catholics and Politics" 1990, p. 9).

This was not a simple warning about the dangers of democracy or licentiousness. Instead, it was an expression of an outlook shared by all the bishops, in agreement with the apprehensions of the larger ecclesiastical conscience, about the advent of democracy. Democracy proposed not only the transformation of the State, but also the liberalization of culture. The bishops' serious reservations stemmed from what they perceived as the "liberalization of customs" (through the loosening of authoritarian attitudes), and the greater "moral relativism" (increased by globalization). In the opinion of the ecclesiastical hierarchy, these changes threatened to unleash a "secularist and immoral" culture.

The words and actions of the Catholic Church during the transition were aimed at promoting understanding on all sides. They were a call for Chileans to remain calm and to support the reestablishment of the rule of law, fundamental liberties, and the democratic values necessary for civic and political coexistence. The actions of the first Concertación government were in harmony with this ecclesiastical position, and the Church had no substantive conflicts with the second administration either. During the democratic consolidation process, the Catholic Church has found its challenges coming less from the State

---

11 "The country is experiencing a process of transition to democracy. This is the main concern of the majority of its inhabitants. It is gratifying to note the seriousness and the moderation with which many pursue constitutional reforms and consensus to assure a peaceful process, one of social and political stability, gathering experiences from the past and seeking out realistic solutions acceptable to all." Bishopric Documents: *Por una transición en paz* [*For a Peaceful Transition*] (April 1989), p. 135.

(which is now more in accordance with its global message), and more from society and the developing culture (which defy its principles and more classical doctrinal guidelines). This helps explain why the Church has been taking a more prominent stand on family issues and sexual mores than on the social agenda.

Overall, the balance sheet for the relations between the Catholic Church and the government from 1990 through 1997 has been positive. From 1990 to 1994, the Church felt that its positions were well-represented by President Patricio Aylwin's administration. Over the course of the second Concertación mandate, the Catholic Church has combined supportive attitudes with a partial distancing from certain governmental actions.

President Frei's administration has developed specific liaison mechanisms with the ecclesiastical hierarchy and has established a dialogue with it various sensitive issues of the Church's agenda: sexual education, educational reform, the fight against AIDS, and legislation on religious organizations and divorce, among other topics. Nevertheless, the bishops retain certain reservations about a government which some see as too "liberal" on cultural and family issues, while other circles criticize its lack of aggressiveness on social matters, because of its difficulties in confronting social grievances and inequalities.

Meanwhile, conservative Catholic circles, which in Chile today enjoy greater access to the media and public opinion, are especially concerned about upholding moral standards and tend to distrust a government which enthusiastically embraces modernization. And this governmental project of modernization clearly includes steps toward the liberalization of society and culture:[12] freedom of information, the abolition of the death penalty, willingness to consider a law on civil divorce, legislation expanding religious freedoms, and so forth.

2. THE CATHOLIC CHURCH'S PUBLIC PERFORMANCE DURING THE DEMOCRATIZATION PERIOD: BETWEEN MORAL DOCTRINE AND SOCIAL ISSUES

During the 1990s, the public actions of the Catholic Church hierarchy have developed along the two lines of ecclesiastical concern — one focused more on doctrine and morality, the other on social teachings and justice — although the media regularly provides greater publicity to the former. These foundations for Church action might be characterized, in their own language, as the "evangelization of culture" on the one hand, and the "preferential option for the poor" on the other.

The guidelines of the Third General Conference of Latin American Bishops in Puebla (1979) set the evangelization of culture as a priority task for the Latin American Catholic Church. These guidelines were confirmed and further developed at the Fourth General Conference of Latin American Bishops held in October 1992 in Santo Domingo. At that gathering, a penetrating diagnosis was made of a "cultural crisis of unsuspected proportions"

---

12 President Frei, speaking in Temuco in January 1997, stated: "Chile will not be fully modern if it does not decisively, boldly, and openly confront the problems faced by the people in their everyday lives. ... The material and spiritual progress of society cannot be based on a fear of liberty and the good judgment of individuals. ... The question is not whether to protect the values of society and family or not, but how to promote them while confronting problems without hypocrisy or cynicism." With that he announced the continuity of the sexual education program and the submission of the Divorce Bill to Congress.

(No. 230) which questions the moral order desired by God in Creation and Redemption and tends toward an autonomous human culture separate from all transcendent authority (Caro 1994). Confronted by the ambiguities and challenges of modern and post-modern culture, the church leaders issued a clear call for a "New Evangelization capable of awakening a new missionary fervor" (No. 124) in order to inculcate the Gospel and return to deeply-rooted Christian values that are present but inhibited, or which have gone into crisis or are beginning to disappear.

The Chilean Catholic Church took up the idea of the "New Evangelization" in its pastoral guidelines. Faced with a cultural diagnosis of increasing secularism, relativism, materialistic hedonism, and the neglect of spiritual values, the Church proposed an evangelization that can recognize the deep thirst for spirituality among the population and quench it with Christian values (Gómez 1995).

Consistent with these guidelines, the Church has expressed deep concern for the manner in which moral values have been expressed in Chilean society through the years. In 1990, while defending politicians' "noble vocation to service" in democracy against an authoritarian culture that had denigrated "politicking" and democratic values, Cardinal Oviedo sought to promote morality in politics. He understood this as a morality dictated by the laws of God, reflected in the laws of nature. Following its principles, a Catholic politician must reject corruption, populism, and totalitarian and sectarian temptations, such as abortion and divorce. An anti-liberal outlook became manifest in the Cardinal's speech as he affirmed that a Catholic politician cannot check his religion at the door to the party or government. Initiating a controversy with several prominent legislators, including self-professed Catholics of both genders, he further stated that "the participation of Catholics in any attempt to legalize abortion or civil divorce dissolving conjugal ties is precluded for serious ethical and social reasons and not only religious ones."[13]

In fact, the bishops' concerns about the defense of life and the family against the dangers of abortion and divorce were manifested even before the inauguration of the new democratic government.[14] At that time, Chilean bishops echoed the guidelines of Pope John Paul II himself and of other Latin American bishops.[15]

The Catholic hierarchy's systematic campaign in defense of the Church's understanding of life and the family has undoubtedly been the action most loudly echoed in the media, which tend to report substantive issues in a more sensationalist than dispassionate style. The Church's position, nevertheless, springs from a long tradition and from teachings which, since Vatican Council II and Paul VI's encyclical Humanae Vitae, insist on the absolute nature of morality and the existence of natural moral laws, "laws that man does not establish for himself, but rather discovers in the depths of his conscience, laws with

---

13 Mons. Carlos Oviedo, *Los católicos y la política* (Sept. 1990), p. 28
14 The April 1989 statement by the Bishops' Conference, *Por una transición en paz* [*For A Peaceful Transition*] (*Documents* p. 135), signed by its President, Fernando Ariztía, and by Secretary-General Sergio Contreras, proposes as central issues the dignity and the rights of every person; support for the Vicariate of Solidarity persecuted by the Military Prosecutor; and the defense of life and the family against abortion and divorce (p.136).
15 For example, *Enérgica advertencia de obispos latinoamericanos* [An urgent warning from Latin American Bishops] was published on June 23, 1994: "An urgent call not to be fooled by birth control campaigns that do not respect life and the dignity of men and women." They denounce abortion bills that "instill the culture of death at the beginning of an innocent and defenseless unborn life." Artificial birth control methods are affirmed to "violate the nature of human beings."

universal features, written into his nature by God."[16] Thus, it is an understanding of moral law — Neo-Thomist in inspiration — which underlies the Church's opposition to various modern and post-modern ethical concepts, and above all to the individualistic ethics of liberalism and laicism,[17] as well as the relativism of the post-modern philosophies that have dethroned the "great legends" which legitimized an objective morality.[18]

This position, supported by a prominent group of bishops wielding considerable influence at the Bishop's Conference, has been reflected on innumerable occasions. It can be seen in statements and pastoral letters, as well as public acts of the Archbishop of Santiago, the Bishop's Conference itself, and several individual bishops. These positions have been invoked in connection with the moral crisis of youth; the problem of AIDS;[19] proposed laws on therapeutic abortion and divorce; the question of educational reform;[20] the sexual education programs and workshops promoted by the Ministry of Education;[21] the immorality arising from obscenity, pornography, sexual promiscuity, contraception, abortion, and divorce,[22] and the manipulation of human life which unduly distorts the laws of nature.

Due to the close relationship between Catholic marriage and civil marriage, based on the indissolubility of the union,[23] the bishops endeavor to uphold the meaning assigned to marriage by the Church. That is, "an alliance by which a man and a woman together constitute a lifetime partnership. This partnership is by its nature for the good of the couple and for the generation and education of offspring." It is an alliance "elevated by Christ Our Lord to the dignity of a sacrament between (those who) are baptized."[24]

The opinion of the ecclesiastical hierarchy, however, is different from that revealed by public opinion surveys. It can be seen that even though a broad majority of Chileans reject

16 Mon. Oviedo, *Moral, juventud y sociedad permisiva* (Sept. 24, 1991), p. 33.

17 "[I]t is frequently said, for example, that morality is a private matter of one's individual conscience, which can only be asserted in the intimacy of the family and interpersonal relations, denying the possibility of an objective and imperative moral standard for economics, politics, and culture." Oviedo (1991), p. 45.

18 "The Church cannot become a part of the growing and destructive moral relativism of our country, which makes of moral law something as variable as cultures, times, temperaments, and even tastes and individual preferences, as if it were not rooted in human nature, where it has been inscribed by the Creator himself." Oviedo (1991), p. 46.

19 Comité Permanente del Episcopado [Standing Committee of Bishops], *El sida: un desafío de dignidad humana y de misericordia* [AIDS: a challenge to human dignity and compassion] (January 1992). Mon. Carlos Oviedo, in Santiago in June 1993, in his pastoral letter *La Iglesia frente al sida* [The Church and AIDS] states that AIDS is a pandemic disease and is a consequence of the world's economic, political, and moral crisis.

20 On May 12, 1994, in a public statement regarding the Law on Education, the bishops stated: "The education area of the Bishop's Conference has been following the situation produced by the draft bill sent to Congress from the Executive Branch with concern..."

21 Statement by the bishops, *Acerca de la educación sexual* [On sex education].

22 Chilean Bishops' Conference, Comisión Nacional de Pastoral Familiar, *First National Congress on the Family: A Workshop on Humanity* (Santiago, 1992).

23 In Chile, civil marriages (Civil Code Art. 102), like marriages in the Catholic Church (Canon Law Code No. 1056), are indissoluble.

24 The Canon Law code on marriage states that its essential properties are "unity and indissolubility" and that its nature is "irrevocable"; that is, "it cannot be dissolved by any human authority, nor for any cause other than death." Marriage as a "sacrament" of the Church means that it is at the same time a sign and a medium to express and strengthen faith, worship God, and achieve sanctification. Canon Law Nos. 840, 1055–1059, and 1141.

abortion, this is not the case regarding a law to permit divorce.[25] The Church's position is that an acceptance of divorce signifies a lack of love, values, and moral strength. Many faithful Catholics, however, look at the real socio-cultural problems confronted by couples in modern society. The most recent development in this debate was the Chamber of Deputies' majority vote in 1997 approving the parliamentary motion on divorce. The reaction from the Catholic hierarchy was swift and scathing. Pressure from the anti-divorce sector finally induced the executive branch not to include this law in the special legislative session of Congress that began in September 1997, thereby indefinitely postponing its discussion in the Senate.

Beyond the controversial issue of indissolubility, the Church has sought to reaffirm marriage as a sacrament involving a sense of community; marriage is also seen as a mutual gift and as the intimate communion of life and love.[26]

Education has been the other central concern of the Church's hierarchy during the democratization period, especially the preservation of religious education in Chile's elementary and secondary schools. Faced with a proposal to make these classes elective, Church authorities reiterate the importance of safeguarding the citizens' right to religious education,[27] consecrated as part of the constitution's guarantees of religious freedom.

It is true that the Church's concern for values is not limited exclusively to family and reproductive morals. They have also shown concern for the pursuit of truth and justice in clearing up the crimes committed under the authoritarian regime.[28] Nonetheless, this concern, strongly manifested during the early years of the decade, has slackened in the face of the public notoriety of its positions on personal and family morals. The lower public profile of the Church's social position has affected its impact on society, in spite of the fact that for the hierarchy the "preferential option for the poor" has been as important as the "evangelization of culture."[29]

Although the "preferential" stance has been subject to diverse interpretations, such as that among some Church circles taking it to mean "not excluding" the poor, and although it has generated some theological and pastoral controversy within the national

25 According to a survey by the Latin American School of Social Sciences (Flacso) carried out in Greater Santiago in 1995 on the degree of acceptance of abortion, 51% responded, "Absolutely not"; 25% "Hardly accept"; 18% "Accept somewhat"; and only 5% "Fully accept." With regard to the degree of acceptance of divorce: 27% said "Absolutely not"; 33% "Accept somewhat; 23% "Hardly accept"; and 16% "Fully accept."

26 See Vatican Council II, *Gaudium et Spes* No. 48. For the current Pope, John Paul II, marriage is above all a design for life based on community. Love in marriage is the "foundation and soul of the conjugal and family community," and "fecundity is the fruit and sign of conjugal love" ("Familiaris Consortio" No. 18 and No. 28).

27 See their *Carta a los profesores de religión* [*Letter to religion teachers*] (October 20, 1995); *Carta a los padres y apoderados de las familias católicas de Chile* [*Letter to parents and guardians of Chilean Catholic families*] (at the end of the Year of the Family); and *Comunicado de la Asamblea Plenaria de Obispos* [*Communiqué of the Plenary Assembly of Bishops*] (December 1994).

28 Note the support given by the Vicariate of Solidarity to the Rettig Commission (1991); the ecclesiastical statements to Judge Milton Juica to help clear up the murder of three professionals (April 1994); the support for the Supreme Court ruling finding General Contreras and General Espinoza to be the masterminds responsible for the assassination of former Foreign Minister Orlando Letelier (May 1995), and so forth.

29 The "preferential option for the poor" was chosen at the Conference of Latin American Bishops in Medellín (1968), but the term was coined by the Conference of Latin American Bishops in Puebla (1979) and reaffirmed by the Conference in Santo Domingo (1992). What is sought is to "serve Jesus Christ through the poor" and "serve the poor as Christ did," (Muñoz 1994).

and international ecclesiastical community, the truth is that the actions and missions of the Chilean Church for decades have been marked by a preferential focus on the poor, because in them the Church sees the very face of Jesus Christ.

During these years, the bishops and the Catholic community have expressed concern in numerous ways for the problems of underdevelopment and for improving the quality of life for Chileans. The issues of poverty and extreme inequality have become especially important.[30] Justice and human rights have also been touched upon, as have the environment, consumerism, and diverse social problems such as those of teachers, rural workers, miners in Lota, health, drugs and AIDS.

In 1994, Chile's bishops returned to the issue of poverty at a seminar where newly-elected President Frei spoke in closing.[31] In May and August of 1995 and May and November 1996, they reiterated their concern for poverty, social problems, the serious inequalities exhibited in the country, and the need to progress toward solidarity in the economy.[32]

Fundamental among the solutions proposed by the prelates are austerity and solidarity, principles that were later taken up by President Frei himself in his speeches on the responsibility of all Chileans to help defeat poverty. The bishops also mentioned the need for the State to reinforce social policies with private support, to focus on the basic education of all Chileans, and to promote job-related training.[33]

3. THE EVANGELICAL CHURCHES AND RELIGIOUS FREEDOM LAWS

During the redemocratization period, the Protestant churches similarly focused upon redefining their role and their institutional legitimacy in the new context of a post-authoritarian State. One of their main concerns was legislative activity on the laws governing religious organizations. The most important legal initiative in the religious field from 1990 to 1997 has been the drive toward legislation on the "Legal Constitution and Operation of Churches and Religious Organizations." On June 1, 1992, the Aylwin administration created a special commission to help draft a bill in this area. The administration sought to "make progress in the application of the principle of equality under the law, giving special consideration to freedom of conscience, belief, and worship, once it is established by law."[34]

---

30 See Mon. Carlos Oviedo, *Los pobres no pueden esperar* [*The poor cannot wait*] (September 1992); Conference of Chilean Bishops, *Superación de la pobreza en Chile* [*Overcoming poverty in Chile*] (March, 1994); Easter Message of the Bishops Conference, *Cristo nuestra esperanza* [*Christ, our hope*] (April 12,1995); as well as several statements in 1995 and 1996.

31 A document cited above contains the conclusions of this seminar, held March 16–18, 1994.

32 See the communiqué issued on May 12, 1995; the statement *Reconciliación y solidaridad* [*Reconciliation and Solidarity*] of August 1995; and the declaration of the Bishops' Conference in May 1996, *¿Es Chile un país equitativo?* [*Is Chile a country of equity?*]. In a document issued in November 1996, the bishops noted: "We are gradually formulating a new style of development, where the logic and structure of an open and competitive market economy take on considerable significance beyond strictly economic activity.... This constitutes an immense challenge for renewed Evangelization," (*Economía y convivencia nacional* [*Economics and the national community*], Working Document of the Doctrine Committee, p. 14). They further denounce unfair, illegal, stressful, and dehumanizing competition; environmental problems; poverty; and persistent misery, as well as intolerable inequality and social exclusion.

33 November 1996, *Economía y convivencia nacional* [*Economics and the national community*], Working Document of the Doctrine Committee, p. 18.

34 Presidential Message to the Chamber of Deputies (October 22, 1993).

FIGURE 11

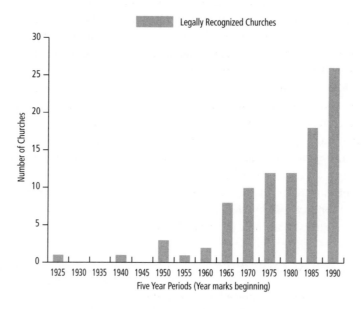

PENTECOSTAL CHURCHES
LEGALLY RECOGNIZED IN THE METROPOLITAN AREA

Source: Ministry of Justice, 1993.

The bill was energetically promoted by the Evangelical churches, who sought institutionalization and legitimization in the eyes of the State on par with the conditions granted to the Catholic Church. The latter enjoys, since the separation of Church and State in the Constitution of 1925, a highly privileged legal and institutional existence,[35] as compared to the Evangelical churches, whose legal identity is more akin to that of private corporations and is regulated separately (by Supreme Decree 110 of 1979).

It is interesting to examine the registration figures for the Christian Evangelical churches, fundamentally Pentecostals. A significant subset of these churches, grouped together in the Council of Pastors, became an important source of endorsement for the military regime. They offered it a substitute religious legitimization, denied by the Catholic Church mainly due to the violation of human rights. Looking at the graph with Ministry of Justice data for the Metropolitan Region through 1994, we see, first of all, that registrations among these churches increased over time. Second, we observe that the largest number of incorporations of Evangelical and Pentecostal organizations occurred between 1974 and 1989: 40, with an average of 2.6 churches registered per year. Nevertheless, the rate of registrations was highest during the Aylwin administration (1990–94), reaching 4.8 churches per year. This suggests that the growth rate of Pentecostal churches was higher during these

---

35 According to current laws and regulations, the Catholic Church enjoys rights, exemptions, and special tax benefits. Only some of these advantages are recognized for Protestant groups and other religious faiths.

years, a logical assumption, since the proportion almost doubles. Or perhaps, with the return to democracy there has been greater confidence in the State, and thus more churches have come forward to regularize their legal and institutional status.

Meanwhile, the government under President Aylwin indicated that broader legislation would be needed to produce a "a better approximation to equality under the law." Thus the proposed text refers to "churches and religious organizations," (p. 4). Nevertheless, in spite of this general intent, the bill was subject to the heavy influence of Evangelical religious groups during the drafting process. It emerged as an almost exclusive recognition of the Evangelical churches themselves,[36] with standards fitting that type of church.

In the hands of the legislature, the bill was explicitly modified, simplified, and clarified, becoming a piece of legislation oriented toward the equal recognition of any type of Church or religious organization representing any faith or religion.[37] The text is careful to affirm that "the exercise of the rights emanating from religious freedom and the freedom to worship are limited by morality, community standards, and public order." The law specifically notes, however, that the law shall not apply to "entities and activities related to the study of and experimentation with psychic or parapsychological phenomenon, magical, superstitious, and spiritist practices or others of a nature that are foreign to or different from religious knowledge and worship." Additionally, "the exercise or development of activities intended for the worship of Satan are prohibited." (Art. 8).

The bill proposes that a religious entity acquires legal protection from the moment it is entered into a public registry maintained by the Ministry of Justice, and that such an entity will "enjoy a legal capacity under public law." In a more highly debated area, Article 10 establishes that "the Ministry of Justice may not deny registration" to a religious entity; it may only state its objection.

Once this legislation was approved in the Chamber, the concern of the Catholic hierarchy became evident, and a public reaction was unleashed by Catholic groups. They pointed to the constitutional basis of the Catholic Church's status, claiming that any new legislation must recognize that status, in the absence of reform to the Constitution. The bill has remained tied up in the Senate, since the Executive did not include it among the priority bills for the special legislative session that ended in 1997.

Senate approval of legislation such as the proposed bill would represent a significant step forward in Chile's legal-institutional regulations regarding freedom of religion. This action would provide suitable legal instruments to the country's diverse religious organizations, assisting them in acquiring a status similar to that of the Catholic Church. It would constitute formal and genuine recognition of the pluralism that increasingly characterizes Chile's religious culture at the end of the century.

---

36 Art.1. of this bill, which was later modified, read: "A Church or Religious Organization is understood to be an entity formed by individuals who profess a determined faith, practice it, teach, and spread it. Especially included in this denomination are the Evangelical Christian churches..."

37 Articles 4 and 5 of the bill approved by the Chamber of Deputies and sent to the Senate on December 1, 1996, establish that "churches, faiths, or religious institutions are understood to mean entities formed by individuals who profess, practice, teach, and disseminate a particular faith." "Religious entities" are defined as "the churches, faiths, and religious institutions of any worship," (Official Letter No. 1,342).

4. FAITH AND POLITICS IN THE 1990S

The globalization of the last decade has been accompanied by the growing dominance of the international capitalist system, strengthened by the crisis of socialism and central planning. The revaluation of democracy as a political system has gone hand in hand with this process, contributing to the collapse of military and authoritarian regimes in Latin America. Both factors have contributed significantly to a profound transformation on the political left. The socialist ideals held by important Latin American Catholic Church circles formed in the 1970s, along with a number of Protestant churches linked to the World Council of Churches, under the influence of Liberation Theology, have also changed.

The disintegration of certain counterparts of popular movements within the Churches can be observed. This disintegration, as Schreiter (1997:105) affirms, "has been driven by rightist pressures within the Church hierarchy, dismantling institutes of learning and research and discouraging grassroots communities. The influx of conservative Protestant groups, especially from North America, has swung the people's focus of attention from the social field to the personal level."

This shift in the general culture, accompanied by the absence of visible alternatives and the crisis of the utopias that mobilized society through the early 1970s, has ended in a de-politicization of society and a lack of motivation for social struggle among youth. These changes affect the religious field in several ways. In fact, one of the main consequences of the cultural transformation at the end of the century, which of course is not limited to Chilean culture, has been the paradoxical rise of a simultaneous "disenchantment" and "re-enchantment" within society. Thus, on the ideological level, we see the relative failure of utopias and social engineering projects, which results in the reinforcement, on another level, of the role of pragmatism in politics and economics.

This crisis has repercussions in the political and religious fields. The "disenchantment" with social and political utopias is associated with the loss of the religious or pseudo-religious feeling of political commitment. This healthy "secularization" of politics shatters the rigid dogmatism and orthodoxy held by both the left and the right, opening the way to cooperation and conciliation. Yet this positive phenomenon in the political field brings about unforeseen consequences in the religious field. Religion — specifically, Latin American Christianity — which in the 1960s and 1970s inspired socio-political activism aimed at liberation, has lost strength and force through the transformation of political practices. The pastoral activity of the 1990s, and the churches themselves, become "disenchanted" with politics, yet feel strengthened by the "re-enchantment" of society through the revitalization of religious and spiritual currents.

The dominant pragmatism in politics and economics, along with the secularism characteristic of the commercialism and materialism of the consumer society, tend to create the perception of a vacuum devoid of meaning. To fill that vacuum, people once again turn to the symbolic field with a powerful history and tradition of providing meaning: religion. This is, however, not simply a return to the religions of the past, with their rigid institutional apparatus. The churches themselves, in their attempt to "evangelize" the world, have perhaps shown excessive attachment to worldly topics, such as the issues of human and political rights, for these new spiritual seekers.

The new quest occurs, moreover, within an intellectual climate marked by the dominance of uncertainty; the crisis of the rationalism of Western modernity; and a lesser role for the established churches, whether Catholic or traditional Protestant. The new paths of this spiritual search take various directions, moving clearly beyond the classic relations between faith and worldliness, or faith and society. Four main currents can be identified:

a) The end of the millennium encourages the hope of an extra-worldly salvation, and a mushrooming of new religious movements with millennarian and sectarian tendencies is unleashed. Public controversy arises around "the sects," intensifying when some of them go to such extremes as collective suicide.

b) The anti-establishment culture of the 1960s, the hippie culture, student revolutions and the "May Revolution" have combined to form a "New Age" movement. Influenced by the "Age of Aquarius," it is centered on the power of the mind, spiritual revitalization, and a turn towards the East and its wisdom and spirituality. "New Age"-style syncretic religious movements have become numerous.

c) The emphasis on spiritual renewal and perception of the presence of the Spirit with new senses, derived from movements outside of the Christian tradition, feeds the Catholic charismatic movements and the Pentecostal currents within Protestantism.

d) Finally, there have been changes in focus within the Catholic Church. The Church has seen the shift from a laity actively committed to social change during the sixties and seventies, to members and supporters of Grassroots Ecclesiastical Communities, who during the years of the dictatorship promoted a commitment to solidarity and human rights, and now to a laity dedicated to an intense spirituality, encouraged by the multiplicity of apostolic movements flourishing in the Church over the past decade.

The consequences of these currents for the members of the churches and other religious groups lead in two directions. People may turn away from the world, because their spiritualizing faith makes them reject its sinful, materialistic, and secularist nature. Alternatively, they may return to a kind of dualism seemingly absent from our society for a time: on the one hand, they are Christians and participate in their churches; and on the other hand, they are citizens and they participate in society, but without any coherent link between the two commitments.

The latter is especially prevalent among Catholic politicians: they have found themselves abandoned by a Church whose concern is centered on spiritual apostolic movements and on the pastoral and parochial life. Even though many were youth activists in movements such as Catholic Action, those times are long gone. These politicians are now immersed in the political field, attempting to uphold their values in a sphere that has become much more specialized and thus not exempt from technocratic characteristics. It is a world with less tolerance for values and humanistic orientations, or at least one which manipulates them with greater ease. It is a world far from the grassroots, since its actions are carried out at the top; in short, it is a world with its own rules, where religious ethics are difficult to apply.

The opposite is true among conservative Catholics. Especially among the upper and upper-middle classes, which have always exhibited a closed and very characteristic Catholicism, we can see a recent strengthening of spiritualizing currents. This direction is reinforced by a Church more focused on family issues and more distanced from political affairs; by apostolic movements such as Opus Dei; and also by the revival, during the authoritarian years, of something resembling the old oligarchical Catholic culture. Its new environment is the successful export economy, where the norms of the consumer society and the media are molding a new culture. Being a successful businessman and a member of the elite goes hand in hand, in this new culture, with Catholicism. "Catholic schools" are multiplying once again, becoming a fashionable educational alternative for the wealthy in the place of disdained public education.

The emerging media culture contributes to the dynamic of "disenchantment" and "re-enchantment." We no longer live in a "mass society," but in an "information society": participation is now more selective than general. Politics has changed, as the relationship between politicians and the public has become filtered through the media. Specialization requires the exclusion of amateurs from political debates and decision-making. The available opportunities for participation are on the local level, or within the framework of the complex processes of globalization and regionalization.

The typical lay figures committed to the Catholic Church today are members of apostolic movements — linked to a specific congregation and a defined spirituality or charisma.[38] Generally recruited from the middle or upper classes, they are sincerely and intensely concerned about defending spiritual and family values as well as charity. Let us remember that the previously dominant type of "lay commitment" was made by apostolic activists from specialized movements: workers, students, rural laborers, professors, etc. These were people with a high social consciousness who were recruited from working-class and middle-income sectors, people actively dedicated to social problems and justice.

It should not seem strange, then, that the range of political options for Catholics has greatly widened, in contrast to the old model, where the Catholic hierarchy played a decisive part in determining the political positions of Christians. Today, clerical tendencies persist, but in a new context. The lay autonomy proclaimed in Vatican Council II has become a reality.

Nevertheless, the Church hierarchy still dispenses influential advice and pastoral counseling, and due to its current orientation and sensibilities, it appears more satisfied to see the laity involved in apostolic spiritual movements — closer to center-right political positions — than independently joining social and political currents that run the gamut from the center to the Left. To this must be added the Church's changing social concerns in recent years. As we have seen, the focus has shifted from human rights to the defense of the family (opposing abortion and divorce). This tendency of the hierarchy to place more emphasis on the socio-familiar than on the socio-political sphere has reduced opportunities for action and responsibility among lay members. Meanwhile, lay Catholics with less social sensitivity and more private concerns now perceive that they are more supported, while potential socio-political activists in the Church feel forsaken.

Among Evangelicals, classic theories of the "social strike" of the Pentecostals (Lalive d'Epinay 1967), seeing these groups as unfailingly apathetic towards politics and upholding conservative attitudes, have been contradicted by the fact that for some time these churches have been establishing diverse socio-political positions (V.A. 1988). These range from fundamentalist views rejecting the sinning world, through those supporting clearly democratic political options, to attempts by various groups to "create their own path" by organizing an Evangelical political party. The latter proposal has enjoyed some success in other Latin American countries.

---

38 These movements include the Legionnaires of Christ, Opus Dei, Neo Catechumenist, the Legion of Mary, the Conference of Saint Vincent of Paul, Schoenstat, Focolares, Charismatic, Christian Short Courses, Communities for a New City, and Communities of Christian Life, among others.

What should not fail to be noticed is that among members of the Evangelical churches, no single predominant political tendency appears; instead, they exhibit a normal distribution over the current spectrum of the Chilean political field. The Evangelical churches belonging to the Council of Pastors, which had lent religious legitimacy to the authoritarian regime, have now adopted moderate positions, fundamentally supporting the democratic system. Evangelical activists can be found in almost all political parties, right, center, and left, including parties such as the Christian Democrats, who in the past were more closely linked to Catholicism, as well as traditionally secular movements such as the Radical and Socialist Parties.

Conclusions: The Outlook for the Church, Globalization, and the Challenges of Democratization

We have analyzed, in general terms, the manner in which the processes of globalization and democratization in the Chilean cultural field have interacted with the religious field. We have examined the new characteristics of the multi-religious reality of our national culture, as well as the public actions and transformations of the main churches in the 1990s. This section will summarize certain ideas and then reflect on the future projections of the panorama we have attempted to lay out.

1. THE CATHOLIC CHURCH: DEMOCRATIZING FACTOR IN THE POLITICAL FIELD AND MODERATING FACTOR IN THE CULTURAL FIELD

The Chilean Catholic Church, as is widely recognized, has been an important factor both in the return to democracy as well as the implementation of the new democratic system. Its commitment to democratic values traces back to the beginning of the 20th century, with its concern for the "social issue" and a timorous defense of a "Christian democracy" — before this term was associated with any party. This can be seen in its ongoing stance, despite the dangers of destabilization that destroyed Chile before the war. This support was clearly manifested in the final stages of Eduardo Frei Montalva's government, during the administration of Salvador Allende and certainly during the military dictatorship (Cleary 1992: 204).

Although the Catholic Church took on a leading role as a mediator between civil society and the authoritarian State, and as a spokesman for that civil society, its role and objectives changed with the advent of democracy. New circumstances and new players came onto the stage, and the Church returned to its place in society determined by its religious nature.

In dealing with religion, the media and culture generally consider it solely from the perspective of the religious field (following the classic social definition of the specialization of functions). Nevertheless, since Vatican II, the Church has defined its field of evangelizing action beyond what is explicitly religious: its concerns encompass the social, cultural, and moral fields, because the Message of the Gospel must reach every aspect of man and all mankind (see Evangelii Nuntiandi). It is for this reason that public opinion's image of the Church's actions, molded by the media, does not correspond to the Church's own view of its mission in the world.

In broad terms, the Church's public image appears to be inclined toward conservatism, reluctant to support processes tending to democratize culture.[39] Nevertheless, it is very important to recognize that the Chilean Catholic Church has been a decisive factor in the consolidation of political democracy, alongside Evangelical, mainline Protestant, and Jewish groups.

However, if between 1990 and 1997 the Catholic Church has been a democratizing factor in the political sphere, it has also been a factor for moderation in relation to the liberalization and democratization of culture and society. Its brave defense of human rights, along with its actions in favor of the country's democratization and reconciliation during the authoritarian years, made it appear, to the public eye, to be a much more "progressive" Church (in its leadership and active membership) than it truly was in its world view and fundamental doctrines.

As can be seen, the teachings and sermons of the Church — more than its practices, which in many aspects continue to reflect a certain social Catholicism — have contributed to lessening the contradictions peculiar to a society in transition from an authoritarian culture toward a liberal and democratic one. Thus, if for many liberalizing circles of Chile's elite the Church appears "conservative" on socio-cultural issues, the truth is that such a stance was never specifically taken — beyond certain isolated incidents involving some radically anti-liberal ecclesiastical figures with an openly restorationist attitude and a tendency toward religious fanaticism. The various degrees of "openness" to the modernization and liberalization of culture and society which have characterized the thinking of various bishops and ecclesiastical currents have never become a real obstacle to these processes. This is true even though Church leaders have sometimes raised legitimate objections, hoping to guide society in its forward motion toward deeper understanding, greater legitimacy, and a higher level of cultural consensus.[40]

All indications are that in the foreseeable future, the Church will continue to play a significant role in the task of consolidating democracy and in the creation of a pro-democratic civic culture. This does not necessarily mean, however, that the Church will support progress toward a modernized and liberalized culture.

Given the Church's prominent role in civil society, it can provide enormous support to the process of democratizing society itself, through the socialization of values such as solidarity, respect for national traditions, respect for human rights, healthy social relations, and peaceful conflict resolution, or reconciliation. This support also takes the form of drawing society's attention to potentially destabilizing issues for the democratic order, such as social inequalities and the lack of social solidarity. In this manner, the Church contributes powerfully, both directly and indirectly, to building a civic culture and strengthening the foundation for national unity.

The Church's contribution of the Church to the democratization and liberalization of culture is a different question. Although in recent years there has been a slight movement

---

39 "Reasonably or not, the Church seems to be less present in society, more concerned with itself, and more spiritualist, which brings about some disenchantment in people who admired it before for its prophetic vigor." Pablo Fontaine, "La herida de Chile y la Iglesia samaritana" [Chile's injury and the Samaritan Church], in *Pastor* (1993:20).

40 Note, for example, the main conclusions of the Synod of the Church of Santiago (IX Synod of the Church of Santiago, Archbishopric of Santiago, 1997).

among most in the Church away from anti-liberal positions toward more open ones, and although the new appointments of ecclesiastical authorities, as well as the latest expressions of pastoral views on controversial issues, seem to be indicating the chance of a new path, it can be predicted that the Church will surely not reach the point of decisive support for a liberalizing culture.

It seems clear that the Catholic Church has been, and probably will remain, a democratizing factor. It will continue to be an element of moderation contributing to stability, and it will continue to be supportive with its social sensitivity. However, it will most likely present itself as an advocate of restraint in the public debate on issues related to the liberalization of culture and social norms. This is aside from the fact, of course, that there is not always agreement between the public voice of the Church — especially that of its hierarchy — and the Catholic faithful as a whole.

2. GLOBALIZATION AND RELIGION IN CHILE: A CHALLENGE TO THE DEMOCRATIZATION OF SOCIETY?

According to the classic theories, modernization on the political-institutional level basically entails the secularization of State institutions; and at the level of conscience, modernization involves the secularization of thinking, which relegates religion to both a limited and private sphere and a tremendously diluted public one. Fundamentally, modernization — with its processes of functional specialization, universalization, the pragmatization of values, and the pluralization of rituals and traditions — is seen as posing a serious risk to religion, threatening to dissolve its very foundation. The response of the religious component in society to these threats is expected to consist of rigid and reactionary measures, preventing it from facing change with the necessary capacity to adjust and adapt.

The sociocultural changes we have analyzed throughout this article, and specifically the phenomenon of globalization, indicate quite a different path. The greater or lesser prevalence of religious beliefs does not constitute an index of greater or lesser "modernity," since we should not mistake the latter for a tendency to secularization in the sense of a loss of beliefs. It involves more the tendency toward the rationalization, abstraction, and pluralization of beliefs. That is, if people in a modern setting consider themselves to be strong believers, this says nothing about the degree of traditionalism to be found in their cultural practices. We know that entering the modern era and achieving a modern awareness in our Latin American countries does not require the abandonment of our beliefs. Catholicism and many other religions have been pillars of traditionalism during many periods of history. Nevertheless, in certain circumstances and situations they have also shown themselves to be powerful social players, defending fundamental values from modernity's excesses in the social and political spheres, as they defend human rights, struggle against oppression, and seek to maintain democratic values within the community of citizens.

The issue of human rights, as well as the issue of democracy taken up by the churches, have undergone conceptual reformulation over time. Anti-modern discourse remains behind, and certain modern issues begin to be taken up, even as elements of critical analysis, to point out gaps and contradictions in the processes of modernization itself.

In the global culture emerging out of post-industrial society (which some mistakenly classify as "post-modern" culture), a new sphere for beliefs and religious expression is

FIGURE 12

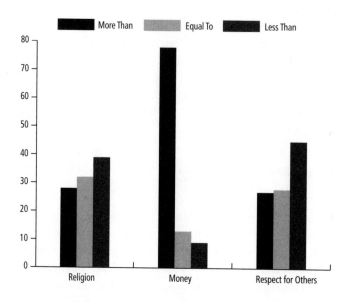

WHAT CHILEANS VALUE ABOVE ALL ELSE?
(percentages)

1995 FLACSO Survey

opening up. Pluralism and diversity are emblematic signs of the changes witnessed by the post-Cold War world. The new culture of differences — developed as a critical response to the hegemonic culture produced by the globalization of markets — not only accepts, but embraces and promotes the new multicultural dynamics emerging in societies ranging from developing countries to highly advanced ones. And this is occurring even though the acknowledgment of the multicultural nature of our societies has been a process marked by conflict.

Religion, as one of the central elements of the symbolic field of society, does not escape from this dynamic. The relative crisis of the mainline religions institutionalized in churches reinforced their anti-modern, reactionary, and fundamentalist sides. Meanwhile, the appearance of new religious movements, mistakenly called "sects" in our Latin American parlance, runs parallel to the growth of more or less individual and diffuse expressions of the so-called "mystical-esoteric nebula."[41] These movements are spreading like a kind of underground intellectual culture with an ambiguous relation to modernity. Therefore, the current religious pluralism in our countries, where the religious field up to this century was the hegemony of the Catholic majority, is no longer situated within the framework of a classic secularization process, and it is not at all similar to the pluralism

---

41 The term "mystical-esoteric nebula" was developed by Françoise Champion. It refers to "New Age"-type, diffuse beliefs, along with charismatic and esoteric movements, and the new syncretism. For an analysis of the Latin American situation, see Imelda Vega Centeno (1995: 61–75).

FIGURE 13

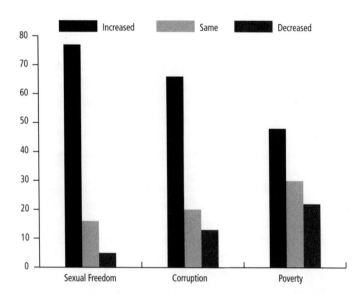

**IN FIVE YEARS, WHAT WILL HAVE
INCREASED OR DECREASED IN CHILE?**
(percentages)

1995 FLACSO Survey

that arose after the Reformation and the religious wars at the birth of modern European and Western society.

Today, modernization processes accentuate the relevance of the symbolic field in the construction of society. It can be said that modernization processes lead to the resurgence of religions (Debray 1996; Parker 1996), because the very contradictions of the moderniz- ing process over the last decades — its incoherence, instabilities, and inequalities — gener- ate human needs unsatisfied by the logic of the market and the reigning pragmatism. Daniéle Hervieu-Léger (1986) states that the distance between what modernity promises as a utopia and what it provides in practice can, at times, overflow the boundaries of toler- ation. This helps explain crises such as the one that can be seen today in the instrumental rationality that arose out of the Age of Enlightenment, above all as an ideology of progress, conquest, and the taming of the universe by man. It also suggests that the flourishing of the "sacred" alongside the contradictions of modernity shows the limits of "seculariza- tion" of modernity itself, since the satisfaction of material needs does not fulfill the need for meaning. This phenomenon is exhibited with greater intensity in our developing coun- tries, where the contradictions of the modernizing process are even more acute, creating fertile ground for pluralization in the religious field and for progress toward a multi-reli- gious society.

In the midst of the cultural crosscurrents at the end of the century, religions, not untouched by these same modernization processes, can be seen to bear values and processes that contribute to secularization. At the same time, they contribute symbolic elements which foster the "re-enchantment of the world." The participants in this "re-enchantment" range from neo-fundamentalist Evangelicals and the current manifestations of popular Catholicism, to charismatic Catholicism and the diverse "New Age" expressions.

During this process, analysts are carefully observing the rise of powerful religious movements or spiritual currents with fundamentalist or reactionary leanings, which tend toward the rejection of modernization and Western society and take refuge in traditionalist models. In Chile, this tendency can be seen in certain Catholic circles, among some Protestants and Evangelicals, and also in the Jewish community. These tendencies are a potential threat to the development and spread of a democratic culture.

The commonly accepted sociology of religions, from Troeltsch (1931) on, has often viewed the religious phenomenon according to the traditional model that established the mainline churches of the West. Now there is a need to analyze diffuse beliefs and the continuity of diverse forms of syncretic beliefs and rituals. As we have seen, alongside people's adherence to certain formally "Christian" credos (God, Christ, the Virgin, the Bible), they articulate popular beliefs and traditions, along with new beliefs of the post-industrial society, often in a disjointed manner.

This represents a challenge to democratic cultures, which seek not only to strengthen freedom of conscience and religion, but also to promote tolerance. This is a tolerance that assumes not only the simple, partial acceptance of the Other, but the radical acceptance of diversity at the center of a multi-religious society. The Chilean democratic State is far from possessing a fully non-confessional policy in this regard, due to its tendency to grant a privileged position to the religions which until now have been in the majority.

The same challenge is posed to the churches, especially the Catholic and Pentecostal ones, although in this case the ecumenical respect for diversity is based upon entirely different reasons from those motivating the actions of the State.

In summary, as the search for spirituality expands because of the effects of globalization, the State must protect religious freedom. This means both supporting religious pluralism and providing the institutional basis for the free development of a range of churches, forms of worship, and faiths. It also means guarding society from religious or pseudo-religious groups which, in the name of religious freedom, pose a threat to the freedom of their followers due to their manipulation of them. The mistakenly-identified "sects" or "Satanism" banned by the bill currently under review by the Senate must be regulated based on objective facts, not on mere suppositions or the simple prejudice of an official culture which for hundreds of years has been shaped by a Catholic-leaning Christianity.

The other challenge to democratic culture resides in the strengthening of an ethical order consistent with democratic principles. Democratic governance requires a more serious exploration of answers to the serious ethical problems faced by society. In the face of such problems, such as the crisis in the family, crime, drug trafficking, corruption, injustice, and social inequality, the churches have something to say and will continue to do so.

These challenges become even more urgent when public opinion, as we can clearly see in Figures 12 and 13, is on a trajectory leading to a lower appraisal of religion, much less respect for others, and on the other hand, a very high regard for money. The same is true when expanding sexual freedom is accompanied by an increase in corruption and, to a lesser degree, poverty. These pressing issues must be emphasized with greater force within a society enjoying positive economic indicators and tending to be complacent about its "successful" culture.

The above are issues of culture, globalization, and the democratization process. These are appeals to the churches, but also to the governments which must seek the common good of their fellow citizens. The greater the gap between what citizens expect from political authorities and what they perceive is delivered, the greater their need to expand their search for meaning beyond the boundaries of the established churches and the institutions of national culture. When the political system faces a crisis of direction, this also affects the religious sphere. The alternatives to a socially-committed faith grow more scarce, while the supply of all kinds of religions is in abundance. The greater the uncertainty induced by the lack of religious and civic leadership, the greater the attraction of emotionally-based religious currents. The greater, also, the appeal of a spirituality detached from all social commitment and distant from the pastoral strategies of the churches attempting to inject Christianity into social, political, and cultural modernity.

We see that society, in highly-developed countries around the world, as well as developing ones, is subjected to the dialectical dynamic of globalization: the tendency toward homogeneous and universal cultural elements brings forth a reaction in favor of heterogeneous and "local" currents. Faced with abstraction and internationalism, traditions rooted in the concrete ties of ethnicity, blood, and religion are revitalized.

The ethical crisis brought on by relativism and pragmatism, as well as the market culture's emphasis on a hedonistic and subjective morality, casts doubt upon the possibility of organizing broad, meaningful, ethically-inspired projects. Even less probable is the social reconstruction of a religion that is reactionary and hegemonic in nature, like that of the already outdated model of traditional Christianity. This same incapacity will perhaps give encouragement to religious fundamentalism and orthodoxy, although the most likely tendency would seem to be toward an increase in diffuse and syncretic beliefs. In any case, it seems probable that the established religions, because of their need to adapt to these changes, will see their activities, rituals, and beliefs transformed in a way that, in the eyes of contemporary peoples, may result in something hitherto unknown.

BIBLIOGRAPHICAL REFERENCES

Acevedo, Rodolfo. 1990. Los mormones en Chile. Santiago: Imp. Cumora.

Araneda, Fidel. 1986. Historia de la Iglesia en Chile, Santiago.

Arroyo, Gonzalo, et al. 1992. Por los caminos de América. Desafíos socioculturales a la Nueva Evangelización. Santiago: Ediciones Paulinas.

Arzobishopric of Santiago. 1995. IX Sínodo Arquidiocesano. Mirada a la realidad. Document Series (November). Santiago.

Barret, David, ed. 1982. World Christian Encyclopedia. London, Nairobi: Oxford University Press.

Berger, Peter et al. 1973. The Homeless Mind: Modernization and Consciousness. New York: Random House.

Bourdieu, Pierre. 1971. "Genèse et structure du champ religieux." *Revue Française de Sociologie* 12, pp. 295–334.

Braudel, Fernand. 1993. A History of Civilizations. New York: Penguin.

Canales et al. 1991. En tierra extraña. Para una sociología de la religiosidad protestante. Santiago: Amerinda, Sepade.

Caro, Mons. Cristián. 1994. "Interpelaciones de Santo Domingo a nuestra Iglesia." En: Cultura, modernidad e Iglesia en Chile. Santiago: Ed. San Pablo, pp. 97–106.

Castillo, Fernando. 1986. Iglesia liberadora y política. Santiago: ECO.

Cleary, Edward L. and Hannah Stewart-Gambino, eds. 1992. Conflict and Competition. The Latin American Church in a Changing Environment. Boulder-London: Lynne Reinner Publishers.

Correa, Enrique y José Antonio Viera-Gallo. 1986. Iglesia y dictadura. Santiago: Ed. Cesoc.

Corvalán, S., ed. 1990. Iglesia, Estado y democracia en América Latina. Santiago: Seminario del Servicio Académico para Extranjeros.

Chaparro, Patricio. 1983. La Iglesia católica y el conflicto político. Santiago.

Debray, Regis. 1996. El arcaísmo posmoderno, lo religioso en la aldea global. Buenos Aires: Ed. Manantial.

Dooner, Patricio. 1989. Iglesia, reconciliación y democracia. Santiago: Editorial Andante.

During, Simon, ed. 1993. The Cultural Studies Reader. New York: Routledge.

Flacso, Área de Educación y Cultura. 1995. Representaciones de la sociedad chilena: Opiniones y actitudes. Survey report. Santiago: Ed. Flacso-Chile.

Frigerio, Alejandro. 1992. "La invasión de las sectas: el debate sobre los nuevos movimientos religiosos en los medios de comunicación argentinos." Sociedad y Religión 10.

Frigerio, Alejandro, ed. 1993. Ciencias sociales y religión en el Cono Sur. Buenos Aires: Centro Editor de América Latina.

Gómez de Benito, Justino. 1995. Proyectos de Iglesia y proyectos de sociedad en Chile. 1961–90. Santiago: Ed. San Pablo.

González, María Adriana. 1997. "Percepción del modelo de familias de los grupos religiosos adventistas y católicos, comuna La Cisterna, Santiago, Chile." Dissertation written for the degree of Masters in Latin American Studies. Instituto Pedro de Córdova, Santiago; P. Universidad Santo Tomás "Angelicum," Rome, Italy.

Guerrero, Bernardo. 1994. Estudios sobre el movimiento pentecostal en América Latina. Centro de Investigaciones de la Realidad del Norte, *Cuaderno de Investigación Social* (Iquique) 35 (November).

Hervieu-Léger, Danièle. 1986. Vers un nouveau christianisme? París: CERF.

Huntington, Samuel. 1993. The Third Wave. Democratization in the Late Twentieth Century. Norman, USA: University of Oklahoma Press.

Houtart, François. 1989. Religión y modos de producción precapitalistas. Madrid: IEPALA.

Irarrázabal, Diego. 1994. Cultura y fe latinoamericanas. Santiago: Rehue.

Lagos, Humberto. 1983. La función de las minorías religiosas: el protestantismo chileno 1973–81 bajo el régimen militar. Santiago.

_____. 1986. Religión y proyecto político autoritario. Santiago: Ed. Presor.

_____. 1987a. La religión en las Fuerzas Armadas y de Orden. Santiago: Ed. Presor-LAR.

_____. 1987b. Sectas religiosas en Chile: ¿fe o ideología? Santiago: Ed Presor-LAR.

_____. 1988. Crisis de la esperanza. Religión y autoritarismo en Chile. Santiago: Ed. Presor-LAR.

Lalive d'Epinay, Christian. 1968. El refugio de las masas. Estudio sociológico del protestantismo chileno. Santiago: Ed. del Pacífico.

Lanternari, Vittorio. 1982. "La religion popu-
laire. Perspective historique et anthro-
pologique." *Archives de Sciences Sociales des
Religions* 53 (1), pp. 121–143.

Levine, Daniel. 1996. Voces populares en el
catolicismo. Lima: CEP.

Levine, Daniel, ed. 1980. Churches and Politics
in Latin America. Beverly Hills: Sage
Publications.

Lowden, Pamela. 1996. Moral Opposition to
Authoritarian Rule in Chile, 1973–90.
Oxford.

Marileo, Armando et al. 1995. ¿Modernización o
sabiduría en tierra mapuche? Santiago: Ed.
San Pablo.

Marx, Karl and F. Engels. 1979 (1844). Sobre la
Religión. Edited by H. Assmann and R.
Mate. Salamanca: Sígueme.

Marzal, Manuel. 1986. "Análisis etnológico del
sincretismo latinoamericano." *Cristianismo
y Sociedad* 24 (88), pp. 27–40.

Mella, Orlando y Patricio Frías, eds. 1991.
Religiosidad popular, trabajo y comu-
nidades de base. Santiago: Primus.

Meneses, Aldo. 1990. Discurso y poder. Santiago:
Ilades.

Mifsud, Tony s.j. 1994. "Principios y ejes temáti-
cos fundamentales del Documento de Santo
Domingo." In: Cultura, modernidad e Iglesia en Chile. Santiago: San Pablo, pp. 11–24.

Morandé, Pedro. 1984. Cultura y modernización
en América Latina. Santiago: Instituto de
Sociología de la Pontificia Universidad
Católica de Chile.

Muñoz, Ronaldo. 1994. "La opción de Santo
Domingo por los pobres." En: Cultura,
modernidad e Iglesia en Chile. Santiago:
San Pablo, pp. 121–145.

Ossa, Manuel. 1992. Lo propio y lo ajeno.
Santiago: Rehue.

Pace, Enzo. 1995. "Tendencias y corrientes de la
sociología de las religiones." *Sociedad y
religión* (Argentina) 13 (March), pp. 3–19.

Pacheco, Luis. 1988. La Iglesia chilena y los cambios sociopolíticos. Santiago: Ed. Pehuén.

Parker, Cristián. 1988a. "La Iglesia en Chile,
1968–88." In: V.A. Chile 1968–88. Los ensay-
istas. Georgia, USA, pp. 51–77.

———. 1988b. "Formas democráticas y participación popular: La experiencia de la Iglesia
en América del Sur." In: R. Alvayay and C.
Ruiz, comps. Participación y democracia.
Santiago: Ed. CERC-Melquíades.

———. 1989. "Autoritarismo, modernización y
catolicismo. Las relaciones Iglesia-Estado
en las últimas décadas en Chile." *Revista
Opciones* (Santiago) 16 (May-August),
pp. 81–106.

———. 1990. "Iglesia Católica, Derechos
Humanos y transición democrática."
Pastoral Popular (Santiago) 198 (May), pp.
27–29.

———. 1992a. Animitas, machis y santiguadoras
en Chile. Santiago: Ed. Rehue.

———. 1992b. "Popular Religion and Modernization in Latin America: A Different
Logic." Maryknoll, New York: Orbis Books,
1996.

———. 1994a. "The sociology of religion in Latin
America." *Social Compass* 41 (3),
pp. 339–354.

———. 1994b. "Iglesia y modernidad: Opciones
del clero sobre los cambios culturales en
Chile." Persona y Sociedad (Santiago:
Ilades) 8 (4), pp. 50–83.

———. 1996a. Las Iglesias y su acción social en
Chile. Santiago: Ediciones Unicef-
Academia.

———. 1996b. Religión popular y modernización.
La otra lógica en América Latina. 2nd. ed.
F.C.E. Santiago, New York: Orbis Books.

———. 1996c. "Trajectoire de la sociologie de la
religion au Chili." *Social Compass. Revue
internationale de sociologie de la religion* 43 (3)
(September). Oxford: Sage, pp. 391–410.

———. 1997a. Religión y postmodernidad. Lima:
Kairos-Perú, CEPS.

Parker, Cristián et al. 1997b. Identidad y diversi-
dad de catolicismos populares urbanos
frente al mercado globalizado (estudio de
caso en San Joaquín-Chile). Final Report.
Santiago: Centro de Estudios de la Realidad
Contemporánea (CERC-UAHC).

Pastor, Aníbal, et al. 1993. De Lonquén a Los
Andes, 20 años de la Iglesia Católica chilena. Santiago: Rehue.

Rammsy, Claudio, ed. 1990. Iglesia y transición
en Chile. Santiago: Centro Ecuménico
Diego de Medellín.

Robertson, Roland. 1992. Globalization: Social
theory and global culture. London: Ed.
Sage.

Salas, Ricardo. 1994. "Modernidad, cultura y
cristianismo en América Latina." In:
Cultura, modernidad e Iglesia en Chile.
Santiago: Ed. San Pablo, pp. 39–60.

_____.1996. "Les sciences sociales face à l'u-
nivers religieux mapuche." Social Compass
43 (3). Oxford: Sage, pp. 367–390.

Salinas, Maximiliano. 1987. Historia del Pueblo
de Dios en Chile. Santiago: Cehila, Ed.
Rehue.

_____.1996. "La recherche d'un lieu sacré: la tra-
jectoire sociale et religieuse des pobladores
au Chili. 1962–92." Social Compass 43 (3).
Oxford: Sage, pp. 353–366.

Salinas, M., H. San Martín, and C. Parker. 1997.
Motivaciones de la población joven chilena
para contraer matrimonio por la Iglesia.
Research report. Santiago: Centro de
Estudios de la Realidad Contemporánea
(CERC-UAHC), Área Cultura y Religión.

Sampedro, Francisco. 1986. Ante las principales
sectas o nuevos movimientos religiosos.
Santiago: Imp. Manantial.

Santagada, Osvaldo et al. 1991. Las sectas en
América Latina. Buenos Aires: Ed.
Claretiana-Celam.

Schreiter, Robert J. 1997. The New Catholicity.
Between the Global and the Local.
Maryknoll, New York: Orbis Books.

Sepúlveda, Juan. 1996. "Reinterpreting Chilean
Pentecostalism." Social Compass 43 (3).
Oxford: Sage, pp. 299–318.

Smith, Brian. 1982. Church and Politics in Chile.
New Jersey: Princeton University Press.

Soneira, Jorge et al. 1996. Sociología de la
religión. Buenos Aires: Docencia.

Tomassini, Luciano. 1995. "El proceso de global-
ización: sus impactos políticos." In:
Seminario Internacional sobre
Transformaciones Económico Sociales y
Políticas Públicas en América Latina."
Santiago: Ed. Universidad de Chile.

Troeltsch, Ernst. 1931. The Social Teachings of
the Christian Churches. New York: George
Allen and Unwin.

Van Kessel, Juan and Bernardo Guerrero. 1987.
"Sanidad y salvación en el altiplano
chileno: Del yatiri al pastor." Cuaderno de
Investigación Social 21. Iquique: Centro de la
Realidad del Norte.

Vega-Centeno, Imelda. 1995. "Sistemas de creen-
cias en la sociedad moderna." Sociedad y
Religión (Argentina) 13 (March), pp. 61–88.

VV.AA. 1988. Democracia y Evangelio. Santiago:
Ed. CERC-Rehue.

Weber, Max. 1964 (1922). Economía y Sociedad.
México: Fondo de Cultura Económica.

DOCUMENTS
(Chronological listing)

Chilean Bishops' Conference

Certeza, coherencia y confianza. Chilean
Bishops' Conference, November 1989.

Con los criterios del Evangelio. Statement of the
Standing Committee of the Conference of
Bishops of Chile, March 7,1991.

Documents of the Bishopric. Chile 1988–91.
Conference of Bishops of Chile, March
1992.

Análisis de la situación del país. Desafíos nacionales. Executive Committee, National
Committee for Justice and Peace, April 1992.

Letter to the Minister of Education, Ricardo
Lagos, from Bishop Carlos González,
Bishop of Talca, President of CECH, June
11, 1992.

Press Release: Aportes del Comité Permanente
del Episcopado a la propuesta del Sr.
Ministro de Educación. August 19, 1992.

Press Release: Sobre el espionaje telefónico y su
gravedad ética. Área Pastoral Social de la
Conferencia Episcopal de Chile. August 27,
1992.

Análisis de la situación y proyecciones del país.
National Committee for Justice and Peace,
April 1993.

Más alegría hay en dar que en recibir. Letter
from the Chilean Bishops' Committee,
April 21, 1993.

Communiqué at the Conclusion of the Plenary
Bishop's Assembly. 65th Plenary Assembly
of Bishops, April 25,1993.

No cometerás adulterio. Bishops' Standing
Committee, May 14,1993.

Press Release: Comunicadores cristianos
reflexionaron sobre la "Aetatis Novae."
Department of Communications,
Archbishopric of La Serena, May 25, 1993.

Reconciliación Nacional: Un urgente desafío
nacional. National Committee for Justice
and Peace, July 1993.

Violación de derechos humanos y casos de
detenidos desaparecidos. Statement by the
President of the Chilean Bishops'
Conference, August 4,1993.

Ocasión para servir. Chilean Bishops'
Conference, August 25,1993.

Para Construir el futuro. Chilean Bishops'
Conference, August 25,1993.

El reencuentro que anhelamos. Chilean Bishops'
Conference, September 8, 1993.

Hoy nos ha nacido un salvador. Chilean Bishops' Conference, December 15, 1993.

Conclusiones Seminario "Superación de la pobreza en Chile." March 16–18, 1994.

Familia camino de amor. Mensaje a las familias de Chile. April 22, 1994.

Familia vida y solidaridad. Mensaje de Santo Domingo, June 18, 1994.

Statement by the President of the Bishops' Conference on the changing of religious holidays, August 5, 1994.

Dar con alegría. Message from the Bishops' Standing Committee on the Day of Solidarity, August 18, 1994.

Algunas reflexiones sobre los jóvenes y la catequesis escolar, October 1994.

Carta a los padres y apoderados de la familias católicas de Chile (at the conclusion of the Year of the Family), December 1994.

Communiqué: Asamblea Plenaria de Obispos, December 1994.

Cristo nuestra esperanza. Easter Message, April 12, 1995.

No nos ha llamado Dios a la inmundicia sino a la Santidad, May 12, 1995.

Declaración, Bishops' Conference President, May 17,1995.

Mejoremos nuestra convivencia nacional, June 14, 1995.

Reconciliación y solidaridad, August 1995.

Obispos piden por los profesores, October 1995.

Carta a los profesores de religión, October 20, 1995.

Navidad camino de esperanza, December 19, 1995.

¿Es Chile un país equitativo? National Committee for Justice and Peace, January 1996.

La colaboración de empresarios y trabajadores: Una urgencia de nuestra hora, March 1996.

Preparemos el año 2000. Letter from the Bishops of the Church to Catholics and to all the people of Chile, April 19, 1996.

¿Es Chile un país equitativo?, May 1996.

Tarea política y bien común, May 16, 1996.

Ante la crisis del carbón, July 17, 1996.

Declaración del Secretariado General del Episcopado sobre el traslado de feriados religiosos a día lunes, September 5, 1996.

Acerca de la educación sexual, September 10, 1996.

Dignidad de la procreación y respeto por la vida humana naciente, September 12, 1996.

Ante el conflicto del magisterio, October 10, 1996.

Economía y convivencia nacional. Elementos para un discernimiento cristiano. Doctrinal Commission, Chilean Bishops' Conference, November 1996.

Declaración del Comité Permanente del Episcopado referente a la cumbre mundial sobre la alimentación, November 13, 1996.

Press release: 72ª Asamblea Plenaria de la Conferencia Episcopal de Chile, November 22, 1996.

Ante el paro de la salud, December 11, 1996.

Press release: 73ª Asamblea Plenaria de la Conferencia Episcopal de Chile, May 6, 1997.

Lota: Problema de todos, May 8, 1997.

PASTORAL LETTERS
(Chronological listing)

Los católicos y la política. Mons. Carlos Oviedo Cavada, Archbishop of Santiago, September 24, 1990.

Moral, juventud y sociedad permisiva. Invitación a una vida evangélica. Mons. Carlos Oviedo Cavada, September 24, 1991.

La Iglesia acoge a todas las familias. Letter from the Archbishop of Santiago, Mons. Carlos Oviedo Cavada, to the families of the Archdiocese. October 1991.

Los pobres no pueden esperar. Pastoral letter, Mons. Carlos Oviedo Cavada, September 24, 1992.

Nacidos para amar. Pastoral letter to youth, Mons. Carlos Oviedo Cavada, April 1993.

Del temor a la esperanza. La Iglesia ante el desafío del sida. Pastoral letter, Mons. Carlos Oviedo Cavada, June 1993.

El amor puede más. Pastoral letter from the Archbishop of Santiago, Mons. Carlos Oviedo Cavada, June 1993.

El cuidado de la casa común. La Iglesia ante el desafío ecológico. Pastoral letter, Mons. Carlos Oviedo Cavada, April 1994.

Revalorizar el domingo. Pastoral letter, Mons. Carlos Oviedo Cavada, August 28, 1994.

Servir como Jesús. Pastoral letter to the youth of the Chilean Association of Scouts, September 1994.

Un sólo rebaño, un sólo pastor. Pastoral letter, Mons. Carlos Oviedo Cavada, September 1994.

Por siempre sea alabado Jesús sacramentado. Pastoral letter, Mons. Carlos Oviedo Cavada, April 4, 1996.

"Vayan y hagan discípulos míos." La catequesis, una educación al servicio de la fe. Pastoral letter, Mons. Carlos Oviedo Cavada, August 10, 1996.

Santidad y vocaciones sacerdotales. Pastoral letter, Mons. Carlos Oviedo Cavada, May 22, 1997.

Vocación y servicio. Pastoral letter to the elderly, Mons. Carlos Oviedo Cavada, June 7, 1997.

Culture Microclimates

Roberto Merino

Although we are creatures of the 1990s, we have no way of knowing how cultural developments from this period will precipitate down to subsequent decades. We have no clue as to what will endure over time and what will be reduced to nothing more than a symptom of the era for historians. Neither do we know whether cultural productions viewed today as dubious or insignificant will be recovered tomorrow by other sensibilities.[1]

For the cultural archaeologist, or even for any curious person, a moment in the past may appear to be more understandable than the mass of confusing and fleeting events which we call the present. Signposts of the past are visible: closed lives, archives, and assessments open to review. It is easy to pinpoint today the cultural schism that Neruda, Huidobro, or Mistral caused around 1920. In fact, if we look back at those years, we find few other recognizable voices, even though the poetic forest of the time was densely filled with trees, and discussions of the day were quite impassioned. Today, however, those other voices have assimilated into the rhetoric of the period and are nearly inaudible for us, as in the cases of Pezoa Véliz and Pedro Prado, considered then "our greatest poets."

Viewed from another vantage point, the situation becomes clear to us: the recovery of democracy brought change in energy, disposition, and cultural framework for those who had labored in "productions of the spirit" in the late 1980s. The change in regime presupposed a transformation of the scenario in which those suffering souls had struggled. The partial unraveling of the authoritarian and oppressive nightmare presumed a new proposal of artistic concerns and "cultural activists." To adjust oneself to the new circumstance became an inevitable necessity. 'What to do now?' became a difficult question for most. Recover the currents cut off by the regime, join in with modernization, cloister oneself within the confines of some private project? Further on, we will attempt to dispel these doubts. For the moment, however, we will take a look at the previous period.

It is more than evident that the 1973 military coup brought a rupture in the life of the country. The change was not only political or institutional; it also affected private,

---

1 In an interview in 1990, José Donoso stated: "I do not believe that anyone with half a brain can conceive of future eternity or that glory will last more than a century. We see how people are forgetting, or have already forgotten, Neruda. Mistral is no longer remembered beyond a group of feminists that are trying to revive her, which is all well and good to me... To think that we write for posterity is absurd. Where will posterity be? We can't know! With the enormous changes we are witnessing, I don't believe that books are going to last more than 20 years. Lasting, in the sense of immortality, is completely irrelevant."

individual lives. Fear, rumor as a source of information, denunciation (that even reached into university classrooms), and darkness in general were the daily fare in the early years of those difficult years.

It is impossible to separate cultural activity of the military era from its authoritarian conditions. Cultural life was severely affected by the coup: its sustenance, the city, had become a place under siege, uninhabitable at night. Many notable figures of national culture were victims of the new power and came to know prison, exile, loss of employment, or ostracism. The scene changed on the streets as well as inside homes. The degree of control reached seemingly petty levels. We remember how, on public streets, just a few days after the 11th of September, military-barber patrols endeavored to cut the hair of long-haired men who failed to heed the hairstyling norms imposed by those who had recently taken power. The concept of citizen had been placed on hold until further notice. Public offices incorporated a figure unfamiliar until that time, technically known as the "sapo" (spy, literally "toad"). These recollections are not simply anecdotal, and, unfortunately, are important.

Meetings were banned and all conversations were subject to vigilance. The press injected the nation with mistrust for the foreigner: evil, in all its expressions, came from a convulsed and mistaken world, for which Chile was an oasis of peace, as a popular slogan affirmed. Outside raged wars and disorder; the ominous "foreign ideologies" came from the outside as did the misinformation schemes aimed against national reality. In this totalitarian spectrum, it is easy to presume that cultural activity was also squelched, not only in its external expressions, but also in its inner-most heart. If art for art's sake is nurtured in some sense by life itself, then it is evident that since September 12, 1973, a page or a blank television screen were no longer what they were before, for those who cared to confront the restrictions once and again. The climate of dirty war, as a spirit prior to and independent of the situation, was even able to find foreboding expression in writings prior to the coup. "Lobos y ovejas," the epic poem by Manuel Silva Acevedo, had announced in 1972 the sacrificial and erroneous scene that would present itself a year later. In 1977, this climate filtered, in an obscure fashion, into "Los helicópteros," a poem which Erick Pohlhammer read in the middle of an extraordinary assembly in Santiago's Caupolican Theater before an expectant crowd. For a long time, those texts were understood as allusions to the coup, although the first described a general situation of human suffering, while the second was meant as a paraphrase of Damaso Alonso's poem about bees.

Political regime and culture, however, are two spheres that are not always harmonious. Despite the dictatorship's cultural confinement, suffocation, and lack of possibilities for civilized man, significant works of poetry were published during its reign. The Chilean tradition of poetry proved to be stronger and able to prevail above the political anomaly of the period. A significant part of the poetry written in that time has survived over the course of years and changing social contexts. The poetry of Enrique Lihn, Raul Zurita, Juan Luis Martinez, and Diego Maquiera are living proof, as are the works on stage of playwrights Rodrigo Lira and Claudio Bertoni. Others will wish to add, and with reason, the work of Alberto Rubio. In none of these cases, did any literary works consume their authors' energies with overt confrontational denunciation of the repressive situation. Rather, it was surreptitiously invoked.

The same thing occurred in the fine arts, although the generation that was active as of 1976 always expressed a clear political orientation. Eugenio Dittborn, for example, with his photographic images of swimmers and athletes, captured in the moment of greatest physical exertion an effective metaphor for a tortured body. Along the same lines, Carlos Leppe exposed his own body to gross mockery in performances before limited groups of audiences, and Raul Zurita and Diamela Eltit, likewise torturously intervened in their own bodies. Carlos Altamirano produced, among other things, a tense video in which he ran through the streets of Santiago repeating incessantly, "Chilean artist Altamirano." Art action was one of the recurrent expressions in concentric circles of culture, which closed in on a space lacking in communicational channels to the rest of the community. Such desperate efforts tended to keep alive, in their own way, what official spheres denied everyone else: the possibility of acting freely and affecting the reality by means of its own linguistic weavings.

The official spheres preferred the cultivation of "meaningless art," in the phrase coined by Enrique Lihn; that is, the merely interpretive art such as ballet, opera, or still life painting. The regime favored art which did not question concrete reality, because it was inconvenient or lacked interest in its own cultural codes.

Around 1978, the idea of the "cultural blackout" (blacking out, others said) began to become more generalized, a diagnosis that was aired even on television, which is blamed every now and then for fostering collective apathy. But, as we have seen, the semi-official sectors of culture themselves came to lament such things as the paucity of Chilean vocabulary, incorrect pronunciation, and lack of general information. A metaphor for the official concept of culture during the years of the dictatorship was the contest-program "Un million para el mejor" ("A million for the best"), where people of different planes of erudition competed for an amount of money before a doubly erudite panel of judges. It was a discrete show, for the living room or set, that applauded participants' capacity to memorize facts, although not to make sense of them. To make sense of the facts would have meant having to talk and thus risk saying (or knowing) too much.

Intellectual limits were opened early on, but under much hardship, by specific people in still strongly controlled places. Important in this regard was the Humanities Studies Department (University of Chile, Engineering School) which under the administration of novelist Cristian Huneeus congregated writers and philosophers who favored freedom of thought. Around 1976, the Humanities Studies Department conducted literary theory workshops of high caliber that employed an extensive bibliographic base. Participants included Enrique Lihn, Adriana Valdes, and Carmen Foxley. In 1975, and already under the administration of Juan de Dios Vial Larrain, this department had produced the magazine "Manuscritos" with advances by Raul Zurita, texts by Nicanor Parra, and a timely resuscitation of the bulletin board newspaper *Quebrantahuesos*, produced in the 1950s by Parra, Lihn, Alejandro Jodorowsky, and other enthusiasts. Only a single issue was published of this remarkably high quality magazine, directed by poet and literary theorist Ronald Kay.

Meanwhile, in 1977 in Villa Alemana near Viña del Mar, Juan Luis Martinez invoked Chilean poetry in his book *La nueva novela*, a work in which Martinez borrowed from the body of European and avant-garde poetry. The work was not strictly original, as one would think. Critics of the press mainly considered its more consumable aspects. The poet Braulio Arenas, a provocative surrealist of yesteryear transformed into a defender of the Pinochet regime, expressed in an essay a certain discomfort with an obscene quote of Francis Picabia, which was printed in the book under the image of a Chilean flag with the caption, "Epigrafe para un libro condenado: la politica" ("Inscription for a condemned book: politics").[2]

That same year comedian Manolo González dared to imitate Augusto Pinochet on television, an act that served as a small escape valve for emotions held back under threat of repression. Still more significant was undoubtedly the publication of *Paris*, a highly exceptional event, considering it was one of the most radical books written by Enrique Lihn. Around the same time, the Ictus Theater presented David Benavente's work "Pedro, Juan y Diego," which for the first time since 1973 dared to address the issue of the marginality of working class neighborhoods that surround Santiago.

When, in 1979, Raul Zurita published his book *Purgatorio*, he reclaimed a few more centimeters of freedom. During an impromptu seminar on poetry and the country's political situation (the Encuentro de Arte Joven at the Las Condes Cultural Institute), which cried out for greater freedom of expression, Enrique Lihn joked with the young poets that what they were winning back was not freedom but licentiousness.

In August 1981, writers Jorge Edwards, Nicanor Parra, Guillermo Blanco, Lihn, Zurita, Francisco Coloane, José Donoso, and others met at CPU headquarters to speak out on issues affecting their trade, and, subsequently, the country's cultural problems. The event gave way to a happening, with Rodrigo Lira taking center stage at the moment Edwards opened the floor to public debate. Strident music provided the signal for Lira (who had donned a clown's nose) and collaborators to break file, passing out copies of a satiric leaflet of the Chamico Group. The episode was a bit flawed since Braulio Arenas did not show up. Lihn had intended to interrupt Arenas, as Arenas himself had done to Neruda 40 years before.

Cultural currents, despite imposed restrictions, began to flow, although it was not apparent in what direction. A basic guide book to visual and literary art of the period must include the work of Carlos Altamirano from 1976 to 1985; Gonzalo Díaz' landmark exhibit in 1982 "Historia sentimental de la pintura chilena," the guerrilla art of the CADA group (Colectivo de Acciones de Arte of Fernando Balcells, Diamela Eltit, Gonzalo Muñoz, and Lotty Rosenfeld) in the early 1980s, and the Juan Domingo Davila exhibit in 1979 in the Epoca Gallery, featuring Zurita's act of public masturbation. And in literature, the corresponding movement was marked by the novels of Adolfo Couve, *La Lección De Pintura* and *El Picadero* (both 1979), and of Diamela Eltit *Lumpérica* (1984) and *Por la Patria* (1986). Other milestones of the era were the books *Exit* (1981) and *Este* (1983) published by Gonzalo Muñoz; Rodrigo Lira's posthumous *Proyecto de Obras Completas* (1984); and the collection of poems *La Tirana* (1983) by Diego Maquiera, Erick Pohlhammer's *Gracias por la Atención Dispensada* (1986), and Claudio Bertoni's *El Cansador Intrabajable* (1987).

In short, although artists had to be on their guard, the cultural blackout was not impenetrable. A government official prevented Oscar Hahn from publishing his poems *Mal de Amor* in 1981, due to an allegedly pornographic poem, but censorship was far more vigorous with newspapers, magazines, and radio news broadcasts. Economic considerations were the major obstacle to getting books published. Most poetry of the period circulated in mimeographed magazines and photocopied sheets, and the poetry recital, characterized by a certain sophistication, became an important cultural expression.

---

2   The quote in question is as follows: "The father and mother have no right over the death of their children, but the Homeland, our second mother, can burn them at the stake to the immense glory of politicians."

We must also note the work of the Ictus Theater group, the literary workshops of the Union of Young Writers at the Society of Chilean Writers (SECH), the ongoing cultural movement in the universities (characterized by the nightly peñas, which interposed theatrical skits, poetry recital, mulled wine, and guitar), and the work of the non-governmental organizations, primarily in the social sciences.

All of this fell short of creating a cultural richness or even a cultural climate. Cultural events were relatively isolated from each other but still managed to create a certain resistance to the cultural paralysis.

I. Deaths and Survivors

The 1990s and the return of democracy were marked from the outset by losses of significant cultural protagonists, some premature deaths, but all of them grievous.

Enrique Lihn had led the cultural movement in May 1988. His funeral in the Parque del Recuerdo cemetery gathered together a large representation of the cultural players of the past four decades. Rumor had it that the mourners included "a 100-year-old lady," a joke very much in line with the poet's sense of humor. Lihn had spent the hard years of the Pinochet regime in Chile, as a poet and critic of the times, which in his mind were inseparable capacities.

Lihn was not only an unpredictable creator, but also an intellectual catalyst in conversation for people of different ages, origins, and disciplines. His voice resounded in books, catalogues, seminars, and a few favorable corners of the press, such as the last page of the daily La Epoca, during the newspaper's early years. Upon his passing, many could have evoked the words Ezra Pound spoke upon the death of Henry James: "I felt there was no one left to turn to when I have doubts." Among his most notable last writings is a cheap broadsheet ("La Aparición de la Virgen", 1987), which artfully used words to transform into poetry one of the major symbolic orchestrations of the military regime: the invocation and miracles of the Virgin Mary in the community of Villa Alemana. His "Diario de Muerte," which Lihn wrote at the end of his life fully aware of his impending demise, was published posthumously in 1989 by Universitaria Press.

The persistence of Lihn's figure even today is striking. As with Juan Luis Martinez and Rodrigo Lira, his presence represents a cultural spectrum of survivors. Interest in his work flourished in unexpected places, fostered by people not necessarily connected to the cultural world. During a conversation following a tribute at a recent Feria del Libro, a young man in the audience, who admitted that he was not drawn by writers, told of how his identification with Lihn's poetry originated when he read "La musiquilla de las pobres esferas." Upon hearing a television newscast announce the poet's death, he shut himself in his room to re-read the book, as a way to protest that untimely passing.

Such examples show that an author's works follow unpredictable courses in search of readers, at times, despite critics' silencing an author or sales strategies of big publishing houses. A book, ultimately, has this advantage: its ability to prevail beyond momentary acclaim or indifference at its launching and re-live the intimacy of each happy reading. Thus, the prestige of Enrique Lihn is a national or, more accurately, a local affair outside the frame of interest stirred up beyond Chile's borders. Lihn's international publications by the New Directions, Hiperion, or Lumen publishing houses, were never remarkable during his lifetime. Such has also been the case of the anthology of Lihn's work, *Porque Escribí*, published in 1996 by the Economic Cultural Fund.

Another survivor has been the poetry and figure of Rodrigo Lira, who committed suicide in December 1981. Books of his work are practically non-existent today. Lira's poetry circulated mainly through photocopies or in fleeting public readings. Only one book, *Proyecto de Obras Completas* (1984), contains the bulk of his work, but the volume is out of print and the publishing companies (Minga/ Camaleon) responsible for his books no longer exist. Yet, Lira's poems, which interpose painful testimony with humor by means of verbal hypertrophy, continue to be read by young readers. At least two efforts have been made in recent years to compile his poetry in an anthology, but for the moment his admirers will have to keep waiting.

The other survivor is Juan Luis Martínez. His book, *La nueva novela* (published in 1977 with a second printing in 1985), still attracts new readers. The book is sold almost entirely by individual vendors in a limited number of places (Martínez had the theory, which he put into practice in his Ediciones Archivo, that a book of poetry should be sold slowly). At some point, before its second printing, it was thought that *La novela nueva* did not really exist, even though people talked about it. Later, literary critic Luis Vargas Saavedra even doubted the existence of its author, believing Martínez to be an invention of Enrique Lihn and Pedro Lastra. "That statement," Martínez remarked in an interview with the El Mercurio Revista de Libros, "moved me immensely. It pleases me to radiate a veiled identity as a poet; the notion of existing or not existing, of being more literary than real." At the conclusion of a conference on the work of Martínez, poets Soledad Fariña and Eduardo Correa unveiled *La poesia chilena*, Martínez' second book, first published in 1978, but stored since then in a warehouse under orders of its author.

Still more admirable writers departed from the world in the dawn of democracy: in 1991 critic and professor Patricio Marchant (another DEH man) passed away, as did Carlos Ruiz-Tagle, narrator of childhood and adolescent intimacies, whose history remains cloaked in silence, not unlike his lifetime. The beautiful tales by Ruiz-Tagle should be published again, to give readers the opportunity to know him. Martin Cerda, possibly the most memorable Chilean essayist, died that same year.

The year 1992 witnessed the demise of the great poet Eduardo Anguita. At the time, Anguita lived in complete isolation in his downtown apartment, voluntarily removed from the written and spoken word. His writings of other times, *Venus en el Pudridero, El Octaedro y el Mar*, and *Poesia Entera*, have survived him commendably. The dazzling metaphysical quality of his words have not lost their gleam.

II. Forms and Symbols

Only by retracing specific events and people is it possible to faithfully distinguish a country's recent cultural movement. General concepts pertain to explanations and to mnemonic techniques of history, often functioning only as mirages of cultural reality.

The advent of democracy in Chile gave rise to a multitude of cultural groups on the fringes of the political scene. The governmental change of 1990 spurred a few limited discussions on the arrival of a so-called modernization to the country, but at first the dominant official esthetic was limited to festive and ecumenical celebration.

An example was the celebration organized in the National Stadium for the inauguration of Patricio Aylwin as president. Its televised broadcast conveyed a type of allegorical nightmare of Chilean identity, albeit quite joyful. In truth, it was a spectacle that should not have been televised, given the disorder that reigned in that overflowing stadium playing field. Cowboys on horseback made their way through wandering vendors hawking their merchandise alongside street break-dancers. Farther down, more cowboys raced while buses carrying more dancers entered the stadium.

The spirit of consensus, or a spirit that tolerates anything, predominated at that celebration and stretched across the nation in those initial hours of the new administration.

A similar outlook, of extreme openness, was installed also in the Fine Arts Museum shortly after Aylwin took office. Its driving force was artist Nemesio Antúnez, who in 1990 recovered his position as curator. Antúnez had held that post at the time of the military coup, which lent his designation a highly symbolic tone. He was, in fact, a figure of consensus, regarded with much prestige by his peers and the new officialdom's cultural world. Years earlier, during day-long cultural events held in Mendoza, Argentina, with the participation of a great number of exiles, Antúnez had been proclaimed in jest President of the Republic, presidential sash and all.

Antúnez' thrust involved the shaking loose, at least in form, of a dark era. There was certainly ample reason for this. The country's main art museum was closed for repairs for several years following the earthquake of 1985. A painter of happy colors and simple messages, Antúnez wanted to "fill Chile with color" and dye the Mapocho River blue. One of his first activities was the exhibit entitled "Open Museum" in which painters of all stripes participated without distinction and with no major consideration for quality or history.

Symbolic restorations continued, and in the case of Antúnez, he returned to National Television (TVN) to take charge of the 1990 version of his program "Ojo con el Arte," another matter that had been interrupted by the coup. Barely had the camera lights come on, when the painter spoke his first words, paraphrasing Fray Luis de Leon: "As we were saying 20 years ago..." The figure of consensus he projected also led him to participate in a television ad in which he appeared in the museum doorway, arms open, calling out to television viewers: "Come one, come all!" Had the previous curator filmed a similar television ad, he would have been obliged to say, "Please, don't come!"

No thought was given to adapting the museum to the demands of modernization or of the market, nor was there a need for that at the time, although since then such change has become urgent in the fine arts. But, initially, the pressing need was for a catharsis to break through the cultural suffocation. Nemesio Antúnez' became the official style.

Theater also staged a festive spirit, as evidenced in the rapid acceptance of "La Negra Ester," with a script based on verse by Roberto Parra and directed by Andrés Pérez. The novelty of this concept was the change in expressive means of portraying marginality. Audiences were not in the mood for portrayals of poverty as in "Tres Marías y una Rosa," which David Benavente had presented on stage a few years earlier. Pathos, in any of its human dimensions, was a theme of the past which, although recent, was already considered remote. "La Negra Ester" was a theater-circus, in which the sordid setting was softened by a rapid and rhymed dialogue, by live music, and by the obvious humor of the situations. Andrés Perez, whose training was grounded primarily, the French theater, staged this work in early 1989, first in an obscure plaza in Puente Alto and soon afterward on one of the terraces of Santa Lucia Hill, in downtown Santiago. It became a hit like no other work of theater, possibly surpassing even "La ronda" or "Deja que los perros ladren." The surroundings of Santa Lucia Hill especially favored the freshness sought in an open air presentation. Years later, "La Negra Ester" retains its freshness and continues to play to a full house, as at its debut. During a recent presentation, the large numbers of government officials in the audience led historian Gonzalo Vial, from his vantage point at the *La Segunda* newspaper, to criticize the humorous treatment of prostitution, which is alarmingly common in Chile.

Young, emerging artists belonging to sectors with little appeal in official media celebrated in gregarious, self-assertive ways, as in the case of the Underground Awards, organized in 1989 by choreographer Vicente Ruiz in a half-demolished mansion in the Bellavista neighborhood. The ceremony got started late and ended badly: the honorees had to climb up to a stage that was no more than a balcony waiting to be torn down and tolerate a rock-throwing public, who joined in on the game of violent hilarity. But we must not let appearances deceive us: the annoyance was not real; everyone knew each other and the crowd favored punk or new wave esthetics, recycled Chilean-style and slightly out of sync with the European models they imitated.

A penchant for curb-side alcohol among young painters of the University of Chile Art School for years, was shared by other art classes at Arcis, Catholic University, and to a lesser degree, the Plaza del Mulato Contemporary Art Institute. The common venue for these volunteers of the arts was the night; and their habitat was mainly the western sector of the city. They were also up on the latest in popular music, especially from Britain. Rather unschooled in their trade, they showed a certain disdain for formal art studies.

Their exhibits in the Matucana International Warehouse, in Buchi Gallery or even in La Maldita Zorra (property of Carlos Bogni, who is now in New York), varied between urban themes and self-portraits. The Santiago these painters portrayed bore no resemblance to the florescent and ostentatious city that was already creeping in. On the contrary, they were more interested in run-down neighborhoods and no less seedy interiors. Notable members of this troupe included Hugo Cardenas and Mauro Jofre, who a year before staged a show in the Santa Ana subway station.

It is curious how commonly used advertising symbols are born, impose themselves, and then quickly become outdated and die. Such will undoubtedly occur with the clouds in vogue today in corporate promotional flyers and other publications. The clouds, easily recognizable by any keen observer, originated in the United States. The computer graphics are copied from the sky over their native Seattle, where Bill Gates, the world's richest man, first used them as a symbolic representation of the Windows computer program.

The brush stroke used in the triumphant esthetics of the 1988 "No" campaign, taken from the painting of Jose Balmes, met a similar fate. The symbol even came to be known as the "Balmes brush stroke" and was soon adopted by officialdom. By the end of 1990, a similar stroke that was free, informal, and agile, reached the redesigned *Apsi* magazine cover, which changed its image in keeping with the new times. The sweeping brush stroke or a similar icon was even borrowed by political camps of the opposition.[3]

---

3   Even in 1991, publicist and editor Francisco Zegers stated in an interview: "I believe that the government could use the opportunity — traditionally given to political officials — to encourage or propose new languages for the social landscape. Enough of Balmes brushstrokes at the heart of "progressive" discourse! These "progressives" are increasingly formal and conservative."

At the other extreme and in relative isolation from other trends, other artists who had been important during the previous era continued their visual work. Eugenio Dittborn, for example, held fast to the system he devised for distributing his work, which he baptized "airpostability." In an effort to transcend the stifling atmosphere of Chilean art of the 1980s, Dittborn adapted his productions to permit them to travel easily for exhibition abroad, thus circumventing the endless red-tape hoops artists were required to jump through to take works of art out of the country. Dittborn's postcard paintings were made upon a light material — initially newsprint and later synthetic interlining fabric — suitable for folding into pleats, stuffed into an envelope, and mailed through the postal service. Dittborn's paintings traveled, and still do, as letters. The itinerary of cities they reached and were unfolded in is extensive, including New York, Helsinki, Sidney, London, and Berlin.

Ever loyal to his ideals, Dittborn mounted several exhibits in Chile in those years. Fleetingly put together in warehouses for a few hours at a time, they were brief farewells for works that began to move about the globe during long periods of time.

The figurative and conceptual model Eugenio Dittborn's paintings set in motion is complex and worthy of greater study than these pages permit. Interwoven in Dittborn's works are references to fragmentation, the painting itself, dreams, and the transitory condition of the work. The artist has also chronicled his paintings in a series of books that combine canvas with poetry, including *Caminoway* (1991), *Mapa* (1993), and *Remota* (1997). Other authors have given account of his works such as Ronald Kay in *Del Espacio de Acá* (1980), and Justo Pastor Mellado in *El Fantasma de la Sequía* (1988).

Whether for lack of official interest in Dittborn's work or his own resistance, he was not included in the initial visual panoramas offered by the new democracy. Only recently, in March 1998, was a retrospective of his work held at the National Fine Arts Museum.

On the other hand, Carlos Altamirano emerged from a self-imposed isolation dating back to 1985, to burst upon the museum in 1990 with his exhibit "Pintor de Domingo." The ironic title made reference to Altamirano's occupational situation, limited to exercising his artistic vocation only as permitted by the work week. The works displayed in that exhibit were violent, not only in the photographic images employed (e.g., a hysterical woman during a crisis or an abduction by unidentified civilians as frequently occurred during the military regime), but also for his unconstrained use of kitsch, such as plastic or printed roses as background decoration.

Altamirano exhibited frequently throughout the 1990s, as evidenced by his "Exposición de Cuadros" (Gabriela Mistral Gallery, 1995) and his most recent show in Chile, ironically and painfully entitled "Retratos" ("Portraits"). The portraits included faces of persons arrested and who subsequently disappeared under the military regime displayed on placards held by mourners. Vulgar television scenes were mounted side by side with harsh scenes of rural life and other views of daily life devoid of poetry.

Also notable is the art of Gonzalo Díaz, another artist of compelling works produced during the military dictatorship. In 1989, Díaz mounted in Arcos Institute's Ojo de Buey Gallery, a dramatic production entitled "Lonquen, 10 years." The gruesome incineration and burial of bodies at critical moments of the repression provided the background and point of departure for the showing. Art unintentionally graced the Lonquen limestone ovens which served as crematorium for numerous people: the vault's arches were pathetically reminiscent of classic architecture. Díaz was able to symbolically connect the tragic discovery of the concealed bodies with the mechanics of dreams. Later, as a professor of art at the University of Chile, Gonzalo Díaz held other exhibits, although primarily abroad. Last January Díaz had his first individual show at the National Fine Arts Museum in which the work "United in glory and in death" intervened the front of the building, stretching inside into the Matta exhibition hall. Achieved with simple elements that considered the installation's monumental proportions, Díaz was able to "awaken the building's subconscious" and suggest a relation with the genesis of art institutions.

III. Prose and Poetry

Prose assumed a new intensity in the days just prior to the restoration of democracy. Until that moment in time, works of prose, particularly the short story and novel had been the result of individual efforts. More than any other literary genre, a significant change was noted in prose and coincided with the arrival of the 1990s in the author's approach, habits, cultural inclination, and above all, in the important role played by medium- and large-sized publishing houses.

A cursory look at the previous literary scene provides a few isolated clues. First, we had the customary publications of Enrique Lafourcade, who always followed a pace of his own with themes that reflected the times, and those of Carlos Ruiz-Tagle, who captured our attention once in a while, with books of short stories and memories of school days. Then there was the work of Diamela Eltit, who had little concern for pleasing the reader, which initially limited the scope of her circulation. Eltit's novel *Lumpérica*, published in 1984 by Sudamericana was not a linear narration of fictional events but an analysis on the pulsation of words. Fragments of deaf urban images were interposed with an unidentifiable, painful experience by means of a language harnessed by its own energy. Though equally indifferent to the public, Enrique Lihn built imaginary and serpentine worlds in *La Orquesta de Cristál* (1981) and *El Arte de la Palabra* (1983). The Buenos Aires-based Sudamericana publishers printed both books, which paid tribute to the power of language but disturbed most readers. Around 1979, Pomaire publishers began to put out a full line-up of Chilean novels, with books by Ximena Sepulveda, Carlos Morandé, and possibly the most beautiful and effective novel by Adolfo Couve, *El Picadero*, with an explanatory prologue by Martin Cerda.

But, as can be seen, there was little else. The most prestigious authors, such as Donoso, Wacquez, and Edwards were better known for their publications abroad, as was Isabel Allende, known to all in Chile as a talented journalist who appeared in the press and whose face appeared on television until 1975. The youngest writers were practically non-existent, or if they did exist, were unknown.

The situation changed radically in 1990, with collections of new fiction from Planeta publishers. Attention shifted from interest in the books themselves to the phenomenon of the resurgence of new works. Planeta published *Las Ganas Locas*, by Sergio Marras; *Santiago Cero*, by Carlos Franz; *Natalia*, by Pablo Azocar; and *Sobredosis*, by Alberto Fuguet. Other names and titles followed.

Mondadori publishers put out a couple of nouvelles by José Donoso, *Taratuta* and *Naturaleza Muerte con Cachimba*, and Jaime Collyer's first novel, *El Infiltrado*. Collyer, a psychologist who resided for several years in Spain, returned to Chile in those days and made the following diagnosis: "I believe a generation of writers between 25 and 40 years of age is germinating. I perceive three characteristics. One is that this generation is born in relative orphanhood, lacking models to follow. The literary boom is long past and the intermediate generation dispersed and, at times, silent. In short, it produces a zeal for internalization that distinguishes it from previous literature of local color. It bets on the cosmopolitan."

Alberto Fuguet is a writer who fits this description well. Reared in the United States and a journalist by trade, Fuguet's world experience was basically automatic sprinklers and shopping malls. He has confessed to feeling out of place when he participated in a literary workshop conducted by José Donoso. Almost all the other participants had Chilean genealogies, complete with mansions and "old ladies coming out of the bathrooms." His own world, he thought at the time, was uninteresting. But such was not the case. His column in *El Mercurio's* Wiken supplement, signed under the pen name Enrique Alekan (the views of an individual who shared his situation), had been read week after week for years, and the book he published about yuppie adventures was a success. In those days, Santiago was rapidly leaving its traditional facade behind, as the culmination of a process over the course of several decades. A new city of bosses from the United States had installed itself in the eastern and southeastern sections of the capital. A gamut of stripes varied from zone to zone, in different shades from upper to emerging middle class. Distant and separate, the two worlds shared, and increasingly continue to share, lifestyles.

Fuguet's entrance into Chile's world of letters was accidental but nonetheless a success. Despite poor reviews from the critics, his name soon became a guarantee of successful sales. Fuguet's fiction is simple, written in language that is direct and easily assimilated by young readers. One of his major achievements is the story "Pelando a Rocio," where he employs banal conversations to form the background of a dramatic world recognizable to all.

The year 1991 brought new publications. Diamela Eltit (*Vaca Sagrada*) and Adolfo Couve (*El Cumpleaños del Señor Balande*) continued to delve into their perpetual concerns. But Elena Castedo also appeared with *El Paraiso* as did Marcela Serrano with *Nosotras que nos Queremos Tanto* (Editorial Los Andes). Both books were hailed as novels of the times, which shot them up in the rankings, especially the latter.

By then, the time was ripe for marketing novels. The old term "readers" was replaced with "book market," as if both terms were synonymous. The old type of writer who edited his own work or financed the publication of his books had been reduced to the dustbin of the absurd.

Marco Antonio de la Parra, the psychiatrist, playwright, novelist, and cultural attaché in Spain, briefly visited Chile and warned: "The way to manipulate writers is to convert them into products and market them. The market is the issue of the end of the century; it is the landscape of the year 2000; not Communism nor anything else; let's not delude ourselves. Things will have to be taken from the market and we will have to be alert to the enormous number of murky elements it contains. Writers in countries like ours will quickly be transformed into clowns. Art is a higher plane of revelation, the portrait of the human being, knowledge of things that a mercantile society does not want to know. The market makes things appear spurious, as fragments of garbage that shine like gold."

Francisco Zegers, editor and publicist, also launched a frontal attack: "Publishing houses are not playing their role in cultural modernization. They deflect the nature of their problems to a legal arrangement (the book law) that is supposed to protect the market, comprised of tools of the past.... The role of an editor in the paradoxical and contradictory society we live in is to keep important material in circulation that ensure a place for social expression of cultures and artistic products not part of the new officialdom, so as to retain their power to question the way the new institutional base functions."

But events that tend to have minds of their own continued their course. The following year Jaime Collyer sparked certain controversy with the publication in magazine of his article, "Casus belli: todo el poder para nosotros," in which he made a somewhat forced yet humorous gesture reaffirming generational independence. According to Collyer, the new writers were already capable of asserting their literary autonomy without having to ask permission of their elders. The defiant tone of the article evoked a response from Jorge Edwards in his column in the *La Segunda* afternoon newspaper.[4]

Other names also emerged from this literary boom: Gonzalo Contreras, who had published his stories in *La Danza Ejecutada* in 1987 and now ventured forth with a successful novel, *La Ciudad Anterior;* and Arturo Fontaine Talavera, who had to his name a couple of books of poems when he published his first novel, *Oir Su Voz.* Fuguet also published his premiere novel that year, *Mala Onda.*

Other young fiction writers were likewise captured by the publishing houses. The wellspring was a literary workshop organized in 1989 by Antonio Skarmeta at the Goethe Institute, later continued by Marco Antonio de la Parra.Some participants continued to write fiction, while journalism absorbed others. Writers spurred on by the workshop included Pablo Azocar, who later wrote *El Señor que Aparece de Espaldas;* Rafael Gumucio, author of *Invierno en la Torre,* Fuguet, and Andrea Maturana.

Poetry, however, became lost in the shadows at the beginning of the new democratic period. Curiously, poetry lost effectiveness with the advent of greater social freedom. It's not that nothing was published; poetry is always published in Chile, but almost all the verse of this period conformed to predictable and highly rhetorical styles.

During previous years, poetry had held an indisputable place in maintaining the flame of national pathos. We mentioned previously the extraordinary occasion in which Erick Pohlhammer read poetry before 8,000 people in the Caupolican Theater, an achievement more common to popular singers. We also mentioned the valuable contributions of Lihn, Zurita, Lira, Bertoni, Maquiera, and Martínez. But nothing, or at least very little, was produced at this time. Most poetry of the early 1990s was combative, self-limiting, which in long paragraphs of verse paid tribute to a hypertrophy of an Id, without evident results.

The scene would have been desolate were it not for the appearance of a few new works of poetry: *Por Ser Vos Quien Sois* in 1989 by Armando Uribe (Uribe had vowed, "I shall not publish again until we have democracy and gentlemen in Chile.") and *Albricia* by Soledad Fariña (published in 1989 by Archivo of Juan Luis Martínez publishers) which suggested an intimate work in a language inaudible from the outset. Others included José Angel Cuevas' *Adiós Muchedumbres* published in 1989 by America del Sur Publishers, an anthology of the author's previous work, characterized by melancholy and sadly humorous observations of

---

4   Collyer further attacked the critics: "Let me say in passing that the Opus Dei critical apparatus does not concern me. We did not forgo our Party ID cards some time ago to have to now render homage and reverence to the apprehensive partisans of tradition. Literary critique, when it is a monopoly and dogmatic, leads to a tyranny of taste and of thinking and we have had quite enough tyranny."

an individual who looks at the various neighborhoods of Santiago; and *Sentado en la Cuneta* by Claudio Bertoni (Carlos Porter Publishers, in 1990), a brilliant poetic memory device by a poet of unconstrained and direct words. That same year, poet Ennio Moltedo of Valparaiso also brought forth his book *Día a Día.*

Another outstanding work of poetry was issued by Carlos Porter publishers in 1991: Bruno Vidal's *Arte Marcial.* A previously unknown writer, Vidal in a fierce and oblique style depicts images of an ominous, nocturnal city, where endless partying alternates with the sordid exercise of power in its most degrading forms. The language originates from the avant-garde poetic tradition, but also from the grassroots and from the upper spheres of power.[5]

IV. The Present

We do not know how long it takes to reconstruct a cultural fabric affected for so many years by social anomaly. The social climate is composed not only of publications, exhibits, and films arranged in chronological order. Work on a more intimate level underlies it; revolving around personal conversation, private dreams, relations of friendship, or complicity between individuals of similar sensibilities.

The *sine qua non* for anchoring a more solid cultural life is time. In every such case, a prerequisite is to allow energies to mature free of pressure.

Despite obstacles and mirages, a favorable cultural climate seems to be appearing on the horizon, one that will bring a bit more freedom so that people may actually take charge of their most personal interests and act upon them.

Obstacles and mirages are numerous, as are extensive areas of indifference. The paranoia of the market, in all aspects of life, emerges as a major enemy of creative indulgence, devaluing creative energies and placing them at the service of consumers' whims.

As has been reiterated to the point of boredom (although nearly always as a monologue to the deaf), television has renounced intelligence. Exceptions are few and far between. But the issue is not television as an abstraction. There are people, or so we imagine, who make decisions about what the majority of viewers should do with their free time. Television messages continue to target the same average mental age; probably around 12 years old. Everything is reduced to a child's level; jokes are the order of the day 365 days of the year. Publicists know it, but won't admit it.[6]

And this is the most curious phenomenon of all. The return to democracy brought great expectations for what television could become in a climate of freedom. However, the arrival of democracy coincided with the assault of liberal policies. In and of itself, this would not be a crime, but the system that finances it has given higher priority to reducing risks than improving product quality.

---

5   Those interested in learning more about Vidal can consult an interview published in *Lo* (Santiago, November 1992). There the poet states: "It is true that the language utilized in the book is that of the CNI (secret police). To know where I learned it you would have to read several books on the psychology of learning, but at the initiative level, I would say in the womb . . ."

6   Reader Sebastián Melmoth wrote to the letters to the editor section of *Apsi* magazine in October 1990: "Are you aware of the new, markedly amateur path that shows like Channel 11's "Extra Jóvenes" or Channel 13's "Más Música" are taking? Nothing more than a collection of simple jokes, off color comments, etc." No, we didn't know it at the time, but the model noted has become the norm over the years.

The situation is even stranger when we recall what used to happen with Pinochet-controlled television. Perhaps because their conscience weighed upon them or maybe out of good intentions, those who ran television in those years once in while allowed themselves to salute viewers with worthy productions. Channel 9, in an experiment of the late 1980s in cultural programming aired the BBC's production of the complete works of Shakespeare over the course of several months. Other channels also offered memorable British series, which gave viewers access to the best English theatrical traditions. Who can forget "Upstairs, Downstairs"; "The Onedin Line"; or "Enemy at the Door"? For many years, Sunday mornings were a cultural haven. During that time slot, television stations transmitted chapters of the Robert Hughes documentary "The shock of the new," on new European trends; and Kenneth Clark's scholarly work, "Civilization." Likewise, Peter Ustinov brought us "The history of Europe."

Such things have become utopian memories or desires. Marcelo's Cachureo children's show, to name but one example, now occupies that time slot and has become nearly as infallible as the Pope. Not only is vulgarity tolerated, but it is cultivated and consumed wholeheartedly. The sole university and the state-run channels have slackened off on transmitting cultural programs to concentrate instead on an excessive quest for mass entertainment.

In keeping up with adjustments of supply and demand, the process has been balanced somewhat by private television business. Cultural fare has primarily come by way of scraps of international programming on cable television. In the midst of cable television's visual bombardment (Babilonia fortunately provides us with excellent foreign productions on a fairly regular basis), a talk show, "La belleza de pensar," moderated by Cristian Warnken, steadily improved and is worthy of the stature of its guests. In this case, the distinctive element has been simply one of the tried and true assets of civilization: knowing how to converse or how to listen. That such a simple notion can produce such an exceptional program is equally exceptional. But one need only look at any number of other talk shows on broadcast television to put this in perspective. These programs are little more than a series of questions from a script and interruptions of the person interviewed, generally from a comedian in between a dance number and contests.

A few initiatives manage to free themselves of this atmosphere and keep interest high. Such has been the case with the journalistic documentary program "Informe Especial" and the anthropological "El Mirador," the concrete work on a national myth in Los Patiperros, and Rock&Pop's effort, particularly in its Plan Zeta program, to take a humorous but biting view of national reality (or at least at its television, which at times appears to stand for national reality).

The general transformations of the social panorama are also accompanied by the loss of cultural assertiveness in the universities. The most notable case is that of the University of Chile, the country's oldest college, which has experienced strong internal turbulence and where a majority of the student body, as well as a great number of the faculty, display what we might prudently term discontent.

The decline in the university as cultural generator and as facilitator of social mobility — a task frequently assigned to it— comes as the result of a long process that incubated during more traumatic days, but which is evident in all its expressions today.

The problem lies essentially in what are called the humanities, which have been left without bridges to the rest of society. Indulgent activity has been left in midstream, far removed from the efficiency models notoriously in fashion today. That studies may be free of charge, paradoxically, does not translate into a measure of solvency anywhere.

However, tradition is not only rhetorical and it may be the weight of tradition which makes it possible to endure difficult moments and reconstruct the path we have lost: the coexistence of different ideas and people, inter-generational conversation, curiosity for the world of the living and of the dead. Perhaps it is the tradition invoked by private universities -entities highly representative of the prevailing cultural and economic model- when, despite their lack of history, they chose as symbols the names of distinguished national heroes of a recognized humanist bent. The choice is not made at random; there is a purpose to it.

While the government has been unable to sustain the cultural role inherent to the universities, its attitude regarding artistic creation has been quite different. The support provided by the governmental Fondart program is the most outstanding example. Since its creation in 1992, this state agency has used public funds to finance a great variety of cultural expressions in Santiago and in the provinces. Publications of books and magazines, art exhibits, theater productions, film festivals, and film production are but a few of the projects Fondart supports. The system is up against great odds, but it works. After evaluation by an appropriate panel of judges, the money reaches the recipients and the work is produced. There is a true desire to support artists, most of whom lack the resources of their own to carry out their projects.

Fondart notwithstanding, we still face a major problem: desirable relations between the state and culture. Precisely because of this necessary plurality, the state's role appears to lack definition. As such, government cultural administration cannot be valued except by way of the relative quality of the projects it finances. Such evaluations will inevitably be made based on fundamentally esthetic considerations, which, like it or not, vary from one individual to another.

Fondart runs the risk of becoming a sort of creation ministry, a term whose components are diametrically opposed, as occurred in the countries on the other side of the iron curtain in a certain moment of history. But an artist does not always work by means of projects or does so with a general idea of the meaning of the word "project." On the other hand, an artist always needs time: time for indulgence, for conversation, contemplation, and even time to make mistakes. Ideally, an artist also needs a cultured family environment. More beneficial than simply financing projects, particularly in the case of film and theater, would be concern to foster a *cultural climate*, which in Chile is endemically impoverished.

An area of concern abandoned in recent years has been that of cultural heritage. No one no one wants to take responsibility for this arena since it links us to a past whose allure fails to attract funding. Lost cultural heritage, unlike other losses, is irrecoverable and individual efforts are generally incapable of arresting its destruction on their own.

Without a living past to turn to, there can be no culture. The capacity to forget, possibly necessary and healthy at certain historic moments, has been exercised with such zeal in Chile that it has brought about what José Donoso described as a "dense veil" which conceals signs of our identity. This process began in the mid-19th century and gathered greater force in the present century. Historians, writers, and architects have harped upon this point, although it is not an issue that belongs to experts but to any citizen with a degree of common sense. During a recent television report on the deterioration and modernization of Santiago, a downtown shoeshine expressed it admirably. In his opinion, the demolition of historic buildings deprives us of an element that helps us know who we are today.

Preservation of the urban heritage must not be left to the vacillations of the market which are capricious and only heed trends of the present. This tacit law justified the destruction of the Cousiño mansion in Valparaíso a few months ago. Monetary interests never sleep and move about faster than purely cultural ones. Once the damage is done, there is no possible way to restore it. The phenomenon is taking place throughout the country, affecting all the oldest cities, but has been most prominent in Santiago and Valparaíso. To learn how our forefathers lived we now have to read chronicles of the era, as it is becoming increasingly less possible to live in their footsteps. The landmarks of the past torn down in Santiago are numerous: the Pedro Prado mansion at the end of the Mapocho River, the Arrieta palace, the Urmeneta palace, the Undurraga palace, the Meiggs house, the Haviland house, the Archbishop's palace, the Clara Sisters' convent, the Carmen Sisters' convent, Providencia Station, the Valdivieso house, and so on. In short, it is not a simple problem of nostalgia. With these unnecessary disappearances has vanished something that belonged to us and the loss undoubtedly leaves us all the more impoverished culturally.

Functional arguments, founded on the prospect of modernization, will always be used to counter this position. But if we review the previous list of vanished landmarks, we will see that the destruction of heritage has never benefited anyone, and, even less so, the poor. It is unacceptable for modernization and collective benefit to be exchanged for historic devastation.

A few isolated efforts have been made to preserve buildings considered national monuments. Fondart, in fact, includes this concern among the situations it supports. But a greater political will is lacking; we need a cultural orientation that is steadfast in the face of the uncontrollable demolition and consequent erasing of memory. Such efforts include those of the Cultural Patrimony Corporation, under leadership of Hernan Rodríguez and Cecilia García-Huidobro since 1996. Financing for protecting and restoring buildings, in this case, comes from the private sector.

The State's cultural mandate could bear better and more solid fruit if it were to give equal attention to our literary and intellectual heritage. That was the course followed in Spain with the return to democracy. The State financed a meticulous review of local culture, century by century, fostering research and publications, as well as outstanding productions of classic Spanish theater. At present, in Chile a similar initiative is underway through several publishers and the National Library's publications department, which we will examine subsequently.

As we were saying, the emerging cultural climate is favorable in several respects. In fact, we could speak of different cultural micro-climates, each one at a reasonable distance from the others.

Poetry, which was nearly extinct at the beginning of the decade, now appears to be recovering its former vitality due to the emergence of a brigade of young poets, all under 25 years of age, who dedicate their all to the creation of poetry, rather than the affirmation of sociological postures. Most do not know each other and are still unpublished, but what they all share is a way of working the traditional forms on the basis of personal intuition. These young poets include, among others, Rafael Rubio, Jorge Mittelman, Matías Rivas, and Cristóbal Joannon. Other, slightly older poets, such as Guillermo Valenzuela and Magdalena Benavente must also be taken into account.

Some years ago, the distrust of others that was quite common in cultural circles in the 1970s began to give way to intellectual curiosity. The Academia Imaginaria, founded in

1994 by Marco Antonio de la Parra and Eduardo Sabrovsky, is a clear example of this new outlook, which fosters the dissemination, discussion, and exchange of cultural information in the context of spiritual freedom. The Academia Imaginaria has neither a programmatic nor confrontational disposition in conferences and other activities. Rather, it allows the persons participating in a seminar to chose their issues and the way they wish to present them to the public.[7]

Recently, there has been insistent discussion over opening the market for Chilean visual arts. The Amigos del Arte Corporation issued a publication that gives account of the place various national artists occupy in the market. The movement to help artists market their work began in the early 1990s with the Supermercar't project, organized by Guillermo Tejeda through the company La Maquina del Arte, offering the public the opportunity to acquire art in medium and small transactions.

Previously, the galleries competed in a limited circuit of exhibits (in which the galleries of Europe and North America remained unrivaled) and that made survival difficult. Today's economic boom and the appearance of an "upwardly mobile middle class" have changed things greatly. The Costanera Norte section of Santiago has become an area favored by commercial galleries. Designed by architects, the galleries bear little resemblance to their forebears of 15 years ago, generally of an alternative or solidarity bent. In 1996, an unprecedented situation occurred with Roberto Matta: three exhibits of the artist's work were held simultaneously in Santiago.

The artists who habitually passed through the gallery circuit — Rojo, Cienfuegos, Carreño, or Carmen Aldunate — were joined by artists of different origins and different concerns: Bororo, Benmayor, Pablo Domínguez, and Omar Gatica. These up and coming artists were formed in the University of Chile Art School and imposed a certain concept of "the pleasure of painting" with colorful and violent expressionism, powerful brushstrokes and layered veils of color. Other painters, of a different style but from the same background are Tacla and Frigerio, who are based outside Chile and whose art is most commonly seen in New York City.

Arturo Duclos was the first to open a niche in mercantile relations for national artists in foreign galleries, skipping the intermediate steps of showing his art at home. Duclos, who was schooled in the avant-garde wave of Catholic University's Art School since the 1980s, had nurtured an iconography of his own consisting essentially of what may be called "quotes." These "quotes" were taken from symbols of the political world and from popular imagination with fragments of cultic texts. Instead of upholding painting as the bastion of personal expression, Duclos put assistants to work at executing some of the figures of his work.

Presently, the market is quite active and less uniform. The Tomás Andreu gallery, for example, has attempted to create a network of buyers for the works of Duclos and Montes de Oca, who has a type of avant-garde style, without the characteristic roughness.

_____

7   In his book *La Mala Memoria*, Marco Antonio de la Parra speaks of the academy: "With Eduardo Sabrovsky we founded the Academia Imaginaria, a spaceless place where we could talk of the century coming to its end and of cultural change. We reviewed the forgotten humanities, the maligned conference format, and the call to build bridges to high culture, and we saw that some people were interested in opening their spheres of knowledge a bit more. Once again, there are more ideas than resources. Fondart helps, we receive support from some companies, we are always taking a loss, but we have the sensation that a shift may take place in a sociocultural system heavily damaged by the very speed of change."

Other artists have remained a bit outside of this ring of enthusiasts and most interest may be centered on their work. Contrary to a certain disparagement painting has come to endure in intellectual circles, these artists insist upon standing by this discipline, and, in fact, the reflections that guide them in each step of their work are evident in their art. The press once catalogued them under the concept of "intelligent art," including in this group Voluspa Jarpa, Pablo Langlois, Natalia Babarovic, Francisco Valdés, Carolina Bassi, and Victoria Polanco, among others. Ignacio Gumucio, who recently appeared on the Chilean art scene, rightly belongs to this group as well.

Those who have acted with greatest freedom in the market and in keeping up with the implicit demands of the previous, radically anti-commercial generation have been Natalia Babarovic and Pablo Langlois. Trained at the University of Chile and a student of Gonzalo Díaz and Adolfo Couve, Babarovic has worked extensively on the theme of the painter's studio, the Chilean rural landscape (a concept always in question), and more recently, the portrait. Her landscapes, profound and lacking in eloquence, try to draw the almost indifferent gaze of the passenger in transit. They always have an unfinished look about them, incorporating blank, raw, or prepared spaces on the canvas. With this device, the artist attempts to represent the apparent analogy or distance between materials employed in painting and nature.

Langlois, who studied art at Arcis Institute, is more concerned with the urban landscape, alternating his parody of copied or even plagiarist images. Langlois' paintings generally consist of patches, painted at different moments in time. Voluspa Jarpa, together with Natalia Babarovic, painted the mural "El sitio de Rancagua," a remarkable commemorative work exhibited in 1994 in the Fine Arts Museum's Matta Hall, which was subsequently hung in the Rancagua train station. Although Voluspa Jarpa paints large-scale works, her major concern is visual installations, as well as traditional techniques in parodic silk-screen imagery and printmaking.

Within a broad freedom of interests, the need has been expressed for reviewing and chronicling the history and small history of the immediate and not-so-immediate past. Far-ranging disciplines and types of work share this concern for delving into our present condition, as seen in the books *Chile Actual: Anatomía de un Mito* by Tomás Moulián; *Historia de las Ideas y de la Cultura en Chile*, by Bernardo Subercaseaux; *La Mala Memoria (Historia personal de Chile contemporáneo)* by Marco Antonio de la Parra; and *El Peso de la Noche (Nuestra frágil fortaleza histórica)*, by Alfredo Jocelyn-Holt.

We must also mention Mónica Echeverría's book *Memorias de una Irreverente* on the writer Ines Echeverría Bello who felt the impact of historical tensions at the beginning of the century; *Dejamé que te Cuente*, a biographical work by Juanita Gallardo on the lost existence of Rosario Puga, one of Bernardo O'Higgins's lovers; and, particularly José Donoso's profound reflections upon the past in *Conjeturas Sobre la Memoria de mi Tribu*. A chronicle of his own literary history, Donoso's book sheds light upon psychological chinks still not healed in the remote foundations of Chilean society. These are contemplative memories that at times approach the realm of fiction to remind us of how the sources of our recollection of real events and literary imagination often become confused with one another. To this spectrum of books, we must add *Ay Mamá Inés*, Jorge Guzmán's historical novel about the life of Inés de Suárez.

The retrospection and analysis of our past, a fundamental condition for a country's cultural consolidation, is an evident trend in these days. Publishers such as Universitaria, Lom, and Sudamericana are printing new editions of Chilean writers, whose works had been attainable mainly in used book stands, such as: Huidobro, Benjamín Subercaseaux, González Vera, Juan Emar, Claudio Giaconi, Merino Reyes, Daniel de la Vega, and Joaquín Edwards Bello. The list is extensive, and confirms our assertion. A novelist in full production, such as Germán Marín, contributes literary creation of a tremendous life experience, where the personal and public lives of Chile's past 30 years meet.

Along another battlefront, Adriana Valdés published a selection of her cultural criticism in *Composición de Lugar* (Universitaria publishers, 1996) and the National Library launched a book of the reflections of Martín Cerda (Escritorio, 1993). Marín also, with tireless dedication, recompiled and edited the key texts of Enrique Lihn, dispersed over 40 years in magazines and minor publications in the book *El Circo en Llamas* (Lom 1997). The height of Luis Oyarzun's literary work, his personal journals, have been published as well as *Diario* (highly edited by Lar publishers of Concepción, 1990) and *Diarios Intímos* (Humanities Studies Department publishers, 1995), allowing us to follow the course of the life and esthetic thought of the great promoter of Chile's cultural protagonists of the 1950s and 1960s.

Grijalbo publishers, for its part, revealed the posthumous "notes on memory" of researcher Oreste Plath in El Santiago que se Fue; Miguel Laborde is editing a collection of photographs accompanied by text which is a valuable citizen archive (Santiago, 1830-1930), and Volodia Teitelboim added *Memorias de un Muchacho del Siglo* 20, an autobiography he added to his collection of recent biographies (on Neruda, Mistral, Huidobro, and Borges).

The spirit of the past has begun to nudge current Chilean culture into motion. The direction it is heading in is unclear, but we have the hunch that there is a promising future ahead. According to Adriana Valdés, as Alfonso Calderón once stated during a seminar on Chilean culture some time back, "Knowledge of the cultural unfoldings and intervals of the past — in this case, those of Chile — contributes freedom and creativity (in addition to distance and humor) to reflections on situations of the present."

V. Omissions

We have finally arrived, prudently, at the conclusion of this chronicle. There are undoubtedly artists and work that have remained folded away in the files or have been erased by the conveniences of memory. We did not mention Juan Domingo Dávila or Alfredo Jaar. Nor did we pause to consider the social, photographic, and bibliographic research of Paz Errázuriz in conjunction with Claudia Donoso and Diamela Eltit. We mentioned painter Ignacio Gumucio, but not photographer Rodrigo Merino, when both have collaborated on a number of occasions. We said nothing about the work of Oscar Bustamante nor that of Jaime Hagel, who have continued to produce throughout this period, as well as José Miguel Varas and Carlos Cerda.

Pablo Oyarzún has forged his own course in his field: philosophy — from lectures to texts — and translations of Kant, Paul Celan, and Swift. We also have just learned that Jorge Eduardo Rivera has completed three translations of Heidegger. Neither must we forget Andrés Claro, who now resides in Paris, or his thesis on "La inquisición y la cabala," nor Manuel Vicuña, based in London, who is the first historian to emerge from a private university.

Other cultural clues we have not analyzed: the impoverishment of AM radio, and the resulting "pleasantness" of FM; the resurgence of the need to see Chile through the eyes of Chileans who are not intellectuals (consider television and the confidence affirmed in a young writer such as Pablo Illanes). Some suggest that we mention also the urban chronicles of Pedro Lemebel, who writes about the everyday world of poverty, often ignoring cultural realms.

Nor have we spoken about the provinces. One might very well get the impression that everything happens in Santiago. The proving ground for cultural activities always seems to have been the capital or abroad, even in the case of outstanding persons of the provinces, as with Claudio Arrau, Joaquín Edwards Bello, and Mariano Latorre.

A phenomenon of these times has certainly been the *Revista de Crítica Cultural*, conducted since 1990 by Nelly Richard, a catalyst and theorist of the artistic line known as "la avanzada." The journal has demonstrated an unprecedented persistence, although its readership in Chile is limited by its use of language, often excessively technical. Besides its Chilean readers, the magazine boasts of followers in intellectual circles in other parts of the continent and at North American universities. The magazine reflects a constant concern for the problem of ethnic, sexual, and cultural minorities, and a sociological perspective for analyzing reality.

We mentioned theater only in passing. In the 1990s, we have observed a tendency in which the role of the playwright has declined to the benefit of the staging. By staging, we refer to two aspects: how a play is mounted on stage and how the script is a collage of texts produced in related fields. Such was the case in the plays "La manzana de Adán" and "Historia de la sangre," produced by Alfredo Castro; as with the works of Ramon Griffero. Most faithful to the theater playwright tradition has been Marco Antonio de la Parra.

Film production in Chile has always presented a problem and a promise. The years of the democracy have not been an exception, in this respect. Expectations upon the inauguration of President Aylwin ended badly last year, with several film producers in debt. State support was evidently insufficient to cover debts contracted in the course of the always highly complicated production of films. Paradoxically, Chilean films produced in these years have been successes in the ratings when shown on National Television, which has encouraged a few young writers such as Marcos Henríquez to work to show his films on television.

A listing of national film producers of recent years must include "Caluga o Menta" of Gonzalo Justiniano; "Imagen Latente" of Pablo Perelmann; "La Luna en el Espejo" of Silvio Caiozzi; and Ricardo Larraín's "La Frontera," all of which premiered between 1990 and 1991. Later "Johnny 100 Pesos" of Gustavo Graeff-Merino and Paloma Blanca, one of few works by Ruiz adapted for commercial film, was discovered and re-edited. The last movie at the box offices was Andrés Wood's "Historias de Fútbol," effective in its telling and simple in structure.

On another sphere, a significant development has been the new openness of *El Mercurio* cultural supplements, which for years were notoriously controlled by ultra- conservatives, with very few connections to the cultural tensions external to an extremely closed set of references. This brought about an increasing impoverishment of these publications while also creating frustrations for their readers, who week after week found only a museum culture, in the worst sense of the word. Changes have been very recent and have come about under the editorial direction of Pedro Gandolfo (Artes y Letras supplement) and Cecilia

García Huidobro M. (*Revista de los Libros* supplement). The new openness has brought a greater circulation of different voices and the beginnings of a few bridges between strains of thought.

Allow us a final thought, in light of the omissions still left out of this fe de omissions. An essay that conveys the cultural life of an era cannot be but incomplete. It is impossible to look at such a diverse area, which is not limited to the framework of officially acceptable entities. Best-selling books, most marketed art, the most applauded theater, and overbearing discussions do not on their own comprise a country's cultural spectrum. On the contrary, often the official versions of culture only disguise the true cultural scene. At this very moment, there are an infinite number of persons who have lost sleep worrying about their works in progress, probably persons who are unknown or known in the intimacy of precarious artistic encounters: people who are trying to translate authors they believe to be significant, who ponder imagery or who make an effort to make sure their writing does not stray from their poetic intuitions. That these endeavors need not respond to anyone or to any preconceived notion of culture is fundamental, and therein lies true creative freedom.

Assessment and Outlook
of the Concertación

The Concertación Coalition of Parties for Democracy:
Assessment and Outlook

Eugenio Lahera
Cristián Toloza

T he Concertación has come a long way from the triumph of the "No" vote to the Congressional elections of 1997. The coalition of today is certainly not that of yesterday. We are beginning to observe the virtues and vices derived from eight years of government: more experience and less enthusiasm, as well as a greater willingness to travel familiar roads than to build new ones. The work of this coalition has been intertwined with our country's fate during the 1990s; whatever one's opinion about it may be, it has certainly left its mark. A complete vision of Chile is impossible without an analysis of the achievements and limitations of this political alliance, as well as its presence and absence in different spheres of national life, and the hopes and frustrations of those who have supported it.

This brief analysis explores one of the least-studied aspects of the Concertación as a political force. Our aim is to look at the nature of the Concertación's internal dialogues, understand its sources of conflict, identify the difficulties that lie ahead and consider new avenues for political and social innovation. Thus, we will summarize and question the coalition's activity, uncover its various layers of complexity, and propose some new fronts for action.[1]

I. Evaluations of the Coalition's Achievements

Two fundamental viewpoints emerge from the Concertación parties' meetings and documents, as well as from the discussions between party leaders and high-ranking government officials. In general terms, one viewpoint emphasizes the coalition's achievements and the other its shortcomings. Although this division has always existed, the debating sides have become increasingly entrenched and critical, and the participants have begun

---

1 The backdrop of this essay is the image of Chile in the 1990s as presented in the articles that make up this book. The work also profited from the discussion workshops held for each chapter, roundtable meetings with the other authors, and the comments of the research team *Direcciones de Estudios y de Contenidos de la Presidencia*. Nevertheless, the political reflections presented here are ours alone.

to affix negative labels to each other. Before we advance to a deeper analysis of the coalition and its challenges, we must hear the basic arguments on each side.

1. FAR-REACHING AND SUBSTANTIVE ACHIEVEMENTS

The first viewpoint argues that the Concertación's two administrations have produced positive results for the country, while holding together a coalition unprecedented in Chilean political history.

The proponents of this view maintain that the first Concertación government implemented a realistic agenda seeking to re-establish democracy, ensure favorable conditions for sustained economic growth, and bring progress to millions of Chileans, thus helping to alleviate the extreme poverty existing under the military regime. They believe that the first administration fulfilled its key objective: bringing political and economic stability to the nascent democracy and thus eliminating the possibility of a return to authoritarianism. The government controlled inflation, significantly increased the country's growth rate and maintained a budget surplus, assuaging the widespread fear that economic disorder would accompany the return to democracy. The country's poverty rate declined markedly, while its competitiveness and international image improved substantially. The new leaders identified the main human rights abuses of the previous regime, as evidenced in the Rettig Report, and took some steps toward reparations.

The second Concertación administration, this side argues, continued the efforts of the first, committing the country to a path of modernization and national integration. According to this viewpoint, the current administration has handled the key issues of the transition wisely. In the case of General Contreras, for example, the administration ultimately carried out the sentence of the courts and imprisoned him, ending a period of national uncertainty. Another highly important issue was the constitutionally-established retirement of the commanders-in-chief, including General Pinochet. The government paved the way for commanders outside the military government's political leadership circles to assume control of the Armed Forces, thus inaugurating a new era for these institutions.

The proponents of this view point out that if the country continues on its current path, the Frei Administration, by the end of its term, will have reduced poverty to half its level at the beginning of the 1990s. In addition, it will have laid the foundation for a far-reaching educational reform; initiated the transformation of the Chilean justice system; created an infrastructure of roads, ports, and airports incomparably better than that existing at the start of the decade; promoted unprecedented economic growth; and integrated Chile into the international system through a wide-ranging network of political and trade agreements. All of these achievements have created the conditions for Chile to progress confidently toward full development.[2]

The positive results of Chile's policies have been acknowledged by the international community as well as by the reports and analyses of international organizations specializing in

---

2   A detailed analysis of the Aylwin administration can be found in Edgardo Boeninger's book, *Democracia en Chile: Lecciones para la gobernabilidad* (Santiago: Editorial Andrés Bello, 1997). For the current government's achievements, see President Frei's annual addresses to the nation each May, known as the *Mensajes Presidenciales del 21 de Mayo.*

economics and development, such as the UNDP, the World Economic Forum, and the International Institute for Management Development.

The Concertación itself, a highly institutionalized political coalition with a common agenda, played a large part in the administration's achievements, supporters say. In these respects, this coalition has been evidently superior to the current political opposition and to past coalitions.[3] As an alliance, the Concertación has acted through the figure of the president. It has thereby avoided numerous problems to which coalitions are susceptible: slowdowns and paralysis derived from a rigid internal power-sharing system; constant transfers of power that prevent the accumulation of experience and the implementation of a coherent program; and explicit or implicit intra-coalition vetoes. In cases where the coalition has faced internal disagreements about administration policies, it has undertaken the necessary dialogue and debate to reach a compromise. Examples include the bills dealing with the country's ports and with water treatment utilities.

Supporters also point to the fact that the coalition has established pacts and mechanisms leading to success in two presidential elections, as well as three Congressional and two municipal ones. It has wisely created methods for integrating its constituent parties' interests and has controlled internal competition when necessary. In the legislative arena, the Concertación has faced a combination of restrictions imposed by the binomial system, especially the special majorities required to pass laws and the presence of the designated senators. The alliance has nonetheless been able to win support for its bills in Congress and see their enactment into law. At times, the entire opposition has joined in passing measures supported by the administration; at other times, the coalition has received support only from the UDI, from Renovación Nacional, or from a portion of the designated senators.

Finally, the Chilean people have demonstrated their approval of the Concertación administrations' achievements, providing the coalition with the support of a majority of voters in all of the elections held during these years.

2. DISSATISFACTION WITH THE COALITION'S ACHIEVEMENTS

The other side of this dialogue about the Concertación focuses on its shortcomings in various areas of governmental action.

This side perceives a lack of attention to the public health care services and those who depend on them, as well as gender-related issues, young people, senior citizens, indigenous groups, and the family. Some members of the business community, these critics allege, seek to impose a labor relations model that denies workers their rights, prevents collective bargaining, and discriminates against those who try to organize unions. In broader terms, these critics maintain that the absence of redistributive measures in Chile is leading to an increasingly unjust allocation of the country's resources. They decry the absence or

---

3   For example, the Radical administrations governed with alliances lasting no more than two or three years. In fact, the Popular Front that elected Pedro Aguirre Cerda was dissolved during his term. President González Videla began his term with a combination of liberals, Communists, and Radicals, which later abruptly disintegrated. Videla then joined the Right for a few years and finally ended up with a cabinet composed of Social Christian conservatives and Falangists.

weakness of public policies aimed at creating truly equal opportunities for lower-income groups; without these, market forces simply tend to accentuate initial differences.

These critics resent the fact that, after eight years of democracy, the so-called "authoritarian enclaves" still persist. On three occasions, the government has submitted a constitutional reform bill to strengthen the country's democratic institutions. These reforms, which include eliminating the designated and lifetime senators and changing the binomial electoral system, have met systematic opposition from the Senate each time. Frustration within the coalition is understandable, since these reforms already represented a scaled-down version of the Concertación's original proposals. Among other things, the coalition called for the election of all members of Congress through moderate proportional representation, alterations in the composition and functions of the National Security Council, and changes to the law that bars the removal of the commanders-in-chief of the Armed Forces. The Concertación's critics believe that while the transition has brought a change in leadership, it has not established a fully democratic system. Consequently, the exercise of democracy is diminished, and its image and dignity are tainted.

From this perspective, there is no reason to expect change from within the system, especially in light of the results of the last Congressional election. These critics reason that the country has not progressed substantially with the help of the democratic Right, that the chances for progress were further diminished with the last election, and that the binomial system has shown itself incapable of self-modification. As there are no further possibilities for change, the strategy of consensus has reached its endpoint, and the time for grassroots social and political mobilization has arrived.

According to this viewpoint, the Concertación asked for the people's support based on a commitment to restoring the dignity of those who felt their country had become foreign to them and who expected a greater participatory role. In practice, however, the alliance has established an elitist political style and a technocratic form of governance. The critics allege that, outside of municipal government, the country's leaders have not created institutional mechanisms to promote greater citizen participation in the formulation, implementation and evaluation of public policy. Politics in general stand in disrepute, and the government has not developed a means of democratic communication to explain what it is doing, the limitations it faces, and what the future may hold. The absence of such communication manifests itself most clearly in the government's failure to attract young people, many of whom do not even register to vote.

From this series of disappointments, strong demands have arisen for improvements in democratic institutions, more genuine citizen participation, and greater social equity and integration. These shortcomings, the critics say, are not merely debating points in discussions among party leaders. Rather, these are the demands of the same electorate that has voted for the Concertación in various elections, an electorate that is becoming more critical of the coalition's performance, both in the executive and legislative branches. This discontent has been expressed in the loss of more than 800,000 votes, with the greatest decline occurring in the last congressional election.[4]

---

4   Comparing the Concertación's level of voter support in the last two congressional elections (1993 and 1997), we find a difference of 860,360 votes.

II. Sensibilities Within the Coalition

The arguments put forth here are reasonable and valid. Feelings of healthy pride in one's achievements and frustration over one's failures normally coexist within the soul of every political movement. From this standpoint, the debate within the Concertación could be a simple one: everyone would agree that both achievements and shortcomings can be seen, while holding different opinions about which are most prominent. The recommended prescription would be to practice humility and transform the shortcomings into new challenges.

Nevertheless, there are two distinct sensibilities within the alliance which make these matters more complex, especially as the Concertación plans for the future. These sensibilities are not exclusive to one party, but rather cut across the coalition.[5] They represent two different ways of perceiving and reacting to situations and events. These positions underlie the debate within the coalition, but they have not been formally acknowledged. We must note that both sensibilities are based on the learning experiences and emotions of people who have been intensively involved in politics over the last several years. We must view these sensibilities through the eyes of the Concertación in order to examine them openly and critically.

1. THE DEMAND FOR STABILITY

One of these sensibilities emphasizes the challenge of economic and political stability. This way of thinking acknowledges the limitations on what it is possible to achieve with political action, while maintaining control of events and preserving social order.[6] People holding this view are highly conscious of Chile's history of agonizing conflicts, and therefore they consider social peace to be a fundamental value. They have the greatest direct knowledge of the conditions imposed by Pinochet's presence as commander-in-chief of the Army, as well as the fact that the Armed Forces remember the military government as a victorious undertaking. They recognize that nothing has been easy during these years, and that everything has been achieved with patience and hard work. This was the dominant sensibility in the Concertación at the start of the 1990s, and at that time the majority of the population clearly subscribed to it.

This viewpoint is naturally tempted to follow a kind of essentialist reasoning: what we have done is the best possible thing, and therefore we should continue to do it. It elevates what it did well to the category of a permanent paradigm for action. It is not particularly conscious of the problems caused by the practice of deal-making among the elite, the constant moderation of expectations, and the consequences of internal discipline. These tendencies have cast their own shadow over society and cultivated a penchant for secrecy, a general rejection of dissenting opinions, the erosion of the coalition's base of support, and

---

5 This clarification is necessary because this term has also been used to refer to splintering within parties.

6 See the article "Desarrollo democrático" by Eduardo Palma, in *Política y Espíritu* Vol. 52, N° 417 (1998), as well as "The Governance of the Chilean Economy since 1990" by Eugenio Lahera, presented at the seminar "Chile: Development Lessons and Challenges," Economic Development Institute, World Bank, December 1997.

a reluctance to promote a policy of education for democracy. Not surprisingly, then, this side is naturally more inclined to make decisions based on poll results than on an interpretation of the interests of social groups.

People holding this perspective approach economics with the view that if the macroeconomic indicators are favorable, then the government is getting the basics right. All else is merely noise or turbulence in a process that is headed in the right direction. They know that macroeconomic management has been a demanding and delicate task, and that there is no such thing as an economy on "automatic pilot." They also believe that they must defend at any cost the hard core of their achievements against populism and unreasonable expectations. In practice, they tend to view the relationship between government and the governed in a traditional management/labor framework, approaching it as if it were a business negotiation. Their greatest problem is believing that macroeconomic achievements in and of themselves are enough to win the people's loyalty, and that there is a strict positive correlation between good economic performance and political success. Consequently, they become perplexed when people display dissatisfaction with their achievements.[7]

2. THE NEED FOR CONVICTIONS

Other sectors of the Concertación are experiencing different emotions. As the dust cloud of the transition clears, they realize that they live in a house they do not like. They perceive that the military government laid many of this home's foundations, through a system imposed by force that abused human rights. Consequently, a cloud of illegitimacy surrounds many of the institutions and policies that emerged from that time and continue to operate today. Those holding this view find it difficult to value the positive elements of the system, or to recognize that even if the military had never taken power, the country would still have needed to carry out structural reforms, as various other Latin American countries have done.

Accordingly, they believe that the Concertación's impulses toward democracy or social justice are not fully expressed. They express an increasingly negative judgment of the transition agreement *(sobrepacto)*,[8] claiming that the negotiators conceded more than necessary and thereby limited future opportunities for change. Sometimes the criticism is more general, such as a basic dissatisfaction with "the (neoliberal) model." The model's presumed achievements, they claim, do not improve daily life for the Chilean people. Further, its commercialist logic destroys social networks and encourages excessive individualism. The result, they say, is a society that is far from desirable from the standpoint of Christian or socialist humanism.

Judging the government's actions in this manner, this focus is more inclined to see shortcomings than progress. It does not fully acknowledge the coalition's achievements, and it sees the specter of privatization behind the government's policies, which would be further proof that the Concertación is simply administering the neoliberal model. Due to

---

7   The team of John Major in Great Britain felt this same bewilderment when, at a time when the British economy had the best indicators in Europe, the Tories experienced the greatest political defeat of the century.

8   The expression "*sobrepacto*" was used by Rafael Otano in the workshop for "Chile in the 90s," in reference to cultural microclimates.

their underlying mistrust, these critics do not fully accept the government's modernizing reforms, and they feel that the modernization currently taking place has little to do with the ideals of liberty and democracy.

Likewise, proponents of this view are acutely aware of a shortage of government assistance for those who need it. They call for a greater governmental role in the life of the people, especially as a counterweight to powerful economic groups. They have difficulty adjusting to government's reduced size and its less paternalistic relationships with social groups. They are disinclined to acknowledge the role of the business community in an open economy like Chile's, and they criticize the excessive influence of the business sector on the government. This view calls for a more populist policy, but it views social categories in a way that is more reminiscent of decades past than representative of the country's current situation.

At its extreme, this sensibility reduces the government to the means for implementing a progressive program. It has little awareness of the fact that a true conservative core has formed in Chilean society. It warns of a concentration of economic power with ideological motives, mainly among UDI supporters who remain loyal to the tenets of the authoritarian regime. Similarly, it decries the Right's prominent role in the formation of social and cultural values through its influence upon churches, universities, and the media. From this standpoint, the government seems to offer the only opportunity for the implementation of freedom-oriented, democratic policies. This sensibility is quite clear about the reasons for its malaise, but it has serious difficulties in offering public policies based on its beliefs. Paradoxically, this view leads to a certain paralysis; if the governing coalition's contributions thus far have been so meager and misguided, it is neither useful nor prudent for it to continue to shape the future.

The dialogue within the alliance thus exhibits divergent emphases on successes and failures, along with different ways of reacting to and perceiving events. These contrasting points of view are the natural result of experiences in different areas of the political arena. The alliance must reconcile these competing views through self-observation and an effort to understand its own limitations. Open discussion will decrease the risk that either of these sensibilities will become isolated in its own internal logic. Confronting its internal differences will enable the Concertación to constructively debate its destiny and inaugurate a new phase of political inspiration.

III. The Concertación and Its Strategic Outlook

One question must be posed before we consider the coalition's direction for the future: Does the Concertación have a future at all? Is it not simply sentimentalism to maintain a coalition that may have already fulfilled the purpose for which it was born? There is no single answer to this question, and it has not yet been debated at length. Therefore, the authors would like to express some thoughts about this essential query.

The Concertación was founded as a coalition of parties aimed at providing a peaceful end to authoritarianism and installing a democracy. In addition, it always harbored a concern, albeit a less explicit and urgent one, about development issues. Since its creation, the alliance has not limited itself to democratizing the political system, broadening the horizons of civic society, and strengthening civil and cultural liberties. It has also promoted economic growth, productive transformation, and sustainable development. In addition to expanding and modernizing the country's productive infrastructure, it has also set all of the following as its goals: Chile's integration into the international system and economy; the elimination of poverty; the modernization and decentralization of the government; the creation of a peaceful and safe environment for Chile's citizens; and the establishment of a new pattern of labor relations.

Looking back over the 1990s, we see that citizens have become increasingly concerned with development issues, including the quality of life, environmental protection, better education and higher-quality services. Gradually, these issues have become part of the language of politics. Politics itself, in repeated references, has come to mean doing things for the people, along with an opportunity for leaders to demonstrate their effective management.

The development of the country has also become a point of dispute, simply because development can take many different forms. The experiences of Asia, North America, and Europe show that there is no set itinerary and no inevitable outcome. Nor are there recipes for guaranteed success, as demonstrated by the recent events in Southeast Asia. The work of development continues to be centered on the education and training of the nation's work force, and its path has become the fundamental focus of the strategic political and cultural struggle. We hold that the Concertación's most far-reaching goal is to guide Chile to national and integral development. "National" here does not refer to a metaphysical quality, but rather to the tangible humanity of Chilean men and women, and to the kind of development that includes our people in both the process and the results. "Integral" means that true development will only be achieved when each of the country's spheres —- economic, social, cultural, and political -— prospers with its own dynamism and direction; when all of these spheres draw strength from one another; and when the objective statistics of development and the subjective experiences of people and communities coincide.

Does the affirmation of this goal mean that the task of strengthening democracy has become less important? On the contrary; the pursuit of this objective does not reduce democracy to the success of two or three reforms. It makes the quality of our democratic life a national issue. It asserts that achieving democracy is not only a matter for politicians, but also a condition for making all of our institutions and social structures stable, effective, and legitimate.

Are we hereby setting aside the aims of the transition? The dilemmas and wounds left by the authoritarian experience will accompany our country for years, no matter how we might try to will them away. We will likely encounter new moments of tension, occasions of collective catharsis, and unexpected changes which might consume the country's attention for a long time. Nevertheless, we must avoid two errors. One is to disregard the historic weight of this legacy and to attempt to escape from our past. That past will return obstinately, again and again, until we have faced it fully. The other error, equally grave, would be to convert a necessary and unavoidable task into an element of strategy. This would leave an opening for the Right to imprint its stamp on development; that is, a combination of "protected democracy," neoliberal economics and cultural conservatism.

1. AN AGENDA FOR DEVELOPMENT

In accordance with these goals, the Concertación must define a domestic agenda that harmonizes the efforts of the government and the rest of society, and one which can enjoy full legitimacy and support.[9]

This initiative has different fundamental goals than the one undertaken at the end of the 1980s. The purpose of that effort was to resolve a domestic conflict and ensure the country's peace and security through a transition arranged by pact. The new agenda, based on the vigorous affirmation of economic and political freedoms, must move toward consensus about the best path toward a strong economic future for Chile; a more effective and more participatory democracy; greater social mobility and real opportunities for the disadvantaged; and a society based on mutual respect and cooperation.

This agenda will require increasing levels of maturity among those involved in the various dimensions of development. In our history, these dimensions have sometimes supported each other in a virtuous circle, and at other times they have worked at cross-purposes, paralyzing progress or creating a perverse dynamic in which one hand destroys the work of the other. As our nation's experience shows, greater democracy without growth is not desirable; nor is growth without political freedom, nor participation without effective government. A more fluid and constructive relationship among these dimensions will help bring about productive synergies among institutions and a more harmonious organization of life in society.[10]

An agenda of this nature would enable us, for example, to move toward a more integrated vision of the economy and macroeconomic equilibrium. It should take inflation control, international competitiveness, and equity simultaneously into account. It should lead to budget agreements providing sufficient funding for recognized social needs. It should emphasize institutional development, promoting competitive markets and not just price stability. Finally, it should allow the economy to be truly flexible in the use of both labor and capital.

This agenda must incorporate the complexity of the changes experienced during the last few decades. If Chile seeks to become a competitive nation in the globalized world, it must take a different approach to the tasks of development. This approach must integrate multiple actors and assist in coordinating the complex interactions between the public and private sectors. The government interacts with the market; local, regional,, and national governments interact with each other; and various civic organizations interact with all of the above.

We must construct this agenda with the consciousness that we face a paradoxical situation: never in our history have we been so close to development, yet we have never been

---

9 Some of these issues are being addressed by organizations like the Productive Development Forum. There have been notable instances of cooperation among various social forces within a community, as in Valdivia. See *Agenda pactada de desarrollo, Provincia de Valdivia* (Gobernación Provincial y Corporación de Desarrollo de la Provincia de Valdivia, 1997).

10 The presidents and heads of state of Latin America clearly recognized this multidimensional approach in the Declaration of Viña del Mar. This document takes a strong stand for integration, making reference to the international, social, economic, and political dimensions of democratic governance. These dimensions are analyzed in detail in *Gobernabilidad Democrática*, by Eduardo Frei Ruiz-Tagle (Santiago: Editorial Andrés Bello, 1997).

more aware of the tremendous chasm we must cross to reach it. What is required is much more than the sum of our individual efforts, since many of these are isolated or contradictory. Our agenda is this: true democracy; a dynamic export sector; modern labor and social security protections; modernization of government; participation in the new, globalized world environment; integrated social and economic policies; and a civic culture characterized by mutual respect. It is clear that to attain any one of these tasks, we must pool the energies of every member of our society.

This agenda would enable us to elevate the level of our national debate and move beyond narrow concerns. During these years, people throughout our nation have been absorbed in their own particular tasks. Politicians have faced the challenge of recovering respect and prestige for their role. The energies of business people have been fully focused on the country's ongoing economic expansion. Citizens have been learning to live within a new economic culture, with new opportunities and burdens. Without a broader vision, the essential questions for our nation will be debated in isolation. The question of the role of government will be reduced to simplistic discussions of privatization; the debate on social issues will be restricted to disputes over the amount of social spending; the question of labor relations will be reduced to disagreements over unemployment insurance; and the examination of our international relations will be narrowed to the expectations for a new trade agreement.

The difference between this agenda and the pact of the late 1980s does not merely lie in their purpose. The method for determining this new agenda is inextricably linked with its success. The new program must emerge from a broad national debate, including contributions from a wide range of perspectives. It must overcome the compartmentalization of national debate, the separation of interests and the isolation of different forces in society. It must not attempt to solve everything at once, but it should establish timetables for resolving the most urgent matters. The agenda resulting from this debate must be formally documented, but this will be a natural consequence of the discussion process rather than a prerequisite for initiating it.

To guide this program to fruition, the Concertación must maintain good working relationships with all segments of society. The coalition has strong historical ties with some of these, but it must bring those relationships up to date. The lower and middle classes, groups that have traditionally supported the alliance, have undergone significant qualitative and quantitative changes in recent years.

The Concertación is ambivalent toward other sectors, especially the business community. Regardless of this community's specific practices and the positive or negative reactions to them among the governing coalition, the fact is that more than two-thirds of the country's economic activity depends on the private initiative of large, medium, and small businesses. Thus, any political effort to lead the country toward development must reach out to these enterprises and include them in a vision that transcends individual interests.

The alliance must firmly establish these new relationships, since they are indispensable for the fulfillment of a national agenda. Refusal to do so would be tremendous political blindness. The struggle for the political center is one of the most dominant themes in Chilean politics today. Winning it requires more than offering a certain set of programs; it demands the ability to cut across class lines. The efforts of the Right in recent years have aimed at an unmistakable goal: making inroads among the lower and middle classes and gaining their sustained support. A highly competitive, strategic fight is being waged over the chance to guide the country in the years to come. In light of this fact, the Concertación's first priority must be to involve the broadest possible spectrum of society (including the business community) in its agenda for national and integral development. It must reach out boldly, confidently, and unambiguously to all Chileans.

IV. Toward New Public Policies

The rejuvenation of a political force does not only imply the broadening of its strategic horizons and the strengthening of its political leadership; it also requires, in particular, the ability to propose and execute more effective public policies. If the Concertación is to reach its objectives, it must move beyond the solid foundation its administrations have established, improving existing policies and initiating new courses of action.

Achieving the objectives of national and integral development will require specific proposals. These specific ideas will not attract the same amount of support as a general program. The coalition must therefore continuously strive to improve its proposals, presenting them to the public and enhancing them with community input. Principles are stable guiding forces, but policies are, by nature, debatable. Policies are the point where the technical, social, and political dimensions of an issue intersect.

Several parties in the coalition will soon hold their programmatic and planning congresses. As the dates for these meetings approach, the authors would like to suggest some angles and examples which might be useful in the creation of new policies.

It is necessary to *re-focus the successful approaches of the past*, for example in macroeconomic and social policy. The government must try to keep inflation low, but it must also strive to minimize the negative impact of these measures on other areas, such as social equity and export development. This calls for a more integrated conception of macroeconomic equilibrium. Budgetary and economic balances must be constructed upon a stable foundation, in order to avoid disruptive corrective measures that undermine equity and competitiveness. Public spending should enjoy clear justification, effective management and transparent evaluation, and funding must be tailored to function. In raising the necessary revenues, the government must insist upon efficiency in collection, as well as equity in its income sources. To prevent a falling exchange rate from strangling export development, the state must settle net capital inflows at a level compatible with a sustainable current account deficit. The government must open the capital account gradually, while preserving the reserve requirement.

In regard to social policy, our leaders must alter their current focus on administration and financing. A new budget agreement must be established, providing more funds for social policies. In the case of retirees, this must be done immediately, not gradually. The public and private sectors should be integrated in order to achieve more effective results. Independent and public evaluation must also become an integral part of social services administration. In the area of regulation, the government must compensate for imperfections in both the market and its own activities in areas such as social security, health care, and housing. Political leaders must decide whether the control of particular services should be autonomous, decentralized, or centralized; but this must be determined according to experience and concerned judgment, not ideological prejudices.

In addition, the government must *redirect the debate over democracy*. Institutional reform can become a dense thicket in which leaders lose their way. The fundamental, universal standard of "one person, one vote" should be the guiding light of this process, leading us toward a democracy of which we can all be proud.

We must establish a proportional electoral system and eliminate the distortions existing today. All legislators should be elected, and Congress should accurately represent the diversity of our political spectrum, without concessions for any party. We must strip non-democratic institutions of their political power and eliminate the military's role as the guardian of our nation's institutions. In the same spirit, political parties must be modernized; they must open their structures to their members, establish clear procedures and submit to various forms of public oversight. The funding of political activities must be transparent; the government must regulate private donations and provide public financing for election campaigns.

In other areas, such as decentralization and public information, our leadership needs *new definitions*. Decentralization is a fundamental aspect of democracy, and yet its success is not yet assured in our country. The barriers encountered in this process must not serve as an excuse to pull back, but rather a stimulus to accelerate and expand our efforts. This will require three lines of action: an increase in regional administrative capacity through a massive training effort; significant funding for the regions; and substantive policy autonomy for regional authorities. The situation also calls for adequately-financed, clear, and effective municipal reforms, which should be approved as quickly as possible.

With regard to communications, we clearly need to increase the quality and quantity of publications and public information programs available to Chilean men and women. Additional forums and media must be establish to disseminate this information. Chile must create a public television channel similar in function, funding, and regulation to those of more developed countries, such as the British Broadcasting Company (BBC) and the Public Broadcasting System (PBS) of the United States. These experiences and others show that it is possible to have quality public television which transcends partisan politics.

In still other areas, the government needs *new criteria*. This is the case in the areas of social equity and government reform. In designating equity as a criterion for public policy, we must eliminate ambiguities and review every area of government action according to its contribution to this goal.

For example, there is a consensus that education is the most effective path to equality. To proceed along this path, we must ensure that all of Chile's young people receive a quality education. This will require differentiated policies reflecting educational standards in various communities. Assuring quality in Las Condes is not the same as assuring quality in poor communities. The criterion for success should be the gradual elimination of the pre-set and unequal educational tracks that hinder the achievement of children in poor communities. There is a consensus in our country about the importance of the family, but we must focus on real families when we formulate social policies, not just on particular indicators such as housing and health care coverage. The same approach must be taken to the protection of our people against violent crime and the threat of drugs.

In addition, the government must apply the criterion of equity to a wide range of social policies, in recognition of our country's great imbalances in economic opportunity. Without development capital, free enterprise is limited, and entrepreneurial talent goes to waste. Without training, productivity stagnates. Without the modernization of companies, a key means of gaining competitiveness is lost. Without fair standards for labor relations, the country's gains do not benefit everyone proportionately. Without unemployment insurance, the labor flexibility required by the economy is one-sided and unjust. All of these variables show that income distribution is not determined at random, nor solely by the particular skills and contributions of each individual.

Government reform also calls for a new focus. With the exception of the reform of the judicial branch currently in progress, the government has thus far done little to establish performance standards and other measures to ensure consistent levels of effectiveness. Although some progress has been made, we must continue to refine the theory and practice in this area. The public sector contributes to national development in numerous ways. We must improve the design, implementation, and evaluation of public policies in order to make them more effective. Specific areas of concern include the budgetary system, social program administration, economic development activities, Chile's participation in the international economy, financial management, and our country's infrastructure. As progress is made in these areas, new challenges will arise in the coordination and integration of governmental institutions and actions.[11] In broader terms, the executive branch must improve institutional design so that each of its divisions has adequate functional capacity; the Congress must strengthen itself technically, in order to fulfill its role of representing the citizenry; and the judiciary must complete the reform it has begun, ensuring that all Chileans have access to justice.

The government must *accept new realities*, such as the need to regulate imperfect or non-competitive markets and to make the economy more flexible.

Some say the best regulation is none at all. For the Concertación, regulation is a tool that, used properly, fulfills basic social functions. We cannot allow markets with distorted or non-existent competition to persist, since they leave consumers unprotected, hinder advances in productivity, and tend toward unequal distribution of any gains achieved.

Regulation must aim primarily at creating conditions for more effective competition. We must modify the non-competitive behavior that arose from the military regime's favoritism in privatizing and deregulating public services. We must also put a stop to non-transparent negotiations and prevent new cases of market concentration. The government must better protect the rights of those who use and consume products and services, whether these are public or private. These rights must be guaranteed expressly and comprehensively by law, and enforcement procedures should be simple and expeditious.

Another urgent area for regulation is the media. The authoritarian state legally sanctioned and financially promoted the media concentration that exists today. It is imperative that the current government counteract this situation and act to diversify the industry. Since an overhaul of the television system is technologically inevitable, the government should conduct an open debate over the content and characteristics of concessions. We must also address the lack of transparency in the media market by improving audience measurement techniques and creating a system to monitor print media circulation.

If our domestic economy is to be flexible in adapting to the challenges of international markets, we must enhance current regulations or create new ones in both the labor and capital markets. The labor market requires better training opportunities and adequate

---

11 See Eugenio Lahera, "Algunos criterios para reformar el Estado," *Documentos de Trabajo No. 45* (Santiago: Cepal, April 1997).

unemployment insurance. In the capital market, we must facilitate bankruptcy procedures for troubled companies, as well as expand financing and development measures to assist in the creation of new private enterprises.

The government must *take a different approach to some classic issues*. A democracy in which people can take pride must have a Charter of Citizens' Rights and Responsibilities. This document would incorporate our past experiences as well as new perspectives. It would help our country transcend the emphasis on rights alone, as well as provide the basis for a civic education program. In the interest of a more humane society, we should abolish the death penalty. Our educational system and our media should also contribute to the ongoing instruction of citizens as to their rights and duties.

One of the greatest weaknesses in Chilean society is the lack of community and private sector participation. We must develop a new approach to this problem. Government ministries and services of all kinds, including decentralized or autonomous entities, must improve their interactions with social groups and individuals. The legislature must establish formal guidelines for organizations wishing to present their opinions, problems, or interests. Promoting participation also means establishing new standards for transparency and the dissemination of information, as well as regulations that facilitate the creation, activities, and public expression of grassroots organizations.

The government must finally *take on neglected tasks*. Society must encourage people to express themselves. Our final frontier is the nation's soul. The best way to explore it is to guarantee freedom of expression and creativity, creating an environment that tolerates diversity and thrives on dialogue.

We propose that the country sponsor or create institutions and social structures that ensure freedom and promote its exercise, while respecting the freedoms of others. Nondiscrimination should be a constitutionally recognized principle with guaranteed legal enforcement. Complete religious freedom also requires that we regularize the recognition of religious organizations and churches.

In the cultural sphere, three areas call out for concrete initiatives: the creative flowering of culture, the dissemination of culture among the people, and the preservation of our rich heritage. Work in these areas will require decisive new policies and new forms of management. The recommendations of the Art and Culture Advisory Commission should be adopted, including the one that streamlines the procedures for implementing cultural projects.

The entire higher education system also requires far-reaching reform, including a new funding policy. The state should make its role in this area more explicit and specify the responsibilities of public universities. State schools must gain a clearer understanding of their mission, which must include commitments to pluralism, equity, and quality in education.

V. Creating Opportunities for Political and Social Dialogue

As we consider all of the issues raised above, an important question arises. Where can a coalition that has held power for eight years obtain the human energy and political force to give it renewed drive? Is it not presumptuous to propose such far-reaching objectives as these? These questions speak to the governing coalition's reason for existence and the passions that drive it.

1. BECOMING A FORCE OF CHANGE

At the end of the 1980s, the Concertación recognized that the nation had had enough of arrogance, divisiveness, cultural mediocrity, and social and political marginalization. There was a collective desire to move from fear to freedom, from helplessness to hope. The coalition's great strength was its proximity to the people and its understanding of their needs and desires. Its great passion has been to represent the common citizens — those without special influence or connections to the elite. In the process of constructing a national agenda, the Concertación has invited the entire country to participate in dialogue and debate. It also possesses the moral obligation to represent those who have not been included in the past, those who have no power, and those who are weak, fragile, and vulnerable. The coalition's central concerns and preoccupations lie with these citizens, and it is to them that it ultimately answers.

The fears and hopes of our people today are different than those of a decade ago. There is the fear of being subject to the whims of a market that seems harsh and unyielding, the fear that a low-paying job will become a lifelong prison. The people clamor for a country in which someone must answer for inefficiency, for services that are advertised and not provided. People hope to see results in their own lifetimes, rather than promises for future generations.

Public emotions, long held in check, are beginning to be unleashed. The call is heard for a more tolerant society, one which celebrates human differences. There is also a demand for greater transparency, especially in the highest circles of power. The shortage of simple friendship, courtesy, and cooperation is lamented in a society that is becoming increasingly competitive in many areas.

We hear these complaints, and many others, in many voices and variations, in our daily conversations. The governing alliance must listen to them, understand them, represent them and guide them. The coalition is a force for liberty, and thus it must open new avenues of change, resist complacency, answer to the people for its promises and results, acknowledge its errors, and work to correct them. We must reopen the dialogue about our collective destiny within the coalition, among party leaders and members, and between the Concertación and all Chileans. Our coalition's capacity for human and political renewal depends on the fruitfulness of this dialogue as well as the full expression of the Concertación's broad social foundation. No leader or party who aspires to political leadership in the coming years can avoid these challenges.

Similarly, the coalition must assert its convictions, but with the flexibility of spirit to reconsider the institutions and arrangements it has created and to change those that must be changed. It needs the energy and imagination to formulate specific public policies, as well as the necessary common sense to find the support to implement them. The Concertación is capable of this. It has brought political and economic stability and effective government to our country because its diverse team of professionals has learned how to make decisions in the face of great challenges. The Concertación is capable of this because it has learned how to persuade the nation, disarming its opponents with public pressure in order to achieve its goals.

The goal is not to implement an exclusive and all-encompassing program, but simply to carry out democratically-selected projects and reforms. The governing coalition has the obligation to respond to and channel feelings of discontent that could give rise to

anarchistic and anti-system movements if left unaddressed. Such tendencies could ultimately produce a confrontational divide between Chile's haves and have-nots, which
would polarize and paralyze the country.[12]

2. BROADENING POLITICAL FORUMS

To renew and strengthen its creative impulse, the Concertación must expand its traditional political outreach and deepen its relationships with the social groups that currently give
it their support. The coalition has experience in this area. By virtue of its very nature and
purpose, it has long practiced the art of harnessing and incorporating the wills of many
individuals and groups. At times it has gained the support of influential figures from other
political currents. At other times it has identified common purposes in order to work in
harmony with others toward specific goals. It has won broad national support for economic and social agreements. All of these tools and experiences can be examined today in a different light.

The alliance has the opportunity to forge agreements with parts of the liberal democratic Right, as well as parts of the Left not represented in Congress, in order to move
toward its goals. The coalition must also consider the possibility of redefining its current
composition; it has no reason to fear such change. The Concertación is so named because
of its practice of constantly seeking agreement in order to move forward. It accomplished
this first among the Christian humanist tradition and the lay Socialist left, and then it tire-
lessly sought accords with the military regime in order to find a democratic solution to the
nation's crisis. The obviously divergent and contradictory interests involved have never
dissuaded it. Meanwhile, the coalition's search for consensus has always served clear and
specific goals. Without these, consensus degenerates into an excuse for maintaining things
as they are.

In addition to expanding its outreach, the coalition must vigorously seek renewed support from those who have voted for it in the past but who now view it with a certain
detachment and skepticism. This is not the time for political inertia. The hour has come
when leaders and groups of a different political stripe are tempted to seize the initiative
and bring about a sweeping reconfiguration of the political landscape.

The coalition that has governed the country for nearly a decade thus faces an urgent
need to broaden its strategic horizons and increase the vitality of its political force. It must
call forth the energies of the nation in order to achieve integral development; that is,
development in which all Chileans can find a place. It must once again become a force for
freedom and change, with leaders who are driven by their convictions and responsive to
the people, in order to meet the challenges faced by our nation.

---

12 This perception is gaining prominence in qualitative studies carried out by the government. A similar idea
is expressed in P. Kirby, *The Impact of Neoliberalism on Chilean Society: A Report for Trócaire* (Trócaire 1996).

The Authors

Jaime Ahumada Pacheco, a political scientist and public administrator, with postgraduate studies in Political Science, Public Administration and International Relations (Latin American School of Political Science and Public Administration, Flacso; and Institute for International Studies, University of Chile), is an external consultant for the Research Department of the Presidency of the Republic, and an international consultant for the United Nations at ECLAC and Ilpes. He is an expert in public administration, decentralization, local development, and social policies, and his published works cover especially these areas.

Raúl Atria Benaprés, a sociologist and doctoral candidate (Columbia University), is the main regional advisor to ECLAC and a professor at the University of Chile. He has been Dean of the Social Sciences Department of the Pontifical Catholic University of Chile and Director of the Institute for Political Science at the same university. His works focus on the areas of higher education, sociological theory, social movements, and political development.

Cristián Belleï Carvacho, a sociologist, serves as Director of Research for the Ministry of Education's Middle-School Program (MECE), and is a professor at the University of Chile and the Academy of Christian Humanism in Santiago. He has published on issues relating to elementary school education in Chile.

Guillermo Campero Quiroga, a sociologist and doctoral candidate (University of Paris), currently works as an advisor to the Labor Ministry. He is also a consultant to various international agencies, a professor at the Pontifical Catholic University of Chile, the University of Chile, and other centers of higher education, and a member of the Directing Committee of the Latin American Council on Social Sciences (Clacso). Formerly he was Director of Research for the Latin American Institute of Transnational Studies (ILET). He has published various works on sociology and social movements.

Enrique Cañas Kirby, a Bachelor of Philosophy and Development Sciences, Master of Political Science (Heidelberg University) and Doctor of Political Science (Friburg University), is an advisor to the Research Department of the Presidency of the Republic. He was previously an advisor to the Research Department of the Ministry of the Secretary General of the Presidency. He is a professor of political development at Ilades, and his publications deal with the issues of political science, sociology, political theory, political development, and development policy.

Carlos Catalán Bertoni, a sociologist with post graduate work at the University of Rome, Italy, is an advisor to the Ministry of the Secretary General of the Government and to the National Television Council. In addition, he is a professor at the Pontifical Catholic University of Chile and at Diego Portales University, a consultant to the Council on Higher Education and a member of the Sociology Commission of Fondecyt. He has served as Director of Research of the National Television Council, Assistant Director of Flacso, Chile, and Executive Director of Ceneca. He has published in the areas of communication, culture, and public opinion.

Flavio Cortés Acevedo, a sociologist, acts as Director of Content for the Presidency of the Republic of Chile. He has published work on youth and labor relations, and has been Assistant Director of the National Institute for Youth, head of the Department of Projects and Organizational Development of the Labor Directorate, and professor at the universities of Chile, Diego Portales, and Andrés Bello National.

Gonzalo de la Maza Escobar, a sociologist, holds a social sciences diploma in *Études Approfondies* from the *École des Hautes Études*, Paris, is an independent consultant on social programs, a member of the National Council for Overcoming Poverty, and a professor at the Academy of Christian Humanism. He was the director of ECO, Education and Communications, and president of ACCIÓN, the Chilean Association of NGOs. His published works cover urban social movements, social programs, international cooperation for development, poor youth, and public education.

Mario Fernández Baeza, an attorney and Master and Ph.D in Political Science (Heidelberg University), is currently the Deputy Secretary of War and a professor de Political Science at the Pontifical Catholic University of Chile and at the University of Chile. He was previously Deputy Secretary of Aviation and editor of the newspaper *La Época*. He has published in the areas of public law and political science.

José María Fuentes Hernández is a civil engineer, Master of Administration (Speyer University of Public Administration, Germany) and Bachelor of Development Sciences (Ilades). He is assistant manager of Public Services for SONDA, a private information technology company, and has published on electoral systems and municipal government.

Gonzalo García Pino, an attorney and Master of Constitutional Law (Pontifical Catholic University of Chile), is currently pursuing his Ph.D. in Law at Carlos III University in Madrid, Spain. He previously acted as cabinet chief of the Ministry of Defense and head of the Civilian and Military Relations Program of the Center for Development Studies. His publications deal with public law and defense issues. He teaches at Andrés Bello National University, and previously taught in the Master's Program for Constitutional Law at the Pontifical Catholic University of Chile, and the Master's Program for Public Safety at the Carabineros police force's Senior Officers Academy.

Eugenio Lahera Parada, a Doctor of Public Affairs (Princeton University), is editor of the ECLAC magazine and a public policy advisor to the Ministry of the Secretary General of the Government. He has been executive director of the Chile 21 Foundation and a regional public policy advisor for ECLAC. He is a professor of Public Administration in the Master's Program for Public Administration and Public Policy of the University of Chile. His published works deal with the design, administration and evaluation of public economic and social policies.

Arturo León Batista, an economist with a graduate degree in Sociology (Flacso), is an expert in Social Statistics at ECLAC. He has published on economic development, social stratification, social policies, income distribution, poverty, and social indicators.

Jorge Manzi Astudillo, a psychologist and Doctor of Psychology (University of California), is director of the School of Psychology of the Pontifical Catholic University of Chile, and adjunct professor of the School of Psychology at the same university. He previously directed the Research Department of the National Commission for Scientific and Technological Research (Conicyt). He has published works on social psychology, political psychology, and psychometrics.

María Pía Martin Münchmeyer is a sociologist and urban development master's candidate (Pontifical Catholic University of Chile), with a degree in Social Planning and Policy (Ilpes/ECLAC). She is an advisor on Social Policies in the cabinet of the Ministry of the Secretary General of the Government, and is in charge of Case Studies in the Master's Program for Public Administration and Policy of the University of Chile. She teaches classes at the University of Chile and at Diego Portales University. Her published papers deal with the area of housing and urban development.

Javier Martínez Bengoa, a Doctor of Sociology, is Director General of QUANTA, Sociología Aplicada Ltda. He has headed up the Institute for Social Sciences of the Catholic University of Valparaíso, was founder and editor of the theory magazine *Proposiciones*, and was executive Director of the SUR Research Center think-tank. He teaches classes at the Catholic University of Valparaíso, Catholic University of Chile and the Autonomous National University of Mexico. He has published extensively on sociology, economic research, social stratification, politics, and public opinion.

Isidora Mena Edwards, a psychologist and Doctor of Education Sciences, (Pontifical Catholic University of Chile), is an academic at the School of Psychology of the Pontifical Catholic University of Chile. She coordinated the Secondary-School Education Program of the University Promotion Corporation, and was vice-coordinator of the Pedagogical Practices Component of the MECE-Secondary School Program, Mineduc. Her published papers deal with the areas of creativity, social coexistence in school, and improving teachers.

Francisco Meneses Mellado, is a business graduate, Master of Public Administration (Harvard University), Master of Economics (University of Chile) and Bachelor of Development Sciences (Ilades). He is executive director of the Corporation for the Promotion and Development of Small and Medium Businesses (Cefope), and a professor at the universities of Chile and Santiago. He has coordinated the Modernization Area of Public Administration under the Ministry of the Secretary General of the Presidency, and was head of the Research Department of the National Institute of Statistics (INE). He has published on statistical methodologies, electoral analysis, productivity, economics and public administration.

Roberto Merino Rojo, a Bachelor of Literature, currently contributes to the magazines *Hoy* and *Capital*, and is a visiting professor in the Master's of Arts Program of the School of Arts of the University of Chile. He has written for the magazines *Apsi*, *Don Balón* and *Paula*, and is an editor at the publishing company Editorial Sudamericana. His published writings relate to literature and the visual arts.

Cristián Parker Gumucio, a sociologist and Doctor of Sociology (Catholic University of Louvain), is a professor and researcher at the University of Santiago de Chile and the Center for Studies of Contemporary Reality at the Academy of Christian Humanism. He has published works on social science methodologies and on the sociology of development, culture, and religion.

Gustavo Rayo Urrutia, a public administrator and Doctor of Public Studies (Institute for Political Studies, University of Grenoble), is currently Chief of Planning and Research at the National Training and Employment Service (Sence), and teaches at the University of Chile. He was previously Head of Planning at the Solidarity and Social Investment Fund (Fosis), and has published papers on social movements, public policies, and reforming government.

Osvaldo Rosales Villavicencio, an economist and Master of Economics (Escolatina), is a regional advisor to ECLAC and a professor at the Academy of Christian Humanism and Diego Portales University. He has taught and researched in the Economics Department of the University of Chile, and was adjunct director of the Training Program at Ilpes. His publications deal with the issues of economic development and international economics.

Fernando Toledo Tapia, an attorney, specialist in Environmental and International Law, Master of Law (Stanford University) and doctoral candidate (Stanford University), is an international partner in the firm Wilmer, Cutler & Pickering in Washington D.C. He was previously a legal advisor to then Senator and later President Eduardo Frei Ruiz-Tagle, and an attaché to the General Consulate of Chile in San Francisco. He taught classes at the Pontifical Catholic University of Chile, and has published research on environmental and international law.

Cristián Toloza Castillo, a psychologist and Doctor of Psychology (University of Exeter), is presently head of the Directorate of Research of the Presidency of the Republic. He was formerly Director of Content of the Presidency and advisor to then Finance Minister Alejandro Foxley. He teaches at the Pontifical Catholic University of Chile and at the University of Chile, and has published works on social psychology.

Tonci Tomic Jakas, an engineer, is director of the Corporation of Environmental Studies and Management for Development. His publications deal with rural development and peasantry, technological innovation in agriculture, the environment, and sustainable development.

Teresa Valdés Echeñique, a sociologist, is Assistant Academic Director of Flacso-Chile and coordinator of the Gender Studies Program of the same institution. Previously she coordinated the regional project "Statistics on Latin American Women" for 19 countries, under the auspices of Flacso Chile. She specializes and writes about public polices for women, sexuality, reproductive health and rights, women's movements in Chile, and political participation of women. She teaches as a visiting professor in the Stanford University Program in Santiago, and at the Christian Humanism Academy.

Alberto van Klaveren Stork, Bachelor of Legal and Social Sciences, Master in International Studies (Graduate School of International Studies, University of Denver) and Doctor of Political Science (Law School, University of Leiden, Holland), acts as Planning Director, with the rank of ambassador, in Chile's Ministry of Foreign Relations. He is also a member of the board of the International Cooperation Agency of Chile. He was formerly lead advisor to the United Nations Development Program (UNDP) and director of the Institute for International Studies of the University of Chile. He teaches at the latter institute, and has published in the areas of foreign policy and international relations.

Joaquín Vial Ruiz-Tagle, a business graduate and Doctor of Economics (University of Pennsylvania), is Budget Director for the Finance Ministry. He formerly acted as coordinator of Economic Policies for the Finance Ministry, and as executive director of Cieplan. He teaches classes at the University of Chile, and previously taught at the universities of Ilades/ Georgetown University, Pennsylvania, and Santiago. He has published works on economics and the environment.